Family Communication

Theory and Research

Lorin Basden Arnold

Rowan University

Boston   New York   San Francisco

Mexico City   Montreal   Toronto   London   Madrid   Munich   Paris

Hong Kong   Singapore   Tokyo   Cape Town   Sydney

Acquisitions Editor: *Jeanne Zalesky*
Assistant Editor: *Jenny Lupica*
Associate Editor: *Deb Hanlon*
Marketing Manager: *Suzan Czajkowski*
Production Editor: *Claudine Bellanton*
Editorial Production Service: *Connie Strassburg, GGS Book Services*
Composition Buyer: *Linda Cox*
Manufacturing Buyer: *JoAnne Sweeney*
Electronic Composition: *GGS Book Services*
Cover Administrator: *Kristina Mose-Libon*

For related titles and support materials, visit our online catalog at www.ablongman.com.

Between the time website information is gathered and then published, it is not unusual for some sites to have closed. Also, the transcription of URLs can result in typographical errors. The publisher would appreciate notification where these errors occur so that they may be corrected in subsequent editions.

Library of Congress Cataloging-in-Publication Data

Arnold, Lorin Basden.
  Family communication: theory and research / Lorin Basden Arnold.
    p. cm.
  Includes bibliographical references and index.
  ISBN-13:978-0-205-45364-1
  ISBN-10:0-205-45364-3
   1. Communication in the family.   2. Communication in the family—Research.   3. Interpersonal communication—Research.   I. Title.
  HQ515.A76 2008
  306. 87—dc22   2007017568

Printed in the United States of America

10 9 8 7 6 5 4 3 2 1   11 10 09 08 07

Contents

7   *Race, Ethnicity, and Family*   *241*

8   *Sexuality and the Family*   *285*

9 *Health, Disability, and the Family*   *318*

10 *The Family in Mediated Contexts*   *367*

Preface

About This Book

As a faculty member or student encountering this book for the first time, you may be wondering what the philosophy is behind its construction, or what it offers that other family communication texts may not supply. The answer to this question is *diversity in stance and voice*. In this text, a wide range of voices in the family communication field are represented both in the literature review chapters and in the specialized research example chapters. It is my hope that this diversity of perspective will give students a better idea of the wide variety of research that is being conducted in family communication and the complexities of this area of study.

This text is divided into content chapters representing some of the major foci in the field of family communication, with each chapter (except for the first and for the conclusion) organized into three sections. In the first section I provide an overview of that aspect of the field and consider some of the more prominent theoretical and empirical findings. The second sections include research examples that delve more deeply into specific aspects of that content area—empirical research being conducted in the field of family communication and critical analysis or response by scholars of family communication. The articles are written by the scholars who completed the work in a format that is more compatible with student reading than the average journal article. In this way, students get an overall view of the breadth of the family communication area while also being exposed to the depth of study being done in specific areas. Finally, each chapter concludes with a third section that briefly considers some ways that students can connect what they have learned to their own understandings and enactments of family.

This format is beneficial to both students and instructors. First, having research examples readily available reduces the need to supplement course material with journal articles. As previously stated, the discussions presented here are written specifically for a student audience unlike journal articles, which are often somewhat inaccessible for student populations. This format also reduces the time and money spent securing and copying articles, and negotiating the challenges of copyright laws.

Second, because the specific empirical and analysis chapters are written by the scholars who are conducting that research in family communication, students can hear scholars speak about their area of specialization. The format also provides students with a variety of voices, rather than a single presentation or point of view. Some students find this social scientific approach to communication particularly convincing and compelling; others are more intrigued by a humanistic or interpretive perspective. Some students learn more easily from narrative examples; others learn more from quantitative visual comparisons. Including several types of empirical or critical study in the text gives students multiple opportunities to find out not only what area of family communication research is most interesting to them, but also what type of communication research they find most useful or believable.

Third, because there are multiple research sections included with each chapter, instructors can select those that meet their needs and the needs of the class in a particular semester. For some chapters, instructors may wish to use all of the research pieces; for others, they may wish to require some as reading and make the others optional for students who are particularly interested in that topic. This makes the text more easily adapted to individual course styles and needs.

Finally, even though this text is written at a level appropriate for undergraduate students, every effort has been made to ensure that students are exposed to concepts and ideas that challenge them and facilitate critical thinking and discussion. For example, though some students may not need to know the precise nature of quantitative research methodology (or interpretive approaches to communication), an exposure to it at a basic level is beneficial to their ability to be critical consumers of the research that they are presented with in academic settings and in other venues.

Given the complexity of family experiences, this text cannot reasonably cover every topic related to family communication. However, topics chosen for this book are those that seem fundamental to a beginning understanding of the family communication phenomenon.

The text begins with a basic introduction to definitions of family. The act of defining, truly a communicative endeavor, is extremely important to how we understand and experience family in our daily lives. Thus, this serves as a starting point for the discussion, which is followed by a discussion of family types. Again, understanding the variety of family forms and types that exist (and are the objects of research in communication) is important to understanding the research done in the field. For students who have taken family sociology or family studies courses, this material should function as a helpful review. For those who are just beginning to study family, these chapters provide the background needed to understand the remainder of the text.

Chapter 3 discusses families as a system. The concept of family systems has become prominent, even when it goes unstated, in studies of family in many fields, including communication. A systems approach is an underlying feature of many theoretical approaches to family communication as well. Thus, this discussion is provided early in the text.

Chapters 4, 5, and 6 address particular communicative aspects of family, such as family rules, metaphors, stories, expressions of intimacy, social support, and conflict. Although this is certainly not an exhaustive list of family communication phenomenon, it represents some of the major study foci.

Chapters 7 through 10 specifically address issues that are important in family interactions and that impact family culture and family behavior. These include race and ethnicity, sexuality, health and disability issues, and how mediated contexts impact (and are impacted by) family processes. These issues also appear in other sections of the text; however, the dedicated chapters provide more complete discussions of the topics.

Additionally, three appendices are provided in the text. Appendix A instructs students how to read the research pieces presented in this text, or other scholarly research pieces they may encounter. Although this may be less necessary for students who have previously taken methods or other courses in communication, it will be particularly helpful for those students who are beginning their study of the communication phenomenon. Appendix B consists of a list of additional sources to which students and faculty may turn for family information and research. Appendix C provides information about each of the contributing authors for the text.

I hope that you find the layout and content of this text both clear and compelling. The study of family communication is a wide-ranging field that cannot possibly be covered completely in any one text or class. However, I believe that this text will serve to introduce students to the field in all of its variety.

Acknowledgments

A large number of people participated in the creation of this text. Without their assistance and contributions, I could not have completed this work.

First and foremost, I owe the contributors of empirical research examples, who held fast and retained their good humor through many revisions. They brought to this work the variety of perspectives, research methods, theories, beliefs, and writing styles that I was hoping for, and that I believe make it both unique and compelling.

Second, I must thank the editorial staff at Allyn and Bacon, who provided immeasurable advice and prompts. In the early stages of the project, Brian Wheel carefully guided me through the proposal and contract process and the start of the "real work," and Karon Bowers and Jenny Lupica truly helped me pull it all together at the end. I also owe a debt to the blind reviewers who provided critiques for Allyn and Bacon. They made constructive suggestions for material inclusion, ordering, phrasing, and examples that make this a better text.

My thanks to Kristin L. Davis, Arizona State University; John Dilworth, Kellogg Community College; Marcia D. Dixson, Indiana University–Purdue University Fort Wayne; Rebecca Dumlao, East Carolina University; Jacki Fitzpatrick, Texas Tech University; Scherrie Foster, Fond du Lac Tribal & Community College; Jean M. Gerard, Bowling Green State University; Robert Harrison, Gallaudet University; Becky Omdahl, Metropolitan State University; Gayle Pesavento, John A. Logan College; J. D. Ragsdale, Sam Houston State University; Thomas J. Socha, Old Dominion University; Renee Stahl, Aquinas College; Alan C. Taylor, Syracuse University; Jason J. Teven, California State University–Fullerton; Jerry Thomas, Lindsey Wilson College; and Marceline Thompson–Hayes, Arkansas State University.

Third, I appreciate the time and effort of the high school and college students who participated in piloting this work. They made astute comments regarding content, reading level, flow, and interest for each chapter and helped create a text that is focused on the needs of the college student reader.

Fourth, I am extremely grateful for the support I received at Rowan University. The time that was provided for research and writing proved invaluable in the construction of this text. The commitment to scholarship and pedagogical advancement shown by both administrators and colleagues has been a great boon to my experience.

Finally, I need to state my appreciation for the friends and family members who were barraged with samples and segments to read, and also shared with me the frustrations and joys of creating a textbook. In particular, I owe a nice dinner out (or at least a pizza) to Joy Cypher and Erica Doran for helping me get through this process. And, I couldn't have done any of this without my spouse, Derek, who served as my "in-house editor" and constant late-night sounding board. He, along with my children Jacob, Devin, Abbigael, Benjamin, Nathaniel, and Emmeline, also participated by providing me with a wealth of examples, a reassuring pat on the back when things weren't moving, and a "way to go" when progress was made. They are the grounding force that makes studying family more than an academic exercise.

1

Communication and the Family

Chapter Outline

What Is Communication?
   Definition of Communication

Why Study Family Communication?

What Is a Family?
   Defining is Communicative
   Medical or Biological Definitions

Legal Definitions
Scholarly Definitions
Personal Definitions

Chapter Objectives

1. To develop a foundational awareness of the nature of communication and the importance of family communication

2. To understand the importance of family communication definitions and the communicative nature of defining

3. To understand some of the basic ways family has been defined in medical, legal, scholarly, and personal domains

4. To be able to critically approach a variety of definitions, seeing both strengths and weaknesses in each

5. To begin creating and understanding your own definition of family

> *What we have here is a failure to communicate.*
>
> —Captain (Strother Martin) in *Cool Hand Luke*, 1967

How many times have you heard someone blame a problem with a spouse, a child, a sibling, or a parent on communication? Even on sitcoms and in hit songs, communication takes the fall for relational problems. We know, from our daily experiences, that communication is important. We also know that when it "works," we feel more at ease than when there is a "breakdown." As important as communication is, however, we often don't stop to think about it until we feel there is a problem. Yet, consideration of how communication functions in our lives, both in the positive moments and in the negative ones, is an important part of understanding and critically analyzing our life experience as humans.

Communicating with others occurs across many types of relational settings, which results in the field of communication studies being extensive in both breadth and depth. In this book, we focus on the communication that occurs in family settings, as well as mediated messages about family. As a starting point, it is important to establish what is meant by *communication*.

What Is Communication?

Communication is talking to each other. Some ways you can communicate are: telephones, cell phones, talking, computers, and kind of TV if you are the President and you want to communicate with the country.—Max, age 8

Communication is people talking together.—Casey, age 11

Communication is when two people talk to each other and you can understand what each other is saying.—KD, age 7

Communication is how people get along with each other and how they talk to each other.—Abbi, age 11

As in these examples of how a group of children defined the word *communication*, we often tend to think of communication as talking. However, it actually encompasses

---

BOX 1.1 • *A Few "Communication" Songs*

INXS—*Communication*
Marianne Faithfull—*Eye Communication*
The Cardigans—*Communication*
Duran Duran—*Communication*
Led Zeppelin—*Communication Breakdown*
Black Eyed Peas—*Communication*
Naked Eyes—*Communication without Sound*
Bela Fleck—*Communication*
Ratt—*Lack of Communication*
Janet Jackson—*Communication*
The Von Bondies—*Lack of Communication*
Spandau Ballet—*Communication*

much more, including verbal elements (spoken and written language), nonverbal elements (such as gestures, facial expressions, and clothing), and the process of interpretation and meaning creation. Even scholars have had difficulty figuring out how to define simply a process that is so complex.

Definition of Communication

Some scholars have created definitions that focus primarily on how communication allows us to share meanings and understandings through the use of shared symbols (the transmission of information). Other scholars have focused more on the process through which communication creates symbols, meanings, and understandings.

We will use a definition that includes both the sharing of meaning or understanding and its creation. **Communication** is the process of creating, negotiating, and sharing meaning through verbal and nonverbal channels. Looking at the parts of this definition can clarify the nature of communication more fully.

- *Communication is a process.* Communication is not a "thing," it is a process. This is why most communication scholars use the word *communication* (a process verb) rather than *communications* (a plural noun) in their discussions. Considering communication as a process puts focus on the continual change that occurs in human encounters and the ways in which those exchanges unfold, rather than simply on the content of the exchange.
- *Communication includes the creation of meaning.* As we engage in interaction with others we develop meanings and understandings. When you were a child, you began to develop meanings for the word *friend* based on the interactions you had with others and what you saw around you.
- *Communication involves the negotiation of meaning.* The communication process is not always without struggle. Various individuals and groups have divergent understandings and meanings for concepts, objects, and so on; the emergence of meaning is a process of negotiation via those different meanings.
- *Communication is a way of sharing meaning.* By communicating with others, we attempt to share our own beliefs and understandings with them. It is not a simple transfer of meaning, but an attempt to influence others to share our meanings.
- *Communication includes both verbal and nonverbal elements.* Verbal elements (language) both oral and written are an important part of the communication process. However, equally important are the nonverbal aspects such as gestures, facial expressions, tone of voice, eye contact, clothing, time management, and even our surroundings.

The process of communication occurs all around us each day, in a variety of forms. The media communicates messages to us as we gaze at billboards, listen to the radio, watch TV, and read magazines. We chat with friends and kiss romantic partners. We hold business meetings and study sessions with classmates. And, we communicate in a variety of ways with and about family. It is that arena of communication that we turn our attention to in this text.

Why Study Family Communication?

There are a variety of reasons why the study of family communication is vital to understanding our human experience (see Vangelisti, 2004, for additional discussion). The importance of family communication in our lives lies both in the connection between communication and family, and in the connection between family communication and the larger culture.

The relationship between communication and family can be visualized (albeit in a simplified fashion) as a circle (see Figure 1.1).

As we communicate with our family members, we create and reflect understandings of the nature of family life, the expectations that go along with family roles, the rules and standards of family behavior, and who we are as a family. In this way, communication produces our understandings of family and our experiences (positive, negative, and in between) of family. But, that is only half of the circle. In addition to communication creating family, family is also a producer of our patterns of communication. In family settings, we learn how to communicate with those close to us. Family members teach us how to communicate in our earliest years. The patterns that we learn in the family are often then reproduced, to some degree, in other relationships throughout our lives. Thus, family is a product of communication, and communication is a product of family.

The impact of family communication is not limited to our individual family settings, or even to the close relationships we have in life. Family is also connected to the larger social structure. In family settings, we learn about the world, what it is like, what we can expect from it, and what it will expect from us. Families teach us about our "place" in the larger culture. Our parents and adult caregivers communicate to us lessons about what is acceptable behavior and what is not. Family is the first institution of socialization (though it is accompanied by other social institutions such as schools, churches, and media). Family is also connected to the larger social structure because the cultural messages we encounter impact our understandings of what families are and what they should be. When we see particular images of family in the media, or learn about family types in school, we develop understandings of family that impact our own experiences of family life. Thus, the connection between family and social structure is a part of communication *in* and *about* family.

For these reasons, studying family communication (including both communication in and about family) is an important part of social scholarship. Scholars from the field of communication—as well as others affiliated primarily with sociology, psychology, and family studies—have studied these important processes, developing a body of theory as well as research findings. (If you are unfamiliar with research studies, see Appendix A for

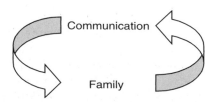

FIGURE 1.1   *Communication and Family Reciprocal Creation*

BOX 1.2 • *Family in the News*

The "baby signs" program, springing from a desire to be able to "speak" to babies sooner than they acquire speaking skills, is a hot topic in the media, featured in magazines, on talk shows, in books, and online. You can read more about baby signs at www.babysigns.com.

a discussion of two prominent perspectives in family communication study and how to read research articles based on those perspectives.) In this text, we consider a variety of family communication issues, including theoretical claims and empirical research that has been conducted by family scholars. To begin, it is important to address how family has been, and continues to be, defined and delineated.

What Is a Family?

- If you were told that you could invite anyone you would like to your college graduation as long as they were family members, whom would you invite? How many people would the group include?
- If you decided to have a family picnic in the summer, whom would you ask? Would you need a lot of sandwiches, or only a few?
- If you won the lottery, and decided that you would share your winnings with your family, whom would that include? How would you decide who got the money?

Looking back on your answers to the previous questions, are all three groups of people you selected the same? For many people, they would not be. The number of people and types of relationships included in each set are also likely to vary widely from person to person. Some individuals would include only parents and siblings in the lottery beneficiaries. Others would also include grandparents, aunts, uncles, or cousins. Some might include close friends they think of as family. The picnic group might include immediate family, extended family, friends, and dating partners. The graduation invitees could be grandparents, siblings, and parents only, or maybe spouses and children, perhaps dating partners, and so on. For any person answering these questions, the composition of the groups is likely to differ from others' responses. All of these differences in what "family" might include point to the difficulty of defining the word *family*.

Defining Is Communicative

To define anything, including family, is a uniquely communicative phenomenon. The communication theory of **symbolic interactionism** states that it is through communication with others that we reach our understandings of any concept, thing, person, and so forth. Once we develop particular meanings, they then impact how we respond to the concepts, things, and people in our environment (Blumer, 1969; Mead, 1934). Thus, as we communicate together about family, and in families, we develop ways of understanding, or defining, family. Those definitions of family then impact how we enact and respond to families, both our own and those of other individuals. For this reason, before discussing the relational practices that occur within family settings, we should begin with thinking carefully about what family "is."

In the next section, we consider various ways of defining family used in four primary domains: medical or biological, legal, scholarly, and personal. We look at the benefits of definitions, as well as what the problematic aspects are (see Table 1.1 for a summary). The

TABLE 1.1 *Definitions of Communication*

Definition	Characteristics	Benefits	Drawbacks
Medical or biological	Defines family on the basis of genetic connection	Allows for study of genetic links to behavioral traits	Restricts family only to those related by blood—limiting
Legal, formal	Defines family on the bases of blood ties or legal ties (marriage/adoption)	Makes it easy to clearly establish family ties for legal issues	Fails to acknowledge familial role of individuals not related by blood or law
Legal, functional	Defines family on the basis of fulfillment of family functions	Places emphasis on familial behaviors rather than legal or genetic ties— broad definition	Creates ambiguity in legal settings; unclear which functions should be used as criteria
Scholarly, traditional	Defines family primarily on the basis of the parent–child unit	Places emphasis on the unit that many individuals view as the most important part of family	Limits consideration of the role of extended family and childfree couples, as well as other groupings
Scholarly, functional	Defines family based on primary functions families fulfill in society	Allows for more cross-cultural comparison and understanding through focus on essential functions	Makes it difficult to fully establish which functions of family are essential and may overemphasize families with children
Scholarly, behavioral or transactional	Defines family by the behaviors that are associated with family groups	Has relatively inclusive focus on behaviors and intimacy building	Makes it difficult to delineate what it means to behave like family, and different behaviors may build intimacy in different cultural settings
Personal	Defines family on the basis of our individual beliefs about who counts as family	Allows for the most variety of family forms—flexible and wide ranging	Makes study difficult as each individual will define family somewhat differently

definitions or types of definitions we consider here will not be exhaustive, merely representative of some of the common ways family is defined. In fact, you should note that these definitions primarily come from twentieth century understandings of family, arising mostly from European and U.S. culture, though some of these views are shared in other cultures. If we were to go back further in time, or delve more deeply into other cultural understandings, we would see many additional understandings of family. As you read this material, begin to develop your own working definition of what family is.

Medical or Biological Definitions

Probably the most restrictive or narrowest way to define family is to use solely biological or "blood" connections. A biological family can be defined by looking at a family tree and tracing the family back through its bloodline. **Biological definitions** of family are principally used in genetic tracing or other medical issues. Researchers and doctors look at how genetic links are implicated in increased risk of breast cancer, manic depression, attention deficit disorder, and other conditions. For physicians or geneticists considering how illnesses may be passed from family member to family member along with genetic material, the biological family is the natural focus.

For research in family communication processes, a biological definition is not the most common. However, some researchers do investigate how genetic traits are related to communication, and how these traits may be passed along family bloodlines. For example, Docherty and colleagues (Docherty, 1993, 2005; Docherty, Grosh, & Wexler, 1996) are interested in the connection between genetic predispositions for schizophrenia and the specific communication patterns that are exhibited by individuals with schizophrenia (for example, disorganized speech and poor sequencing). Other researchers have considered how heredity might be more generally related to communication styles for issues such as verbal aggressiveness, social adaptability, and communication apprehension (Beatty, 2005; Beatty, Marshall, & Rudd, 2001; Horvath, 1995). These scholars use a biological definition of family in order to address communication issues thought to be primarily related to the blood/genetic connection between family members. A scholar studying communication from this perspective might also be interested in the extent to which genetics influence an individual's ability, or desire, to interact with others (what we often call "shyness").

A positive aspect of using a biological definition to define family is the clarity that it has. From this view, it doesn't matter whether individuals perceive themselves, or others, as part of the family. The sole criterion is the blood relationship of the family members and therefore it is easy to define who is "in" a family and who is "out." In addition, for communication study, a biological definition of family allows researchers to focus on genetic influence in communication processes.

Although a biological family definition can be useful in understanding how health issues or communication tendencies follow genetic lines, it results in the omission from "the family" of adoptees, stepparents, and even marital partners who did not procreate within that family line. Biological definitions also may prevent a full consideration of the effects of environmental factors on communication phenomenon. If a study did find that communication reticence (shyness) seemed to be common in particular families, there could be a genetic connection. However, it is possible that family members who share this trait have learned it from each other, rather than passing it along genetically. Thus, biological definitions may seem too restrictive to many researchers.

Legal Definitions

Systems of law are generally quite complicated. Thus, it is probably no surprise that legal definitions of family are diverse and complex. Documents and legal bodies at varying levels have defined family in different ways, across different time periods. How family is defined legally can have serious implications for important family issues like custody of children, inheritance, public services, insurance, and so on. Because legal issues involving family definition vary widely across the world, we will focus on the legal system of the United States in this discussion. However, it is important to understand that legal decisions made in the United States are based on cultural heritage. This means that they are not necessarily any more or less accurate or better than those made in other systems.

Formal.   As discussed in the *Harvard Law Review* ("Looking for a Family Resemblance," 1991), the legal system in the United States has recently taken two primary approaches to the definition of family. The first approach is to use a formal, **traditional legal definition.** This typically means defining family in terms of biological and/or formalized legal connections. One example of this type of definition can be seen in how the U.S. federal government defines families in the census: "A group of two or more people who reside together and who are related by birth, marriage, or adoption" (www.census.gov/dmd/www/glossary/ glossary_ f.html). This definition requires the sharing of a household and either a blood (birth) or formal legal (marriage or adoption) connection between the individuals. In many cases, formal legal definitions do not include the stipulation of shared dwelling, but typically retain the aspects of a marital, adoptive, or blood relationship between the members. This definition is based on a model of the nuclear family as including a married couple and their children.

Functional.   In other instances, the legal system has chosen to adopt a **functional legal definition** of family. Such an approach looks at the functions of a traditional family (economic cooperation, affection between family members, the maintenance of long-term relationships, the rearing of children, etc.) and then uses those functions as criteria for defining family units (Hickman, 1999). The focus is on how the members interact with each other, what they do for each other. Families are groups of people that do the things a family is supposed to do.

A functional approach to family is sometimes used in legal forums when making decisions about particular family groups. For example, if a widowed stepfather and a biological father were debating the custody of a child, this standard or definition might be applied. If the judge decided that the biological father had not "functioned" as a father to the child, whereas the stepfather had, the custody may be awarded to the stepfather. In the same situation, application of a formal traditional definition would result in custody being awarded to the biological parent. It should be noted that the functional approach is typically taken by individual judges or other members of the legal system, and is somewhat rare. At this time, this view of family has not become an extensive part of official legal code in the United States.

Both the formal and functional approaches have benefits and limitations that can impact the lives of families as they take part in legal processes. Formal definitions of family are relatively clear and can be applied with ease across cases and time periods. Additionally, this type of definition places a strong emphasis on the value of marriage, adoption, and blood relation, which is consistent with the moral and ethical beliefs of large segments of the U.S. population.

As indicated by Hickman (1999) and others, the most problematic aspects of formal legal definitions are that they marginalize those individuals who participate in nontraditional family groupings and prioritize the morals and ethics of one segment of society over others. By this definition, if a man lives with a woman and her children for many years, he would still not be considered a part of her family because there is no legal bond. If the couple decides to separate, the "parent" without legal or blood ties to the child may lose all opportunity to interact with that child again and will hold no further responsibility for the care or upbringing of the child.

In legal settings, the primary benefit of the functional approach is its inclusiveness. Individuals who act as a family, yet may not qualify under a formal approach, can be considered a family, with the legal rights and privileges, when a functional definition is applied. For example, a homosexual couple living together and co-raising children would be considered a family when applying a functional definition. They would likely not be considered a family if using a traditional formal definition. This means that those individuals who operate in nontraditional family forms can still receive the legal benefits of family status under a functional definition, which can be very important in issues such as child custody, inheritance, dwelling ordinances, adoption, and divorce settlement.

As noted in *Harvard Law Review* (1991), the difficulty of the functional definition lies in its vagueness. There are no clear guidelines as to which functions of traditional families should be applied to nontraditional groupings in order to define them as families. Individual courts or judicial agents may apply standards very differently, thus resulting in unfair or uneven application of law. Additionally, you need to know a lot about the day-to-day interactions of a family to understand what functions an individual is fulfilling.

As legal environments change, so too do the definitions of family in those settings. One example of this can be seen in the ongoing discussions of same-sex relationships and laws applying to them. As countries and other municipalities around the world respond to issues such as the question of sexuality in family law, formal definitions of family are likely to change.

BOX 1.3 • *Internet Connection*

The American Bar Association provides up-to-date information about family law in the United States on its Web site at www.abanet.org/family/familylaw/tables.html

Scholarly Definitions

Like those in the legal field, scholars who study family often face challenges in their attempts to define it. Anthropologists, sociologists, philosophers, family communication theorists, and others have defined families in various ways in an attempt to reach a definition that covers the essential elements of family.

Traditional.   Some scholars take a relatively **traditional definition** of family. One example of this is provided by Lévi-Strauss (1956), a French social anthropologist:

> Let us try to define the family. . . . It would seem that this word serves to designate a social group offering at least three characteristics: (1) it finds its origin in marriage; (2) it consists in husband, wife, and children born out of wedlock, though it can be conceived that other relatives may find their place close to that nuclear group; and (3) the family members are united together by a) legal bonds, b) economic, religious, and other kinds of rights and obligations; c) a precise network of sexual rights and prohibitions, and a varying and diversified amount of psychological feelings such as love, affection, respect, awe, etc. (pp. 266–267)

In his attempt to delineate what the term *family* means, Lévi-Strauss rooted the definition in the relationship between a married man and woman and their children. Thus, this definition is considered traditional. The bonds between the family members are legal, marital, and genetic.

Another, slightly expanded yet still traditional definition was provided by Murdock, an American anthropologist and sociologist, in 1949:

> The family is a social group characterized by common residence, economic cooperation, and reproduction. It includes adults of both sexes, at least two of whom maintain a socially approved sexual relationship, and one or more children, own or adopted, of the sexually cohabiting adults. (p. 1)

In this definition, Murdock attempts to account for the varying legal forms that may exist in different cultures. Thus, he does not indicate that the adults must be married: rather, he states that their relationship should be "socially approved." In cultures, like the United States, where marriage is the most socially approved type of sexual relationship, you might assume this to be a married couple. Additionally, Murdock allows for the possibility that there might be more than two adults involved in the relationship. This accounts for cultures where polygamy is practiced and families are composed of more than two adults. Although Murdock's definition does not rule out homosexual relationship per se (that is, he does not say that the two sexes need to have sex with one another), his definition does seem to imply that the sexual union is primarily heterosexual. And, the socially approved sexual relationship between the adults and the production or adoption of offspring are still key.

Traditional definitions primarily proceed from the idea of the union between man and woman as the root of family. Such definitions focus on the heterosexual nuclear family (parents and their biological children). They do not typically include others who may reside in or out of the household, such as grandparents, aunts, uncles, and so on. As such, this type of definition is relatively rare in family communication scholarship (Whitchurch, 1993).

In attempts to address the intergenerational nature of family, some scholars turn to other definitions. Beutler, Burr, Bahr, and Herrin (1989) use the term *family realm* to differentiate the family experience from other human endeavors. They define the family realm as

> the realm that is created by the birth process and the establishment of ties across generations. The irreducible parameter of this realm is the biological, emotional, social, and developmental processes that are inherent in the procreation and the nurturing of dependent children. (p. 806)

As you can see from this definition, Beutler et al. widen the scope of family somewhat from the definitions of Lévi-Strauss and Murdock. In defining a family realm, Beutler and colleagues focus primarily on the actions involved in the rearing of children. Therefore, in its focus on the blood or adoptive relationships implied by childrearing, this view does not completely depart from the more traditional definitions. However, this view does include more generations in the "family realm" than the nuclear family referred to by traditional definitions. Additionally, in its focus on the function families perform in the nurturing of dependent children, this definition begins to hint at a more functional view of families.

Functional. Previously, we considered how the legal system sometimes relies on a functional view of families in attempting to define who and what "count" as family. Some family researchers also utilize **functional definitions** in the attempt to delineate family. Murdock (1949), whose traditional definition of family was mentioned previously, also argued that families performed four primary functions: Families act to socialize the young, represent the economic cooperation of members, fulfill the sexual needs of the adults, and result in the reproduction of the species. Murdock argued that, whereas families provide other functions, these four are universal across cultures. Additionally, he claimed that though other social institutions may participate in some of these functions (for example, schools act to socialize children), they are not as important as the family to those functions.

Not all scholars agree with Murdock's claims. In response to his work, Reiss (1965) states that "the family institution is a small kinship structured group with the key function of nurturant socialization of the newborn" (p. 449). "Nurturant socialization" refers to the process of caring for and raising a child and teaching him or her the socially accepted behaviors of the cultures in which he or she exists. Reiss argues that, although families may provide other functions as well (depending on the culture), this is the universal function that defines family. Thus, for Reiss, the family can principally be defined by social groupings that function to socialize children (see also Lerner & Spanier, 1978).

Functional views attempt to define the primary functions that all families perform. This allows the definitions to be more easily applied across cultures, because marriage arrangements, household structures, and so on. vary from culture to culture. However, to designate which functions of family are the most important or most crucial is quite difficult. Additionally, because functional definitions, like traditional definitions, often place a significant emphasis on childrearing, couples that do not have children seem to exist outside the framework of family provided by these views.

Behavioral or Transactional.   In an attempt to avoid some of the pitfalls of both traditional and functional approaches to defining family, some scholars operate from a more **behavioral or transactional definition.** Wegar (2000) argues that a more appropriate way to consider family is to look at how individuals behave toward each other and impact each other. Being part of a family means behaving like a family member. Fitzpatrick and Caughlin (2002) state that transactional approaches consider how the interactions between family members over time stem from and create commitment, intimacy, and family identity. This type of definition allows for a much broader and more inclusive concept of family. Same-sex couples, childfree couples, and large groups of adults living communally with or without children could all be considered family in this approach. What becomes complex about this view is that it requires consideration of what it means to "behave" like family and how various types of communicative interaction may contribute to the establishment of family identity.

Some communication scholars blend together bits and pieces from functional, behavioral, and genetic definitions in an attempt to create an understanding that is more inclusive. An example of this can be seen in Baxter and Braithwaite (2006), where a family is defined as "a social group of two or more persons, characterized by ongoing interdependence with long-term commitments that stem from blood, law, or affection" (p. 3). This definition reaches into the legal realm, acknowledges the blood/genetic realm, considers the interdependent functions of family, reflects the notion of the commitments of behavior that family may include, and also approaches the idea of the highly personal dimension of affection and feelings in how we define family (for similar definitions, see DeGenova & Rice, 2002; Galvin, Bylund, & Brommel, 2004). This is important because, as other authors would argue, our beliefs about who is and is not family, and what family members should and should not do may be highly personal.

Personal Definitions

A variety of authors, including Jorgenson (1989), have noted that family members may define their families differently than theorists or researchers do. In fact, individuals may consider their families to be composed of others who are not related by blood or legal means. Weston (1991) discussed the concept of **families of choice** as applied to homosexual men and women. Weston argued that, often, homosexual men and women are separated from families of origin (the family in which an individual was raised) due to the social stigma of having a gay or lesbian relative. Additionally, they have been generally prohibited from marrying and thus creating a new family. Therefore, gay men and lesbian women select members of their friendship community to function as a sort of substitute family (see also Allen, 1997; Allen & Demo, 1995).

The same phenomenon has been noted in other situations as well. McRae (1992) considers how older men and women select **fictive kin** to replace family members who may not be accessible to them. In retirement communities and nursing homes, older adults form family-like relationships that offer support as well as the opportunity to express affection and provide comfort and care for another. Karner (1998) discusses how health care workers can adopt a family role for the older adults they attend. These workers may take on the role of son or daughter, grandson or granddaughter, to the older adults in their care. In exchange for the care and attention they provide, the older adult provides affection, advice, and encouragement.

The concept of fictive kin has also been applied to understanding the lives of individuals who are homeless. In their study of homeless adolescents, McCarthy, Hagan, and Martin (2002) found that "kin" groups are formed among the street population. These groupings, often designated by use of familial terms like *sister*, *uncle*, *mom*, or *dad*, become replacements for the absent family of the homeless youths. Such associations provide the youths with mechanisms for support, affection, a sense of responsibility, and even increased safety on the streets.

As homeless individuals or gay or lesbian persons may adopt fictive kin because they have been physically or emotionally separated from their families of origin, so too immigrants might form strong familial relationships with people who are not related by blood or legal ties. Ebaugh (2000) discusses the development of fictive kin relationships among immigrant populations. Individuals who immigrate find themselves facing the challenges of a new culture. In many cases, they may have few, if any, family members available to support and aid them through this acclimation process. Fictive kin may then provide that group cohesiveness that is needed.

In addition to the populations mentioned here, fictive kin can be found in many other situations. Perhaps you have a godparent (or more than one). Godparents are ritualized examples of fictive kin. In some cases, godparents may be related by blood to their godchildren, but in other cases they are not. However, once the ritual of godparenting is completed, they may assume a familial relationship to the child. Or, you might have a family friend that you call "Aunt" or "Uncle." That individual is not really related to you, but you have developed a relationship with him or her that seems more similar to a family relationship than friendship.

None of the types of personal families discussed in this section would be adequately accounted for by the many definitions we have discussed in this chapter. This points to the inherent difficulty in defining family. In order to study any social phenomenon, including family and family communication, it becomes necessary to reach some sort of definition of what that phenomenon is. The act of defining something, a truly communicative behavior, is at the root of how we understand and respond to that thing. However, family is not an easy phenomenon to define. Each definition we have studied here has its benefits and its drawbacks. This doesn't mean they don't have utility; it simply means that they aren't perfect. This is partly because of the multitude of family forms that exist throughout the world. And, how we understand what counts as family is deeply embedded in our cultural mores and expectations. Additionally, it is difficult for researchers, theorists, legal agents, and even students like you to separate personalized understandings of family from the attempt to define what family is.

Think back on your answers to the questions at the start of this section. Whom did you select to include in the three events mentioned? How did you make that selection? The answers likely indicate something about how you would define family. As you read the remainder of this text, you will encounter research being done from a variety of perspectives. As you do so, I encourage you to consider the ways in which each author seems to define and discuss family. Think about some of the ways family has been defined in this chapter as they apply to your life understandings and the readings you encounter here. Compare what you read with your own definitions of family and ponder where your definitions come from. Most people would agree that family is vitally important, but like other social concepts including love and friendship and trust, it is sometimes extremely hard to pin down. Perhaps in the end, you will find that a family is simply a group of people who consider themselves to be family and are somehow bound together by that belief.

Questions for Consideration and Discussion

1. What is your definition of family? Who is included and who is left out of your definition?
2. What is an example of how family communication impacted your understanding of the world?
3. Thinking about your most recent family communication encounters, how were both verbal and nonverbal elements important parts of the interaction?
4. How possible, or appropriate, do you think it is for definitions of family to be developed that apply across cultures worldwide? Why?
5. What do you see as the utility (usefulness) of attempting to clearly define family? What do you see as the drawbacks of such an attempt?

Key Terms and Concepts

behavioral or transactional
    definition (scholarly)
biological definition
communication

families of choice
family realm
fictive kin
functional definition (legal)

functional definition (scholarly)
symbolic interactionism
traditional definition (legal)
traditional definition (scholarly)

References

Allen, K. (1997). Lesbian and gay families. In T. Arrendell (Ed.), *Contemporary parenting: Challenges and issues* (pp. 196–218). Thousand Oaks, CA: Sage.

Allen, K., & Demo, D. H. (1995). The families of lesbians and gay men: A new frontier of family research. *Journal of Marriage and Family, 57*, 111–127.

Baxter, L. A., & Braithwaite, D. O. (2006). Introduction: Metatheory and theory in family communication research. In D. O. Braithwaite & L. A. Baxter (Eds.), *Engaging theories in family communication: Multiple perspectives*. Thousand Oaks, CA: Sage.

Beatty, M. J. (2005). Fallacies in the textual analysis of the communibiological literature. *Communication Theory, 15*(4), 456–467.

Beatty, M. J., Marshall, L. A., & Rudd, J. E. (2001). A twins study of communicative adaptability: Heritability of individual differences. *Quarterly Journal of Speech, 87*(4), 366–377.

Beutler, I. F., Burr, W. R., Bahr, K. S., & Herrin, D. A. (1989). The family realm: Theoretical contributions for understanding its uniquens. *Journal of Marriage and Family, 51*(3), 805–816.

Blumer, H. (1969). *Symbolic interactionism: Perspective and method.* Englewood Cliffs, NJ: Prentice Hall.

DeGenova, M. K., & Rice, F. P. (2002). *Intimate relationships, marriages, & families* (5th ed.). Boston: McGraw-Hill.

Docherty, N. M. (1993). Communication deviance, attention, and schizotypy in parents of schizophrenic patients. *Journal of Nervous and Mental Disease, 181*, 750–756.

Docherty, N. M. (2005). Cognitive impairments and disordered speech in schizophrenia: Thought disorder, disorganization, and communication failure perspective. *Journal of Abnormal Psychology, 114*(2), 269–278.

Docherty, N. M., Grosh, E. S., & Wexler, B. E. (1996). Affective reactivity of cognitive functioning and family history in schizophrenia. *Biological Psychiatry, 39*, 59–64.

Ebaugh, H. R. (2000). Fictive kin as social capital in new immigrant communities. *Sociological Perspectives, 43*(2), 189–209.

Fitzpatrick, M. A., & Caughlin, J. P. (2002). Interpersonal communication in family relationships. In M. L. Knapp & J. A. Daly (Eds.), *Handbook of interpersonal communication*. Thousand Oaks, CA: Sage.

Galvin, K. M., Bylund, C. L., & Brommel, B. J. (2004). *Family communication: Cohesion and change (6th ed)*. New York: Allyn & Bacon.

Hickman, L. A. (1999). Making the family functional: The case for legalized same-sex domestic partnerships. *Philosophy of the Social Sciences, 29*(2), 231–247.

Horvath, C. W. (1995). Biological origins of communicator style. *Communication Quarterly, 43*(4), 394–407.

Jorgenson, J. (1989). Where is the "family" in family communication?: Exploring families' self-definitions. *Journal of Applied Communication Research, 17*(1–2), 27–41.

Karner, T. X. (1998). Professional caring: Homecare workers as fictive kin. *Journal of Aging Studies, 12*(1), 69–82.

Lerner, R. M., & Spanier, G. B. (Eds.) (1978). *Child influences on marital interaction: A lifespan perspective*. New York: Academic Press.

Lévi-Strauss, C. (1956). The family. In H. L. Shapiro (Ed.), *Man, culture and society* (pp. 278–286). New York: Oxford University Press.

Looking for a family resemblance: The limits of the functional approach to the legal definition of family. (1991). *Harvard Law Review, 104*(7), 1640–1659.

MacRae, H. (1992). Fictive kin as component of social networks of older people. *Research on Aging, 14*(2), 226–247.

McCarthy, B., Hagan, J., & Martin, M. J. (2002). In and out of harm's way: Violent victimization and the social capital of fictive street families. *Criminology, 40*(4), 831–865.

Mead, G. H. (1934). *Mind, self, and society*. Chicago: University of Chicago Press.

Murdock, G. P. (1949). *Social structure*. New York: Macmillan.

Reiss, I. L. (1965). The universality of the family: A conceptual analysis. *Journal of Marriage and Family, 27*(4), 443–453.

Vangelisti, A. L. (2004). Introduction. In A. L. Vangelisti (Ed.), *The handbook of family communication* (pp. xiii–xx). Mahwah, NJ: Erlbaum.

Wegar, K. (2000). Adoption, family ideology, and social stigma: Bias in community attitudes, adoption research, and practice. *Family Relations, 49*(4), 363–370.

Weston, K. (1991). *Families we choose: Lesbians, gays, kinship*. New York: Columbia University Press.

Whitchurch, C. G. (1993). Designing a course in family communication. *Communication Education, 42*, 255–267.

2

Family Types and Structures

Chapter Outline

Chapter Objectives

1. To understand the basic types or structures of family
2. To learn about significant issues and research findings for each family type
3. To see the diversity and similarity across and between family types
4. To consider three specific examples of research related to particular family types or structures
5. To consider the importance of thinking about family type, as well as the potential drawbacks in utilizing typology
6. To see the role of stereotypes in the creation of your understandings of family types

Section 1: Overview of Family Types and Structures _____

Which of the following apply to your family?

- You were raised by two biological parents.
- You were raised by two adoptive parents.
- You were raised by one parent (biological or adoptive).
- Your parents are married to each other.
- Your parents are divorced.
- Your parent or parents are remarried.
- You have siblings (how many?).
- You have half-siblings (how many?).
- You have stepsiblings (how many?).
- Your parents are in a heterosexual relationship.
- Your parent or parents are gay or lesbian.
- You have cousins, aunts and uncles, and grandparents.
- You have godparents or other nonrelatives that you consider family.

In all likelihood, if you looked at the answers to these questions for the people around you, you would see as many different sets of answers as there are people in the room. This reflects the multitude of family types and structures that exist for people, even within just one classroom. Just as it is difficult to establish a single definition of family that fits all family types, it is also difficult to generate an exhaustive list of family types or structures.

In this chapter, you will read about some of the common typologies assigned to family as it is studied, and some of the research and theories related to those family types and their communication issues. As you read, however, it is important to note that there will be overlap between the categories. There will also be families that are impossible to pin neatly into one category.

This overview section considers intact nuclear families, single-parent families, blended families, gay- and lesbian-parented families, and families whose type or structure does not fit into any of the other categories. Before beginning that discussion, it is important to note the difference between family of origin and family of procreation. Your **family of origin** is the family (or families) you grew up in as a child. Your **family of procreation or cohabitation** is the family that you inhabit as an adult, when you become a parent or develop a long-term committed familial relationship. These two families may be of the same or different types or structures. Additionally, you have an **extended family** composed of family members beyond parents and siblings that may or may not reside with you. Extended families will be considered here as well.

In 1975, Cogswell discussed variant family forms—that is, those families that did not correspond to the traditional image of the nuclear family. Included in the definition of variant families were gay- and lesbian-parented families, and also single-parent families. At that time, these family forms were considered quite unusual. Today, we know that families other than the two-parent biological family are quite common. However, we still seem to consider the "mom, dad, and the kids" family type to be the ideal family within our culture.

Thus, this overview begins with the family type that is most often represented in our media images and idealized notions of what a family is: the intact nuclear family.

Intact Nuclear Families

A study of college students (Ford, 1994) indicated that, when asked what constituted a family, the predominant family form that college students counted was the intact nuclear family. This is probably not surprising. Even though there are many types of family forms, the image suggested by the word *family* still seems to be a mother, a father, and their children. However, even intact nuclear families can be different. Some arise through birth, and others through adoption. In some intact nuclear families the parents are married, and in others they cohabitate. Some families have 1 child; others may have 10. The **intact nuclear family** can be generally defined as a family composed of a married or cohabitating mother and father and their biological or adopted children.

Nuclear families have been frequently studied in family communication because they are seen as the "normal" or usual family. Thus, many of the findings in family communication study have been made largely by studying intact nuclear families (Koerner & Fitzpatrick, 2004). We will return to some of those findings and studies throughout the text. For this section, let's focus on one particular way that intact nuclear families have been studied as an exemplar.

One theoretical approach to studying family communication in the intact nuclear family that has been very influential is consideration of the extent to which a family has a conformity orientation, and the extent to which a family has a conversation orientation (Fitzpatrick & Ritchie, 1994; Koerner & Fitzpatrick, 1997, 2004). Though this approach can be applied to nonintact families, its primary use has been in the study of intact nuclear families.

Conformity orientation refers to how much family members' communication indicates that they share the same beliefs and values. Families who have a high orientation toward conformity tend to downplay conflict. Children in high-conformity-orientation families are expected to obey their parents without discussion. Children in low-conformity families are allowed more flexibility to make their own choices.

Conversation orientation is how much the climate of the family encourages (or discourages) members to participation in communication about many different topics. Families with a high conversation orientation have frequent interaction and discussion of both individual and family activities and decisions. Families with a low conversation orientation tend to exchange less communication, and decisions are made with less family input.

Based on these two orientation scales, families can be divided into four basic categories (Koerner & Fitzpatrick, 2004) (see Table 2.1). **Consensual families** have high conversation and conformity orientation. Although they want to maintain harmony and agreement, they also display an open communication pattern. **Pluralistic families** have a high conversation orientation, but their conformity orientation is low. The families engage in much discussion, but they do not feel the need to agree and parents

TABLE 2.1　*Family Types Model*

	Low Conformity	*High Conformity*
High Conversation	Pluralistic	Consensual
Low Conversation	Laissez-faire	Protective

do not desire as much control over children. **Protective families** have a low degree of conversation orientation, but a high degree of conformity. These families value obedience to parents more highly than open communication. Parents in such families do not feel the need to explain their actions or rules to the children. Finally, **laissez-faire families** have a low conversation orientation and a low conformity orientation. These families maintain a high degree of privacy. They do not communicate with great frequency, or about many topics, and they allow both parents and children much freedom in making their own decisions.

Although these family pattern labels allow us to distinguish between intact families, and see some of the differences within this broad grouping, they do not tell us that one family type is better than another. Each of these family patterns has positive qualities and drawbacks for family relationships and the individual family members. Studying intact nuclear families in terms of conformity and conversation orientations is just one way they can be considered. Additionally, we must proceed with extreme care in making overall assumptions about them. A family with two biological children has likely had vastly different experiences in family creation and enactment than a family with two children who were adopted as preteens. Though the general family category of intact nuclear allows us to group families for study, this does not mean that families within that type are more similar than different. The same is true for other family forms.

Single-Parent Families

Like intact families, single-parent families can be very different from one another. In general, a **single-parent family** is a family comprised of one parent (mother or father) and his or her biological or adopted children. However, within that general definition there are multiple possibilities for the origin of a single-parent family. Some single-parent families occur through divorce or separation; others result from parental death. In these instances, the parents were married or cohabitating at some time in the family's past. Finally, some single-parent families consist of a mother or father who is raising children without ever cohabitating or marrying. This section addresses these single-parent family types and some of the research that has been done regarding them. In some cases, families that are technically intact nuclear or blended may function more like single-parent families on a day-to-day basis, as work or other constraints cause one parent to be separated geographically from the family. In those situations, a family may have characteristics and outcomes similar to both single-parent families and intact nuclear or blended families.

Divorced Single-Parent Families

One of the biggest worries of divorcing parents and others is the effect that divorce has on children. We fear that children may suffer both from the divorce itself (and surrounding conflict) and from not having one parent living in the home.

The general effects of divorce on the child, as well as the parents, are complex. A variety of factors—such as conflict before the divorce, the suddenness of the divorce, postdivorce parental communication, the economic resources available, and the age of the child at divorce—all contribute to the end outcomes. Because of the complexity of the divorce process, this section focuses on research and theory that has accumulated related to the divorced single-parent family itself, rather than the divorce process.

Studies related to divorced single-parent family relationships have resulted in conflicting and complex findings. An example of this can be found in the work of Guttmann and Rosenberg (2003). The authors studied children in intact families, as well as in single-mother divorced families. Their goal was to consider how family status affected emotional intimacy, and how that in turn related to academic, social, and emotional adjustment. The researchers found that the children in intact families, as expected, did seem to be somewhat more adjusted. However, the difference was quite small. The only large difference found was related to the quality of the children's relationships with their noncustodial fathers. In Guttmann and Rosenberg's study, those children from the divorced single-mother families who had low levels of intimacy in their relationship with their fathers were more likely to have difficulties in the psychological, social, and academic areas than children from intact families. The children from divorced families that had good relationships with their fathers did not have more problematic outcomes than those from intact families (see also Amato, 1994). Although this is only one study, it suggests the importance of family relationships and the communication patterns that sustain them, rather than family forms per se, in child outcomes.

Another example of mixed findings can be found in research related to parent and child roles in the single-parent divorced family. Glenwick and Mowrey (1986), Johnston, (1990), and other researchers (for an overview, see Peris & Emery, 2005) argue that one of the problems that may happen when families are headed by a single parent is that the child–parent relationship is disrupted. This happens because the parent begins to communicate with the child more as a peer and confidant, rather than as a child. The child is then driven to act more like an adult, and possibly even take over some of the caretaking in the family. These authors argue that such a role shift may lead to problems for the child (such as psychosomatic physical conditions or poor academic performance). However, in a study of 58 undergraduate students whose parents had divorced, Arditti (1999) found that these young adults generally had close, satisfying, and supportive relationships with their divorced mothers. This study also suggests that when mothers turned to their children for emotional support it was not problematic for the relationship. Instead, it contributed to the sense of closeness and equality. The experiences of these young adults indicates that the caretaking they provided for their mothers had not been detrimental to them (see also Mayseless, Bartholomew, Henderson, & Trinke, 2004).

Some authors suggest that many of the problems that have been seen in divorced families (i.e., social and academic adjustment issues) relate more to economic issues than family status. Single-parent families may experience economic decline after a divorce, and lower socioeconomic status can have problematic effects for children (Afifi & Keith, 2004; Furstenberg, Morgan, & Allison, 1987; Nelson, 1993). Amato and Booth (2001a, 2001b) and other researchers also argue that the negative outcomes that are sometimes seen in divorced families and in future relationships of children from those families may relate more to communication issues such as conflict between parents than the divorce or single-parent family status itself (Afifi & Keith, 2004; Afifi & Schrodt, 2003; Amato & Afifi, 2006; Amato & Booth, 1991). Additionally, causality is often hard to assess. For example, in Guttmann and Rosenberg's (2003) study, negative relationships with noncustodial fathers were correlated to psychological, social, and educational issues. However, it was not completely clear whether some aspect of the divorce led to the negative outcomes (for the child and the child–father relationship), the child–father relationship had an effect on the negative outcomes, or the negative child outcomes impacted the child–father relationship.

Thus, you can see that assessing the effect of divorce and living in a divorced single-parent family is not easy. In all likelihood, the characteristics of the individual family, family relationships, and the communication patterns that occur within that family setting have a large impact on the outcomes. After divorce, the child and parents will communicatively negotiate their relationships through the process of becoming and being a single-parent family. The patterns that develop therein affect the outcomes of being in a single-parent divorced home.

Widowed Single-Parent Families

The loss of a parent through death is likely to have a strong effect on family processes and communication. As in divorce, families going through the process of coping with death have much with which to contend. Grieving processes, anger, and the need to fulfill the functions of the lost parent are bound to create changes in the family.

It might seem that in a family where a death has occurred the outcomes for children would be worse than in families of divorce, due to losing a parent so completely. Biblarz and Gottainer (2000) studied this issue to determine whether single-mother families produced by divorce would fare better, worse, or the same as single-mother families resulting from death of the father. They considered the long-term effects of the family status on the children through adolescence and into adulthood. Based on their analysis, Biblarz and Gottainer concluded that children from widowed single-mother families seemed to fare better than children from divorced single-mother families in educational attainment, occupation, and psychological health. In addition, children of widowed-mother families did not have significantly different results on these measures than children from intact families. In terms of the two types of single-mother families, the authors found no evidence that the mothers themselves were different in terms of health (physical or psychological), values, religiosity, gender roles, or social behavior. Acock and Kiecolt (1989) and Amato and Keith (1991) had similar findings in their comparison of children from divorced and widowed single-parent families. So, why the difference in outcomes?

Biblarz and Gottainer (2000) argue that the source of the difference may be in economic changes that occur after divorce and widowhood. Although both divorce and spousal death can result in a loss of income and reduced opportunities for parent and child, there are more governmental benefits available to widowed parents than to divorced parents. Even if a widowed mother's own income is substantial, her children are still provided benefits through Social Security, based on the income of the deceased parent. This is not the case for divorced mothers. Though they may receive child support, the regularity of child support payments is more difficult to ensure than the regularity of Social Security payments. Thus, our social system may help protect the children of widowed families from some of the outcomes that can result in divorced single-parent families.

Of course, this argument may not be representative of all families after parental death. There are many factors that impact the family, such as the availability of extended family (to help fill in for the missing parent), overall income level, circumstances of the death, general family communication practices, how the family copes with and communicates about the loss, and so on. However, studies such as Acock and Kiecolt (1989), Amato and Keith (1991), and Biblarz and Gottainer (2000) help show how environmental forces contribute to family functioning. What goes on within a family is not just about the family itself. The larger cultural setting in which the family exists has a profound influence on family processes.

Solo Mother or Father Single-Parent Families

Not all families become single-parent families through divorce or separation or the death of a spouse or partner. For some families, only one parent raises the child or children from the start. Some solo-parent families are created through pregnancy, when one of the biological parents does not participate in the family. Other solo-parent families are created through adoption, when a single man or woman decides to raise a child alone. However the family is created, a **solo-parent family** is a family where a parent raises his or her child or children without ever being married to or living with another parent.

As with any other family type, solo-parent families can be very different from one another. The family life of a 16-year-old solo mother is likely to be quite dissimilar from the family life of a 40-year-old solo mother. Issues like economic status, family support, parent education level, and participation of the extended family all contribute to the life of solo parents (Weinraub, Horvath, & Gringlas, 2002). Thus, you can't make any broad generalizations about solo parents.

The influence of contextual factors on the success of solo-parent families can be seen in a study conducted by Mannis (1999). Mannis interviewed solo mothers who had selected to become solo parents, were over the age of 35, and were financially independent. The mothers in Mannis's study all noted that being a solo parent can be difficult. However, while discussing the difficulty of this situation, all of these mothers spoke of the rewards.

BOX 2.1 • *Family in the News*

In 1992, the TV series *Murphy Brown* contained a story line in which the lead character elected to have a baby without being married. Then Vice President Dan Quayle spoke out against the show, indicating that it was contributing to the decline of family values. Today, such a story would likely seem more commonplace.

They all additionally noted that financial security and support (from family and friends) for their choice to become solo mothers were important parts of their happiness and success. Such financial and social benefits are not always readily available to solo parents (see also Weinraub et al., 2002).

Generally, when people think of solo parents, they envision young women or teenagers who become mothers by accident, or older women who choose to single parent. However, men also act as solo parents. In fact, being a solo father may be more difficult in some ways than being a solo mother because of the societal perception that men are less suited to child-rearing than women. Hamer and Marchioro (2002), in their study of low-income African American solo fathers, argue that solo fathers are themselves frequently uncertain about their ability to be full-time parents. Additionally, the fathers in their study found that the culture around them did not support them in this role. For example, employers did not understand that they would occasionally need time off for child care issues. They also often did not receive information indicating the various types of governmental support available to them as single fathers, and when they sought such public assistance, they were met with suspicion. Additionally, these fathers generally did not receive support from the mothers of their children. Even given these problems, all fathers in the sample indicated that they were glad to be parenting their children on a full-time basis. Whereas these fathers experienced difficulties partly because of their low socioeconomic status, Weinraub and colleagues (2002) note that, generally, solo-parent fathers have a better economic position than solo-parent mothers, because of income differentials between men and women. Thus, some of the issues experienced by these African American fathers would not be as likely to impact other solo fathers.

From the studies noted here, it is clear that the choice to solo parent a child or children can be challenging. Contextual factors such as gender expectations, financial security, and the social support of others may make this process easier or more difficult. This finding can also be seen in the research related to other single-parent family types. Identifying overall features and outcomes of single-parent families will never be simple because the internal and external factors affecting the family are part and parcel of the outcomes for family members.

Blended Families

A **blended family** can be defined as a family in which one or more of the children is residing with a stepparent. So, blended families may include biological or adopted children from one or both spouses' previous relationship(s), and biological or adopted children of that couple. The term *blended family* has replaced *stepfamily* in much scholarly research because it has fewer negative connotations and also is more encompassing. *Stepfamily* suggests that all children in the house are being raised by a stepparent, whereas *blended family* represents the reality that there may also be adopted children and biological children of the married couple in the home. Blended family also represents the idea that these families are a bringing together of previously existing family structures. The 2000 U.S. Census indicated that at least 3.2 million households include stepchildren. This means that a minimum of 7 percent of American households are blended family homes. The number from the census, however, may be low because how children were identified depended on who filled out the census form (parent or stepparent). This suggests that there are likely significantly more blended households than indicated by the census.

Blended families are becoming a common part of our lives; thus, study of these family forms has also increased. Much attention has been paid to the difficulties family members may face when adapting to a stepfamily and the factors that may help or prevent that adjustment process. Because blended families bring together two or more families into one new system, this causes adjustments, both major and minor, to be required of the family members. New relationships are created and developed as the blended family comes together, and as it continues across time. Additionally, social beliefs and expectations about blended families, even the use of the term *step* to describe the relationships in blended families, may create negative expectations for new family members (Ganong & Coleman, 1983, 1994). Due to these difficulties, research about blended family has often focused on the processes that facilitate or prevent relational development and adaptation (Hetherington & Stanley-Hagan, 2002).

As a blended family forms, members in it may know varying amounts about each other's histories, beliefs, values, and preferences. The **social penetration theory** of Altman and Taylor (1973) suggests that as we learn more about another person, it becomes easier to communicate with him or her and feelings of relational closeness increase. This was supported by the work of Martin, Anderson, and Mottet (1999) when they looked at the effect of **self-disclosure** (revealing information about the self to others that they would not likely discover on their own) on stepfamily relationships. They found that as disclosure increased, feelings of understanding also increased (see also Golish, 2000). The finding was even stronger for stepdaughters than stepsons. The authors suggest that this relationship could be because disclosure increases understanding. However, it could also be because increased feelings of being understood increase disclosure.

In addition to disclosure of information about self, people in blended families may do other things to attempt to create positive relationships within the family. Ganong, Coleman, Fine, and Martin (1999) consider the behaviors that stepparents engage in to encourage their stepchildren to like them, and to maintain liking once it is created. These strategies communicate a desire for affection and connection. Such behaviors are called **affinity-seeking** and **affinity-maintaining** communication strategies. In their study, Ganong et al. found that some stepparents did not really do much to try to encourage their stepchildren to like them. Although these stepparents were not cruel to their stepchildren, they did not feel it was particularly important to develop a warm relationship with them. A second group of stepparents tried to encourage the children to like them early in the relationship (often before the marriage), but mostly stopped later. The authors argue that these individuals saw themselves as new or replacement parents for the stepchildren. Because affinity seeking is not something that is usually considered a part of parenting, they stopped once they became "official" parents to the children. Finally, the third group of stepparents engaged in affinity seeking both early in the relationship and after the marriage. There was a decrease in the behaviors as the relationship progressed, but they still continued over time.

Based on their research, Ganong and colleagues (1999) argue that stepparents who engaged in continuous affinity seeking had better relationships with their stepchildren, and the stepchildren were more likely to reciprocate the affinity-seeking behaviors. The stepparents who did little to create affinity had the most distant relationships with their stepchildren, and the children were least likely to attempt to create liking from the stepparent. Based on this study, it seems that actively attempting to create and maintain a good relationship in a blended family may have a positive outcome for the family members (see also Hetherington & Stanley-Hagan, 2002).

A variety of factors contribute to the ease or difficulty that a blended family experiences while adapting to the new relationship. Some of the factors may have little to do with the behavior of the family members (things like financial issues, cultural acceptance, and space concerns). Others, like affinity seeking and disclosure, are directly related to how the family members communicate with each other before and after the blending takes place.

Gay- and Lesbian-Parented Families

Gay- and **lesbian-parented families** are those where the parental figures (whether single-parent or a couple) are gay or lesbian. In this section we specifically consider the research related to families where there are two parents living in the home, and those parents are the same sex. Though this family type is certainly less common than the types discussed previously, it is not a rarity in the United States. Census 2000 indicated that over 600,000 families in this country are headed by same-sex parents, and that number is probably lower than the actual count.

Millbank (2003), Patterson (2002), and Allen and Burrell (1996) review and summarize much of the scant research about gay and lesbian families (see also Gartell, Deck, Rodas, Peyser, & Banks, 2005; Golumbok et al., 2003; Vanfraussen, Ponjaert-Kristoffersen, & Brewaeys, 2002). They indicate that people are often concerned about gay/lesbian families and their effects on children; however, based on their analysis of previous research, these authors argue that there is little to suggest that being in a gay/lesbian family is detrimental to the social or psychological development of the child. These authors do note, however, that gay and lesbian families face some challenges that are not present for heterosexual-parented families. Such problems include the legal issues of parenthood and social stigma.

Legal issues can play an important part in the lives of gay- and lesbian-parented families. As of this writing, most states still have policies that discriminate against adoption by same-sex couples, although only Florida has laws that explicitly *forbid* it. More states allow adoption by one gay or lesbian individual. However, this means that the other partner would have no legal parenting right over the adopted child. In some states, it is possible that the second partner can later file for adoption as well. Although these legal issues are outside the family, they can certainly impact family life in terms of stress and fear.

In 2001, the Henry J. Kaiser Family Foundation, a nonprofit organization that primarily focuses on and gathers information about health issues including those related to family life, published the results of a public opinion study about gay and lesbian families. In this study, 40 percent of adults surveyed disagreed with the idea that gay and lesbian couples could parent as well as heterosexual couples, and respondents were evenly split as to whether gay/lesbian couples should be legally allowed to adopt. As we have discussed previously in this text, how we communicate about a concept or issue impacts how we define and understand it and thus how we respond to it. This study suggests that there remains social stigma for gay and lesbian families in the United States, and that stigma is likely to affect life in a gay or lesbian family.

Gay/lesbian parents have to consider the ways that others may respond to them and their children in public settings, in school, and even among extended family.

From the research that exists thus far, there is no evidence that the structure of gay- and lesbian-parented families is harmful to children. However, the legal problems and social stigma experienced by gay/lesbian parents and their children can contribute to stress and other problems for the family members. Research related to gay/lesbian families is ongoing in the communication field, and we will return to this topic in Chapter 8.

Other Family Forms

The list of family forms considered so far is only partial; however, they tend to be the most common family types in the United States. This section addresses two additional family forms that are less common, but still an important part of the lives of many individuals. Of course, this list is also not exhaustive.

Foster Families

A **foster family** can be defined as a state-licensed family unit that provides temporary care for a child whose biological or adoptive parents are unable to care for him or her. Foster care may be short or long term, and may precede a legal adoption. According to the U.S. Department of Health and Human Services, there were more than 130,000 foster families in the United States in 2004. Whereas a foster family may at times represent only a short-term situation for a particular child, the communication patterns can have a long-term impact on the future of the family members.

A study by Vuchinich, Ozretich, Pratt, and Kneedler (2002) indicated that communication in foster families was not significantly different from communication in biological low-risk families (families where children had not previously had elevated levels of behavior problems). However, this study also indicated that there was a correlation between parental negative communication behavior (such as using insults, criticizing, and displaying anger) and child behavior problems in foster families. This means that higher levels of negative communication behaviors from foster parents are associated with higher levels of child behavior problems (and vice versa). This correlation did not exist as strongly for low-risk or at-risk biological families. Although child behavior problems could have led to the negative communication, these authors argue that it is likely that the communication behavior and child behavior affected each other. That is, when children behave poorly, parents or caretakers are more likely to respond negatively, and when parents/caretakers are negative, children are more likely to behave poorly. Therefore, it is important for foster parents to have positive communication with their foster children in order to help decrease or prevent child behavior problems.

In addition to communication that occurs within the foster family setting, communication with the biological (or adoptive) parents is also a concern. The goal of foster care is often reunification with the parents; thus, it is important to maintain that parent–child relationship and the communication between the family members. Leathers (2003) considers the way loyalty to the biological parents, and visits with them, may affect children's adjustment to foster family settings. In a study of 1,999 adolescents (12 or 13 years old) who had been in foster care between 1 and 8 years, Leathers found that increased visitation with the biological mother was related to increased loyalty to her. For most of the children, a high level of loyalty to the biological mother was related to a low level of connection or loyalty with the foster family. However, when these adolescents had a high level of loyalty to both the biological mother and the foster family, it was associated with more emotional and behavioral problems. It is possible that this is because the teens felt some degree of guilt or anxiety about having strong connections to both their foster and biological parents. Though the study did not clearly indicate that this relationship was causal, it does point to some of the difficulty of creating good, strong relationships within the foster family while still maintaining the biological family bonds in hopes of reuniting with that family.

Polygamous Families

Polygamy can be defined as a social system in which an individual has more than one spouse. Thus, a **polygamous family** is composed of more than two parents and the biological or adopted children of those parents. Although somewhat uncommon yet certainly not nonexistent in the United States today, polygamous families have been a frequently occurring phenomenon throughout history and remain a typical family form in more than 800 different societies across the world (Elbedour, Onwuegbuzie, Caridine, & Abu-Saad, 2002). Therefore, most recent studies of polygamous families have been conducted outside the United States.

Polygamy is a common family form in many cultures for a variety of reasons (Elbedour et al., 2002). These include a desire for more children, uneven numbers of men and women in a society, increased socioeconomic status produced by older or adult children becoming part of the workforce (more spouses leads to more children, and more children leads to more family money), and religious beliefs. So, there are many reasons that people may have polygamous family forms, but how do such forms affect the family members? It is somewhat difficult to fully assess this because polygamous families, being less common than monogamous families in most cultures, have been less researched. However, there have been some findings regarding this family form.

One issue that may be a concern in polygamous families is marital conflict and distress (Elbedour et al., 2002). Al-Krenawi, Graham, and Slonim-Nevo (2002) found a higher level

BOX 2.2 • *Did You Know?*

Polygyny (a man having multiple wives) was a sanctioned and promoted practice in the Mormon church (Church of Jesus Christ of the Latter-day Saints) in the nineteenth century, stemming from religious beliefs. However, the practice did not fit in well with U.S. social standards at that time. In the late 1800s, the U.S. government indicated that it would begin seizing temples if the practice continued. The church announced a formal discontinuation of approved polygyny in 1890, though some splinter groups that formed after that declaration have continued the practice.

Learn more at www.lds.org.

of tension and dysfunction in polygamous families and that seemed to be connected to adolescent mental health issues. They argue that this tension may have come from internal disagreements and anger over unequal distribution of resources (primarily among wives in this study). Additionally, mothers in polygamous families may have lower self-esteem, particularly if they feel additional wives have replaced them. This could then affect the self-esteem of the children. Other studies have also indicated that marital problems may be heightened in polygamous families (Elbedour et al., 2002). This does not suggest that polygamy itself is harmful, but, if family functioning is compromised, there may be negative outcomes.

Another issue of concern in polygamous families may be financial stressors (Elbedour et al., 2002). The large size of the family may cause more economic stress. Additionally, the marital partners may have lower education levels, and therefore have more difficulty obtaining secure and financially rewarding employment. Al-Krenawi and colleagues (2002) argue that socioeconomic status and education level of parents may have a large impact on children's educational attainment in polygamous families. Elbedour, Bart, and Hektner (2003) agree that it is not the polygamous family form per se that affects intelligence or academic achievement; rather, it is some of the other factors that may impact polygamous families that then are related to these intellectual outcomes.

Based on their meta-analysis of polygamous family research, Elbedour et al. (2002) suggest that, on the whole, research into polygamous families, although limited, indicates that this family form may face more obstacles, particularly within some cultural settings, than other forms. However, the extent and effect of those obstacles for a particular family are tightly connected to the specific cultural dynamics in which that family exists.

Childfree Families

As discussed in Chapter 1, definitions of family often presume the presence of children in the home (or at least that children were present at some point). However, as you know, not all individuals have or raise children. Some data seem to indicate that the number of adults who select to not have or adopt children has been rising (Downs, 2003; Somers, 1993). Adults living together in a home (married or otherwise) often consider themselves to be family without the presence of children. We often think of having children as a normal or natural part of adulthood (Hoffman & Levant, 1985), but there are many reasons why couples decide to live without children.

Having no children may be a choice made, or it may result from factors outside the control of the adult partners. Some couples may be **involuntarily childfree;** that is, they have experienced infertility issues that prevent birthing a child and are unable or unwilling to adopt a child. Other couples may be **voluntarily childfree,** having chosen not to raise children in their household. There can be many reasons for such a choice that are unique to the particular circumstances of the couple (Weston & Qu, 2001).

Studies have indicated that members of childfree families are no less socially adjusted and happy in their lives generally and in their relationships with their life partners than members of families with children (Callan, 1987; Hoffman & Levant, 1985; Somers, 1993). The reasons for being childfree do seem to have some impact on the outcomes for men and women. Those individuals who are childfree due to infertility may feel less happy with their lives overall than those individuals who are childfree by choice (Cain, 2001;

Callan, 1987). This makes sense because these individuals may see themselves as "childless" rather than "childfree," which certainly makes a difference.

Because most research and scholarship about family communication operate on the presumption that family includes parents and children, the work that you see in this textbook typically does not focus on the childfree family. However, it is important to remember that families that do not have children are still families. Additionally, bear in mind that individuals who elect not to have children may still be fundamental parts of the lives of children around them (whether in professional capacities, via extended family, or through friends).

Extended Family

For most of this chapter we have been considering the family composed of parents and children, the immediate family. However, for most of us this is not the boundary of family. Our extended family consists of grandparents, stepgrandparents, aunts and uncles, cousins, godparents, and in-laws, among others. In this section we consider some of the research related to extended family, with a focus on grandparents as that is the most heavily researched extended family relationship.

The way in which we communicate with and about extended family members is partly about the relationships we have within our particular families. However, extended family patterns are also related to cultural differences (Aaron, Parker, Ortega, & Calhoun, 1999; Georgas et al., 2001; Smith & Drew, 2002). In some cultures, extended family is central to daily life. In others, the immediate family is the focus of daily life and interaction with extended family is more of a rarity. Extended family members may be closer or further away geographically, and relationally as well. For example, Bahr (1994) found that conceptions of grandparents and their roles are different in Native American and Anglo cultures in the United States. Grandparents in Native American culture are expected to be a more prominent part of the day-to-day life of the family and an important part of the childrearing process, whereas for Anglo families, grandparents are generally less participative in the daily activities of raising children.

Family culture impacts how a family understands extended family relationships, and this then affects how those relationships are developed, facilitated, and maintained. In her study of the role of grandparents, Gauthier (2002) notes that how grandparents interacted with their grandchildren was largely dependent on how the parent facilitated or blocked

BOX 2.3 • *Internet Connection*

Many people are interested in researching their extended family history (family tree). Some good places to start researching your genealogy include:

www.ancestry.com
www.familysearch.org
www.freesurnamesearch.com

that relationship (see also Mueller & Elder, 2003; Smith & Drew, 2002). This points to the intergenerational nature of family relationship dynamics.

Because culture is so important in our enactment of family and how we think about and respond to extended family relationships, as cultures change, there may be changes in family enactments as well. In a study of family life in Korea, Yoo (2006) found that, whereas the traditional Korean family had an orientation toward the past and a focus on the role of ancestors, and thus older extended family members were of primary importance, more contemporary urban families focus on future generations instead. Thus, we can see how a cultural shift can create a shift in understanding of family relationships.

Although extended family relationships differ across time periods, families, and cultures, one of the most common functions served by extended family is support. The role of extended family in providing support varies from family to family. However, in many cases, extended family members are relied on to provide some degree of support, whether emotional, instrumental, or both. Block (2002) considers the degree to which a stepgrand-mother's support for a college student is similar to or different from that of a biological grandmother. In her study of 106 college students, Block found that grandmothers continue to be a source of support for their grandchildren into young adulthood. The grandmothers and stepgrandmothers in Block's study provided their grandchildren primarily with emotional support, guidance, and social interaction. Less frequently, grandmothers provided financial support, and part of this may be related to the financial situations of the grandmothers themselves. Although the stepgrandmothers in Block's research did provide support for their grandchildren, it was significantly less than that provided by the biological grandmothers. Block notes that this may in part be due to the parents not fostering a close relationship between their children and stepgrandparents (see also Gauthier, 2002; Smith & Drew, 2002).

At times, extended family may take on even more substantial support roles, such as when grandparents become custodial caregivers for their grandchildren. Kropf and Burnette (2003) note that, as of the 2000 census, over four million children in the United States were living in households headed by grandparents. This does not necessarily mean that the parents were not present in the home as well, but it does suggest that there are a significant number of children in the United States being raised by their grandparents. Additionally, studies have indicated that, for grandparents, taking on a parental role can be quite stressful and problematic for their mental and physical health, social relationships, and financial status (Glass & Huneycutt, 2002; Smith & Drew, 2002). Thus, such behavior is a significant example of the support offered by extended family members.

We have considered a wide variety of family forms, and we haven't even managed a complete list! The possible combinations of family, both immediate and extended, are almost limitless. Although the research and theory suggests that some family types may have issues related in part to their structure, it is also quite clear that what goes on within the family, the family functions and communication patterns, is more predictive of family health and outcomes than the family type.

In Section 2 of this chapter you will read three examples of research related to particular family types, followed by Section 3 which discusses how you might apply the material to your own life. Before you begin reading the research articles, you may wish to take some time reviewing the material in Appendix A for insight about how to read scholarly research reports. Even if you are familiar with such work, you may still find a refresher helpful. The research exemplars chosen for this chapter relate to the material we have already addressed and also represent research about three common family forms you have likely had experience with, either in your own life or in the lives of those close to you. The first study focuses primarily on intact nuclear families and considers how family communication type can be related to the communication competencies of the child or children. The second study considers at single-parent divorced and blended families and addresses issues of coping and resilience, and the third study addresses extended family and the role of grandparents.

References

Aaron, V., Parker, K. D., Ortega, S., & Calhoun, T. (1999). The extended family as a source of support among African Americans. *Challenge: A Journal of Research on African American Men, 10*(2), 23–36.

Acock, A. C., & Kiecolt, K. J. (1989). Is it family structure of socioeconomic status? Family structure during adolescence and adult development. *Social Forces, 68*(2), 553–571.

Afifi, T. D., & Keith, S. (2004). A risk and resiliency model of ambiguous risk in postdivorce families. *Journal of Family Communication, 4*(2), 65–98.

Afifi, T. D., & Schrodt, P. (2003). "Feeling caught" as a mediator of adolescents' and young adults' avoidance and satisfaction with their parents in divorced and non divorced households. *Communication Monographs, 70*(2), 142–173.

Al-Krenawi, A., Graham, J. R., & Slonim-Nevo, V. (2002). Mental health aspects of Arab–Israeli adolescents from polygamous versus monogamous families. *Journal of Social Psychology, 142*(4), 446–460.

Allen, M., & Burrell, N. (1996). Comparing the impact of homosexual and heterosexual parents on children: Meta-analysis of existing research. *Journal of Homosexuality, 32*(2), 19–35.

Altman, I., & Taylor, D. A. (1973). *Social penetration.* New York: Holt, Rinehart & Winston.

Amato, P. R. (1994). Father–child relations, mother–child relations, and offspring psychological well-being in early adulthood. *Journal of Marriage and Family, 56*(4), 1031–1042.

Amato, P. R., & Afifi, T. D. (2006). Feeling caught between parents: Adult children's relations with parents and subjective well-being. *Journal of Marriage and Family, 68*(1), 222–235.

Amato, P. R., & Booth, A. (1991). Consequences of parental divorce and marital unhappiness for adult well-being. *Social Forces, 69*, 895–914.

Amato, P. R., & Booth, A. (2001a). The legacy of parents' marital discord: Consequences for children's marital quality. *Journal of Personality and Social Psychology, 81*(4), 627–638.

Amato, P. R., & Booth, A. (2001b). Parental predivorce relations and offspring postdivorce well-being. *Journal of Marriage and Family, 63*(1), 197–212.

Amato, P. R., & Keith, B. (1991). Separation from a parent during childhood and adult socioeconomic attainment. *Social Forces, 70*, 43–58.

Arditti, J. A. (1999). Rethinking relationships between divorced mothers and their children: Capitalizing on family strengths. *Family Relations, 48*(2), 109–119.

Bahr, K. S. (1994). The strengths of Apache grandmothers: Observations on commitment, culture and caretaking. *Journal of Comparative Family Studies, 25*, 233–248.

Biblarz, T. J., & Gottainer, G. (2000). Family structure and children's success: A comparison of widowed and divorced single-mother families. *Journal of Marriage and Family, 62*(2), 533–548.

Block, C. E. (2002). College students' perceptions of social support from grandmothers and step-grandmothers. *College Student Journal, 36*(3), 419–432.

Cain, M. (2001). *The childless revolution.* New York: Perseus.

Callan, V. J. (1987). The personal and marital adjustment of mothers and of voluntarily and involuntarily childless wives. *Journal of Marriage and Family, 49*(4), 847–856.

Cogswell, B. E. (1975). Variant family forms and life styles: Rejection of the traditional nuclear family. *The Family Coordinator, 24*(4), 391–406.

Downs, B. (2003). *Fertility of American women: June 2002.* Retrieved March 14, 2003, from the U.S. Census Bureau Web site: www.census.gov/prod/2003 pubs/p20-548.pdf

Elbedour, S., Bart, W. M., & Hektner, J. (2003). Intelligence and family marital structure: The case of adolescents from monogamous and polygamous families among Bedouin Arabs in Israel. *Journal of Social Psychology, 143*(1), 95–110.

Elbedour, S., Ongwuegbuzie, A. J., Caridine, C., & Abu-Saad, H. (2002). The effect of polygamous marital structure on behavioral, emotional, and academic adjustment in children: A comprehensive review of literature. *Clinical Child and Family Psychology Review, 5*(4), 255–271.

Fitzpatrick, M. A., & Ritchie, L. D. (1994). Communication schemata within the family: Multiple perspectives on family interaction. *Human Communication Research, 20*, 275–301.

Ford, D. Y. (1994). An exploration of perceptions of alternative family structures among university students. *Family Relations, 43*(1), 68–73.

Furstenberg, F. F., Morgan, S. P., & Allison, P. D. (1987). Paternal participation and children's well-being after marital dissolution. *American Sociological Review, 52*, 695–701.

Ganong, L., Coleman, M., Fine, M. A., & Martin, P. (1999). Stepparents' affinity-seeking and affinity maintaining strategies in stepfamilies. *Journal of Family Issues, 20*, 299–327.

Ganong, L. H., & Coleman, M. (1983). Stepparent: A pejorative term? *Psychological Reports, 52*(3), 919–922.

Ganong, L. H., & Coleman, M. (1994). *Remarried family relationships*. Thousand Oaks, CA: Sage.

Gartrell, N., Deck, A., Rodas, C., Peyser, H., & Banks, A. (2005). The National Lesbian Family Study: 4. Interviews with the 10-year-old children. *American Journal of Orthopsychiatry, 75*(4), 518–524.

Gauthier, A. (2002). The role of grandparents. *Current Sociology, 50*(2), 295–307.

Georgas, J., Mylonas, K., Bafiti, T., Poortinga, Y. H., Christakopoulou, S., Kagitcibasi, C., et al. (2001). Functional relationships in the nuclear and extended family: A 16-culture study. *International Journal of Psychology, 36*(5), 289–300.

Glass, J. C., Jr., & Huneycutt, T. L. (2002). Grandparents parenting grandchildren: Extent of situation, issues involved, and educational implications. *Educational Gerontology, 28*(2), 139–161.

Glenwick, D. S., & Mowrey, J. D. (1986). When parent becomes peer: Loss of intergenerational boundaries in single parent families. *Family Relations, 35*, 57–62.

Golish, T. D. (2000). Is openness always better?: Exploring the role of topic avoidance, satisfaction, and parenting styles of stepparents. *Communication Quarterly, 48*, 137–158.

Golombok, S., Perry, B., Burston, A., Murray, C., Mooney-Somers, J., Stevens, M., et al. (2003). Children with lesbian parents: A community study. *Developmental Psychology, 39*(1), 20–33.

Guttmann, J., & Rosenberg, M. (2003). Emotional intimacy and children's adjustment: A comparison between single-parent divorced and intact families. *Educational Psychology, 23*(4), 457–472.

Hamer, J., & Marchioro, K. (2002). Becoming custodial dads: Exploring parenting among low-income and working-class African American fathers. *Journal of Marriage and Family, 64*(1), 116–129.

Henry J. Kaiser Family Foundation. (2001). *Inside-OUT: A report on the experiences of lesbians, gays and bisexuals in America and the public's views on issues and policies related to sexual orientation* (publication #3193). Washington, DC: Author.

Hetherington, E. M., & Stanley-Hagan, M. (2002). Parenting in divorced and remarried families. In M. H. Bornstein (Ed.), *Handbook of parenting* (Vol. 3, pp. 287–316). Mahwah, NJ: Erlbaum.

Hoffman, S. R., & Levant, R. F. (1985). A comparison of childfree and child-anticipated married couples. *Family Relations, 34*, 197–203.

Johnston, J. R. (1990). Role diffusion and role reversal: Structural variations in divorced families and children's functioning. *Family Relations, 39*(4), 405–413.

Koerner, A. F., & Fitzpatrick, M. A. (1997). Family type and conflict: The impact of conversation orientation and conformity orientation on conflict in the family. *Communication Studies, 48*, 59–76.

Koerner, A. F., & Fitzpatrick, M. A. (2004). Communication in intact families. In A. L. Vangelisti (Ed.), *Handbook of family communication* (pp. 177–195). Mahwah, NJ: Erlbaum.

Kropf, N. P., & Burnette, D. (2003). Grandparents as family caregivers: Lessons for intergenerational education. *Educational Gerontology, 29*, 361–372.

Lansford, J. E., Ceballo, R., Abbey, A., & Stewart, A. J. (2001). Does family structure matter?: A comparison of adoptive, two-parent biological, single-mother, stepfather, and stepmother households. *Journal of Marriage and Family, 63*(3), 840–851.

Leathers, S. J. (2003). Parental visiting, conflicting allegiances, and emotional and behavioral problems among foster children. *Family Relations, 52*(1), 53–63.

Mannis, V. S. (1999). Single mothers by choice. *Family Relations, 48*(2), 121–128.

Martin, M. M., Anderson, C. M., & Mottet, T. P. (1999). Perceived understanding and self-disclosure in the stepparent–stepchild relationship. *Journal of Psychology, 133*(3), 281–290.

Mayseless, O., Bartholomew, K., Henderson, A., & Trinke, S. (2004). "I was more her mom than she was mine": Role reversal in a community sample. *Family Relations, 53*(1), 78–86.

Millbank, J. (2003). From here to maternity: A review of the research on lesbian and gay families. *Australian Journal of Social Issues, 38*(4), 541–600.

Mueller, M. M., & Elder, G. H. (2003). Family contingencies across the generations: Grandparent–grandchild relationships in holistic perspective. *Journal of Marriage and Family, 65*(2), 404–417.

Nelson, G. (1993). Risk, resistance, and self-esteem: A longitudinal study of elementary school-aged children from mother custody and two-parent families. *Journal of Divorce & Remarriage, 19*(1–2), 99–119.

Patterson, C. J. (2002). Lesbian and gay parenthood. In M. H. Bornstein (Ed.), *Handbook of parenting*, (Vol. 3, pp. 317–338). Mahwah, NJ: Erlbaum.

Peris, T. S., & Emery, R. E. (2005). Redefining the parent–child relationship following divorce. *Journal of Emotional Abuse, 5*(4), 169–189.

Smith, P. K., & Drew, L. M. (2002). Grandparenthood. In M. H. Bornstein (Ed.), *Handbook of parenting* (Vol. 3, pp. 141–172). Mahwah, NJ: Erlbaum.

Somers, M. D. (1993). A comparison of voluntarily child-free adults and parents. *Journal of Marriage and Family, 55*, 643–650.

Vanfraussen, K., Ponjaert-Kristoffersen, I., & Brewaeys, A. (2002). What does it mean for youngsters to grow up in a lesbian family created by means of donor insemination? *Journal of Reproductive and Infant Psychology, 20*(4), 237–252.

Vuchinich, S., Ozertich, R. A., Pratt, C. C., & Kneedler, B. (2002). Problem-solving communication in foster families and birthfamilies. *Child Welfare, 81*(4), 571–594.

Weinraub, M., Horvath, D. L., & Gringlas, M. B. (2002). Single parenthood. In M. H. Bornstein (Ed.), *Handbook of parenting*, (Vol. 3, pp. 109–140). Mahwah, NJ: Erlbaum.

Weston, R., & Qu, L. (2001). Men's and women's reasons for not having children. *Family Matters, 58*, 10–15.

Yoo, G. (2006). Changing views on family diversity in urban Korea. *Journal of Contemporary Family Studies, 37*(1), 59–74.

Section 2: Research Examples

Family Communication and Interpersonal Communication Competence

Joy Koesten

> In this article, Koesten considers the relationship between the family communication patterns discussed in Section 1 (related to conformity and conversation orientation) and the development of particular interpersonal communication skills. The communication model she uses in this analysis, although it has often been applied to intact nuclear families, can be applied to families of origin of all types. As you read, consider the extent to which you can see Koesten's findings reflected in your own experiences.
>
> *L.B.A.*

Developing meaningful relationships is a lifelong endeavor and yet none of us are given a handbook at the beginning of our lives that explains what skills we need to possess in order to do just that. Interpersonal relationships (which can generally be defined as ongoing, personal, mutual, voluntary relationships between two or more people) become especially important as an individual enters adolescence (Buhrmester, 1990) and continue to be vital to our success later in life. In fact, interpersonal competence is one of the top five qualities that employers seek in new recruits (Job Outlook, 2003). According to Koerner and Fitzpatrick (2002), much of what an adolescent knows about interpersonal relationships and how to communicate in those relationships has been established by watching family members interact. Although family communication patterns have previously been linked to many other areas important to adolescent socialization, little exploration has been pursued concerning how family communication patterns help or hinder the development of specific interpersonal communication competencies for adolescents. To that end, I decided to conduct a study that would explore these relationships. In addition, I wanted to see if the sex of a person had any bearing on how these communication skills were employed. First, I explain the theoretical foundations that framed my study, explain the variables examined, and discuss the study itself. In addition, I discuss the implications of my findings.

Theoretical Foundations

Because I was interested in exploring the relationship between family communication patterns and how young people learn certain communication skills, it was important to begin with a strong theoretical base. A theory simply helps us explain and understand a phenomenon and a number of theories guided my research: theories about communication, theories about interpersonal communication competence, and theories about differences between men and women.

Three theories of communication were especially helpful in developing the ideas for my study: Koerner and Fitzpatrick's (2002) theory of family communication, Wilson's (1990, 1995) goals–plans–action (GPA) theory, and Berger's (1997) theory of planning. Together these theories help explain how adolescents begin to formulate successful and meaningful relationships.

Koerner and Fitzpatrick's (2002) theory posits that as family members interact, individuals within the family develop mental maps, or schema, about how certain relationships "work." Their framework defines three specific levels of relational schema: general social schema (the most general social schema), relationship-type schema (for example, romantic relationships or sibling relationships), and relationship-specific schema (such as the individual's relationship with his or her mother, or father). Once these schemas begin to develop, the individual can draw from various pools of information stored in his or her cognitive map to make sense of interactions that have already occurred (i.e., "I forgot that Mom doesn't like surprises; I won't do that again") and to guide them through future interactions (i.e., "Mom's birthday is next week; maybe I'll ask her to go to dinner with me"). As young people continue to interact with family members, they also begin to formulate goals and plans for future interactions with people outside their family (Koesten, 2004). These interactions help adolescents create what Spitzberg (2003) calls an anticipatory mind-set, which Spitzberg says is fundamental to becoming competent communicators. Spitzberg argues that competent communicators should be able to understand and anticipate what will happen to them and the other person if they choose one action over another. Additionally they should be able to employ the best strategy in their response so that they can ultimately achieve their own communication goal (Spitzberg, 2003).

A second set of theories that shaped my study centered on what constitutes "competent" communication for adolescents. According to a number of GPA theories, people form relevant interaction goals for each situation they encounter. They then enact those goals, monitoring and adjusting their subsequent plans according to how the person they are interacting with responds. The more competent communicators are, the more adaptive they are to the responses of the individual they are interacting with and the more options they have to draw on for planning future interactions. Wilson (1990, 1995) argues that people store specific cognitive rules in their long-term memory. These rules are linked to a wide variety of interaction goals and situations the individual might encounter. Extending this idea, Berger's (1997) theory of planning posits that people not only formulate strategic plans for interactions, but they also develop fluidity for maneuvering within a situation as it becomes more and more complex. These contingency plans for action, or mental representations of goal-directed action, prepare the individual for multiple options should they encounter a more complex communication environment. From these fundamental ideas, I speculated that family communication patterns should shape this anticipatory mind-set, setting the stage for a person's abilities to engage in future interactions.

In her research, Samter (2003) identifies a number of specific communication skills that are particularly important for developing successful adolescent relationships. The ability to initiate interactions and relationships is a prerequisite for developing successful relationships.

Without this fundamental skill adolescents aren't likely to assimilate into new groups where they can develop new relationships. The ability to disclose personal information is another important skill necessary to develop close relationships. Self-disclosure can allow individuals to enhance their relational intimacy with other people; it can also cause irreparable harm or create unnecessary tension if people reveal unnecessarily hurtful information for no apparent reason (Bochner, 1982; Parks, 1982; Pawlowski, 1998). Consequently, managing this communication skill is critical to developing relationships that can provide support in times of crises.

In order to maintain a healthy relationship, it often becomes necessary to be able to tell someone that you are unhappy with something he or she has done. So the ability to assert your personal rights and displeasure with someone is another important communication skill necessary for maintaining healthy and successful relationships. Additionally, the ability to offer comfort to others is important to developing relationships. Comforting strategies are attempts to use communication in an effort to alleviate or soothe someone in a state of distress. The ability to use comforting strategies has been determined to be an important influence in a person's social adjustment and social acceptance (Burleson, 1984; Kunkel & Burleson, 1999). So being a friend who can listen empathically to another's concerns and offer emotional support when appropriate is a critical skill when someone you care about needs help to manage life's ups and downs. Finally, the ability to manage conflict is another important communication skill necessary for successful relationships. Studies have indicated that the ability to articulate ideas and argue constructively dramatically improves problem solving and results in less verbal and physical aggression (Rancer, Whitecap, Kosberg, & Avtgis, 1997).

As you can see, the core competencies required for developing and maintaining successful relationships during adolescence are not simple skills—especially when you consider that not only do the goals in each interaction change, but each person and each situation encountered is different. Consequently, in order to be truly competent communicators, adolescents need a broad repertoire of communication strategies from which they can draw. Based on this assumption, I speculated that individuals coming from a family where they had many opportunities to develop a broad range of communication skills would be more likely to develop these five core competencies and to be able to employ them with both same-sex friends and romantic partners.

In addition to these theories, a number of studies have offered evidence that supports the idea that men and women have different expectations about interpersonal relationships and that they engage in different communication skills depending on the sex of the person they are interacting with. Consequently, these studies formed a theoretical base of understanding about differences between men and women as they relate to interpersonal relationships, which shaped my study as well. Although sex and gender cannot be completely separated, many people who study differences between men and women make the distinction that sex differences have to do with biological sex (male versus female) and gender differences have to do with socially constructed norms of behavior for men and women (masculine versus feminine). In my study, I was concerned only with whether the subject identified himself or herself as a man or woman. Based on prior research on sex differences, I speculated that men and women would employ different communication strategies depending on their family communication environment and depending on the sex of the relational partner.

Instruments for Measurement of Constructs

In order to measure these different constructs (family communication patterns, communication competence, and sex differences), I had to find survey instruments that had been previously used to measure each construct and found to be reliable as assessed by Chronbach's alpha. Scores for scale reliability range from zero (meaning the items measuring the construct are not related at all to one another) to 1.0 (meaning the items are perfectly related to one another). For the first construct of family communication patterns I used the Revised Family Communication Pattern (FCP) scale (McLeod & Chaffee, 1972; Ritchie & Fitzpatrick, 1990). The Revised FCP scale (Ritchie & Fitzpatrick, 1990) consists of 15 statements that measure an individual's perceptions that his or her family communication is conversation oriented and 11 statements that measure an individual's perceptions that his or her family communication is conformity oriented (see the discussion in Section 1 of this chapter). Individuals completing the 26-item measure get two scores, one for the degree to which they perceive their family communication patterns as conversation oriented and one for the degree to which they perceive their family communication patterns as conformity oriented. These two dimensions are not mutually exclusive, but the tendency is that as the score for conversation orientation goes up the score for conformity goes down, and vice versa. For this study, Chronbach's alpha was computed to be .89 for the 15 statements relating to conversation orientation and .71 for the 11 statements relating to conformity orientation.

For the second construct of communication competence, I used the Interpersonal Competence Questionnaire (ICQ), which was developed by Buhrmester, Furman, Wittenberg, and Reis (1988). The ICQ allowed me to measure the five specific interpersonal communication competencies relevant to adolescent development for relationships with same-sex friendships and romantic partnerships. The subject is asked to respond to 40 questions describing common interpersonal situations by indicating how comfortable he or she is in each situation (uncomfortable to extremely comfortable). The five competencies measured include the ability to initiate a relationship, the ability to assert displeasure with others, the ability to disclose personal information, the ability to offer emotional support to others, and the ability to manage conflict. Reliabilities for each of these competences ranged from .79 to .86. Each question is answered twice, once for a same-sex friend and once for a romantic partner. Consequently each subject ends up with 10 scores, 5 for competencies with same-sex friends (SSF) and 5 for competencies with romantic partners (RP).

Finally, to account for sex differences, I simply coded the male subjects as a "zero" and the female subjects as a "one" to differentiate between the two. This meant that I had 13 distinct variables to test in this study: 3 independent variables (the conversation orientation score, the conformity orientation score, and the sex of subject variable) and 10 dependent variables (5 scores for competencies relating to ICQ-SSF and 5 scores for competencies relating to ICQ-RP).

Analysis

The students who participated in this study were all enrolled in undergraduate communication courses at a large midwestern university; 169 were women and 130 were men. The subjects were between the ages of 18 and 25 ($M = 20.82$, $SD = 1.61$). Each subject completed both the FCP and the ICQ scales, and answered some demographic questions. Because this was a quantitative study, all data were entered into the SPSS statistical program (Green, Salkind, & Akey, 2000) to conduct the appropriate statistical analyses.

Correlations

My first task was to explore whether there were any statistically significant relationships between the 13 variables, so Pearson product-moment correlation coefficients were computed among these variables using SPSS. Pearson product-moment correlation simply tests the difference between two mean scores to see if there is a relationship. A correlation of 0 would indicate that there is no relationship between the two variables; a correlation of 1 would indicate a perfect relationship or that the two variables measure the exact same thing. In this study a number of important statistically significant relationships were revealed. First, sex of subject was correlated with family communication patterns. Men (coded 0) reported higher scores of conformity orientation ($-.20$), whereas women (coded 1) reported higher scores of conversation orientation (.20). Both relationships are relatively small, but they do support the notion that men and women interact differently within their families. We are unable to discern, however, why these differences exist based on data from this study. Additional correlational findings relating to the sex of the subject included that women were more likely to report being comfortable with asserting personal rights and displeasure with someone of the same sex (.13), whereas the men in this study were less likely to report the ability to self-disclose ($-.30$), offer emotional support ($-.40$), or manage conflict ($-.19$) with a same-sex friend.

The correlational analysis also revealed that as an individual's conformity-oriented score increased, regardless of sex, his or her ability to offer emotional support ($-.14$) and manage conflict ($-.21$) with a same-sex friend diminished. Conversely, as conversation-oriented scores increased, regardless of sex, an individual's perceived ability to employ all five skills with a same-sex friend increased (correlations ranged from .13 to .28). Finally, the analysis revealed that the five interpersonal competencies had statistically significant positive relationships with each other, indicating that as one skill increases, so too do the other skills.

Similar analyses were conducted to examine the relationships for FCP, sex of subject, and the ICQ scores for romantic partners. As in the first analysis, men were more likely to report their family communication patterns as conformity oriented ($-.20$), whereas women were more likely to report their family communication patterns as conversation oriented (.20). In this second analysis, however, men were less likely to be able to offer emotional support ($-.20$) to their romantic partners. There were no statistically significant relationships between the conformity-oriented scores and any of the five competencies relating to romantic partnerships. The conversation-oriented score, however, had statistically significant positive relationships (ranging from .12 to .23) with all five competencies related to romantic partners, indicating that as an individual's score on conversation orientation increased, regardless of sex, his or her ability to employ these five skills with a romantic partner increased.

Family Communication Patterns and Sex of Subject as Predictors of ICQ

The discovery of these statistically significant relationships led me to explore the data further. Because I was interested in how family communication patterns and the sex of the subject interacted to influence one's ability to employ certain communication skills, I needed to conduct a series of multiple regression analyses to see which variable was the stronger predictor of whether an individual would garner these skills. Multiple linear regression analysis allows us to test the relationship between the mean scores of two or more predictor variables and one dependent variable. Specifically, I wanted to find out if I could predict the extent to which each interpersonal competency could be attributed to family communication patterns, sex of subject, or to a combination of these variables. In order to conduct such an analysis, however, I first had to create four new variables that would account for the interaction effect of family communication pattern and sex of subject. I created these new interaction variables by multiplying each set of scores together. The four new variables were sex and conversation orientation; sex and conformity orientation; conversation and conformity; and the three-way interaction of sex, conversation, and conformity. Additionally because these variables were already correlated, the new scores had to be "centered" to reduce problems of multicollinearity (Cohen, Cohen, West, & Aiken, 2003). Now I could examine the unique relationship of each domain of interpersonal competence with each of the seven predictor variables. A total of 10 regression analyses were conducted. In each analysis the seven predictor variables (i.e., the three original predictor variables, the three two-way interaction terms, and the three-way interaction term) were regressed onto one of the 10 competency scores (dependent variables).

Regression analyses revealed a number of statistically significant predictive relationships, based on the adjusted R^2 and beta (β) weights of each analysis. In a regression analysis, the adjusted R^2 indicates the overall strength of the predictive model. Then, by exploring the beta weights you can determine which variable carries more weight in the prediction equation. The higher the beta weight, regardless of whether it is positive or negative, the more important that specific variable is (in relationships to the other variables in the model) for predicting a specific outcome. In this case, I was interested in understanding which variable or variables were most influential in predicting communication competence in same-sex friendships and romantic partnerships. The predictive strength of the seven variables combined (R^2) on the five competencies for same-sex friendships ranged from 7% to 24%, meaning that in some cases the combined variables were less powerful predictors than in other cases. The key to understanding regression analyses, however, is to examine the overall pattern of your findings. In this study, two important patterns emerged. For relationships with same-sex friends, sex of subject was more important to gaining the ability to self-disclose ($\beta = .23$), to offer emotional support ($\beta = .35$), and the ability to assert displeasure with others ($\beta = .21$) than any other variable. In only one case was family communication patterns a stronger predictor and that was in the model analyzing the ability to manage conflict. In this analysis, conformity orientation emerged as the stronger predictor ($\beta = .21$). Individuals growing up in a conformity-oriented family were less likely to report having this skill in same-sex friendships. Whereas the ability to initiate a same-sex friendship was predicted by the overall regression model, no one variable emerged as a stronger predictor than the others.

The predictive strength of the seven variables combined (R^2) on the five competencies for romantic partnerships ranged from 7% to 12%, indicating that the same set of predictor variables were weaker when it came to explaining how individuals gained competencies relating to romantic partnerships. Relative to the other variables, however, family communication patterns (conversation orientation) were more important in predicting the ability to self-disclose ($\beta = .23$) and the ability to assert displeasure with others ($\beta = .25$) in romantic partnerships. With regard to the ability to offer emotional support, sex of subject made a more important contribution to the prediction ($\beta = .15$). The ability to manage conflict in a romantic relationship, however, was best predicted by the interaction of sex and conformity orientation ($\beta = .21$). Men growing up in a conformity-oriented family were less likely to develop this skill. Similar to the analyses on same-sex friendships, the ability to initiate a romantic partnership was predicted by the overall regression model, but no one variable emerged as a stronger predictor than the others.

It is important to remind you here that this study was focused on sex differences (i.e., male versus female), not gender differences and that I had speculated that men and women would use different communication strategies depending on their family communication environment and depending on the sex of the relational partner. To examine that notion additional tests were needed.

Communication Competence and Sex of Relational Partner

Because the regression analyses confirmed sex of subject did influence interpersonal competence in some interesting ways, I wanted to explore even further by conducting a test that would allow me to discern whether individuals used interpersonal skills differently depending on the sex of his or her relational partner. Using sex of subject as the independent groups factor, I performed a 2×2 mixed analysis of variance (ANOVA). The five subscales of the ICQ served as the dependent variables. A number of interesting sex-of-subject by sex-of-partner interactions were present (see Figure 2.1). Both men and women were more comfortable initiating relationships with people of the same sex rather than people of the opposite sex. Men reported being more comfortable asserting displeasure with a same-sex friend, whereas women reported being more comfortable asserting displeasure with a romantic partner. Men reported being more comfortable self-disclosing to a romantic partner, whereas women reported being more comfortable self-disclosing to a same-sex friend. Overall, women were more likely to report the ability to offer emotional support than were men, regardless of the type of relationship. Additionally, men reported being more comfortable offering emotional support to a romantic partner, whereas women reported being more comfortable offering emotional support to a same-sex friend. Finally, men reported being more comfortable managing conflict with a romantic partner, whereas women reported being more comfortable managing conflict with a same-sex friend.

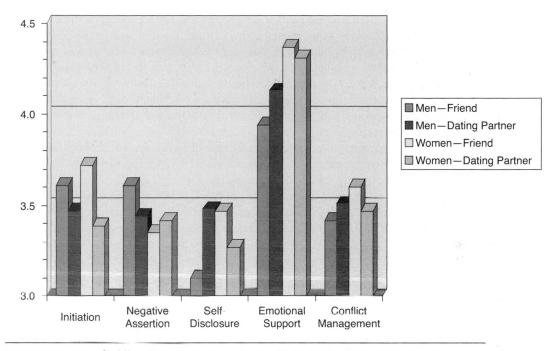

FIGURE 2.1   *Level of Comfort with Communication Skills for Same-Sex Friend and Cross-Sex Dating Partners.*

Conclusion

This study clearly demonstrates that family communication and sex of subject influence how the individuals develop and employ certain interpersonal communication skills. These findings have important implications for both personal satisfaction and healthy relationship building. Here and elsewhere there is considerable evidence that a conversation-oriented family communication environment is the optimal environment for adolescent development. Families who encourage lots of discussion and who encourage many opinions are more likely to raise individuals who possess a broad range of communication strategies that they can use with others they encounter in the future. This may be especially important considering the findings of another study (Koesten & Anderson, 2004) which discovered that interpersonal communication competence was linked to certain risk behaviors (e.g., drinking, smoking, and sexual behavior). The data were not conclusive, but they did shed light on an important idea: managing risk behavior is inherently an interpersonal task. This line of reasoning has been substantiated by others in the communication discipline. For example, Alberts, Miller-Rassulo, and Hecht (1991) found that a young person typically receives offers to drink alcohol or smoke marijuana from friends either at home or in social situations. In fact, the authors found that 81% of the persuasive offers to consume controlled substances and 95% of the offers to consume alcohol came from either friends or acquaintances. With friends like that, young people today need to be armed with a broad range of communication strategies that will allow them to say no and at the same time continue to function within their peer group.

The question becomes this: How does a parent successfully create and maintain a conversation-oriented communication environment? Most parents are not equipped to continuously negotiate new boundaries and ideas with their adolescents over the course of adolescent development; parental communication skills are limited too. In order to engage in the type of open-ended discussion that encourages pluralistic thinking, parents have to relinquish certain types of control while providing boundaries and guidelines that will keep adolescents safe and aware of consequences for their choices. In a world where there are so many outside influences and threats, it's much easier for parents to simply say no to a request that pushes beyond their comfort level. Yet, those are exactly the type of negotiations that broaden adolescents' understanding of relationships and the world around them, broadening their relationship schema in general and building a repertoire of possible communication goals and plans for future interactions. These are developmental skills that are required in today's rapidly moving world and without a broad repertoire of communication skills, it's unlikely that adolescents will be fully equipped to interact with others successfully as they mature.

Questions for Consideration and Discussion

1. Koesten found that a higher conformity orientation in families was associated with less comfort managing conflict with friends and romantic partners. What might be the cause of this relationship?
2. In this study, a higher conversation orientation was associated with a greater comfort self-disclosing to romantic partners and expressing displeasure. Why might this be the case?
3. Koesten's work revealed that both men and women were more comfortable initiating conversations with same-sex friends than with romantic partners. What cultural expectations might be related to this finding?
4. For these respondents, men were more comfortable self-disclosing and managing conflict with romantic partners, whereas women were more comfortable self-disclosing and managing conflict with same-sex friends. Does this resonate with your experiences? If yes, what might be the reasons for these findings? If no, why do your experiences diverge from these findings?
5. This study was completed with a subject group of 299 undergraduate students (between 18 and 25 years of age) at a large midwestern university. What limitations does this sample suggest for the generalizability of this study, and why?

References

Alberts, J. K., Miller-Rassulo, M., & Hecht, M. L. (1991). A typology of drug resistance strategies. *Journal of Applied Communication Research, 19*, 129–151.

Berger, C. R. (1997). *Planning strategic interaction: Attaining goals through communication action.* Mahwah, NJ: Erlbaum.

Bochner, A. P. (1982). On the efficacy of openness in close relationships. In M. Burgoon (Ed.), *Communication yearbook* (Vol. 5, pp. 109–124). New Brunswick, NJ: Transaction Press.

Buhrmester, D. (1990). Intimacy of friendship, interpersonal competence, and adjustment during preadolescence and adolescence. *Child Development, 61,* 1101–1111.

Buhrmester, D., Furman, W., Wittenberg, M. T., & Reis, H. T. (1988). Five domains of interpersonal competence in peer relationships. *Journal of Personality and Social Psychology, 55*(5), 991–1008.

Burleson, B. R. (1984). Age, social-cognitive development, and the use of comforting strategies. *Communication Monographs, 51*, 140–153.

Cohen, J., Cohen, P., West, S. G., & Aiken, L. S. (2003). *Applied multiple regression/correlation analysis for the behavioral sciences* (3rd ed.). Mahwah, NJ: Erlbaum.

Green, S. B., Salkind, N. J., & Akey, T. M. (2000). *Using SPSS for Windows: Analyzing and understanding data* (2nd ed.). Upper Saddle River, NJ: Prentice Hall.

Job Outlook. (2003). *Jobweb.* Retrieved June 26, 2003, from www.jobweb.com/joboutlook/outlook2.htm

Koerner, A. F., & Fitzpatrick, M. A. (2002). Toward a theory of family communication. *Communication Theory, 12,* 70–91.

Koesten, J. (2004). Family communication, sex of subject, and interpersonal competence. *Communication Monographs, 71*(2).

Koesten, J., & Anderson, K. (2004). Exploring the influence of family communication patterns, cognitive complexity, and interpersonal communication competence on adolescent risk behavior. *Journal of Family Communication, 4*, 99–121.

Kunkel, A. W., & Burleson, B. R. (1999). Assessing explanations for sex differences in emotional support: A test of the different cultures and skill specialization accounts. *Human Communication Research, 25*, 307–340.

McLeod, J. M., & Chaffee, S. H. (1972). The construction of social reality. In J. Tedeschi (Ed.), *The social influence processes* (pp. 50–59). Chicago: Aldine-Atherton.

Parks, M. R. (1982). Ideology of interpersonal communication: Off the couch and into the world. In M. Burgoon (Ed.), *Communication yearbook* (Vol. 5, pp. 79–107). New Brunswick, NJ: Transaction Press.

Pawlowski, D. R. (1998). Dialectical tensions in marital partners' accounts of their relationships. *Communication Quarterly, 46*, 396–412.

Rancer, A. S., Whitecap, V. G., Kosberg, R. L., & Avtgis, T. A. (1997). Argumentativeness and argumentative behavior in adolescents. *Communication Education, 46*, 273–286.

Ritchie, L. D., & Fitzpatrick, M. A. (1990). Family communication patterns: Measuring intrapersonal perceptions of interpersonal relationships. *Communication Research, 17*, 523–544.

Samter, W. (2003). Friendship interaction skills across the life span. In J. O. Greene and B. R. Burleson (Eds.), *Handbook of communication and social interaction skills,* (pp. 637–684). Mahwah, NJ: Erlbaum.

Spitzberg, B. H. (2003). Methods of interpersonal skill assessment. In J. O. Greene and B. R. Burleson (Eds.), *Handbook of communication and social interaction skills* (pp. 93–134). Mahwah, NJ: Erlbaum.

Wilson, S. R. (1990). Development and test of a cognitive rules model of interaction goals. *Communication Monographs, 57*, 81–103.

Wilson, S. R. (1995). Elaborating the cognitive rules model of interaction goals: The problem of accounting for individual differences in goal formation. In B. R. Burleson (Ed.), *Communication yearbook* (Vol. 18, pp. 3–25). Thousand Oaks, CA: Sage.

Strong Families' Use of Communicative Coping in Postdivorce Families

Tamara D. Afifi

> Afifi's work presented here is related to two of the types of families discussed in Section 1: single-parent families from divorce, and blended families. Rather than taking a deficit approach (focusing on what is problematic about the divorce process for families), she focused on the communication strategies engaged in that make families stronger after divorce. Whether you have experienced divorce in your own family life, or just observed the process in someone else's family, as you read ponder whether you see the communication strategies she discusses in that family, and how those strategies seem to be related to family outcomes.
>
> *L.B.A.*

When I was still young, my father began having an affair with a woman at his workplace. My mother found out, and my parents got counseling, but my father didn't seem to want to be married. He wanted to be free to do his own things. The marriage was dead, and had almost no chance for revival. So my father decided to leave, and my mother decided to hold him to his word. On a December day of my third-grade year, my father rented a U-Haul truck and moved his pitifully few possessions to an apartment several blocks away. I didn't understand what impact his absence would have on my life. It was almost a relief from some of the tension that had been wearing at our nerves for the past several months. So my mother got the house, the car, and the kids, and my father got his freedom and a lot of regret.

Those first few years, adjusting to life as a single-parent family, were very difficult. We all struggled with emotional baggage and confusion, wondering how to right a world that had been turned upside down. My fourth-grade year was the worst of my life, being fatherless and friendless. I learned about pain that year. I learned, as I would cry myself to sleep, what it meant to be hurt, what it meant to be poor in spirit. . . . I grew up fast those first years of the separation and it changed me forever.

One of the things I will always be thankful for is the way my mother took care of us all. She joined the workforce after being a homemaker for twelve years, left alone with four children, all under thirteen. She went to church for our sake even when she didn't feel like it, waited up for us more times than I can count, insisted on meeting my first date before I went out, and always kept a supply of jokes on hand. My mother taught me about sacrifice, about giving because of love. She read stories and books to us, forced us to practice piano, and made me eat enough liver and red beets to conquer my anemia. She came to a myriad of concerts and recitals, always encouraging, always listening carefully to offer her most thorough advice.

My family has had its ups and downs, as all families do, some being more traumatic than others. But I would not trade this family, my family, for anything in the world. I wouldn't even trade my father, who is still distant. My family has taught me about pain, about struggling, but I have also learned from them loyalty and love. They have given me roots, lifelong friends, protectors, and mentors, and I am forever their debtor.

—Dana, a 17-year-old girl writing about her parents' divorce

As a researcher who studies and talks with a lot of families in their homes or in the lab about their divorce, I have a lot of vivid memories of their divorce accounts. Everyone's experience is unique and is usually filled with both pain and a sense of renewal. As this letter (that was written for a school assignment) from one of my participants illustrates, divorce is a heart-wrenching process and one that has a rippling effect on the whole family. Even though divorce has become very common in our society, one has to be careful never to dismiss the pain and sadness that comes with it. Divorce is often a very stressful experience that influences everyone involved. You most likely have friends whose parents are divorced or your own family may have experienced a divorce. If so, you probably know how stressful it can be and how much it can challenge the very essence of family relationships.

As Dana pointed out in her letter, one of the reasons that divorce is so stressful is because a family's everyday life is turned upside down and everyone is forced to cope with a lot of different stressors simultaneously. Some of these stressors include a decrease in income, less time spent with one another, balancing new rules and roles between households, moving to a new neighborhood, the loss of social networks, uncertainty and loss regarding one's relationships and family, and conflict (Afifi & Keith, 2004; Afifi & Schrodt, 2003a, 2003b; Amato, 2000; Hetherington, 1993, 1999; Lamb, Sternberg, & Thompson, 1999). Because many of these stressors affect the whole family, family members must learn how to communicate with one another and cope with them together in order to function effectively.

Although divorce is often a stressful experience, most families learn to function quite well and many even grow from it. As Dana's letter also illustrates, even though it takes time and a lot of perseverance, many families learn to thrive in the face of adversity. Other families have a more difficult time with the divorce. For instance, you may know some friends who say that their parents' divorce had a devastating impact on them and still does many years later. You may have other friends, however, who think that the divorce was the best choice for their family because their parents get along better now than they did when they were married. Research indicates that individuals vary considerably in how they respond to divorce, with some experiencing long-term difficulties from which they may never recover and others faring better after divorce because they are removed from a conflict-ridden home environment (Amato, 2000; Hetherington, 1993, 1999). Just as there is significant diversity in how individuals cope with divorce, there is also diversity in how different families cope with divorce. Some families suffer considerable losses and experience a lot of difficulty adapting to divorce. Other families are able to adapt more easily to it and learn to thrive from the challenges they face.

Many times we also focus so much on the negative aspects of divorced families that we forget about the behaviors and practices that make them function effectively (Coleman, Fine, Ganong, Downs, & Pauk, 2001; Golish, 2003). Just as many people in the general public tend to associate divorce (and stepfamilies) with negativity, so do many scholars. Researchers often adopt what Ganong and Coleman (Coleman, Ganong, & Fine, 2000; Ganong & Coleman, 1997, 2000) refer to as a "deficit approach" to studying postdivorce family life. No one would deny that divorce is a painful process, but it is also important to remember that there are behaviors, attitudes, and actions that families engage in that can help them cope effectively with divorce and build resilience against the stressors that come with it.

Rather than focus only on the problems that divorced families experience, a more effective way to think about them may be from what researchers call a "normative-adaptive perspective" (Visher & Visher, 1979). Instead of comparing divorced families *only* to "continuously intact" families or focusing exclusively on the behaviors that make them problematic or deficient, researchers who use this perspective examine the interaction patterns and beliefs that help make some divorced families function better than others. Research on family strengths, for instance, has found that strong families differ from other families in many ways. In particular, researchers have found that strong families, when compared to families having greater difficulty, tend to engage in more activities together, are religious, foster an open communication environment, are committed to one another, listen to one another, and reserve judgment (DeFrain & Stinnett, 1992; Golish, 2003; Kelley & Sequeira, 1997; Stinnett, 1979; Stinnett & DeFrain, 1985).

Communication is an incredibly important part of the coping process because family members often cope through their interaction with one another. Their communication can also help build resilience or protection against divorce-related stressors. After a divorce, parents and children often lose some of their friendship networks (Leslie & Grady, 1988). Having access to friends for social support, however, has been shown to help people manage the stress of divorce. For instance, research suggests that custodial mothers and children who have greater access to friends, neighbors, and family to talk to after a divorce are more likely to adapt and cope effectively with the divorce process than mothers and children whose social networks diminish (Cowen, Pedro-Carroll, & Alpert-Gillis, 1989). Research also indicates that families who are able to problem solve together and work through their stressors as a family are better able to adapt to divorce and remarriage (e.g., Afifi, Hutchinson, & Krouse, 2005a, 2005b; Braithwaite, Baxter, & Harper, 1998; Braithwaite, Olson, Golish, Soukup, & Turman, 2001; Golish, 2003). These initial studies point to the need for further research on how family members use communication to help each other cope with divorce and how it influences their family's ability to adapt to the divorce.

If you think back to the people you know whose families have experienced a divorce, you may wonder why it is that some families are able to get through the divorce better than others. An important question to consider is: what is it about the coping of some families, particularly the way that they communicate with one another, that helps them function better than others with a divorce? Also, is there something about the communication patterns of families that consider themselves "strong" that makes them better able to cope with divorce? Two studies were conducted to examine these questions. The first study (Golish, 2003) consisted of 90 face-to-face interviews and telephone interviews with one young adult (aged 18–22), one stepparent, and one parent from 30 stepfamilies that experienced divorce. The majority of the participants were White and from the midwestern part of the United States. The goal of this study was to better understand the challenges that stepfamilies face, how they use communication to cope with these challenges, and the communication strengths of their family.

The second study (Afifi et al., 2005a, 2005b) was a more extensive attempt to identify the stressors that divorced families experience and how they use their communication to cope with them on a regular basis. We conducted series of face-to-face group and individual interviews with 60 divorced families. We interviewed 60 adolescents (aged 10–18), 60 custodial parents, and 10 dating partners/stepparents. The majority of the respondents were White and were from the northeastern part of the United States. They represented a wide range of socioeconomic statuses, with roughly a quarter of the sample below the poverty level.

For both studies, we used a qualitative approach to analyze most of the data. At times, we used surveys to supplement or provide additional insight into the data. However, only a brief look at some of the themes that surfaced from the interviews is provided here. An interpretive or qualitative method promotes an in-depth understanding of the meaning of a phenomenon, through individuals' lived experiences of it (Creswell, 1998; Moustakas, 1994; Strauss & Corbin, 1990). The goal is to provide depth and richness to a phenomenon, such as coping, by attempting to understand and articulate people's personal experiences with it. The processes that comprise individuals' experiences must also be placed within the larger circumstances in which they occur (Strauss & Corbin, 1990), such as the length of time since the divorce, the reasons for the divorce, the degree of conflict, and the age and gender of the participants.

After we coded the qualitative data, we assessed the perceived strength of each family, which was accomplished in four ways. We asked the participants to circle the item that best represented the strength of their family from 1 to 7 with 1 being "very strong" and 7 being "really struggling." Next, the researcher who interviewed the family assessed the strength of the family based on this same scale. We also determined the closeness and satisfaction of the family members with one another with closeness and satisfaction scales that each family member completed. Both of the samples were then separated into families that were considered "strong" and families that were "having greater difficulty" coping as a family.

Numerous themes emerged from the interviews to help explain how the families, particularly strong families, used their communication to cope together with the stress of divorce and remarriage. Because we cannot cover all of the themes here, only a few of the most important themes are emphasized. In addition, because stepfamilies often deal with issues that are very different from divorced families that have not formed a stepfamily, only themes that are relevant to divorced families in general (and not stepfamilies per se) are discussed. Overall, seven themes seem to capture distinct differences in the coping strategies of strong families compared to families that were having greater difficulty adapting. These themes include family practices, communal coping, regulating of privacy boundaries and separating of personal issues from family issues, affection and affirmation of strengths, openness and direct confrontation, clear boundaries and rules, and good conflict management skills. These themes are described in the following text.

A major distinction between strong families and families having greater difficulty coping was their use of *family practices* to cope with the divorce. Strong families reported that they were more likely to engage in family rituals and activities together as a way to cope with the divorce. For instance, many of the families noted that they went on family vacations, attended each other's sporting events, and had "family nights" where they watched their favorite television program or played a game together. Although these activities promoted consistency and stability in the families, it was more about the *talk* that happened during them that promoted the "family making" (Bella, in press) process. That is, talking about what they did during their day and problem solving while they engaged in the activities with one another was the glue that solidified their family and helped them reestablish their family identity. For instance, dinner was often a time when family members sat down and talked to one another about the things that were going on in their lives. As one mother noted:

> I think communication is huge. . . . It sounds kind of goofy, but I think this dinner thing is really big. Because I hear about so many families who say, "Oh man, we never eat dinner together." It's almost. . . . They're almost talking as if it is . . . almost like a badge. . . . "Oh, we're so busy that we never have dinner together and aren't we just wonderful because we're so busy." It's like "no."

Strong families were also more likely than other families to engage in *communal coping*. Communal coping involves "the pooling of resources and efforts of several individuals (e.g., couples, families, or communities) to confront adversity" (Lyons, Mickelson, Sullivan, & Coyne 1998, p. 580). It consists of family members coming together and helping one another cope with similar stressors through problem solving and other proactive measures. As one child mentioned, "We stick together. You know, we make decisions together. Or, my mom will say 'Oh, that's a great idea' and she'll talk to me about it. Or, you know, we work together on our problems, not separate." Some divorced families held family meetings where they problem solved together about how to address their stressors. Communal coping also involved families communicating about their stressors as "family owned" or as "our problem" rather than simply "my" or "your" problem. Children also often protected their parents from unnecessary stress by doing extra work around the house, making dinner, and not asking for things they couldn't afford. Communal coping also meant that the families used positive reframing when communicating about their stressors, confronted their stressors as a group, attempted to move forward together as a family, communicated resolve, and attempted to structure their family life into manageable units. Sometimes, however, communal coping can make coping worse, not better. For instance, sometimes children can assume too much responsibility for their parent's stressor; the stress may become "our" problem when it really should be the parent's problem.

Another distinction between strong postdivorce families and families having greater difficulty coping was their ability to *regulate the type of private information they revealed and concealed* to one another. From a communication privacy management perspective (see Petronio, 1991, 2000, 2002), strong families seemed to be better able to create appropriate privacy rules for sharing personal information with other family members. Because parents' social networks tend to decline after a divorce, parents sometimes turn to their children as confidants. They can reveal too much personal information to their children about the divorce, the other parent, their grief, and their sadness. Although some information is valuable and necessary in order to reduce children's uncertainty about the divorce process (Thomas, M. Booth-Butterfield, & S. Booth-Butterfield, 1995), too much information, especially if it is negative (e.g., talking bad about one's former spouse), can make children anxious and depressed (Afifi, 2003; Buchanan, Maccoby, & Dornbusch, 1991). Parents in strong divorced families were better able to regulate issues that should be kept private from those that should be shared as a family compared to other parents.

Still another distinguishing characteristic of the coping skills of strong families compared to families experiencing greater difficulty coping was the *ability to affirm one another, show affection, and communicate about their strengths* as individuals and as a family. One way that family members were able to work through their stress was to tell one another how much they respected and appreciated each other as individuals. They emphasized the characteristics that made each other unique and also the aspects that made their family special. They also often hugged and kissed one another, demonstrating their caring through their nonverbal displays of affection. When we were conducting the interviews, for instance, some of the family members of the strong families showed their love for one another by playing footsie underneath the table, touching each other on the shoulder or leg, and using direct eye contact. Family members also supported one another, reserved judgment, and listened actively. As one father stated about his communication with his children:

> I'll support you. I'm not going to judge you. I'm not going to do that. Be supportive: I tell them I'm proud of them even when they fail, that I care about them, that there's a lot of learning to do. Point out when there was some failure that there are all these incidences that you know—Babe Ruth struck out 4,000 times and all that other stuff so that they feel . . . I don't want them to ever feel like they are a failure.

In addition to communicating about the strengths of their family, family members in strong families also reported engaging in *greater openness and direct confrontation* of their stressors. Although avoidance can be an effective coping strategy at times, because it can allow people time to gather resources and provides temporary relief from chronic stress (Herman-Stahl, Stemmler, & Petersen, 1995; Holahan & Moos, 1987; Lazarus & Folkman, 1984), it is often not as productive as more proactive forms of coping. Strong families often recognize the need to be open about their problems, recognize they exist, and attempt to problem solve through them as a family. As one woman noted in a group interview about her family's need to work together on the housework, "I would try to tell them [her children], 'You know what, there is just the three of us and we have to work together or we are never going to survive around here.'" Rather than avoid their problems, these families directly confronted them as a family through family meetings and one-on-one discussions.

Divorce often sets in motion a series of changes within families that require not only openness, but also *clear boundaries and rules*. When families undergo divorce, there may be different rules that are established for each household. This can be incredibly stressful for parents and children alike. In order to cope with this, parents and children in strong families often report that they set clear, consistent boundaries and rules within and between households. Parents must maintain an authoritative parenting style in which they are firm in their decision making and rules, while providing children with rationales for why certain actions were taken. They must also communicate consistency in their rules and discipline between households so that children know what to expect and what will result if the rules are broken. Strong families also mentioned that they created predictability between households by establishing a weekly calendar where they identified the activities for each day at each household. Children also mentioned that they got their clothes and books ready the night before they went to their other parent's house in order to better facilitate traveling between households.

Finally, strong families often had *good conflict management skills* that characterized their relationships. These skills often included compromise, direct confrontation, problem solving, empathy, collaboration, and collective resolve. More specifically to postdivorce family life, however, parents were able to limit the amount of interparental conflict and learned to coparent effectively together. Parents in strong postdivorce families were able to communicate more directly with each other and construct disciplinary rules with one another about their children. They made purposeful attempts not to place their children in the middle of their disputes or prevented them from "feeling caught" between them (Afifi, 2003; Afifi & Schrodt, 2003b; Buchanan et al., 1991). If the parents had a lot of conflict in their relationship, they were still able to maintain an effective coparental relationship by reducing the amount of face-to-face contact with one another in order to lessen the emotions they felt. In these situations, email proved to be a rather productive form of communication.

These were only a few of the themes that emerged in the two studies of coping and family resilience. The results illustrate that there may be certain characteristics of strong families that make them more apt to coping effectively with the divorce process. On the other hand, engaging in certain proactive coping strategies, such as communal coping, can also build resilience. Consequently, it may be the case that strong families use certain coping strategies that build resilience and that these strategies foster strength in families (in families that may not be strong to begin with). Future research is necessary to further delineate these associations. Additional work is also required to tap into the communicative nature of coping. Many of the coping strategies that are used by postdivorce families are interactive and jointly constructed. Yet, much of the work on stress and coping is highly individualistic in nature and often assumes that people cope alone with their stressors. As these data suggest, divorce is a stressful process that often demands that family members cope together through their communication with one another in order to function effectively.

Questions for Consideration and Discussion

1. In this study, Afifi takes a normative-adaptive approach to studying families of divorce, focusing on the communication behaviors of these families and how those contribute to family functioning. What are the potential positives and negatives of this type of approach?
2. The results discussed here came from two studies, both of which had a majority of White respondents. How might this have impacted the studies' results (if at all)?
3. As qualitative interpretive work, these studies use self-report (via survey and interview) from members of divorced families. What are the advantages of this sort of research method for studying families of divorce?
4. Afifi discusses how families of divorce use communal coping. In what other situations might we find families using this communicative practice and how so?
5. In Afifi's work, she found that regulation of privacy (what information to reveal or conceal) was very important in these families. All families must deal with privacy issues. Why is privacy a more heightened concern in families of divorce?

References _____

Afifi, T., & Keith, S. (2004). A risk and resiliency model of ambiguous loss in post-divorce stepfamilies. *Journal of Family Communication, 4,* 65–98.

Afifi, T. D. (2003). "Feeling caught" in stepfamilies: Managing boundary turbulence through appropriate privacy coordination rules. *Journal of Social and Personal Relationships, 20,* 729–756.

Afifi, T. D., Hutchinson, S., & Krouse, S. (2005a). *Communicative ways of coping: Variations in individual, social, and communal coping and resilience in post-divorce families.* Manuscript submitted for publication.

Afifi, T. D., Hutchinson, S., & Krouse, S. (2005b). *A context-specific examination of communal coping in post-divorce families.* Manuscript submitted for publication.

Afifi, T. D., & Schrodt, P. (2003a). Uncertainty and the avoidance of the state of one's family/relationships in stepfamilies, post-divorce single parent families, and first marriage families. *Human Communication Research, 29,* 516–533.

Afifi, T. D., & Schrodt, P. (2003b). "Feeling caught" as a mediator of adolescents' and young adults' avoidance and satisfaction with their parents in divorced and non-divorced households. *Communication Monographs, 70,* 142–173.

Amato, P. R. (2000). The consequences of divorce for adults and children. *Journal of Marriage and Family, 62,* 1269–1287.

Bella, L. (Ed.). (in press). *Family making.* Halifax, Nova Scotia, Canada: Fernwood Press.

Braithwaite, D. O., Baxter, L. A., & Harper, A. M. (1998). The role of rituals in the management of the dialectical tension of "old" and "new" in blended families. *Communication Studies, 49*(2), 101–120.

Braithwaite, D. O., Olson, L., Golish, T., Soukup, C., & Turman, P. (2001). Developmental communication patterns of blended families: Exploring the different trajectories of blended families. *Journal of Applied Communication Research, 29,* 221–247.

Buchanan, C. M., Maccoby, E. E., & Dornbusch, S. M. (1991). Caught between parents: Adolescents' experience in divorced homes. *Child Development, 62,* 1008–1029.

Coleman, M., Fine, M. A., Ganong, L. H., Downs, K., & Pauk, N. (2001). When you're not the Brady Bunch: Identifying perceived conflicts and resolution strategies in stepfamilies. *Personal Relationships, 8,* 55–73.

Coleman, M., Ganong, L., & Fine, M. (2000). Reinvestigating remarriage: Another decade of progress. *Journal of Marriage and Family, 62,* 1288–1307.

Cowen, E. L., Pedro-Carroll, J. L., & Alpert-Gillis, L. J. (1989). Relationships between support and adjustment among children of divorce. *Journal of Child Psychology, 31,* 727–735.

Creswell, J. W. (1998). *Qualitative inquiry and research design: Choosing among five traditions.* Thousand Oaks, CA: Sage.

DeFrain, J., & Stinnett, N. (1992). Building on the inherent strengths of families: A positive approach for family psychologists and counselors. *Topics in Family Psychology and Counseling, 1,* 15–26.

Ganong, L. H., & Coleman, M. (1997). How society views stepfamilies. *Marriage and Family Review, 26,* 85–106.

Ganong, L. H., & Coleman, M. (2000). Remarried families. In C. Hendrick & S. S. Hendrick (Eds.), *Close relationships: A sourcebook.* Thousand Oaks, CA: Sage.

Golish, T. D. (2003). Stepfamily communication strengths: Understanding the ties that bind. *Human Communication Research, 29,* 41–80.

Herman-Stahl, M. A., Stemmler, M., & Petersen, A. C. (1995). Approach and avoidant coping: Implications for adolescent mental health. *Journal of Youth and Adolescence, 24,* 649–665.

Hetherington, E. M. (1993). An overview of the Virginia longitudinal study of divorce and remarriage with a focus on early adolescence. *Journal of Family Psychology, 7,* 39–56.

Hetherington, E. M. (1999). Family functioning and the adjustment of adolescent siblings in diverse types of families. In E. M. Hetherington, S. H. Henderson, and D. Reiss (Eds.), Adolescent siblings in stepfamilies: Family functioning and adolescent adjustment. *Monographs of the Society for Research in Child Development, 64,* 1–25.

Holahan, C. J., & Moos, R. H. (1987). Risk, resistance, and psychological distress: A longitudinal analysis with adults and children. *Journal of Abnormal Psychology, 96,* 3–13.

Kelley, D. L., & Sequeira, D. L. (1997). Understanding family functioning in a changing America. *Communication Studies, 48,* 93–107.

Lamb, M. E., Sternberg, K. J., & Thompson, R. A. (1999). The effects of divorce and custody arrangements on children's behavior, development, and adjustment. In M. E. Lamb (Ed.), *Parenting and child development in "nontraditional" families* (pp. 125–136). Mahwah, NJ: Erlbaum.

Lazarus, R. S., & Folkman, S. (1984). *Stress, appraisal, and coping.* New York: Springer.

Leslie, L. A., & Grady, K. (1988). Social support for divorcing mothers: What seems to help? *Journal of Divorce, 11,* 147–165.

Lyons, R. F., Mickelson, K., Sullivan, J. L., & Coyne, J. C. (1998). Coping as a communal process. *Journal of Social and Personal Relationships, 15,* 579–607.

Moustakas, C. (1994). *Phenomenological research methods.* Thousand Oaks, CA: Sage.

Petronio, S. (1991). Communication boundary management: A theoretical model of managing disclosure of private information between marital couples. *Communication Theory, 1,* 311–335.

Petronio, S. (2000). The boundaries of privacy: Praxis of everyday life. In S. Petronio (Ed.), *Balancing the secrets of private disclosures* (pp. 37–49). Mahwah, NJ: Erlbaum.

Petronio, S. (2002). Boundaries of privacy: Dialectics of disclosure. Albany, NY: State University of New York Press.

Stinnett, N. (1979). In search of strong families. In N. Stinnett, B. Chesser, & J. DeFrain (Eds.), *Building family strengths* (pp. 23–30). Lincoln: University of Nebraska Press.

Stinnett, N., & DeFrain, J. (1985). *Secrets of strong families.* Boston: Little, Brown.

Strauss, A., & Corbin, J. (1990). *Basics of qualitative research: Grounded theory procedures and techniques.* Newbury Park, CA: Sage.

Thomas, C. E., Booth-Butterfield, M., & Booth-Butterfield, S. (1995). Perceptions of deception, divorce disclosures, and communication satisfaction with parents. *Western Journal of Communication, 59,* 228–242.

Visher, E. B., & Visher, J. S. (1979). *Stepfamilies: A guide to working with stepparents and stepchildren.* New York: Brunner/Mazel.

Developing and Maintaining Grandparent–Grandchild Relationships

Sherry J. Holladay

In this article, Holladay considers her work related to the grandparent–grandchild relationship, an important part of the extended family network. Much of the work focuses on how situational factors (life turning points, influence of other family members) impact this extended family relationship. While reading, consider the extent to which situational factors (such as how your parents responded to extended family, geographic distance, life changes) have impacted your relationships with extended family members.

L.B.A.

Relationships between grandchildren and grandparents often seem to be idealized in our culture. We have visions of the loving role model who offers unconditional acceptance and spoils grandchildren. Grandparents often are portrayed as indulgent, fun-loving, and wise. We may believe we can turn to our grandparents for solace and assistance when we feel our own parents "just don't understand." Grandparents often are depicted as taking great joy in their grandchildren. They may be jokingly described as enjoying their grandchildren so much that they would have had them before their children if they had known how much fun they would be.

Researchers have examined issues such as the roles, types, or styles of grandparenting (e.g., Cherlin & Furstenberg, 1986; Neugarten & Weinstein, 1964; Szinovacz, 1998; Wood & Robertson, 1976) in order to identify typical behaviors associated with the grandparenting role. An underlying assumption of this research is that grandparents seem to embrace a certain style of grandparenting and that their styles are invariant across relationships with different grandchildren (i.e., grandparents enact a particular style of grandparenting with every grandchild). However, this view, which tends to be grounded in sociological, role-based approaches, seems to run counter to what we typically think about communication in relationships. It neglects the dynamics of the relationship and the role of communication in relationship development and maintenance.

Two research projects reported here focus on the grandmother–granddaughter dyad. Past research suggests the bonds between granddaughters and their maternal grandmothers may be especially close (Hyde & Gibbs,1993; Kennedy, 1992; Kostelecky & Bass, 2004). The explanation for this is that mothers typically are close to their own mothers and provide the connection between generations. If the grandchild's mother and grandmother have a close relationship, then it is expected that the grandchild and grandmother will, too. Another reason for focusing on grandmother–granddaughter dyads stems from a practical concern associated with the research process. In conducting pilot research for these studies we found that our college-aged male participants had much greater difficulty than females in describing their relationships with both grandmothers and grandfathers. Although we tried to obtain detailed descriptions of their relationships, they struggled with the task. Describing their relationships did not come easily to them and no males were included in the first two studies described here.

Our research on grandparent–grandchild relationships attempts to acknowledge that the relationship is embedded within the larger family system. The family system is comprised of various relationships, and what transpires within some relationships may impact other relationships. Our research also tries to explore the dynamics of grandparent–grandchild relationships by identifying communicative events that enhance or detract from the development and maintenance of the relationships.

The Role of Parental Mediation in Grandmother–Granddaughter Relationships

Our study of granddaughter–grandmother dyads reflects a concern with the role of the middle generation in influencing the quality of the relationship (Holladay et al., 1997). Parents are described as "mediators" of the grandparent–grandchild relationship. Parental mediation can take many forms. Especially when grandchildren are young, parents control opportunities for communication and the nature of the interaction that can take place. For example, parents may allow the grandchild to go on vacation alone with the grandparents. Parents may encourage the grandchild to spend time with the grandparent. They provide physical opportunities for visits by driving to the grandparent's house for Sunday dinner, for example. Parents also are likely to influence the grandchild's perceptions of and attitudes toward the grandparent through conversations about him or her or through the behaviors they condone and restrict. Although some parents encourage a great deal of interaction with grandparents, other parents discourage relationship development. For instance, if one of the parents has a poor relationship with the grandparent, he or she may offer negative comments about the grandparent and limit interaction opportunities. If one of the parents often criticizes the behaviors of the grandparent, the grandchild may develop less than positive impressions of him or her. Whereas the influence of the parent may wane as a grandchild becomes more independent and can, for example, drive alone to see the grandparent, by that age negative attitudes may be entrenched and be resistant to change. In sum, the attitudes and behaviors of the parents may have a positive or negative impact on their relational development.

One of our studies explored the role of the middle generation in mediating the relationship between grandmothers and granddaughter. We examined granddaughters' perceptions of their parents' mediation of their relationships with their maternal grandmothers and the impact of the mediation on their feelings of closeness to those grandmothers. We drew upon Robertson's (1975) work on dimensions of parental mediation and developed nine questionnaire items to reflect aspects of mediation. Items asked the granddaughters to report how frequently nine forms of mediation were used by their parents.

The participants were 94 females aged 17 to 27 who reported on parental mediation in their relationships with maternal grandmothers. The great majority (93.6%) were Caucasian. The participants completed the parental mediation questionnaire. Then 48 of the granddaughters participated in face-to-face interviews designed to help us learn more about the mediation process. Trained graduate students conducted the audio-taped interviews, which covered general issues about their relationship with their grandmother, more detailed information about the nature of parental mediation, their perceptions of specific events that affected their relationships, and their feelings of closeness toward their grandmother. The interviews ranged in length from 30 minutes to over 1 hour. Interviews were transcribed and the data were used in two research reports, one focusing on the quantitative and qualitative data pertaining to parental mediation and the second focusing upon the role of turning points in relational development.

Questionnaire responses pertaining to the ways in which parents affected the grandmother–granddaughter relationship revealed which forms of mediation were more commonly used as well as which forms granddaughters perceived to be most important to the relationship development. The most frequently reported forms of parental mediation included (1) parents telling them that the grandmother was an important person in their lives, (2) visiting the grandmother alone, and (3) favoring one grandmother over another (e.g., showing preferential treatment). Correlational analysis, which examines the association between variables, revealed that feelings of relational closeness with the grandmothers were significantly and positively related to the first two types of parental mediation. In fact, visiting the grandmother alone was the most important predictor of overall relational closeness and suggests that the opportunity to develop a relationship independent of the parents has a significant, positive influence on the quality of the relationship.

Some parental mediation behaviors were associated with granddaughters feeling less close to their grandmothers. Feelings of closeness were negatively associated with (1) parents using threats, rewards, or persuasion to influence the granddaughter's behavior with respect to the grandmother (e.g., bribing them, preventing them from engaging in certain activities); (2) parents influencing or mediating the conversations (e.g., controlling their ability to make contact, telling them what to and what to not discuss); and (3) granddaughters hearing that the grandmother was wrong in the way she (the grandmother) behaved (e.g., parents criticizing the grandmother). In other words, granddaughters were likely to report a more distant relationship when their parents engaged in those mediation behaviors.

The information gained through the interviews was used to shed light on granddaughters' perceptions of the mediation process and helps reveal how their parents influenced their relationship with grandmothers. As these excerpts reveal, parents may have a positive or negative effect on the relationship development. For example, one granddaughter reported positive mediation by both parents:

> I think that since I was always able to see her, they always wanted me to be close to her . . . by always taking us there or always planning things with her.

Another granddaughter described how her parents always chose her grandmother to watch her when she was younger. She interpreted this as a push to get to know her and a signal that she was an important person in their lives. Many granddaughters recounted specific conversations with their parents that communicated the message that the grandmothers were important and beloved family members and that they should get to know them well.

In contrast, several granddaughters reported that parents had a negative impact on the relationship and mediated in ways that prevented relationship development. Granddaughters may be aware of a poor relationship between their parents and the grandparent and see that as a roadblock to their own relationship development. It also is important to note that fathers and mothers may differ in their views of the grandmother and the relationship.

For instance, some interviewees described fathers who had poor relationships with their mothers-in-law and limited contact or offered negative comments about the grandmothers. In many cases the parents were in agreement about the desirability of the relationship.

The account provided by this granddaughter indicated she was not close to her grandmother because of her own mother's relationship with her. She explained:

> When my mom was young they [the mother and grandmother] had some problems, like I think my grandmother and my grandfather didn't pay as much attention to them as children. . . . My mother just holds a grudge. I mean I'm mad at my mom for holding such a grudge because that makes me, you know, in the middle. There's a wall there on account of my mom so I don't get to see her so we aren't as close as we could be.

Another granddaughter described how her mother had explained her own relationship with the grandmother and how that affected her expectations of the relationship:

> [When she was a kid] my mom always felt that my grandma was kind of distant. You couldn't really talk to her that much. My mom kind of made it clear that when she was little my grandma was really nice to her and all that but they didn't really discuss anything personal. So my mom probably influenced my views of her and my closeness.

In several cases the granddaughters attributed the absence of a relationship to their mothers who would otherwise serve as the link to the maternal grandmother. They also seem to view this as abnormal or undesirable. Other accounts were very matter of fact and discussed how they were not close because the grandmother was not really welcomed into the family due to some family problems or that the grandmother's alcoholism or "extreme" religious beliefs posed a barrier. It was clear that these granddaughters really did not want or expect to have a close relationship with these grandmothers. Overall, granddaughters' accounts of mediation attempts revealed that both their mother's and father's relationships with the maternal grandmother could have a strong impact on relationships with their grandmothers.

In sum, the parental mediation study was important because it provided insight into how granddaughters viewed the parental generation to have influenced their relationship and identified three specific aspects of parental mediation as especially important to feelings of closeness to the grandmothers. The interviews enriched our understanding of the ways in which parents communicated in order to influence the relationship. The qualitative analysis provided rich descriptions of the granddaughters' subjective experiences that could not be gained through traditional quantitative analysis. We learned that the parental generation does make a difference, how the mediation attempts are experienced by the granddaughters, and how they see the mediation as affecting their relationships.

Analysis of Turning Points in Grandmother–Granddaughter Relationships

Interview data collected from 42 granddaughters from the larger study were used to explore another facet of relationship development. Granddaughters were asked to account for the development of their relationships over time by describing specific "turning points"

(Holladay et al., 1998). Baxter and Bullis (1986) describe a turning point as "an event or occurrence that is associated with a change in a relationship" (p. 470). In the interviews, turning points were described as memorable specific events or behaviors that were experienced or expressed by them, their grandmothers, or other parties that caused them to become closer or more distant from their grandmothers. So, these turning points could have a positive or negative effect on the relationship.

The study of turning points draws upon the communication literature on relational development. We were interested in illuminating the types of events granddaughters identified as turning points, how types of turning points were related to changes in the relationships, and which types of turning points were perceived to have the most significant impact on the relationships.

In reflecting on the course of their relationships, the granddaughters reported from 0 to 8 turning points, with an average of 4. Based on the interviews, we identified 10 categories of turning points. They are reported in terms of decreasing frequency: (1) participating in shared activities (e.g., going on vacation together, weddings, memorable holidays, visiting for extended periods); (2) death or illness in the family (e.g., the death of the grandfather, the grandmother's stroke, death of another family member); (3) moving away to attend college (which signaled not only geographical separation but also the granddaughter's increased autonomy); (4) granddaughter's entering adolescence and developing an increased peer orientation (e.g., wanting to spend time with friends rather than family); (5) negative experiences with the grandmother (e.g., negative evaluations of the grandmother's behaviors as they affected her or her family, family disagreements attributed to the grandmother, the grandmother passing judgment on the granddaughter or family members); (6) decreases in geographic distance separating them (e.g., grandmother or granddaughter's family moving closer, grandmother moving in with the family, daughter moving in with the grandmother); (7) increase in geographic distance (e.g., grandmother or granddaughter's family moving away); (8) family disruptions (e.g., divorce, separation, marital problems, remarriage); (9) mature insight into the grandmother (e.g., a trigger event that caused the granddaughter to see the grandmother as a "real person" or in a different light); and (10) miscellaneous (i.e., could not be classified into any other category).

The most frequently reported turning points were those involving shared activities and deaths and serious illnesses. These two types were reported about four times as often as other types of turning points. It is interesting to note that some turning points involve the larger family system and do not pertain solely to the grandmother–grandparent dyad. For example, a granddaughter's parents might divorce, a sibling might die, or a parent might chose to accept a job in another city. These represent turning points that are outside the control the dyad but affect them nonetheless.

To examine how the turning point content was associated with changes in feelings of closeness, relational change scores were computed by subtracting the closeness score for each turning point from the closeness score associated with the preceding turning point. Three types of turning points were typically associated with reduced feelings of closeness: moving to college, increasing geographic separation, and having a negative experience with the grandmother. Two types of turning points, increased peer orientation and developing a mature insight into the grandmother, did not, on average, tend to produce relational change. Increased closeness tended to be associated with participation in shared activities and death or serious illness.

When asked to identify what they felt was the most significant turning point in the relationship, a little over one-third (35.9%) reported turning points associated with death or serious illness, whereas 30% reported shared activities. The same category of turning point could have different effects on the relationships. For example, the death of the grandfather might make the granddaughter feel closer to the grandmother. However, in another case a granddaughter reported that the death seemed to make the grandmother much "needier." She became too clingy and self-centered and their relationship suffered because of it.

Overall, the study of turning points in the grandmother–granddaughter relationship helps us appreciate that relationships are dynamic rather than static, and that certain events or behaviors—many of which are unexpected—can impact the relationship. This encourages us to adopt a more complex view of relationships. This type of research is not without weaknesses, however. We asked granddaughters to provide retrospective accounts of their relationships. In other words, they had to think back and try to remember significant events. They also had to try to recall their feelings of closeness. They recreated their relationships. This method may be associated with "misremembering." We cannot be certain that their reports reflect what actually happened at that time. Often the present influences how we think about the past. Their accounts do indicate how they personally remember the relationship, and that may be what is most important for understanding their present relationship.

Considered together, these two studies of grandmother–granddaughter relationships contribute to our understanding of factors both within and beyond the relationship that may affect its quality. Parental mediation as well as turning points can influence relational development and feelings of closeness. Like other relationships, grandparent–grandchild relationships can have their ups and downs.

Questions for Consideration and Discussion

1. Holladay makes a point that U.S. culture idealizes the grandparent–grandchild relationship. Do you agree with this assertion? If yes, why? If no, why not? If such idealization exists, what might be some of the outcomes for family members?
2. In this work, Holladay found that college-aged male respondents found it very difficult to discuss or describe their grandparental relationships. Why might this be the case?
3. These studies represent a combination of quantitative (numerical analysis) and qualitative (thematic analysis of language) research. What are the advantages of such an approach? What are the drawbacks?
4. Holladay found that parental mediation was influential in the grandparent–grandchild relationship. What do you think parents should do to help facilitate the most positive grandparent–grandchild experiences?
5. The second study here focused on turning points in grandparent–grandchild relationships. What turning points can you recall in your extended family relationships? How did they impact the relationship? Why do you think those turning points are moments you remember?

References

Baxter, L. A., & Bullis, C. (1986). Turning points in developing romantic relationships. *Human Communication Research, 12,* 54–77.

Cherlin, A., & Furstenberg, F. (1986). *The new American grandparent.* New York: Basic Books.

Holladay, S., Denton, D., Harding, D., Lee, M., Lackovich, R., & Coleman, M. (1997). Granddaughters' accounts of the influence of parental mediation on relational closeness with maternal grandmothers. *International Journal of Aging and Human Development, 45,* 23–38.

Holladay, S., Lackovich, R., Lee, M., Coleman, M., Harding, D., & Denton, D. (1998). (Re)constructing relationships with grandparents: A turning point analysis of granddaughters' relational development with maternal grandmothers. *International Journal of Aging and Human Development, 46,* 287–303.

Hyde, V., & Gibbs, I. (1993). A very special relationship: Granddaughters' perceptions of grandmothers. *Ageing and Society, 13,* 83–96.

Kennedy, G. (1992). Quality in grandparent/grandchild relationships. *International Journal of Aging and Human Development, 35,* 83–98.

Kostelecky, K. L., & Bass, B. L. (2004). Grandmothers and their granddaughters: Connected relationships. *Journal of Intergenerational Relationships, 2*(1), 47–61.

Neugarten, B. L., & Weinstein, K. K. (1964). The changing American grandparent. *Journal of Marriage and Family, 26,* 199–204.

Robertson, J. F. (1975). Interaction in three-generation families, parents as mediators: Toward a theoretical perspective. *International Journal of Aging and Human Development, 6,* 103–110.

Szinovacz, M. (Ed.). (1998). *Handbook on grandparenthood.* Westport, CT: Greenwood.

Wood, V., & Robertson, J. F. (1976). The significance of grandparenthood. In J. Gubrium (Ed.), *Time, roles and self in old age* (pp. 278–304). New York: Human Sciences Press.

Section 3: Conclusions and Application—How Can Understanding Family Type Impact You?

Discussing and categorizing family type is both simple and incredibly complex. Once you know about the different types of families, it may seem easy to conclude what type your family fits into. However, often it is not that simple. One reason for the complexity is that each of us may belong to more than one family (for example, family of origin, family of procreation, and extended family). Additionally, issues such as adoption, divorce, and remarriage can lead to greater complication in assigning one label for a family type.

Although considering and identifying family type, your own or those of others, is not always easy, it can still be a worthwhile endeavor, particularly in terms of studying family. One benefit of discussing family type, in terms of understanding family processes and communication patterns, is that it *allows us to make comparisons of similarity and difference between the family experiences of individuals*. All family experiences are different, but the configuration of family is a part of family experience. Thus, studying family type may allow some insight into particular experiential elements that may be impacted by the family type or configuration. We can see that reflected in the studies presented here. Afifi's work provides insight into some of the specific communication habits experienced by postdivorce families who are strong. Holladay's article reveals important aspects that impact the extended family relationships between grandparents and grandchildren. Though gaining understanding about the experiences of particular family types and relationships is important, we also need to remain careful not to assume that there will necessarily be similarity between two families of the same type, or particular differences between two families that are not of the same type.

A second reason to ponder family typology in a more formal way is that we can consider our preconceived notions about family types that come from culture and the ideas that we learn as we grow from infancy through adulthood. As indicated by the theory of symbolic interactionism discussed previously, one of the ways we cope with the immense amount of information that bombards our senses is to categorize that information and then form understandings of those categories (for example, every dog is different, yet we develop understandings about the whole category of "dog" that inform our response to this animal). Likewise, images that are communicated by the media, ways we hear people talk about family create meanings about family type. Start with the idea of an intact nuclear family. What sort of words spring to mind when you think of such a family. Are they words like *happy, secure, stable, normal, mainstream*? Those are some of the images that are shown on television and in other media with regard to nuclear families. They are so common that it is hard to avoid having these ideas become part of our stereotyped understanding of nuclear families. What about single-parent families? What sort of ideas do you associate with that? Do you think of poverty, stress, latchkey children? Again, such concepts are common in the media representations of single-parent families and thus often become a part of our understandings or beliefs. You could continue this exercise for each of the family types discussed in this chapter. Although such stereotypes are a part of our socially developed understandings of families, research indicates that in any one family, those stereotypical representations are as likely to be false as true. In Koesten's work, intact nuclear families, often stereotypically assumed to be the healthiest and most likely to result in well-functioning offspring, have a wide variety of communication patterns that influence the socialization experiences of their members.

Once we have considered some of the stereotypes we have about different family types, this allows us to interrogate those stereotypes, both positive and negative, and such perceptions about how they function in our lives and in our interactions with others (as well as in our understandings of self). Categorical *stereotypes* are a natural phenomenon. We categorize the things in our environment to help us cope with the enormous amount of diversity that we encounter every day. However, although stereotypes help us in that way, they can also be harmful to us (as both social interactants and family scholars). Carefully thinking through what our stereotypes are and how they operate in our lives (as well as where those stereotypes have come from) allows us the critical distance we need to begin making changes to our stereotyped beliefs in a way that allows us to truly appreciate difference. In the case of our understanding of family, it is through interrogating our own preconceived notions of how family type relates to family process and outcome that we can open a door to more fully understanding how truly unique each family is and that no one family type is "better" or "worse" than any other. As we will see throughout this text, it is the communication (which includes behavior) that occurs in family settings that has the most impact, not the family form or number of members.

Questions for Consideration and Discussion

1. Why is it helpful to categorize families according to type?
2. How do your own experiences of the benefits and drawbacks of your specific family type compare to the research considered here?
3. How would you classify your family on the conformity and conversation dimensions? Why? How does that orientation impact you?
4. Given the positive effects that can result from the grandparent–child relationship, to what extent should parents be held responsible for facilitating those relationships?
5. In what ways do you see understanding family types impacting your life as a student of family communication, a family member, and possibly even in your occupation?

Key Terms and Concepts _____

affinity-maintaining
affinity-seeking
blended family
conformity orientation
consensual family
conversation
   orientation
extended family
family of origin

family of procreation or
   cohabitation
foster family
gay- and lesbian-parented
   family
involuntarily childfree
intact nuclear family
laissez-faire family
pluralistic family

polygamous family
polygamy
protective family
self-disclosure
single-parent family
social penetration theory
solo-parent family
stereotypes
voluntarily childfree

3

The Family as a System

Chapter Outline _____

Chapter Objectives _____

1. To understand the systemic nature of family
2. To be able to state, define, and apply the concepts of systems theory (including those related to the nature of system, regulation of systems, and roles)
3. To understand the idea of relational dialectics
4. To be able to state, define, and apply the basic concepts of dialectics, some examples of dialectical tensions, and dialectical management strategies
5. To be able to state, define, and apply the basic concepts of the circumplex model of family
6. To see how the systems perspective can be applied to understanding your own family experiences

Section 1: Overview of the Family as a System _____

- If you went home from school in a bad mood today, how would your family know?
- Once your family knew you were in a bad mood, what would they do? How would they respond?
- How would your bad mood impact the general atmosphere of the family setting?
- How would the atmospheric change, and the responses of your family, impact your mood?

The scenario you imagined above points to the systemic nature of family interactions. In a family, the behaviors of one member don't just affect that member, they also impact the other members of the family. The responses of those members then come back to affect the individual. Outside influences are brought into the family system as we interact with others and then bring the results of those interactions into our family lives. This entire process creates the general "atmosphere" and patterns of behavior and communication for the family. In this chapter, we investigate this idea of family as a system.

Systems Theory

Systems theory as applied to families and other interpersonal relationships came largely from the general systems theory proposed by von Bertalanffy (1968). He argued that the same basic principles can be used to understand a variety of systems, and focused on the interaction between system parts, rather than the characteristics of individual parts of a system. Thus systems theory, when applied to relational systems like families, considers the behavior that goes on between system members, rather than the individual traits or feelings of the members. This means that, in a family system, a mother may love her children, but it is how she does or does not indicate that love behaviorally that will affect the other parts or members of the system. For example, the parent–child relationship of a mother who shows love only through gifts will be different from that of a mother who shows love through physical and verbal expressions of affection as well, despite the fact that they may love their children equally.

Family systems theory has been foundational in the study of family communication (Broderick, 1993; Galvin, Dickson, & Marrow, 2006; Stamp, 2004). Although scholars do not always explicitly use the terminology of systems theory, the worldview it suggests is an underlying feature of much family communication research. As such, some scholars consider family systems to be more of an approach or perspective to be used in combination with other theories and concepts, rather than a specific theory of family interaction (Galvin et al., 2006). Thus, in this chapter we consider the basic ideas suggested by a family systems viewpoint, as well as two more specific theoretical concepts (relational dialectics and the circumplex model) that spring from a systems approach. From the perspective of systems theory, the way a family functions together creates a system, and that system has certain standard characteristics.

Characteristics of a Human System

A **system** can generally be defined as a set of elements that are connected and interrelated. Based on the work of von Bertalanffy (1968) and other scholars, we can say that human systems, including family systems, are characterized by several features (for an additional discussion of family systems see Galvin et al., 2006). In this textbook we focus on five characteristics.

The first characteristic is wholeness. **Wholeness** refers to the way that the individual parts of the system (i.e., family members) come together to form a whole. Think about your family for a moment. The fact that you can consider your "family" as a thing in and of itself, which goes beyond the individual members who make it up, is reflective of wholeness. If your family were to gain or lose a member, it would still be a family, even though it would be changed.

A second characteristic of a human system is interdependence. **Interdependence** means that the members or features of a system affect each other. When you were a child, and you got the flu, your sickness had an impact on your parents or caretakers, even though the sickness was not in their bodies. They may have had to rearrange their work or other schedules to care for you or take you to the doctor (or arrange for someone to do so). What they cooked might have been altered. They probably spent some time worrying about you and your health (thus not thinking about other issues). They may have had to do extra laundry. The impact can be large, or it can be small, but the behavior of one member of a system, or one part of a system, will affect other parts of that system. Different features or issues within a system also affect one another. A couple having disagreements about financial issues may end up arguing about what to have for dinner, even if they don't really care that much about dinner. One issue affects the other.

A third characteristic of human systems is **nonsummativity.** Literally, this means that humans are not additive, or the whole is more than or different from the sum of the parts. Just because two people are "nice" does not mean you can add them together and get a nice system. Similarly, a group of people who are pretty unpleasant when taken individually may create a very positive and healthy family.

Fourth, human systems have hierarchy. **Hierarchy** refers to the idea that systems exist within other systems. So, a family system exists within a community system, but that community system also exists within larger societal systems. When we study family, we need to attend to how larger systemic forces impact family interaction. Inside the family, there are smaller systems composed of pairs or sets of people (the marital system, the sibling system, parent and child systems). Therefore, we can focus study on a particular smaller system (or **dyad,** as a system of two is called); nonetheless, we must attend to the fact that that system is affected by (and affects) the others in the family.

Finally, human systems are also characterized by equifinality. **Equifinality** means that the path of a human system cannot be predicted. Additionally, this characteristic indicates that human systems are not bound by their historical conditions. Systems may start in the same basic condition, but end up in different places. They can also start in different conditions, and end up in similar places. Although we are affected by the past, we are not totally constrained by it. A family that has very stressful and unhappy interactions today can still make changes that will lead to a better future.

BOX 3.1 • *Did You Know?*

Even though equifinality means relationships aren't predictable, we still like to believe we can find a perfect match. Online dating services (like match.com and eharmony.com) boast of scientific compatibility tests that will ensure a happy relationship. Studies estimate that over 20 percent of single individuals in the United States have used online services, and that, in 2007, more than $640 million will be spent for online dating services (Houran, Lange, Rentfrow, & Bruckner, 2004).

This brings us to the notion of how systems do make changes, or how they maintain their functioning over time. The study of this process is known as cybernetic systems theory.

Self-Regulation in a Family System

A number of scholars, including Bateson (1972), von Bertalanffy (1968), and Laing (1972), have considered how human systems "self-regulate." **Self-regulating systems,** also called **cybernetic systems,** provide their own internal feedback in order to produce stability or change.

The calibration of a system is also sometimes called the "norm" or the "set point." **Calibration** refers to the pattern of behavior that is typical for that system. Some family systems scholars, for example Minuchin (1974), refer to calibration as **homeostasis.** Calibration does not assume a constant steady state. Instead, the system exhibits some degree of variation around that calibration level (often called the "range of variation"), but will tend to remain within that range of variation and resist moving away from it. Calibration also does not mean that the norm for the system has to be what we might consider a "normal" or "happy" situation. If a family is usually engaged in a pattern of abusive behavior, then that is the calibration for that family. It does not mean that every behavior in that family must be abusive, just that the general pattern of interaction they engage in is abusive. Similarly, another family may have a calibration that is characterized by behaviors exhibiting mutual love, respect, and tolerance. On an everyday basis, members can say or do things that don't quite live up to that calibration, but still are within the range of variation for that system. For example, if a child in this family calls his brother a "whiney crybaby," it wouldn't be a very respectful thing, but it would probably still be within the normal range of behavior for the family. On the other hand, if that child were to shred all of his brother's clothing in a fit of rage, that would probably fall well outside the range of variation and would require some strong response from the other family members in order to return things to the normal range. When the calibration of a family system changes, we can refer to this as *recalibration.*

In order to maintain calibration or to produce change, systems engage in the sharing of information called feedback. *Feedback* occurs in the form of behavior (which includes verbal and nonverbal communication). Feedback may be positive or negative. **Positive feedback** is behavior that encourages movement away from the calibration (that is, positive feedback is behavior that attempts to induce change in the system). **Negative feedback** is behavior that discourages movement away from the calibration (that is, negative feedback is behavior that attempts to maintain the norm of the system). While operating within the range of variation, a system will exhibit both positive and negative feedback. If enough positive feedback occurs within a system, the system will eventually recalibrate, or develop a new norm of behavior. In the previous example, when one brother called the other a name, this was probably a mild form of positive feedback because it moved away from the calibration of respectful behavior. When the boy cut his brother's clothing to pieces, this was an extreme example of positive feedback. In the first case, very little may have been needed to correct the direction of the system behavior. In the second case, a more dramatic form of negative feedback (perhaps a visit to family therapy or anger management for the offending boy) might have been needed.

To clarify, positive feedback is not always "good" or "nice" and negative feedback is not always "bad." Positive feedback just encourages movement away from the norm. Let's say your family system behavior includes the giving of moderately sized gifts for special occasions. This is part of your calibration. If, one year, your father got you a Mercedes for your birthday, this would be positive feedback in the system (and probably a nice thing!). On the other hand, if that year your father got you a broken CD for your birthday, that would also be positive feedback (but probably not so nice). Both examples are positive feedback because they represent movement away from the norm, regardless of whether they seem nice or not. By the same token, negative feedback is feedback that discourages deviation from the norm. If, after your father gave you the Mercedes, your mother said, "You have got to be kidding me! That is far too much to spend," and then took the keys and gave you a beautiful sweater instead, it would be negative feedback (and you might be sad). If, after your father gave you the CD, your mother said, "Now, dear, that is no kind of present," and then took the CD and gave you a beautiful sweater instead, it would be negative feedback (and you might be happy). Both of these examples represent negative feedback because they attempt to return the system to the norm, whether they make individual members feel happy or sad. Understanding what types of behaviors in a system represent positive feedback, and what types represent negative feedback requires a careful analysis of the system and its communication patterns. Thus, cybernetic systems theory is a communication-based way of looking at family functioning.

Communication/Behavior Patterns in a Family System

As noted, scholars who use a systems approach, as in Watzlawick, Beavin, and Jackson's (1967) classic work, often look at how behaviors within a system relate to one another. In order to do this, streams of behavior can be separated into pairs (so we look at how behavior 1 relates to behavior 2, and then how behavior 2 relates to behavior 3, etc.). In studying pairs of behaviors, we can identify symmetrical pairs of behaviors and complementary pairs.

Symmetrical behaviors occur when behavior A calls forth a similar behavior B. That is, if behavior A is an assertion of power, behavior B is also an assertion of power. If behavior A is an attempt to give power to the other, behavior B is also an attempt to give power to the other. An example of a power-taking symmetrical set might be a disagreement over where to go for dinner: "I want Mexican food tonight"; "Well, I want Thai food." Both parties are attempting to assert power with their communication. An example of a power-giving symmetrical exchange might be the trading of compliments: "That's a beautiful sweater"; "Thanks, I love your boots." Both parties here are attempting to give power through their communication.

Complementary behaviors occur when behavior A calls forth an opposite, but fitted, behavior B. That is, if behavior A is an attempt to take power, behavior B is an attempt to give power to the other. If behavior A is an attempt to give power to the other, behavior B is an attempt to take power. In the discussion about where to go to dinner, if the conversation had been "I want Mexican food tonight"; "Okay, let's have Mexican," then that would have been a complementary exchange. The first party was asserting power and the second party was granting it. The conversation that began with the compliment regarding the sweater could have also been complementary (note here that *compliment* and *complementary* are two different words and concepts): "That's a beautiful sweater." "Yes, it is!" In that circumstance, the first person would have been giving power, and the second person would have been accepting it. Table 3.1 compares symmetrical and complementary behaviors.

Like positive and negative feedback, symmetrical and complementary behaviors are not, in and of themselves, good or bad. A symmetrical exchange can be pleasant (you give your friend a gift; she gives one back to you), or unpleasant (you punch your cousin in the nose; he punches you back). As long as both behaviors are power taking or power giving, then the exchange is symmetrical. Likewise, a complementary exchange can be nice (you tell your roommate that you would like pizza for dinner; she agrees to get pizza), or not very nice (your roommate suddenly screams, "Give me the stupid remote control!" and you give it to him). As long as one behavior is power giving and the other is power taking, the exchange is complementary.

By studying behavior in pairs, we can consider how one behavior is related to the other behaviors that go on in the system. Recent examples of work that use this approach to

TABLE 3.1   *Symmetrical and Complementary Behaviors*

Symmetrical Behaviors	*Complementary Behaviors*
A behavioral pair that is the same in terms of power:	A behavioral pair that is opposite, but fitted, in terms of power:
• Person 1 asserts power and Person 2 also asserts power ("I want to watch *Sex and the City*." "Well, I want to watch *Law and Order!*"). • Person 1 grants power and Person 2 also grants power ("What would you like to watch tonight?" "Oh, I don't care; whatever you want to watch is fine.")	• Person 1 asserts power and Person 2 grants power ("I want to watch *Sex and the City*." "Okay, that sounds great."). • Person 1 grants power and Person 2 asserts power ("What do you want to watch tonight?" "I really want to see this episode of *Law and Order*.").

research family communication processes include Caughlin and Malis's (2004) consideration of communication between parents and adolescents, and the relationship of communication patterns to satisfaction; Koerner and Fitzpatrick's (2002) exploration of how family of origin affects the way romantic couples engage in conflict; and Olson's (2002) study of violent behavior in heterosexual relationships. Studying behavioral patterns in this way relates back to the systems theory idea that we can't really understand one behavior or person in a system out of its context. In order to fully comprehend the communication within a family, we have to study patterns of behavior. Studying family interaction patterns in this way can give us a sense of how particular family groupings, or the family as a whole, typically communicate with each other, and the types of power moves that go on within that communication. Although behavior patterns in a particular system are complex and related to many factors, one of the things that affect them is the roles that individuals play in that family setting.

Family Roles

Within a family system, members perform certain roles. A **role** can be defined generally as a group of behaviors that are patterned or recurring. Often, we give labels to the roles that people fulfill in a system. For example, we label the two partners of the heterosexual marital relationship as husband and wife. Within a family system, there are role labels such as mother, father, husband, wife, son, daughter, sister, brother, grandparent, grandchild, cousin, aunt, uncle, stepmother, stepchild, stepfather, and so on. Some family roles may not have formalized labels, for example the breadwinner, the nurturer, the peacekeeper, but they refer to behavior sets that are performed within the family. Each individual member of a family fulfills a variety of roles within that family system (Huston & Holmes, 2004; Stamp, 2004).

Role expectations are those behaviors that are considered the norm for that particular role (i.e., in the United States, we expect that the mother role will consist in part of nurturing behaviors). Drawing from the theory of symbolic interactionism (Blumer, 1969; Mead, 1934), discussed previously in the text, which says in part that our understandings and meanings about self and others are created through social interaction and interpretation, Goffman (1959) argues that role expectations like these are created through a process of negotiation at the societal or cultural level and also within a particular family or system. The process of negotiating role expectations occurs through communication. You weren't born knowing what a parent is or what to expect from a parent. But, through communication within your family and with the larger society, you have probably developed certain role expectations about how parenting is, or should be, accomplished. This results in roles being enacted in a variety of ways across families and family types. For example, Mosley-Howard and Evans (2000) note that the cultural beliefs and values of African American families result in greater role flexibility and role sharing than in White families. Likewise, as cultures shift and change, the expectations of particular roles will also shift. Holloway, Suzuki, Yamamoto, and Mindnich (2006) studied the mother role in Japan and found that, for young women in contemporary urban Japan, the beliefs about that role are shifting to include career opportunities, as well as childrearing. Thus, we see that what is the norm for a role may be different both across cultural settings and across time periods.

According to Turner (1962), **role acquisition,** or the process of assuming a particular role, consists of two parts. First, we engage in **role taking,** or learning about what the expected parts of a role are. Second, we enact **role making,** in which we negotiate how to fulfill those expectations within our own personal meanings. As a child, you learned about the concept of a "friend" and started to learn what the expectations were for friends and friendship. Then, in your individual friendships, you negotiate how to enact those expectations. The same is true in families, where the general cultural expectations for family roles are negotiated in the daily accomplishment of role making (see, for example, Medved, 2004; Mormon & Floyd, 2002).

Sometimes, our roles come in conflict with each other. There are many examples of **role conflict** that can be found within a family system. The roles that are in conflict may be two roles within the family setting. For example, the role of wife assumes some degree of sexuality and sexual availability. The role of mother is typically thought of as largely devoid of sexuality. So, a new mother may find herself struggling with how to fulfill both of these roles at the same time (Friedman, Pines, & Weinberg, 1998; Johnson, 2001). Similarly, as the role expectations of fatherhood have shifted to call for more intensive child care efforts, but men are still expected to be devoted to their careers and successful, fathers may also experience conflict while attempting to fulfill their roles as family breadwinner and father (Garcia & de Oliveira, 2005; Wille, 1995). At times, the roles that are in conflict are not both family roles. The conflict arises from how our other roles impact our functioning within the family. A young adult may find that his or her work obligations are quite large. This may prevent him or her from doing the things that are expected in the role as grandchild, child, or sibling.

It is through communication that we learn family roles, and it is through behavior (which is communicative) that we enact them. We use communication to renegotiate and recreate the roles, and we learn, through feedback, when we have violated or failed to fulfill the roles. When we have role conflicts, management of the conflicts is often a process of engaging in some communicated renegotiation of the roles themselves. Thus, roles, communication, and family systems are intimately connected.

Dialectics

As we have already considered in terms of role conflict and the cycling of positive and negative feedback, systems theory does not assume everything in families is neat, tidy, and easy. The **dialectical perspective,** which is a type of systems approach, explicitly focuses on the "messiness" and contradiction inherent in human relationships, including family.

The dialectical approach is most often associated with the work of Baxter and Montgomery (Baxter, 1988, 2003, 2006; Baxter & Montgomery, 1996; Montgomery & Baxter, 1998). This approach acknowledges the constant presence of contradiction in relationships. However, these authors, and other dialectical scholars, aren't exactly speaking of contradiction in relationships the way we do in casual conversation (as in two people fighting). They mean something slightly different.

The dialectical approach starts from four basic ideas (Baxter & Montgomery, 1996; Montgomery & Baxter, 1998; Rawlins, 1989, 1992). Although different dialectical scholars

BOX 3.2 • *Balancing Family and Work*

Finding a way to do your job effectively or to advance your career while also fulfilling family role expectations isn't always easy. Role conflict can also be said to occur when the roles we have in the home and those of the workplace collide with one another in a way that makes fulfilling both sets of obligations difficult.

The conflict between family roles and work roles has been considered by a variety of scholars who, among other things, have addressed how gendered expectations of men and women impact the extent and intensity of work–family role conflict. Huston and Holmes (2004) found that in the United States, working mothers seem to experience more negative effects from work–family role conflict than working fathers. They suggest that this may be because they are responsible for the majority of the household and child care tasks, even given the increase over the last few decades in men's household participation (see also Buzzanell et al., 2005; Hill 2005; Kulik, 2004; O'Laughlin & Bischoff, 2005). Aycan and Eskin (2005), Kulik (2004), and Kinnunen, Geurts, and Mauno (2004) found similar results for men and women in Turkey, Israel, and Finland. Thus, overall it appears that when caretaking of children and household are generally associated with a particular family role, the individual who fulfills that roll may experience greater work–family role conflict if he or she also has a paying job.

In addition to considering the causes of role conflict, attention has also been given to aspects of family, social, and work cultures that may contribute to or decrease work–family conflict. Scholars have found that when families have supportive social networks (friends to help with picking up after school or doing household tasks, extended family to assist with child care issues, etc.) or organizations to help facilitate family roles (for example, by offering days off to care for a sick child, onsite child care, family leave for new parents, etc.) work–family role conflict is reduced (Aycan & Eskin, 2005; Hill, 2005; Thompson, Kirk, & Brown, 2005; Voydanoff, 2002).

Recently, attention has been given to the issue of telecommuting and how working from home may impact work–family conflict and balance. On the surface it may seem that working from home would only reduce conflict, as parents could be in the household, taking care of the children, while also completing their job tasks. However, research suggests that the possible outcomes are more complex than that, with individuals experiencing both benefits and drawbacks in terms of work–family balance.

There are several benefits to telecommuting (Manochehri & Pinkerton, 2003; Mirchandani, 2000; Potter, 2003; Robertson, Maynard, & McDevitt, 2003). Studies have indicated increased employee satisfaction due to more feelings of control, flexible working hours, and feelings of less pressure and more productivity. Additionally, time and money spent commuting is reduced, allowing more of the day to be spent in home or on work tasks. Workers also feel that there are fewer distractions, including less office politics. The drawback of telecommuting is mostly related to a concern about how to separate work time from family time (Desrochers, Hilton, & Larwood, 2005; Kurland & Bailey, 1999; Mirchandani, 2000; Tietze, 2002). When people work in the home, they may find it more difficult to complete job tasks because their attention is diverted by household and child care responsibilities. Similarly, they may find it difficult to ever fully be "off work" because the occupational tasks are always there.

As work practices continue to shift and change, along with cultural expectations, family members will continue to need to devise ways to balance work and home requirements and cope with the potential role conflicts of being an organizational actor and family member. Continued attention to this issue, on the part of scholars and business leaders, can help organizations create strategies that ease work–home conflict, and help individuals find their own ways to achieve greater role compatibility.

label them slightly differently, they mean fundamentally the same four things. These ideas should sound familiar to you, as they come from a systems perspective.

Totality

The first idea is totality. **Totality** refers to the fact that the relationship operates as a whole. The members of the relationship affect each other. The different parts of the relationship affect each other. We can't understand one part of a relationship in isolation from the other parts. This is basically the same as the concepts of wholeness and interdependence that we addressed earlier in the chapter.

Change

The second concept is change or motion. **Change** refers to the idea that relationships never stay the same. This does not mean that relationships can't have patterns, but even within pattern there is still some change. If you and your family have had the same fight every year about where to go on vacation, that is a pattern. But, each year the fight is still somewhat different. You are a year older every time you have it. You've had the fight one more time every time you have it. You have had a year's worth of new experiences every time you have it. So, there is pattern, but there is also change.

Contradiction

A third concept, and possibly the most important for your understanding of dialectics, is **contradiction.** As I noted previously, this is not the contradiction between people, necessarily. Instead, it is the overall idea of contradiction. As humans, we think of things often in contradiction. Many of our meanings for ideas or concepts require opposition for true understanding. What is darkness? The absence of light. What is happiness? The absence of sadness. We even have more terms for opposites than for what lies in the middle (if something isn't good, and it isn't bad, it is average; if someone isn't tall, and isn't short, he or she is average). So, from the dialectical perspective, contradiction is not about *either/or* (either you are happy or you are sad), but about the *both/and* (you know and understand both happiness and sadness at the same time).

Praxis

Finally, dialectics also rests on the concept of praxis. **Praxis** means that, as humans, we are simultaneously reactive and proactive in the world around us. We make choices for our behavior and we are affected by the behavior of self and others. We make choices and then we react to them. If you behave in a mean way to your sibling (your choice), then your sibling might behave in an unpleasant way toward you and you will be affected by that.

Relational Dialectics

Starting from these basic assumptions, dialectical theorists discuss relational dialectics. A **dialectic** is a pull, tension, or contradiction between oppositions that individuals experience within relationships (Baxter & Montgomery, 1996; Montgomery & Baxter, 1998; Rawlins, 1989, 1992). Tension is not necessarily a bad thing. Instead, it is an inherent part of a relationship, like the tension in a spring. For a spring, tension isn't bad; it is what makes it a spring. So, dialectic tensions aren't bad, they just *are*. When we are in relationships, we want things that seem contradictory, but we want them at the same time. As in the previous discussion of contradiction, the two parts of the dialectic are a unified opposition. They require each other for existence and understanding. Thus, dialectics is not about the either/or of the two pulls, but rather about the both/and. Some examples of common relational dialectics that can be found in families as well as other types of interpersonal relationships should clarify this idea.

Autonomy/Connection.   One relational dialectic is the urge or pull to be an individual, coupled with the urge or pull to be a part of relationships with others. This dialectic permeates family life. From the very earliest years, children seek to differentiate themselves from their parents ("I can do it myself!"), but at the same time, they depend on their parents to be there and they need their parents' love and affection. This continues throughout childhood and the teen years. Adolescents want to be treated as adults. They want to make decisions on their own ("Curfew is stupid. Why can't I decide when to come home?"). However, these same adolescents would likely be appalled if their parents completely stopped worrying about them or taking care of them. As adults in families, we still feel this dialectic. Our family roles (mom, dad, sister, brother) sometimes seem to compete with our other roles outside the relationship. We want to be individuals apart from the family, but we still want to be a part of the family. This is the dialectic of autonomy and connection.

Privacy/Openness.   Frequently, when speaking of our close relationships, we say, "I can tell her or him anything." It may or may not be the case that we can tell our friends or family anything, but it would be rare for us to really tell them everything. Even as we reveal information to those we are close to, we keep other information inside. Sometimes we do this to protect the other. For example, if your grandmother gets a really horrible haircut, and then asks you how it looks, you probably wouldn't say "It looks awful!" You would find some other way to remark on it ("It certainly is a change.") to avoid hurting Grandma's feelings. Sometimes, we withhold information to protect ourselves. There may have been things you did as a child or young adolescent that you won't ever tell your parents because you don't want to experience their disappointment, or because you are embarrassed.

BOX 3.3 • *Family in the News*

Learning what information to keep private, with family and others, is a skill developed as we mature. Recently, media stories suggest increasing parental concern about blog sites. Parents worry that these sites encourage adolescents to disregard privacy rules and engage in inappropriate openness. Adolescents may feel that the site is not really "public" because they anticipate it being read by friends. Web sites like wiredsafety.com provide parents with information about helping adolescents stay safe on blog sites, and advice for family talk about blogging. You can read more at www.wiredsafety.org/internet101.

However, even though we keep some information private, we also share information with others we are close to. This is one of the ways that we create closeness, and one of the ways that we exhibit that degree of intimacy. This is the dialectic of privacy and openness.

Novelty/Predictability.   Imagine a life where every day was exactly the same. It would be boring. On the other hand, imagine a life where nothing was ever predictable or patterned. That would be confusing, even scary. The same is true for our relationships with others. If every interaction we had in our families was completely repetitious of previous interactions, we would get bored, and probably irritated. Total predictability isn't even possible because we, as individuals, change as we age. But, if we were never sure from one minute to the next how our family members would behave, how they would respond to us, how they would feel about us, this would also be upsetting. Thus, we want both predictability and novelty in our family relationships. We want some patterned behaviors ("I know that Mom will always send me a birthday present"), but we want some change ("I don't want Mom to get me the same CD for my birthday every year"). This is the dialectic of novelty and predictability.

Dialectic Management Strategies

From a dialectical perspective, these dialectics never go away in relationships. They are always there, but at times we don't think about them. This is because we have managed the dialectic in a way that works for that particular relationship. Sometimes we concentrate more on one pole of the dialectic and less on the other. This is a management strategy known as **selection** (Baxter, 1990). For example, when college students go away to school, they may be focusing more on the autonomy end of the autonomy–connection dialectic in their relationship with their parents, at that time. In this way, they are "selecting" one part of the dialectic urge to satisfy, and ignoring the other need.

Sometimes we try to divide the relationship into parts and we satisfy the poles differently in different parts. So, you might tell your father everything about your classes, but be very private about your romantic relationships. This is called **segmentation** (Baxter, 1990). In one part of your relationship, you satisfy one need (discussing class satisfies a need for openness), and in another part, you satisfy the other need (keeping quiet about your romance satisfies a need for privacy).

Or, maybe you try to satisfy each urge somewhat all of the time. In the dialectic of predictability and novelty, you may have no pattern to when exactly you are predictable and novel, but some of each happens. Sometimes you eat at the same restaurant you frequently go to, but other times you spontaneously try something new. This can be called **neutralization** (Baxter, 1990).

Another possibility is that you try to think about the contradiction of the dialectic in a way that makes it seem less contradictory. A college student might choose to live away from home during college (which seems like autonomy) because he or she believes that not being together physically with his or her parents all of the time will actually solve some relationship problems and make them all closer (which is connection). This is a strategy known as **reframing** (Baxter, 1990).

There is no one way to handle dialectics that is better than the others; it depends on the particular relationship and what is going on in that relationship at that time. Management strategies change over time as relationships change, and in each relationship multiple strategies are used. At times, we may find a particular dialectic is at the forefront of the relationship as we seek a new way to manage that tension.

It is important to note that the dialectics mentioned here are not all of those that are possible within a given family. The management strategies noted are also a partial list. A variety of scholars have considered dialectics in family issues such as stepfamily formation (Braithwaite, Baxter, & Harper, 1998), adoption (Shank-Krusiewicz & Wood, 2001), marital life (Hoppe-Nagao & Ting-Toomey, 2002), the transition to motherhood (Foster, 2005), and romantic and marital conflict (Erbert, 2000; Olson & Braithwaite, 2004) and have noted many different dialectics and dialectical processes and there are likely more that will be chronicled as this work unfolds. It is also imperative that you understand that, from the perspective of dialectics, these tensions are an important and inherent part of human relationships. They are not something we can cure, and we wouldn't even want to. They are a part of our being and being together.

The Circumplex Model of Family Systems

The **circumplex model** of family systems, developed by Olson and colleagues, is another way of considering family relationships built upon the general principles of family systems theory (Olson, 1997, 2000; Olson, Russell, & Sprenkle, 1983; Olson, Sprenkle, & Russell, 1979). This model (see Table 3.2) considers the interactions of family cohesion, family adaptability, and communication and how those relate to family stress.

Family Cohesion

Family **cohesion** is the sense of emotional bonding that family members have with each other. The model specifies four levels of family cohesion (listed here from least to most cohesive). **Disengaged families** have extreme separateness; they feel little sense of family belonging or loyalty to the family unit. **Separated families** are relatively emotionally independent, but they do have some sense of belonging for the family and do have some involvement with each other. **Connected families** attempt to have emotional closeness and involvement, while still maintaining a sense of individuality. **Enmeshed families** experience extreme closeness and loyalty, to the extent that individuality is virtually nonexistent.

TABLE 3.2   *Circumplex Model Family Types*

Level	*Family Cohesion*	*Family Adaptability*
Highest	Enmeshed families	Chaotic families
	Connected families	Flexible families
	Separated families	Structured families
Lowest	Disengaged families	Rigid families

Olson and colleagues note that families are most functional when they operate at the two middle levels, because they are able to maintain a feeling of belongingness while also having a sense of their own individuality.

Family Adaptability

Family **adaptability** refers to the amount of change that exists in a family's leadership patterns, roles, and rules; it relates to how the system manages both stability and change. The model indicates four levels of adaptability (listed here from least to most adaptable). **Rigid families** tend to have very strict roles and rules, decisions made only by the adult(s) in power, and a dislike of change. **Structured families** tend to have relatively stable roles and rules, but allow for some flexibility within the general guidelines; the adult(s) still tends (tend) to make the final decisions, but somewhat more input is given to all family members. **Flexible families** have roles and rules that are easily changed based on the circumstances, but still maintain some underlying predictability in them; their decision-making tends to be characterized by negotiation between family members. **Chaotic families** have little in the way of specific rules and roles; their decision-making patterns are widely varying, and they have almost nonexistent leadership. Olson and colleagues argue that the two middle levels are healthier for family members because they allow for change when it is needed, but also give families a sense of stability.

Communication is the third part of the model. It is through communicative processes that family systems facilitate change and stability in the cohesion and adaptability of the family. As families communicate together, they may change their level of cohesion or adaptability to respond to the changing circumstances of their lives, or they may act to maintain the level of adaptability and cohesion that they currently exhibit.

Scholars utilizing the circumplex model to understand family processes have approached it in a variety of ways. Schrodt (2005) considered the extent to which expressiveness, traditionalism, and conflict avoidance related to cohesion and adaptability. He concluded that expressiveness was positively correlated to both dimensions (as expressiveness increased, so too did cohesion and adaptability), whereas traditionalism and conflict avoidance were negatively correlated to both dimensions (as they increased, cohesion and adaptability decreased). Gauze, Bukowski, Aquan-Assee, and Sippola (1996) researched the interaction among family patterns of cohesion and adaptability, adolescent friendships, and adolescents' assessment of their own well-being and adjustment. They found that, for adolescents without a close friend, the family measures were more predictive of adjustment than they were for adolescents with close friendship. The reverse was also true, such that in families with the lowest levels of adaptability and cohesion, friendship was more predictive of adolescent well-being. This study suggests that for adolescents, friendship and family patterns interact to affect adjustment (for other examples of the circumplex model in research, see Farrell & Barnes, 1993; Lavee & Olson, 1991; Mathijssen, Koot, Verhulst, DeBryn, & Oud, 1997; Pink & Wampler, 1985).

Whether considering the basic notions of a family as a system, how a system regulates itself to either remain the same or to change, the roles of the members within the system, how relational dialectics create and are created by family systems, or the adaptability and cohesion of family systems—these ideas all relate to how different elements of the family come together and affect each other. The parts of a system, from these views, are so connected and related to each other that it is impossible to separate them out and study them in isolation. Therefore, from this perspective, when studying family we have to take a broad view of the family as a whole, rather than focusing on any one individual or issue. We have to understand how complex families and family interactions are and recognize that to oversimplify them would be to portray them inaccurately.

Section 2 presents three pieces of family communication research that address some of the issues we have considered here. In the first article, the authors address the impact of the college transition on family roles and the family system. In the second reading, the authors consider the role of father and the expectations that attach to that role for fathers and sons. In the third article, the authors apply the notion of dialectics to a consideration of how divorced and stepfamilies manage and renegotiate their relationships. Finally, Section 3 briefly considers how all of this material may be used to help you understand your life experiences.

References

Aycan, Z., & Eskin, M. (2005). Relative contributions of childcare, spousal support, and organizational support in reducing work–family conflict for men and women: The case of Turkey. *Sex Roles, 53*(7/8), 453–471.

Bateson, G. (1972). *Steps to an ecology of mind.* New York: Bantam.

Baxter, L. A. (1988). A dialectical perspective on communication strategies in relationship development. In S. Duck, D. F. Hay, S. E. Hobfoll, W. Ickes, & B. Montgomery (Eds.), *Handbook of personal relationships* (pp. 257–273). New York: Wiley.

Baxter, L. A. (1990). Dialectical contradictions in relationship development. *Journal of Social and Personal Relationships, 7,* 69–88.

Baxter, L. A. (2003). Couple perceptions of their similarities and differences: A dialectical perspective. *Journal of Social and Personal Relationships, 20,* 491–515.

Baxter, L. A. (2006). Relational dialectics theory: Multivocal dialogues of family communication. In D. O. Braithwaite & L. A. Baxter (Eds.), *Engaging theories in family communication: Multiple perspectives* (pp. 130–145). Thousand Oaks, CA: Sage.

Baxter L. A., & Montgomery B. M. (1996). *Relating: Dialogues and dialectics.* New York: Guilford Press.

Blumer, H. (1969). *Symbolic interactionism: Perspective and method.* Englewood Cliffs, NJ: Prentice Hall.

Braithwaite, D. O., Baxter, L. A., & Harper, A. M. (1998). The role of rituals in the management of the dialectical tension of "old" and "new" in blended families. *Communication Studies, 49,* 101–120.

Broderick, C. (1993). *Understanding family process: Basics of family systems theory.* Newbury Park, CA: Sage.

Buzzanell, P. M., Meisenbach, R., Remke, R., Liu, M., Bowers, V., & Conn, C. (2005). The good working mother: Managerial women's sensemaking and feelings about work–family issues. *Communication Studies, 56,* 261–285.

Caughlin, J. P., & Malis, R. S. (2004). Demand/withdraw communication between parents and adolescents as a correlate of relational satisfaction. *Communication Reports, 17*(2), 59–71.

Desrochers, S., Hilton, J. M., & Larwood, L. (2005). Preliminary validation of the work-family integration blurring scale. *Journal of Family Issues, 26*(4), 442–466.

Erbert, L. A. (2000). Conflict and dialectics: Perceptions of dialectical contradictions in marital conflict. *Journal of Social and Personal Relationships, 17*(4–5), 638–659.

Farrell, M. P., & Barnes, G. M. (1993). Family systems and social support: A test of the effects of cohesion and adaptability on the functioning of parents and adolescents. *Journal of Marriage and Family, 55*(1), 119–132.

Foster, E. (2005). Desiring dialectical discourse: A feminist ponders the transition to motherhood. *Women's Studies in Communication, 28*(1), 57–83.

Friedman, A., Pines, A. M., & Weinberg, H. (1998). Sexuality and motherhood: Mutually exclusive in perception of women. *Sex Roles: A Journal of Research, 38,* 781–790.

Galvin, K., Dickson, F. & Marrow, S. R. (2006). Systems theory: Patterns and (w)holes in family communication. In D. O. Braithwaite & L. A. Baxter (Eds.) *Engaging theories in family communication: Multiple perspectives* (pp. 309–324). Thousand Oaks, CA: Sage.

Garcia, B., & de Oliveira, O. (2005). Fatherhood in urban Mexico. *Journal of Comparative Family Studies, 36*(2), 305–327.

Gauze, C., Bukowski, W. M., Aquan-Assee, J., & Sippola, L. K. (1996). Interactions between family environment and friendship and associations with self-perceived well-being during early adolescence. *Child Development, 67,* 2201–2216.

Goffman, E. (1959). *The presentation of self in everyday life.* Edinburgh, Scotland: University of Edinburgh, Social Sciences Research Centre.

Hill, E. J. (2005). Work–family facilitation and conflict, working fathers and mothers, work–family stressors and support. *Journal of Family Issues, 26*(6), 793–819.

Holloway, S. D., Suzuki, S., Yamamoto, Y., & Mindnich, J. D. (2006). Relation of maternal role concepts to parenting, employment choices, and life satisfaction among Japanese women. *Sex Roles, 54* (3/4), 235–249.

Hoppe-Nagao, A., & Ting-Toomey, S. (2002). Relational dialectics and management strategies in marital couples. *Southern Communication Journal, 67,* 142–159.

Houran, J., Lange, R., Rentfrow, P. J., & Bruckner, K. H. (2004). Do online matchmaking tests work? An assessment of preliminary evidence for a publicized "predictive model of marital success." *North American Journal of Pyschology, 6*(3), 507–526.

Huston, T. L., & Holmes, E. K. (2004). Becoming parents. In A. L. Vangelisti (Ed.), *Handbook of family communication* (pp. 105–133). Mahwah, NJ: Erlbaum.

Johnson, F. L. (2001). Ideological undercurrents in the semantic notion of "working mothers." *Women and Language, 24*(2), 21–27.

Kinnunen, U., Geurts, S., & Mauno, S. (2004). Work-to-family conflict and its relationship with satisfaction and well-being: A one-year longitudinal study on gender differences. *Work & Stress, 18*(1), 1–22.

Koerner, A. F., & Fitzpatrick, M. A. (2002). You never leave your family in a fight: The impact of family of origin on conflict-behavior in romantic relationships. *Communication Studies, 53,* 234–251.

Kulik, L. (2004). Strategies for managing home–work conflict and psychological well-being among Jews and Arabs in Israel: The impact of sex and sociocultural context. *Families in Society, 85*(1), 139–147.

Kurland, N. B., & Bailey, D. E. (1999). Telework: The advantages and challenges of working here, there, anywhere, and anytime. *Organizational Dynamics, 28,* 53–64.

Laing, R. D. (1972). *The politics of the family.* New York: Vintage.

Lavee, Y., & Olson, D. H. (1991). Family types and response to stress. *Journal of Marriage and Family, 53*(3), 786–798.

Manochehri, G., & Pinkerton, T. (2003). Managing telecommuters: Opportunities and challenges. *American Business Review, 21*(1), 9–16.

Mathijssen, J. J. J. P., Koot, H. M., Verhulst, F. C., DeBryn, E. E. J., & Oud, J. H. L. (1997). Family functioning and child psychopathology: Individual versus composite family scores. *Family Relations, 46*(3), 247–255.

Mead, G. H. (1934). *Mind, self, and society.* Chicago: University of Chicago Press.

Medved, C. E. (2004). The everyday accomplishment of work and family: Exploring practical actions in daily routines. *Communication Studies, 55*(1), 128–135.

Minuchin, S. (1974). *Families and family therapy.* Cambridge, MA: Harvard University Press.

Mirchandani, K. (2000). "The best of both worlds" and "Cutting my own throat": Contradictory images of home-based work. *Qualitative Sociology, 23*(2), 159–182.

Montgomery, B. M., & Baxter, L. A. (1998). *Dialectical approaches to studying personal relationships.* Mahwah, NJ: Erlbaum.

Morman, M. T., & Floyd, K. (2002). A "changing culture of fatherhood": Effects on affectionate communication, closeness, and satisfaction in men's relationships with their fathers and their sons. *Western Journal of Communication, 66*(4), 395–411.

Mosley-Howard, G. S., & Evans, C. B. (2000). Relationships and contemporary experiences of the African American family: An ethnographic case study. *Journal of Black Studies, 30*(3), 428–452.

O'Laughlin, E. M., & Bischoff, L. G. (2005). Balancing parenthood and academia: Work/family stress as influenced by gender and tenure status. *Journal of Family Issues, 26*(1), 79–106.

Olson, D. H. (1997). Family stress and coping: A multisystem perspective. In S. Dreman (Ed.), *The family on the threshold of the 21st century* (pp. 259–282). Mahwah, NJ: Erlbaum.

Olson, D. H. (2000). Circumplex model of marital and family systems. *Journal of Family Therapy, 22,* 144–167.

Olson, D. H., Russell, C. S., & Sprenkle, D. H. (Eds.). (1983). *Circumplex model: Systematic assessment and treatment of families.* New York: Haworth Press.

Olson, D. H., Sprenkle, D. H., & Russell, C. S. (1979). Circumplex model of marital and family systems: Cohesion and adaptability dimensions, family types, and clinical applications. *Family Process, 18*, 3–28.

Olson, L. N. (2002). Exploring "common couple violence" in heterosexual romantic relationships. *Western Journal of Communication, 66*, 104–128.

Olson, L. N., & Braithwaite, D. O. (2004). "If you hit me again, I'll hit you back": Conflict management strategies of individuals experiencing aggression during conflicts. *Communication Studies, 55*, 301–315.

Pink, J. E., & Wampler, K. S. (1985). Problem areas in stepfamilies: Cohesion, adaptability, and the stepfather–adolescent relationship. *Family Relations, 34*, 327–335.

Potter, E. (2003). Telecommuting: The future of work, corporate culture, and American society. *Journal of Labor Research, 24*(1), 73–84.

Rawlins, W. K. (1989). A dialectical analysis of the tensions, functions, and strategic challenges of communication in young adult friendships. *Communication Yearbook*, (Vol. 12, pp. 157–189).

Rawlins, W. K. (1992). *Friendship matters: Communication, dialectics, and the life course*. Hawthorne, NY: Aldine.

Robertson, M., Maynard, W., & McDevitt, J. (2003). Telecommuting: Managing the safety of workers in home office environments. *Professional Safety, 48*(4), 30–36.

Schrodt, P. (2005). Family communication schemata and the circumplex model of family functioning. *Western Journal of Communication, 69*(4), 359–376.

Shank-Krusiewicz, E., & Wood, J. T. (2001). He was our child from the moment we walked in that room: Entrance stories of adoptive parents. *Journal of Social and Personal Relationships, 18*, 785–803.

Stamp, G. H. (2004). Theories of family relationships and a family relationships theoretical model. In A. L. Vangelisti (Ed.), *Handbook of family communication* (pp. 1–30). Mahwah, NJ: Erlbaum.

Thompson, B. M., Kirk, A., & Brown, D. F. (2005). Work based support, emotional exhaustion, and spillover of work stress to the family environment: A study of policewomen. *Stress and Health, 21*(1), 199–207.

Tietze, S. (2002). When "work" comes "home": Coping strategies of teleworkers and their families. *Journal of Business Ethics, 41*(4), 385–396.

Turner, R. H. (1962). Role-taking: Process versus conformity. In A. Rose (Ed.), *Human behavior and social processes: An interactionist approach*. Boston: Houghton Mifflin.

von Bertalanffy, L. (1968). *General systems theory*. New York: Braziller.

Voydanoff, P. (2002). Linkages between the work–family interface and work, family, and individual outcomes: An integrative model. *Journal of Family Issues, 23*(1), 138–164.

Watzlawick, P., Beavin, J., & Jackson, D. D. (1967). *Pragmatics of human communication: A study of interactional patterns, pathologies, and paradoxes*. New York: Norton.

Wille, D. E. (1995). The 1990s: Gender differences in parenting roles. *Sex Roles: A Journal of Research, 33*, 803–817.

Section 2: Research Examples _____

Going Away to College: A Family Turning Point

Jo Anna Grant

Annette L. Folwell

> In this reading, Grant and Folwell consider the ways in which family systems change, or resist change as their life situations shift. Thus, the work focuses on the calibration (homeostasis) and recalibration of the family system. Additionally, as in the circumpex model discussed in Section 1, this article also addresses the issue of cohesion in the family setting. As college students, you are well positioned to consider the ways in which the change from high school to college impacted your family system, and how that is (or is not) reflected in this work.
>
> *L.B.A.*

Have you ever wondered why you feel closer to some family members than you do to others? Are some members of your family more powerful than others? Have you noticed that the way you feel about your family has changed over the course of your lifetime? This investigation looks at how families change when young adult children move away from the family home to attend college. Additionally, it also looks at how people explain their family relationships.

Going away to college is a big step into adulthood. Students have a chance to be more independent and make their own decisions. Their parents do not have as much control as before and these new college students do not see their family members as much as they did when they lived in the family home. These changes cause the family system to change over time. Because of this, we expect that entering first-year students will differ from juniors and seniors in the way they see (a) family power, (b) family closeness, (c) personal power, (d) who feels the closest, (e) who feels most distant, (f) who is most powerful, and (g) who is least powerful.

We also expect to find differences in how first-year students, sophomores, and juniors and seniors explain (a) why someone is the most powerful, (b) why someone is the least powerful, (c) why two people feel the closest, and (d) why two people feel the most distant.

Methods

Participants

We recruited 162 students: 52 first-year students, 55 sophomores, and 55 juniors and seniors. All of them met the following conditions:

a. They started college right after high school.
b. They moved away from home when they started college, and had not moved back.
c. They were in college continuously since beginning or had not taken off more than one semester.
d. They were single.

The students came from general education and communication classes. Eighty-three percent of the students were White, 12% were African Americans, and two students were Hispanic. Only one student checked "other" for race. Women outnumbered men almost two-to-one (women = 69.7%, men = 30.3%). Their ages ranged from 18 to 25 years and the average age was 19.8 years old.

We identified five different types of families in this study. Ninety-nine students came from nuclear families; 31 came from blended families; 25 came from single-parent families; 2 students had adopted families; and 5 students had grandparents or other family members serving the parent role.

Measures

We used the Family System Test (FAST) (Gehring & Feldman, 1988) to measure how students perceived family closeness and power. Students placed figures on a board to show how close each person in their family felt toward the other family members. Then, the participants raised the figures on blocks to show how much power each person had (see Figure 3.1). We used the FAST because it had demonstrated validity and reliability in past studies.

Next, students explained how they set up the board and we recorded their answers. First, they identified their two closest family members, and then they described why these

FIGURE 3.1   *The Family System Test (FAST) measures family closeness and power. Courtesy of JoAnna Grant.*

two people felt so close. Next, they identified the most distant pair of family members and explained why they felt distant. Finally, the students identified the most powerful and least powerful members of the family and described why they held these positions.

Data Analysis

We measured family power by calculating an average of how much each family member's representative figure on the board differed in height from the others. This number is the Perceived Family Power Score (PFPS). The PFPS assumes that people compare themselves to the most powerful person in the family (Kahn & Meier, 2001). A large PFPS meant a bigger power difference in the family.

We measured the overall family closeness with the Perceived Family Cohesion Score (PFCS). The PFCS equals the longest distance between two contiguous pieces divided by the shortest distance between contiguous pieces (Kahn & Meier, 2001). The pieces were contiguous if a line drawn between them did not cross a square occupied by another piece. A PFCS close to one meant the family felt as close as possible. A larger PFCS showed more family distance.

Next, we made a codebook using themes from students' answers. The codebook identified each theme, defined it, and gave specific examples. By developing a codebook, we could count the number of times each theme appeared in a student's answer.

We trained three research assistants to use the coding scheme. These research assistants coded the same 10 surveys. We compared their answers to make sure they agreed with each other; this consistency is referred to as *intercoder reliability*. We measured intercoder reliability with a formula called Scott's Pi, which measures the percentage of agreement between coders. Good intercoder reliability is generally considered to be 70% or higher. Once the research assistants achieved good intercoder reliability (Scott's Pi = .87), they divided the remaining surveys and coded them separately. Then, we added up the research assistants' findings to determine the most frequent themes.

Results

Family Power and Closeness Scores

A student's year in school had a significant effect on family power. Juniors and seniors felt their families were more powerful when compared to first-year students. There was not a significant effect on closeness for year in school.

Family power and closeness did show a significant positive correlation. This finding means that the more powerful a family is, the closer its members feel to each other. The less powerful the family is, the more distant its members feel.

We did not find any differences in family power or closeness based on sex, family type, or age. Age and year in school did not affect how students perceived their personal power.

The mother's power predicted the student's power. In other words, students with more powerful mothers felt more powerful themselves. Students with less powerful mothers felt that they had less personal power.

Most and Least Powerful Family Members

Parents held the most power in the family, whereas children had the least power. The student's year in school did not make a difference in this perception. Class did affect the explanations for why the most powerful family member had power (see Table 3.3). First-year students saw the most powerful family member as the one who controlled finances. Sophomores identified the decision maker as the most powerful. Juniors and seniors were more likely to see the authority figure as most powerful. The explanations students gave for the least powerful family member also differed by class (see Table 3.3). Juniors and seniors ascribed a lack of power to personality characteristics more often than first-year students or sophomores.

Students saw the mother as the most powerful family member, followed closely by the father. Students thought the mother has a wider basis of power. Mothers were seen as more powerful because they are decision makers, parents, essential family members,

TABLE 3.3 *Reasons for Being Most Powerful and Least Powerful Person in the Family by Class*

	First-Year Student	Sophomore	Junior/Senior	Totals
Reasons for Being Most Powerful (MP)				
Authority	4	7	16	27
Controls finances	15	15	9	39
Decision maker	17	28	19	64
Essential family member	9	5	12	26
Good communicator	3	6	5	14
Male dominance	6	3	7	16
Parental power	10	15	8	33
Personality	4	8	8	20
Other reasons	6	3	3	12
Totals for MP	74	90	87	251*
Reasons for Being Least Powerful (LP)				
Age	23	29	25	77
Family changes	1	2	0	3
Independent person	3	5	6	14
Lacks involvement	9	10	14	33
No biological tie	1	1	1	3
Personality changes	7	7	16	30
Some power	6	5	8	22
Rebellion	4	6	5	15
Other reasons	14	7	6	27
Totals for LP	68	75	81	224*

*Students could give more than one reason for MP and for LP.

$\chi^2_{MP} = 32.20$, $df = 16$, $p < .01$; $\chi^2_{LP} = 35.87$, $df = 14$, $p < .01$.

controllers of finances, and good communicators. The father's basis of power was viewed as more concentrated in two main areas: the students saw fathers primarily as decision makers and controllers of finances. College students most often cited themselves as the least powerful, followed by their sister or brother. Age was the most common reason for low power.

Closest and Least Close Family Members

Who do students think are the closest and most distant family members? The mother–self relationship is most often the closest (45.2%), followed by the father–self relationship (17.8%) and the mother–father relationship (8.9%). Students included themselves as a member of the closest pair most of the time (79.4%). For the most distant relationship, students' responses were spread across more relationships than for the closest relationship. The self–father relationship was most often identified as the most distant relationship (17.6%), followed by the sister–self relationship (11.8%) and the brother-self relationship (9.8%). The mother–self and the father–mother relationships tied as the most distant relationship (7.8%). Again, students often included themselves in the most distant relationship (56.9%).

Why do family members feel close? Most students gave the following reasons: (a) commonalities (24.5%); (b) proximity/contact (16.7%); (c) good communicator (15.1%); (d) parental role (10.3%); (e) friendship; and (f) longevity of the relationship. Students had more explanations for why people felt distant: (a) lack of proximity/contact (16.9%); (b) lack of commonalities (14.3%); (c) power struggles between individuals (14.3%); (d) personality characteristics (13.9%); (e) poor communicator (12.2%); and (f) age (8%).

Discussion

Family Power Differences

Moving away from home to attend school allows students to have more autonomy. Family systems theory (Minuchin, 1974) predicts that this change will cause a change in their family relationships. However, in this study, we found that students' perceptions of family relationships remained stable throughout the college experience.

First-year students, sophomores, and juniors and seniors did not differ significantly from each other in their views of personal power within their families. This finding might change if we measured personal power outside the family. Although students might feel growing levels of power *outside* their family as they continue through college, power *within* their family seems to remain steady.

We expected that living outside the family home would lead to a decrease *in the perceived power* of students' families. Instead, juniors and seniors actually felt that their families had *more* power than first-year students did. Students may gain more appreciation for their parents' power the longer they live away from home. They can observe the power their parents have from a new perspective.

Juniors and seniors were more likely to see the most powerful person in the family as the one who acted as an authority figure. Why is this so? Do parents step up the pressure on juniors and seniors? As professors, we see parents pushing students to interview for jobs and internships. Parents try to get students to declare a major, and they even try to direct the students' career choices. These pressures may explain the increase in family power that juniors and seniors feel.

The link between closeness and power is in harmony with the concept of *referent power* (French & Raven, 1959). Someone has referent power to persuade others because they want that person to like, admire, or respect him or her. In this study, referent power and emotional closeness are related. This connection explains why close families have more power, and distant families have less power. The relationship of closeness and power also explains why students depict "power struggles" as a leading reason for feeling distant.

Explaining Family Power

How do students explain power in their families? A student's year in school affects the reasons given for having the most power. All three class standings listed "decision maker" as the top reason for being powerful. However, first-year students and sophomores referred to the reason of "controlling finances" more than juniors and seniors. Juniors and seniors cited "authority figure" more than the other two classes.

Students also gave a very traditional picture of family power. All students saw power as a function of being a decision maker, controlling finances, having authority, and being a parent. Mothers, however, get power from being good communicators. Fathers have power because of male dominance. These differences show that students still have some conventional ideas of gender roles and power. Parents and children also have very typical power roles. Mothers and fathers have the power in the family. The children have the least power because of their age. This power difference between parents and children does not change with time. Power differences may be constant because the age and status differences between parents and children are constant.

Family Closeness Stability

Why did students not grow more distant from their families the longer they lived away from home? This finding is more difficult to explain. Several studies show that people feel more distant when they live farther away (Folwell, Chung, Grant, Nussbaum & Sparks, 1997; Folwell & Grant, 1999). Families who live closer to each other also feel closer. However, in this study, students moved away and yet felt the same closeness no matter how long ago they moved.

Cicirelli's (1991) work supports this finding. He says that people can feel emotionally close even when they have no physical contact. Students may be paying more attention to their feelings of closeness than to their physical experiences of closeness. So even though they have lived away for a long time, it does not affect the feelings of closeness.

Another reason for this finding is that students may not live far enough away from their families to change their experiences of closeness. They may be living close enough to home to keep their relationships the same; for example, they live only a few miles away and still see their families regularly. Students that moved out of state or far from home could have another approach to maintain their family relationships; they may think of the family home as their "real" home. In this case, students and their families do not recognize a need to renegotiate their relationships because the student still "lives" at home.

Family systems theory (Minuchin, 1974) gives another reason. Minuchin says that families react to change in ways that keep family relationships the same. Families oppose change, and Minuchin calls this opposition homeostasis. Here, we see homeostasis in action. Students and their families react to the stress of a family member leaving home by finding other ways to keep up their relationships. They may stay close through contact by calling or visiting often. They may stay close through giving objects such as cards, gifts, money, and care packages. Other family members may play a role, too. A nearby aunt, uncle, cousin, or grandparent may give students a sense of still being linked, thus still close to their families.

Another way to explain this finding is that students have not accepted the change yet. Their families have become more distant, but the students do not know it. They may notice the change only when they go home for a long visit. For example, things may be very different when they go home for summer break.

Maybe students became more distant from their families before they left home. Many high school students work and take part in extracurricular activities. They may be away from their families so much in high school that when they attend college their family relationships have already changed.

Explaining Closeness

Students gave three reasons for why their family members felt close: commonalities, proximity/contact, and communication skills. They gave the same reasons for feeling distant. All three are on a dichotomous scale. Students name more commonalities, more proximity/contact, and good communication as contributors to close relationships. Students blame their distant family relationships on a lack of proximity/contact, a lack of commonalities, and poor communication. These results are consistent with other studies. We have seen similar examples in adult grandchild–grandparent relationships (Folwell & Grant, 1999) and in older adult sibling relationships (Folwell et al., 1997).

Students had a very self-focused point of view in this study. Students see themselves as a part of the closest relationship 79.5% of the time. They are part of the most distant relationship 56.9% of the time. Most students feel closest to their mothers and most distant from their fathers. Only 10.3% of the students showed that their parents have the closest relationship in the family. This is surprising given the high number of students in this sample that come from nuclear families. Students are also likely to see themselves as the least powerful person in the family. After themselves, students listed sisters and brothers as having the least power.

These findings may imply that students may be overly self-centered, but they also may be a product of how we asked the questions. We did not permit ties in closeness or power, so students had to choose. This method may have led them to select relationships that involve themselves, which makes sense: they have firsthand knowledge of their own relationships. The feelings of others are only guesswork.

In summary, we can conclude that the college students reported different levels of power in their families. Juniors and seniors felt that families were more powerful than first-year students and sophomores. The variables of power and closeness positively correlated with each other. In other words, the more powerful a family is, the closer they feel to each other. All college students, regardless of year in school, chose a parent as the most powerful family member and a child as the least powerful member. Mothers had a wider base of power than fathers did, and students' year in school affected the different explanations for why mothers and fathers had the most power. Overall, students felt that their relationship with their mother was the closest relationship in the family, whereas their relationship with their father was the most distant.

Questions for Consideration and Discussion

1. Grant and Folwell's respondents indicated that the closest relationship in the family was between themselves and their mother. What cultural phenomenon might help explain this finding?
2. In this study, junior and senior students felt that a lack of power was more attributable to personality characteristics than did first-year and sophomore students. Why do you think this might be the case?
3. Juniors and seniors also saw the person in an authority position as being the most powerful. Grant and Folwell suggest this may be because parents pressure students more (with regard to grades, getting a job, etc.) as they progress through college. How would you respond to this claim?
4. Overall, the study indicated a lack of change in familial closeness. The authors suggest this may be the result of homeostasis in action. How can you explain this lack of change with homeostasis? What alternative explanations can you see?
5. Most of the respondents in this study were White. In what ways, if any, do you think this may have impacted the results?

References

Cicirelli, V. G. (1991). Attachment theory in old age: Protection of the attached figure. In K. Pillemer & K. McCartney (Eds.), *Parent–child relations throughout life* (pp. 25–42). Hillsdale, NJ: Erlbaum.

Folwell, A. L., Chung, L., Grant, J. A., Nussbaum, J. F., & Sparks, L. (1997). Differential accounts of closeness in older adult sibling relationships. *Journal of Social and Personal Relationships, 14*, 842–849.

Folwell, A. L., & Grant, J. A. (1999, November). Differential accounts of closeness in adult Grandchild–Grandparent relationships. Paper presented at the annual meeting of the National Communication Association, Chicago, IL.

French, J., & Raven, B. (1959). The bases of social power. In D. Cartwright (Ed.), *Studies in social power* (pp. 150–167). Ann Arbor, MI: Institute for Social Research.

Gehring, T. M., & Feldman, S. S. (1988). Adolescents' perceptions of family cohesion and power: A methodological study of the Family System Test. *Journal of Adolescent Research, 3*, 33–52.

Kahn, J. S., & Meier, S. T. (2001). Children's definitions of family power and cohesion affect scores on the Family System Test. *American Journal of Family Therapy, 29*, 141–154.

Minuchin, S. (1974). *Families and family therapy*. Cambridge, MA: Harvard University Press.

What Does It Mean to Be a Good Father?

Kory Floyd

Mark T. Morman

> As discussed in Section 1, family roles are an important part of understanding family systems. The meanings and expectations we have for particular roles come from the cultures in which we participate, as well as our own role negotiation processes. In this article, Floyd and Morman discuss the results of a study considering how men and boys understand the father role. While reading this article, consider your own beliefs about fathering, and how those beliefs coincide with, or depart from, the points made by these respondents.
>
> *L.B.A.*

You don't have to read many self-help books or watch many talk shows these days to get the impression that most men aren't very good at fathering. Lots of attention has been paid to the negative aspects of ineffective or distant fathering, focusing on things like alcoholism (Whipple & Noble, 1991), physical punishment (DeKlyen, Speltz, & Greenberg, 1998; DeVet, 1997), aggressiveness (Moss, Mezzich, Yao, Gavaler, & Martin, 1995), conflict (Comstock, 1994), and dysfunction (Lee, 1987). No one would disagree that fatherhood is a demanding role and that problems like these are tough for fathers and their families to deal with. However, when we focus only on the problems of fatherhood, this can take our attention away from the fact that many men work hard to be good fathers to their children.

Society's ideas about what it means to be a good father seem to be shifting with the times, too. For example, a 1996 survey found that American men are becoming more committed to fathering—more than half of the men in the survey said that being a father is more important to them than it was to their own fathers. About 70% also said they spend more time with their children than their fathers spent with them (Adler, 1996). In another study, 74% of men said that balancing work and family life was a major priority in their lives (Shellenbarger, 1997). On the same note, research by Kindlon and Thompson (1999) found that most men want to do a good job raising their children and want to do a better job than their fathers did raising them.

It's great that men want to be better fathers, but what exactly does that mean? What makes a man *a good father*? To find out, we asked 572 boys and men for their opinions about what makes a father a *good* father. The males who took part in our survey were as young as 12 years old and as old as 87, with an average age of just over 40 years old. They came from all regions of the United States. We recruited the participants by giving questionnaires to college students and asking them to find boys and men to be in the study.

For those who said they'd take part in our survey, we gave them a questionnaire with the following question:

> Think for a few minutes about being a father. What does being a "good father" mean to you? Below, please describe your thoughts on what it means to be a good father. (You might think specifically of instances in which you felt like a particularly good father, or about men you know whom you think of as good fathers.) What does it mean to be a good father?

Each person was given a page of lined paper on which he could write out a response to the question. This gave us 572 pages of handwritten answers to the question about good fatherhood. Our job, then, was to go through what the men and boys said and figure out if we could group their answers into themes. We each went through a process of figuring out what the themes might be, first by ourselves and then together. What did the males say was important for good fathers? We found 20 different themes, which we talk about here in alphabetical order.

The first was that a good father *admits when he makes mistakes.* For instance, one man said "sometimes you have to be willing to say to your son, 'I blew it. I'm sorry.'" Second, some participants said that a good father *shows affection* to his children. One father commented that "a good father loves his son and communicates to him that he loves him, hugging, things like that." A third theme was that good fathers must be *available when needed.* This theme communicated the idea that good fathers are always there when their children need them.

The fourth and fifth themes focused on the responsibilities of fatherhood. Good fathers must *exercise control* by setting limits and boundaries for their children's lives, and they must *provide discipline* when their children need it. For example, one father noted that "a father needs to be a loving disciplinary instrument in his son's life." However, the boys and men in the study also saw good fatherhood as having a softer side. The sixth theme evident in the narratives was that a good father *exercises forgiveness.* One participant commented that "a good father may not always agree with his son's actions, but must always be willing to forgive him." Similarly, the seventh theme was that a good father *is a good friend* to his kids, someone his children can turn to and confide in.

Good fathers must also *be involved*, according to the eighth category. Participants in the survey thought that good fathers must take an active role in their children's lives and interests. On a similar note, the ninth category suggested that good fathers are *good listeners.* One man said of his son, "I want to be open and listen when he needs to talk." In addition, the tenth category was that good fathers *provide love* to their children. For instance, one father indicated that "a good father loves his son as much as he can."

Males in the survey also talked about a father's obligations to his children. According to the eleventh category, a good father *protects.* One participant noted that "a good father makes his kids and wife feel safe and protected." Similarly, a good father *provides for his family*, according to the twelfth category.

The importance of a father's relationship with his children's mother was the focus of the thirteenth category: a good father *maintains a good relationship with the mother.* For example, one father noted that "a good father loves his wife and teaches his children to do the same." Others noted, in the fourteenth category, that a good father *relinquishes control appropriately.* This theme reflects that idea that parents must adjust their rules as their children age, giving their children more freedom as they grow older.

The fifteenth category was that a good father is a *role model* for his children. Many books and articles have been written about the importance of parents being good role models; participants in our study also thought that it was an important part of good fatherhood.

Good fathers also *sacrifice for their children*, according to the sixteenth category. As one participant noted, "being a good father has meant self-sacrifice for the betterment of my children." Also, some participants felt that good fathers *seek their children's approval*. In particular, according to the seventeenth category, good fathers should behave in ways that make their children proud of them. Moreover, according to the eighteenth category, a good father *supports his children*. Unlike the twelfth category, this theme had to do with providing emotional and instrumental types of support, rather than providing for children financially.

The final two categories had to do with a father's teaching role. The men and boys in our study seemed to talk about teaching in two ways: teaching about life skills and teaching about religion, ethics, or morals. We put these into separate categories. The nineteenth category said that a good father *teaches his children skills and information*. For instance, good fathers might teach their children how to drive a car, how to balance a checkbook, or about their family history. Finally, the twentieth category said that a good father *teaches his children about morals and beliefs*. One father noted, for instance, that "a good father loves God and teaches his son to do the same."

The categories that were mentioned the most were (1) providing love, (2) being a role model, (3) being available, (4) being involved in children's lives, and (5) being a good provider. Older men were more likely than younger men and boys to mention forgiveness and admitting mistakes as characteristics of good fathers. We thought this might be the case because forgiveness and admitting mistakes might become more important over time as men get more experience as fathers.

To recap: we asked men and boys about what it means to be a good father, and we found 20 different themes in their answers. The categories of love, availability, and role modeling were mentioned the most often as characteristics of good fathers. Many of the boys and men in our study simply wrote one or two sentences in response to the question; however, several others wrote paragraphs or filled the entire page with comments, suggestions, and insights into the role of fathering. We think one of the best parts about this approach is that it leaves the question open for people to decide what to write, how much to write, and how many suggestions they would make. Of course, this study is only a first step, and we think it's important to go further by looking at how men become good fathers and why some men get better at fathering over time whereas others don't. We also want to look at how children benefit from good fathering, and how good fathering is the same as—or different from—good mothering. These are questions that can help each of us understand the positive and negative parts of fatherhood a little better.

Questions for Consideration and Discussion

1. In Section 1 we discussed how culture contributes to our understandings of roles. How do you see mainstream U.S. culture (in which the study was done) impacting the 20 characteristics of fathering mentioned?
2. Some of these characteristics might be harder than others for fathers to enact, depending upon the cultures in which they participate. Thinking about the cultures you are a part of, which do you see as most difficult, and why?

3. This particular analysis used self-report (asking respondents to talk about what they think). What might be the problems associated with this type of research? The benefits?
4. Given that all research methods have drawbacks and benefits, what are some alternative methods that might have been used in a study of father roles?
5. Floyd and Morman note that future research is needed about this issue. In addition to the streams of research they suggest, where do you think this research should or could go in the future, and why?

References

Adler, J. (1996, June 17). Building a better dad. *Newsweek*, pp. 58–64.

Comstock, J. (1994). Parent–adolescent conflict: A developmental approach. *Western Journal of Communication, 58*, 263–282.

DeKlyen, M., Speltz, M. L., & Greenberg, M. T. (1998). Fathering and early onset conduct problems: Positive and negative parenting, father–son attachment, and the marital context. *Clinical Children and Family Psychological Review, 1*, 3–21.

DeVet, K. A. (1997). Parent–adolescent relationships, physical disciplinary history, and adjustment in adolescents. *Family Process, 36*, 311–322.

Kindlon, D., & Thompson, M. (1999). *Raising Cain: Protecting the emotional life of boys*. New York: Ballantine Books.

Lee, J. (1987). *The flying boy: Healing the wounded man*. Deerfield Beach, FL: Health Communications.

Moss, H. B., Mezzich, A., Yao, J. K., Gavaler, J., & Martin, C. S. (1995). Aggressivity among sons of substance-abusing fathers: Association with psychiatric disorder in the father and son, paternal personality, pubertal development, and socioeconomic status. *The American Journal of Drug and Alcohol Abuse, 21*, 195–208.

Shellenbarger, S. (1997, April 30). These top bosses may signal move to more family time. *The Wall Street Journal*, p. B1.

Whipple, S. C., & Noble, E. P. (1991). Personality characteristics of alcoholic fathers and their sons. *Journal of Studies on Alcohol, 52*, 331–337.

Dialectic Characteristics and Shadow Realities in Postmarital Relationships

Elizabeth E. Graham

Autumn P. Edwards

We don't always think of ex-spouses as having a "relationship," and yet they do. In the work considered here, Graham and Edwards use the concepts of dialectics to consider the ways in which postmarital partners construct understandings of their relationship that are comfortable to acknowledge in the open, but often maintain other understandings that are unspoken (shadow realities). As the authors note, shadow realities are not only a part of divorce relationships. As you think about the study discussed here, and your own relational dialectics, you may gain a clearer sense of how shadow realities operate in your family systems.

L.B.A.

The purpose of this article is to illuminate the communication challenges former spouses face as they as they create and manage long-term postmarital relationships with one another. Specifically, this research focuses on how postmarital (divorced) couples experience dialectical characteristics and shadow realities. Shadow realities are manifest in unprivileged thoughts and topics and contradict the shared postmarital reality. The characteristics of relational dialectics (contradiction, change, praxis, and totality) serve as the framework for discussing postmarital relationships. Recognizing that postmarital relationships are viable relational forms, with dialectical characteristics and shadow realities, prompts us to reconsider divorce as relationship transition rather than termination.

Shadow Realities

In marriage, as in postmarriage, couples create a reality that reflects the way they want to view their relationship. This shared reality can be seen in couples' communication with and about each other. Thus, people in relationships make choices about which subjects or topics to privilege and deal with and which to ignore and cast aside. These unprivileged topics, according to Rosenblatt and Wright (1984), make up what is known as a "shadow reality." Specifically, a shadow reality is an "alternative reality" that directly threatens the reality that has been negotiated by relational partners.

A shared reality presupposes a shadow reality. When a shadow reality does emerge—whether in words spoken or unspoken, gestures recognized, or glances interpreted—a revision of reality might be required. As a consequence, former spouses are prompted to confront, through communication, the contradictions between their shared reality and the reality that has been lurking in the shadows.

Perhaps uninvited and unappreciated, shadow realities creep into the fabric of relationships, often in times of crisis. Shadow realities can ultimately provide insight into important relationship dynamics by bringing particular characteristics of the relationship into focus. Couples work together to avoid shadow realities, because if a shadow reality surfaces it may involve "ending of the marriage, a radical revision in sense of self, a shattering of all that one has believed in, or embarrassment over having lived a lie" (Rosenblatt & Wright, 1984, p. 48). It is important to note that not all relationship partners "shun" shadow realities. As Rosenblatt and Wright point out, "there are . . . marriages with a marriage reality that includes shadow illumination as a legitimate, even desired, part of the relationship" (p. 50). In these relationships, shadow realities can be liberating and perhaps serve as a motivator for positive relational change.

Shadow realities are particularly significant for former spouses as they sift through and choose behaviors appropriate to their new postmarital reality. These shadow realities are present as individuals work to transform their once spousal relationships into viable postmarital or coparenting relationships. For example, a shared postmarital reality may be that each former spouse has moved on with his or her life separate from the other, whereas the shadow reality may include acknowledgment of ongoing dependency, interconnectedness, and intimate feelings remaining after the marriage ended. Or, consider a couple whose shared postmarital reality is that they are equal partners in parenting their children. Their shadow reality may contain recognition that the children seem to relate better to one parent, that one parent may contribute more time or financial resources to the children, or that one parent has the privilege of making more childrearing decisions. In both of these hypothetical cases, it is clear that an entirely different postmarital relationship would emerge if the shadow reality came into the light.

A Dialectic Framework

Shadow realities are closely related to dialectics in that both involve a perceived contradiction. Although there are many conceptualizations of dialectics (Altman, 1993), there are four characteristics that capture the essence of a dialectical framework: contradiction, change, praxis, and totality (Baxter & Montgomery, 1996).

Although shadow realities might be confused with dialectics, there are distinctions to be drawn. Dialectical tensions involve a contradiction of relational forces; shadow realities involve a contradiction between an agreed upon and a subverted or unprivileged reality. Dialectical tensions likely emerge from the incongruity between the postmarital reality and the accompanying shadow realities. Conversely, potential realities may be pushed into the shadows or brought into the light for the very purpose of managing dialectical tensions. Perhaps the defining link between shadow realities and dialectics is one of reflexivity. Indeed, the very existence of one prompts the existence of the other.

In an effort to understand how shadow realities are communicatively managed in postmarital relationships, accounts offered by participants in postmarital relationships are examined through the framework of these four defining characteristics of dialectics: contradictions, change, praxis, and totality.[1]

Method

Participants for this study were 35 divorced individuals (25 women and 10 men) who had been divorced for at least one year, were a parent of a biological or adopted child, and were actively involved in childrearing. All participants were White and most were middle-aged, middle class, college educated, and employed. Participants had an average of 2 children. On average, participants had been divorced about 8 years. Many had subsequently remarried or were living with someone, but several participants indicated that they were not currently in a romantic relationship.

They had been recruited to participate in this study by responding to advertisements featured in local newspapers, email, community access cable television, as well as personal knowledge and network sampling (Granovetter, 1976). The participants were informed of the purpose of the study and asked to participate in interviews, which took place in participants' homes, restaurants, and private offices. The interviews concerned participants' experience with relational dialectics.[2] We asked participants to talk with us about their experiences with dialectical contradictions and to describe how they managed their relationship with their former spouse. Their responses were then examined through a dialectical framework consisting of contradiction, change, praxis, and totality.

Results

Through discussions with participants, we were able to identify relational dialectics and shadow realities. We organized our thoughts by employing the framework of the four defining characteristics of relational dialectics: contradiction, change, praxis, and totality.

Contradiction

The search for dialectical contradictions in postmarital relationships has been the subject of previous research (see Graham, 1997, 2003; Masheter 1994, 1997; Masheter & Harris, 1986). The outcome of these efforts points to the presence of contradictions, which means there are real relationships between divorced individuals. Simply put, there are no relationships without contradictions; thus, the manifestations and articulation of contradictions by former spouses is indicative of some form of after-divorce partnership.

The dialectical contradiction termed autonomy and connection is the most central to the study of relationships (Rawlins, 1983) and will, thus, be a theme woven throughout subsequent discussions. However, the relationship between former spouses requires specific terminology to express the complex web of relationship pushes and pulls. Therefore, the autonomy-connection contradiction will be recast as a contradiction between "separate and together" and a "separate togetherness" (Masheter, 1997). Consistent with the notion that contradiction encompasses both negation and unity (Altman, Vinsel, & Brown, 1981), responses provided by the participants are organized according to the principle of negation and are termed *establishing separateness* and *establishing togetherness*. The principle of unity is encompassed in the dialectical contradiction termed *establishing a separate-togetherness*.

Establishing Separateness.   Shadow realities are perhaps most evident when postmarital couples attempt to establish a separateness from their former spouse so that they might develop a new life for themselves. Perhaps the most tangible evidence that a divorce has occurred can be found in the efforts that postmarital couples engage in to untangle the web of jointly constructed identities, physical and emotional boundaries, and even habitual behaviors and activities (Madden-Derdich & Arditti, 1999).

In commenting on her desire for separateness from her former spouse, Joan, a 42-year-old homemaker and mother of three, explained: "I just really want to keep things at arms' distance. I don't want things to appear to be coming back together." She went on to describe her feelings of discomfort in an experience that she felt violated the separateness that she was trying to establish between the two of them:

> It was going to see his dad. It was the two of us showing up together. That was the first time anybody had seen us together; it was the first time we had gone anywhere together for months and so yeah, I think that that was definitely disturbing to me because I spend a lot of time trying to keep it just "me" and all of a sudden it was "us" going to see him. Well it was more than that; we stopped and did some shopping and bought some things for my truck and then [he] takes me down to drop the truck off and brings me home. That whole day was like us doing things together and it was just very uncomfortable for me after awhile.

Clearly the event of "appearing" to be together threatened Joan's reality and she felt that this was a digression from the agreed-upon separateness that they had worked so hard to develop.

Establishing Togetherness.   Contrary to traditional thoughts about relationships, not all relationships are based on liking and affection (Hess, 2000). Hess suggests that we think of liking as just one of the many factors that contribute to relational maintenance. Indeed, sometimes people are compelled to maintain a relationship with a disliked other. Nonvoluntary relationships are quite common. Examples include relationships with coworkers, siblings, in-laws, stepfamilies, and former spouses. It is important to note, however, that not all postmarital relationship are regarded as nonvoluntary. As in marriage, postmarriage is also characterized by relative degrees of closeness and distance. But clearly, many postmarital couples struggle with the necessity of maintaining a relationship with a person whom they have chosen to no longer be married. It seems then that the desire and responsibility one might feel to stay connected to one's former spouse is fraught with contradiction. Indeed, other factors such as the presence of children may influence a partner's desires to maintain a friendly relationship with his or her former spouse. As one participant named Debbie explained:

> I realized that as parents we're still very useful for each other because I need to deal with the kids every day and when major events occur, like the kids getting in trouble with grades

or trouble with anything, I can call him up and he adds his input. It has to be over the telephone, but still we come together over anything that has to do with the kids.

Establishing a Separate-Togetherness.   Attention to one polarity of the contradiction (i.e., separate or together) is more readily recognizable and retrievable than the unity of the contradiction termed separate-togetherness. A search for a separate-togetherness comprises the both/and quality of dialectical contradiction. Participants provided several personal reflections that could be characterized as a struggle to achieve a state of a separate-togetherness.

For instance, Sue, a 38-year-old accountant, commented on her attempt to establish a separate-togetherness with her former spouse:

> He would come to my house for visitation to pick her up or drop her off or to visit with her there while I left and I had trouble getting rid of him. And so it was a very difficult situation; we all lived in the same small community and I just wanted out of that. I needed to get a fresh start, which is why I came here. But we continue to have a relationship that I would characterize as being friends, where we talk with each other about what is going on in your profession and funny things that have happened and that kind of thing. Staying away from family issues pretty much, but talking about more other global things. I have done that by choice, that's been a really hard thing for me to do.

In grappling with the tension inherent in creating a separate-togetherness, this woman exercised a choice to devote attention to some topics and ignore others. This account is demonstrative both of the considerable effort often required to push portions of reality to the shadows and the active role of relationship partners in doing so.

Another participant, Jay, spoke quite movingly about his awkward feelings toward his former spouse when they would meet up at their son's wrestling match:

> It does seem strange when we are together and we were together at the wrestling match on Wednesday and every once in a while you look and say "do I even know this person?" We were married for all those years and we have not had any contact, I mean physical, a hug, a kiss, any of that stuff. Nothing, absolutely nothing and that has been really her doing and I think it is hard for her. Because she is doing what she thinks she needs to do which is probably what you need to do.

Postmarital couples perhaps find themselves "suspended between opposite relational identities" (Baxter, Braithwaite, Golish, & Olson, 2002)—separate as husband and wife, together as mom and dad. Perhaps there are stages or phases that characterize one's movement through the divorce process, both legal and emotional (e.g., Ahrons, 1994). As previously suggested, divorce is not a finite moment, but rather a process of continuing renegotiation of roles and relationships.

Several participants spoke about the relatively enduring close relationship they have with their former spouse. They report little trouble balancing a separate togetherness. Tim, a participant in his late 50s, detailed how his former wife asked for his approval of the man she was about to marry:

> She wanted my reaction on how her marriage would influence our relationship . . . she wanted approval of him as my son's stepfather. I approve. I think that if I would have had

some reservations about this fellow, then she would have taken them seriously. I don't know if she would have not married him, but I think she would have taken seriously or closely examined what my concerns were and checked it out. As it turns out he is a fine fellow.

To summarize, participants expressed clear indications of a desire for separateness, togetherness and instances of a separate-togetherness as a means of managing postmarital shadow realities. The results of this study illustrate the complexities of postdivorce relationships, particularly those that involve children.

Change

Change is closely tied to contradictions as contradictions prompt change and change prompts contradictions. Consider the words of Martin, a divorced father of two, who described the process by which he and his former spouse agreed to focus the communication in the relationship to the children. He explains:

> We came to a crossroads about nine years ago. When we first got divorced, our communication had a lot to do with being friends. Then, we went through a period where we couldn't talk to each other about anything because it was always accusatory. And we finally agreed to keep the communication focused on our child, and forget about who did what back then. It wasn't always easy but we did make an effort to do that. . . . I think we were able to work our way from where we were to where we are now.

This postmarital couple's originally shared reality involved friendship and stressed togetherness. This reality was followed by a period of antagonism, separateness, and inability to connect, but finally evolved into a functional state of separate-togetherness. Running as an undercurrent in this account is a story of individuals struggling to achieve a satisfactory shared reality by agreeing to push certain aspects of their relationship out of the light. Despite the fact that these former spouses have a relational history that is larger than the sharing of a child and remember and feel anger for things that transpired earlier in that relationship, they have decided not to privilege topics unrelated to their children. Rosenblatt and Wright (1984) note that shared realities are often constructed to exclude the memory of considerable hurt in the relationship. Shadow realities are then avoided, because moving into them may bring a pain that is difficult to forget.

Praxis

The third characteristic of a dialectical framework, praxis, refers to the notion that future actions are influenced by past actions. Essentially, communicative choices made at one point frame future communications. Thus, fragments of other realities remain as constant undercurrents of the relationship and merge to form postmarital shadow realities.

Participants' awareness of the relationship between their marital histories and postmarital realities was evident. One woman named Pat reported being very connected to her former spouse and described a shared reality between the two of them where "we do not discuss who we are dating or what our involvement is." In the shadows, however, is her remembrance that, at times in the past, both have been open about their suspicions, jealousy, and concern regarding individuals seeking relationships with the other. She felt and voiced her concern over "gold-digging women, you know, with a couple kids that aren't really interested in him" and recalled what her former spouse said about the first man she dated after the divorce: "he told me he thought he was a drunk and stuff like that." She went on to express her certainty that her former spouse was aware of her current relationship with her new boyfriend. However, despite the things this couple thought of, said, did, or hoped for at one time, they have constructed a shared postmarital reality in which they do not make the romantic lives of the other an issue. Their fears, concerns, and feelings were banished to the shadows in order to forward a reality in which spouses share a closeness revolving around their children and each others' nonromantic lives.

In addition, several participants clearly stated that there is a link between their past and present actions by admitting that though their marriages were unsuccessful, their postmarital relationships could be successful. One woman, a physical therapist named Jeanne, recounted how she and her former spouse came to realize that though they had failed as spouses, they could succeed as coparents.

> We went to a family counselor at the time, and the counselor was a husband–wife team and we decided that they were more screwed up than we were. So, we stopped seeing them and decided that we both loved our son and that even though we weren't good spouses to each other, we could still be good parents and we had one of the first joint custody settlements in the state.

In explaining her belief that she and her former spouse were unsuccessful in marriage but successful afterward, another female participant remarked: "I'm surprised as much as we did fight and those horrible things we said to each other and as mean as we were to each other when we were married. It's surprising that now we can be so cordial and friendly and so like it didn't even happen." Clearly, aspects of this couples' shared past have been pushed to the shadows so that they could successfully coparent. Even as she expressed surprise that their past could so easily be cast into the shadows *as if it never happened*, she spoke of the marital and postmarital realities as connected—linked in history and tied to the future.

Totality

The last quality, totality, refers to the interconnectedness and fluidity as a defining characteristic of relational life. Although the focus of this research has been the management of dialectics between former spouses, as Montgomery (1992) reminds us, "relationships exist in the context of a larger social order" (p. 475). Thus, larger society must be considered as an important influence on all personal relationships, including the postmarital variety. This study demonstrates the need to recognize postmarital relationships as legitimate family forms rather than treating them as deviant and undesirable.

Although divorce is generally thought of as an unfortunate relationship outcome, once the divorce has occurred, there is societal pressure to terminate any and all relationship between former spouses. Indeed, former spouses are pressured by society to rid themselves of any emotional attachment to one another because continued attachment represents a failed divorce (Kressel, Lopez-Morillas, Weinglas, & Deutsch, 1978). Prior to the early 1990s, divorce was pathologized, such that any ongoing attachment to a former spouse was deemed "unhealthy." The only advice for former spouses to engage in a healthy divorce was to completely terminate the relationship. This might be necessary and helpful to accomplish the transition to a new identity; however, there is minimal guidance for those former spouses willing and capable of maintaining a relationship with each other. As previously evidenced, just as there is a need for couples to establish a quality marriage, there too is a need to establish a quality postmarital relationship. Unfortunately, it is possible for former spouses to experience a failed marriage and a failed divorce—perhaps the ultimate contradiction.

Discussion

As former spouses grappled with establishing separateness, togetherness, and a separate-togetherness as part of their postmarital realities, they sometimes found themselves pushing fragments of reality that did not fit well out of the light. This was often accomplished with a conscious awareness and a considerable amount of time and effort. The existence of shadow realities in postmarital relationships provides powerful additional impetus for treating the relationships between former spouses as viable continuing relational forms subject to ongoing renegotiation, reconstitution, and coconstruction throughout the lifetime of the family. By peering into the shadows of a couple's relationship reality, we may gain important insight into how individuals go about constructing postmarital realities that help them meet their needs and manage the dialectical tensions of relational life.

The effort to rename postdivorce relationships as postmarital relationships has implications for the study of dialectics—specifically, the assumptions of contradiction, change, praxis, and totality. Though much previous research and popular discourse has conceptualized divorce as relationship termination, the identification of relational contradictions between former spouses in this and other investigations (e.g., Graham, 2003; Masheter, 1994, 1997; Masheter & Harris, 1986) prompts a treatment of divorce as instead a marker of relational transition. Participants in the present study demonstrated that postmarital relationships are often fraught with contradictions (e.g., reality/shadow reality; separate/together).

Furthermore, the term *postmarital* affirms praxis as characteristic of relational life. A postmarital reality is one that is constrained, enabled, and *literally* made possible only by a marital history. Each relationship is answerable to the other. Yet, all too often our terminology in framing this relationship (e.g., *divorced*) suggests only the termination of a previous relationship and denies the accountability of and inextricable link between marital and postmarital life. Rethinking our terminology may go a long way in giving validation and support to individuals in this relational system. An awareness of dialectical characteristics and shadow realities is particularly informative as we continue to investigate this ever-growing family form.

Questions for Consideration and Discussion

1. Graham and Edwards argue that shadow realities can serve as motivators for positive change in relationships. In what ways might this be so?
2. The results of this analysis and the dialectical perspective suggest that separating past experiences and choices from present interaction is impossible (praxis). Why is this particularly important to understand in the context of postmarital relationships?
3. The dialectical perspective was used in this study as a framework for creation and analysis. What particular benefits do you see in examining family relationships from a dialectical perspective? What drawbacks do you see?

4. The respondents for this study were primarily women, and all White. In what ways, if any, might this have impacted the results?

5. For a participant in a family of divorce, or a professional interacting with divorced families (i.e., teacher, therapist, minister, caseworker, lawyer, etc.), what might this study add to the understanding of relationships after divorce?

Endnotes

1. This data set served as the basis for two articles written by the first author, Elizabeth Graham, and appeared in *Communication Monographs, 64,* 350–368 and the *Journal of Family Communication, 3,* 193–214.

2. One female participant was unable to recall any dialectical contradictions characteristic of her relationship with her former spouse. She indicated that she was suffering from a lack of memory rather than a resistance to comply with the requirements of the research project. She did not differ in any discernable way from the other participants. Therefore, dialectical contradictions were analyzed for 34 respondents rather than 35.

References

Ahrons, C. R. (1994). *The good divorce*. New York: HarperCollins.

Altman, I. (1993). Dialectics, physical environments, and personal relationships. *Communication Monographs, 60,* 26–34.

Altman, I., Vinsel, A., & Brown, B. (1981). Dialectical conceptions in social psychology: An application to social penetration and privacy regulation. In L. Berkowitz (Ed.), *Advances in Experimental Social Psychology* (Vol. 14). New York: Academic Press.

Baxter, L. A., Braithwaite, D. O., Golish, T. D., & Olson, L. N. (2002). Contradictions of interaction for wives of elderly husbands with adult dementia. *Journal of Applied Communication Research, 30,* 1–26.

Baxter, L. A., & Montgomery, B. M. (1996). *Relating: Dialogues & dialectics*. New York: Guilford Press.

Graham, E. E. (1997). Turning points and commitment in post-divorce relationships. *Communication Monographs, 64,* 350–368.

Graham, E. E. (2003). Dialectic contradictions in post-marital relationships. *Journal of Family Communication, 3,* 193–214.

Granovetter, M. S. (1976). Network sampling: Some first steps. *American Journal of Sociology, 81,* 1287–1303.

Hess, J. A. (2000). Maintaining nonvoluntary relationships with disliked partners: An investigation into the use of distancing behaviors. *Human Communication Research, 26,* 458–488.

Kressel, K., Lopez-Morillas, M., Weinglas, J., & Deutsch, M. (1978). Professional intervention in divorce: The views of lawyers, psychotherapists, and clergy. *Journal of Divorce, 2,* 119–155.

Madden-Derdich, D. A., & Arditti, J. A. (1999). The ties that bind: Attachment between former spouses. *Family Relations, 48,* 243–249.

Masheter, C. (1994). Dialogues between ex-spouses: Evidence of dialectic relationship development. In R. Conville (Ed.), *Uses of structure in communication studies* (pp. 83–101). Westport, CT: Praeger.

Masheter, C. (1997). Former spouses who are friends: Three case studies. *Journal of Social and Personal Relationships, 14,* 207–222.

Masheter, C., & Harris, L. M. (1986). From divorce to friendship: A study in dialectic relationship development. *Journal of Social and Personal Relationships, 3,* 177–189.

Montgomery, B. M. (1992). Communication as the interface between couples and culture. In S. A. Deetz (Ed.), *Communication yearbook* (Vol. 15, pp. 475–507). Newbury Park, CA: Sage.

Rawlins, W. K. (1983). Negotiating close friendship: The dialectic of conjunctive freedoms. *Human Communication Research, 9,* 255–266.

Rosenblatt, P. C., & Wright, S. E. (1984). Shadow realities in close relationships. *American Journal of Family Therapy, 12,* 45–54.

Section 3: Conclusions and Application—Thinking about the Systemic Nature of Your Own Family

When I teach family communication theory and research, students often approach systems theory with some trepidation. First, the very word *theory* can be frightening to students who have learned that theory means something difficult (which, really, it doesn't—a **theory** is simply an understanding about the way the world does or will work; we all operate with our own theories of the world every day). Second, some of the terminology and concepts in the systems perspective (for example, positive and negative feedback) seem very complex or counterintuitive when first encountered. However, even with these drawbacks, systems theory is most often mentioned on student evaluations as the concept that students found most revealing and compelling.

Why do you suppose that is? I believe the reason is that systems theory is so applicable to any relationship, or any family at any time and place. Systems theory and cybernetics call upon ideas and understandings of relationships that we already intuitively know, and develop these in such a way that we can increase our understandings of our family and relational processes. They allow us to put names to the experiences that we have on a daily basis and to see the operation of our own relational systems as normal.

Within a family system, we operate in particular roles and *systems theory can help us analyze those roles*. Our family roles emerge partly through our own family negotiation (who cleans the bathroom . . . Mom, Dad, or the kids?) but also via the messages that we are socialized by in a particular culture (whom do you picture "kissing the booboo" and applying the bandage?). Floyd and Morman consider how a group of men and boys describe the role of a good father. Think about your family of origin and the roles played by each member. How do you see the impact of society in those roles? In what ways did your family "go against" the societally expected role divisions? Why do you think that might be? Now consider the shifts that happened in your family as you grew from childhood to adulthood. How did you experience the negotiation of roles as time and space changes occurred in the family?

As you consider your family of origin, social expectations of the culture in which you live, and your own beliefs about fulfillment of family roles, you may find yourself thinking about your future family cultures. What family roles would you hope to repeat in future family situations, perhaps in your family of procreation? What roles might you hope to let go of? Conducting this type of personal analysis into our family role behaviors is useful because it gives us a chance to reaffirm the positive value of some role enactments. It also gives us the opportunity to think about the kind of changes we would like to see and how we might make those changes, rather than simply recreating the same role patterns over again.

In addition to helping us see the roles that are maintained in our family settings, a *systems perspective can also provide insight into how our family operates and the successes and problems the family experiences*. Because the United States is such an individualistic culture, the urge to understand relationships and families in terms of individual behavior is intense. We are sometimes tempted to blame the problems in a family on the behavior of one member ("If Mom wasn't so controlling, there wouldn't be so many arguments!"). And yet, under the surface we know that although a particular behavior may (or may not) seem to be the province of one relational member, the overall outcome of a relationship is developed through the interaction of all relational members, and thus cannot be narrowed down to one member's contributions. Systems theory encourages and develops this understanding.

Not only does systems theory prompt us to think about how each member of the family system impacts the family and is part of the intricate family process, but it also *encourages us to remember the complexity of connection between the many "parts" of being family*. Have you ever been upset with one family member and directed that anger toward another family member? After being punished by parents or adult caregivers for a particular behavior (let's say breaking curfew), have you ever treated those family members differently about what seems to be a very separate issue (let's say household chores)? A change in any part of the system—for example, when a student enters college and maybe even moves out of the family home—creates changes in other parts of that family system, sometimes in unexpected ways. Family systems theory and cybernetics press us, as family members and family scholars, to remember that what happens in one domain of family will have impacts (small or large) on other domains, even if those domains seem to be distinct.

This complexity of interactional forces in the family system is related to why making changes to a family system is sometimes so hard. Intentionally changing a family, even when you believe that change to be for the better, is difficult. *Family systems theory and cybernetics help us understand why change can be so hard*. Positive and negative feedback within a family system are ongoing. As we attempt to introduce positive feedback (away from the norm) to induce change, it is likely that negative feedback will emerge to counter the changing force. Although an individual may want change, the system tends to act to maintain the norm. Grant and Folwell saw this in operation in their study of college students and their family systems. The negative feedback may come from individual members of the family, or from the system more generally, and individual members may not even be aware that they are resisting change. This is what makes change so hard for family systems. If you have ever resolved, in a family relationship, to intentionally alter the relationship in some way, you understand this. Even if we tell ourselves that we, for example, won't fight with our siblings any more, the system, and the patterns of behavior that we have learned to enact within it, tends to push us back toward that norm of behavior and true change is difficult. This concept can ultimately help us understand, in our own family as well as for other families, why behavioral patterns that seem negative aren't stopped by the family members. Often it isn't as simple as just stopping one set of behaviors—and such change is likely to have unexpected consequences on other parts of the family system.

The idea that intentionally changing a family in a specific way is difficult may seem discouraging. And yet, *systems theory also functions to reassure us that change is ultimately possible*. Systems theory tells us that family systems are never just sitting still; even in the midst of pattern, there is still change. Additionally, the principle of equifinality tells us that the path of a human system is not bound by its historical conditions. What happened in the past affects us, and perhaps makes change more difficult. However, changing a system (for better or worse) is not impossible.

Of course, all of this is tied to the idea of dialectics. We know the world through contradiction and we desire contradictory things in our relational systems, including family. This too may make change both inevitable and difficult. We might want to become more independent from our parents (change), but we may also want to maintain our dependence upon them (stability). Again, *concepts from a systems perspective, specifically dialectics, can help us understand that such contradiction is normal and that, although it will never go away, we can think about how best to manage it in our particular relationships* as we analyze the ways that we have managed it over time. Considering the unspoken dialectics of a relationship, like the shadow realities discussed by Graham and Edwards, may help us move forward in our relationships, and also to understand their complexities.

As you read the rest of this text, keep the concepts that you have learned in this chapter close at hand. The ideas of systems theory form an important part of the study of family communication. Many family communication scholars, even those who may not specifically invoke the notion systems or cybernetics in their writing, operate with an underlying idea that families are complex systems that are difficult, yet invigorating, to study because of the many interwoven aspects that affect the family dynamic.

Questions for Consideration and Discussion

1. From a systems perspective, each system is embedded within other systems. This presents family scholars with a dilemma of where to "stop" the research. When studying family relationships and systems, how important do you believe it is to also study the cultures in which the family exists, and why?
2. How do you see the dialectics of autonomy and connection, privacy and openness, novelty and predictability operating in your family systems?
3. As our culture changes, expectations for the roles of father, mother, and children within the family also change. What changes have you observed in these roles over the course of your life and what are some of the factors within the culture at large that you believe have lead to changes in family roles?
4. Family systems also change as the lives of individual family members shift. What is one important change that has happened in your family system and how did it impact the system?
5. Family systems approaches suggest that you cannot separate out one part of a family and really understand it, nor can you place responsibility for family success or failure upon one member. What are the potential consequences of this view for your understandings about personal responsibility?

Key Terms and Concepts _____

adaptability
calibration
change
chaotic families
circumplex model
cohesion
complementary
   behavior
connected families
contradiction
dialectic
dialectical perspective
disengaged families
dyad
enmeshed families

equifinality
flexible families
hierarchy
homeostasis
interdependence
negative feedback
neutralization
nonsummativity
positive feedback
praxis
reframing
rigid families
role
role acquisition
role conflict

role expectations
role making
role taking
segmentation
selection
self-regulating (cybernetic)
   system
separated families
structured families
symmetrical behavior
system
systems theory
theory
totality
wholeness

4

Family Rules, Rituals, and Stories

Chapter Outline

Chapter Objectives

1. To understand the importance of studying family communication processes
2. To be able to define family rules and discuss the familial elements that contribute to the creation of rules
3. To be able to define family rituals and explain and apply the functions of family rules
4. To be able to define family stories and discuss and apply the purposes they serve in families
5. To understand the role of culture in family communication processes
6. To apply this material to assessing your own family rules, rituals, and stories, understanding their origins, and planning for your future interactions

Section 1: Overview of Rules, Rituals, and Stories in the Family

- What is your favorite family holiday? What things do you do with your family on that day?
- What stories does your family tell when you get together?
- What were the grown-ups allowed to talk about (or hear about) in your family that children were not allowed to talk about (or hear about)?

The foundation of this textbook is family communication. So, everything we discuss in the book relates to family communication. It's amazing to think about the role of communication in the family. Without communication, families wouldn't exist at all. Interaction is required to bring people together, form connections, and coordinate behavior. Thus, without communication parents would never court or marry; children would not be born and could not be parented. Communication is primary. The interaction patterns developed in a particular family are complex, and affected by a variety of things including the culture in which the family is situated, the past history and interactions of the members, and the relational dynamics that have developed among members. To study family communication patterns is therefore quite complicated. There are many types of communication that occur in the family setting. In the next few chapters, we will consider several of these. In this chapter, we focus on three communication processes: family rules, family rituals, and family stories. Later chapters address other processes, such as conflict management, social support, and the display of affection. As discussed in Chapter 1, family communication processes are important to study because how a family interacts affects the members of that family in both positive and negative ways. Let's talk about three specific impacts of family communication patterns: attachment, child or adolescent behavior patterns, and socialization.

One of the ways that family communication practices impact us as we go through life is via the development of family attachments. **Attachment theory** (Bowlby, 1969, 1973, 1988) argues that when children, as infants and toddlers, develop a belief that their parents can be counted on to be there when needed, they are then more psychologically able to explore their world and feel safe doing so. When this occurs, according to the theory, children are more likely to grow into adults who have good psychological health and are capable of maintaining functional adult relationships (for example, Bachman & Bippus, 2005; Hollist & Miller, 2005; Jones, 2005). Various studies have indicated that it is the interactions that occur between parents and children that lead to a healthy attachment (see Ainsworth, Blehar, Waters, & Wall, 1978; Belsky, 1999; Cummings & Cummings, 2002). Thus, we need to consider how family communication may increase or decrease healthy attachment.

Scholars have also found a relationship between family communication processes and child or adolescent behaviors (see, for example, Gosebruch, Sánchez, Delva, Wagner, & Anthony, 2003; Vazsonyi, Hibbert, & Blake Snider, 2003) such as smoking, drinking, school misconduct, anxiety, and depression. Earlier in this text, Koesten considered how family communication patterns contribute to children learning, or failing to learn, particular communication skills. The acquisition of communication skills can affect children and their behaviors and opportunities throughout the rest of their lives, and even be carried on to future generations of children. Therefore, family communication patterns are important to address because they impact child or adolescent behavior both inside and outside the family setting.

Family communication patterns and processes also serve a **socialization** function. They socialize children into their cultures. Family communication teaches children (of all ages) about the values and lessons their parents and grandparents have learned and would like to pass on. For example, Knafo and Schwartz (2003) found that how parents communicated with their children affected the extent to which adolescents were able to accurately perceive and understand the values that their parents would like them to adopt, regardless of what specific values the parents were promoting (see also Baxter, Bylund, Imes, & Scheive, 2005; Fingerson, 2005; White & Matawie, 2004). It isn't only children and adolescents who are socialized by family messages. Holladay (2002) investigated communication about aging and its effects. She found that most people receive their memorable messages about aging from family members, and these messages impact how they feel about and respond to the aging process. Children even socialize their parents; this is called **reciprocal socialization** (Boxer & Cook, 1991; Peterson & Hann, 1999; Stafford, 2004). Think back to your young adolescence, were there slang phrases, items of dress, habits, or media programs, that had become a large part of the culture that you educated your parents about? As they grow, children often have a significant impact on their parents' socialization, as well as the other way around. Socialization is an extremely important part of family communication.

Thus, family communication processes are important to consider (that's a good thing for us, because this is a family communication textbook). At the start of the chapter, three questions were posed. These questions asked you to reflect on your family rules, rituals, and stories. It is to these particular family communication processes that we now turn. Subsequent chapters address additional family communication processes. As you consider some of the theories and research discussed in the remainder of this chapter, continue to think about your answers to those questions raised earlier, as well as the other examples of family rules, rituals, and stories that you remember in your family.

Family Rules

Satir (1972, 1988), as well as many other family systems scholars, argues that rules are an inherent part of family life. As stated by Shimanoff (1980), a **rule** is a "prescription that indicates what behavior is obligated, preferred, or prohibited in certain context." (p. 57).

BOX 4.1 • *Internet Connection*

Because it primarily emanates from teens and young adults, children often teach slang to their parents. Though often not "official" terms, slang is culturally powerful. You can read more about slang at www.pbs.org/speak/words/sezwho/slang/.

All families have rules. These rules *may be explicit or implicit.* **Explicit rules** are recognized rules that are stated out loud (rules like curfews or no cursing). **Implicit rules** are unstated rules that are just understood by family members (perhaps no one tells you not to comment on Grandad's poor hearing; you just know that you aren't supposed to because no one else ever does). Families also have metarules. **Metarules** are rules about rules and rule making. So, for example, a family may have a somewhat implicit rule that only the rules Mom states count and that when Dad makes rules, those can be safely ignored. Or, a family may have a rule that explicit rules will be made only about issues of safety, and other behavior will be left to individual family members' discretion. When you consider your own family experience, you can probably think of many rules that were expressed to you over the years, from no jumping on the bed, to chores, to grades, to dating rules, to curfew. Many family rules are directly related to communication, including who can communicate with whom, about what, and how. Some common areas for family communication rules include differences in adult–child communication (i.e., "children can't say that word"), sexuality communication (see Chapter 8 for further consideration), discipline rules, conflict management rules (see Chapter 6), and affection rules (see Chapter 5). Because there are so many different issues that are rule-bound in family life, and because we consider some of these in subsequent chapters, we focus now on two types of communication rules: privacy rules and media rules.

Family Communication and Privacy Rules

One communication area where rules arise relates to what issues can or should be talked about within or outside the family (Caughlin & Petronio, 2004; Petronio & Caughlin, 2006). **Communication privacy management theory** (Petronio, 2000, 2002) argues that people conceal particular information for two primary reasons. First, they may feel that the information "belongs to them." Thus, they should have control over who knows it. Second, they may believe that to reveal the information would make them vulnerable to some sort of harm. By either granting or refusing access to certain types of information, family members maintain **privacy boundaries.** The privacy boundary may exist around the individual (when the information not shared "belongs" only to him or her). But, often, the information not revealed is shared by two or more people in the family, thus creating a boundary around that family subsystem with regard to that information. For example, parents typically maintain a boundary related to their relational sexuality that excludes the children in the family. In addition to these boundaries around individuals or sets of individuals in the family (termed **interior boundaries**), families also maintain **exterior boundaries** that protect family information from those outside the family system.

Caughlin and Petronio (2004; see also Petronio & Caughlin, 2006) note that knowing what to talk about, or not talk about, is complex. The dialectic of openness/closedness (discussed in Chapter 3) is in operation. This also relates back to the impact of disclosure on stepfamily relationships discussed in Chapter 2. Sharing information with others is a way to create closeness. Often, the more you know about someone, the closer you feel to him or her. Yet, some information may harm relationships. Someone might tell you something that you wish you didn't know, thereby making you feel less close to him or her. Similarly, maintaining a sense of individual identity requires privacy. If your parents know every single thing about you and about your life, you may feel too exposed and as if you don't have a life of your own. Yet, too much privacy can create barriers in relationships. If you don't tell your parents much of anything about your life, they might feel shut out and as if you don't care about them.

According to Caughlin and Petronio (2004; see also Green, Derlega, & Petronio, 2003), the factors of culture, gender or sex, and motivations are important in what family rules are created with regard to privacy and disclosure. First, culture affects what privacy rules are important because different groups believe that different types of information should be kept private. For example, Caughlin and Petriono (2004) note that, in the past in North America, adoption of a child was considered a private issue and even adopted children frequently didn't know they were adopted. As culture has changed and adoption has become more acceptable, and even admirable, it is more openly discussed. Most children of adoption now are aware of their history, and many adoptions are conducted with an open relationship between the birth parent(s) and the adoptive parent(s).

Second, the gender or sex of family members affects what types of communication rules are created (Caughlin & Petronio, 2004; see also Green et al., 2003). Research suggests that children and adolescents are more open with their mothers than they are with their fathers (Caughlin & Petronio, 2004; Golish & Caughlin, 2002). This could have something to do with the fact that mothers still spend proportionally more time with children than fathers do in the average household. Gender expectations can also affect disclosure. Men and boys may be discouraged from talking about their weaknesses or fears, and may be encouraged to speak of their successes and their interests in "manly" topics like sports or cars. Women and girls may be discouraged from communicating about sexuality, and may be encouraged to discuss their feelings.

Finally, individuals in families may have different communication rules due to different motivations (Afifi, 2003; Caughlin & Afifi, 2004; Caughlin & Petronio, 2004; Green et al., 2003). Sometimes privacy is maintained in order to avoid conflict. In some family settings, conflict is considered a bad thing in general, and something to be avoided. A priority is placed on getting along (a high-conformity orientation). In some families, individuality is more important than connection, and privacy may be maintained to create a sense of separation. In still other family settings, privacy may be maintained in certain dyads or groups because of a fear that information will be used against the speaker or out of fear. For example, Afifi, Olson, and Armstrong (2005) and Affifi and Olson (2005) found that their respondents often keep negative secrets because they fear the response of an aggressive family member or because they believe that revealing the secret will result in punishment. Revelation of information can also stem from different motivations. Sometimes, family members share information because it creates a sense of connection. In other situations, speaking your mind is considered the norm, even when it will cause an argument, and disagreement is not feared. At times, information may even be shared as a way of punishing another. (You may remember convincing your sibling not to tell Mom that the two of you did something wrong, and then when he or she was mad at you, the secret was revealed.) Thus, the issue of what can be talked about in a family, and to whom, is very complex. Family communication is bound by privacy rules and expectations related to culture (larger culture or family culture), gender or sex, and motivations.

Family Communication and Media Rules

Another area where communication rules often arise is in the consumption and use of media. When you were growing up were there any rules about how much, or what kind, of television (TV) or movies you could watch? Or maybe your parents monitored the amount of time you could be online. Families often establish policies about what members can use what media forms, how, and how often. Wilson (2004) argues that, in consideration of general control over the TV, a **patriarchal** family power model is most commonly in effect. Fathers are most likely to be the family members who control the television programming that the family watches (Gantz, 2001; Wilson, 2004). Mothers also tend to have more control than children over TV viewing (Wilson, 2004). This means, not too surprisingly, that children are generally the family members with the least control over TV programming.

The extent to which parents engage in rule making specific to media viewing depends upon a number of factors, including the age of the children, the parents' education level, the nature of the parent–child relationship, and parental attitudes about media (Warren, 2003, Warren, Gerke, & Kelly, 2002). Frequently, parental rules about TV or movie viewing for children are designed to prevent the negative effects of children viewing "inappropriate" programs. Chang (2000) addressed one of the most common areas of media use where rules arise—that of violent TV programming. Because of the general public's concern over how media images of violence contribute to the violence perpetrated by children and adolescents (for example, the shootings at Columbine High School in 1999), parenting self-help books, magazines, and parenting seminars have increasingly focused on how to set effective rules for the viewing of violent media. In her research, Chang considered three of the recommendations that are commonly given to parents with regard to rule making and violent media: (1) children's viewing should be limited to educational programming; (2) parents should closely monitor viewing and turn off the TV if there is any violence in the program; and (3) parents should not buy toys, games, or books related to violent TV shows. In her analysis, Chang suggests that such rules related to violent media may, in fact, increase the child's urge to watch violent TV programming, and also create confusion as to why such shows are not allowed. Instead, Chang argues that parents need to talk more with children about media viewing, asking the children questions about the show, about the violence, and about the outcomes of violence, in order to help children develop better reasoning skills related to such behavior. Additionally, Chang suggests that if parents and children work together to establish the rules, children are more likely to see the rules as fair, understand the reasoning behind the rules, and obey the rules. Although Chang's work relates to TV rules, similar rule systems may be developed with relation to Internet use, music exposure, and other forms of media.

What can be revealed or concealed, and how media are to be used are two examples of family rules related to communication. There are many other areas of family interaction that can be rule based (how affection can be shown, how anger can be displayed, what language can be used by adults and children, what types of communication are expected from males and females, how people can engage in conflict, what names and terms family members use for each other, etc.). Additionally, rules may operate in ways that are helpful to particular family members or hurtful to them (for example, a rule that a child cannot discuss sexuality in the home may ultimately be detrimental to his or her own growth). We cannot discuss all of the variations of family rules here, but they all are interesting areas for study and reflection. As Satir would remind us, family rules are an inevitable part of family life.

Family Rituals

As defined by Schuck and Bucy (1997), "**family rituals** are repetitious, highly valued, symbolic social activities that transmit the *family's* enduring values, attitudes, and goals" (p. 478). So, family rituals are the things that we do as a family, over and over again, that mean something special to us in some way, and say something about who we are as a family. Wolin and Bennett (1984) divided family rituals into a typology that included celebrations, traditions, and patterned daily interactions. **Celebrations** are the sort of ritualized behaviors that correspond with cultural practices (Christmas, Hanukah, Thanksgiving, etc.). **Traditions** are more personalized events that a particular family group enacts (family reunions, birthday celebrations). **Patterned daily interactions** are the things that we do in our families on a daily basis that come to represent something special and important to the family (always talking about school at dinner, singing a special song at bedtime). What makes a ritual a ritual, rather than just a routine or habit, is the meaning that the ritual has for the family members. Sometimes we may not even realize that a particular set of behaviors is important to us until it becomes disrupted in some way, and then we recognize its significance. Schuck and Bucy (1997), Wolin and Bennett (1984), Jorgenson and Bochner (2004), and other scholars argue that family rituals provide a variety of functions in the family. They provide stability, they create and maintain family identity, and they provide socialization.

Because families are continually changing as children grow and parents age, new members join, and older members leave, family rituals can offer a way to find stability in family life (Jorgenson & Bochner, 2004; Leon & Jacobvitz, 2003). Parents often continue "tucking in" a child at night well after the child could get into bed on his or her own. That special moment provides stability in the changing world of the child's life. Moriarty and Wagner (2004) considered the way that single-parent families use rituals. They concluded that one of the purposes of rituals in a single-parent family is to provide a sense of cohesion, and thus stability, for the family members who may feel a lack of stability due to family changes following divorce or separation.

Family rituals also help provide family members with a sense of identity for the family, and a feeling of belongingness in that family (Jorgenson & Bochner, 2004; Schuck & Bucy, 1997; Wolin & Bennett, 1984). In her study of marriage as a ritual, Kalmijn (2004) found that one of the functions of marriage for the couple is the establishment of identity as a couple for themselves and for their friends and family. This helps provide for the transition that

---

BOX 4.2 • *Did You Know?*

The ritual of men's wedding rings in the United States was not always common. In the 1920s, jewelers responded to the threat of mass retailers' cheap prices with a campaign promoting men's engagement rings. That campaign was not very successful, but a subsequent effort, in the 1940s and 1950s, to popularize the "double ring" wedding ceremony was and a wedding ring for the groom gradually became an expected part of the ritual (Howard, 2003).

accompanies marriage. The ritual of the marriage ceremony helps create an identity for the new family. Another example of family rituals creating identity can be found in religious observance. When families engage in religious celebrations together, the way that they do so can carry meaning about the family's identity in relation to religion. Family traditions can provide a sense of identity and belonging as well. Having a birthday party thrown for you shows that you belong in the family. What type of party is thrown says something about the family identity (gift-giving expectations, socioeconomic status, closeness to extended family). Oswald (2002) considered how rituals can create, or diminish, a sense of belongingness for gay and lesbian adults. Based on her research, she concluded that participating in rituals, particularly celebrations, is correlated with a greater sense of belongingness in the family. The opposite was also true in her research. Not being invited to family celebrations was related to participants having less of a feeling of belongingness. Thus, we can see that family rituals can say something about the family identity and who belongs in that family.

Finally, family rituals help socialize young people into family expectations and values. Sutton (2004) looked at family reunion rituals of African Caribbean transnational families. Because these families are spread across countries, family reunions provide a particularly useful way of socializing the younger generation into family values and traditions. Reunions like this, and those of families in closer proximity, allow older family members to connect with and teach younger members. Additionally, the fact that the reunion is held communicates a value for family connection. Similarly, Friedman and Weissbrod (2004) found that young adults whose same-sex parents engaged in more ritual initiation were more likely to plan to continue those family rituals into their families of procreation. A ritual as small as saying a bedtime prayer socializes young children into the expectations that that family has and teaches the child what the values of the family are.

Continuation of family rituals, or the development of new rituals in a new family, is important not only because of the functions it serves in the family system, but also because such rituals have been found to be related to other issues. Family rituals have also been associated with many positive outcomes for family members (Leon & Jacobvitz, 2003). Studies have found a relationship between marital happiness and family rituals, as well as finding positive outcomes for children in families with healthy rituals (Kiser, Bennett, Heston, & Paavola, 2005; Leon & Jacobvitz, 2003). For example, Eaker and Walters (2002) studied adolescents and young adults and found that family rituals were associated with the development of psychosocial maturity. Fiese and Marjinski (1999) found an association between positive child behavior and pleasant dinnertime rituals. Leon and Jacobvitz (2003) suggest that family rituals may act to create secure attachment between parents and children, and the effects of that positive relationship may then be associated with the adult child developing healthy rituals with his or her own children.

Although rituals can have many positive outcomes in family settings, it is important to note that families may have **negative rituals** as well. Rituals are enacted repeatedly because they provide satisfaction to family members, but it does not mean that all family members will derive satisfaction from each ritual. At times, families may have negative rituals that are unpleasant, hurtful, or even dangerous to particular members. For example, if a family had a ritual that involved repeated extreme unwanted teasing of one member, that ritual may be experienced as fun, and bonding, for the teasers, but the person being teased would experience hurt and possibly self-esteem issues as a result.

Rituals thus act in a number of ways in the family. They create a sense of stability and cohesion, show the family identity and who belongs to it, and socialize the younger members (or new members) of the family into family beliefs and attitudes. Additionally, having healthy rituals in the family can be related to other positive outcomes for all family members; however, although rituals may often have positive functions in the family setting, some rituals operate in a more harmful way for individual family members.

Family Stories

In the book *Black Sheep and Kissing Cousins: How Our Family Stories Shape Us*, Elizabeth Stone (1988) considers the role of stories in the creation and maintenance of family. In general, a **family story,** or narrative, can be defined as an account of an event or series of events involving the family that has significance to the family members. In her text, Stone argues that stories are important because they create a shared belief in a particular reality. It doesn't much matter whether the stories are "really true," if the family members believe them to be, because the purpose of family stories isn't really about the telling of an accurate life history (see also Jorgenson & Bochner, 2004). Due to the commonality of family stories, and narratives in general, in understanding life experiences and beliefs, narrative analysis is frequently used as a method for studying family understandings, patterns, and processes. Narrative analysis can take many forms, but the basic effort is to study the stories told in and about families to see what themes and patterns they reveal.

The stories that a family tells shift and change over time. This isn't because the family members are "lying" or have forgotten their past. Rather, at different times families tell different stories because those stories serve a function for the family at that point in time. Though the telling of family stories is usually not an explicit attempt to accomplish a particular function, Stone and other scholars (Bylund, 2003; Jorgenson & Bochner, 2004) have found that family stories do serve a variety of purposes in the family.

A first purpose of family stories is to describe and define the family itself and provide information about what type of behavior is acceptable or common within that family (Jorgenson & Bochner, 2004; Leeds-Hurwitz, 2005; Stone, 1998). Family stories, in this sense, help us understand who "we" are. For example, Stone, Gomez, Hotzoglou, and Lipnitsky (2005) researched the stories of immigrant families in the United States. In their research, they found that these families, though appearing to have completely assimilated to American culture, were able to retain their sense of affiliation with their home country through storytelling. Thus, the stories helped family members define that culture as still being a part of who they were. While telling identity, family stories frequently indicate the "ground rules" for the family. They tell members how they are expected to behave and what their responsibilities are toward each other. Some of the behaviors that can be part of family stories may include proximity (how close members should stay), how courtship and marriage should proceed, how members should handle their finances, religious obligations, and educational expectations. Family stories also provide information about, and assist family members in coping with, the negative issues that occur in family life, like anger and violence, illness and injury, death and suicide (Bosticco & Thompson, 2005; Stone, 1988). While defining the family, family stories often provide us with myths that explain some

BOX 4.3 • *Internet Connection*

Would you like to know more of your family's stories? Story Arts Online discusses how to find out your family stories and even provides some story-eliciting interview questions at www.storyarts.org/classroom/roots/family.html#questions.

particular historical issue within the family (Stone, 1988). The myths tell tales of fantastic successes (or horrible failures or traumas) of family members and the outcomes of those events. These myths may not be, and likely are not, fully accurate, but they allow family members to understand or assign cause to an event.

In addition to providing information about events within the family, family stories also give advice about the outside world and how to deal with it. Family stories indicate where that family "fits" in the larger social and power structure and how the family has responded to that place (Bylund, 2003; Jorgenson & Bochner, 2004; Stone, 1988). Such family stories might focus on issues like racial, ethnic, or religious prejudice and how it has affected family members. Or, they might explain how the family has succeeded in a certain arena and the impact the family has had on the community at large. Family stories also talk about the family's financial status in the world. These stories sometimes operate as cautionary tales, giving the message that family members should be careful because there are dangers in the world. They may be encouraging stories that indicate that hard work of family members has been met with success and that future members should continue to work and keep that success. They can also be celebrations of where the family stands in relation to other families.

Finally, family stories function to socialize the individual, and provide understandings about his or her place in the family and in the world (Bylund, 2003; Jorgenson & Bochner, 2004; Stone, 1988). Stories about an individual may focus on a particular trait that the family has "assigned" to that person. Frequently, birth or adoption stories about individuals indicate how the new child affected the family (good or bad) and say something about the expectations that the family has for that child in the future. Family stories may also provide individuals with someone to look up to or emulate (Stone, 1988). If you think about the stories that are told about your childhood, they probably say something about the way the family sees you. Maybe all of the stories are about the trouble you got in (but how cute you were doing it). Maybe most of the stories are about how smart you were, or how much of a tomboy, or your sports prowess. Whatever the specific content of the stories, they indicate how the family sees you, and how they see you in relation to other members of the family.

Though family stories do work to socialize children into certain expectations, as families and the individuals in them grow and change, they can select which family stories they will maintain, or focus on, and which stories they will let go (Jorgenson & Bochner, 2004; Stone, 1988). Additionally, family members can negotiate the meaning of the family stories. If your parents told a story about you that was meant to indicate that you were stubborn, you could opt to reframe that story into an indication that you are determined and willing to work hard to accomplish what you want. Thus, family stories can show us who we are as a family and the rules for interaction within the family; they can tell us how we should respond to the world around us; and they can describe to us who we are and who we are meant to be. But, as the subjects of family stories, we also participate in creating and shaping their meanings and can alter those meanings as we grow and create our own lives.

In addition to the "why" of family storytelling, the "who" and "how" have importance in family settings. Langellier and Peterson (2006) discuss how, in some family settings, intergenerational storytelling is most often accomplished by the middle generation (parents, aunts, and uncles), directed toward the younger generation (children), and is subject to correction by the older generation (grandparents). Storytelling may also be structured by gendered expectations (Langellier & Peterson, 2006; Stone, 1988). For example, women may tell and hear more stories that relate to the "relational" aspects of family like births, deaths, celebrations, meals, and so on, whereas men may tell and hear more stores that relate to adventures, finances, and work (Fiese & Bickham, 2004; Thorne, McLean, & Dasbach, 2004). Storytelling may also be primarily the act of one individual, a series of individuals each contributing separately, or a group of individuals cotelling the story (Fivush, Bohanek, Robertson, & Duke, 2004; Koenig Kellas & Trees, 2006). In their study of storytelling about difficult family experiences, Koenig Kellas and Trees (2006) found that when family members cooperatively participated in telling a story together, they were more likely to reach a shared family understanding of the meaning of that story (see also Fivush et al., 2004). How a story is told, and by whom, may relate to the type of the story, the purpose of the telling, and the outcome of the storytelling experience.

Family rules, family rituals, and family stories are just some of the communication processes that occur in families that are addressed in this text. Section 2 includes three pieces of research that focus on these issues. The first article discusses a study related to family rules for media use. The second reading considers the role of rituals after the death of a family member. Finally, the third article discusses orphans and their stories about both being orphaned and being adopted into a family. As you read these selections, think about your own family and the rules, rituals, and stories you have encountered in your life.

References

Afifi, T. D. (2003). "Feeling caught" in stepfamilies: Managing boundary turbulence through appropriate communication privacy rules. *Journal of Social and Personal Relationships, 20*(6), 729–755.

Afifi, T. D., & Olson, L. (2005). The chilling effect in families and the pressure to conceal secrets. *Communication Monographs, 72*, 192–216.

Afifi, T. D., Olson, L. N., & Armstrong, C. (2005). The chilling effect and family secrets examining the role of self protection, other protection, and communication efficacy. *Human Communication Research, 31*, 564–598.

Ainsworth, M. D. S., Blehar, M. C., Waters, E., & Wall, S. (1978). *Patterns of attachment: A psycholo-gical study of the strange situation.* Hillsdale, NJ: Erlbaum.

Bachman, G. F., & Bippus, A. M. (2005). Evaluations of supportive messages provided by friends and romantic partners: An attachment theory approach. *Communication Reports, 18*(2), 85–94.

Baxter, L. A., Bylund, C. L., Imes, R. S., & Scheive, D. M. (2005). Family communication environments and rule-based social control of adolescents' healthy lifestyle choices. *Journal of Family Communication, 5*(3), 209–227.

Belsky, J. (1999). Interactional and contextual determinants of attachment security. In J. Cassidy & P. R. Shaver (Eds.), *Handbook of attachment: Theory, research, and clinical applications* (pp. 259–264). New York: Guilford Press.

Bosticco, C., & Thompson, T. (2005). The role of communication and story telling in the family grieving system. *Journal of Family Communication, 5*(4), 255–278.

Bowlby, J. (1969). *Attachment and loss: Vol. 1. Attachment.* New York: Basic Books.

Bowlby, J. (1973). *Attachment and loss: Vol. 2. Separation: Anxiety and Anger.* New York: Basic Books.

Bowlby, J. (1988). *A secure base: Parent–child attachment and healthy human development.* New York: Basic Books.

Boxer, A. M., & Cook, J. A. (1991). Double jeopardy: Identity transitions and parent–child relations among gay and lesbian youth. In K. Pillemer & K. McCartney (Eds.), *Parent–child relations throughout life* (pp. 59–92). Hillsdale, NJ: Erlbaum.

Bylund, C. L. (2003). Ethnic diversity and family stories. *Journal of Family Communication, 3*(4), 215–236.

Caughlin, J. P., & Afifi, T. D. (2004). When is topic avoidance unsatisfying? Examining moderators of the association between avoidance and dissatisfaction. *Human Communication Research, 30*(4), 479–513.

Caughlin, J. P., & Petronio, S. (2004). Privacy in families. In A. L. Vangelisti (Ed.), *Handbook of family communication* (pp. 379–412). Mahwah, NJ: Erlbaum.

Chang, N. (2000). Reasoning with children about violent television shows and related toys. *Early Childhood Education Journal, 28*(2), 85–89.

Cummings, E. M., & Cummings, J. S. (2002). Parenting and attachment. In M. H. Bornstein (Ed.), *Handbook of parenting* (Vol. 5, pp. 35–58). Mahwah, NJ: Erlbaum.

Eaker, D. G., & Walters, L. H. (2002). Adolescent satisfaction in family rituals and psychosocial development: A developmental systems theory perspective. *Journal of Family Psychology, 16*(4), 406–414.

Fiese, B. H., & Bickham, N. L. (2004). Pin-curling Grandpa's hair in the comfy chair: Parents' stories of growing up and potential links to socialization in the preschool years. In M. W. Pratt & B. H. Fiese (Eds.), *Family stories and the life course: Across time and generations* (pp. 259–278). Mahwah, NJ: Erlbaum.

Fiese, B. H., & Marjinsky, K. A. T. (1999). Dinnertime stories: Connecting family practice with relationship beliefs and child adjustment. *Monographs of the Society for Research in Child Development, 64*(2), 52–68.

Fingerson, L. (2005). Do mothers' opinions matter in teens' sexual activity? *Journal of Family Issues, 26*(7), 947–974.

Fivush, R., Bohanek, J., Robertson, R., & Duke, M. (2004). Family narratives and the development of children's emotional well-being. In M. W. Pratt & B. H. Fiese (Eds.), *Family stories and the life course: Across time and generations* (pp. 55–76). Mahwah, NJ: Erlbaum.

Friedman, S. R., & Weissbrod, C. S. (2004). Attitudes toward the continuation of family rituals among emerging adults. *Sex Roles, 50*(3/4), 277–284.

Gantz, W. (2001). Conflicts and resolution strategies associated with television in marital life. In J. Bryant & J. A. Bryant (Eds.), *Television and the American family* (2nd ed., pp. 289–316). Mahwah, NJ: Erlbaum.

Golish, T. D., & Caughlin, J. P. (2002). "I'd rather not talk about it." Adolescents' and young adults' use of topic avoidance in stepfamilies. *Journal of Applied Communication Research, 30*, 78–106.

Gosebruch, G., Sánchez, M., Delva, J., Wagner, F., & Anthony, J. C. (2003). Family attention and tobacco smoking among adolescents in Central America, Panama, and the Dominican Republic. *Substance Use & Misuse, 38*(8), 1037–1062.

Green, K., Derlega, V. J., Yep, G. A., & Petronio, S. (2003). *Privacy and disclosure of HIV in interpersonal relationships: A sourcebook for researchers and practitioners.* Mahwah, NJ: Erlbaum.

Holladay, S. J. (2002). "Have fun while you can," "You're only as old as you feel," and "Don't ever get old": An examination of memorable messages about aging. *Journal of Communication, 52*(4), 681–696.

Hollist, C. S., & Miller, R. B. (2005). Perceptions of attachment style and marital quality in midlife marriage. *Family Relations, 54*(1), 46–57.

Howard, V. (2003). A "real man's ring": Gender and the invention of tradition. *Journal of Social History, 36*, 837–856.

Jones, S. M. (2005). Attachment style differences and similarities in evaluations of affective communication skills and person-centered comforting messages. *Western Journal of Communication, 69*(3), 233–249.

Jorgenson, J., & Bochner, A. P. (2004). Imagining family through stories and rituals. In A. L. Vangelisti (Ed.), *Handbook of family communication* (pp. 513–538). Mahwah, NJ: Erlbaum.

Kalmijn, M. (2004). Marriage rituals as reinforcers of role transitions: An analysis of weddings in the Netherlands. *Journal of Marriage and Family, 66*(3), 582–594.

Kiser, L., Bennett, L., Heston, J., & Paavola, M. (2005). Family ritual and routine: Comparison of clinical and non-clinical families. *Journal of Child and Family Studies, 14*(3), 357–372.

Knafo, A., & Schwartz, S. H. (2003). Parenting and adolescents' accuracy in perceiving parental values. *Child Development, 74*(2), 595–611.

Koenig Kellas, J., & Trees, A. R. (2006). Finding meaning in difficult family experiences: Sense-making and interaction processes during joint family storytelling. *Journal of Family Communication, 6*(1), 49–76.

Langellier, K. M., & Peterson, E. E. (2006). Narrative performance theory: Telling stories, doing family. In D. O. Braithwaite & L. A. Baxter (Ed.), *Engaging theories in family communication: Multiple perspectives* (pp. 99–114). Thousand Oaks, CA: Sage.

Leeds-Hurwitz, W. (2005). Making marriage visible: Wedding anniversaries as the public component of private relationships. *Text, 25*(5), 595–631.

Leon, K., & Jacobvitz, D. B. (2003). Relationships between adult attachment representations and family ritual quality: A prospective, longitudinal study. *Family Process, 42*(3), 419–432.

Moriarty, P. H., & Wagner, L. D. (2004). Family rituals that provide meaning for single-parent families. *Journal of Family Nursing, 10*(2), 190–210.

Oswald, R. (2002). Inclusion and belonging in the family of origin rituals of gay and lesbian people. *Journal of Family Psychology, 16*, 428–436.

Peterson, G. W., & Hann, D. (1999). Socializing children and parents in families. In M. B. Sussman, S. K. Steinmetz, & G. W. Peterson (Eds.), *Handbook of marriage and the family* (2nd ed., pp. 327–370). New York: Plenum Press.

Petronio, S. (2000). The boundaries of privacy: Praxis of everyday life. In S. Petronio (Ed.), *Balancing the secrets of private disclosures* (pp. 37–49). Mahwah, NJ: Erlbaum.

Petronio, S. (2002). *Boundaries of privacy: Dialectics of disclosure.* Albany: State University of New York Press.

Petronio, S., & Caughlin, J. P. (2006). Communication privacy management theory: Understanding families. In D. O. Braithwaite & L. A. Baxter (Ed.), *Engaging theories in family communication: Multiple Perspectives* (pp. 35–49). Thousand Oaks, CA: Sage.

Satir, V. (1972). *People making*. Palo Alto, CA: Science and Behavior Books.

Satir, V. (1988). *New peoplemaking*. Palo Alto, CA: Science and Behavior Books.

Schimanoff, S. B. (1980). *Communication rules: Theory and research*. Beverly Hills, CA: Sage.

Schuck, L. A., & Bucy, J. E. (1997). Family rituals: Implications for early intervention. *Topics in Early Childhood Special Education, 17*(4), 477–493.

Stafford, L. (2004). Communication competencies and sociocultural priorities of middle childhood. In A. L. Vangelisti (Ed.), *Handbook of family communication* (pp. 311–332). Mahwah, NJ: Erlbaum.

Stone, E. (1988). *Black sheep and kissing cousins: How our family stories shape us.* New York: New York Times Books.

Stone, E., Gomez, E., Hotzoglou, D., & Lipnitsky, J. Y. (2005). Transnationalism as a motif in family stories. *Family Process, 44*(4), 381–398.

Sutton, C. R. (2004). Celebrating ourselves: The family reunion rituals of African–Caribbean transnational families. *Global Networks, 4*(3), 243–257.

Thorne, A., McLean, K. C., & Dasbach, A. (2004). When parents' stories go to pot: Telling personal transgressions to teenage kids. In M. W. Pratt & B. H. Fiese (Eds.), *Family stories and the life course: Across time and generations* (pp. 187–212). Mahwah, NJ: Erlbaum.

Vazsonyi, A. T., Hibbert, J. R., & Blake Snider, J. (2003). Exotic enterprise no more: Adolescent reports of family and parenting processes from youth in four countries. *Journal of Research on Adolescence, 13*(2), 129–160.

Warren R. (2003). Parental mediation of preschool children's television viewing. *Journal of Broadcasting & Electronic Media, 47*(3), 394–417.

Warren, R., Gerke, P., & Kelly, M. A. (2002). Is there enough time on the clock?: Parental involvement and mediation of children's television viewing. *Journal of Broadcasting & Electronic Media, 46*, 656–663.

White, F. A., & Matawie, K. M. (2004). Parental morality and family processes as predictors of adolescent morality. *Journal of Family Studies, 13*(2), 219–233.

Wilson, B. J. (2004). The mass media and family communication. In A. L. Vangelisti (Ed.), *Handbook of family communication* (pp. 563–591). Mahwah, NJ: Erlbaum.

Wolin, S., & Bennett, L. (1984). Family rituals. *Family Process, 23*, 401–420.

Section 2: Research Examples

Family Home Media Rules and Interactions

Chrys Egan

Developing rules for communication practices, including the use of media, is an important part of the family, and particularly the parent–child relationship. In Section 1, we briefly considered this issue. In this article, Egan expands upon the concerns parents have about media use, and provides an analysis of a study examining children's understandings of media and media rules. The results of this study could be important for parents as they formulate family rules for media use. While reading this article, consider both the media rules of your family of origin, and how you might change or adapt those rules in your future family settings.

- Think back to your childhood. What rules did your family have about your media use? Could you watch only a certain number of hours of TV or certain shows? Did your parents control what CDs you bought or radio stations you heard? Would they forbid movies or video games with certain ratings? Were there parental controls on your computer?
- How aware were your parents of what media you used? How often did they use media with you? Did they directly discuss with you media content or why they had certain rules?

L.B.A.

There is a long-standing debate in our culture over the content of and access to television, radio, recorded music, movies, video games, the Internet, and print. Much of the present concern focuses on whether children should be exposed to adult subjects in the mass media, and who is ultimately responsible for shielding children from material that may not be suitable for them. This is an extremely difficult debate to resolve, which may be why it's been fought for generations. One side of the debate centers on rights, mainly the First Amendment guarantee of free expression and public dissemination of ideas; the other side of the argument focuses on the responsibility to protect citizens, particularly children, from controversial or objectionable material. Parents, the government, special-interest groups, and the media industry have said much in the continuing debate about children's exposure to adult content.

Surprisingly, although children are at the heart of this issue, almost no one has asked children for their input. Certainly children know what media they are using, including things that their parents may not know about. Children also are the best experts on what media content attracts or repels them, and why this occurs. Plus, children are the only ones who can tell us if parental guidelines really work when Mom and Dad are not home, how parents can better explain media content and family rules to kids, and what guidance they need from family members to understand the amazing array of media choices that are easily accessible to them.

Therefore, this article takes a different approach to the children and media debate by asking over 300 children about their television and computer use. In this study, children explain (1) what rules their parents have for appropriate television and computer use, (2) what factors determine whether they obey their parents' rules, and (3) how parents use media with them, including explaining media content and ratings.

Introduction to Children and Media Concerns

Concern over children's exposure to "adult" media stems from two basic fears. One fear is that, like the mythical Pandora's box, evil content lurks in media "boxes" such as television and the computer. The other fear is that, like Pandora, children will be irresistibly drawn to the forbidden content of television and the computer. This study investigates the legitimacy of these parental fears by asking children about their understanding of family media rules, factors influencing likelihood of obeying such rules, and parent–child communication about media content and usage.

Studying television and the Internet and parent–child interactions is useful for several reasons. Television is an established medium, present in American society prior to the birth of today's children and omnipresent in our culture. The Internet is a newer medium, still establishing its place in our culture, and perhaps perceived differently by those introduced to it as children or as adults. Although there are censoring technologies available for both media (i.e., television V-chips and Internet filters), this study is more concerned with child–parent and child–media interactions because censorship technologies are not on every television set and computer, they become obsolete, and they can be overridden by clever children. More enduring are lessons taught by parents and those learned through media experience. Therefore, this study aims to determine what television and computer restrictions children acknowledge, understand, and obey, plus more important, *why*. Attempting to address these issues is potentially significant for parents, children, educators, the media, government, and anyone interested in children's media use.

Related Work on Children and Media

"All over the world, a growing number of governments, schools, special interest groups and families are struggling to find acceptable ways of tapping into the riches of the [media] without also hitting the darker veins" (Lewis, 1996). But the combined resources of governments, schools, special-interest groups, and families have not created a foolproof method to keep children from accessing adult information. One approach is to determine what family rules and restrictions are in place, and why children do or do not obey them. To address these considerations, we will examine three theoretical areas: (1) diffusion of innovation; (2) Turkle's children, self, and technology; and (3) the domestic paradigm.

To summarize the complex theory of diffusion of innovation, Rogers (1995) defines diffusion as the "process by which an innovation is communicated through certain channels over time among the members of a social system" (p. 10), and an innovation as "an idea, practice, or object that is perceived as new by an individual or other unit of adoption" (p. 11). The diffusion of innovation process has four main considerations: the innovation (i.e., television rating system and Internet); communication channels (television, computer, and people); time (newness of innovation to children); and the social system (family). By examining all of these elements, the intricate process by which a new idea or technology makes its way into the mainstream culture, and thereby impacts individuals, can be better understood.

The diffusion of innovation theory can be more narrowly examined in the work of Turkle (1984, 1995), whose books *The Second Self* and *Life on the Screen* focus on how children psychologically and socially understand and use media differently than adults. Where the diffusion of innovation deconstructs complex systems into their simplest parts, Turkle challenges the romantic notion of the simplicity of childhood by exploring how children relate to complex machines, how technologies internally influence children, and how children's interpersonal relationships change as a result of interacting with machines. Through observations and interviews with hundreds of children, Turkle develops several claims about these complex child–media–interpersonal relationships. First, today's children have a unique understanding of technologies and the rules that govern them. Second, Turkle's observations mirror Marshall McLuhan's "The medium is the message" philosophy. In Turkle's words, "it is the medium itself and not the content of a particular program that produces the more powerful effect" (1984, p. 93). Third, there is a "technological generation gap," not simply between the sophistication of the technology children use at their age as compared to their parents, but in the way parents and children understand the world as a result.

Although Turkle's approach to the diffusion of innovations focuses on the self and relations, the domestic paradigm specifically examines how technology affects the family. At its foundation, the domestic paradigm explains family "activity as powerfully mediated by the social, economic, political, and technological systems and structures of everyday life" (Sinclair, 1993, p. 2). The domestic paradigm stresses the importance of researching innovations within their context in order to determine the social ramifications. For instance, "most media consumption occurs in the domestic space, within the context of familial relations" (Wotring, Kayany, & Forrest, 1995, p. 4). It therefore seems logical to question children about media use where it most frequently occurs: the home.

In addition to these three guiding theories, a body of media research shapes this study. An exhaustive amount of research has been conducted on the topic of children and media involving contradictory findings, inconclusive results, varied subtopics, different methods, unique populations, and all types of media. Because all these studies cannot be discussed here, two current and closely related projects will suffice: children and media studies (Egan, Gehrs, & Kemp, 1996; Kahn-Egan, 1996, 1997) and the ratings and advisory TV study (Cantor & Harrison, 1997).

The children and media studies of third graders generated results that both supported previous findings and broke new ground. Three relevant findings about children's television and computer habits are summarized: use, rules, and favorite/least favorite things. First, as expected, children watched television more than they used computers; however, there was a smaller amount of difference than anticipated. Second, children reported "how long they could watch" as the television rule they were most likely to follow, yet "watching with an adult" as the one they were least likely to follow. For computers, the three most likely rules to be followed were equally "getting permission," "when you can use it," and "what can be done on the Internet." As with television, the rule least likely to be followed for computers was being "with an adult." In general, the television rules are broken more often. Third, not surprisingly, children's favorite thing about television was their favorite show, whereas their least favorite thing was their least favorite show. Children's favorite thing about the computer was that it was fun, whereas their least favorite thing was when it would "freeze" or "crash." In general, children liked using both media for entertainment rather than education.

The ratings and advisory television study also generated a few major conclusions relevant to this study. One, the number of children who selected television shows and films with warnings is higher than researchers expected to find by chance. Two, gender and age were indicators of the likelihood of choosing media with warnings. Boys were more likely than girls to chose restricted programming in all instances, and older children were more likely than younger children to chose restricted programming in all instances. Three, children do not necessarily understand warnings the same way adults do. Children saw no real differences between the television discretion warnings, and often misinterpreted the restrictiveness of MPAA film warnings. Four, although most children were able to interpret a warning as requiring parental consent, children still chose these programs on their own, without any parental input. Five, parental involvement strongly reduced the likelihood of children choosing restricted shows. However, slightly more than a third of the parents watched television with their children most of the time, and parents were more likely to regulate television amount than content.

My Study's Results

Based on this previous work, there were several questions left unanswered and a few hypotheses to test. With the help of research assistants, school teachers, and a local principal, I had 310 children complete the nine-page survey over a few hours on a school day. Children and their parents had to consent to be in the study. The children ranged from third through eighth grade and ranged from 8 to 15 years olds (based on age, some students were obviously moved up or held back grades). They were of diverse ethnicities including White, African American, Hispanic, and Asian Indian.

In each classroom, the teacher and research assistant instructed the students to independently complete the survey booklet by answering questions on their family home media rules and use, personal television and Internet use, understanding of content ratings and warnings, and experience of adult content. The completed surveys were qualitatively and quantitatively analyzed to determine children's perceptions of family media rules, each medium's impact, clarity of rating and warning systems, correlation of age and gender with likelihood of following media rules, use of adult content, and parental involvement in their media use. Statistical comparisons and students' quotes were used to summarize the following findings.

Family Rules

Children reported that in their homes, from most common television and computer rule to least common rule were "sharing it," "not eating/drinking near it," "acceptable content," "when children could use it," "length of time allowed," and "needing adult supervision." In diffusion of innovation terms, parents seem to have adapted rules for the TV and simply applied them to the computer when they bought one.

The order of the rules themselves is also interesting for several reasons. First, it seems amazing that parents were more likely to regulate sharing of the television or computer and having food near it, than to regulate the content; in other words, more parents told their children not to drink juice by the computer than told them not to view adult material on it. Second, it is surprising that more parents regulate *when* children can watch television or use the computer than for *how long*. This rule likely stems from regulating television content during prime time or late night, typically geared for older audiences. Third, the ratings and advisory TV study concluded that parents were more likely to regulate *how long* children could watch rather than *what*. However, almost half of the children in this study report that their parents regulate content and only about one-quarter said their parents regulate length of time. Finally, although evidence in this report suggests that children need parental input to interpret media content, the least likely rule was requiring children to use media with an adult. The commonness (or lack of) of media rules paints an interesting picture of priorities, or at least children's perceptions of those priorities, in these children's homes.

Each Medium

As expected, based on the children and the media study, children reported they were more likely to follow the computer rules than the television rules. Based on the diffusion of innovation theory, because the computer is a newer and more complex technology, children may be less able to use it or misuse than they are television. Children may not yet have as much access to computers or technical knowledge of them. In fact, some children claimed the reason they did not use restricted sites was that they did not have access to the Internet, but certainly this trend is changing.

Another explanation for the greater likelihood of obeying computer rules relates to both Turkle and the domestic paradigm's discussions of interactivity. In a sense, children seem to be both captivated and intimidated by the interactivity of the computer. Because computers, particularly the Internet, require active participation, children may feel more guilt about actively seeking adult content on the Internet than more passively seeing it on television. Further, some children justified their use of restricted television shows by claiming they were not watching for the content indicated in the warnings, but for something else in the show. For instance, they were passively viewing a show and it happened to contain harsh language, but they were not actively seeking a show with harsh language. By contrast, most Internet users are actively seeking a particular kind of content. Although some children indicated they found restricted Internet material "on accident," most children who claimed to use restricted sites gave very purposeful reasons for doing so, like "wanting to get my freak on." Whatever their personal reasons, children were more willing to break the television rules.

The medium itself also impacted which specific rules children followed. For instance, the rule most likely to be followed for television, having to use it with an adult, was the least likely rule to be followed for the computer. The computer rule requiring children to use it with an adult was also the most broken rule in the children and media study. Perhaps this difference in rule-following behavior is explained by the domestic paradigm. Because families already use television together, the rule that children must watch with an adult is more common in their experience, and may be more likely to be followed. Also, media seem to be divided into personal and shared categories. Personal media, such as headphones, are not meant to be used in groups. It seems logical, then, to expect that rules requiring shared use of those media would not likely be followed. Even though more than one person at a time can see the computer screen, it would be difficult to share the keyboard, therefore, whereas the computer can be a shared medium, it tends to lend itself more to personal use. After all, they are called "personal" computers.

In general, most of the children who report having a rule also report typically following it. However, children may overestimate their general likelihood of following the rules because they have a difficult time answering more abstract questions.

Rating and Warning Confusion

Notably, the ratings and warnings sections of the survey proved to be the most difficult for the children to complete. During the survey, younger children had to ask the researchers many questions about ratings and warnings, plus the older children wanted to check their answers with or brag about illicit content to fellow classmates. Although children were instructed by the principal and the researchers not to discuss their answers, when they reached this section, conversation sprouted. Also during the survey, a surprising number of children claimed they had never seen TV ratings, had no recollection of ever viewing codes in the corner of their television screens, and so on. Finally, without a doubt, the most common question posed to all members of the research team was "What's dialogue?" (concerning the "Dialogue" warning for television), with children as old as 15 not recognizing the terminology. This observation of children's confusion helps demonstrate that the ratings may not be especially useful for children.

With the television content warnings ("D = Dialogue," "L = Language," "S = Sex," and "V = Violence"), the largest number of children correctly recognized that the warnings were intended to caution parents about content. The unusual finding is that fewer than half of the children could agree on any one meaning for the warnings. Also, as high as one-quarter (for the "Dialogue" warning) thought it meant "anyone can watch." In general, children had only a vague understanding of what the warnings meant on a practical level.

Children were also asked to interpret the television ratings codes ("TV-G," "TV-PG," "TV-14," and "TV-MA") in the same fashion as the television warnings. Although as many as three-quarters of the children agreed on interpretations of the television ratings, responses still ran the gamut, indicating that there was some confusion about the ratings. For example, the largest group of children believed "G" and "PG" meant the same thing. Although in some of the open-ended responses children correctly identified "G" as "general audiences," other open-ended responses indicated a belief that "G" meant "guidance." It is therefore not surprising that some children mistakenly equated "G" and "PG" ratings. This finding is consistent with the ratings and advisory TV study's conclusion that children often misinterpret the hierarchical nature of ratings. However, children seem to be able to understand and interpret the television rating codes better than the content warnings because of the similarity with the more familiar MPAA film ratings. In fact, many children made reference to movies rather than television in their open-ended interpretations of the ratings, even though the questions clearly asked about *television* ratings. For instance, children might quote the exact language used for a "PG" movie, "parental discretion is advised," or say that the "*movie* contains violence." Children apply the meanings of the MPAA codes to the television ratings codes because of familiarity with the film system.

In addition to television, children were asked to interpret who should use certain Internet sites with warnings. At least some children selected every given interpretation for every Internet warning, and no more than two of five children ever agreed on what a warning meant. For example, many children thought that a "parental" warning meant that "people shouldn't see it," rather than parental discretion. Also, children interpreted "adults only" and "over 18" warnings differently, although these warnings are likely similar because people over 18 are legal adults. Children felt the "adults only" sites could still be accessed by children (contrary to the name) if they sought adult permission. Children believed the "over 18" warning was for adults to determine their own viewing, and not as a warning to protect children. These findings indicate that the intent of the warnings was not explicitly clear, and that children often were unsure if they should get parental permission to visit a site with a warning.

As a final note, children's comprehension of warnings and ratings did not necessarily decrease the likelihood of their using restricted material. Evidence indicates that even when children understand that ratings or warnings involve parental permission, children chose this type of restricted content without adult consent anyway. Without parental consent or guidance the majority of children (ranging from about half to almost 9 in 10) use various types of restricted content.

Gender and Age

The results indicated that more children used restricted television than restricted Internet content, with boys and older children most likely to use restricted media of both types. Boys were much more likely than girls to use restricted Internet content and slightly more likely to use restricted television. Teens (13–15 years old) were significantly more likely than preteen (11–12) or younger (8–10) children to use restricted media, and likewise, preteens were more likely to use it than younger children. The trend appears to be that boys use more restricted media, particularly computers, and that as children age, they are more curious and adventurous in their restricted media use.

Interest, Ease of Access, and Presence of Adults

Other factors such as interest in content, the ease of access, and the presence of adults help determine children's use of restricted media. The most common reason given for attraction to television shows with restricted warnings was that those shows are "interesting," "entertaining," or "funny." The most common reason for children being repelled by higher ratings and warnings was that they simply did not like those types of shows. Children who were attracted to Internet sites with warnings were most likely to indicate they "like them," "want to see them," or use them because they "can get away with it." The children repelled by those sites most likely indicated that they did not like those kinds of sites. Not surprisingly, children's interest in particular content helps determine what they look for, even if restricted.

To some degree, ease of accessing adult content revealed that (1) children are attracted to restricted media because it is restricted, but still accessible; and (2) finding adult content is not difficult. First, some of the open-ended responses indicated that children accessed adult content because they "could." These responses tended to be very general comments where children simply said they liked media with those warnings, wanted to see them, or were able to see them. Responses like these may indicate that children were attracted more to the rating or warning than anything specific about that type of media content. These types of open-ended responses may relate to the Pandora's box notion, which suggests that children seek out restricted content because they know they are not supposed to. A second conclusion about access is that locating adult material is not terribly difficult for children, with the majority claiming that accessing adult Internet material is "easy" or "very easy." Some children further claimed that finding such material is so easy that they had found certain material "on accident."

A surprising result from this section of the study was that almost three of five children who reported being repelled by television warnings also indicated that they would choose restricted programs with no adult present, and about one in five who reported being repelled by Internet warnings indicated that they would visit restricted Web sites if no adult were present. So, even children who expressed their disdain for adult media content sometimes would still choose to use it when no adult was around. This finding suggests, as discussed previously, that children do not have a solid understanding of the various restriction systems. It illustrates that at least some children do not understand the connection between content and warnings and may not be making the choices parents would hope in their absence. Also, this finding may suggest that children are paying lip-service to reasons they heard from their parents or others concerning restricted media.

Perception of Parental Involvement

Children reported that they did not often use media with their parents in general, with about one in five claiming their parents "never" or "almost never" watched television with them and over half saying their parents "never" or "almost never" used the computer with them. As for explaining the family rules, content, and ratings and warnings, children believe there is not significant parental guidance. Fewer than half of the children claimed their parents had ever clearly explained the importance of the family media rules. Just over half of the children said their parents did not discuss media content with them. As evident with the children's mass confusion over ratings and warnings, parents, in general, have not sufficiently explained these systems either. Results further indicate that as parents watch more television with their children, the children are less likely to watch restricted shows, which makes sense, yet the same could not be proven for computer use, because so few parents do this with children. Also, as might be expected, sharing media with a child seems to have less impact than discussing content and the importance of rules.

What seems telling from these findings is how often children use media without their parents. Astonishingly, almost 9 of 10 children claim their parents did not have too many media rules, and that their parents could do more to help them understand media. Although the domestic paradigm notes that most media use occurs in the home, it appears it does not necessarily occur routinely with parents and children truly engaged together.

Real-Life Implications of This Study

First, this study has direct implications for parents. Children both use and misuse television more than computers. The good news for parents is that if their children are going to use restricted media, television seems to be the safer medium, because the sexual and violent content is less graphic than on the Internet. The potentially bad news is that, as computers diffuse further into the culture, their likelihood of being misused by children probably increases. Parents concerned about their children's exposure to adult content should evaluate their media rules and the clarity of those rules. Further, based on the likelihood of having certain rules, parents send the message that their concern for sharing and avoiding food near media override their concern for their children's exposure to content. If children are mistaken about the commonness of these rules, then parents are not being clear. Almost 9 in 10 of these children were willing to have more guidance. Because children whose parents seldom used or discussed media with them were more likely to use restricted media, concerned parents should spend more time doing this with their children. Parents may need to reinforce positive media habits in girls and younger children, and to discourage negative habits in boys and older children. It will be interesting to observe how parents respond to this evidence.

The study also can be used to improve the TV ratings. Based on the multiple problems with the system, as indicated by the children's responses, some suggestions for improvement can be made. The proponents and designers of rating systems first need to determine the intended users of the system: adults and/or children. If adults, then adults need to explain this information to their children. The major problem with this approach is that it relies on adults taking the time to learn the ratings and explain them to their children, yet about half of the children in this study claim their parents do not do this. The number of children who were unsure if they had seen the rating system, and the number who could not correctly explain the meanings, suggest that their parents had not explained the system to them, or not in a comprehensible way. So, whereas a rating system based on adult comprehension and explanation to children might release the television industry from further responsibility, it does not appear to help children understand the rating system. If the rating system is meant to be comprehensible both to adults and children, a significant improvement must be made. To begin, the text needs to be larger and remain on the screen longer so children can read the words. The language used should be more familiar to children. Also, a voice-over that reads the warning could be used either all of the time, when shows had certain ratings or warnings, or when young children (especially those who could not read) typically watch television. Using a voice-over, complete-sentence, full-screen explanation of the rating and content is currently used before some shows. It would not be unreasonable for all channels to adopt this approach, either all or part of the time. This approach, combined with information disseminated to parents about explaining the rating system to children, would eliminate many of the problems cited previously.

As with the TV rating system, this study can be used to improve the Internet warning system. Internet warnings tend to be infrequent, unsystematic, not related to ease of accessibility, more for the site sponsor's legal protection than for the user's benefit, and possibly more of an enticement than repellent. Obviously, then, the first place to begin improvements is by creating a system that has the opposite characteristics from the negative trends currently seen (i.e., a format that is uniformly applied, systematic, related to the degree of access, more user-friendly, and less sensational). Based on the results of this survey, adults are not likely to use the Internet with children or interpret its warnings for them, so a more clear system like the improved TV system suggested would be more useful.

Summary

Children believe their parents are more concerned about sharing the television or computer and not eating near media than any other concern, such as appropriate content. Because parents tend to report that they monitor their children's media, they would likely be surprised by their children's claims.

Factors affecting the likelihood of obeying parents' rules included the medium itself, ratings and warnings, gender, age, content, presence of adults, and ease of access. Children were more likely to follow family computer rules than television rules. Also, boys were more likely to use adult media, and older children more likely than younger children. Findings on content reveal that children were attracted to restricted television because the shows were "interesting," "entertaining," or "funny"; children were attracted to restricted Internet sites because they "like them," "want to see them," or because they "could." Further, with no adult present, the majority of children use restricted TV and computer content. The majority also claim that finding adult Internet material is "easy" or "very easy."

Fewer than half of the children thought their parents had explained the importance of media rules, and just over half said their parents did not discuss media content with them. About one in five said their parents "never" or "almost never" watched television with them and over half said their parents "never" or "almost never" use the computer with them.

These findings suggest that these children believe their parents do not have too many media rules, they are curious about content and will view what they can, and that better communication with their parents would help their understanding of media.

Questions for Consideration and Discussion

1. Parents worry about children's exposure to media. From your experiences, what things should they be concerned about, and why? What things should they not be concerned about, and why?
2. The respondents for this study were children and adolescents aged 8 to 15. What are the advantages of this? What are the disadvantages?

3. Egan found that children were unclear about the meaning of television and Internet ratings. How could the ratings be changed to clarify them for children?

4. This study indicated that boys were more likely to break media rules than girls. What cultural factors might explain this finding?

5. Based on the results of this study, what recommendations would you make to parents and media executives regarding children and their exposure to media?

References

Cantor, J., & Harrison, K. (1997). Ratings and advisories for television programming: University of Wisconsin, Madison study. *National Television Violence Study, 1,* 363–409.

Egan, C. (2002). *Children speak up: Children's views of their families' home media rules and interactions.* Unpublished manuscript, NCA Family Division.

Egan, C., Gehrs, D., & Kemp, P. (1996). *Children and media.* Unpublished manuscript, Florida State University.

Kahn-Egan, C. (1996, November). *Diffusion of innovations research employing the domestic paradigm: How families use new computer technologies.* Paper presented at the meeting of the Speech Communication Association, San Diego, CA.

Kahn-Egan, C. (1997, October). *Generation net: Computers in education according to third-grade students.* Paper presented at the meeting of the Florida Communication Association, Melbourne, FL.

Lewis, P. H. (1996). Limiting a medium without boundaries: How do you let the good fish through the net without blocking the bad? *NY Times* News Service On-line. http://select.NYtimes.com

Rogers, E. M. (1995). *Diffusion of innovations.* New York: Free Press.

Sinclair, J. (1993). *The domestic paradigm: Researching the use of communication and information technologies in the home.* Victoria Australia: Victoria University of Technology.

Turkle, S. (1984). *The second self.* New York: Simon & Schuster.

Turkle, S. (1995). *Life on the screen.* New York: Simon & Schuster.

Wotring, C. E., Kayany, J. M., & Forrest, E. J. (1995). *Consuming technologies at home: New consumer research techniques.* Tallahassee, FL: Florida State University.

Collective Remembering and Ritualized Communication about the Deceased Parent in Postbereaved Stepfamilies

Leah E. Bryant

Rituals can serve many purposes in the family, including helping members cope with difficult issues. In this work, Bryant discusses a study of stepfamilies that were formed after the death of a parent. Drawing from the accounts of children who lost a parent, she considers the communicative behaviors of the family, and what types of communication aided, or hindered, the grieving and remembering process for these children. Thinking about the loss of a family member is hard to do, but this article sheds light on some behaviors that may help family members cope with such a loss.

L.B.A.

Stepfamilies are common family structures that usually form following divorce (Coleman, Fine, & Ganong, 2001). However, divorce and remarriage is not the only precursor to stepfamily creation. Sometimes stepfamilies form as a result of parental death and remarriage of the surviving parent (Griswald, 1995). Currently, it is unknown how many children in stepfamilies formed postbereavement. What is known is that approximately 5% of children under 15 (or 1.5 million children), in the United States live in single-parent families because the other parent is deceased (Tellerman, Chernoff, Grossman, & Adams, 1998; U.S. Bureau of the Census, 1989).

Sometimes, talk about the former family is difficult to enact in the new stepfamily (Braithwaite, Baxter, & Harper, 1998). Furthermore, communicating about the deceased parent is difficult among surviving family members, largely due to a lack of experience with loss (Weber & Fournier, 1985). This lack of communication is likely to continue into the stepfamily. However, family therapists state that children should be encouraged to be open with the surviving parent about parental death, as it is associated with better psychological outcomes in children (Christ, 2000; Hurd, 1999; Worden, 1996). Yet, there is a tendency for surviving parents to withhold information about parental death to protect children from the pain associated with loss (Baker, Sedney, & Gross, 1992).

It is important for children to be able to express grief and talk openly with family members, especially their surviving parent, about the deceased parent. An ability to talk about the deceased parent and the death in general is important because it aids in the bereavement process and decreases the likelihood of depression later in life (Rosenblatt & Elde, 1990; Saler & Skolnick, 1992). Furthermore, sharing reminiscences, keeping mementos of the deceased parent, hearing stories about the deceased parent, and visiting the grave was also associated with less risk for subsequent depression. This highlights the importance of communication about the deceased parent.

Many children worry about not being able to remember their deceased parent (Tellerman et al., 1998). Memory is created and preserved around physical objects and spaces. Photographs and artifacts particularly capture and preserve memories, enabling the past to be recalled and reinterpreted because they provide a symbolic connection to the lost parent (Radley, 1990; Riches & Dawson, 1998). Silverman and Worden (1992) found that 76% of the children they studied kept something personal that belonged to their deceased parent either on them (such as jewelry) or in their rooms.

The need to publicly discuss the deceased parent partially compensates for the inability of the parent to actually respond. This provides bereaved children the opportunity to exchange information with others which helps them construct internal images, or mental picture, of their parent (Riches & Dawson, 1998). Talking about memories (the happy times, the funny times, and the sad times) will help fix the parent in the child's mind and helps the children preserve their memories and come to terms with their grief (Tellerman et al., 1998).

Collective Remembering

Clinicians and researchers who treat and study bereaved children recognize the importance of communicating about the deceased parent to help provide an enduring memory. Middleton and Edwards (1990) describe this process as collective remembering, where the notion of memory has been extended beyond a conceptualization of it as the property of individuals. Instead, memories are described as highly variable and socially constructed, where they emerge between people as a social act through conversation (Middleton & Edwards, 1990). Families who discuss the deceased parent engage in conversational remembering, which is a process where past events are reconstructed and revised.

The purpose of collective remembering is not to provide an objective factual account of past events. Rather than constructing a story in sequential order, it is recalled in pieces, specifically the parts that are poignant or significant. Therefore, memories are personal reactions and evaluations based on the communication about the event being remembered (Middleton & Edwards, 1990). Instead of verbatim recall, where the goal is word-for-word accuracy, gist remembering is getting the essential features of an event correct even if there are omissions and errors (Neisser, 1981). Individual memory contributions are negotiated, evaluated, and validated in the context of conversation, which contributes to the construction of a version of what occurred (Bangerter, von Cranach, & Arn, 1997).

Collective remembering is similar to shared reminiscence. However, shared reminiscence involves people "remembering common experience or one telling the other of events that the listener has not experienced but can appreciate and integrate with personal memories because of knowledge of the players and related events" (Rosenblatt & Elde, 1990, p. 207). During collective remembering, individuals who were not participants of a particular event can be integrated into it through the sharing of information. Therefore, it is through shared reminiscence that collective remembering can occur.

Researchers of collective remembering recognize that personal objects, mementos of the deceased parent, can be used to invoke a sense of the past. Therefore, artifacts of the deceased parent (e.g., pictures, jewelry, clothing) function as a boundary between individual and social that links personal memories with communal ones (Middleton & Edwards, 1990). Middleton and Edwards explain that when families look at photographs and recount shared experiences, they are recalling and commemorating events that extend beyond any one family member's memory; what is jointly recounted in that interaction is what is remembered and serves as the basis for future recollection.

Moos (1995) argued that communication patterns that are already established within families influence the extent of conversation about the deceased person, noting a link between healthy grief and open family systems. This suggests that if the deceased parent is discussed and remembered prior to remarriage, this will continue to occur after the remarriage. Therefore, in order to continue a dialogue about the deceased parent, families need to develop a norm of talking about the deceased to maintain a memory of him or her. Somehow, issues surrounding communicating about the deceased parent must be addressed for the stepfamily to establish its own identity and for children to be able to adjust to the new family.

Given the difficulty for stepfamilies of communicating about the deceased parent and about the previous family, the question guiding the current study is as follows:

> *RQ:*   How do stepfamilies formed postbereavement communicate about and remember the deceased parent?

Methods

In order to participate in the present study, participants had to meet five criteria. First, the participants' parents must have been married or cohabiting at the time when the other parent died. Second, the participants must have been at least 2 years old when the parent died. Third, they must have been living at home when the stepfamily began. The fourth criterion for participation in the study was that the surviving parent's partner must have been the same individual from the original stepfamily following parental death. The fifth and final criterion was that the participants must have been at least 19 years old.

A total of 31 ($N = 31$) participants were interviewed about communication in their family before and after their parent died. The interviews for this study occurred face-to-face or over the telephone and followed a semistructured focused format (Kvale, 1996; McCracken, 1988; Stewart & Cash, 2000). Each interview was audio-recorded and transcribed verbatim.

The purpose of the study was to better understand communication in stepfamilies that form postbereavement. When not much is known about a particular experience or phenomena, qualitative or interpretive methods are especially suited for this type of inquiry— to describe recurring patterns, meanings, and behaviors of stepfamily members in order to make sense of the family experience (Cissna, Cox, & Bochner, 1990; Creswell, 1998; Miles & Huberman, 1994).

The transcribed data were first read to achieve a general understanding of the participants' experience. In order to answer the research question, the data were then analyzed using an open coding technique to identify the ways participants communicated and remembered the deceased parent (Strauss & Corbin, 1990). The data were then organized in descriptive categories. The categories continued to undergo refinement until a conceptual framework for the results was designed.

Results

All of the stepchildren in the study expressed a desire to be open with their family about their deceased parent. The deceased parent is a part of who the participants are, and because the parent is not physically present in their life, they want communication about the parent to maintain their memories. However, nearly all of the participants (27 of 31) reported difficulty initially communicating with family about the deceased parent. Yet, each of the participants recognized the importance of communication about the deceased parent to create and maintain and enduring memory of that person; therefore, they developed ritualized ways of communicating about him or her.

Desire to Know about the Deceased Parent

All of the adult children interviewed reported a desire to know about their deceased parent. A 24-year-old female participant, who was 2 years old when her mother died and 3 when her father remarried, explained: "I was so curious when I was little. I think I must have asked him [her father] a zillion questions, like how did you guys first meet? What was her favorite food, you know, her favorite color." The children are curious and they want to know everything they can about their deceased parent. This information becomes the basis of their knowledge about the deceased parent to help them remember him or her.

Surviving family members were often not open with the children about the deceased parent. The participants explained the difficulty involved in learning information about the deceased parent. The children also experienced discomfort in having to ask surviving family members about the deceased parent. Instead, they wished that there was a norm of openness. One participant explained the need

> to be open and honest for sure about everything and the more that I found that my dad was keeping from me that he should have told me I thought, the more angry I got with him, so if this would happen to them, like with my daughter and say that my husband had died and she got old enough to know what was going on, I think I would tell her as much as I could in a way that she would understand it. I think instead of me having to ask.

Another participant reported the frustration she felt about the lack of communication about her deceased father. She stated, "people get, everyone gets on with their lives and that's a sad thing. I wish that we could talk about it more and celebrate his life more. You know?" The previous participant echoed the sentiment of everyone interviewed in the study. Almost all of them wished there was more communication about the deceased parent. This is why the development of ritualized remembering serves such an important function in families. It provides a way for the surviving children to learn about their parent and develop memories of him or her without feeling like they are upsetting their surviving parent.

Difficulty Involved in Talking about the Deceased Parent

Though almost all of the participants reported the need to communicate about their deceased parent to create and enduring memory of him or her, they also recognized the difficulty the surviving family members had in doing so. A participant who was 8 when his father died and 10 when his mother remarried explained the trouble he had trying to talk with his surviving parent about his deceased parent:

> Uhm, probably bringing it up was kind of hard, talking with them. We just didn't want to bring it up. We just kind of went on without . . . we didn't ignore it, but we just kind of went on with life and really never brought it up much.

For this participant, it was difficult for him to talk to his surviving parent about his deceased parent, so he discontinued further questions.

The topic of the deceased parent was often a taboo topic in the family. However, this was not always the case. One 24-year-old female participant said, "I was thinking, okay, he's mad at me because I talk about her and ask questions about her . . . so for a long time, I didn't talk about her at all." The participant wanted her dad to be open about her deceased mother, but still he refused. She went on to explain:

> My dad, every time I ask him a question [about the deceased parent], it's yes or no. Yeah, she did or no, she didn't. I came upon that article about her tumor and all that stuff by accident and he was like, "Throw it away." He didn't even want me to keep it.

Clearly, it was too painful for her father to talk about her mother, but the participant's need to know about her mother continued. She went on to say, "I want to know the truth. I'd like to know everything." All of the participants were aware of the pain their surviving parents felt after the loss, but still wanted to be able to communicate with them about their deceased parent.

Because families tended to be less open than the participants wanted, they expressed their frustration in opening the lines of communication. This frustration stems from the need for communicating about the deceased parent to keep a working memory of the person.

Ritualized Talk about the Deceased Parent

The participants understood the importance of communicating about the deceased parent in order to remember him or her. Many of the adult children explained that it was talking with family members about the deceased parent that allowed them to have memories of him or her. One participant explained how her stepfather would talk about her deceased father:

> *E:* I guess my mom would bring it up somewhat, but actually after my mom remarried, married Wally, I think he probably talked more than anyone.
>
> *I:* Wally did?
>
> *E:* Yep. Cause he did know him.
>
> *I:* Yeah. Well, were you all comfortable with Wally talking about your dad?
>
> *E:* Well, yeah, because we were remembering the past and stuff like that.

This participant knew that by communicating with his stepfather about his father, he could remember him better.

Some of the participants explained how it was difficult to remember what their deceased parent looked like. Upon the realization that her sons did not remember their father, one participant's mother made it explicit that her sons should not forget their dad. The participant explained:

> I remember a couple of times when we'd go into my mom and just. . . . Me and my brother would come and talk to each other and be like, "We drew a picture of him because we really don't remember his face." And that was one of the things that she did not want us to grow up or just to forget about him, so she went and got this picture, blew it up and put this big old picture in the picture frame and put it in our room so that we never would forget him and never forget what he looks like and just always kind of remember where we came from, that type of thing.

Having the picture of the deceased parent enabled the participant and his brother to communicate with their mother about their father. This open communication persisted on into the stepfamily.

Whether it is casual conversation, or during major life events, the ability to talk about the deceased parent is paramount to the surviving children. One participant explained the vital role of communication about her deceased father:

> Well, you know, we talk about [him] even now, you mention. . . . My sister says, well, yeah dad used to do this. . . . We sit around and you always are bringing up, you're bringing up the past or whatever, when you're talking about family. It might be at Thanksgiving . . . but even if they're gone they're still just a huge part of your life. So you talk about them . . . with love and how you remember them and the things that they used to do.

The purpose of her conversation with her sibling was not to recount specific events, but rather to vocalize her feeling about her deceased father and memories she had of him. This vocalization allowed her to continue to remember her father, long after he passed away. Holidays provided an event that facilitated communication about her deceased parent. The development of ritualized communication about the deceased parent during major life events, namely holidays, allowed the participants to talk about him or her comfortably.

Another participant explained how her mother communicated that her father would be proud of her for her accomplishments. The 26-year-old female participant who was eight when her father died explained:

> Like if I was, had some performance, or sporting event that I excelled in, um, my dad always used to say when he was proud of us, he'd always say, "I'm so proud of you the buttons on my shirt almost popped off." So Mom would always say, "I'll bet your dad's buttons are popping off right now." And for example when I graduated from high school, uh, Mom sent me a little card, left me a little card, and she just signed her name, and she had uh, some buttons inside of it, you know a kind of to symbolize, uh you know that my dad would be proud of me for that.

Throughout her life, following her father's death, her mother would reference how her father's "buttons would be popping off" as a way of communicating about the deceased parent. This ritualized way of bringing him up allowed the participant and her mother a way to remember the deceased parent. The mother also created a standardized way to communicate about her increased household responsibility following her husband's death—which allowed the participant to better understand the role her father played in the household. She explained:

> Mom would say things a lot of times because she, we were grown to teenagers, and Mom she had always been the typical housewife, she did everything inside, and Dad took care everything outside. Um, so she learned how to do all the stuff which meant learning to ride the tractors, and mow the grass, and all this other stuff. So she'd always talk about it. When she'd get in some situation that she didn't know how she was going to get out or if she didn't know what she was doing, and she'd always say, "oh Charlie, you've got to help me now" or this or that, um and different things like that.

The contexts of the participant's accomplishments and the housework her mother had to assume following parental death were events that provided the opportunity for the deceased parent to be addressed. This stylized way of communicating about him allowed the participant and her mother a way to address the parent in a way that was comfortable for both of them.

For another participant, the family members (surviving parent, stepparent, and brother) used daily events as a ritualized way to talk about the deceased father. The participant explained:

> Sometimes Mom will say, "I wonder what Dad would think about this" or like we'd read something. . . . Like the Enron, my dad was a big accountant and so we'd always be like, "Well I wonder what he thinks about this," but Jeff talked about him too cause Jeff [stepfather] kind of asked once about him like what kind of person was he. What are the kind of things you remember? But us being at that age, we really don't have that many memories of him. So we kind of told him all the things we really know, so he kind of knows it all.

Not only did the surviving family members talk about the deceased father, but the stepfather also joined in the conversations about him. The participant described that he does not have many memories of his father; however, communicating with his family members provides a way to remember him.

Most of the participants acknowledged that the memories of the deceased parent come from what they communicate, or are told about him or her. Although some expressed frustration that the memories were not "their own," others explained how appreciative they were that their family members were willing to share stories and feeling about the deceased parent. One participant explained how her stepmother played an instrumental role in her ability to remember her deceased mother:

> My mom now is never ever not able to answer any questions I have about my real mom. There's no jealousy between her and my dead mom. It's very open that way. That's the only reason why I remember things is because they saved many things that she had that I have now.

The participants understood that their memories were socially constructed. That is why the most prevalent piece of advice the adult stepchildren gave concerned the importance of open communication about the deceased parent. When this participant was asked what advice he would give to the surviving parent in a blended family, he said, "Be open with your children. Bring up things that have happened in the past with them and kind of keep it open." He explained how children long for openness about their deceased parent. Another participant further explained the importance of being open with children about their deceased parent:

> That parent is as much a part of them [surviving children] as you [parent] are, the parent that's left. They need to know who that person is. And the thing is my mother now probably doesn't have a lot of memories. I mean probably she's let them go. So now for me to get stuff out of her, even when we talk to my aunt, their memories were vague. You know, we would ask questions and they would say, "Well, let's see now. How did that go?" And none of them would remember something one way and one the other. So you need to have those memories . . . you need to talk about it [the deceased parent] with them [children] from day one if you can. That's what I would say, talk about them [the deceased parent]. Tell them everything you know. Whether you think it's interesting or not because I would like to know anything about my dad. I would like to know like what was his favorite color? What was his favorite food? . . . So tell them everything, everything. They need to know that because that person is part of them. . . . Never quit talking about that.

The participants expressed how important it was for the surviving parent to be open with them about their deceased parent in order for them to remember him or her. Following the death of their parent, the participants expressed feeling as if part of them was missing, and the more information they had about their deceased parent the more it helped fill that gap.

Discussion

The results reported in this article reflect the common experiences among all the participants—wanting to know about the deceased parent, having difficulty talking about the deceased parent, while understanding the importance of communicating about him or her, and the creation of ritualized ways to remember the deceased parent. Stepfamilies formed postbereavement have to manage the difficulty of making the transition into a new family structure, while also finding a way to communicate about the deceased parent. From the children's point of view, that difficulty is compounded by knowing that memories are dependent upon communication about the deceased parent. Therefore, the development of ritualized ways of communicating about the deceased parent allows family members to talk about the deceased parent in order to create and sustain memories of him or her.

One of the participants who reported that talk of the deceased parent was immediately welcomed had a much different experience than the other participants. She said it was one of the first things she discussed with her stepmother. At their first meeting, the stepmother explained that a train hit and killed her husband. This began the normative process of discussing deceased family members. This was much the same experience for the few ($N = 5$) participants who had open communication about their deceased parent. Conversely, there was one participant whose family rarely, if at all, discussed the deceased parent. Her memories were limited entirely to the experiences that others (outside the family) had shared with her. Furthermore, she did not have access to her deceased mother's belongings or pictures, which made it even more difficult for her to remember her mother. And in this case, she had no recollection of experiences with her mother and could not remember what she looked like. These are two extreme examples, one where the talk about the deceased parent was immediately open and one where no talk about the deceased parent was ever allowed. The range of communicative experiences family members have communicating about deceased members deserves further inquiry.

All of the individuals interviewed reported a healthy adjustment to the stepfamily, even if it was not a pleasant experience. Furthermore, none of the stepchildren interviewed reported intense animosity toward their stepfamily; but as previously stated, some had siblings who did. This may be an artifact of self-selected sampling. The individuals who were interviewed were willing to participate. Perhaps those who had a positive experience volunteered.

The sample size of this study is relatively small ($N = 31$). Certainly, before any definitive statements can be made about stepfamily adjustment after the death of a parent, there must be more research on this family structure. However, it can be said that there are important differences between stepfamilies that form postdivorce and those that form postbereavement. Communication scholars are uniquely positioned to study the interaction of family members who experience loss.

Questions for Consideration and Discussion

1. Why do you think scholars suggest that an objective, factual account is not the goal of collective remembering?
2. This study focuses on communication about parental death in a stepfamily formed after the loss. What other family situations might this information apply to?
3. Death, serious illness, financial problems, alcoholism, and abuse are among the topics that many people find difficult to discuss with family or friends. Why is this the case?
4. Based on this study, what advice would you give to adult caretakers of a child or adolescent whose parent or other close family member has died?
5. Bryant's thematic analysis was based on respondent memories of family experience. What limitations and benefits of this method can you see?

References

Baker, J. E., Sedney, M. A., & Gross, E. G. (1992). Psychological tasks for bereaved children. *American Journal of Orthopsychiatry, 62,* 105–117.

Bangerter, A., Cranach, M. von, & Arn, C. (1997). Collective remembering in the communicative regulation of group action: A functional approach. *Journal of Language and Social Psychology, 16,* 365–388.

Braithwaite, D. O., Baxter, L. A., & Harper, A. (1998). The role of rituals in the management of the dialectical tensions of "old" and "new" in blended families. *Communication Studies, 49,* 101–121.

Christ, G. H. (2000). Impact of development on children's mourning. *Cancer Practice: A Multidisciplinary Journal of Cancer Care, 8*(2),72–81.

Cissna, K., Cox, D., & Bochner, A. (1990). The dialectics of marital and parental relationships within the stepfamily. *Communication Monographs, 57,* 44–61.

Coleman, M., Fine, M., & Ganong, L. (2001). Reinvestigating remarriage: Another decade of progress. *Journal of Marriage and Family, 62,* 1288–1307.

Creswell, J. W. (1998). *Qualitative inquiry and research design: Choosing among five traditions.* Thousand Oaks, CA: Sage.

Griswald, S. (1995). Communication-family characteristics: A comparison between stepfamilies (formed after death or divorce) and biological families. *Journal of Divorce & Remarriage, 24,* 183–196.

Hurd, R. (1999). Adults view their childhood bereavement experiences. *Death Studies, 23,* 17–41.

Kvale, S. (1996). *InterViews: An introduction of qualitative research interviewing.* Thousand Oaks, CA: Sage.

McCracken, D. (1988). *The long interview.* Newbury Park, CA: Sage.

Middleton, D., & Edwards, D. (1990). Conversational remembering: A social psychological approach. In D. Middleton & D. Edwards (Eds.), *Collective remembering* (pp. 23–45). London: Sage.

Miles, M. B., & Huberman, A. M. (1994). *Qualitative data analysis* (2nd ed.). Thousand Oaks, CA: Sage.

Moos, N. L. (1995). An integrative model of grief. *Death Studies, 19,* 337–364.

Neisser, U. (1981). John Dean's memory: A case study. *Cognition, 9,* 1–22.

Radley, A. (1990). Artifacts, memory, and a sense of the past. In D. Middleton & D. Edwards (Eds.), *Collective remembering* (pp. 46–59). London: Sage.

Riches G., & Dawson, P. (1998). Lost children, living memories: The role of photographs in processes of grief and adjustment among bereaved parent. *Death Studies, 22,* 121–140.

Rosenblatt, P., & Elde, C. (1990). Shared reminiscence about a deceased parent: Implications for grief education and grief counseling. *Family Relations, 39,* 206–210.

Saler, L., & Skolnick, N. (1992). Childhood parental death and depression in adulthood: Roles of surviving parent and family environment. *American Journal of Orthopsychiatry, 62,* 504–516.

Silverman, P. R., & Worden, J. W. (1992). Children's reactions in the early months after the death of a parent. *American Journal of Orthopsychiatry, 62,* 93–104.

Stewart, C. J., & Cash, W. B. (2000). *Interviewing: Principles and practices* (9th ed.). Boston: McGraw-Hill.

Strauss, A. & Corbin, J. (1990). *Basics of qualitative research: Grounded theory procedures and techniques.* Newbury Park, CA: Sage.

Tellerman, K., Chernoff, R., Grossman, L., & Adams, P. (1998). When a parent dies. *Contemporary Pediatrics, 15,* 145–150.

U.S. Bureau of the Census. (1989). *Marital status and living arrangements: March 1989* (Series P-20, No. 445). Washington, DC: U.S. Government Printing Office.

Weber, J. A., & Fournier, D. G. (1985). Family support and a child's adjustment to death. *Family Relations, 34,* 43–49.

Worden, J. W. (1996). *Children and grief: When a parent dies.* New York: Guilford Press.

Storytelling as a Means to Communicate within the Family—The Orphan Stories

Dennis Alajandro Vegas Leoutsakas

Family stories function to provide us with a sense of belongingness and identity in the family. Orphans, however, are in a somewhat unique situation with regard to their family experience, and, thus, that feature may be simultaneously heightened and diminished. In this work, Leoutsakas discusses his work with orphan stories, and the ways in which these stories can illuminate both the experience of orphans and the functions of family stories.

L.B.A.

Twenty years of experience as a mental health counselor, juvenile probation officer, and a family therapist has led me to define *identity* as the sum of our experiences that makes us who we are, and as a result, influences what we do. Restated, we are everything that has happened to us. If this is true, then one of the most natural ways to express ourselves is through story and storytelling. Storytelling is a method for relating experiences and placing them in context. My friend, Michael Arrington (2002), who uses stories as a practical tool to analyze the way men with prostate cancer perceive their illness, writes,

> Storytelling allows people to contextualize themselves and their actions. It is through this process that we discover who we really are. . . . We use stories to shape our identities, not only in the mundane aspects of our daily lives, but in the midst of adversity, as well. (p.25)

The use of stories to make sense of our lives is not a unique idea.[1] The scholar, Coste (1989), claims there are three very specific purposes for narrative: they help explain cultural realities, they provide examples for us to imitate, and they can be used to persuade our thoughts or actions. Kirkwood (1992) suggests an additional function of narratives: they open our eyes to the realm of possibilities. In addition, the use of stories by all civilizations is undeniable. Writer and scholar Roland Barthes discusses the prevalence of stories:

> The narratives of the world are numberless. . . . Narrative is present in every age, in every place, in every society; it begins with the very history of [humankind] and there nowhere is nor has been a people without narrative. (Quoted in Polkinghorne, 1988, p. 14)

Because stories are so commonplace, and they are willingly embraced by humans, it follows that stories are an important vehicle of family communication. Stories help us with understanding family interactions and determining our places in family configurations. By slightly altering the ideas forwarded by Coste and Kirkwood, I suggest that the following relationships exist between stories and family communication: (1) Stories help us explain what is happening in our families. (2) Stories are used by primary caretakers in families to provide examples of beliefs, values, attitudes, and behaviors. (3) As individuals, we use stories to convince other family members to recognize our points of view. (4) Stories help us dream, both as individual family members and as family units.

Ironically, having stated the importance of stories to family communication, I turn my attention to a single family member, the orphan (defined as a child with absent biological parental figures). Having read or heard the stories of hundreds of orphans, I think they give us a unique perception of the family. Through these orphan stories (often told by adults), I can show how stories are used to explain family circumstances, forward ideas within the family, convince family members of a point of view, and finally, help family members imagine a different set of circumstances for their families.

The Orphan Narratives

Stories of the orphaning experience are spellbinding. Like horrendous disasters, orphan narratives compel us to stare (or at least peek) at the tragic aftermath of a life in disarray.[2] Along with weaving a background for themselves through their stories, orphans also use stories to provide a structure through which their experiences can be understood by others. Furthermore, it is through these stories that others learn what life is like for orphans. For orphans, this means that the stories they tell themselves, the stories they tell others, and the stories they are told, shape both self-perceptions and social impressions of orphaning

Although the work in this article does not seek to scientifically identify the origins of all stories told under familial circumstances, it does seek to better understand the use of stories through the conditions of orphaning. Its research locus is in uncovering the reflections of those who have been orphaned. The research captures pieces of inner conversations through a thematic analysis of 14 formal interviews of self-identified orphans and an informal survey of anecdotal material gathered from documents and textualized material (e.g., books, newspapers, magazines, audio documentaries, film, etc.) forwarded by orphans. This article is designed as an in-depth analysis, utilizing narrative interviews of a small population ($N = 15$) of orphans, supported by readings from orphan-related material, and self-revelations and observations from my own orphaning and consequential family-related experiences. This research augments available family communication research about the utilization of storytelling within the family by taking the time to listen to stories told by contemporary orphans.

As a family communication researcher, I collect stories told by orphans because I do not find representations of orphans in the media or popular culture to be at all convincing. By using oral histories and open-ended interviewing, rather than surveys and statistical analysis that are commonly used by social scientists, I explore the depths of orphaning through the stories orphans tell about their childhoods and family-life happenings. Bringing these stories out into the open provides a more culturally complete picture of the orphaning experience. It is a picture that contrasts sharply with the fictional and pop-cultural images of orphaning.

The remainder of this article uses narrative accounts from self-identified orphans to examine the relationships of stories to individuals, family units, and family communication. In addition to providing examples of family communication, the stories are used to enhance existing characterizations of contemporary orphans and orphaning processes. From the stories that follow, I show that there is a strong relationship between stories and family communication.

1. Stories help us explain what is happening in our families.

Every intact family has stories about family members (remember crazy Aunt . . .) or the development of the family (Grandma and Grandpa can trace their roots back to . . .). Orphans, whether adopted or not, also have riveting stories to tell. Many people who did not grow up with their biological parents use stories to describe the circumstances of their orphaning. This is a story narrated by a young woman whose father was fatally shot in front of her when she was a child, and who was totally orphaned as a teenager when her mother died from AIDS. She talks about her father:

> My best memories were always going to Puerto Rico in the summer time to visit my family. I got to spend time with my father and see my father. I loved being with my father. I lived in New York City. When my mom and dad split up, my mom went with my step-dad and went to New York. . . . When me and my mom left my dad I was three years old. I didn't feel like I left him completely, because of the fact that every summer I'd go see him. When my father was killed it changed. . . . It was okay, I mean he was in and out of drug rehab and trying to clean up, and trying to straighten himself up. But, uhm, he was really good. He cared for me a lot. He made me feel comfortable and safe around him.

Here is another story from a young woman who was adopted as an infant. She talks about her adopted grandmother:

> I don't think that my grandmother liked my brother and I very much. Especially because I wouldn't eat her chicken soup. Because she put chicken feet into it! Which was hideous! As a child it freaked me out. I didn't think it [the differences in our taste in food] had anything to do with [my grandmother] being Slovak or having it [Mexican] in my blood. So, I used to run around and she would chase me. To get even, just to spite her, I was sort of a bratty kid, I would eat the dog biscuits. She thought that was horrendous—a Slovak child would never do that!

From these stories we can get a sense of a father–daughter relationship and an adoptive grandmother–granddaughter relationship. Thinking back to our childhood, we all have such stories. In this way we rely on stories to help explain what did happen or what is happening in our families.

2. Stories are used by primary caretakers in families to provide examples of beliefs, values, attitudes, and behaviors.

Stories help forward or teach these beliefs, values, attitudes, and behaviors that we hold dear. When we read or hear stories of those who do poorly because of drugs or alcohol, the message to us is "don't do drugs or drink excessively." When we hear or read stories about people who excel in their fields because they are educated, the message to us is "stay in school because education is important." These lessons are taught through the process of sharing our own beliefs, values, attitudes, and behaviors consistently. Naturally, some of these qualities are cultural values and are often reinforced by society (i.e., don't lie, don't steal, don't kill, etc.) because they generally benefit the entire society. Others are more subtle and may play out in the family, but not hold true for general society (e.g., if your father really loved you, he'd . . . ; Mother didn't care about me because she was more interested in . . .). In family relationships where blood relations are not available, some of the beliefs, values, attitudes, and behaviors are more subtle still, but orphan children get the messages. The first story is from an adult woman reflecting back on her adoptive parents. She first talks about the messages she received about her biological family, and then describes the values she received from her adoptive family:

> I know that my adopted mom was bitter about not being able to have children. . . . She fed me some things, I think that they were true from her perspective. This idea that the biological family personally hated me. . . . I didn't get a sense of any kind of hatred [when I contacted them]. [However] I learned a lot of really great things from them [my adoptive parents], . . . a great work ethic, loyalty, [and] a sense of commitment. You take something on, you do it. [I guess the word is] stick-to-it-ness.

The second story is considered "the great adoption story" by orphans. Adopted children are often told they are special because their adoptive parents picked them out of all the orphan children in the world. One of the problems with this story is that, when the children grow older, it is difficult to reconcile the mythology with adult issues (e.g., Why did my biological parents abandon me? In a racially divided culture, why must I look so different than my adoptive family? etc.). Here is an example of how the story was communicated to a young Asian woman growing up in a White home.

> This [my adoption] was really a great thing and this was something special, something unique. And my family and my church family and all of our friends, and sort of the people just around me were always reminding me that I was special, I was unique. You know, . . . really instilling in me that something really wonderful happened, and it was a blessing, and this wasn't something bad. But I do remember people treating it as if it were [really sad], and then being retold that wasn't the issue, and so I never saw it like that [as bad]. . . . I remember going into the bathroom, and turning on the light and looking in the mirror, and noticing there was something very different between the way I looked and the way they looked! . . . I look Asian, but I think, and was brought up, as White American. . . . so—I'm treated one way because of my physical appearance. There is always like this reminding that I am different. . . . It's hard because I find myself trying to identify with the Asian side of my heritage, and that's so foreign.

From these stories we can get a sense of the many values that can be imparted by the narratives in our family relationships. In the two brief scenarios described, issues of parenting, work ethics, family loyalty, personal commitments, adoption, and race all surfaced. Thinking back to your childhood, you too can probably remember a time when a story was used to teach you a value, or pass on a belief. From religious stories to personal stories we are surrounded by such stories. In this manner, stories are used by primary caretakers in families to provide examples of beliefs, values, attitudes, and behaviors to be followed by other family members.

3. As individuals, we use stories to convince other family members to recognize our points of view.

Can you remember a time when you came home and used this line on your parents or caretakers, "My friend . . . , so I should . . ."? In a sense we were telling the story about our friend to convince our primary caretaker to be more like our friend's primary caretakers. This type of narrative reasoning is found throughout the family constellation. At times it is adults trying to convince children or other adults; other times it's children trying to persuade adults or other children. Although we can all come up with lighthearted persuasive stories we've witnessed, it should be remembered that many children and caregivers use stories as incendiary devices in very serious family situations or as a means to realign the family. For instance, in the first scenario presented here, a grandparent uses the stories of her daughter's poor relationships, her granddaughter's truancy from school, and the girl's relationship with a boyfriend to force the teenage girl from the home:

> My grandmother was very dictating, very traditional, very—in some ways, she could be very mean. She was mad at my father [who was murdered], she was mad at my sister's father [who died from AIDS], she took it out on us. We're the closest thing to them so she would take it out on us. The day after my mom died [from AIDS], she's [grandmother] telling me how awful I am, and how I have so much to do with it [her mother's death], because *I couldn't be a better kid*! . . . She told me never to come back. That I could [only] go back to see my sister's dead body [when she too died from AIDS], because I need to see what I did to my sister, that's what she told me! My grandmother just says things without thinking—hurtful things.

The second story has a different tone and outcome. A 19-year-old boy told me the story to illustrate how he and his sister prompted a turnaround in his biological mother's behavior just before she died:

> My mother started drinking when we moved back to Tampa. She would burn dinner when she was drunk. And, she would drive drunk and get into accidents. And at times I would have to drive her home when I was too young, 14 or 15, to have a license. One time me and my sister wrote her a letter [explaining everything that was happening] and we were like, "hey look, it's either the alcohol or us." And, she finally gave it up . . . . She started being real good with us. . . . At the end [before she died from AIDS], my mom was real good with us.

From these narratives we can get a sense of how imposing a member of the family can be with the use of stories as a major tool for persuasion. Thinking back to our own childhoods, I'm sure we all remember times when we or someone else in our family used stories to convince other family members to think or do things. In this way, we use stories to convince other family members to recognize our points of view.

4. Stories help us dream, both as individual family members and as family units.

Stories from the past help us plan for the future. If we can place an experience, or several experiences, into a narrative form, then we can decide what to do differently or similarly in the future. Because of the difficult circumstance that many orphaned children experience, they often dream of a better future. In addition, they more clearly understand that their dreams rest on their actions as opposed to relying on family guidance. The first story here is from a teenage Vietnamese refugee, who grew up in poverty. His story and dreams are similar to the immigrant stories we have grown up hearing as children in the United States:

> [Because I grew up in poverty] I just want to concentrate on my goal, you know, in the medical profession. I want to become a doctor one day. . . . Right now I try not to worry too much about girls. . . . I feel like my goal is more important and when I become the person I want to be, you know, when I become independent and financially independent, maybe then I can start dating. Right now, it's just not a good time.

Many orphaned children fantasize about what their parents must be like. They look and listen for the slightest hints about their biological families. Even when information is limited they can create idealized pictures of their biological parents in their minds from the few stories they've heard. Here a young woman talks about her biological mother and father. She never met either of them and all the information she received about them came from her adoptive parents:

> Oh yes, I remember, I have that conversation [about my orphaning] with her [my mother] a lot, because I would, I guess, talk to her, think about her, try to relate to her, because I felt like maybe this was the only person that could have understood me; that could have helped me make some sense of some stuff, but, she's dead.
>
> But the father, that's always been a thing. I think the reality has always scared me so much about who he might have been. I guess, I hoped realistically that he was just a high school boy, maybe a senior or a little bit older, but not in his thirty's or forty's or something like that. Hopefully not related or anything like that. But, I always had silly fantasies about people like Paul McCartney or Jim Morrison. . . . I thought, "maybe it could have happened, why not?, you know." . . . It's that whole kind of hero mythology or fantasy that I created about him. But in reality I know—hopefully—he was just some slightly older teenage dweeb, who may or may not have known that he got her pregnant. Who probably, if he did know, did exactly what I would expect a young guy to do, which is run for the hills. I mean, she was only fourteen. . . . I seriously doubt I will ever put any effort into trying to find him. Because I'm really scared about who he could turn out to be in reality.

From these excerpts we get a sense that there is a perception of a future for the speakers. The young man is contemplating his career based on the poverty in his past, and the young woman is contemplating searching for her extended biological family based on the stories she's created in her head from the few bits and pieces of information she has about her biological parents. Again, considering our own childhoods, it's only natural to set our goals based on the experiences we've had. We think of the stories we hold (e.g., how well we did at . . . , what happened to . . . .) and we know our strengths, or likes, or fears, and the such. From this knowledge, we can plan for the future. This is the way we use stories to help us dream, both as individual family members and as family units.

I have one final comment about the storytelling process within families. Every family unit has its codes that trigger often-repeated stories. For example, when my niece's children call me their "*Great* Uncle Dennis" it is the code to remember the stories of how I played with their mother when she was a child; the stories of my wild side as an adolescent; the stories of me as a child growing up with their greatgrandparents (my foster parents); more recent stories of the past few Thanksgivings that I've spent with them, and so forth. These code statements are found in all families. The simple mention of a name can trigger the stories that surround that person, or a mere remark about an event causes all the old experiences of that event to surface. Often these are fun conversations because we are looking backward in time. We do not have to cope with the stress we felt at the time of the event. Even the trauma of orphaning can be minimized by adult orphans when the orphaning is treated historically. These code words and comments are wonderful vehicles for rich and fulfilling family conversations. Use them often and then sit back and enjoy the stories that emerge.

Questions for Consideration and Discussion

1. Leoutsakas notes that orphan stories are not accurately represented in the media. What do you think this claim refers to? Why do you think this might be the case?
2. This study shows how family stories are used to pass on values. Why are stories such a good mechanism for teaching values in the family?
3. Leoutsakas also argues that stories are frequently used to persuade family members. What makes storytelling a good way to engage in persuasion?
4. Having read this article, what advice would you give to friends and family members of orphans about how to use storytelling for positive impacts in the life of the orphan?
5. This interpretive study uses personal narrative as a research methodology. Do you think this method is appropriate for study of orphan experience? Why or why not?

Endnotes

1. Storytelling, in narrative form, as a means of inquiry is critically examined by a growing number of contemporary scholars who strongly advanced the value of narrative analysis in research. A few of the more well-known communication scholars, who have laid the foundations for these contemporary critical studies, include Bateson (1989); Bruner (1987, 1990); Burke (1968); Coles (1989); Davis (1999); Fisher (1984); Frank (1995); Gergen (1992); Gergen and Gergen, (1983, 1988); Goffman (1959); Polkinghorne (1988); and Richardson (1990, 1992).
2. The narratives used in this chapter were all collected between 1996 and 2002. All interviewees in this research have allowed their comments to be used for my continued work, but for the purposes of anonymity, I have not used the actual names of any participants.

References

Arrington, M. I. (2002). *Recreating ourselves: Stigma, identity changes, and narrative reconstruction among prostrate cancer survivors*. Unpublished doctoral dissertation, University of South Florida, Tampa.

Bateson, M. C. (1989). *Composing a life*. New York: Plume/Penguin.

Bruner, J. (1987). Life as narrative. *Social Research, 54*(1), 11–21.

Bruner, J. (1990). *Acts of meaning.* Cambridge, MA: Harvard University Press.

Burke, K. (1968). Psychology and form. In *Counterstatement* (pp. 29–44). Berkeley: University of California Press. (Original work published 1925)

Coles, R. (1989). *The call of stories.* Boston: Houghton Mifflin.

Coste, D. (1989). *Narrative as communication.* Minneapolis: University of Minnesota Press.

Davis, C. A. (1999). *Reflexive ethnography: A guide to researching selves and others.* New York: Routledge.

Fisher, W. R. (1984). Narration as a human communication paradigm: The case of public moral argument. *Communication Monographs, 51,* 1–22.

Frank, A. (1995). *The wounded storyteller: Body, illness, and ethics.* Chicago: University of Chicago Press.

Gergen, K. J., & Gergen, M. M. (1983). Narrative of the self. In T. R. Sarbin & K. E. Scheibe (Eds.), *Studies in social identity* (pp. 254–273). New York: Praeger.

Gergen, K. J., & Gergen, M. M. (1988). Narrative form and the construction of psychological science. In T. R. Sarbin (Ed.), *Narrative psychology: The storied nature of human conduct* (pp. 22–94). New York: Praeger.

Gergen, M. M. (1992). Metaphors for chaos, stories of continuity: Building a new organizational theory. In S. S. R. Fry (Ed.), *Executive and organizational continuity: Managing the paradoxes of stability and change* (p. 374). San Francisco: Jossey-Bass.

Goffman, E. (1959). *The presentation of self in everyday life.* New York: Doubleday.

Kirkwood, W. G. (1992). Narrative and the rhetoric of possibility. *Communication Monographs, 59,* 30–47.

Polkinghorne, D. (1988). *Narrative knowing and the human sciences.* Albany: State University of New York Press.

Richardson, L. (1990). Narrative and sociology. *Journal of Contemporary Ethnography, 19,* 116–135.

Richardson, L. (1992). The consequences of poetic representation: Writing the other, rewriting the self. In C. Ellis & M. G. Flaherty (Eds.), *Investigating subjectivity: Research on lived experience* (pp. 125–137). Newbury Park, CA: Sage.

Section 3: Conclusions and Application—
Reflecting on Your Family Rules, Rituals,
and Stories _____

In this chapter we've talked about family communication processes, specifically in relation to rules, rituals, and stories. Hopefully, as you have read the examples provided in Sections 1 and 2 you've begun to think about your own family experience in these three arenas.

Every family has rules. This is a rather basic concept, and yet, as a family member (particularly when you were a young one) you may have felt that other families had no rules—or at least far fewer than yours. However, as discussed in this chapter, the existence of a family system indicates the presence of rules, created through communication and often regulating communication. I once heard a story of a woman who grew up in a household where there were no beds, and no bedtimes. When someone (adult or child) was tired, he or she simply laid down on a couch or futon and napped for a few hours until ready to get up again. The woman who told the story, as a child, felt odd growing up in this environment and requested that her parents get her a bed and establish a bedtime (like all of her friends had). They would not, they indicated, because in their house the schedule was regulated by bodily needs, not by the clock. Thus, we can see how what seems like the absence of a rule is, in fact, the presence of a different rule.

Because family life is rule bound, it makes sense, as scholars and as family members, to spend some time thinking about our family rules, particularly those rules related somehow to communication (like the media use rules discussed by Egan). Doing so may *help us understand what family rules were conducive to a positive familial environment and/or personal development, and which family rules were less so*. Such an *analysis can also give us the tools that we need for future operation in the family*. Perhaps you believe that the rules your parents had about television watching, when you were a teenager, were completely unreasonable. Some careful consideration of those rules and how they came to be could provide more insight. Maybe the rules were appropriate for an eight-year-old; however, they was never discussed or renegotiated as the family system changed (i.e., as you grew older) and that was how they became so burdensome to you. In this case, the rules themselves are not the issue, so much as how those rules were handled by the family members. In the future, should you be in a parenting or caregiving role for a teenager, this information could help you understand the value of carefully reassessing communication rules frequently based on age, developmental changes, and other family system issues.

As with family rules, family rituals are present in all family system. However, what is a ritual for one family may simply be a habit for another. When I ask students to read about ritual, they often begin by thinking that they have no rituals in their family of origin. This is usually because they are only considering "big" events (i.e., religious ceremonies) to be ritualized. However, as we have covered in this chapter, rituals can range from complex behaviors, like organizing a family reunion, to very simple behaviors. Bryant's work is a good example of the later. Collectively reminiscing about a family member who has died is not a big event, but it can still become a ritual. It is not what the repeated behavior consists of that makes it a ritual; it is the meaning that the members of the system give to that behavior or set of behaviors that turn it into a ritual. After carefully considering the concept of family rituals, students can typically think of many rituals that were engaged in by their family members. One student told the class that her mother had always packed notes in her lunchbox, all through elementary school and junior high school. By junior high, she was rather embarrassed by the notes and would just glance at them and throw them away. Sensing her embarrassment, her mother stopped packing the notes around the time her daughter was about to enter high school. The student told us that, though she had been somewhat annoyed by the notes, she was very upset when they stopped. Something as simple as a small slip of paper with a few words on it, even when it was a bit embarrassing, had become a ritual that reassured her of her importance to her mother.

Considering the rituals present in your family systems can operate to give you a clearer idea of the values that you, and the other members of your family system, hold as important. Think about the behaviors you do repeatedly with family members. Now, for each behavior, think about what family members, including you, might feel if that behavior was lost. For some behaviors, you may think that the family members wouldn't feel much (or might be relieved) if the behavior were not reproduced. (For example, you might clean house on Saturday mornings; if someone else came and cleaned your house on Saturday, the members of the family might feel only happy.) In that case, the behavior is likely just a habit, or a scheduled repetition, rather than a ritual. For other repeated behaviors, however, you may note that if the behavior were lost, family members would be upset, confused, feel less loved, be angry, and so on. If members of the family had a strong emotional response to the loss of the behavior, then it must have some significance. This opens the door for you to consider what that significance is. What is the underlying value of the repeated behavior for family members? Such thinking may allow us to avoid upsetting rituals that are precious to family members, or at least give us the tool to understand why a particular person (or people) is upset when a repeated behavior gets disrupted. Additionally, *thinking about the rituals in operation in our family systems may even allow us to plan future ritualized behaviors in an effort to emphasize the beliefs and values we hold most dear.*

Of course, family rituals are not the only family phenomenon that speaks to the values and beliefs of family members. The stories we tell in a family system do this as well. As considered in previous sections of this chapter, family stories are an important part of the creation of understanding that happens in a family system. Like the orphans in Leoutsakas's work, through telling and hearing family stories we learn about ourselves, the family system, and the world. We create our realities and attempt to influence and shape the realities of others. What family stories are told in your family systems? Think about what those family stories say about you, about the other members of the family, about the family in general, and about the world in which the family operates. Sometimes, it is hard to focus on what the story is really emphasizing. "Oh, we just tell that story because it's funny." That may be true, but over the course of a family lifetime there are thousands of funny things that happen (when there are small children in the house, funny things tend to happen several times a day). So, why are the particular stories that get told and retold the ones selected for remembering, revisiting, and sharing with others? This has to do with the family culture and the beliefs the family has about self and others (and the beliefs that adult members hope to socialize their young into). *By thinking about the family stories we tell, both within and outside the family setting, we can get a better sense of what family reality we have created and, perhaps, why.* Such an effort can give us added insight into how history is an issue of creating, not simply fact, and may provide impetus for telling different stories (or affirm that the stories we are telling are useful) or understanding of how the stories we have heard have created our realities and impacted our lives.

Family rules, rituals, and stories are three important dimensions of communication in the family system. However, these are not the only types of communication that goes on in families: we will spend time discussing some other communication processes in upcoming chapters. But these three forms of family communication are very important in the creation of family culture and in the lives of family members. Family culture is important in their creation, as well. Attention paid to the processes and meanings involved in these family communication phenomena is certainly not wasted effort.

Questions for Consideration and Discussion

1. Family rules can be implicit or explicit. Some scholars argue that families should make rules as explicit as possible and discuss them openly with all members. What do you see as the advantages and disadvantages of this approach?
2. Privacy rules in the family are an important part of family culture. The privacy/openness dialectic may become even more heightened as children become teenagers. What sort of information do you think parents and teens should keep private? Why? What sort of information should be shared? Why?
3. What are some of the rituals your family observed concerning birthdays? What do you think those rituals taught you about family?
4. Family rituals may be positive or negative. If a ritual is negative, why do you think the family continues to engage in it?
5. What stories do you remember about joining your family (through birth or adoption)? What is the significance of those stories to you?

Key Terms and Concepts

attachment theory
celebrations
communication privacy
   management theory
explicit rules
exterior boundaries
family rituals

family stories
implicit rules
interior boundaries
metarules
negative rituals
patriarchal
patterned daily interactions

privacy boundaries
reciprocal socialization
rule
socialization
traditions

5

Communicating Intimacy, Affection, and Social Support

Chapter Outline

Chapter Objectives

1. To be able to define intimacy, affection and social support in families

2. To develop understanding of some of the factors that contribute to intimacy, affection, and social support patterns in families

3. To understand some of the outcomes that have been associated with intimacy, affection, and social support patterns in families

4. To be able to apply this material to assessing and planning your own family patterns

Section 1: Overview of Intimacy, Affection, and Social Support in Families

- If you had to explain your feelings for family members, what kind of words would you use?
- Pick two people in your family and imagine expressing your positive feelings about them (to them). How would you do it?
- If you needed help with a serious issue, whom would you turn to?

> *The best thing about having a family is that a family takes care of you and helps you out a lot . . . and even though you might get in fights with them, they will still try and be nice and love you.*
>
> —Response of a nine-year-old asked what the best thing about a family is

One of the things that often springs to mind as we think about family is the love we expect family members to feel for each other, and the ways that they express that love. Hopefully, one of your early memories of childhood is experiencing affection and support given to you by your family members. Responding to such positive displays starts soon after birth. We know from research and common experience that babies are soothed and comforted by affection, and by an early age, children learn to appreciate affection being shown to others as well. In their 1981 study, Cummings, Zahn-Waxler, and Radke-Yarrow concluded that children as young as one year old responded positively to displays of affection between others, and were likely to respond with signs of pleasure and their own displays of affection. Based on this study, others that we consider as the chapter proceeds, and our own experiences, it seems that affection, intimacy, and social support are an important part of the family system from birth throughout life.

Intimacy, Affection, and Social Support Defined

Let's begin by defining these three terms and considering the similarities and differences between them. ***Intimacy,*** a word originating from the Latin word *intimus*, meaning "inner", can be defined as the degree to which individuals feel a sense of closeness and connection to one another, a feeling that we can or have revealed our inner self to the other (Baumeister & Bratslavsky, 1999). The intimacy that we have with others is developed through the interactions in that system. Although in casual conversation we often use the word *intimate* to refer to sexual intimacy, intimacy can actually be divided into a variety of types (Kouneski & Olson, 2004; Schaefer & Olson, 1981). We use a typology developed by Schaefer and Olson that is commonly used both to understand intimacy and to evaluate it using methodological tools (see also Kouneski & Olson, 2004; Laurenceau, Barrett, & Rovine, 2005; Laurenceau, Rivera, Schaffer, & Pietromonaco, 2004). This typology classifies intimacy as emotional, intellectual, recreational, social, or physical intimacy (see Table 5.1).

TABLE 5.1   *Types of Intimacy*

Emotional intimacy	Shared sense of closeness and shared emotion
Intellectual intimacy	Shared ideas and worldview
Recreational intimacy	Enjoyment of shared leisure time
Social intimacy	Overlapping social networks
Physical intimacy	Comfort with physical expressiveness

Emotional intimacy is the sense of closeness that you have with others on an emotional level (Schaefer & Olson, 1981). It represents the extent to which you believe that you can tell other persons about your emotions, and he or she can do the same with you.

Intellectual intimacy is the degree to which you feel connected to another because you share a similar worldview and ideas about how things are or should be (Schaefer & Olson, 1981). You experience a sense of closeness because you share these ideas, and you find it easy to talk to each other about your thoughts.

Recreational intimacy refers to the extent to which you and another enjoy time together and participate in recreational activities together (Schaefer & Olson, 1981). For families, this could include watching television, going to a park, playing sports, and so on.

Social intimacy is sharing of social networks and doing things with others as a family; for example, a married couple going out to dinner with friends (Schaefer & Olson, 1981). The more your social networks overlap, the more opportunity you may have for engaging in social activities with both family members and others outside the family system.

Physical intimacy relates to how comfortable you feel being physically expressive with another (Schaefer & Olson, 1981). Types of physical intimacy can range from feeling okay about a pat on the back, to giving a hug, to sexual intercourse. In some relationships, physical expressions may be shown without indicating a great deal of intimacy (e.g., the social kiss on the cheek), whereas in other relationships, the same behavior indicates more closeness (e.g., kissing a grandmother on the cheek). The behavior itself isn't necessarily indicative of the level of intimacy felt; it is how that behavior is understood and interpreted by the members of the relationship that indicates the importance of that behavior in establishing, maintaining, and reflecting intimacy.

These five types of intimacy don't necessarily correspond in a relationship. In some relationships we have a high degree of emotional intimacy, but a low degree of physical intimacy.

BOX 5.1 • *Did You Know?*

Physical affection is not only enjoyable for babies, but also good for them! Studies have indicated that caring touch has a positive impact on the physical and psychological development of babies (Caulfield, 2000).

In other relationships we may have a high degree of physical intimacy, but little or no emotional intimacy. Intimacy is a feeling experienced by family members and degrees of intimacy are negotiated in relational systems. Thus, each family will experience and negotiate intimacy in its own way. Likewise, the individual members of the family may feel differently about the amount of intimacy they experience in the system.

Affection is similar to emotional intimacy in that it refers to the degree of caring, closeness, and positive regard that individuals have for one another (Floyd & Morman, 1998). Generally, we can consider affection to be the positive feelings (i.e., love, caring) that we have for those we are close to. Because affection is a feeling that we have, it is experienced differently by different people, even within one family. This makes it somewhat difficult to define. In research, however, the focus is often on how that affection is displayed, rather than how it is felt (Floyd & Morman, 1998; Floyd & Morr, 2003; Floyd & Ray, 2003), because it is very difficult to accurately assess a complex feeling like affection or love. Affection can be displayed verbally (saying "I love you"), and nonverbally (a hug, a kiss, a favor done) in ways that are very similar to the types of social support we consider next.

Social support can generally be defined as communication that makes people feel that they are valued and cared for within their particular group as the members of that group offer them assistance in some way (Burleson & MacGeorge, 2002; Cobb, 1976). There are various types of social support that can be offered within families and other social systems. Some of the types that have been identified by scholars include instrumental support, emotional support, and informational support (House, 1981) (see Table 5.2).

Instrumental support is doing something practical to help someone (Braithwaite & Eckstein, 2003; House, 1981). When you carry boxes for family members as they move from one house to another, give them a ride to the airport for a trip, or loan them a car if theirs is broken down, you are engaging in instrumental support.

Informational support is providing someone with additional knowledge about a topic in order to help out him or her (House, 1981; MacGeorge, Samter, & Gillihan, 2005). If you've ever explained something to a child you care for, given a family member directions to get somewhere, or warned a friend about a particular computer virus, you've offered informational support.

Finally, **emotional support** is the way that we caretake others with regard to their feelings (MacGeorge, et al., House, 1981). When family members are particularly unhappy or stressed, we may offer a sympathetic ear, give a hug, or just spend time with them. These are all forms of emotional support. Some studies have indicated that emotional support messages are seen as more helpful by receivers than other types of support (Burleson & MacGeorge, 2002).

TABLE 5.2   *Types of Social Support*

Instrumental support	Providing practical help for others
Informational support	Supplying needed information to others
Emotional support	Caretaking the feelings of others

From these various examples, we can see that social support amounts to providing some sort of "aid" to those we care about. In family settings, social support is both common and important.

Although intimacy, affection, and social support are theoretically somewhat distinct, in our daily lives they are expressed in similar ways and experienced as interwoven aspects of our relationships. They are developed through our communication with family members; they impact how we feel about and understand our relationships; they create our family cultures; and then, through our communication, they reflect those cultures. Thus, in this chapter we address these three factors of family communication simultaneously.

Factors Affecting the Expression of Intimacy, Affection, and Social Support

At the start of this chapter, you were asked to think about how you might express your affection to different members of your family. Let's continue to investigate the expression of positive regard here. As you grew up, was there a difference between how your female and male caregivers expressed their affection and support for you? How do you show affection and support for your romantic partners? Do you see similarities or differences from the way your parents or other adult caregivers expressed emotion to their romantic partners?

Sex and Gender Differences

Our life experiences suggest that not everyone shows their affection and intimacy for others in the same way. At one time or another, we have probably all been surprised by how someone else indicated his or her feelings of intimacy and affection for us. There are a variety of factors that may influence how family members express their caring. Research indicates that one thing that affects our expression of emotions is the sex (being male or female) of the communicators.

In a study of the families of college students at Brigham Young University, Barber and Thomas (1986) found that fathers were more likely to display physical affection (hugging and kissing) with their daughters than with their sons. Mothers tended to display affection in a physical manner equally with both sons and daughters. But, both mothers and fathers tended to pick up, or hold on their lap, girls more than boys. In addition to their findings with regard to physical displays of affection, Barber and Thomas concluded that mothers and fathers were more likely to show companionship affection (time spent together doing things) with children of the same sex.

Gender differences can be seen in the behavior of marital partners as well. Aylor and Dainton (2004), in a study of relational maintenance behaviors, found that feminine people are more likely to engage in more routine openness (being open as a matter of course, not for a particular purpose), whereas masculine people are more likely to engage in strategic openness (openness to reach a particular end goal). Other scholars have also found that the sex or gender of the affection recipient, and the affection giver, has an impact on how much and in what ways these positive emotional messages are provided (see, for example, Lytton & Romney, 1991; Stafford, 2003; Tucker, McHale, and Crouter, 2003).

It is likely that some of these differences can be attributed to cultural expectations about men and women and their behavior (Brody, 1997). Men in U.S. culture are generally discouraged from showing a lot of physical affection for others, except within the confines of heterosexual romantic relationships. Thus, fathers may feel more discomfort showing physical affection for sons. With regard to companionship affection, our cultural expectation in the United States is largely that women have more in common with other women, and the same is true for men. Therefore, it is probably not surprising that companionship affection between parents and children tends to align along sex lines. Likewise, in the United States femininity is associated with open expression of positive emotion, whereas masculinity is not. Thus, it seems reasonable that masculine people would be less likely to routinely engage in openness, without a goal in mind.

Other scholars would likely suggest that there are "inherent" (or natural) tendencies for men and women to behave in certain ways. **Evolutionary psychologists** argue that our ancestral history from thousands of years ago and the evolution that followed have impacted how we interact with one another today, and have influenced behavioral and psychological differences between men and women (Kenrick & Luce, 2000). These scholars would argue that, because of these evolutionary differences, men and women have an innate tendency toward different relational behaviors and expressions, such as the expressions of affection considered here.

Whether the differences in affection/intimacy behavior are biologically based or culturally developed (or some combination of the two), research seems to clearly suggest that within most family settings there are differences between how men and women (and boys and girls) express their affection and support. This does not suggest that all men or women show their intimacy in these ways or that this pattern will be represented fully in your individual family experience; rather, these are tendencies that seem to be common for men and women.

Position or Role in the Family

Research has indicated that a person's position or role in the family can also affect how he or she shows affection (or receives it) (Taylor, Chatters, & Jackson, 1993; Vogl-Bauer, 2003). Not surprisingly, these scholars found that children often receive the most social support in families, and that support frequently comes in the form of advice, encouragement, or financial assistance from parents and grandparents. Grandparents also receive support from family members, and common forms of support they receive are companionship,

---

BOX 5.2 • *Family in the News*

Recent news reports, television programs, and even movies have focused on the fact that adult children in their 20s and 30s seem to be more likely to live at home than in the past, in the United States. Media reports suggest that this is because of an increased comfort with that situation. Read a news example at www.usatoday.com/printedition/life/20060316/d_cover16.art.htm.

services (picking up groceries, housecleaning, etc.), transportation, and help when sick. Parents indicated that they receive support from extended family members, including grandparents, and some common types of support they receive are child care help and assistance during illness.

Here, too, we can see the effects of cultural expectations, as well as pragmatic factors, on how social support is exhibited. In the United States, we expect support between parents and children to primarily be provided from parent to child, rather than the reverse. This is partly pragmatic when children are young, because their access to resources is limited and they are in more need of financial and emotional assistance. Additionally, our cultural expectation is that parents will care for and provide guidance to children until they become adults, and even beyond formal adulthood until the children establish homes of their own.

As children become adults, parents often continue to serve a supporting function by providing babysitting services or advice for their adult children. At this point, the child and parent may have relatively equal access to monetary resources, so financial assistance is less needed by either party. Culturally, adulthood is also thought of as the time when we more completely "strike out on our own" and establish ourselves, which is the final stage of a process of gaining independence that begins in adolescence. This, too, may explain why less support is provided to the parental generation.

When an adult reaches his or her elder years, the pragmatic need for assistance may return as health becomes less robust and mobility more inhibited. Additionally, to some extent we have a cultural expectation that family members will help care for the elderly in their midst (though this is less the case in the United States than in some other cultures). Thus, it is not particularly surprising that the grandparent generation in the family experiences increased social support.

Relationships between Members

In addition to the sex or gender of communicators and family roles, the relationships that develop between family members, including the behavior of the recipient of affection, impact how much and what type of affection is shown. Russell (1997) found that when children behaved toward their parents in a way that was warm and affectionate, both mothers and fathers were more likely to also behave in such a way. This is somewhat like the question of the chicken and the egg, because causal direction cannot be claimed (that is, are children warmer and more affectionate because parents are, or is it the other way around?). However, what is apparent from this study is that reciprocity is active in the parent–child relationship in terms of warmth and affection. When we receive warmth and affection from a family member, we are more likely to reciprocate that behavior. Similarly, Brody, Stoneman, and McCoy (1992) found that when children had a more difficult temperament, parents were less likely to be affectionate toward them. Tucker, McHale, and Crouter (2003) note that, in their study, children who were particularly emotional received less affection than children who were less emotional. Additionally, they indicate that when children displayed the characteristics commonly associated with their position in the family (for example, firstborns being more independent, the youngest child being less brave), they were likely to receive more affection than if they did not display such characteristics, or displayed characteristics that seemed counter to their role. From these examples, we can see that the relationships and patterns of behavior developed between the partners affect how intimacy is shown in the family.

Not only does the relationship between the two individuals (affection giver and affection receiver) affect that process, but so too do the other family relationships that exist in the family system. White (1999) found that a parent's affection for a child was not only correlated with his or her relationship to the child, but also with the other parent's relationship to the child and to the marital relationship of the parents or stepparents. Similarly, in this study White discovered that a child's affection toward one parent was related to his or her feelings toward the other parent. This isn't surprising when we consider the argument of family systems scholars that all relationships within the family are interconnected.

From these studies, we can see that there are many factors (not limited to those discussed here) that impact how and to whom support, affection, and intimacy are directed. The outcomes of those communicative behaviors also proceed in a variety of ways.

Outcomes Related to Intimacy, Affection, and Social Support

How others treat us leaves an impression and affects both us and our relationships. Thus, it isn't surprising that the ways in which family members treat each other with regard to affection, intimacy, and social support can have an impact on how they feel about and assess their relationships.

Parental/Romantic Relationship Outcomes

The parental/romantic relationship that often is a part of family life can be affected by the way these communicative elements are displayed. Xu and Burleson (2004) found that emotional support from a spouse was correlated to marital satisfaction for both men and women, in both Chinese and American marriages (see also Gardner & Cutrona, 2004; Wan, Jaccard, & Ramey, 1996). Similarly, in a study of young dating and married couples, Gulledge, Gulledge, and Stahmann (2003) concluded that displays of physical affection between young couples (not including sexual intimacy) were connected to more relational satisfaction and better ability to manage conflict.

Other Family Relationship Outcomes

But, it is not only the parental relationship in the family that is affected by how closeness is exhibited. This same finding has been seen in other family relationships. For example, Floyd and Morr (2003) considered displays of affection in the relationships of siblings, spouses, and siblings-in-law (see also Gardner & Cutrona, 2004). Not surprisingly, they found that affection in these relationships was correlated positively to satisfaction. Similar results have been obtained relating to how children and parents understand and evaluate their relationships with each other (Gardner & Cutrona, 2004; Morman & Floyd, 2002; Punyanunt-Carter, 2005). For example, Lang and Schütze (2002) found that the relational satisfaction of elderly parents was increased when their children showed more affection and emotional support.

It isn't always clear which factor is affecting the other (that is, do we express more social support when we are satisfied, or are we more satisfied when we express more social support?). But, the correlation between these elements and relational satisfaction is clear. It is likely that these two aspects (how we show intimacy, affection, and support and how satisfied we are with the relationship) have some sort of reciprocal effect on each other.

Individual Outcomes

The benefits from these positive communication phenomena can be individual as well as relational. Support from family members has been found to be correlated with better mental health (Burleson & MacGeorge, 2002; Gardner & Cutrona, 2004). Bal, Crombez, Van Oost, and Debourdeaudhuij (2003) studied the role of family support in adolescent well-being after a stressful and traumatic life event. They found that, generally, increased family support was correlated to less trauma-related symptoms for these adolescents. Barber and Thomas's (1986) study found a connection between parental displays of affection in childhood and the self-esteem of young adults. As parents' displays of various types of affection for their son or daughter in childhood increased, there was a correspondent increase in the positive self-esteem that child had when he or she became a young adult. Social support also affects the mental functioning of adults. Postpartum depression is a common occurrence for new mothers. It affects the mother, impacts her relationship with the new child, and also has outcomes for other familial relationships. Cutrona and Troutman (1986) concluded that social support helped reduce postpartum depression by helping new mothers feel more capable about their parenting. Similarly, Arnold (2003, 2005) found that supportive interactions contributed to positive and empowered feelings about parenting for pregnant women and parents of large families. Thus, such support can improve the lives of parents, children, and other family members.

In addition to positive impacts on mental health, social support has also been associated with physical health benefits, or helping people cope with health issues (Berkman, Glass, Brissette, & Seeman, 2000; Burleson & MacGeorge, 2002; Gardner & Cutrona, 2004). There are far too many such studies to detail here, so a few examples will suffice. Some studies have focused on cancer patients and how they deal with the disease and the associated

BOX 5.3 • *Internet Connection*

Studies have indicated the value of social support for individuals with medical conditions. In the absence of (or in addition to) support from family and friends, online discussion forums may provide a venue for advice and support. You can find many health related bulletin boards at www.healthboards.com.

medical interventions. For instance, Manne et al. (2003) concluded that, particularly when the husband was unsupportive, social support from family and friends helped women with breast cancer more effectively cope with the disease. Other medical issues have been considered as well. Holtzman, Newth, and Delongis's (2004) study of adults with rheumatoid arthritis revealed that increased social support had an impact on pain levels and pain management. Similarly, scholars have found an association between heart health and social support, particularly for individuals who have had a heart attack (see, for example, Janevic et al., 2004; Pedersen, Van Domburg, & Larsen, 2004).

Factors Affecting Outcomes

Although findings such as these suggest that displays of social support, intimacy, and affection have very real effects in the lives of family members, those effects can vary depending on how the messages are constructed and understood, as well as the sender (and the receiver) of the positive messages. Some communication scholars have focused their attention on the effectiveness of positive relational messages, with respect to the elements of the message itself. Applegate, Burleson, and colleagues (for a review see Burleson & MacGeorge, 2002) argue that messages intended to offer emotional support and comforting are most effective when they are person centered. **Person centeredness** is the extent to which a message communicates both an understanding of and adaptation to the perspective of the message receiver. Burleson and colleagues state that comforting messages that are highly person centered (explicitly recognize the emotions of the other, indicate the legitimacy of those emotions, discuss the reasons for the emotions, and offer new ways to understand the emotions) are most effective. Messages that reject or ignore the perspective of the other are the least effective and can be problematic for the recipient, the sender, and their relationship. Holmstrom, Burleson, and Jones (2005) found, in a study of undergraduate students, that senders who offered low person-centered support messages were evaluated more negatively and liked less than those who offered highly person-centered messages (see also Goldsmith, McDermott, & Alexander, 2000). They found this to be even truer for women comforting other women, and the authors suggest that this may be because of cultural expectations that women are good at supporting others.

In outcomes, as well as in factors contributing to affection, there are sometimes gender differences. According to Lawton, Silverstein, and Bengtson (1994), greater affection for the mother tends to lead to more frequent contact between adult children and their parents. In relation to the father, however, greater affection is not associated with increased contact. This could be because fathers are less likely to initiate contact, perhaps due to their social role having less of an expectation of being relationship experts (Lawton et al., 1994). Or, it could be that children feel less compelled to contact their father than they do their mother, perhaps because of childhood relational patterns. In a similar finding, Jorm, Dear, Rodgers, and Christensen (2003) argue that, in their sample of adults, individuals whose parents had shown more affection had fewer mental health problems. However, when fathers showed more affection and mothers showed less, there were increased family interaction problems and also increased mental health problems for the adult children. The authors contend that this could be because family problems cause fathers to show more affection and mothers to show less. Alternately, it may be that, because mothers are expected to be more affectionate in behavior than fathers, when that role is reversed it is problematic for the family system. Thus, we can see that the sex or gender of the family members may impact how affection, support, and intimacy affect members (see also Gardner & Cutrona, 2004).

In addition to gender or sex effects, the culture in which the family exists can impact how these communicative elements impact family members. Some research suggests that in families where members are overly "attached" to one another (enmeshed), problems for the children may result (Olson, 2000). Additionally, as noted previously, research often finds that in Western cultures, affection and support displays are important to satisfaction in a marital relationship. However, it is likely that the impact of these family aspects varies based on the culture in which the family lives. Rothbaum, Rosen, Ujiie, and Uchida (2002) argue that in Japanese culture extremely close relationships exist between mother and child, and less affectionate marital relationships are expected and common. Thus, this type of pattern does not have negative impacts on the family members or the family system in Japanese culture.

Whereas social support has generally been found to have positive impacts on physical and psychological health, as discussed earlier in this section, Dressler, Balieiro, and Dos Santos (1997) found that these effects are also impacted by cultural expectations. In their study, participants who were receiving social support most closely resembling that expected in the culture had the biggest health benefits. Similarly, Burleson and Mortenson (2003) and Mortenson (2006) found that support needs, expectations, and outcomes showed both similarities and differences for undergraduate students from the United States and undergraduate students from China. Thus, in different cultures different amounts or types of social support may be needed to see the positive benefits of support.

From these examples, we can see that as culture and gender affect how social support, affection, and intimacy are displayed, they also are related to how these aspects of relational communication impact the family members. Additionally, the construction of such messages impacts their outcomes. All of these factors point to the complexity of these aspects of family life.

In this section, we have considered definitions of social support, intimacy, and affection. We've also addressed some of the research on factors that impact how these phenomena are displayed and how they affect participants. Section 2 discusses a study using conversational analysis (a common methodology of family studies in communication) to understand how intimacy is cocreated in a mother–daughter relationship. It also addresses the use of positive relational messages and gender differences in marital relationships, and looks at social support and family communication patterns. Finally, in Section 3, I address how what you have learned in the chapter might be applied in your own life experiences.

References

Arnold, L. B. (2003). Delivering empowerment: Women's narratives about the role of pregnancy bulletin boards. *Qualitative Research Reports in Communication, 4,* 45–52.

Arnold, L. B. (2005). Don't you know what causes that?: Advice, celebration, and justification in a large families bulletin board. *Communication Studies, 56*(4), 331–351.

Aylor, B., & Dainton, M. (2004). Biological sex and psychological gender as predictors of routine and stategic relational maintenance. *Sex Roles, 50*(9/10), 689–697.

Bal, S., Crombez, G., Van Oost, P., & Debourdeaudhuij, I. (2003). The role of social support in well-being and coping with self-reported stressful events in adolescents. *Child Abuse & Neglect, 27*(12), 1377–1395.

Barber, B. K., & Thomas, D. L. (1986). Dimensions of fathers' and mothers' supportive behavior: The case for physical affection. *Journal of Marriage and Family, 48,* 783–794.

Baumeister, R. F., & Bratslavsky, E. (1999). Passion, intimacy, and time: Passionate love as a function of change in intimacy. *Personality and Social Psychology Review, 3,* 49–67.

Berkman, L. F., Glass, T., Brissette, I., & Seeman, T. E. (2000). From social integration to health: Durkheim in the new millennium. *Social Science and Medicine, 51,* 843–857.

Braithwaite, D. O., & Eckstein, N. J. (2003). How people with disabilities communicatively manage assistance: Helping as instrumental social support. *Journal of Applied Communication Research, 31*(1), 1–25.

Brody, G. H., Stoneman, Z., & McCoy, J. K. (1992). Parental differential treatment of siblings and sibling differences in negative emotionality. *Journal of Marriage and Family, 54,* 643–651.

Brody, L. (1997). Gender and emotions: Beyond stereotypes. *Journal of Social Issues, 53(2),* 369–393.

Burleson, B. R., & MacGeorge, E. L. (2002). Supportive communication. In M. L. Knapp & J. A. Daly (Eds.), *Handbook of interpersonal communication* (3rd ed., pp. 374–422). Thousand Oaks, CA: Sage.

Burleson, B. R., & Mortenson, S. R. (2003). Exploring cultural differences in evaluations of emotional support behaviors: Exploring the mediating influences value systems and interaction goals. *Communication Research, 30,* 113–146.

Caulfield, R. (2000). Beneficial effects of tactile stimulation on early development. *Early Childhood Education Journal, 27*(4), 255–257.

Cobb, S. (1976). Social support as a moderator of life stress. *Psychosomatic Medicine, 5,* 300–314.

Cummings, E. M., Zahn-Waxler, C., & Radke-Yarrow, M. (1981). Young children's responses to expressions of anger and affection by others in the family. *Child Development, 52*(4), 1274–1282.

Cutrona, C. E., & Troutman, B. R. (1986). Social support, infant temperament, and parenting self-efficacy: A mediational model of postpartum depression. *Child Development, 57,* 1507–1518.

Dressler, W. W., Balieiro, M. C., & Dos Santos, J. E. (1997). The cultural construction of social support in Brazil: Associations with health outcomes. *Culture, Medicine and Psychiatry, 21*(3), 303–335.

Floyd, K., & Morr, M. C. (2003). Human affection exchange: VII. Affectionate communication in the sibling/spouse/sibling-in-law triad. *Communication Quarterly, 51*(3), 247–251.

Floyd, K., & Morman, M. T. (1998). The measurement of affectionate communication. *Communication Quarterly, 46*(2), 144–162.

Floyd, K., & Ray, G. B. (2003). Human affection exchange: IV. Vocalic predictors of perceived affection in initial interactions. *Western Journal of Communication, 67*(1), 56–73.

Gardner, K. A., & Cutrona, C. E. (2004). Social support communication in families. In A. L. Vangelisti (Ed.), *Handbook of family communication* (pp. 495–512). Mahwah, NJ: Erlbaum.

Goldsmith, D. J., McDermott, V. M., & Alexander, S. C. (2000). Helpful, supportive and sensitive: Measuring the evaluation of enacted social support in personal relationships. *Journal of Social and Personal Relationships, 17,* 369–391.

Gulledge, A. K., Gulledge, M. H., & Stahmann, R. F. (2003). Romantic physical affection types and relationship satisfaction. *American Journal of Family Therapy, 31,* 233–242.

Holmstrom, A. J., Burleson, B. R., & Jones, S. M. (2005). Some consequences for helpers who deliver "cold comfort": Why it's worse for women than men to be inept when providing emotional support. *Sex Roles: A Journal of Research, 53*(3/4), 153–172.

Holtzman, S., Newth, S., & Delongis, A. (2004). The role of social support in coping with daily pain among patients with rheumatoid arthritis. *Journal of Health Psychology, 9*(5), 677–695.

House, J. S. (1981). *Work stress and social support.* Reading, MA: Addison-Wesley.

Janevic, M. R., Janz, N. K., Dodge, J. A., Wang, Y., Lin, X., & Clark, N. M. (2004). Longtitudinal effects of social support on the health and functioning of older women with heart disease. *International Journal of Aging and Human Development, 59*(2), 153–175.

Jorm, A. F., Dear, K. B. G., Rodgers, B., & Christensen, H. (2003). Interaction between mother's and father's affection as a risk factor for anxiety and depression symptoms: Evidence for increased risk in adults who rate their father as having been more affectionate than their mother. *Social Psychiatry and Psychiatric Epidemiology, 38*(4), 173–179.

Kenrick, D. T., & Luce, K. L. (2000). An evolutionary life-history model of gender differences and similarities. In T. Eckes & H. M. Trautner (Eds.), *The developmental social psychology of gender* (pp. 35–63). Mahwah, NJ: Erlbaum.

Kouneski, E. F., & Olson, D. H. (2004). A practical look at intimacy: ENRICH couple typology. In D. J. Mashek & A. Aron (Eds.), *Handbook of closeness and intimacy* (pp. 117–135). Mahwah, NJ: Erlbaum.

Lang, F. R., & Schütze, Y. (2002). Adult children's supportive behaviors and older parents' subjective well-being: A developmental perspective on intergenerational relationships. *Journal of Social Issues, 58*(4), 661–680.

Laurenceau, J.-P., Barrett, L. F., & Rovine, M. J. (2005). The interpersonal process model of intimacy in marriage: A daily-diary and multilevel modeling approach. *Journal of Family Psychology, 19*(2), 314–323.

Laurenceau, J.-P., Rivera, L. M., Schaffer, A. R., & Pietromonaco, P. R. (2004). Intimacy as an interpersonal process: Current status and future directions. In D. Mashek & A. Aron (Eds.), *Handbook of closeness and intimacy* (pp. 61–78). Mahwah, NJ: Erlbaum.

Lawton, L., Silverstein, M., & Bengston, V. (1994). Affection, social contact, and geographic distance between adult children and their parents. *Journal of Marriage and Family, 56*, 57–68.

Lytton, H., & Romney, D. M. (1991). Parents' differential socialization of boys and girls: A meta-analysis. *Psychological Bulletin, 109*, 267–296.

MacGeorge, E. L., Samter, W., & Gillihan, S. J. (2005). Academic stress, supportive communication, and health. *Communication Education, 54*(4), 365–372.

Manne, S., Ostroff, J., Sherman, M., Glassman, M., Ross, S., Goldstein, L., et al. (2003). Buffering effects of family and friend support on associations between partner unsupportive behaviors and coping among women with breast cancer. *Journal of Social and Personal Relationships, 20*(6), 771–792.

Mormon, M. T., & Floyd, K. (2002). A "changing culture of fatherhood": Effects on affectionate communication, closeness, and satisfaction in men's relationships with their fathers and their sons. *Western Journal of Communication, 66*(4), 395–411.

Mortenson, S. (2006). Cultural differences and similarities in seeking social support as a response to academic failure: A comparison of American and Chinese college students. *Communication Education, 55*(2), 127–146.

Olson, D. H. (2000). Circumplex model of marital and family systems. *Journal of Family Therapy, 22*, 144–167.

Pederson, S. S., Van Domburg, R. T., & Larsen, M. L. (2004). The effect of low social support on short-term prognosis in patients following a first myocardial infarction. *Scandinavian Journal of Psychology, 45*(4), 313–318.

Punyanunt-Carter, N. M. (2005). Father and daughter motives and satisfaction. *Communication Research Reports, 22*(4), 293–301.

Rothbaum, F., Rosen, K., Ujiie, T., & Uchida, N. (2002). Family systems theory, attachment theory, and culture. *Family Process, 41*(3), 328–350.

Russell, A. (1997). Individual and family factors contributing to mothers' and fathers' positive parenting. *International Journal of Behavioral Development, 21*(1), 111–132.

Schaefer, M. T., & Olson, D. H. (1981). Assessing intimacy: The PAIR Inventory. *Journal of Marital and Family Therapy, 7*, 47–60.

Stafford, L. (2003). Maintaining romantic relationships: A summary and analysis of one research program. In D. J. Canary & M. Dainton (Eds.), *Maintaining relationships through communication: Relational, contextual, and cultural variations* (pp. 51–78). Mahwah, NJ: Erlbaum.

Taylor, R. J., Chatters, L. M., and Jackson, J. S. (1993). A profile of familial relations among three generation Black families. *Family Relations, 42*, 332–341.

Tucker, C. J, McHale, S. M., & Crouter, A. C. (2003). Dimensions of mothers' and fathers' differential treatment of siblings: Links with adolescents' sex-typed personal qualities. *Family Relations, 52*, 82–89.

Vogl-Bauer, S. (2003). Maintaining family relationships. In D. J. Canary & M. Dainton (Eds.), *Maintaining relationships through communication: Relational, contextual, and cultural variations* (pp. 31–50). Mahwah, NJ: Erlbaum.

Wan, C. K., Jaccard, J., & Ramey, S. L. (1996). The relationship between social support and life satisfaction as a function of family structure. *Journal of Marriage and Family, 58*, 502–513.

White, L. (1999). Contagion in family affection: Mothers, fathers, and young adult children. *Journal of Marriage and Family, 61*, 284–294.

Xu, Y., & Burleson, B. R. (2004). The association of experienced spousal support with marital satisfaction: Evaluating the moderating effects of sex, ethnic culture, and type of support. *Journal of Family Communication, 4*(2), 123–145.

Section 2: Research Examples _____

Negotiating Intimate Family Ties in Ordinary Family Interaction

Shirley A. Staske-Bell

> Intimacy is a relational creation, developed through interaction. In this work, Staske-Bell uses conversational analysis, which is a prominent methodological tool in interpersonal and family study, to look at how intimacy is negotiated in the everyday interactions of a mother and daughter. Although this example is about a particular dyad, it points to how conversations that are not explicitly about relationships can carry messages about relational factors such as intimacy. As you read, consider the last few conversations you have had with family members and what they may have "said," without necessarily ever speaking it, about your relationships.
>
> *L.B.A.*

If you don't- (0.3) ↑te:ll me: (0.9) those things, . . .
the:n (0.3) ↑guess wha:t. There becomes a little stagnant
↑part in our re↑la↓tionship. (1.5) >Know wha' I mean?<

—Mother to her young adult daughter

Mommy hates you.

—Snookie, a stuffed animal, speaking *for* one adult sister, his "mommy," to her twin sister

That's all you've been saying since the day I was ↓born.

—Young adult daughter to her father

These utterances come from ordinary, naturally occurring conversations between members of three families who are at the launching stage in the family lifecycle (Fitzpatrick & Badzinski, 1994). The speakers of the utterances are involved in rather different conversational activities—a mother–daughter relationship talk, a sibling advice episode, and a heated father–daughter conflict. However, that they are talking with an intimate conversational partner is evident even without the speaker identification provided at the end of each quotation. Clearly, these interactants know their conversational partner well, they share a significant relational history, and the conversations from which these utterances were taken contribute to their ongoing negotiation of intimate relational bonds. Intimacy and distance, like other relational properties, are coconstructed by conversational partners' verbal and nonverbal actions in their ordinary, everyday interaction. It is in the doing of conversation that relational partners negotiate a power distribution of some sort (e.g., by making, confirming, and challenging claims of authority), affectionate and hostile relational ties (e.g., by using terms of endearment and insult), and intimacy and distance. The construction and reconstruction of these relational properties is an ongoing, interactional task to which close relational partners attend whenever they interact (Staske, 2002a). Although we often speak of "having" or "being in" an intimate relationship, these phrases are but a shorthand or gloss for the interactional work collaboratively accomplished by close relational partners across multiple conversations over some period of time.

This conceptualization of intimacy is fundamentally social in that it locates this relational property in the interactive communicative behavior of two (or more) people in an interpersonal encounter (see Baxter, 1998; Tracy & Haspel, 2004). As such, investigating intimate family relationships requires the close analysis of family members' everyday, naturally occurring conversations (i.e., both partners' sequentially organized conversational actions must be examined if we are to explain how they go about coconstructing intimate [or distant] relational bonds). The particular social approach taken in my investigations of interpersonal relationships begins with Conversation Analysis (CA) of close partners' ordinary interaction, and then theory and research findings from the more traditional, psychological study of interpersonal communication are utilized to explore how conversational actions work to address relational concerns (see Staske, 2002a, on this approach and Metts & Planalp, 2002, and Tracy & Haspel, 2004, for discussion of it).

Data collection for this study of family intimacy therefore began with the collection of naturally occurring conversations between family members and was accomplished with the help of students who completed my Family Communication course. The major paper assignment for that course requires students to audiotape four hours of ordinary conversation between themselves and one or more family members, transcribe four minutes of that using Jefferson's (1984) transcript notation system, and then analyze the conversation. Students are advised to tape the ordinary, everyday things families do together (e.g., eating meals, traveling, working on projects or hobbies, "catching up" since their last visit home). At the end of the course, I ask students if they want to contribute their tapes to my Conversation Analytic Family Communication database and the students who choose to do so are assured of anonymity, obtain signed research release forms from all family members on the tapes, and provide ethnographic information about their family. Thus, the mother–college-aged daughter conversation analyzed in this study was selected after listening to and analyzing hundreds of ordinary family conversations between parents or stepparents and their adult and younger children, siblings, and, sometimes, husbands and wives or extended family members.

Connecting across Miles and Milestones: Mother and Daughter Negotiating Changing Relational Boundaries

The conversation examined in this study occurred during the launching stage of the family lifecycle and Mother and adult Daughter are negotiating changes in what has been, according to Daughter, a very close mother–daughter relationship. Being an adult child and being the parent of one can be challenging as mothers, fathers, sons, and daughters reconstruct relational bonds to achieve a more equal, voluntary, adult relationship than the one they have coconstructed over two decades of shared interactional history (Staske, 2002b). Being an adult means fulfilling one's obligations as one sees fit, and constructing a more equal adult relationship requires that both relational partners acknowledge and act upon one another's rights to determine its nature and conduct. That is what is being negotiated in the conversation investigated here and, as will be seen, although sharing intimate information (including "problems") is the mother's method of maintaining intimate ties with her daughter, as an adult, the daughter has the right to decide whether and to what extent she will employ similar practices.

The conversation discussed here was audiotaped during the spring semester of 1999. Mother, Daughter, and Don, the man the mother has lived with for the last three years, are traveling home from a restaurant where they had dinner. They have stopped at a gas station, Don has exited the car, and Mother and Daughter converse during the 21 minutes before his return. According to the ethnographic data obtained from the daughter, her mother and father are separated and her mother and two younger siblings have been living with Don for the last three years while she lived with her father and attended a community college close to home. Daughter is now enrolled in her second semester at a university far enough away to require on-campus residence, and so has been home during the previous eight months only during the main college break times. Before reading the analysis to follow, please review the transcript notation conventions and mother–adult daughter conversations in the text boxes that follow. Note that, in the talk between Mother and Daughter, each conversational turn is numbered, to make following the analysis easier.

TEXT BOX 5.1 • *Transcript Notation Conventions Adapted from Jefferson's (1984) Notation System*

The purpose of transcribing conversation is to obtain a detailed description of the talk as it is actually said and heard by the interactants, so utterances are transcribed as they are heard, up to the point of unrecognizability or presumed reader confusion. Turns of talk are numbered consecutively and speakers are identified by their family relational identity (e.g., *M* = Mother).

[ ] Brackets mark simultaneous utterances (overlaps) at the start and end of the overlap.
= Equal sign marks contiguous utterances—no pause between turns.
(·) Micropause marks pauses, which are timed in tenths of a second—for example, a pause less than three-tenths of a second is marked (0.3)
- Hyphen marks a short, abrupt stop at the end of a word.
: Colon following a sound marks the speaker's extension of that sound.
· Period indicates a stopping fall in tone.
, Comma indicates a continuing intonation.
? Question mark indicates the rising inflection typically accompanying yes/no questions.
↑ Up arrow marks raised pitch on the syllable or word following it.
↓ Down arrow marks lowered pitch on the syllable or word following it.

underline marks stress.

CAPITALS mark the talk as louder than surrounding talk.

° ° Degree symbols enclose talk that is lower in volume than surrounding talk.

(( )) Double parentheses mark sounds where they occur (e.g., laughs).

> < Greater than and less than symbols enclose speech that is spoken at a faster rate than surrounding speech.

( ) Parenthesis mark transcriptionist uncertainty due to auditory difficulties.

. . . Ellipses indicate that part of an utterance has been left out.

TEXT BOX 5.2 • *Mother–Daughter Conversation*

M: Mother; *D*: Daughter, 21 years old; Eric, Daughter's boyfriend of six years; Aunt Wanda, her great-aunt; Dotty, her grandmother; both on her father's side of the family. The radio is playing Rock Oldies in the background throughout the conversation.

(14-second pause prior to first transcribed utterance)

1 M: Oh. (0.6) ↑I know:. There was somethin' I wanted ta tell ya.

2 D: Ye:ah.

3 M: U:m (2.4) rememer when you ↑ca:lled me:?

4 D: °(Uh huh   too)° ((laughs))

5 M: And um (1.2) I talked ta ya 'bout (2.3) u:m (3.9) you know my ↑heart.

6 D: Y:[eah.]

7 M: [(An:)] that deal. (1.6) Well (0.6) I just wanchu ta know: that- (2.1) I'm just gonna have that looked into: an (everything).

8 D: Mm hm.

9 M: An um: (2.3) but- (1.6) I din't- (0.3) tell ya tha:t (1.2) the only reason- I don't know why: I told you that. (1.3) Huh- (0.9) Just because I was ↑tal↓kin' to you. (0.5) You kno::w an (1.7) >lettin- ya kno:w everything.< (1.1) Okay? (1.3) And (0.7) the ↑po:int i:s tha:t (1.4) if you have a ↑problem at scho:ol? (3.1) or you have a- (0.9) ↑problem with Er:ic (1.1) or: some: body or some↑thing:,

10 D: ([ )]

11 M: [Tea]cher- whatever- (0.8) ya know: ah (1.0) if you don't- (0.3) ↑te:ll me: (0.9) those things,

12 D: Ye:ah?

13 M: U:m (0.5) the:n (0.3) ↑guess wha:t. There becomes a little stagnant ↑part in our re↑la↓tionship. (1.5) >Know wha' I me:an?<=

14 D: =Mm hm.=

15 M: =There becomes kind of like a: (2.4) It gets <u>wo:rse.</u> (0.7) Like. (0.6) Like I did that with Aunt Wanda?

16 D: [Yeah]

17 M: [Becau]se I ↑thou:ght (.) that- >she didn't-< (.) cause at one time she ↑sa:ys (0.5) she ↑sa:id- <u>I</u> didn't wanna ↑<u>he:ar</u> anything about- (.) what ↑Do:tty's (0.5) I didn't wanna hear ↑Dot↓ty's ↑pro↓blems cause it up<u>set</u> me too much an (besides) (0.5) yaknow: (0.5) I have hea:rt problems an this:, that, an >the other-.< (0.6) But what ↑happened wa:s, then ↑I stopped ↑talkin' to her. (1.0) About any problems? (2.3) Well you know life- (0.4) isn't a bowl of ↑cherries. (2.3) (So) if you don't discuss the ↑<u>pro:</u>↓<u>blems,</u> (1.3) well ↑<u>wha:t</u>- (0.4) you're just <u>ma:sking.</u> (0.4) >Yaknow an then:< (.) even the ↑happy part's unre:al. (1.0) °Ya understa::nd?°

    (1.5)

18 D: °Ye:ah.°

19 M: So: um: (1.1) °ya know > (tellin' to think about that, what you think about that)°<

20 D: °(Whadaya mean.)°

21 M: ↑Kinda ↑think↓ing that a liddle? (0.8) Didn't wanna ↑bo:ther ↑<u>Mo::m</u>:. (1.5) You know,=

22 D: =°No[:]°

23 M: [Sh]e has these ↑pro::blems, she's

24 D: I just wantedju ta go: an ↑<u>check</u> it.

25 M: Okay:. (0.6) We:ll (0.4) I have an appointment, twenty ninth, (to check it). (0.5) Ka:y?

26 D: Cool.

27 M: °>Okay.<°

28 D: °(I don't have a) problem.°

29 M: °But- I <u>do</u> wantcha to tell ↑<u>me</u>:. (.) I don't care: if it's twelveaclock at night. (1.3) Ya can't ↓sleep.

30 D: M ↓mm.

31 M: You have a ↑pro:↓blem. (2.2) You know, you can ↑ca:ll me. (4.1) You: are my ↑<u>daughter</u>.

32 D: I ↑<u>kno:w</u>: I am- (0.3) I haven't- (0.6) °(well)° (0.5) [thought different.]

33 M: [(You don't-)] If you: like- (0.9) if you feel like crying all night, 'er somethin'. (0.5) I mean (0.8) ↑<u>why:</u> would you feel like °crying all night.° We:ll, (.) I don't know, we can ↑TALK ↑ABOUT ↑I:T. Yaknow I might not be able ta (1.7) ↑<u>SOLVE</u> your ↑<u>PRO:</u>↓blems. (0.5) 'Er whatever:, (.) or: whatever but- (.) yaknow, (.) jus' talkin' about it's ↓great. (1.6) Oka:y:? (4.5)

34 D: °(Yeah)°

    (36-second pause during which a new song, "Little Diana," comes on the radio)

Twenty-one Minutes of Mother–Daughter Time

Transcribing the entire 21-minute episode made it possible to locate the relationship talk contained in turns 1–34 in the real time of Mother–Daughter interaction. Turn 1 begins 5 minutes and 15 seconds after Don exited the car and, during this time, Mother and Daughter have engaged in three very brief exchanges of talk. The transcribed conversation is not the first topic discussed in the 21-minute episode nor is it the last because Daughter's turn 34, which closes this topic, is followed by a 36-second pause and then the introduction of a new topic about the song playing on the radio. Thus, this mother–daughter relationship talk is clearly demarcated from their other talk. It is preceded and followed by unrelated topics and by extended (many seconds or minutes) pauses. It is also unlike the prior and subsequent topics in that it is fully developed and both Mother and Daughter make multiple contributions to it.

As the transcript also makes evident, Mother not only initiates this topic, her contributions to it are longer and more substantive than Daughter's. Seven of Daughter's 17 turns consist solely of acknowledgment tokens (*Yeah, Mm hmm, Mmm*) and only two (turns 4 and 32) of her other 10 contain more than one conversational action. This is the case despite (1) the many pauses within Mother's turns that provide an opportunity for Daughter to respond; (2) three turns (9, 17, and 21) Mother makes with questions within them; and (3) the six turns (3, 13, 15, 17, 25, 33) Mother completes with questions or question intonation that overtly solicit a response from her daughter. Mother does much more of the interactional "work" (Fishman, 1983) of this conversation—initiating topic, elaborating topic, directly and indirectly soliciting Daughter's response—and although Daughter does participate in the conversation in important ways, development of the mother-initiated topic is largely dependent upon Mother's conversational actions. At any rate, afforded a 21-minute unplanned (but perhaps not unforeseen) opportunity for private, two-party talk, Mother and Daughter close out talk about the dinner they shared with Don, mark their immediate shared context with talk about that context (gas station activities, radio content), and, after another extended pause, make entry into what will become a 3-minute, 17-second conversation about the vitality and intimacy of their relationship. Importantly, addressing concerns about intimacy in this particular interactional space works, in part, to redress them because private, two-party talk about closeness in a relationship can be taken to be evidence of closeness in that relationship.

Mother begins turn 1 with "Oh." which, as Heritage (1984) demonstrates, marks a change in the speaker's state of knowledge or awareness—in this case, a remembrance of "somethin'" Mother wanted to tell her daughter. After a short pause this is followed with "↑I know:.", a claim of existing knowledge that is routinely employed as a responsive action, often to a prior speaker's informing, assessment, or offering of advice (Gornick, 2004). This claim, however, is clearly not a response to prior talk because it follows an extended pause in interaction. Although arguable, this "↑I know:." can be seen to mark Mother's orientation to an interactional difficulty that her upcoming utterance will remedy. Recall that Mother and Daughter have been alone in the car now for more than 5 minutes and they have engaged in only brief exchanges of talk about matters that neither acted to elaborate in any depth. Fishman (1983) has demonstrated that "making conversation" can be problematic because for an initiated topic to become a topic of conversation, one's partner must provide uptake on it and the brief exchanges preceding and following this conversation suggest that uptake alone may not be enough. Without multiple contributions by both interactional partners, a proffered topic can be quickly exhausted and when interactants remain in one another's presence following such an eventuality, they confront what can be a problematic pause in activities (i.e., an "awkward silence," until a new topic is located). The Mother's "Oh. (0.6) ↑I know:." can, therefore, be seen to mark both her remembrance of "somethin'" she wanted to tell her daughter and the locating of a topic that is likely to enjoy full development and so resolve the problematic silence preceding it. This analysis is supported by the finding by Duck, Rutt, Hurst, and Strejc (1991) that the mere presence of talk, regardless of content, is taken by relational partners as a sign of the healthy continuation of their relationship. The Mother has, then, with the first three words of her first utterance marked both the lack of conversation with Daughter as problematic and, with the higher pitch on "I," underscored her part in resolving the difficulty.

The third item in Mother's first turn, "There was somethin' I wanted ta tell ya," is a "pre"—the first in a sequence of utterances that project a future action, an announcement in this case, by the speaker of the "pre" (Levinson, 1983; Terasaki, 1976). The standard, full pre-announcement format consists of four positions that are often, not always, performed in four consecutive turns where turns 1 and 3 are performed by the initiator of the sequence and turns 2 and 4 are performed by the other speaker; for example, A: "Guess what."; B: "What."; A: "I got the job."; B: "Terrific." Position 1 turns prefigure the action to be performed in position 3 by serving notice to the hearer of the upcoming action and checking the hearer's ability or willingness to respond to that action. Position 2 in the standard format is slotted for the second speaker to provide either a "go-ahead" (i.e., perform the action) or to discourage performance of the action. Daughter's turn 2, "Ye:ah," is a go-ahead, whereas discouragements (or outright blocks) would include utterances like "Wait a minute, I can't hear," or "I don't wanna hear about it." Position 2, then, fully involves the second speaker in his or her partner's projected action: "Forewarned is forearmed"; and if speaker B is disinclined to participate in the action speaker A has projected, he or she has, in position 2, the opportunity to decline to do so.

Thus, "There was somethin' I wanted ta tell ya" projects the telling of a particular but as yet unspecified item and, prefaced as it is with the change-of-state token ("Oh") and the locating of a topic to repair the most recent silence, Mother projects an announcement of some import. It is important to note that the format of this first turn significantly influences conversational development. Mother could have told Daughter the things she eventually does tell her and made the request she eventually does make of her by simply continuing her talk in turn 1 with these actions; for example, she could have said, "I'm concerned because you haven't been talking to me about your problems and I'm asking you to tell me about what's going on in your life." Such an utterance is clear and efficient; however, it also places tighter constraints on Daughter's response. That is, a direct request creates an immediate and expectable "slot" for a grant or refusal of the request (see Sacks, Schegloff, & Jefferson, 1978). Consequently, Daughter's alignment on this issue, or lack thereof, would be quite visible. Moreover, Daughter's response to this kind of utterance would not provide for her collaboration in the upcoming action in the way that the position 2, go-ahead slot of a preannouncement sequence does. Mother's "Oh. (0.6) ↑I know:. There was somethin' I wanted ta tell ya." therefore not only serves to mark her solution to the problematic silence Mother and Daughter have experienced, but it also makes the achievement of that solution a shared activity. Importantly, then, despite Daughter's clear go-ahead in turn 2, in neither of the mother's next *two* turns does she offer the announcement she prefigured (i.e., turns 3 and 5 are done in question and quasi-question form and they concern additional background information about the "somethin'" rather than the "somethin'" itself). Both also receive go aheads from Daughter. Consequently, in six turns and a few seconds of mother–daughter time, barring recourse to direct refusals to engage (e.g., "I don't want to talk about it") the daughter in this conversation has collaborated in the construction of a conversation about a topic whose nature is not yet clear and which her mother has prefigured as relationally important and troublesome.

Turn 7 is, therefore, an ideal location for delivery of the announcement because mutual tracking of the conversation has been established with the go-aheads in turns 4 and 6 (i.e., Daughter does recall the phone call Mother is referencing and she does recall the discussion about her mother's heart problem). The announcement projected in turn 1 could, then, be delivered here and Mother does report in this turn her intention to have her heart problem "looked into." However, if this report is the announcement, the construction of the turn makes recognizing it as such problematic. The turn begins with And-Prefacing (Heritage & Sorjonen, 1994)—"(An:) that deal."—and it interrupts Daughter's third go-ahead. It's constructed, then, as a continuation of Mother's turn 5 (she's still backgrounding) and the report of her intention to have her heart problem "looked into:" is positioned at the end of the turn after three short pauses, a "Well," and the beginning of an utterance that is aborted ("I just wanchu ta know: that-"). Consequently, although this report could be the announcement Mother projected in turn 1, it may not be that and Daughter's "Mm hm." in turn 8 treats it accordingly ("Mm hm" is routinely used as a "continuer" which acknowledges and invites continuation of the prior speaker's talk [see Schegloff, 1982], unlike a news receipt [Maynard, 1997], which receipts the news and may comment on it, such as "Oh" or "That's good.")

Like her two prior turns, Mother begins turn 9 with And-Prefacing, so Mother and Daughter have now coconstructed turn 7 as not the "somethin'" Mother wanted to tell her daughter. This "An" is followed, after a short pause, with a stressed "but-" and the account that follows is interesting in multiple respects. First, it is an unsolicited account of Mother's reasons for discussing her heart problem with her daughter which is (again) located in an interactional space where the important and troublesome announcement could be told. Second, the account follows (1) multiple brief pauses; (2) two clear restarts following the "but-" which concern something that was not the reason she discussed the heart problem with her daughter; (3) a claim of insufficient knowledge (Beach & Metzger, 1997) about her own actual motivation; and (4) the very interesting "Huh-" that, as a responsive action, appears to mark Mother's "just found" discovery of that which actually did motivate her disclosure. Finally, this account of Mother's reasons for discussing her heart problem with her daughter—"Just because I was ↑tal↓kin' to you. (0.5) You kno::w an (1.7) >let-tin- ya kno:w everything.<"—references the phone call previously mentioned such that it can be seen and treated as an instance where Mother disclosed (">lettin- ya kno:w") or "shared" her concerns about her heart problem with her daughter. This is important because, as it turns out, it is this kind of mother—daughter interaction that becomes the primary topic for the remainder of this conversation.

The rest of turn 9 and Mother's next four turns are devoted to the explication of a theory, of sorts, about intimacy and distance in family relationships. Mother's "And (0.7) the ↑po:int i:s tha:t" is heavily marked (note the sound extensions, pitch change, and stress) and it directly claims that the upcoming utterance is what her prior turns have been "leading up to," so the delayed announcement appears about to be delivered. This is followed by a series of utterances, completed in Mother's turn 13, which are constructed as an "if-then" narrative that outlines multiple potential problems Daughter could be having and might not be telling her mother about. Importantly, the daughter does not receipt Mother's explanation, which creates the one and a half second pause that follows the "then" part of the narrative (i.e., "There becomes a little stagnant ↑part in our re↑la↓tionship.") In fact, Daughter provides no uptake at all until Mother directly solicits a response by asking ">Know wha' I me:an?<."

Daughter's "Mmhm" in turn 14 acknowledges understanding of her mother's explanation without taking a position (agreement or disagreement) on it and this is responded to by Mother with renewed efforts to explain and support her theory of intimacy. She begins, in turn 15, with an emotion narrative (a narrative where a character's emotional experience is the point of the telling—Staske, 1994, 1998) that is completed in turn 17. This narrative illustrates the intimacy theory outlined in turns 9–13, supports the account Mother offered for telling Daughter her concerns about her heart, and it legitimates that telling. The gist of the story is that Mother once "stopped ↑talkin'" to her sister-in-law about the problems in her life and, as a result, they lost genuine closeness in their relationship (they were "just ma:sking" and even the happy times became "unre:al"). Goodwin (1993) has described young girls' tactical use of stories as "a preliminary stage" (p. 129) in the accomplishment of larger conversational activities and this story appears to function similarly in that it sets the stage for Mother's upcoming request (the larger action) that her daughter talk to her about her problems.

As in the previous set of mother–daughter turns, Daughter does not respond to the story and so Mother again directly solicits a response with "°Ya understa::nd?°" which, after another significant pause, Daughter affirms with "°Ye:ah.°" Goodwin (1993) notes that in conflict interactions between young girls, taking up alignments to story characters' actions can be "interpreted as commitments to undertake future action for which parties may be held responsible by others" (p. 127). Daughter's turn 18 can, then, also be seen as tactical: "°Ye:ah.°" claims understanding of the distance created when her mother and Aunt Wanda stopped talking about problems, but it does not take up an alignment to their actions and so does not commit Daughter to sharing her own problems with her mother. Mother's turn 19 is not entirely recoverable; however, it appears to be the first open-ended (as opposed to yes/no questions) solicitation of her daughter's response made in this conversation, so, Daughter is free to address Mother's prior talk as she sees fit. It's interesting then that her response "Whadaya mean." is a clarification question and repair initiator (Schegloff, 1992) which work to narrow her options for appropriate response. In turn 21, Mother responds accordingly by offering a candidate answer (Pomerantz, 1988) to her own query which is immediately (note the equal sign) disconfirmed by Daughter first with "°No:°" (i.e., she was not avoiding discussing her problems with her mother because of the heart problem), and then with a statement asserting what she did think about that (i.e., she wanted her mother to go and "↑check it").

This is important in that it redirects the conversation to what should be done about that problem rather than following the topic Mother identified as "the ↑poi:nt" of this conversation and the one she asked about (i.e., Daughter telling her mother about her problems). Mother's turn 25 aligns with the topic shift (with the "Okay") and then continues with an utterance that is unambiguously an announcement of news: She has made an appointment on the twenty-ninth to have her heart problem "checked." This is met with a pause, so Mother (again) solicits Daughter's response with "Ka:y?" whereupon the daughter issues a clear and positive news receipt: "Cool." Mother's following "Okay" completes the news report and, perhaps, the presequence with which Mother initiated this conversation.

Daughter's "(I don't have a) problem." in turn 28 is, again, ambiguous due to auditory difficulties for me but apparently not the interactants, and it apparently claims a current lack of problems in Daughter's life. Mother does not address this seemingly positive state of affairs in turns 29 and the continuing 31 and, instead, requests her daughter to tell her about her problems ("I do wantcha to tell ↑me:.") and offers to hear them regardless of sleep needs and distance ("You know, you can ↑ca:ll me"). The pause following this utterance is important because it's long (4.1 seconds is much longer than the typical few tenths of a second gap between speakers' turns) and because it follows an offer; thus, it constitutes the slot for Daughter's acceptance or declination of that offer. Mother herself ends this long pause with an utterance that deserves more analysis than can be here provided: "You are my ↑daughter." is interesting in many respects. First, it violates a conversational rule that one not tell one's partner things one has reason to believe he or she already knows. Clearly, Daughter already knows she is her mother's daughter and the relevance of those identities has been referenced in prior talk—see, especially, turns 13 and 21—and so informing or reminding are not good explanations of the work the utterance accomplishes.

"You are my ↑daughter." is located in this conversation after (1) Mother's discussion of intimacy and the role that talking about problems plays in maintaining it, (2) her request that Daughter tell her about her problems, and (3) her offer to talk about such problems even in the middle of the night (i.e., "I don't care: if it's twelveaclock at night."). Importantly, Daughter has not taken up any kind of alignment to any of these actions. The heavily stressed "You are my ↑daughter." underscores the importance of this relationship in Mother's life and, located after Mother's report of her concerns, her request, and her offer, it works to summarize these actions such that Mother's relationship with her daughter can be seen as one where, despite time, geographical distance, and significant changes in family life, Mother remains ever-available and talking about Daughter's problems is not only acceptable, but it is expected and desired.

Daughter's response to this utterance is her longest in the entire conversation; it contains the most substance (two complete actions—"I ↑know." and "I haven't- (0.6) °well° (0.5) [thought different.]"), and it was not overtly solicited by a question. It is, then, unlike nearly all of her prior utterances and constitutes an unqualified agreement—daughter claims existing knowledge of her mother's ongoing interest in her life and reports not having thought otherwise. Mother overlaps the last part of the utterance to, again, restate her willingness and desire to talk about her daughter's problems even if she cannot solve them. And, again, given no immediate uptake, she issues a question to which, after another significant pause, Daughter apparently responds with another acknowledging "°(Yeah)°." This mother–daughter relationship talk is then jointly terminated with the 36-second pause that follows and the introduction of an unrelated topic, derived from the new song playing on the radio.

Discussion

The findings of this study demonstrate that explaining the construction, maintenance, and change in relational processes over the many years of the family lifecycle requires examination of the conversational practices family members employ in the natural interactional settings that constitute family life. That is where and how family relationships and the relational identities appropriate to them are made, negotiated, and renegotiated. Mother's use of the conventional presequence format and her delay of the announcement projected by that action made it possible for her to develop a "theory" of intimacy in family relationships and to tell an emotion narrative that legitimated the disclosure of her problem to her daughter and supported the request she eventually makes that her daughter reciprocate such disclosures. The presequence, repeated pauses within turns, and overt requests for response, actively solicited Daughter's involvement in the relationship talk and, thus in the coconstruction of their changing relational boundaries. Daughter's repeated use of continuers and acknowledgment tokens made it possible for her to claim understanding of her mother's concerns and desires without committing herself to as yet unperformed and, perhaps, undecided future actions.

Sharing intimate information (including "problems") is one index of an intimate relationship, but it is only one and it is not an unproblematic one (Bochner, 1982). Consequently, the relatively indirect and preliminary conversational practices employed here are a good fit for the emerging and ongoing (it's not a done deal) relational changes that mother and daughter are addressing in this launching stage conversation. As the parent in this conversation, one could hardly lay claim to having settled an important relational problem and, as the adult daughter, one could hardly consider the matter one that will not come up again. Mother did tell her daughter some things she was concerned about and she did make a request of and offer to her daughter. Daughter did listen to and claim understanding of her mother's talk; however, plans and promises regarding future action on this issue were not proffered and they were not interactionally pursued. Clearly, passing up a 21-minute opportunity to address and perhaps redress a problematic distance between mother and daughter would count as a lost opportunity; at the same time, "pushing too hard" in that 21 minutes would compromise, rather than facilitate, the achievement of intimacy between this mother and her adult daughter. Hence, the presequence, pauses, and soliciting questions; stories and theories about family relationships and continuers; withholding uptake; and claims of understanding but not agreement can be seen as useful conversational resources in the ongoing negotiation of intimate ties in a more equal, voluntary, adult relationship between this mother and the young woman who is, as they both affirm, her "↑daughter."

Questions for Consideration and Discussion

1. Staske-Bell's work presented here is based on the idea that intimacy is primarily created and negotiated in everyday conversation. What other relational factors are created or negotiated in the same way?
2. This analysis focuses on a mother–daughter pair, where the daughter is in college. Why does the shift from high school to college tend to call for a renegotiation of intimacy? What examples of this renegotiation can you see in your own relationships?
3. In addition to the shift from an adult/child to an adult/adult relationship, what other life changes might call for a renegotiation of intimacy in the parent–child relationship? How so?
4. What are the advantages of studying intimacy through an examination of everyday talk?
5. Conversational analysis considers not only the verbal element of conversation, but also the nonverbal vocal elements, such as pauses and vocal inflection. What do you see as the benefits and drawbacks of this approach?

References

Baxter, L. A. (1998). Locating the social in interpersonal communication. In J. Trent (Ed.), *Communication: Views from the helm* (pp. 60–64). Boston: Allyn & Bacon.

Beach, W., & Metzger, T. (1997). Claiming insufficient knowledge. *Human Communication Research, 23,* 562–588.

Bochner, A. (1982). On the efficacy of openness in close relationships. In M. Burgoon (Ed.), *Communication yearbook* (Vol. 5, pp. 109–124). New Brunswick, NJ: Transaction Press.

Duck, S., Rutt, D., Hurst, M., & Strejc, H. (1991). Some evident truths about conversation in everyday relationships: All communications are not created equal. *Human Communication Research, 18,* 228–267.

Fishman, P. (1983). Interaction: The work women do. In B. Thorne, C. Kramarae, & N. Henley (Eds.), *Language, gender, and society* (pp. 89–101). Rowley, MA: Newbury House.

Fitzpatrick, M. A., & Badzinski, D. M. (1994). All in the family: Interpersonal communication in kin relationships. In M. L. Knapp & G. R. Miller (Eds.), *Handbook of interpersonal communication* (2nd ed. pp. 726–771). Thousand Oaks, CA: Sage.

Goodwin, M. (1993). Tactical uses of stories: Participation frameworks within girls' and boys' disputes. In D. Tannen (Ed.), *Gender and conversational interaction* (pp. 110–143.). New York: Oxford University Press.

Gornick, M. (2005). *Sibling interaction: Sisters' use of advice episodes in the construction of relational identities.* Unpublished master's thesis, Eastern Illinois University, Charleston, IL.

Heritage, J. (1984). A change-of-state token and aspects of its sequential placement. In J. Atkinson & J. Heritage (Eds.), *Structures of social action* (pp. 1–16). Cambridge, England: Cambridge University Press.

Heritage, J., & Sorjonen, M.-L. (1994). Constituting and maintaining activities across sequences: And-prefacing as a feature of question design. *Language in Society, 23,* 1–29.

Jefferson, G. (1984). Transcript notation. In J. Atkinson & J. Heritage (Eds.), *Structures of social action* (pp. ix–xvi). Cambridge, England: Cambridge University Press.

Levinson, S. (1983). *Pragmatics.* Cambridge, England: Cambridge University Press.

Maynard, D. W. (1997). The news delivery sequence: Bad news and good news in conversational interaction. *Research on Language and Social Interaction, 30*(2), 93–130.

Metts, S., & Planalp, S. (2002). Emotional communication. In M. L. Knapp & J. A. Daly (Eds.), *Handbook of interpersonal communication* (3rd ed., pp. 339–373). Thousand Oaks, CA: Sage.

Pomerantz, A. (1988). Offering a candidate answer: An information seeking strategy. *Communication Monographs, 55,* 360–373.

Sacks, H., Schegloff, E., & Jefferson, G. (1978). A simplest systematics for the organization of turn taking for conversation. In J. Schenkein (Ed.), *Studies in the organization of conversational interaction* (pp. 7–55). New York: Academic Press.

Schegloff, E. (1982). Discourse as an interactional achievement: Some uses of "uh huh" and other things that come between sentences. In D. Tannen (Ed.),

Analyzing discourse: Text and talk (pp. 71–93). Washington, DC: Georgetown University Press.

Schegloff, E. (1992). Repair after next turn: The last structurally provided defense of intersubjectivity in conversation. *American Journal of Sociology, 97*, 1295–1345.

Staske, S. (1994). *The instantiation of emotion in conversations between romantic partners, male friends, female friends, and cross-sex friends.* Unpublished doctoral dissertation, University of Illinois at Urbana–Champaign, Department of Speech Communication.

Staske, S. (1998). The normalization of problematic emotion in conversations between close relational partners: *Inter*personal emotion work. *Symbolic Interaction, 21*, 59–86.

Staske, S. (2002a). Claiming individualized knowledge of a conversational partner. *Research on Language and Social Interaction, 35*(3), 245–276.

Staske, S. A. (2002b). *Multi-party "family conflict": Now, again, and (ever?) after.* Paper presented at the annual meeting of the National Communication Association, Atlanta, GA.

Terasaki, A. (1976). *Pre-announcement sequences in conversation* (Social Science Working Paper No. 99). Irvine: School of Social Science, University of California.

Tracy, K., Haspel, K. (2004). Language and social interaction: Its institutional identity, intellectual landscape, and discipline-shifting agenda. *Journal of Communication, 54*(4), 788–816.

Sex and Gender in Relational Maintenance

Marianne Dainton

As discussed in the Section 1, research has indicated that there are sex or gender effects at work in how intimacy, affection, and social support are expressed, and those sex/gender effects are thought primarily to be cultural, though some theorists also argue a biological cause. In this article, Dainton looks at relational maintenance behaviors, communicative practices that help increase feelings of affection, intimacy, and satisfaction, and the gender/sex influence on those behaviors. Consider your own relational maintenance behaviors while reading, and the extent to which they do, or do not, fit with Dainton's findings.

L.B.A.

In the 1990s, for every two marriages in the United States one ended in divorce (Hughes, 2004). In fact, 40% of people born in the 1970s can expect to get divorced during their life span (Hughes, 2004). Given the high divorce rate in the United States, it is surprising that relatively little research centers on answering the question of which communication strategies work to keep relationships together. The research spotlighted in this chapter focuses specifically on relationship maintenance, which is defined as communicative efforts to keep a relationship satisfactory (Dindia & Canary, 1993).

A series of research studies has identified seven behaviors that people use to maintain a satisfying relationship (Stafford & Canary, 1991; Stafford, Dainton, & Haas, 2000). The techniques include *openness*, which means self-disclosure and direct discussions of the relationship (e.g., "I tell my partner what I want or need from the relationship"); *assurances*, which refer to verbal and nonverbal reassurances of commitment to the relationship and to the partner ("I say I love you"); *positivity*, which means being optimistic and pleasant ("I am cheerful and positive around him or her"); *social networks*, which means relying on common friends and family members for support ("I spend time with our same friends"); *shared tasks*, which means engaging in housework, child care, and other joint responsibilities ("I do my fair share of the work we have to do"); *conflict management*, which includes proactive and positive ways to resolve conflict ("I apologize when I am wrong"); and *advice*, which means counseling the partner ("I give him/her my opinion about things going on in his life").

Research indicates that these techniques are consistent and strong predictors of relationship satisfaction, commitment, love, and liking (e.g., Dainton, Stafford, & Canary, 1994; Stafford & Canary, 1991). Positivity and assurances seem to be of particular importance in relationship maintenance, as they are more strongly related to satisfaction, commitment, and love than other strategies. Surprisingly, openness does not seem to be very important; in virtually every study using these seven maintenance strategies, openness is a negative predictor of satisfaction, meaning the more open you are, the less satisfied you are with your relationship (e.g., Dainton, 2000). Of course, there are many reasons for this, including the possibility that people are more likely to talk about the relationship when they are unhappy. Nevertheless, the importance placed on self-disclosure in the popular press might be overstated.

The two studies reported in this chapter focus on why people choose particular maintenance techniques. Previous research has focused on sex differences as the explanation for the type and amount of maintenance activity performed. Results are fairly consistent, with women performing more maintenance than men (e.g., Canary & Stafford, 1992; Dainton & Stafford, 1993; Ragsdale, 1996). The fact that women use more maintenance strategies than men is probably not surprising to you. However, the issue is a fairly complex one that taps into the classic "nature versus nurture" debate. Do women perform more maintenance because they are biologically programmed to do so? Or are the differences based on the way that people are raised to behave?

The first study reported in this chapter asks whether the differences are really based on biology (e.g., sex differences) or whether differences are based on gender role (e.g., differences due to the way people are raised). Note that although the terms *sex* and *gender* are often used interchangeably, scholars have precise meanings for the terms. As alluded to previously, sex is biological (male vs. female) and gender is the way people are raised to behave (masculine vs. feminine).

Popular treatment of the topic emphasizes a biological explanation (Gray's 1992 book argues that men are from Mars and women are from Venus), treating men and women as different species. However, a growing body of scholarly research seems to indicate that biology alone explains very little about why people communicate in particular ways (Canary & Hause, 1993). The researchers in the following study hypothesized that femininity would be a stronger predictor of the frequency of using maintenance behavior than would be masculinity or biological sex.

Study One

Stafford and colleagues (2000) had 520 married people fill out a survey that asked them how frequently they performed the seven maintenance behaviors described earlier in this article. Each of the measurement scales was reliable as assessed by Chronbach's alpha. Reliability means the consistency of the measurement. If a measurement is not reliable, you should not trust the results of the study. Chronbach's alpha is a particular statistical tool that assesses reliability. Scores range between 0 (meaning no consistency) and 1.0 (meaning perfect consistency). In general, researchers look for a reliability score between .70 and 1.0. Think of these numbers as percentages on an exam—typically you want to score above 70%, and the closer to 100% you get the happier you will be. In this study, the lowest reliability score was for advice, with .70, and the highest was for assurances, with .92.

In addition to filling out the maintenance measures, the participants also filled out Bem's (1974) Sex-Role Inventory (SRI), which measures gender (masculinity and femininity). The SRI asks people to assess their own personality characteristics on a Likert-type scale (with 1 = never true and 7 = always true). For example, personality characteristics that are used to measure masculinity include *independent*, *ambitious*, and *competitive*. Personality characteristics that are used to measure femininity include *affectionate*, *sensitive*, and *sincere.* Note that all people filling out the survey receive both a masculinity score and a femininity score. The average masculinity score (regardless of sex) was 5.75 on the seven-point scale, and the average femininity score (regardless of sex) was 5.70 on that scale.

To determine whether males were more likely to have higher masculinity scores and females were more likely to have higher femininity scores, the researchers ran a point biserial correlation between sex and gender. A point biserial correlation is a statistical technique that is used to determine the strength of the relationship between two variables. A correlation of 0 would indicate absolutely no relationship between the two variables (meaning that being female bears no relationship to being feminine). A correlation of 1.0 would indicate a perfect relationship between the two variables (meaning that being female and being feminine are exactly the same thing). In this study the correlation was .13, which indicates a relatively small relationship between sex and gender; men were not necessarily masculine and women were not necessarily feminine.

The major purpose of this study was to find out the relative importance of sex and gender in relationship maintenance. Do people perform more or less maintenance because of biology (sex), or do they perform more or less maintenance because of the way they are raised (gender), or is it some combination of the two? To answer these questions, the researchers ran a series of multiple regression equations. Multiple regression is a statistical technique that allows a researcher to use a set of variables to predict another variable. For example, college admissions officers use things like high school class rank, high school grade point average, and SAT scores to predict the likelihood of success in college. In this study, the researchers ran seven different equations, each predicting a different maintenance technique. The variables used to make the predictions were sex (male or female) and gender (masculinity and femininity). Results are reported in Table 5.3, p. 176.

To understand these results, look at the numbers for each of the maintenance strategies. Two statistics help us answer the research questions: *beta* and *adjusted R^2*. The beta score indicates how important a variable is relative to other variables in that same equation—the bigger the number the more important it is for the prediction (whether the score is positive or negative doesn't matter in terms of importance). If you look at assurances, femininity got a .46 and masculinity got a .14. That indicates that femininity is a stronger predictor of assurances than masculinity—feminine people are more likely to use assurances than masculine people. The beta for sex is zero, which means that the sex of the person (whether they are male or female) isn't important at all in determining if a person is going to use assurances or not.

Adjusted R^2 indicates how strong the prediction is overall. Once again, scores range from 0 to 1.0, with 1.0 being a perfect prediction. Low scores mean that it is something other than sex and gender that predicts maintenance enactment, and higher scores indicate that sex and gender provide a lot of information when predicting maintenance enactment. In this study, the strongest prediction is for conflict management, with an adjusted R^2 of .33. This means that knowing someone is feminine gives you about 33% of the information you need to predict exactly how much conflict management a person will use. The weakest prediction is for social networks; in this case, knowing someone is feminine explains only 8% of the information you need to predict how much the person will rely on social networks.

The most important thing for you to understand related to these results is the overall pattern. As the researchers hypothesized, femininity was the best predictor for every equation. That means that people high in femininity are most likely to use all seven of the

TABLE 5.3   *Results of Regression of Sex and Gender on Each Maintenance Behavior*

Advice	**Assurances**	**Conflict Management**
Feminine beta = .26 Masculine beta = .26 Sex beta = .00 *Adjusted R^2 = .13*	Feminine beta = .46 Masculine beta = .14 Sex beta = .00 *Adjusted R^2 = .24*	Feminine beta = .58 Masculine beta = .00 Sex beta = .00 *Adjusted R^2 = .33*
	Networks Feminine beta = .28 Masculine beta = .00 Sex beta = .00 *Adjusted R^2 = .08*	
Openness	**Positivity**	**Tasks**
Feminine beta = .46 Masculine beta = .17 Sex beta = −.18 *Adjusted R^2 = .23*	Feminine beta = .37 Masculine beta = .20 Sex beta = .00 *Adjusted R^2 = .17*	Feminine beta = .23 Masculine beta = .00 Sex beta = −.22 *Adjusted R^2 = .11*

relationship maintenance behaviors (and therefore have a more satisfying marriage). This isn't surprising, because femininity is defined as being sensitive and affectionate. Being masculine was a less powerful predictor, but also appeared in several of the equations. Accordingly, things like independence and assertiveness also facilitate maintenance activities (especially giving advice and being positive).

Biological sex appeared in only two of the equations, however. This means that sex is relatively unimportant in predicting the use of relational maintenance communication. In both cases where sex appeared in the equation, being female predicted the use of the maintenance behavior. Earlier I indicated that whether the beta score was positive or negative didn't matter for importance; it is important for what is known as "dummy coding." Because sex is a single variable with two possible responses (male or female), the statistical procedures require you to mathematically indicate being male or female. In this study, being female was a negative score and being male was a positive score. The fact that the beta scores were negative both times that sex appeared indicates that the prediction is for women. It seems that being a female makes you slightly more likely to pursue open discussions about the relationship, and also makes you slightly more likely to do household chores. However, when looking at the betas, sex is not as important as gender in predicting these behaviors. And, recall that sex appears in only two of the seven predictions, meaning that it is not very important overall in predicting maintenance communication.

The results of Stafford and colleagues' (2000) study have profound implications for stereotypes about who does what in marriage. The results indicate that relationship maintenance is not biologically driven; women are not "programmed" to use more maintenance than men, it is a learned behavior. Despite Gray's assertions, men are not from Mars and women are not from Venus. As such, advice for married people should shift from a focus on what men can or should do and what women can or should do, and instead should focus on how developing feminine qualities—regardless of whether you are a man or a woman—can enhance marital success.

The notion that both gender roles and relationship maintenance can be learned leads to a second study linking sex, gender, and relationship maintenance. One of the central controversies in maintenance research is the extent to which maintenance is performed strategically versus routinely. According to Dainton and Stafford (1993), strategic maintenance refers to behaviors performed at a high level of consciousness, and for the explicit purpose of relationship maintenance. Routine maintenance refers to behaviors performed at a low level of consciousness (perhaps because they are overlearned), and without the specific intention of relationship maintenance (i.e., the married person does not think "I should do this for the sake of my marriage"). Dainton and Aylor (2002) found that both strategic and routine maintenance are important for relationship satisfaction, but that routine maintenance is slightly more important.

At issue is whether there are sex or gender variations in the extent to which maintenance is performed strategically or routinely, and what such variations might mean. Aylor and Dainton (2004) asked three research questions:

RQ1:   Are there sex differences in the use of strategic and routine maintenance behaviors?

RQ2:   Are there gender differences in the use of strategic and routine maintenance behaviors?

RQ3:   Is biological sex or psychological gender a better predictor of routine and strategic maintenance?

Study Two

Aylor and Dainton (2004) collected survey data from 189 individuals in romantic relationships. The measurements were exactly the same as those described under study one, and the Chronbach alpha scores were all above .80, indicating the measurements are reliable. In this study, participants filled out the maintenance questions twice. First, they reported how frequently they had used each behavior strategically during the past two weeks, and then they reported how frequently they had used each behavior routinely during the past two weeks.

The first research question, which asked about sex differences in the use of routine and strategic maintenance, was assessed using a statistical technique known as multivariate analysis of variance, or MANOVA. This tool allows you to calculate the average scores for groups (males and females) and determine the likelihood that differences between the groups are due to chance, or whether they reflect real ("significant") differences. The result of the MANOVA indicated only one sex difference; women reported using openness more routinely than did men. Notice that this result supports and builds upon the results of study one, which found that one of the few sex differences in maintenance is related to openness. Aylor and Dainton's (2004) findings indicate that the difference between men and women when it comes to self-disclosure is not one of conscious intent, but that self-disclosure seems to be a part of women's interaction routines, whereas it doesn't seem to be a part of men's interaction routines.

The second research question asked about gender differences in routine and strategic maintenance. This requires a different statistical test because there are no groups to compare—every individual has both a masculinity and a femininity score. In this case, a multivariate multiple regression (MMR) was used. The MMR combines multiple regression, which was described in study one, and MANOVA, described previously. Two MMRs were run, one for routine maintenance and the other for strategic maintenance.

The first analysis found that femininity was significantly related to routine maintenance; feminine individuals were more likely than masculine individuals to use openness, positive conflict management, and advice as part of their interaction routines. The second analysis found that masculinity was significantly related to strategic maintenance; masculine individuals were more likely than feminine individuals to strategically use openness and tasks to maintain their relationship.

Aylor and Dainton's (2004) final research question asked whether sex or gender was more important when considering routine and strategic maintenance. Because there was only one sex difference found in this study, the clear answer is that gender is more important than sex. More important, the results of this study indicate that masculine people perform maintenance strategically and feminine people perform maintenance routinely.

The results are consistent with explanations of gender that suggest that masculine individuals tend to be more task-oriented when confronted by problems—they recognize a problem and then consciously decide on a course of action to "fix" the problem (Huston & Houts, 1998). Such an orientation would lead masculine individuals to treat relationship maintenance as a task that needs to be accomplished. Feminine individuals, on the other hand, are more likely to be relationally oriented, and so are more likely to incorporate relational maintenance into their everyday communication routines. The behavior happens more naturally and without great effort for them.

The results of the Aylor and Dainton (2004) study also allow us to explain the Stafford et al. (2000) study presented as study one in this article. Recall that the authors found that a combination of femininity and masculinity predicted four of the seven maintenance techniques. It may be that feminine people are performing the behavior routinely and masculine people are performing the same behavior strategically—which is why both masculinity and femininity predicted the behavior.

In the end, however, it doesn't matter whether the behavior is performed routinely or strategically; it matters only that the behavior is performed. And it seems that gender, rather than sex, provides the ultimate explanation for what is done and how it is done within a marriage. Combined, the two studies presented in this article suggest that there are dangers associated with the stereotypes of sex differences that appear so often in the popular press. As Aylor and Dainton (2004) argue, the more an individual believes that "men are like this and women are like that" the more likely that person is going to be disappointed and disillusioned when such stereotypes do not hold true. Instead, people interested in maintaining their marriage should learn and reinforce both feminine and masculine gender roles in their relational partners, because femininity would encourage the routine use of maintenance and masculinity would encourage the strategic use of maintenance.

Questions for Consideration and Discussion

1. Studies have indicated that increased openness in marital relationships is not associated with increased satisfaction. Dainton suggests that one explanation may be that we are more open when we are unhappy. What other explanations might there be for this finding?
2. Do you think that more advice giving in a relationship would be associated with more satisfaction? Why or why not?
3. Dainton notes that sex and gender are not the same concept. However, the two are somewhat difficult to separate in our actual experience. Why is that the case?
4. Are you surprised that Dainton found femininity to be associated with greater use of maintenance behaviors? Why or why not?
5. All of the research reported here is self-report. That is, participants filled out questionnaires regarding their relational behavior. What are the benefits and drawbacks of this technique?

References

Aylor, B., & Dainton, M. (2004). Biological sex and psychological gender as predictors of routine and strategic relational maintenance. *Sex Roles, 50,* 689–697.

Bem, S. L. (1974). The measurement of psychological androgyny. *Journal of Consulting and Clinical Psychology, 45,* 195–205.

Canary, D. J., & Hause, K. S. (1993). Is there any reason to study sex differences in communication? *Communication Quarterly, 41,* 129–144.

Canary, D. J., & Stafford, L. (1992). Relational maintenance strategies and equity in marriage. *Communication Monographs, 59,* 243–267.

Dainton, M. (2000). Maintenance behaviors, expectations, and satisfaction: Linking the comparison level to relational maintenance. *Journal of Social and Personal Relationships, 17,* 827–842.

Dainton, M., & Aylor, B. (2002). Routine and strategic maintenance efforts: Behavioral patterns, variations associated with relational length, and the prediction of relational characteristics. *Communication Monographs, 69,* 52–66.

Dainton, M., & Stafford, L. (1993). Routine maintenance behaviors: A comparison of relationship type, partner similarity, and sex differences. *Journal of Social and Personal Relationships, 10,* 255–272.

Dainton, M., Stafford, L., & Canary, D. J. (1994). Maintenance strategies and physical affection as predictors of love, liking, and satisfaction in marriage. *Communication Reports, 7,* 88–98.

Dindia, K., & Canary, D. J. (1993). Definitions and theoretical perspectives on maintaining relationships. *Journal of Social and Personal Relationships, 10,* 163–173.

Gray, J. (1992). *Men are from Mars, women are from Venus: A practical guide for improving communication and getting what you want in your relationships.* New York: HarperCollins.

Hughes, R., Jr. (2004, April 5). The demographics of divorce—United States and Missouri. Retrieved November 24, 2004, from the University of Missouri Extension Web Site: http://missourifamilies.org/features/divorcearticles/divorcefeature17.htm

Huston, T., & Houts, R. (1998). The psychological infrastructure of courtship and marriage: The role of personality and compatibility in romantic relationships. In T. Bradbury (Ed.), *The developmental course of marital dysfunction* (pp. 114–151). New York: Cambridge University Press.

Ragsdale, J. D. (1996). Gender, satisfaction level, and the use of relational maintenance strategies in marriage. *Communication Monographs, 63,* 354–369.

Stafford, L., & Canary, D. J. (1991). Maintenance strategies and romantic relationship type, gender, and relational characteristics. *Journal of Social and Personal Relationships, 8,* 217–242.

Stafford, L., Dainton, M., & Haas, S. (2000). Measuring routine and strategic relational maintenance: Scale revision, sex versus gender roles, and the prediction of relational characteristics. *Communication Monographs, 67,* 306–323.

Family Communication Patterns
and the Socialization of Support Skills

Ascan F. Koerner

Laura Maki

> In this chapter, we have considered how displays of affection, intimacy, and social support are influenced by both family practices and the larger culture. Here, Koerner and Maki present the results of research investigating how family communication patterns impact the development of support skills. Reflecting on your own family experiences as you read the article may provide you insight with your support behaviors and skills.
>
> *L.B.A.*

During your interactions with friends and romantic partners, you have probably noticed differences in the way individuals communicate. These differences arise in part because of the different ways in which families communicate. How parents communicate with their children influences the communication skills children acquire and later use in their own interpersonal relationships with friends and romantic partners. More formally, it can be said that family communication is the primary means by which children are socialized to communicate; that is, to interpret their own and others' behaviors, to experience emotions, and to develop and maintain their interpersonal relationships (Koerner & Fitzpatrick, 2002a, 2004; Noller, 1995). One important communication behavior affected by family communication is social support. In this article, we discuss two studies that investigated how family communication patterns affect social support in families and how family social support affects the social support children experience in their romantic relationships as adults.

Social Support

Social support refers to interpersonal behaviors that have positive outcomes for the targets of such behaviors and is best defined in terms of these positive outcomes. Cutrona and Russell (1987) identified six such outcomes: guidance, reliable alliance, attachment, reassurance of worth, social integration, and opportunity for nurturance. *Guidance* refers to receiving advice or information from the other on how to think or behave. *Reliable alliance* refers to receiving assurance that others can be counted on for tangible assistance, such as money or shelter. *Attachment* refers to a sense of emotional closeness to others from which one derives a sense of security. *Reassurance of worth* refers to others' ιccognition of one's competence, skills, and values. *Social integration* refers to a sense of belonging to a group that shares similar interests, concerns, and recreational activities. Finally, *opportunity for nurturance* refers to the sense that others rely upon one for their own well-being. This final outcome of social support differs from the other five outcomes of social support in that it places the individual in the provider role as opposed to the receiver role.

Family Communication Patterns and Social Support

Family communication patterns are consistent and pervasive ways in which families communicate and, as discussed in Chapter 2, can be defined by two underlying dimensions, conversation orientation and conformity orientation (Fitzpatrick & Ritchie, 1994; Koerner & Fitzpatrick, 2002b, 2002c, 2004). Conversation orientation is the extent to which family members engage in frequent, open, and spontaneous interactions with each other, unconstrained by topics discussed or time spent communicating. Conformity orientation is characterized by a uniformity of beliefs and attitudes within the family. Interactions focus on maintaining harmonious relationships that reflect obedience to the parents (Koerner & Fitzpatrick, 1997, 2002b, 2002c).

Previous research supports the idea that different family communication patterns are associated with different interpersonal communication skills and that children acquire those skills that they experience in their own families. For example, Koesten and Anderson (2004) examined the role of family communication patterns in fostering the development of emotional support. They found that conversation orientation was positively correlated with emotional support in same-sex friendships and adult children's romantic relationships, whereas conformity orientation was negatively correlated with emotional support, but only in same-sex friendships.

Similarly, Koerner and Cvancara's (2002) investigation of specific speech acts suggesting a speaker's orientation toward another's thoughts and feelings found that high-conformity orientation is associated with speech acts that are less concerned with the feelings and thoughts of others. Low-conformity orientation, by contrast, is associated with the validation of others' attitudes and beliefs. Being able to take another person's perspective, however, is a necessary condition for providing social support to them (Burleson & Kunkel, 1996). Consequently, Koerner and Cvancara's research suggests that conformity orientation in families is negatively associated with children's learning of social support skills.

To better understand the effects of family communication patterns on family social support and children's learning of social support skills, we conducted two studies that examined the influence of families on children's social support skills. Based on existing research, we predicted that family conversation orientation would result in higher levels of social support in both the family of origin and in children's romantic relationship as adults. A second prediction was that family conformity orientation would result in lower levels of social support in the family of origin and in adult children's romantic relationships.

Study 1—Method

Participants and Procedure

Participants were 268 undergraduate students at the University of Minnesota in romantic relationships that on average had lasted 2.2 years. Participants completed a Web-based questionnaire asking for demographic information, information about communication in their current romantic relationships and in their families during childhood and adolescence.

Instruments

Family Communication Patterns.   Ritchie and Fitzpatrick's (1990) Revised Family Communication Patterns (RFCP) instrument was used to measure the two dimensions of family communication: conversation orientation and conformity orientation. The RFCP asks participants to rate their agreement on five-point scales (1 = completely disagree; 5 = completely agree) with 26 statements such as "My parents encourage me to express my feelings" (for conversation orientation) and "My parents often say things like 'My ideas are right and you should not question them'" (for conformity orientation).

Social Support.   Cutrona and Russell's (1987) social provisions scale (SPS) was used to measure social support in families of origin and in adult children's current romantic relationships with two relationship-specific versions of the SPS (i.e., for participants' relationships with parents and for participants' romantic relationships). The SPS consists of 24 items asking respondents to agree or disagree on five-point scales (1 = completely disagree; 5 = completely agree) with statements regarding the six types of social support discussed earlier. Each type of social support was measured with 4 items, whose averages were used as scores for each type of social support. The average of all 24 items was used as a score for overall social support.

Study 1—Results

We used linear regression analysis to test the prediction that family communication patterns affect social support in the family. The result of the analysis was that family communication patterns explained 68% of the variance in overall family social support. Specifically, conversation orientation ($\beta = .73$, $p < .001$) had a strong influence on family social support, whereas conformity orientation ($\beta = -.03$, *ns*) had no measurable influence. The interaction between conversation orientation and conformity orientation, however, was significant ($\beta = .18$, $p < .001$). This means that for participants from high conversation orientation families, level of conformity orientation did not affect social support, which was uniformly high. For participants from low conversation orientation families, however, increased conformity orientation was associated with a decrease in social support. Results for the six social provision subscales essentially replicated the findings for the overall score, with the exception of reassurance of worth. Here, in addition to the significant effects of conversation orientation and the interaction, conformity orientation had a significant negative association with social support ($\beta = -.16, p < .01$).

Thus, the data collected in study 1 provided strong support for the hypothesis that conversation orientation is positively associated with social support in families. Support for the second hypothesis, that conformity orientation is negatively associated with social support, was supported only for families low in conversation orientation. In regard to our prediction that family communication patterns predict social support in adult children's romantic relationships, in this study we did not find any consistent correlations between family communication patterns and social support in adult children's romantic relationships. Thus, the idea that social support is learned in families was not supported in this study.

Study 2

The results of study 1 supported our prediction that family communication patterns affect social support in families, but not our prediction that family communication patterns affect social support in adult children's romantic relationships. One possible explanation for why we failed to support the second prediction is that how much social support adult children receive in their romantic relationships is not just determined by what they have experienced in their own families, but also by what their partners have experienced in their families. Thus, we decided to conduct a second study involving both partners in a couple to further examine the association between family communication patterns and social support in adult children's romantic relationships. We predict that family communication patterns will affect social support in adult children's romantic relationships in two different ways. First, family communication patterns will affect the social support experienced in families of origin and subsequently, how social support is experienced in adult children's romantic relationship. In addition, rather than having an effect only on participant's own perceptions of social support in their romantic relationships, we predict that family social support also affects partners' reports of social support. The reason for this prediction is that if social support is a communication skill learned in the family, than the person benefiting from that skill is the partner of the child and not only the child herself, because it is the child that is using the skill in the relationship with the partner. Finally, because social support should affect relationship satisfaction, we also predict that social support in adult children's romantic relationships will be associated with relationship satisfaction of both child and partner.

Study 2—Method

Participants and Procedure

Participants were 54 undergraduate students from the University of Minnesota and their romantic partners. The procedure for study 2 was identical to that of study 1; participants completed a Web-based questionnaire with the same instruments along with a relationship satisfaction instrument.

Instruments

The instruments for study 2 included the RFCP and the SPS as described previously and a measure of relationship satisfaction—Huston, McHale, and Crouter's (1986) version of the Marital Opinion Questionnaire. The measure consists of 10 semantic differential items (e.g., miserable-enjoyable) that asks respondents to rate how they feel about their relationship, as well as one overall indicator ranging from "completely satisfied" to "completely dissatisfied."

Study 2—Results

We collected data from romantic couples in study 2 to test the associations between family social support, social support in adult children's romantic relationships, and relationship satisfaction in adult children's romantic relationships. A path analysis was used to test all of our predictions simultaneously in one causal model (see Figure 5.1). The path analysis also allowed us to investigate gender differences, which was appropriate because past research has established some gender differences in perceived social support and relationship satisfaction.

The first interesting outcome of the path model analysis was that when separated into gender groups, the interaction between conversation orientation and conformity orientation no longer predicted family social support. Instead, we found different effects of family communication patterns on social support for men and for women. For men,

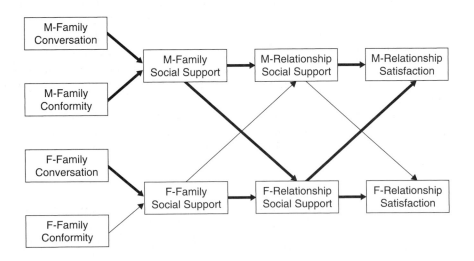

FIGURE 5.1   Associations between Family Communication, Social Support, and Relationship Satisfaction for Couples in Romantic Relationships.

Note: Statistically significant paths are indicated by thick arrows; hypothesized but statistically nonsignificant paths are indicated by thin arrows; M = males; F = females.

conversation orientation was positively correlated and conformity orientation was negatively correlated with perceived social support in families, as we predicted. For women, however, there was only one significant main effect for conversation orientation, whereas conformity orientation had no correlation with perceived social support. In other words, for males, greater conformity orientation leads them to perceive their families as less supportive, whereas females' perceptions of family social support are not affected by their families' conformity orientation. This is consistent with a society in which independence from parents is more important for males than for females, and consequently males, but not females, react negatively to parental pressures to conform (Fitzpatrick & Ritchie, 1994).

Our analysis also showed some significant gender differences between family social support and social support in adult children's romantic relationships. For both men and women, their own families' social support was associated with the social support they reported receiving in their own subsequent romantic relationships. As far as the social support of their partners' family is concerned, however, only the link between male partners' perceived family social support and females' perceived social support was statistically significant. The link between females' family social support and male partners' social support in their subsequent romantic relationship, however, was not. In other words, how supportive females are in their romantic relationships is independent of how much support they received in their own families, whereas how supportive men are in their romantic relationships depends on how much support they received in their own families.

A similar pattern emerged for the association between social support in adult children's romantic relationships and relationship satisfaction. For both men and women, we observed a large direct effect for social support and their own relationship satisfaction. The more social support they reported, the more satisfied they were. At the same time, men's relationship satisfaction, but not women's, was also affected by the social support their partners reported receiving in their relationships. In other words, men were happier if their partners reported more social support in their romantic relationship. Women's satisfaction, however, was not affected by how supportive they were perceived by their partners.

It is important to note that these interesting gender differences were observed only for associations among variables. As far as variable means are concerned, there were no differences between men and women regarding how they perceived their families and their own romantic relationships (see Table 5.4).

TABLE 5.4   *Summary of Variable Means for Couples Data from Study 2 (N = 54)*

Variables	Men	Women
Conversation orientation	4.8	5.1
Conformity orientation	4.0	3.9
Family social support	5.7	6.0
Relationship social support	6.1	6.3

General Discussion

Family Communication Patterns and Perceived Social Support in the Family

Results of both studies were consistent with the prediction that family communication patterns are associated with family social support. In both studies, conversation orientation was positively associated with all aspects of social support in families. Families that value open communication and the free exchange of ideas are more supportive than families that place less value on open communication. The predicted negative association of conformity orientation on family social support was more complicated. In study 1, it was supported as a direct effect only for one dimension of social support, reassurance of worth. Statistically significant interactions, however, revealed that conformity orientation had the predicted negative effect on the other dimensions of social support when conversation orientation was low. In study 2, we observed the negative correlation between conformity orientation and family social support for men, but not for women. Thus, the results showed that family communication patterns overall affect social support in families. The effect of conversation orientation is consistently positive, whereas the effect of conformity orientation is generally negative, but less consistent.

Family Social Support and Support in Adult Children's Romantic Relationships

In study 2, we investigated a sophisticated causal model linking family communication patterns to adult children's social support in subsequent adult children's romantic relationships and their satisfaction in those relationships. The finding that family social support affects how supportive adult children's romantic relationships are is consistent with a dyadic definition of social support. In a dyadic definition, social support refers to two interrelated interpersonal skills: (1) the ability to provide social support to others and (2) the ability to recognize and utilize the social support others provide. The ability to provide social support includes perspective taking, empathizing with the distressed person's situation, and providing symbolic and instrumental support. The ability to utilize social support includes acceptance of what others say and the assistance they offer. Thus, the ability and motivation to provide social support in a relationship is a necessary but insufficient condition to guarantee its benefits; recipients must also possess the ability and the desire to utilize social support by others if the need arises (Coble, Gantt, & Mallinckrodt, 1996). Our results suggest that experiencing social support in families allows adult children to experience it in their subsequent adult relationships as well.

Another very interesting finding was that only men's ability to provide social support is affected by how supportive their families are. We expected both partners' reports of how supportive their partner is to be a function of that partner's family social support. Instead, only women's perceptions of their male partner's supportiveness were correlated to the male partner's family social support. Men's perceptions of their female partners' supportiveness did not correlate with females' reports of their families' supportiveness.

This finding cannot be explained by gender differences in how supportive partners are, because participants of both genders perceived their partners to be equally supportive.

This suggests that the family is a more important socialization agent for social support for boys than for girls. Women seem to be able to acquire social support skills independently from how supportive their own families are, potentially from their female friends or from a culture that often defines being female in terms of being supportive. In contrast, men are more dependent upon their families of origin for these important interpersonal skills. If they do not acquire these skills in their families, in a culture that does not value social support in males, they do not acquire them at all before entering into romantic relationships as adults. Given that our sample consisted of predominantly young couples, our data do not address the issue of whether men are able to learn to be more socially supportive in their romantic relationships. Future research will have to address this important question.

Gender Differences in Social Support and Relationship Satisfaction

A final interesting gender difference we observed was that only men's relationship satisfaction was affected by how supportive their female partners perceived them to be, but not women's relationship satisfaction. A possible explanation is that women care more about having supportive partners and somehow communicate their satisfaction or dissatisfaction with their male partners to them in a way that affects the male partners' relationship satisfaction. As a result, men who are more supportive are more satisfied than men who are not as supportive. Because we did not observe actual communication between partners, this explanation is very speculative and needs to be investigated in a further study.

Conclusion

Our research has demonstrated the importance of family communication patterns for children's experience of social support in families and their acquisition of this important interpersonal communication skill. Results of both studies show that conversation orientation in families is strongly associated with family social support for children. We also observed a number of negative correlations between conformity orientation and social support. These correlations, however, were never entirely consistent and appeared to be limited to children of families low in conversation-oriented families (study 1) or to boys (study 2). Still, even if the results for conformity orientation are not always consistent, it is clear that when conformity orientation has an effect, it is always a negative correlation with social support, never a positive one.

In addition to creating family environments that differ in the social support they provide for children, family communication patterns also play an important role in socializing children to be supportive in their own romantic relationships. For both men and women, growing up in a supportive family leads them to identify supportive partners and to elicit supportive behaviors from them. In regard to their own behaviors of supporting their partners, men are much more affected by their families than are women, whereas women seem able to learn supportive behaviors outside their families, men do not. Thus, it is particularly important for families with boys to provide them with social support because they are unlikely to acquire this important interpersonal skill outside the family. Both boys and girls, however, are happier in supportive families and this happiness translates into healthier and more supportive relationships as adults.

Questions for Consideration and Discussion

1. Koerner and Maki note the connection between parental (or other adult caregivers) social support expression and how children express support. What examples of this do you see in your experiences?

2. This article discussed six outcomes of social support (drawing from the work of Cutrona and Russell). What outcomes of social support have featured most prominently in your experiences, and how has that changed over time?

3. These scholars used the Revised Family Communication Patterns instrument that requires participants to rate statements about family communication. What are the benefits and drawbacks you see in this research design?

4. The studies here found conversation orientation to be more important in explaining later social support than conformity orientation. What might be the reason behind this relationship?

5. Koerner and Maki looked at how family communication patterns (conformity and conversation orientation) related to social support. What larger cultural effects may be in operation here?

References

Burleson, B. R., & Kunkel, A. W. (1996). The socialization of emotional support skills in childhood. In G. R. Pierce, B. R. Sarason, & I. G. Sarason (Eds.), *Handbook of social support and the family* (pp. 105–140). New York: Plenum Press.

Coble, H. M., Gantt, D. L., & Mallinckrodt, B. (1996). Attachment, social competency, and the capacity to use social support. In G. R. Pierce, B. R. Sarason, & I. G. Sarason (Eds.), *Handbook of social support and the family* (pp. 141–172). New York: Plenum Press.

Cutrona, C. E., & Russell, D. W. (1987). The provisions of social support and adaptation to stress. In W. H. Jones & D. Perlman (Eds.), *Advances in personal relationships* (pp. 37–67). Greenwich, CT: JAI Press.

Fitzpatrick, M. A., & Ritchie, L. D. (1994). Communication schemata within the family: Multiple perspectives on family interaction. *Human Communication Research, 20,* 275–301.

Huston, T. C., McHale, S. M., & Crouter, A. C. (1986). When the honeymoon's over: Changes in the marriage relationship over the first year. In R. Gilman & S. Duck (Eds.), *The emerging field of personal relationships* (pp. 109–132). Hillsdale, NJ: Erlbaum.

Koerner, A. F., & Cvancara, K. E. (2002). The influence of conformity orientation on communication patterns in family conversations. *Journal of Family Communication, 2,* 133–152.

Koerner, A. F., & Fitzpatrick, M. A. (1997). Family type and conflict: The impact of conversation orientation and conformity orientation on conflict in the family. *Communication Studies, 48,* 59–75.

Koerner, A. F., & Fitzpatrick, M. A. (2002a). Toward a theory of family communication. *Communication Theory, 12*(1), 70–91.

Koerner, A. F., & Fitzpatrick, M. A. (2002b). Understanding family communication patterns and family functioning: The roles of conversation orientation and conformity orientation. *Communication Yearbook, 26,* 37–69.

Koerner, A. F., & Fitzpatrick, M. A. (2002c). You never leave your family in a fight: The impact of family of origin on conflict behavior in adult children's romantic relationships. *Communication Studies, 53,* 234–251.

Koerner, A. F., & Fitzpatrick, M. A. (2004). Communication in intact families. In A. Vangelisti (Ed.), *Handbook of family communication* (pp. 177–195). Mahwah, NJ: Erlbaum.

Koesten, J., & Anderson, K. (2004). Exploring the influence of family communication patterns, cognitive complexity, and interpersonal competence on adolescent risk behaviors. *Journal of Family Communication, 4,* 99–121.

Noller, P. (1995). Parent–adolescent relationships. In M. A. Fitzpatrick & A. Vangelisti (Eds.), *Explaining family interactions* (pp. 77–111). Thousand Oaks, CA: Sage.

Ritchie, L. D., & Fitzpatrick, M. A. (1990). Family communication patterns: Measuring intrapersonal perceptions of interpersonal relationships. *Communication Research, 17,* 523–544.

Section 3: Conclusions and Application— Intimacy, Affection, and Social Support in Your Life

We all experience aspects of intimacy, affection, and social support in our relationships. Whether the material you read here seemed very like your experiences, or very divergent, you can apply the understandings gained here to your family experiences: assessing patterns of intimacy, affection, and social support; considering how those patterns relate to the relationships and the culture in which they are embedded; and planning for the future of your relationships.

Assessing Your Family Patterns

There are many dimensions of intimacy, affection, and social support that you might consider as you assess the patterns present in your own family (or families). As you read in this chapter, families and family members express affection in varying ways. The readings and research reported here suggest that mothers tend to be more physical in expressing affection to their children, whereas fathers tend to show less physical affection. However, both mothers and fathers show affection more to their daughters than to their sons. Dainton's writing also argued that women tend to do more routine maintenance of relationships, whereas men tend to do more strategic maintenance. How are these patterns reflected in your family setting? If they are not reflected in your family setting, you might consider why that is the case. If they are reflected in your family, knowing that these patterns are common may provide you some idea of why your parents or adult caregivers may have related to you and/or your siblings in these ways.

You also read in this chapter that social support provided in family settings tends to vary by the roles occupied by family members. Children tend to receive the most support. Grandparents get less support than children. Parents are the least likely to be provided with social support, but are the most likely to provide it to the other two groups. Does this seem similar to your experiences of family? What types of social support do your parents or adult caregivers provide you? What types do you provide them? If you provide less, why? How much social support do you provide to your grandparents or other older relatives? How much do they provide you? Are the types similar or different?

Staske-Bell argued that intimacy is something that is negotiated in communication with family members. As you consider your own family relationships, think about some times that you have recently engaged in the negotiation and creation of intimacy with family members. Do the ways that you negotiate intimacy vary from family member to family member? As you have grown up and developed more autonomy in your familial relationships, has this impacted the ways that intimacy is negotiated?

These questions are just a few that you might consider as you assess intimacy, social support, and affection in your family (or families). Thinking about and analyzing your family patterns may provide you with a new window of understanding for the family inter-action patterns you have experienced.

Thinking about How Your Family Patterns Relate to Your Relationships and Culture

In addition to analyzing the patterns of behavior your family has in relation to intimacy, affection, and social support, you may also wish to consider how those patterns relate to the relationships in that family and the larger cultural settings in which your family is embedded.

Koerner and Maki argued that many of our family communication patterns are passed down from parent to child, and then continue on into future romantic relationships, potentially resulting in a new family of procreation, where those patterns will be learned anew by a new generation. After you have assessed the patterns displayed in your family, consider how those patterns may have developed. One way to do this is to look at the inter-generational transmission of patterns within your family settings. Are the ways that your parents communicate with you similar to the ways that their parents communicated these positive emotions to them? You might also wish to take time to think about how you have replicated the patterns you learned from your parents in your own romantic relationships.

In addition to the intergenerational transmission of communication patterns, the readings in this chapter considered the impact of culture on how we show affection, inti-macy, and social support. Dainton's work indicated that the patterns she saw with relations to maintenance behaviors were not sex based—that is, they did not occur because women naturally behave one way and men naturally behave another way. Instead, these aspects related to the gendered expectations of men and women (masculinity and femininity). In terms of the expression of social support, the fact that children receive the most support is probably at least partly due to culture. In U.S. culture, we place a high value on children, and have low expectations of them providing support to others (even as they get older). We tend to see adults as very self-sufficient, and thus do not necessarily view them as needing much support from either their parents or their children. These are cultural beliefs that are likely impacting our relationships. How can you apply these cultural understandings to how your family members interact? If your family patterns do not seem to represent what is being discussed in this chapter, consider the possibility that other cultural settings than the mainstream (racial culture, ethnic culture) are impacting your family patterns.

As we interact with others, we often think of the way that we do things as the natural way that interaction should happen. "Of course," we might say, "women are more affec-tionate, because that is how women are." "The way my family interacts and shows affection is the normal way to do so." "Children get more social support because they just need it, and parents don't." Considering how intergenerational transmission and cultural expecta-tions impact the way these elements of family interaction are created allows us to engage in critical analysis of our own behaviors and the behaviors of others. It helps us stop taking for granted the patterns that have become so normal to us and consider the possibility of other options (or to celebrate our own patterns for what they are).

Planning for Your Future and Making Changes(?)

Engaging in assessment of our relational patterns and critical analysis as to how and why we have developed those patterns provides us with the information we need to think about our relational futures. At times, this may mean planning to attempt changes in our interactions. At other times, it may mean feeling comfortable that the way we are doing things is a good way and we should just stick to the same path.

As you saw throughout this chapter, research has suggested a positive relationship between affection, intimacy, social support, and the relational and individual health of family members. Affection in marital and other family relationships has been associated with satisfaction in those relationships. Likewise, emotional and other forms of social support have been shown to be correlated with satisfaction for particular family dyads and members. Although it isn't clear which element causes the other, it seems clear that these aspects of family relationships are connected.

Similarly, social support has been shown again and again to be positively correlated to better mental health for parents and children. The effects of social support on physical health have also been widely supported by research in communication, health fields, sociology, and so on. So, what do we do with this knowledge?

I think we would probably all like to have more relational satisfaction, have better mental health, and have increased physical health. Even if the causality of these relationships is not always clear, it stands to reason that increasing the extent to which we offer affection and social support to family members is probably a good idea. If, by doing so, we can increase the positive outcomes for loved ones, that's a good thing. Additionally, reciprocity is at work in family affection displays and negotiation of intimacy. If we exhibit more affection and social support to family members, they are likely to do so for us, and this may increase our own relational satisfaction, mental health, and physical health.

Of course, this process is not always easy. We need to carefully think about the analyses we have made of our family patterns, and where they come from (including both cultural and intergenerational elements). Bucking the trend is difficult to do. Care must be taken to not alienate family members or suggest that their ways of showing affection, intimacy, and support are wrong or bad. We need to remember that these patterns are processes of negotiation between family members.

Thinking about how we want to respond to (and replicate or not) cultural expectations of us as men and women is another part of how we can plan for our familial future in terms of affection, intimacy, and social support. The patterns of expectation in culture do shift and change over time, but change is slow and comes from the changes that individuals make in their own interactions. After considering the extent to which culture has impacted our displays of these positive family elements, we are better prepared to address whether we want to support gendered patterns of behavior in our relationships, or if we would like to move in the direction of considering what is most helpful to the relationship, and engaging in those behaviors regardless of our sex and the expectations thereof.

Although changing our current family patterns may be difficult and slow, it can be rewarding. Our future relationships can be impacted by these considerations. Additionally, because the transmission of these patterns is intergenerational, changes we make in our own lives can have long-term impacts on future generations, and that deserves some attention.

Questions for Consideration and Discussion

1. As you have grown from a child, to an adolescent, to an adult, how have your intimacy, affection, and social support been renegotiated in the relationships you have with your family members?
2. In your family of origin, what types of affectionate displays were most common? How do you think that has affected your own affection behaviors?
3. Were there differences between how men and women (or boys and girls) in your family showed affection? How can the work presented in this chapter help you understand those differences (or the lack thereof)?
4. What type of role models did you have for romantic affection when you were a child? How do you think those models affected your behavior in your own relationships as an adult?
5. Most researchers argue that person-centered support messages are more effective than those which are not person centered. Can you think of any situation in which a person-centered message may not be most effective?

Key Terms and Concepts

affection
emotional intimacy
emotional support
evolutionary psychologists
informational support

instrumental support
intellectual intimacy
intimacy
person centeredness
physical intimacy

recreational intimacy
social intimacy
social support

6

Power and Conflict in the Family

Chapter Outline

Chapter Objectives

1. To understand the nature of conflict
2. To understand the nature of power and its sources
3. To become aware of familial and cultural roots of family conflict and power processes
4. To see the outcomes of family conflict and power processes
5. To apply the material to your own understandings of conflict and family interactions

Section 1: Overview of Power and Conflict in Family Life _____

- When you hear the word *conflict*, what is the image that comes to your mind?
- If you envision a "perfect" family, how much conflict is there?
- How do you think your family experiences have shaped the way you think about and respond to conflict?

As a child, I vividly remember hearing my mother say "I am *sick* and *tired* of hearing you two argue!" Now, as a mother of six children, I know exactly what she meant. Hearing the arguments or squabbling of others isn't particularly enjoyable. And yet, conflict is an inevitable and even beneficial part of family life. In this chapter, we consider what conflict is, its relationship to power, the factors that affect how family members engage in conflict with one another, and the outcomes of conflict. Additionally, we address what happens when conflict becomes violent or otherwise abusive.

What Is Conflict?   *discursively*

Often, our conflicts with others stem from what we perceive as difference. It might be difference of opinion, difference in desires, difference in plans or goals, and so on (Koerner & Fitzpatrick, 2002). However, conflict is not simply about two people wanting different things, or one person being right and the other being wrong. Instead, **conflict** is a perception of difference developed in the interaction between relational partners as they discursively create positions and realities to which the other interactants respond (Sinclair & Monk, 2004). As we engage in communication with others, we cooperatively participate in creating our own position or reality about a point of disagreement, and we interact with others to do the same. This is why conflicts and the positions of the participants shift in the course of the interaction. At times, we may start a conflict about one issue, only to have it shift to something else. Or, we may believe that we know how we feel about a particular problem, only to realize that our position has changed in the course of a conflict. This is the interactive nature of the creation of conflict.

Every relationship has conflict (Sillars, Canary, & Tafoya, 2004). Conflict may occur in the form of argument, but it may not. Sometimes conflict goes unstated, yet it is still there in the interaction. Even when we don't acknowledge the conflict explicitly, it nonetheless exists. Conflicts can vary in their intensity and length, as well as in the number of relational members who participate. They can also have varying levels of impact on the participants and other members of the relational system. Family relationships are certainly no exception to these ideas.

Though we often think of conflict as a "bad" thing, it can actually be beneficial for the family system when it is managed constructively (Deutsch, 1973; Sillars et al., 2004). It is frequently through discussing our disagreements that we stimulate needed change in the family. If parents have established a 9:00 P.M. curfew for their child, and don't change that curfew as the child grows older, a conflict may prompt a reassessment of the age appropriateness of the time and possibly a change that is beneficial to family members. Conflict between family members can also serve to help members understand each other better. Although we tend to think that we know what our family members think about things (and this, in itself, sometimes produces conflict), at times it takes an argument to learn that a family member has an opinion or view that is surprising to us. And, as we have conflict with others, it often helps us understand our own ideas and beliefs more clearly (and to create those ideas and beliefs). While we talk to others about what we believe, and listen to and think about their responses, we clarify for ourselves what our own positions and opinions are. Thus, conflict should not be seen as something to be squashed in a family environment. Rather, we need to appreciate that conflict is as normal as (maybe even more normal than) peaceful agreement, and is an important part of family process.

How Is Power Related to Conflict?

Power can be defined as one's ability to influence others to act in a desired manner. Like other family phenomenon, power is relational. This means that an individual in a family has power to the extent that other family members grant or enable that power. Power is also not a unitary concept. There are different "sources" of power (but remember that regardless of source, power is only power if others grant it). Power can be based on "official" position in a system; this is called **legitimate power** (French & Raven, 1959). Power can stem from knowledge or things that a person knows how to do; this is called **expert power** (French & Raven, 1959). Power can be related to a person's attractiveness, whether that is physical, emotional, or otherwise, and how much we like that person; this is **referent power** (French & Raven, 1959). Power can also be related to ability to reward or punish others; these power bases are **reward power** and **coercive power** (French & Raven, 1959). So, different people can have power from different bases at different times. Generally, most people in a family system have some sort of power, even the people we might think of as being the "weaker" members.

Think about your family relationships. When you were just a baby, though you were ostensibly the weakest person in the family, you had power over your parents or adult caregivers because you could reward or punish them with your cries and coos. You also had power because of your baby cuteness (awwwww!). On the other hand, they had power over you because they had legitimate power (as parents), and also power based on knowledge and expertise. As you grew, power may have shifted. You gained some knowledge and expertise, so that provided an additional base of power to you. Your parents wanted your love and affection, so that too gave you a base of power. Your parents gained more ways to reward and punish you. (It's hard to really influence a newborn with rewards, but as a child ages, he or she becomes much more susceptible to reward offers.) When you became an adult, your parents lost some of their power over you (they can't ground you, or send you to your room: you've gained knowledge and expertise in some areas, and you have some of your own resources), yet, they can still affect you through rewards (gifts, affection, etc.), or punishment (withholding money, ignoring you, being upset with you). And, in your particular situation, your parents may have expertise or knowledge in specific areas that you don't have. Finally, parents maintain some sort of power because of their culturally defined position as parents. So, given the different bases on which power can rest, power is a negotiable concept within a particular family. Who is seen as having the most power, and when he or she has that power, is created through the interaction between family members and the acceptance or rejection of power moves.

Although power is negotiated within a particular family, cultural expectations of family roles also impact who has power in a family. We expect that adults will be more powerful, and have more control of resources that can be used to reward or to punish, than children. Therefore, it is not surprising that studies tend to show that parents typically do have more relational power than children or adolescents (Barber & Haddock, 2003). However, age is not the only cultural expectation that affects power. In American culture, we still maintain an expectation that men are more powerful than women. Barber and Haddock's (2003) research suggests that this is also true in family settings, where husbands, grandfathers, and even sons feel relatively more powerful than mothers, grandmothers, and daughters. This does not, of course, mean that children do not have some power over parents or that women don't have any power in their relationships with men. At times, we gain power through what is seen as a weakness (if you've ever said "but I don't know how to . . ." and gotten someone to do something for you, you've seen this in action). However, this study, and others like it, suggest that, on the whole, men feel themselves to have more power than women, and parents believe themselves to have more power than children (and these beliefs are relatively culturally supported).

The impact of such cultural beliefs about power is extensive. Culturally, we restrict parents' ability to punish children in some ways, but parents can still engage in corporal punishment in the United States. In no other relationship is hitting or spanking another considered appropriate or acceptable, but in the parent–child relationship, this is still culturally supported to some degree. In male–female relationships, physical punishments are no longer legal (though that hasn't been the case for a particularly long time). However, some scholars argue that physical punishment of women by men is still tacitly approved, or at least overlooked unless it gets "too bad" in many parts of American culture (Bent-Goodley, 2004; Locke & Richman, 1999). Additionally, the relative power of men over women in our culture can be seen in issues such as the distribution of household work. Even in homes where both partners work, women are likely to be responsible for the majority of household tasks and child care (Davis & Greenstein, 2004; Kroska, 2004). This is related to the power of men in U.S. culture.

Given all of these many issues that affect who has power, how, and in what ways, it is important that we think about power when considering conflict. After all, it is the power that is granted to us within relationships that affects who is more (or less) likely to achieve his or her final goals in a conflict situation.

In addition to the power that family members hold, how particular members handle conflict (often called **conflict management**) also impacts the outcomes of conflict within the family. Different families exhibit different arguing styles and, even within one family, various members will manage conflict at different ways at different moments in the relationship.

What Factors Affect How Family Members Engage in Conflict?

As you might guess, some scholars believe that individual characteristics impact how conflict management strategies are selected and used. For example, Jensen-Campbell, Gleason, Adams, and Malcolm (2003) studied the role of the personality characteristic of agreeableness in children. They found that children who had more agreeable personalities were better able to handle conflict in a constructive manner. Lee-Baggley, Preece, and DeLongis (2005) also found agreeableness, in addition to other personality factors, to be associated with effective conflict coping styles for adult partners in stepfamily relationships.

Cognitive Complexity

Another factor that has been seen as related to conflict management is how complex an individual's cognitions are. Scholars who follow a **constructivist** viewpoint argue that different people are more or less cognitively complex. A **social construct** is a descriptor of a characteristic that we believe another to have (e.g., nice, tall, teacher). Our constructs about others can be more or less abstract (for example, to say someone is nice is a more abstract construct than to say he or she is tall), can vary in number (a young child may have only a few constructs about another individual, whereas an adult may have many), and can be more or less connected or integrated to one another (you know someone is a teacher because he or she likes children . . . you have connected two constructs). People who are more **cognitively complex** have constructs that are more differentiated (numerically more), more abstract, and more integrated than those who are less complex (see Delia, O'Keefe, & O'Keefe, 1982). As individuals become more complex, they are able to create person-centered messages that are specifically oriented to their relational partners (Burleson, 1989; Clark & Delia, 1977) and thus those messages should be more successful. Because of this, constructivist scholars argue that cognitively complex individuals are able to handle conflict more effectively (Applegate, Burke, Burleson, Delia, & Kline, 1985; Applegate, Burleson, & Delia, 1992; Samter, 1994). Although cognitive complexity does not guarantee that an individual will produce effective messages, these scholars argue that this individual factor means that a person is capable of doing so.

Attributions

How individuals attribute responsibility for behaviors is an additional arena of social judgment that may impact conflict management. **Attribution theories** involve the way in which we explain our own behavior and the behavior of others (Manusov, 2006). In general, when we observe someone engaging in a particular behavior, either ourselves or someone else, we are often motivated to think about why that person did what he or she did. At times, we may think that the cause of a behavior is external to the individual (he or she did it because of a situational force out of his or her control), whereas other times we may believe that the behavior was caused by internal factors (he or she did it because of his or her personality or desires). As you might guess, how attributions are made can be important in conflict situations. If my son behaves poorly (let's say he says something extremely rude to his brother), I can attribute that behavior to the situation (his brother provoked it; he isn't feeling well today) or I can attribute that behavior to him (he's just rude). Which of these attributions I make will impact the character of the conflict to follow. Some research has indicated that more satisfied couples tend to attribute negative events to external causes, rather than to their partners. More dissatisfied couples or couples with violent relationships, on the other hand, tend to attribute negative events to their partners (Henning, Jones, & Holdford, 2005; Manusov, 1995, 2006; Sillars, Leonard, Roberts, & Dun, 2002). Similar results have been found with relation to how parents and children evaluate each other's behaviors (Fincham, Beach, Arias, & Brody, 1998; Wilson & Whipple, 2001) and for siblings (Matthews & Conger, 2004). Tendencies toward assigning particular types of attributions under particular circumstances are individual traits; however, scholars argue that those traits may stem in part from learned cultural and family patterns (Bugental & Johnston, 2000; Fincham et al., 1998; Matthews & Conger, 2004).

Parent Modeling and Couple Types

Various authors argue that family culture and how parents model and respond to emotional displays impact how children deal with conflict (Dumlao & Botta, 2000; Koerner & Fitzpatrick, 2002; Ramsden & Hubbard, 2002). In one research example of this, Rinaldi and Howe (2003) found that parental conflict management styles seemed to impact both parent–child conflict management and sibling conflicts. This suggests that the parental relationship both sets a tone for and models conflict behavior in other family relationships.

Given the impact that marital conflict management can have on the partners and the children in the family, understandings of marital conflict patterns are important to family communication study. Thus, some communication scholars have conducted research about marital conflict specifically, and based on that research have developed typologies of marital types. The basic argument here is that couples develop particular relational cultures that impact and are impacted by communication, and conflict management is an important part of that communication process. Two such scholars are Fitzpatrick and Gottman.

Fitzpatrick (1988) argues that heterosexual married couples can generally be divided into three types, based on their relational culture. Those types are traditionals, independents, and separates. **Traditional couples** tend to have a high degree of conformity with traditional sex-role expectations in the relationship; they are very interdependent with one another, and although they dislike conflict, they will engage in it when necessary to produce agreement. **Independent couples** tend to be more flexible with regard to sex roles; they are more independent of one another, though they still share (in terms of time and communication). They do not fear conflict and expression of personal difference. **Separate couples** tend to be fairly conservative in their views about sex roles, but live somewhat separate lives with little sharing. They try to avoid conflict when possible. Fitzpatrick argues that some couples may be a combination of the three, with one partner expressing more of one style, and the other one another. The couple types designated by Fitzpatrick tend to respond to conflict in a way that corresponds to how they understand intimacy and roles in the marriage (Sillars et al., 2004).

Gottman's (1994) work focuses even more strongly on conflict in his classification of marital styles. Gottman argues that successful couples are those that tend to exhibit one of

BOX 6.1 • *Internet Connection*

Based on their work with couples, researchers at the Gottman Institute believe they can predict marital success and help couples be more satisfied with their relationships. You can read more about it at www.gottman.com/.

three types of conflict styles. He terms these validating, volatile, and conflict avoiding. **Validating couples** are couples that "fight nice." These couples tend to have medium levels of both conflict and passion in their relationships. When they argue, they do so with respectfulness and strong attention to the relationship over personal needs (this type of conflict style might be expected from Fitzpatrick's traditional type). **Volatile couples** are those that have high levels of conflict, but also high levels of passion. They hold strong personal opinions and like to "win" an argument, but they also express high levels of affection for their partners at nonconflict times (this is parallel to Fitzpatrick's independent type). **Conflict avoiding couples** do not like conflict and prefer to ignore areas of disagreement. They often have low levels of both conflict and passion (this would be like Fitzpatrick's separate type). Gottman argues that it doesn't matter what style of conflict management is used; they can all be successful. What is important, he claims, is that the two partners are both using the same style, and that overall the positive communication moments in the relationship far outweigh the negative ones. Table 6.1 summarizes Fitzpatrick and Gottman Couple types.

The conflict styles parents develop may have far-reaching effects in the family system. As noted previously, when children observe their parents arguing in a certain fashion, they may understand this to be the way that people, or at least people in their family, deal with conflict (Sillars et al., 2004). And, the impact of this learning goes even further Koerner and Fitzpatrick (2002) note that the patterns we develop in our family of origin, with regard to conflict management, are often carried into our later romantic relationships (see also Andrews, Foster, Capaldi, & Hops, 2000). This means that these patterns may

TABLE 6.1 *Couple Types and Conflict*

Fitzpatrick's Couple Types	*Gottman's Couple Types*
Traditional couples—conservative sex roles, very interdependent, will conflict when necessary	Validating couples—medium level of passion and conflict; fight nicely when needed
Independent couples—flexible sex roles, more independent but still sharing, not afraid to conflict	Volatile couples—high level of passion and conflict; fight more frequently and with high intensity
Separate couples—conservative sex roles, very independent, avoid conflict	Conflict avoiding couples—lower levels of passion and conflict; avoid fighting if possible

then be reproduced for our own children, and so on. At times, the patterns we learn in the family may be constructive patterns that will help us in our future relationships. Unfortunately, children sometimes learn negative patterns of conflict in the family of origin and then carry those patterns into their families of procreation.

Research suggests that if children are exposed to parental violence they are more likely to reproduce that violence in their later romantic relationships (Kinsfogel & Grych, 2004; Lichter & McCloskey, 2004). It may seem odd that someone who sees violence as a child (and possibly even experiences that violence visited upon himself or herself) would then become violent with others, but we probably should not be surprised. The things that we see and hear when we are children have a strong impact on us throughout our lives and can become what we revert to when we are unsure of how to proceed. This does not mean that those individuals who were exposed to poor, or even violent, conflict management strategies as children cannot overcome that as adults and choose better ways to handle conflict. They can, and often do. What it does mean is that it is more difficult for people who have not had good conflict management modeled for them as children to "come up" with their own better strategies.

Cultural Patterns

In addition to the impact of family culture on how we "do conflict," the larger cultures in which the family is embedded are also related to conflict patterns. For example, gendered expectations of behavior developed through cultural socialization impact the use of particular conflict strategies. Boxer (2002) suggests that women, being less powerful in the U.S. culture, are more likely to engage in "nagging" than men. This finding is certainly compatible with our commonsense stereotype of women as "nags." From Boxer's (2002) perspective, women are more likely to have their first request ignored, dismissed, or overlooked. Thus, they feel pressed to repeat the request in order to get the desired behavior enacted. When it is again ignored, they are again pressed to repeat. Because women are not expected to be as vocally aggressive as men, each request may be fairly calmly stated (though some degree of increasing frustration is likely reflected in the tone used). So, women become the nags of the relationship. Men, on the other hand, are less likely to nag and more likely to use forceful requests. Because their requests get responded to more quickly, they are not put in a position of needing to repeat themselves again and again (Boxer, 2002). Again, it should be noted that studies that make claims about sex or gender differences are generalized statements. This does not mean that every woman nags or that no man does. Instead, this study simply indicates that, due to our cultural expectations about men and women, women are put in a position that makes it more likely that they will resort to nagging more often.

BOX 6.2 • *Did You Know?*

British Labour politician Lady Edith Summerhill once said: "Nagging is the repetition of unpalatable truths" (www.bartleby.com).

Cultural views about gendered behavior are not the only way that culture affects our conflict management techniques. In a study of individuals in Germany, Japan, the United States, and Mexico, Oetzel and colleagues (2003) found that national culture had an impact on how family members engaged in conflict with one another. Their study indicated that people in more individualistic cultures, like the United States and Germany, tend to be more concerned with maintaining their own face (how they appear to others and their sense of individual power) in conflict and are more defensive than people from collectivist cultures, like Japan and Mexico. Even within the individualistic culture pair and the collectivist culture pair, the researchers found specific differences in conflict management that appeared to be culturally created. German participants were more direct and confrontational in their conflict style than participants from the United States. Japanese participants were more expressive in conflict style than were the participants from Mexico (see also Ting-Toomey, Oetzel, & Yee-jung, 2001).

Differences in culture may also affect how abusive or violent conflict tactics are used and responded to in a family setting. In her 2004 report of research, Gill argues that the South Asian women she studied were reluctant to report violent behaviors in their marital relationships, or even to define these behaviors as abusive. Gill notes that cultural concepts of shame and honor in relation to family were largely responsible for the silence of these women about their situations. Similarly, West (2004), Bent-Goodley (2004), and Kasturirangan, Krishnan, and Riger (2004) argue that sociodemographic, socioeconomic, and sociopolitical factors affect the amount and type of familial abuse experienced by women of minority racial or ethnicity status, as well as impacting how that abuse is responded to by the victims. Anderson (1997) found that cultural expectations of masculinity seemed to be a part of the creation of violent relationships within families. In the families she studied, when men were less economically powerful within their marital relationships (that is, their wives made more money), the likelihood of them becoming violent increased (see also Harrell, 1990). She suggests that this is because manliness, in American culture, is associated with the provider role. When men are unable to take on that role, they may more strongly exhibit other "masculine" characteristics (such as aggression) in order to compensate. In a similar finding, Harrell found that husbands who were less masculine (and therefore perhaps less likely to feel the need to prove that masculinity behaviorally) exhibited less relational aggression and violence. Thus, we can see that culture affects not only how conflict is handled, in general, but also impacts when and if more violent or abusive strategies are implemented within family settings and how that violence is responded to by family members.

The way that family members engage in conflict is impacted by a variety of factors. These factors include individual abilities or differences, family culture and socialization, and the socialization we receive from the larger cultures in which the family is embedded. As you will see in the next part of the chapter, similar issues are in action in how conflicts affect the family members.

What Are the Outcomes of Conflict?

Many researchers suggest that it is not the amount of conflict, or even the issues under discussion, that most impacts how conflict affects our relationships overall. Instead, how conflict is managed and how relational partners respond to that management style are extremely influential with regard to conflict effects (Sillars et al., 2004).

Couple Conflict

In addition to the consideration of overall conflict style, scholars have noted that some conflict management techniques seem to be more effective and positive for couples. In this body of work, they conclude that the use of positive affect messages, like the use of humor and showing verbal and physical affection, both during and preceding conflict, was correlated with better relational stability and satisfaction. Additionally, expressions of support and reassurance for the partner, the use of problem solving, and calm discussion have been found to be effective strategies overall in couple conflict management (for discussions see Cummings & Davies, 1994; Driver & Gottman, 2004; Gottman, Coan, Swanson, & Carrere, 1998; Gottman, Markman, & Notarius, 1977; Julien, Chartrand, Simard, Bouthillier, & Begin, 2003; Notarius & Markman, 1993; Stanley, Markman, and Whitton, 2002).

Researchers have also found particular behaviors to be ineffective in management of couple conflict. For example, the use of negative affect messages was correlated with poorer stability and more dissatisfaction. Other negative strategies noted in research include verbal and nonverbal hostility, threats, physical aggression, personal insults and defensiveness (see, for example, Cummings & Davies, 1994; Driver & Gottman, 2004; Notarius & Markman, 1993). One particular negative management strategy that has received extensive attention is the use of demand–withdraw patterns in conflict. A **demand–withdraw pattern** occurs when one relational partner attempts to talk about an issue ("demands" communication), while the other partner refuses to discuss it ("withdraws" from communication). Scholars such as Caughlin and Vangelisti (1999, 2000), Caughlin and Malis (2004), and Gottman and Levenson (2000) argue that this pattern of conflict management can be harmful to the happiness of relational members. Caughlin and Malis (2004) studied conflicts between adolescents and their parents. Their research revealed that, regardless of the amount of conflict present in the relationship, adolescents and parents reported less relational satisfaction as the incidence of demand–withdraw patterns of conflict management increased. When demand–withdraw patterns exist, one member of the relational dyad repeatedly makes criticisms or requests with regard to the conflict issue, sometimes called nagging (Boxer, 2002), while the other relational partner attempts to avoid discussing the conflict issue at all. This type of pattern is unsatisfactory for both partners in the interaction. The person who is doing the repeated demanding (or nagging) sees the issue as something important that needs to be discussed, and may feel ignored or like the other person doesn't care. The individual doing the withdrawing does not want to talk about the problem (perhaps he or she sees it as a nonissue, or as not solvable) and likely feels that he or she is being pestered by the other in an annoying manner. So, it isn't too surprising that such a pattern isn't good for the satisfaction of either partner.

Which strategies are most effective in particular couple conflict situations is complex and dependent upon a variety of factors. One factor that may impact conflict effects is the sex, or gender, of the participants. Some research has suggested that, in the demand–withdraw pattern, women may be more likely to demand, whereas men may be more likely to withdraw (Caughlin & Vangelisti, 1999). Caughlin and Vangelisti (2000) argue that this may be related to the fact that women, in general, are culturally taught to have greater need for connection, whereas men are taught to have greater need for autonomy. Thus, women are more likely to attempt to discuss the issues, whereas men withdraw from such discussion. Similarly, Roberts (2000) found that men and women were affected differently by various conflict management styles of their spouses. Women's marital satisfaction was more associated with their husband's hostility of response (that is, as husbands' hostility in conflict management increased, wives' satisfaction decreased). Husbands, on the other hand, were more affected when their wives withdrew from the conflict (that is, their satisfaction level tended to decrease as their wives withdrawal increased). This response is probably partly due to our cultural expectations. Women are expected to be emotionally available to others, so men may be particularly surprised when their wives don't want to talk about problems. From findings like this, it appears that, within the adult partner dyad, conflict management styles are more important than the amount of conflict in terms of the health of the relationship. Similar outcomes have been found in relation to how the parental conflict affects children in the family.

Scholars have found that the problem behaviors of youths are more associated with how their parents handle conflict than with the amount of conflict the parents have. That is, having parents that argue frequently does not seem related to poor child behaviors, but having parents who argue destructively does seem to be related to poor child behaviors. Buehler and colleagues (1998) found that hostile parental conflict styles were most predictive of both internalizing (i.e., depression, anxiety) and externalizing (i.e., disruptive behavior) problem behaviors for youth, regardless of whether they were boys or girls, preadolescents or adolescents, in divorced or intact families, or were poor or not poor. Katz and Woodin (2002) also found a strong effect on children and families based on how parents managed marital conflict. They applied one of three classifications to each parental couple, based on conflict style. Hostile–couples were those who showed negative speaker behaviors in conflict. Hostile-withdrawn couples were those who exhibited both negatives speaker and negative listener behaviors in conflict. Engaged couples were those who showed positive behaviors in both speaking and listening. In their study, Katz and Woodin encountered significant differences in the families of these couples. Couples who enacted hostile–withdrawn behaviors during conflict were most likely to have families that were less cohesive and playful. The parents had more problems coparenting their children as well. These couples' children were, as in the Buehler et al. (1998) study, more likely to also exhibit behavioral problems. On the other hand, couples who utilized constructive conflict management strategies were more likely to have happier families and more behaviorally, socially and psychologically well-adjusted children (Beuhler et al., 1998; Cummings, Goeke-Morey, Papp, & Dukewich, 2002; Katz & Woodin, 2002).

Parental Discipline and Decision Making

Another area of conflict management and power negotiation between family members relates to parental discipline and decision making. Disciplining of children is fundamentally related to conflict, as disciplinary moments often arise when there is a perceived conflict between the desires or tendencies of the child and those of the parent (even if the discipline involves a proactive strategy on the part of parents to prevent a child from engaging in particular behaviors in the future). Studies indicate that parents discipline and monitor children using a variety of styles, and that different styles tend to have different impacts on children and on the parent–child relationship (see Wilson & Morgan, 2004, for a review). The four primary parenting and discipline styles that are often referred to in research are authoritarian, authoritative, permissive, and rejecting-neglecting parenting (Baumrind, 1971, 1991). **Authoritarian parenting** is parenting with very high levels of control, but low levels of warmth and responsiveness.

Authoritative parenting is parenting characterized by consistent, warm, and accepting parenting with firm discipline strategies that involve clear explanation of standards for behavior. **Permissive parenting** involves parenting with high levels of warmth, but very low levels of control or discipline. **Rejecting-neglecting parenting** is parenting that has low levels of warmth and acceptance and also discipline and control. Studies have indicated that, generally, authoritative parenting strategies have the most positive outcomes for children and adolescents in psychological, relational, and educational domains (Bronte-Tinkew, Moore, & Carrano, 2006; Dornbusch, Ritter, Leiderman, Roberts, & Fraleigh, 1987; Kauffman et al., 2000; Lamborn, Mounts, Steinberg, & Dornbusch, 1991). However, here too we see the impact of culture, with some studies indicating that very high levels of control (which would generally be seen as authoritarian) may be most effective in African American family settings, and this may be related to socioeconomic issues leading to residing in communities that hold more dangers for children. Additionally, these studies suggest that the extremely strict control is most beneficial when paired with a greater degree of warmth in the mother–child relationship, which would be a style sort of "in between" authoritative and authoritarian (Wilson & Morgan, 2004). Overall, these results suggest that, although discipline is often a source of conflict between parents and children, firm and consistent discipline, if paired with warm and responsive parenting it is helpful to outcomes for children and adolescents in many cultural settings. Of course, that doesn't always mean that the children and teenagers will like it!

Family Violence

When conflict escalates to violence, outcomes can be both troubling and dramatic, **Family violence** can be defined as physical, psychological, or sexual abuse occurring between family members. This definition includes partner violence, child abuse, sibling abuse, elder abuse, and child-to-parent abuse. It also includes violence that occurs both nonverbally (hitting, punching, sexual assault), and verbally (name calling, belittling, threatening). We would all hope that the extent of violence in family settings is limited, but studies suggest that this is not the case.

Family violence is a hidden part of the family experience that occurs throughout the world. The National Center for Injury Prevention and Control (NCIP, a division of the Centers for Disease Control and Prevention) in the United States indicates that over 20 percent of Americans have experienced partner violence (NCIP, 2006). Cantalupo, Martin, Pak, and Shin (2006) note that approximately one in three women in Ghana have experienced physical abuse from a partner, and similar findings have been reported in Spain (Ruiz-Pérez, Plazaola-Castaño, & del Rio-Lozano, 2006) and Tanzania (McCloskey, Williams, & Larsen, 2005). In a study of different countries conducted by the World Health Organization, between 20 percent and 75 percent of women across the countries had experienced intimate partner violence (Fathalla, 2005). Child abuse in family settings is also common. Statistics for child abuse rates are somewhat more difficult to obtain, as the reporting and standards of child abuse varies from culture to culture, and children are less often the participants in research studies. However, in 2004, almost 900,000 children were found to have been abused in the United States, and this number is likely significantly lower than the number of children actually experiencing familial abuse (Administrartion for Children and Families [ACF], 2004). As considered previously in this chapter, many scholars argue that, in part, the level of family violence in various settings has arisen from cultural acceptance of familial violence, or at least a refusal to acknowledge its existence, that serves to facilitate its continuation. Thus, cultural understandings about family, family roles, and family practices are an important consideration in the study of family violence and abuse.

The potential outcomes of family violence are startling. Violence between domestic partners or from parent to child can lead to physical problems ranging from stress-related illnesses to death (Arias, 2004; Bent-Goodley, 2004). Psychological difficulties, including chronic depression, posttraumatic stress disorder, and suicidal thoughts are also common for victims of domestic violence (Arias, 2004; Bent-Goodley, 2004). For children, domestic abuse and violence is also associated with behavioral problems (Moran, Vuchinich, & Hall, 2004; Salzinger et al., 2002). Family violence impacts how children understand the nature of family as well. Winstok, Eisikovits, and Karnieli-Miller (2004) argue that adolescents who have seen father-to-mother violence in the home are unable to form a coherent mental understanding of their family and its members. Additionally, as the violence escalated, the adolescents studied became more distant from the father. As noted previously, children who observe negative conflict patterns, including violent behavior, in their families of origin are more likely to go on to reproduce those same patterns with their own families (Kinsfogel & Grych, 2004; Lichter & McCloskey, 2004). Cottrell and Monk (2004) also note that adolescents who become abusive to their parents have likely either been abused by them or have witnessed abuse between their parents. So, an additional problematic effect of violent behavior exhibited by parents is that it may then be replicated in other family relationships.

Abusive behaviors in family are not always between adults or perpetrated on children or adolescents by adults. At times, adolescents and children may abuse each other or abuse their parents (Cottrell & Monk, 2004; Eckstein, 2004; Paulson, Coombs, & Landsverk 1990). Eckstein (2004) and Cottrell and Monk (2004) indicate that adolescent-to-parent abuse makes it difficult for parents to feel good about their role as parents. When parents are abused by their children, they may feel both shame and guilt. Shame may stem from the sense of embarrassment that their child (one whom they should have power over) is taking power over them. Guilt can come from feeling that they have done something in the upbringing of the abusive child to make him or her violent in this way. Child-to-parent abuse may be unlikely to be reported due to this combination of shame and guilt, in addition to the love and loyalty the parent feels for the child.

From this portion of the research about conflict effects on family members, it is clear that those effects are rather complicated. Conflict is not, in and of itself, dangerous or problematic to a family and its members; however, how that conflict is managed or enacted can have significant impact on the participants and those around them.

BOX 6.3 • *Family in the News*

Elder abuse, neglect, or violence directed toward the elderly made national news again in July 2006, as the son of Brooke Astor, a 104-year-old multimillionaire and former socialite, was accused of neglecting and abusing her. Although elder abuse in the family is not frequently talked about, it is not as uncommon as you may think. Visit the National Center on Elder Abuse Web site for additional information, at www.elderabusecenter.org/.

Power and conflict in the family setting is an inevitable, and functional, part of life. Families encounter conflicts for a variety of reasons, deal with them in many ways, and the outcomes of those interactions are multiple. In Section 2, you will read about specific research that has been done with regard to family conflict. The articles consider family roles in conflict; adolescent abuse of parents, and how parents attempt to manage and avoid abusive interaction; and the role of culture in the creation of conflict management strategies. As you read these articles, and think about your own conflict interactions and the impact that your family of origin has had on your views of the appropriateness of particular types of conflict styles, and how effective (or not) you find those styles in your own relationships.

References

Administration for Children and Familes. (2004). *Child maltreatment 2004*. Retrieved August 1, 2006, from the U.S. Department of Health and Human Services Web site: http://www.acf.hhs.gov/programs/cb/pubs/cm04/index.htm

Anderson, K. L. (1997). Gender, status, and domestic violence: An integration of feminist and family violence approaches. *Journal of Marriage and Family, 59*(3), 655–669.

Andrews, J. A., Foster, S. L., Capaldi, D., & Hops, H. (2000). Adolescent and family predictors of physical aggression, communication, and satisfaction in young adult couples: A prospective analysis. *Journal of Consulting and Clinical Psychology, 68*, 895–915.

Applegate, J. L., Burke, J. A., Burleson, B. R., Delia, J. G., & Kline, S. L. (1985). Reflection-enhancing parental communication. In I. E. Sigel (Ed.), *Parental belief systems: The psychological consequences for children* (pp. 107–142). Hillsdale, NJ: Erlbaum.

Applegate, J. L., Burleson, B. R., & Delia, J. G. (1992). Reflection-enhancing parenting as antecedent to children's social-cognitive and communicative development. In I. E. Sigel, A. V. McGillicuddy-Delisi, & J. J. Goodnow (Eds.), *Parental belief systems: The psychological consequences for children* (2nd ed., pp. 3–39). Hillsdale, NJ: Erlbaum.

Arias, I. (2004). The legacy of child maltreatment: Long-term health consequences for women. *Journal of Women's Health, 13*(5), 468–473.

Barber, C. E., & Haddock, S. A. (2003). Self-perceptions of comparative power and worth in three generational families. *Contemporary Family Therapy, 25*(2), 229–245.

Baumrind, D. (1971). Current patterns of parental authority. *Developmental Psychology Monograph, 4*, 1–103.

Baumrind, D. (1991). Parenting styles and adolescent development. In J. Brooks-Gunn, R. M. Lerner, & A. C. Petersen (Eds.), *The encyclopedia on adolescence* (pp. 746–758). New York: Garland.

Bent-Goodley, T. (2004). Perceptions of domestic violence: A dialogue with African American women. *Health and Social Work, 29*(4), 307–316.

Boxer, D. (2002). Nagging: The familial conflict arena. *Journal of Pragmatics, 34*, 49–61.

Bronte-Tinkew, J., Moore, K. A., & Carrano, J. (2006). The father–child relationship, parenting styles, and adolescent risk behaviors in intact families. *Journal of Family Issues, 27*(6), 850–881.

Buehler, C., Krishnakumar, A., Stone, G., Anthony, C., Pemberton, S., Gerard, J., et al. (1998). Interparental conflict styles and youth problem behavior: A two-sample replication study. *Journal of Marriage and Family, 60*(1), 119–132.

Bugental, D. B., & Johnston, C. (2000). Parental and child cognitions in the context of the family. *Annual Review of Pyschology, 51*, 315–344.

Burleson, B. R. (1989). The constructivist approach to person-centered communication: Analysis of a research exemplar. In B. A. Dervin, L. Grossberg, B. J. O'Keefe, and E. Wartella (Eds.), *Rethinking communication: Vol. 2. Paradigm exemplars.* Newbury Park, CA: Sage.

Cantalupo, N., Martin, L. V., Pak, K., & Shin, S. (2006). Domestic violence in Ghana: The open secret. *Georgetown Journal of Gender and the Law, 7*, 531–597.

Caughlin, J. P., & Malis, R. S. (2004). Demand or withdraw communication between parents and adolescents as a correlate of relational satisfaction. *Communication Reports, 17*(2), 59–71.

Caughlin, J. P., & Vangelisti, A. L. (1999). Desire for change in one's partner as a predictor of the demand-withdraw pattern of marital communication. *Communication Monographs, 66*, 66–89.

Caughlin, J. P., & Vangelisti, A. L. (2000). An individual difference explanation of why married couples engage in demand/withdraw pattern of conflict. *Journal of Social and Personal Relationships, 17*, 523–551.

Clark, R. A., & Delia, J. G. (1977). Cognitive complexity, social perspective-taking and functional persuasive skills in second- to ninth-grade children. *Human Communication Research, 3*, 128–134.

Cottrell, B., & Monk, P. (2004). Adolescent-to-parent abuse: A qualitative overview of common themes. *Journal of Family Issues, 25*(8), 1072–1095.

Cummings, E. M., & Davies, P. T. (1994). *Children and marital conflict: The impact of family dispute and resolution*. New York: Guilford Press.

Cummings, E. M., Goeke-Morey, M. C., Papp, L. M., & Dukewich, T. L. (2002). Children's responses to mothers' and fathers' emotionality and tactics in marital conflict in the home. *Journal of Family Psychology, 16*(4), 478–492.

Davis, S. N., & Greenstein, T. N. (2004). Cross-national variations in the division of labor. *Journal of Marriage and Family, 66*(5), 1260–1271.

Delia, J., O'Keefe, B. J., & O'Keefe, D. J. (1982). The Constructivist approach to communication. In F. E. X. Dance (Ed.), *Human communication theory: Comparative essays* (pp. 147–191). New York: Harper & Row.

Deutsch, M. (1973). *The resolution of conflict: Constructive and destructive processes*. New Haven, CT: Yale University Press.

Dornbusch, S. M., Ritter, P. L., Leiderman, P., Roberts, D., & Fraleigh, M. (1987). The relation of parenting style to adolescent school performance. *Child Development, 58*, 1244–1257.

Driver, J. L., & Gottman, J. M. (2004). Daily marital interactions and positive affect during marital conflict among newlywed couples. *Family Process, 43*(3), 301–314.

Dumlao, R., & Botta, R. A. (2000). Family communications patterns and the conflict styles young adults use with their fathers. *Communication Quarterly, 48*(2), 174–199.

Eckstein, N. J. (2004). Emergent issues in families experiencing adolescent-to-parent abuse. *Western Journal of Communication, 68*(4), 365–388.

Fathalla, M. F. (2005). When home is no longer safe: Intimate-partner violence. *Lancet, 366*(9501), 1910–1911.

Fincham, F. D., Beach, R. H., Arias, I., & Brody, G. H. (1998). Children's attributions in the family: The children's relationship attribution measure. *Journal of Family Psychology, 12*, 481–482.

Fitzpatrick, M. A. (1988). *Between husbands and wives: Communication in marriage*. Newbury Park, CA: Sage.

French, J. R. P., Jr., & Raven, B. H. (1959). The bases of social power. In D. Cartwright (Ed.), *Studies in social power* (pp. 150–167). Ann Arbor, MI: Institute for Social Research.

Gill, A. (2004). Voicing the silent fear: South Asian women's experiences of domestic violence. *Howard Journal of Criminal Justice, 43*(5), 465–483.

Gottman, J. (1994). *What predicts divorce: The relationship between marital processes and marital outcomes*. Hillsdale, NJ: Erlbaum.

Gottman, J., Coan, J., Swanson, C., & Carrere, S. (1998). Predicting marital happiness and stability from newlywed interactions. *Journal of Marriage and Family, 60*, 5–22.

Gottman, J., Markman, H., & Notarius, C. (1997). The topography of marital conflict: A sequential analysis of verbal and nonverbal behavior. *Journal of Marriage and Family, 39*(3), 461–477.

Gottman, J. M., & Levenson, R. W. (2000). The timing of divorce: Predicting when a couple will divorce over a 14-year period. *Journal of Marriage and Family, 39*, 461–477.

Harrell, W. A. (1990). Husband's masculinity, wife's power, and marital conflict. *Social Behavior and Personality, 18*(2), 207–216.

Henning, K., Jones, A., & Holdford, R. (2005). "I didn't do it, but if I did I had a good reason": Minimization, denial, and attributions of blame among male and female domestic violence offenders. *Journal of Family Violence, 20*(3), 131–139.

Jensen-Campbell, L. A., Gleason, K. A., Adams, R., & Malcolm, K. T. (2003). Interpersonal conflict, agreeableness, and personality development. *Journal of Personality, 71*(6), 1059–1085.

Julien, D., Chartrand, E., Simard, M., Bouthillier, D., & Begin, J. (2003). Conflict, social support, and relationship quality: An observational study of heterosexual, gay male, and lesbian couples' communication. *Journal of Family Psychology 17*(3), 419–428.

Kasturirangan, A., Krishnan, S., & Riger, S. (2004). The impact of culture and minority status on women's experience of domestic violence. *Violence and Abuse, 5*(4), 318–332.

Katz, L. F., & Woodin, E. M. (2002). Hostility, hostile detachment, and conflict engagement in marriages: Effects on child and family functioning. *Child Development, 73*(2), 636–652.

Kaufmann, D., Gesten, E., Santa Lucia, R. C., Salcedo, O., Rendina-Gobioff, G., & Gadd, R. (2000). The relationship between parenting style and children's adjustment: The parents' perspective. *Journal of Child and Family Studies, 9*(2), 231–245.

Kinsfogel, K. M., & Grych, J. H. (2004). Interparental conflict and adolescent dating relationships: Integrating cognitive, emotional, and peer influences. *Journal of Family Psychology, 18*(3), 505–515.

Koerner, A. F., & Fitzpatrick, M. A. (2002). You never leave your family in a fight: The impact of family of origin on conflict-behavior in romantic relationships. *Communication Studies, 53*(3), 234–251.

Kroska, A. (2004). Division of domestic work. *Journal of Family Issues, 25*(7), 900–931.

Lamborn, S., Mounts, N., Steinberg, L., & Dornbusch, S. M. (1991). Patterns of competence and adjustment among adolescents from authoritative, authoritarian, indulgent, and neglectful families. *Child Development, 62*, 1049–1065.

Lee-Baggley, D., Preece, M., & DeLongis, A. (2005). Coping with interpersonal stress: Role of the big five traits. *Journal of Personality, 73*(5), 1141–1180.

Lichter, E. L., & McCloskey, L. A. (2004). The effects of childhood exposure to martial violence on adolescent gender-role beliefs and dating violence. *Psychology of Women Quarterly, 28*(4), 344–357.

Locke, L. M., & Richman, C. L. (1999). Attitudes toward domestic violence: Race and gender issues. *Sex Roles, 40*(3–4), 227–247.

Manusov, V. (1995). Intentionality attributions for naturally-occurring nonverbal behaviors in intimate relationships. In J. E. Aitken & L. J. Shedletsky (Eds.), *Intrapersonal communication processes* (pp. 343–353). Plymouth, MI: Midnight Oil.

Manusov, V. (2006). Attribution theories: Assessing causal and responsibility judgments in families. In D. O. Braithwaite & L. A. Baxter (Eds.), *Engaging theories in family communication: Multiple perspectives* (pp. 181–196). Thousand Oaks, CA: Sage.

Matthews, L. S., & Conger, R. D. (2004). "He did it on purpose!" Family correlates of negative attributions about an adolescent sibling. *Journal of Research on Adolescence, 14*(3), 257–284.

McCloskey, L. A., Williams, C., & Larsen, U. (2005). Gender inequality and intimate partner violence among women in Moshi, Tanzania. *International Family Planning Perspectives, 31*(3), 124–130.

Moran, P. B., Vuchinich, S., & Hall, N. K. (2004). Associations between types of maltreatment and substance use during adolescence. *Child Abuse & Neglect, 28*(5), 565–574.

National Center for Injury Prevention and Control. (2006). *Intimate partner violence: Fact sheet.* Retrieved August 1, 2006, from the Centers for Disease Control and Prevention Web site: http://www.cdc.gov/ncipc/factsheets/ipvfacts.htm

Notarius, C., & Markman, H. J. (1993). *We can work it out: Making sense of marital conflict.* New York: Putnam.

Oetzel, J., Ting-Toomey, S., Chew-Sanchez, M. I., Harris, R., Wilcox, R., & Stumpf, S. (2003). Face and facework in conflicts with parents and siblings: A cross-cultural comparison of Germans, Japanese, Mexicans, and U.S. Americans. *Journal of Family Communication, 3*(2), 67–93.

Paulson, M. J., Coombs, R. H., & Landsverk, J. (1990). Youth who physically assault their parents. *Journal of Family Violence, 5*(2), 121–133.

Ramsden, S. R., & Hubbard, J. A. (2002). Family expressiveness and parental emotion coaching: Their role in children's emotion regulation and aggression. *Journal of Abnormal Child Psychology, 30*(6), 657–667.

Rinaldi, C. M., & Howe, N. (2003). Perceptions of constructive and destructive conflict within and across family subsystems. *Infant and Child Development, 12*, 441–459.

Roberts, L. J. (2000). Fire and ice in marital communication: Hostile and distancing behaviors as predictors of marital distress. *Journal of Marriage and Family, 62*(3), 693–707.

Ruiz-Pérez, I., Plazaola-Castaño, J., & del Rio-Lozano, M. (2006). How do women in Spain deal with an abusive relationship. *Journal of Epidemiology & Community Health, 60*(8), 706–711.

Salzinger, S., Feldman, R. S., Ng-Mak, D. S., Mojica, E., Stockhammer, T., & Rosario, M. (2002). Effects of partner violence and physical child abuse on child behavior: A study of abused and comparison children. *Journal of Family Violence, 17*(1), 23–52.

Samter, W. (1994). Unsupportive relationships: Deficiencies in the support-giving skills of the lonely person's friends. In B. R. Burleson, T. L. Albrecht, & I. G. Sarason (Eds.), *Communication of social support: Messages, interactions, relationships, and community* (pp. 195–214). Thousand Oaks, CA: Sage.

Sillars, A., Canary, D. J., & Tafoya, M. (2004). Communication, conflict, and the quality of family relationships. In A. L. Vangelisti (Ed.), *Handbook of family communication* (pp. 413–446). Mahwah, NJ: Erlbaum.

Sillars, A. L., Leonard, K. E., Roberts, L. J., & Dun, T. (2002). Cognition and communication during marital conflict: How alcohol affects subjective coding of interaction in aggressive and nonaggressive couples. In P. Noller & J. A. Feeney (Eds.), *Understanding marriage: Developments in the study of couple interaction* (pp. 85–112). Cambridge, England: Cambridge University Press.

Sinclair, S. L., & Monk, G. (2004). Moving beyond the blame game: Toward a discursive approach to negotiating conflict within couple relationships. *Journal of Marital and Family Therapy, 30*(3), 335–347.

Solomon, D. H., Knobloch, L. K., & Fizpatrick, M. A. (2004). Relational power, martial schema, and decisions to withhold complaints: An investigation of the chilling effect on confrontation in marriage. *Communication Studies, 55*(1), 146–167.

Stanley, S. M., Markman, H. J., & Whitton, S. W. (2002). Communication, conflict, and commitment: Insights on the foundations of relationship success from a national survey. *Family Process, 41*(4), 659–675.

Ting-Toomey, S., Oetzel, J. G., & Yee-jung, K. (2001). Self-construal types and conflict management styles. *Communication Reports, 14*(2), 87–104.

West, C. M. (2004). Black women and intimate partner violence. *Journal of Interpersonal Violence, 19*(12), 1487–1493.

Wilson, S. R., & Morgan, W. M. (2004). Persuasion and families. In A. L. Vangelisti (Ed.), *Handbook of family communication* (pp. 447–471). Mahwah, NJ: Erlbaum.

Wilson, S. R., & Whipple, E. E. (2001). Attributions and regulative communication by parents participating in a community-based child physical abuse prevention program. In V. Manusov & J. H. Harvey (Eds.), *Attribution, communication behavior, and close relationships* (pp. 227–247). Cambridge, England: Cambridge University Press.

Winstok, Z., Eisikovits, S., & Karnieli-Miller, O. (2004). The impact of father-to-mother aggression on the structure and content of adolescents' perceptions of themselves and their parents. *Violence Against Women, 10*(9), 1036–1055.

Section 2: Research Examples

An Exploratory Investigation into Family Conflict Roles

Patrick C. Hughes

Chelsea A. H. Stow

> In Chapter 3, we considered the nature of family roles. In addition to family roles based on positions (mother, father), families also exhibit other roles in their communication processes. In this article, Hughes and Stowe consider the group roles that develop in family conflict situations, and how those roles may serve to diffuse or facilitate conflict situations. An awareness of the roles we play in family conflict, and how those roles impact conflict resolution, can help us develop more effective patterns of conflict management.
>
> *L.B.A.*

Family relationships are not always easy, and can be extremely challenging and difficult; however, the fact that relationships in general, and specifically family relationships, are complicated is nothing new. Baxter and Montgomery (1996), for example, suggested that all relationships are "messy," or "less logical and predictable than we might expect, and rife with tensions of different sorts" (p. 86). Furthermore, family life itself "is varied and complex and this variation and complexity is very difficult to study" (Bernardes, 1993, p. 41). One aspect of family life that is often difficult to understand is members' experiences during family conflict. This work expands on the discussion of the influences and dimensions of family conflict to include an empirical investigation of the emergent roles during family conflict. First, we briefly point out the many different conceptualizations of "family" from the literature. Second, we describe our method for looking into the emergent family conflict roles. Third, we present our results and analysis, which reveal the role dynamics during family conflicts as recalled by our participants. Finally, we conclude with suggestions for new directions of research on emergent family roles.

Family Types

Many scholars have provided valuable information about different types of families; for example, Afifi and Schrodt (2003) have identified family types such as step- or remarried families, traditional nuclear families, single-parent families, postdivorce families, and first marriage families, to name a few. Although many of these families are considered common in our society, scholars like Turner and West (2003) argue that we should "think outside the box" of commonality to include diverse family configurations like gay and lesbian families, adopted families, and interracial, interclass, or interethnic families. Therefore, whether your personal definition of family is similar to or different from these scholarly definitions, we can be sure that family life is both consistent and changing, both stable and chaotic, and both predictable and emergent.

One conceptualization of family that has received less attention is that of a family as a small group (Whitchurch & Constantine, 1993). Communication in small groups is best characterized as naturally occurring, or "emergent," communication behaviors that are socially constructed through group processes. One area of research in small-group communication that could explain a similar phenomenon in families is the concept of emergent small-group roles. Much of the communication that takes place during the life of a group is called "role formation talk," which is dedicated to the development and assignment of the roles that each member of the group will have (Cragan & Wright, 1993); examples of these roles include the Task Leader, Social-Emotional Leader, Tension Releaser, Central Negative/Devil's Advocate, and Information Provider. Additionally, to the extent that these emergent roles help groups construct their identities, complete tasks, establish rules for interaction, and formulate problem-solving talk (Pavitt & Curtis, 1990), we might also expect *family members* to develop group-type roles during their communication because the family can be considered a small group. That is, we would expect to see roles emerge as in other groups, but to differ in content from nonfamilial group communication (Whitchurch & Dickson, 1999).

Family Conflict and Family Roles

One area in which the emergence of family group roles might be instructive is during family conflict. The family is a unique context for study because "its influence has great longevity. . . . Long after people have moved away from family members geographically, they still feel psychologically and emotionally connected to them" (Sabourin, 2003, p. 39). Relationships with family members have ongoing impacts, and illustrate the importance of the roles filled by those around us (Vuchinich, Emery, & Cassidy, 1988). Regardless of how these roles are formed, the family environment provides its members with a source of support during times of conflict, and often supplies a conflict "template" upon which a person can draw in other stressful situations.

Although there seems to be a general American cultural perception that engaging in conflict is detrimental, conflict often produces beneficial results (McCarthy, Lambert, & Seraphine, 2004; Smetana, 1989). In fact, the presence of conflict has been shown to be less threatening to the relationship than *how* the conflict is managed communicatively (Gottman, 1994). The perception of conflict as nonbeneficial often stems from negative conflict experiences such as role identity confusion, when the family structure changes and individuals are uncertain how to change with it or how to respond to events in their new environment (Marsiglio, 2004). For example, in blended families it is typical for children to be unsure about which parent (the biological parent or the "new" parent) is responsible for discipline (Baxter, Braithwaite, & Bryant, 2004).

Family disagreements are inevitable, and effective conflict management has been recognized as an integral part of family life research (Vuchinich, 1987). Further, some research has pointed to the impact roles may have on promoting or ending conflict; however, this research focuses only on the *structural* aspects of family roles, meaning that little research has been done regarding how family members *socially construct* roles during conflict. Therefore, the purpose of this study is to explore the roles that family members construct during family conflict. The guiding research question of this study is: *What roles emerge for family members during family conflict?*

Method

Participants

One hundred undergraduate students ($n = 46$ males, $n = 54$ females) from a large university in the southwestern United States participated in this study. The participants ranged in age from 19 to 22 years ($M = 21.30$ years). At the time of these interviews, all participants were full-time college students. The cultural backgrounds of the participants were European American (75%), Hispanic (15%), and African American (10%). Most participants were single (90%), but a few were married or engaged (10%). At the time of this study, most of the participants reported that their parents' marital status was married (80%), with fewer being divorced (15%) or widowed (5%).

Procedures

Participants were recruited from the basic public speaking course in the authors' department, and through snowballing procedures (Reinard, 1994); participants were offered extra credit for their participation in the study. Data were collected using an open-ended questionnaire, and participants responded to five questions asking them (1) who they considered members of their families; (2) to recollect a recent family conflict, and describe what each person did and said during that conflict; (3) if they felt the conflict was resolved; (4) how family members participated in this resolution, and if conflicts were typically resolved in this manner; and (5) to describe their family communication patterns since the conflict. All questionnaires were completed during participants' regularly scheduled class time, and took approximately 50 minutes to complete. Data collection continued until saturation was reached—when similar themes in additional questionnaires emerged (Strauss & Corbin, 1990).

Data Analysis

Consistent with the grounded-theory design (Lincoln & Guba, 1985) and following the analytical induction procedures recommended by Glaser and Strauss (1967) and Strauss and Corbin (1990), transcripts and field notes were read for an overall impression of the data. Second, transcripts were read again, and the data were coded into smaller units based on participants' conflict experiences with their families. Third, these units were combined to generate family conflict role themes. Finally, using the constant comparative method of analysis (Strauss & Corbin, 1990), when new themes emerged old themes were reviewed and revised accordingly.

Results and Discussion

The research question guiding this study asked: What roles emerge for family members during family conflict? Our analysis revealed four emergent themes during family conflict: the Avoider role, Mediator role, Instigator role, and Role Construction Contradictions. Examples in support of each theme are given; however, in an effort to be concise, we included only the most representative excerpt for each theme.

Theme 1: Avoider Role

One of the open-ended questions in this study prompted participants to describe what each person in the family did and said during a recent family conflict. Interestingly enough, most of the respondents indicated that many family members (including themselves) wanted to "stay out of it," or otherwise distance themselves from the situation. For example, one participant disclosed:

> There was a fight when my sister decided to drop out of school and my mom was very much against it and my dad wanted to know why she wanted to drop out of school because my sister was a good student. Our parents wanted to involve me because I would be going to school next and they thought that this would set a bad example for me but I just wanted to stay out of it even though it involved my education to a degree because it wasn't my issue and it wasn't my life even though my parents wanted me to talk to my sister about it. I did what I could to not get involved or talk about it with my family.

There are many possible reasons why people avoid conflict, including protecting their relationships and family conflict dynamics. First, Avoiders might distance themselves from a conflict because they feel that their involvement might threaten or jeopardize an aspect of their relationship with the family members involved. Further, avoiding conflict may also reveal a subtle family conflict dynamic. That is, because conflict often temporarily disrupts family life, many family members might avoid conflict in an attempt to maintain homeostasis, or balance. However, research shows that conflict avoidance is an ineffective means of conflict management (Sillars, Canary, & Tafoya, 2004), and family members who avoid conflict to "keep the peace" are probably worsening the situation and causing more imbalance. Further, conflict avoidance in families may also be influenced by a greater cultural need to avoid conflicts in general.

Theme 2: Mediator Role

Participants also reported that someone (themselves or another family member) was often called on to act as a Mediator between conflicting family members. One participant recalled when her mother was mediating a disagreement between her father and herself:

> In my family, the fights were usually just little outbreaks but we would fight a lot. One time I was fighting with my dad, we have a lot of conflicts because we're both stubborn, and I really can't remember what it was we were fighting about but I remember my mom trying to get me and dad to be calm and restate our points of view. I really think she thought we

could figure out what was bothering me and dad, but mom kept trying to get us to "bargain" for what we wanted.

Many responses revealed the Mediator role, and analysis of these excerpts showed that other family members (not just mothers) act as Mediators.

From a family systems perspective, the Mediator role may emerge for similar reasons as the Avoider role: to restore order in the family. However, where the Avoider stays out of it and often increases family disruption, the Mediator gets involved in the conflict to diffuse the situation. Mediation seems to be a more effective tool than avoidance in conflict management, maintaining balance in the family system, and helping family members better understand each others' point-of-view (i.e., find shared meaning). Further, this direct and cooperative form of family communication is considered a highly effective conflict communication strategy (Knudson, Sommers, & Golding, 1980), which suggests that, even though family members may "fight a lot," as the last participant disclosed, a role exists in the family system to help maintain family equilibrium.

Theme 3: Instigator Role

So far, these themes have revealed the relative involvement (or lack thereof) of members during family conflict. Whereas the Instigator role also reveals a level of involvement in family conflict, this role emerged as someone who purposefully contributes to or escalates a situation by manipulating or baiting family members into a conflict with each other. One participant noted:

> Not just in one conflict, but in others we had in our family, there always seems to be someone (especially my brothers and sisters) who whispers in my parents' ears when my mom and dad are having a fight. One time, my brother knew that my mom and dad were fighting about how much time he [Dad] was spending at work because he's in sales and is out of town a lot. My brother overheard my dad talking with his partner about having to miss my sister's game, and my brother told my mom about this before my dad could and started a huge fight because mom thought that my dad wasn't going to tell her. This happens all of the time, my brothers and sisters saying things like "hey mom, guess what Gail is doing?" just to start a fight or keep one going.

This clearly reveals a darker side of family conflict processes. The emergence of the Instigator role in our data suggests that these families may be characterized by a pattern of competition. For example, Gottman (1994) demonstrated that competitive couples often repress ongoing conflicts for a period of time, as the parents seem to do in the previous excerpt, but when one person feels provoked the partners engage in a series of arguments marked by the presence of negative and competitive communication. Therefore, in many cases this competition originates with the parents and is then modeled by their offspring because "children learn how to manage conflicts indirectly by watching their parents and model their behavior and style" (Sillars et al., 2004, p. 426). As seen in the previous example, the children's involvement in this competitive pattern seems almost like a "communication rule" of their family, as "taught" by their parents, which could explain the emergence of an Instigator within the family.

Theme 4: Role Construction Contradictions—Symmetrical versus Complementary Roles

In addition to the Avoider, Mediator, and Instigator roles, our data revealed that the development of roles during conflict may not be as clear-cut as we might think. For some participants, the role they filled during conflict was different from the family's role expectations for that person. For example:

> We were staying home for the summer with our parents and my sister and I forgot we were living under my parents' roof. My sister and I got into a fight with our parents about the curfew issue because we believe we are adults who can come and go as we please, but mom and dad think we are their children still and as long as they are paying the bills we follow their rules.

It is clear from the example that this family is constructing contradictory roles: the children symbolize the construction of symmetrical roles between parent and child, and the parents represent the attempt to enact complementary roles (see Chapter 3 for discussion and definition of symmetrical and complementary behaviors). First, the children claim that they are adults, and have as much authority or power over their lives as their parents (symmetrical roles). However, the parents argue that they have more power over the rest of the family, first by virtue of their "place" as parents in the family structure, and second as having reward power over their children because they "still pay the bills" (complementary roles).

Other occurrences of this theme centered on conflicts between participants' parents that often stemmed from different constructions of power and equality, typically with the father constructing a complementary role and the mother constructing a symmetrical role. Furthermore, in the case of adult dependent children, several excerpts showed that some parents constructed symmetrical roles for certain children and complementary roles for others in the same family, in spite of the similarity in age among the adult children. Therefore, although there is not a clear pattern of these Role Construction Contradictions, it is important to note that these contradictions *can* emerge during family conflicts, often with lasting effects.

Conclusions

The purpose of this study was to conduct an exploratory investigation into the emergent roles during family conflict. Our data revealed four patterns of role development during family conflict: Avoider role, Mediator role, Instigator role, and Role Construction Contradictions; these findings seem to suggest that family members *do* develop particular roles during family conflict. Future research could improve upon and extend this study in at least three ways. First, future research might explore the general pervasiveness of these roles and seek to uncover more types of emergent roles. Second, future research might look at these roles more closely in order to distinguish between the well-being of families in which the various roles emerge (relative [un]happiness, etc.). Finally, the contradiction between the construction of symmetrical and complementary roles could be studied further, especially in the context of parents and their adult dependent children: does the presence of this tension mark the structural transition of a family from one in which the power and authority falls specifically on the parents, to one in which adult children become self-reliant (i.e., adjustment during life changes)? Future research might also ask if this tension helps or hinders this transition.

Questions for Consideration and Discussion

1. In this article, Hughes and Stow use concepts from small-group research and apply these to family communication processes. How well do you think small-group concepts apply to family, and why?
2. This work addresses the emergent nature of roles during conflict. Considering your most recent conflicts with family members, what examples of emergent roles do you see? What causes roles to emerge in conflict situations?
3. The discourse from the participants in this study indicated a divergence in the construction of symmetrical and complementary roles between parents and children. Do you believe this is because these participants are college students, or might this be explained by other factors?
4. This study asked participants to recollect a recent family conflict and base their responses on that recollection. What are some benefits and drawbacks to this method?
5. The participants in this work were college students. How might their age and/or education level have impacted their perceptions of family conflict?

References

Afifi, T. D., & Schrodt, P. (2003). Uncertainty and the avoidance of the state of one's family in stepfamilies, post-divorce single-parent families, and first-marriage families. *Human Communication Research, 29*(4), 516–532.

Baxter, L. A., Braithwaite, D. O., & Bryant, L. (2004). Stepchildren's perceptions of the contradictions in communication with stepparents. *Journal of Social and Personal Relationships, 21*, 447–467.

Baxter, L. A., & Montgomery, B. M. (1996). *Relating: Dialogues and dialectics*. New York: Guilford Press.

Bernardes, J. (1993). Responsibilities in studying postmodern families. In T. C. Sabourin, *The contemporary American family: A dialectical perspective on communication and relationships*. Thousand Oaks, CA: Sage.

Cragan, J. F., & Wright, D. W. (1993). *Theory and research in small group communication: A reader*. Edina, MN: Burgess.

Glaser, B., & Strauss, A. (1967). *The discovery of grounded theory*. Chicago: Aldine.

Gottman, J. M. (1994). *What predicts divorce? The relationship between marital process and marital outcomes*. Hillsdale, NJ: Erlbaum.

Knudson, R. M., Sommers, A. A., & Golding, S. L. (1980). Interpersonal perception and mode resolution in marital conflict. *Journal of Personality and Psychology, 38*, 751–763.

Lincoln, Y. S., & Guba, E. G. (1985). *Naturalistic inquiry*. Newbury Park, CA: Sage.

Marsiglio, W. (2004). When stepfathers claim step children: A conceptual analysis. *Journal of Marriage and Family, 66*, 22–39.

McCarthy, C. J., Lambert, R. G., & Seraphine, A. E. (2004). Adaptive family functioning and emotion regulation capacities as predictors of college students' appraisals and emotion valence following conflict with their parents. *Cognition & Emotion, 18(1)*, 97–124.

Pavitt, C., & Curtis, E. (1990). *Small group communication: A theoretical approach*. Scottsdale, AZ: Gorsuch Scarisbrick.

Reinard, J. C. (1994). *Introduction to communication research*. Dubuque, IA: Brown & Benchmark.

Sabourin, T. C. (2003). *The contemporary American family: A dialectical perspective on communication and relationships*. Thousand Oaks, CA: Sage.

Sillars, A., Canary, D. J., & Tafoya, M. (2004). Communication, conflict, and the quality of family relationships. In A. Vangelisti (Ed.), *Handbook of family communication* (pp. 413–446). Mahwah, NJ: Erlbaum.

Smetana, J. G. (1989). Adolescents' and parents' reasoning about actual family conflict. *Child Development, 60*, 1052–1067.

Strauss, A., & Corbin, J. (1990). *Basics of qualitative research: Grounded theory procedures and techniques*. Newbury Park, CA: Sage.

Turner, L. H., & West, R. (2003). Introduction. Breaking through silence: Increasing voice for diverse families in communication research. *Journal of Family Communication, 3*, 181–186.

Vuchinich, S. (1987). Starting and stopping spontaneous family conflicts. *Journal of Marriage and Family, 49*, 591–601.

Vuchinich, S., Emery, R. E., & Cassidy, J. (1988). Family members as third parties in dyadic family conflict: Strategies, alliances, and outcomes. *Child Development, 59*, 1293–1302.

Whitchurch, G. G., & Constantine, L. L. (1993). Systems theory. In P. G. Boss & W. J. Doherty (Eds.), *Sourcebook of family theories and methods: A contextual approach* (pp. 325–355). New York: Plenum Press.

Whitchurch, G. G., & Dickson, F. C. (1999). Family communication. In M. B. Sussman, S. K. Steinmetz, & G. W. Peterson (Eds.), *Handbook of marriage and the family* (2nd ed.). New York: Plenum Press.

"What Do *You* Do When Your Teenager Hits You?": Exploring Conflict Tactics Used by Parents in Adolescent-to-Parent Abuse

Nancy J. Brule

We often think of abuse as occurring between adult partners, or visited upon children by adults. However, there are numerous instances where teens and adult children abuse their parents or other familial elders. In this article, Eckstein considers the conflict strategies used by parents during teen abusive episodes. Even if you never experience this type of situation, you may find that the same tactics are used in other conflict situations, even those which are not abusive.

L.B.A.

Daily interactions between parents and adolescents often result in conflicts. Family members assume different roles when contributing to the development and enactment of conflict episodes and the basic skills required to resolve conflict involves utilizing a variety of communication tactics (Canary & Spitzberg, 1987, 1989; Cupach & Canary, 1997; Messman & Canary, 1998). An individual's conflict tactics are often reinforced by other family members' responses, and individuals develop patterns of behaviors that others come to expect. These patterns of conflict behaviors may be either constructive or destructive—promoting cooperation and relational growth or power struggles, competition, and unresolved conflicts (Rueter & Conger, 1995; Smetana, 1995). Some destructive conflict between adolescents and parents may escalate into abuse.

Adolescent-to-parent abuse is defined as "actual physical assaults or verbal and nonverbal threats of physical harm" (Harbin & Madden, 1979, p. 1288) directed toward parents by their adolescent children. The National Family Violence Survey reported that adolescents victimized 18% of parents at least once a year; 2.5 million parents are struck by their adolescents, 900,000 of these experiencing severe physical abuse (Cornell & Gelles, 1981; Straus, Gelles, & Steinmetz, 1980). Yet, not all adolescent-to-parent abuse is physical in nature; parents also experience verbal and emotional abuse (Eckstein, 2004, 2005; Price, 1996). Although adolescent-to-parent abuse exists, there is little research in this area of relational violence and as a result the problem often goes unnoticed and more likely unreported.

Because societal norms hold parents responsible for the behavior of their children, parents experiencing abuse often blame themselves for their own abuse (Eckstein, 2004, 2005; Schuett, 1999). Many abused parents fear public victimization (being judged as poor parents), and as a result, become prisoners in their own home, avoid talking about the abusive episodes, minimize the seriousness of the behavior, and are unable to punish the behavior. However, narratives by abused parents reveal that they do attempt to negotiate interactions with their teens in efforts to prevent adolescent-to-parent abuse (Eckstein, 2004, 2005; Price,

1996). The purpose of this study is to identify the specific conflict strategies and tactics used by parents to manage or prevent episodes of abuse.

Defining Abuse

This study defines abuse within a relationship as an "ongoing, repetitive pattern—psychological, emotional, or behavioral—of pain infliction" (Spitzberg, 1997, p. 177). Abuse is conceptualized to include verbal (attacks the self-concept of another individual), physical (acts resulting in physical harm against a person), and emotional (impacts the ability to function in a relational role) behaviors that inflict hurt upon another individual and which violate socially accepted standards.

Conflict and Strategies

Defining Conflict

Interpersonal conflict is defined here as an "expressed struggle between at least two interdependent parties who perceive incompatible goals, scarce resources, and interference from others in achieving their goals" (Wilmot & Hocker, 2001, p. 34). Communication is central to this definition because conflict must be expressed to be an interpersonal conflict. Certain verbal and nonverbal behaviors often lead to, reflect, and express conflict, and can be used to manage or prevent the escalation of conflict (Canary & Spitzberg, 1987, 1989, 1990; Wilmot & Hocker, 2001). When participants are faced with a conflict situation, they consciously or subconsciously make a decision to avoid or engage in conflict.

Strategies and Tactics

Strategies and tactics are the general way individuals behave in a conflict situation. A strategy is an overall plan made up of communication tactics (specific observable actions) that move a conflict in a direction that helps achieve an outcome (Lulofs & Cahn, 2000). Researchers have identified three strategies individuals often use to engage in conflict. First, the integrative strategy (i.e., cooperative confrontation, supportive comments, listening in a supportive manner) encourages both parties to identify and share the goals of conflict and is often considered to have a positive impact on a relationship. Second, the distributive strategy (i.e., threats, demands, coercion, intimidation) is often considered to have a negative impact on a relationship (Sillars, 1986; Wilmot & Hocker, 2001). Third, the avoidance strategy (i.e., giving in to the demands of others, physically withdrawing from the conflict, not voicing thoughts) tries to keep tension at a low level and can have either a positive or negative relational impact. Because tactics are the communicative behaviors that shape conflict strategies, identifying the tactics parents use in attempts to manage and prevent escalation of conflict into adolescent-to-parent abuse becomes important. Thus, the research question is:

> *RQ:*   What conflict tactics do parents use when managing and attempting to prevent conflict episodes from escalating into adolescent-to-parent verbal, physical, and emotional abuse?

Methods

Participants

Participants were 20 (male = 7; female = 13) European American parents located in the Midwest, who met the criteria of having been verbally, physically, and emotionally abused by an adolescent child who was living in the home at the time of abuse. Via phone, I contacted 3 parents who met the criteria and asked them if they would be willing to be interviewed. These parents then suggested other parents they knew, and using the purposive snowball sampling method, 10 additional participants were recruited. The final 7 participants were located through a social worker that contacted parents who met the criteria and, if parents consented to being interviewed, I was forwarded their contact information.

Participants ranged in age from 35 to 55 (*m* = 42). These families averaged 3.4 children; 19 of the families only had one child who was abusive. Nine of the participants were in first marriages (*m* = 25 years), 9 in second marriages (*m* = 9 years), and 2 participants were divorced at the time of the interview. Thirteen participants had experienced abuse by biological children, 5 by stepchildren, and 2 by adopted children. Each of the participants had participated in multiple family counseling programs.

Data Collection and Analysis

This study used a qualitative or interpretive approach to data analysis. A semistructured, open-ended interview instrument was developed (Holstein & Gubrium, 1995; McCracken, 1988) composed of questions that asked participants to explain, from start to finish, one experience of each type of abuse episode (verbal, physical, emotional). Before beginning the interview, the three different types of abuse were clearly defined and examples provided for the participants. The use of follow-up questions helped parents provide a full description of each type of abuse episode. Interviews were audio recorded and lasted between 1 and 1 ½ hours yielding 753 pages of 1.5-spaced data.

Data were analyzed in four phases. First the transcripts were listened to and read simultaneously in their entirety to verify the accuracy of the transcription, develop an overall picture of the participants' perceptions, and to start the analysis procedure. Second, Sillars's (1986) conflict strategy and tactic typology guided this analysis. Data were analyzed for the presence or absence of conflict tactics; tactics that did not clearly fit the typology were set aside for further analysis. Third, findings that did not fit the typology were analyzed and additional categories were developed (Creswell, 1998; Miles & Huberman, 1994). Fourth, the transcripts were read again, confirming the findings and locating examples for this study (Miles & Huberman, 1994). For verification of these findings, I performed a member check, which involved presenting my findings to eight of the participants in written form. Participants supported the analysis and stressed the consistency of these tactics, discussing how similar the excerpts were to their own experiences.

Results

Distributive Tactics

Few distributive tactics emerged when analyzing these data, possibly because of the destructive nature of these types of conflict tactics. Regardless of the reasons, the distributive tactics that emerged included personal criticism, ridicule, hit and run, sarcasm, and mirroring.

Personal Criticism, Ridicule, Hit and Run, and Sarcasm.   When personal criticism, ridicule, hit and run, and sarcasm tactics were used, it was often at a point in the conflict episode when parents grew frustrated and had lost control of their emotions. As a result, parents believed these tactics to be reactionary responses and were troubled when using them with their adolescents. A mother reported, "I would try not to ever lose my cool. And as many times as I would get up in the morning and say, 'Today, when he aggravates me I am going to maintain it'. . . . I just couldn't do it. Push that button and bam, gone." Parents also reported that personal criticism, ridicule, hit and run, and sarcasm were ineffective during a conflict and played a role in escalating the conflict into abuse.

Mirroring.   A tactic emerging that was not previously identified as a distributive tactic was mirroring. The mirroring tactic involves parents mimicking, verbally and nonverbally, an adolescent's words and behaviors. Although the initial use of mirroring often was effective in stopping the conflict episode from escalating, parents eventually came to view mirroring as a negative tactic. A mother explained:

> One of the good things is that he would use the language on me and I'd use it back on him. And he'd be shocked, intensely hearing his mother talk in the same language he talked. And that bothered him. . . . He'd bang his fists on something so I'd bang it, and he didn't like that. . . . And in the beginning, when I would do that with him, he would back off. . . . But then he hit a point where that didn't bother him anymore.

Although mirroring was effective when first used, over time it was ignored and thought to contribute to the escalation of the conflict.

Avoidance Tactics

Parents also used a number of avoidance tactics in attempts to prevent escalation of conflict into abuse; tactics included not voicing thoughts, physically withdrawing, giving in to demands, and ignoring.

Not Voicing Thoughts.   Parents frequently used the tactic of not voicing thoughts. A father shared this rationale: "Even though it's hard to do, you have to sit there and take the abuse. I could yell and swear at them back again, but it wouldn't do any good." Participants believed that responding to verbal abuse was not only ineffective, but also contributed to its escalation into more severe forms of abuse.

Physically Withdrawing.   Professional counselors often suggested to parents that they remove themselves from the proximity of the conflict so the adolescent would be unable to escalate it into abuse. Although intuitively this seems like a simple solution, parents reported that, because adolescents often followed parents throughout the house in attempts to continue the conflict, this tactic was extremely difficult to implement. When parents would lock themselves in a bathroom or bedroom, adolescents often pounded or kicked the door while screaming, swearing, and demanding the parent let them in. A parent summed up the failure of this tactic, "Well, unfortunately, it comes with you. It's on the other side of the door pounding. So they [counselors] don't tell you that part of it." Many parents reported these abuse episodes would often escalate and the doors would get broken.

Giving In to Demands.   These parents did not like giving in to the demands of their adolescents. However, parents' emotional exhaustion as well as the length of abuse episodes made this tactic a realistic one. A mother reported:

> He'd be in my face for anywhere from ten minutes to two, three hours . . . he wouldn't leave me alone . . . and he kept on and on. . . . He just wouldn't leave it alone. And I couldn't just let him keep talking to me and not get pulled back. . . . And I'd say, "Yeah, well, whatever." Because I was tired. I didn't want to do it anymore.

Implementing the tactic of giving in to demands was very simple: the adolescent asked for something, the parent said no, the teen verbally abused the parent, and the parent gave in to the adolescent's demands. After years of abuse, these parents reported not having the energy or desire to invest in the conflict episode.

Ignoring.   A tactic that emerged from these data not previously identified as an avoidance tactic was the ignoring tactic; this involved ignoring the verbal, and at times physical abuse taking place during a conversation or activity with the adolescent. For example, a mother who was washing dishes reported continuing to wash dishes even while her adolescent was punching her in the arm. On reflection, parents concluded that this tactic might have contributed to the escalation of the conflict into abuse because adolescents' behaviors become more intense in attempt to get their own way.

Integrative Tactics

Abused parents used integrative tactics the least, even though this strategy is considered a positive approach to dealing with conflict. Parents reported using supportive listening and comments and specific issue tactics.

Supportive Listening and Comments.   These parents used supportive listening and comments to focus on the needs of their adolescent. After an abuse episode, parents arranged a specific time to go for a soda, walk, or lunch with the adolescent. Parents used this time to address conflict issues, using positive verbal and nonverbal language, listening to the frustrations of the adolescent, and encouraging them to "hang in there." One father reported, "that's the times he's staring at you in the eyes, he's talking to you, he's looking at you, you've got your eye contact. . . . Their guard gets totally dropped so you can talk—get them to talk about a bunch of different things." Although this tactic provided opportunity for calm discussion and connection, having a positive effect on the adolescent–parent relationship, it had no evidence of preventing future abuse episodes.

Specific Issue.   A new integrative tactic identified from these data was the specific issue tactic that involved using verbal cues that keep refocusing the parent and the adolescent on the issue of the conflict rather than the behavior of the adolescent. Implementation of this conflict included the use of deflectors such as "nevertheless," "regardless," or "anyway." A mother provides an example of the use of this tactic during a verbal abuse episode when she told her son he could not go out for the night:

> So I said, "no, you can stay home tonight if I don't know who you are going to be with." And he said, "You are such a fuckin' whore, you never trust me, you never let me do things," and things like that. So I simply said, "Nevertheless, you are still staying home tonight." And he kept on verbally abusing me, calling me things, going off on a rampage, and when he finished his statement I would say, "Regardless, you are still staying home tonight." It always made him so mad, he had no response to it and regardless of what he said, I wasn't going to get into it with him and my answer was still no.

Parents viewed the specific issue tactic as being surprisingly effective in preventing the escalation of verbal abuse into either physical or emotional abuse episodes. This tactic allowed parents to maintain control of their emotions, showing adolescents that the parents had heard what they said, but still pointed the interaction back to the issue under dispute.

Engagement Tactics

When placing conflict tactics into the specific context of abuse, a number of conflict tactics emerged that are not previously identified in the conflict typology; these were categorized and labeled as an engagement strategy. The engagement strategy is best defined as tactics used by parents when they have no other option but to engage their adolescent in a conflict situation and are particularly focused on preventing the escalation of conflict into abuse. In fact, these parents believed they were abused because they made decisions that the adolescent did not agree with such as curfew times, not granting permission to go to certain activities, forcing completion of chores, or requiring attendance at certain functions. Engagement tactics identified included (a) warning, (b) good-cop-bad-cop, (c) strategic confrontation, (d) manipulation of physical space, (e) tag-team arguing, (f) physical compliance and restraint, and (g) repetition tactics.

Warning.   These parents learned that although a conflict between one parent and adolescent may have ended earlier in the day, this did not necessarily mean it would not be revisited with the other parent. The warning tactic was used to inform an absent parent of a conflict that had occurred earlier in the day. For example, if earlier in the day a mother and adolescent had engaged in a serious conflict over an issue, the mother would call the father to inform him of what had occurred to prepare him if he was faced with the same question when he got home that evening. When adolescents did engage the other parent, this was the last opportunity to get a yes and often the confrontation with the second parent over the same issue escalated into abuse. A father reported:

> You communicate [with your spouse], because if the kid comes in and says "I want to talk to you," you look at, you know, your husband or wife . . . across the room. . . . But you don't say nothing. You just kind of look . . . and you know this is what the call earlier in the day was about. So you can support each other and kind of be on the same side on this.

Although these episodes often escalated into abuse, the warning tactic helped parents maintain a united front and prevented adolescents from manipulating parents against each other.

Good-Cop-Bad-Cop.   A unique tactic that emerged from these data was labeled the good-cop-bad-cop tactic—a tactic specifically focused on preventing verbal abuse from escalating into physical or emotional. Participants realized that, when having to make decisions that are unpopular with the adolescent, the news was often better received when given by the parent not in the same proximity as the adolescent. When a teen asked a parent to do something, the parent present (good cop) advised the teen to ask the parent who was absent (bad cop). The teen would then call the bad cop on the phone to ask for permission to do something. If the bad cop said no, the conflict episode often escalated into verbal abuse over the phone. Interestingly, these teens focused on only one parent at a time during episodes of abuse. The argument on the phone would continue until the adolescent would either hang up or, in many cases, break the phone. The teen then verbally abused the bad cop to the good cop, who would be supportive of both the teen and the bad cop, using deflectors such as "nevertheless, he is your father and he has made his decision," or "I know this is frustrating for you but you need to just hang in there." A mother explained this tactic:

> My husband and I decided that one of the best ways to deal with him at times . . . was to have the other person call on the phone and be the bad guy. So, say he wanted to go somewhere and we were going to say, "no." I would say, "You'll have to chat with your father about that," so he would call dad at work and dad would say, "No, I've decided you can't go. . . ." And I would be the one at home with him, listening to all of this taking place. . . . He would cuss and he would swear. . . . And they'd go through the argument back and forth like they normally do [on the phone]. But then he was so upset finally he would throw—or hang up the phone and then he'd proceed to beat the phone into a million pieces, throw it and break it. And it was very interesting because the person at home, even though you would hear this outrage and this swearing and this breaking of the phone, it was never directed at you. So, we learned a good way to deal with this type—and to control the level of intensity and keep it from becoming physical abuse toward a person was to have—use the phone. And we went through fourteen, fifteen, more, maybe twenty phones in order to accomplish it.

Parents reported this tactic worked surprisingly well and often diffused what could have been a more serious situation.

Strategic Confrontation.   Another engagement tactic parents used was strategic confrontation. Because the location of the conflict often played a role in how severe a conflict became, some parents strategically chose the location of where to address an issue. For example, if adolescents were more likely to abuse their parents in private, parents often waited to address an issue in public. Other adolescents had a history of being verbally abusive in public so these parents would choose to address the issue in a private setting. Although strategic confrontation did not stop a conflict from escalating, parents believed it helped prevent escalation into physical or emotional abuse.

Manipulation of Space.   When participants were engaged in a conflict episode with an adolescent that had the signs of escalating into physical abuse, they reported being careful to manipulate their physical space. For example, if an adolescent was being verbally abusive, parents would physically position objects (e.g., table, counter, chair) between themselves and the teen to prevent the teen from being able to grab the parent. If a teen moved closer to the parent during an episode, parents often stepped back. Using the manipulation of space tactic often prevented verbal abuse from escalating to physical abuse.

Tag-Team Arguing.   Many times adolescents and parents were engaged in conflict episodes that often lasted up to three hours. Participants used the tag-team arguing tactic rather than give in to an adolescent's demands. Tag-team arguing involved participants taking turns engaging the adolescent so that one parent would not get worn out or overly frustrated. The goal of tag-team arguing was to enable parents to maintain their composure while at the same time wearing out the adolescent until he or she stopped the conflict.

Physical Compliance and Restraint.   The physical compliance and restraint tactic was the use of physical measures to gain compliance or control an adolescent's behavior. This tactic was problematic because adolescents were often larger and stronger than parents and the use of it many times escalated conflict. For example, if a parent asked an adolescent to get in the car and the adolescent refused, the only way the parent was able to get the adolescent into the car was to lead the teen and physically put his or her limbs into the car; this tactic was usually used with girls as they were less likely to respond physically to the parent.

However, parents often used physical restraint when the adolescent was physically abusing a parent or damaging property. Parents may have sat on, lay on, or held the adolescent in a bear hug or hold that prevented him or her from moving until calmed down. As a mother described:

> And he would have to be in holds all the time, where I would have to have him on my lap and wrap my legs around his legs and my arms around his body. . . . And so I ended up laying on him on the floor for like an hour. And the whole time he was hitting me, punching me, biting me, kicking me. And I finally told my little [other] kid, I said, "You need to call the cops." And so he did.

Participants reported using physical compliance when they believed there was no other way of getting the adolescents to comply with their wishes; physical restraint was used to prevent the adolescents from physically harming parents, property, or themselves.

Repetition.   Finally, the tactic of repetition involved parents repeating over and over to an adolescent the reasons for saying no to a request. Participants reported that when they used the repetition tactic, they focused on using calming nonverbal cues such as a soft voice, relaxed body tension, or a slow vocal rate. A mother stated, "And I calmly went over and over the discussion with him, softly and really slowly retelling him why he couldn't do something, over and over while he is yelling until he calms down." Participants reported that the repetition tactic required very deliberate verbal and nonverbal communication and although at times proved effective, at other times, regardless of how long repetition was used, the conflict eventually escalated into other forms of abuse.

Discussion

First, it is important to note that the tactics used by these parents were used in attempts to prevent the escalation of conflict into verbal, physical, and emotional abuse and appear to be unique to adolescent-to-parent abuse episodes. When verbal abuse occurred, it was viewed as an indicator that the conflict was escalating and if not stopped or diffused, then physical or emotional abuse often resulted (Eckstein, 2004, 2005; Price, 1996). These parents considered tactics successful if a verbal abuse episode did not escalate into physical or emotional abuse and were willing to try numerous tactics in attempts to prevent abuse.

Second, the identification of the engagement strategy and its tactics is an important contribution to understanding adolescent-to-parent abuse. Because parents believed it was necessary to engage in some conflict episodes, engagement tactics were specific attempts to maintain parental authority as well as prevent escalation of verbal abuse into physical or emotional abuse. Parents' choice of a conflict tactic was based on the previous history of adolescent-to-parent abuse interactions. Parents realized stopping verbal abuse was virtually impossible and used it as an indicator that a tactic needed to be implemented if escalation of the abuse was to be prevented.

Finally, these parents' reports of conflict episodes reveal the rapid and extreme escalation of conflict into verbal abuse. Participants were very specific in the description of their efforts used to prevent abuse; this may be a sign that experiencing abuse makes parents hypersensitive to the communicative behaviors that play a role in escalating conflict in intensity and as a result, parents may be more willing to experiment with different conflict tactics in attempts to prevent abuse. Because all these participants sought outside counseling and attended parenting classes, they may approach an adolescents' abusive behavior as a puzzle that they should be able to solve. Unfortunately, the majority of these parents were unable to change the behavior of their abusive adolescent and the abuse continued until the adolescent left home.

Limitations and Future Research

All studies have areas that can be improved upon and this study is no exception. First, the homogeneity of the sample is both a limitation and strength. Although generalizability is a problem, because of the early stage of research on adolescent-to-parent abuse, having a homogeneic sample actually provides a strong basis for branching off for future research. Second, these data use retrospective self-reports, and issues of accurate recall may be a consideration. The ideal research situation would be to observe adolescent–parent dyads engaged in conflict episodes escalating into abuse; however, ethical dimensions prevent researchers from doing this.

Finally, these reports are from only one perspective—the abused parent—and do not represent the whole adolescent–parent relationship. I specifically asked these parents to describe a verbal, physical, and emotional abuse episode and as a result, we see only the abusive side of these relationships. Many of these parents expressed great affection for, and gave indications of the good times they experienced with, these teens. Future research should provide descriptions of the entire adolescent–parent relationship such as reports from abusive adolescents, siblings, and others in the family network, the impact on the family, and relational satisfaction.

This study is just a brief glimpse into a phenomenon that impacts many families and yet, family counselors, researchers, and professionals have a long way to go in helping victims of adolescent-to-parent abuse. These parents' reflections on their attempts to prevent abuse episodes should enable us to better understand families experiencing such abuse.

Questions for Consideration and Discussion

1. Brule draws upon research that indicates the superiority of integrative conflict strategies over distributive and avoidance strategies. Based on what has been discussed in this chapter and your own experiences, why do you think integrative strategies are more effective?
2. The parents in this study reported using few distributive tactics with their teens. What might be some causal factors for this choice?
3. Professional counselors had recommended physical withdrawal to many of these parents; however, they found it ineffective. What would be the advantages of physical withdrawal in abusive conflict (i.e., why might counselors recommend it?) and why might these parents have found it ineffective?
4. Brule's study resulted in the creation of a group of tactics she calls "engagement." In these examples, engagement allowed the parent to engage in the conflict, while preventing escalation to abuse. What of other engagement strategies could be used and what are other times when engagement might be useful (besides in parent–teen abuse situations)?
5. Each participant in this study had previously been involved in multiple family counseling programs. What kind of impacts might this have had on the findings of this study?

References

Canary, D. J., & Spitzberg, B. H. (1987). Appropriateness and effectiveness perceptions of conflict strategies. *Human Communication Research, 14*, 93–118.

Canary, D. J., & Spitzberg, B. H. (1989). A model of perceived competence of conflict strategies. *Human Communication Research, 15*, 630–649.

Canary, D. J., & Spitzberg, B. H., (1990). Attribution biases and associations between conflict strategies and competence outcomes. *Communication Monographs, 57*, 139–151.

Cornell, C. P., & Gelles, R. J. (1981, November). *Adolescent to parent violence.* Paper presented at the annual meetings of the American Society of Criminology, Washington, DC.

Creswell, J. Q. (1998). *Qualitative inquiry and research design: Choosing among five traditions.* Thousand Oaks, CA: Sage.

Cupach, W. R., & Canary, D. J. (1997). *Competence in interpersonal conflict.* New York: McGraw-Hill.

Eckstein, N. J. (2004). Emergent issues in families experiencing adolescent-to-parent abuse. *Western Journal of Communication, 68*, 365–388.

Eckstein, N. J. (2005). *Adolescent-to-parent abuse: Abused parents' perceptions of the meaning and goals of adolescents' verbal, physical, and emotional abuse.* Manuscript submitted for publication.

Gelles, R. J. & Straus, M. A. (1988). *Intimate violence.* New York: Simon & Schuster.

Harbin, H. T., & Madden, D. J. (1979). Battered parents: A new syndrome. *American Journal of Psychiatry, 136*, 1288–1291.

Holstein, J. A., & Gubrium, J. F. (1995). *The active interview.* Thousand Oaks, CA: Sage.

Lulofs, R. S., & Cahn, D. D. (2000). *Conflict: From theory to action*. Boston: Allyn & Bacon.

McCracken, G. (1988). *The long interview*. Newbury Park, CA: Sage.

Messman, S. J., & Canary, D. J. (1998). Patterns of conflict in personal relationships. In B. H. Spitzberg & W. R. Cupach (Eds.), *The dark side of personal relationships* (pp. 121–152). Mahwah, NJ: Erlbaum.

Miles, M. B., & Huberman, A. M. (1994). *Qualitative data analysis: A sourcebook of new methods* (2nd ed.). Thousand Oaks, CA: Sage.

Price, J. A. (1996). *Power and compassion: Working with difficult adolescents and abused parents*. New York: Guilford Press.

Rueter, M. A., & Conger, R. D. (1995). Antecedents of parent-adolescent disagreements. *Journal of Marriage and Family, 57*, 435–448.

Schuett, D. (1999, February 25). "I wanted him to be a good child." *Post Bulletin*, p. 7B.

Sillars, A. L., (1986, April). *Procedures for coding interpersonal conflict (revised)* [Manual]. Missoula: University of Montana, Department of Interpersonal Communication.

Smetana, J. G. (1995). Conflict and coordination in adolescent–parent relationships. In S. Shulman (Ed.), *Close relationships and socioemotional development* (Vol. 7, pp. 155–184). Norwood, NJ: Ablex.

Spitzberg, B. H. (1997). Violence in intimate relationships. In W. R. Cupach & D. J. Canary (Eds.), *Competence in interpersonal communication* (pp. 174–201). New York: McGraw-Hill.

Straus, M. A., Gelles, R. J., & Steinmetz, S. K. (1980). *Behind closed doors: Violence in the American family*. New York: Anchor Press.

Wilmot, W. W., & Hocker, J. L. (2001). *Interpersonal conflict* (6th ed.). New York: McGraw-Hill.

Enacting Conflict as Resistance: Urban Indian Women in Hindu Arranged Marriages

Devika Chawla

As considered throughout the text, culture has a strong impact on our family communication patterns. In this article, Chawla considers how cultural factors are a part of family conflict that occurs in the arranged marriages of urban Indian women. The narratives here express how cultural conflict (i.e., the more traditional Hindu family practices meeting more liberal modern urban views of family and individual power) can become an important factor in family experiences, and exhibit the attempts of family members to cope with this conflict. As you read, consider the ways in which culture, as well as cultural changes, have affected family conflict in your experiences.

L.B.A.

The Context: Hindu Arranged Marriages

Arranged marriages are a norm in Asian cultures such as India, China, Japan, and Korea (Applbaum, 1995). Premised upon similarity of social standing, which often includes the caste, class, religion, and education of the prospective couple, the arranged marriage is the most popular form of organizing a marital relationship among Hindu Indians in India (Mullatti, 1995). Despite forces of modernization, urbanization, and liberalization, the number of arranged marriages in India far outnumbers "love" marriages. In fact, an estimated 95% of all Hindu marriages in India are still arranged marriages, thus making them a norm rather than an exception (Bumiller, 1990; Kapadia, 1958; Kapur, 1970; Mullatti, 1995).

Contemporary arranged marriages are generally organized by parents and elderly kin (Sur, 1973). In earlier times, intermediaries called sambhalas, or traditional matchmakers, were employed to keep the genealogical history of each family, and make sure that the bride and groom were not related from five to seven generations (Sur, 1973). In more recent times, these criteria have stretched to include other characteristics. Mullatti (1995) outlines seven criteria that are currently followed by matchmakers, kin, parents, and relatives: caste, social structure, moral value compatibility, academic compatibility, occupational compatibility, the family's moral history, and horoscope compatibility (though not necessarily in this order). In the past two decades, parents have begun looking for matches for their children through matrimonial columns in newspapers, magazines, and now even the Internet (Mullatti, 1995).

Originally, the most appropriate form of Hindu marriage was a union arranged by parents and kin, and is said to be derived from laws interpreted in the *Dharmashastras* which in turn have their roots in the 3,000-year-old hymns called *Vedas* and *Smritis*, the oldest surviving documents of the Indian civilization recorded between 4000 B.C. to 1200 A.D. (Kapadia, 1958). A general theme across these scriptures was that marriage was a duty and a religious sacrament that was required of all human beings for the well-being of the community. In fact, marriage and procreation are one of the four necessary stages in a

Hindu's life. Marriage constitutes the second stage, *grahastha*, aimed at progeny and sexual activities.

However, there is no evidence that any of these life stages were structured toward women. Therefore, although marriage was required of all Hindus, its advantages were enjoyed only by men, who benefited from both the spiritual and economic understandings of the Hindu marriage (Mukherjee, 1978). Spiritually, men benefited because they married in order to beget sons who would light their funeral pyre. This ensured the male line a place in heaven, rebirth in the next life as a human being, as well as the liberation of future generations of the family (*moksha*). The need for a male heir was also an economic necessity—a male heir was desired because he alone could continue the family line and inherit ancestral property.[1] Therefore, historically, the Hindu arranged marriage was "male-emphasized" (Mukherjee, 1978). It has even been suggested the word *wife* was often used interchangeably with *household* (Mukherjee, 1978; Sastri, 1972, 1974). In other words, a woman's role in her own home as well as in her marital home was largely objectified.

Once married, an Indian woman would typically enter a joint family system. An ideal Hindu joint family in contemporary India consists of a man and wife, their adult sons, their wives and children, and younger children of the parental couple (Gore, 1968; Sharma, 1997). A joint family can often be looked upon as a multiplicity of genealogically related nuclear families living under the same roof and sharing in worship, food, and property.[2] Very often, a joint family has been described as a group of adult male coparceners and their dependents—the dependents being wives and children (Gore, 1968). For instance, if a father has two sons and one daughter, the sons would be considered joint heirs (coparceners); but, a daughter would not inherit property (see endnote 1). According to Hindu law, an adult male and his sons were coparceners in ancestral property (Gore, 1968).

The very structure of the joint family contributed to an overall subordinate status of women. Formal authority was always centered on the oldest male and thereby hierarchically bound by age. This hierarchy occurred on many levels. Women were married and brought into the family that consisted of men who were all related by blood. They were not only biologically on the outside, but also they were treated as "symbolic-outsiders" until they gave birth to a son. Daughters-in-law would be completely included in the family only once they begot a son. And, if they did not beget a son, then a new wife could be *brought into the family* (although this changed with the Hindu Divorce Bill in 1952; Kapadia, 1958). Once married, the conjugal relationship between couples was discouraged from becoming too romanticized because the emphasis was on the socioeconomic welfare of the family. This contributed to the degradation of women's status in the family, which in turn was supported by denial of property rights to women and by women's inability to achieve economic independence (see endnote 1). Role and authority segregation of men and women were therefore essential to the economic well-being of a joint Hindu family. Even though women remained necessary to the family, they remained powerless, property-less, and dependent within the household which they symbolized.

It is evident from this discussion that women were largely seen as an instrument of procreation in the Hindu marriage system. Not only were they a "silent" voice in the historical literature, but their experiences of marital life remain largely unexplored. This is true even of social scientific literature which has continued to focus on variable-analytical studies that explore marital adjustment, attitudes, marital satisfaction, comparisons to love marriages, and so on (see Chandak & Sprecher, 1992; Dhyani & Kumar, 1996; Kapadia, 1958; Kapur 1970; Rao & Rao, 1975; Ross, 1961; Yelsma & Athappilly, 1988). Moreover, many of these studies are dated. The most recent longitudinal study to focus on arranged marriages was a sociopsychological survey published by Promilla Kapur in 1970, now over three decades old.

Given the scarcity of literature on the marital experiences of Hindu women in arranged marriages, I designed a narrative study that would access marital narratives of women who had been involved in arrange marriages in the last three decades. In the following section, I briefly describe the research practices that I undertook for the study. Following this, I explore the main sites of conflict and negotiation in the family that emerged from the interview narratives of my participants. Finally, I offer a brief discussion of the implications of such conflict in the study of diverse family systems.

Research Practices and Thematic Analysis

Aided with this historical and sociological knowledge, I traveled to Delhi, India, in the summer of 2003 to conduct life-history interviews with urban middle-class north Indian women who had chosen to have their marriages arranged for them. Broadly described, I centered my research practices around an ethnographic qualitative interviewing framework. Such approaches are especially sensitive to context, dynamic processes, and subjective perspectives, and allow us to understand experiences that are inaccessible from survey methods (Denzin & Lincoln, 2000; Strauss & Corbin, 1998).

My participants included 20 urban, working and nonworking, middle-class women who ranged in age from 27 to 44 and were married either in the early 1980s, the 1990s, or the early 2000s. I accessed the groups using a word-of-mouth and snowball strategy. A majority of the women were referred to me by families in the Delhi community where I myself reside. Their occupations ranged from homemakers to corporate executives, medical doctors, teachers, special education counselors, sexual rights activists, journalists, day care workers, and private entrepreneurs.

I designed a chronological interview protocol that was structured around three broad domains—girlhood, premarriage, and marriage. It comprised 25 open-ended questions that focused on socialization processes, family interactions, events, and turning points. Once completed, each interview was treated as a case. The interviews were all audiotaped and transcribed by me. After doing so, I conducted a thematic analysis to search for shared experiences that were common to the stories.

Seven broad themes, two of which focused upon conflict, emerged from my analysis. Through my participant's narratives, I found that family and marital conflict seemed to be rooted in one authority figure, that of the mother-in-law. Therefore, addressing the mother-in-law as a power-authority figure emerged as the primary site of conflict in the women's marital stories. My participants named her as a threat and coped with her by "performing resistance" which emerged in the form of a "material embodied resistance" and "silence." In the following section, I rely on my participants' self-stories to explore the aforementioned themes.

Addressing the Mother-in-Law

When a Hindu woman marries and moves to her new home, she joins a world in which all men are related by blood and the women are unrelated to each other (unless one is the daughter of the house who eventually does leave home). Within this world of the women, there exists a matriarchal hierarchy with the mother-in-law as the most significant person in terms of authority. In fact, a woman's marital experience often begins with encountering the mother-in-law. At least 60% of my participants were married into joint or semijoint families (see endnote 2), and the mother-in-law was invariably the first person they encountered. This figure merged as the first site and figure of conflict in my participants' narratives. All participants, regardless of age or year of marriage, spoke about the persisting presence of the mother-in-law. They portrayed her as a "monstrous" character who dominated their marital relationship. Her presence was so continuous that there seemed to be an acceptance of her interfering presence.

This process can be seen in Anita's story.[3] Twenty-nine-year-old Anita, who was married into a very traditional extended family, repeatedly referenced her mother-in-law in her story. In the course of her marriage, Anita's parents-in-law had disapproved of her wearing non-Indian or Western clothes. Anita explained that, although her mother-in-law never verbalized her disapproval, Anita nevertheless sensed the disapproval in her silence. Addressing this, she explained:

> No, she doesn't say anything, but you can make out. Because my mom-in-law is like that, no? I don't know sometimes I feel that she doesn't say anything, because she knows that I will not take any nonsense. That's why she doesn't speak up. But, it's okay because I don't like to cross her. If I cross her I cross him [my husband], and I don't want to do that. His whole happiness is connected with the parents. If I keep his parents happy he is very happy, you know?

In this exchange, Anita illustrated the importance of her mother-in-law in her marital life. In fact, as the interview progressed her relationship with her mother-in-law took more space in the story than her own marital relationship.

A resonating experience was related by Reema, a 37-year-old woman who had been married for 18 years. Reema's narrative was saturated with stories about her mother-in-law. She charted a trajectory that spanned a description, an explanation, and the consequence of the mother-in-law's presence in her life. Upon speculating on the "whys" of the conflict with her mother-in-law, Reema explained that the troubles were rooted in the beginning years of her marriage:

> Maybe because my husband is the only son (male) as my father-in-law expired very early. My mother-in-law must have been very attached to him or something. Then after the marriage the husband looks after more about the wife, that is there among newlyweds anyway. So she must be feeling that thing—left out. Maybe the problem started that way.

By suggesting that the problem starts "that way," Reema was generalizing that perhaps this was the reason for mother-in-law conflicts in most homes. Describing her verbal altercations with her mother-in-law, Reema attributed them to power struggles in the home:

> Yeah there are many. It's always a little thing, of no consequence. The fight starts about just anything. If I reply back then it becomes big. Then she says, "She doesn't listen to anyone, she doesn't agree with anything." Then they call up [my parents] and say, "She replied back and she did this." So they [my parents] used to say that, "We will make her understand, we can take her home for a while." Even now it's still there, but very less. I keep myself very busy. Now I don't involve in these things. I make it a point to go out, have my kitty parties

and all. Otherwise I go to the Avon store. I do this to make myself busy. There is not much money in it. You don't have any earning, but it keeps me occupied.

Reema's mother-in-law was a discipliner in the home, and if Reema did not "behave well," her "misdeeds" were reported to her parents. In whatever verbal or nonverbal ways the conflict occurred, there was a sense of foreboding about this matriarchal presence. Only some of the participants had been able to make spaces for themselves, both symbolically and physically, in their own homes. However, most of them were bitter about their continuing struggles with their mothers-in-law. This bitterness shadowed Suparna's story.

Thirty-seven-year-old Suparna's story was more old-fashioned. She had been married to her husband for spiritual reasons. Her mother's guru had suggested a match with a man who was one social class lower than her natal family, but belonged to the same religious community. Blindly believing the spiritual consul, her mother had urged her to marry this man not realizing that Suprana was unaccustomed to doing household chores. Suparna's mother-in-law expected a daughter-in-law who knew how to manage the household. Describing her inability to work in her in-law's kitchen, which was small and dirty compared to the one in her parental home, Suparna described some early altercations with her mother-in-law:

> She would say, "Why don't you work in the kitchen? Did your parents not see initially that we don't have a servant? Did they not prepare you for this?" I was like all young girls. I would like to get up late. I would get up at eight and I would find her scary eyes looking at me. I was asked not to get out of my room without taking a bath and I could not get out in a dressing gown. I had to get up early in the morning. They would get up at five, so I was expected to do the same. Things like that, you know? My husband would not say anything, and ours was not a very pleasant relationship. We used to have a lot of fights because of my in-laws. He would not accept his parents' mistakes. He thought that they were the best. She is my husband's soft spot. You know he never said "no" to her for anything. That's something very wrong I feel for my husband.

Suparna's story involved power struggles with her mother-in-law over chores, space, and her husband's attention. These eventually led to a property split in the family, leading to the literal emergence of two spatial units as they each moved into different family homes. During the time of the interview, her struggles with her mother-in-law continued.

Anita, Reema, and Suparna's stories illustrate that the mother-in-law is a power-authority figure in the Hindu joint family. A conflict with her is comparable to a conflict with the entire family. Not only is she the first matriarchal figure that a daughter-in-law encounters, but she also becomes a conduit to the rest of the family. Rather than get involved in overt conflict with her, my participants utilized and enacted a strategy of resistance to her interference.

Performing Resistance

In my study, I used the term *resistance* as a conflict resolution and negotiation strategy employed by my participants. Even though none of the participants used the terms *negotiation* or *resolution*, their stories seem to suggest that they had performed resistance to accomplish these very goals. In other words, they used resistance to carve literal and emotional spaces for themselves in their homes. As a response to conflict in the stories of my coparticipants, I defined resistance very loosely—it constituted material embodied resistance and silence against filial structure. Both qualities of resistance were articulated in distinct ways by the participants.

Material Embodied Resistance

By a material embodied resistance I am implying that some participants relied on external objects to enact resistance. As already explored, Anita had been discouraged from wearing Western clothes such as jeans, skirts, or dresses. As a new bride, the north Indian traditional dress, such as a sari or the salwar kameez, had been imposed upon her by her mother-in-law. For about five years, Anita adhered to these rules, but on occasion she would slip outside the house unnoticed in her jeans. She was materially resisting filial norms. On one such occasion she was caught by her father-in-law, who complained to her husband. Revealing her response to being disciplined about clothing, Anita told me:

> I didn't say anything, but I told my husband, look I am married to you, I'm not married to them. I will wear what I want. He said, "Okay agreed." He was agreeable to the idea that a human being should be able to wear clothes of their choice.

This negotiation with her husband was a resistant act against material norms which Anita successfully accomplished. Such material resistances might seem small, but they seemed to shape Anita's story.

Later on in the interview, Anita spoke of other restrictions that she had encountered. When single, she was used to dining out. Both her mother- and father-in-law had imposed a rule that required every family member to eat dinner together. Not one to be deterred by this, Anita began a bodily rebellion against the rule and was able to negotiate new rules of dining out with her husband. In doing this, she was able to make her marriage take precedence over the family. She reflected on this when she said:

> I just kept losing weight. There was a time when I was 38 kilograms [84 pounds] because I stopped eating at home. I don't like eating at home, and on top of it, it was a sort of rebellion. I was trying to show my husband that I will not eat at all.

This embodiment of material resistance was a recurrent theme in the narratives. Meena, a 27-year-old doctor, was married into a semijoint family. At the time of the interview she was living alone with her husband, but her in-laws often stayed with her. Meena spoke of beginning to wear "cut-sleeve" blouses even though her mother-in-law disapproved. Wearing those clothes in front of her husband's family was a resistant act through which she was sending the message that she was a "differentiated self," and that she would make her own rules while adhering to some of theirs.

> My own father never stopped me from wearing any type of dresses. My mother-in-law thinks that girls shouldn't wear jeans and sleeveless blouses. Once I shifted to my own home, I started wearing my normal clothes. I loved wearing shorts. When they are here, to not make them unhappy, I wear a nightgown over them.

Meena felt that she was able to resist because of the support she received from her husband.

> When they asked me not to wear these clothes, I told my husband, "So what should I do?" He said, "You wear whatever you want, don't worry I'll talk to them." He was supportive. He could have said, "No, my parents don't like it, so you shouldn't wear it." Instead he said, "No I like it and you should wear what everyone is wearing nowadays."

There were two factors that influenced Meena's resistance—support from her husband and beginning to live in her own home. Both Anita and Meena had involved their husbands in their resistant acts, thus garnering support from them. Although Anita and Meena embodied resistance in material ways, other women told stories of performing resistance through silence.

Silent Resistance

Neeta, a 44-year-old woman entrepreneur, was married into a joint family in which she was required to live not only with a mother-in-law, but also a grandmother-in-law. Her personal history as a single person had been a source of conflict with her mother-in-law. As an unmarried woman, Neeta had been "picky" about whom she would marry. Word of this had reached her husband's home. Her grandmother-in-law and mother-in-law were aware that she was "outspoken," and that she had rejected many men before she chose their son. Therefore, when Neeta got married they were determined to keep her "in check." They imposed rules on her that involved learning how to cook, how to obey them, and how to do household chores. Neeta coped with these rules via silence. Describing this, she said:

> I already knew that I was known to be very "outspoken." I did not want to do anything that would aggravate this. Yet I did not know what to do. I was not happy. Then my grandmother-in-law came to stay with us and that was a major adjustment because she was very clever and she had heard that I was sharp. She knew that if they don't keep me suppressed then I will speak out too much. So, the initial year was very difficult. I would cry sometimes—in hiding.

In trying to disprove her previous reputation to her in-laws, Neeta remained silent. In those early years she grew closer to her husband, who had been a stranger to her. Her silence with his family pushed them closer, and she gained his emotional support. In her silence, Neeta managed to shift the focus from family to marriage. In becoming closer to her husband, she had started helping him out in his business, which was undergoing a rough patch. During all this time, she carried on working in the household and also took over the reins of the business. In starting to help her husband economically, Neeta had emerged from the silence, and/or defeated the silence that had been imposed upon her. Neeta explained this transformation and her new self very succinctly:

> I think after marriage for a few years I really tried hard to be like a typical wife. Later, I was just trying to survive. I was busy with my house, my work, my children and I was trying to run the whole show. I think I was trying to be a superwoman, but at that time I was trying to be the best at whatever I was doing. My children had to be the best. In my work whatever I could do, even at home *I tried you know to do all the work that I can do.*

Silence emerged as strength in Neeta's narrative. Along similar lines, 44-year-old Naina, an economically independent corporate executive, was married into a joint family in which her mother-in-law tried to keep her in check. Naina utilized silence as a deliberate resistant strategy in dealing with conflict with her mother-in-law and other members of the family.

Naina entered her marriage as a confident and financially independent woman. However, she soon began to be harassed by her husband's family because they expected a traditional Indian wife. At first, she responded by replying and fighting back. When this did not solve the problem, she addressed the issue with her husband, thus shifting their story from family to marriage. She stopped overt resistance and handed the conflict over to her husband, thereby attaining a silent resistance:

> He took over and that was the only way we saved our sanity. Whenever I tried doing things on my own it never used to work. His family used to outplay me. They are much sharper, more politically minded, wiser about silly games. I think Mahesh latched on to the fact that I was cracking up. He told me, "You may be a communications expert, but you don't know how to communicate with this clan and I know how to communicate with them, so now you stay out. If they ask you anything just keep quiet and either you say we'll talk in front of Mahesh or don't say anything, just keep quiet."

Both Neeta and Naina used silence as a shield against the mother-in-law, which in turn brought them closer to their husbands. Anita and Meena used a material embodied resistance, with a similar goal—to garner support from their husbands. Resistance worked in a two-dimensional way in these marital stories. First, it shielded these women against the mother-in-law. Second, resistance brought these women closer to their husbands because they began confiding in their spouses to resist the matriarchal figure.

Final Thoughts

It is evident from the previous examples that the structural configuration of the Hindu joint (and semijoint) family creates two concentric circles of power in the household. The outer circle consists of the male line in which all men are bound by blood. The inner circle or the interior world of women, with the mother-in-law as the ruling matriarch, consists of women unrelated not only to each other but also to the men. In a typical situation, a daughter-in-law first experiences the inner circle and encounters the mother-in-law. This allows us to understand a type of marital conflict that is located outside the husband–wife relationship. It resides in a figure of authority in the family. Interestingly, even as this figure comes to represent conflict, it is clear that in resisting the mother-in-law, women gain access to marital support from their husbands, thus solidifying their marriage. The mother-in-law, even as she creates conflict, opens up channels for the daughters-in-law, allowing them access into the outer circle of men in which their husbands reside.

Questions for Consideration and Discussion

1. The topic considered in this research is somewhat sensitive in nature. What elements of the methodology do you think might have made participants more at ease discussing these issues?
2. Chawla's work considers, in part, a cultural conflict between more conservative mothers-in-law and their less conservative daughters-in-law. What would be other examples of times when cultures may conflict within family settings?
3. The narratives of these participants reflect upon issues of family power and the importance of the mother-in-law in Hindu family culture. In your family experiences, what specific family roles or positions have been culturally established as powerful, and why do you think that is the case?
4. Chawla's respondents used both silence and material embodied resistance in their efforts to reject the power of the mother-in-law. What examples of these strategies have you seen in family settings?
5. What do you see as the overarching value of this type of research for our understandings of family?

Endnotes

1. Hindu women were not entitled to any property rights until 1956, and therefore were economically dependent on their fathers, husbands, and later sons (Gore, 1968; Kapur, 1970). With the amendment of Hindu property laws in 1956 that allowed for female inheritance, and increased levels of women entering the workforce by choice in the latter half of the twentieth century, there was some change in gendered roles within families (Gore, 1968; Kapadia, 1958; Kapur, 1970). Further, in the 1980s and 1990s the liberalization of developing world economies created new jobs for women throughout the world, including India (Government of India, 2001). In particular, the last two decades saw an upsurge of women in both the urban and rural workforces. Of the 314 million Indians currently in the workforce, 89 million are women (Government of India, 2001). Despite the promise and arrival of economic independence, many urban Hindu women continue to choose arranged marriages. It would seem that the breakdown of economic disparities would lead to an increase in self-arranged or love marriages, yet that has not been the case.

2. In this study I have used the words *joint* and *semijoint* to refer to family structure and cohabitation patterns. A semijoint family could mean one in which one son and his family live together with his parents while the other siblings live elsewhere.

3. In this chapter, all the women's names have been changed to pseudonyms in order to protect their privacy.

References

Applbaum, K. D. (1995). Marriage with a proper stranger: Arranged marriage in metropolitan Japan. *Journal of Ethnology, 34*, 37–51.

Bumiller, E. (1990). *May you be the mother of 100 sons: A journey among the women of India*. New York: Fawcett Columbine.

Chandak, R., & Sprecher, S. (1992). Attitudes about arranged marriage and dating among men and women from India. *Free Inquiry in Creative Psychology, 20*(1), 59–69.

Denzin, N. K., & Lincoln, Y. S. (2000). *Handbook of qualitative research* (2nd ed.). Thousand Oaks, CA: Sage.

Dhyani, J., & Kumar, P. (1996). Marital adjustment: A study of some related factors. *Indian Journal of Clinical Psychology, 23*(2), 112–116.

Gore, M. S. (1968). *Urbanization and family change*. New York: Humanities Press.

Government of India. (2001). National Commission for Women Report. New Delhi, India: Ministry of Education and Social Welfare, 2001.

Kapadia, K. M. (1958). *Marriage and family in India*. Calcutta, India: Oxford University Press.

Kapur, P. (1970). *Marriage and the working woman in India*. Delhi, India: Vikas.

Mukherjee, P. (1978). *Hindu women: Normative models*. New Delhi: Orient Longman Ltd.

Mullatti, L. (1995). Families in India: Beliefs and realities. *Journal of Comparative Family Studies, 26*(1), 11–25.

Rao, V. V., & Rao, N. (1975). Arranged marriages: An assessment of the attitudes of college students. *Journal of Comparative Family Studies, 7*(3), 433–453.

Ross, A. D. (1961). *The Hindu family in the urban setting*. Bombay, India: Oxford University Press.

Sastri, H. C. (1972). *The social background of the forms of marriage in ancient India* (Vol. 1). Calcutta, India: Sanskrit Pustak Bhandar.

Sastri, H. C. (1974). *The social background of the forms of marriage in ancient India* (Vol. 2). Calcutta, India: Sanskrit Pustak Bhandar.

Sharma, K. L. (1997). *Social stratification in India: Issues and themes*. New Delhi, India: Sage.

Strauss, A., & Corbin, J. (1998). *Basics of qualitative research (2nd* Ed.). Thousand Oaks, CA: Sage.

Sur, A. K. (1973). *Sex and marriage in India*. Bombay, India: Allied.

Yelsma, P., & Athappilly, K. (1988). Marital satisfaction and communication practices: Comparisons among Indian and American couples. *Journal of Comparative Family Studies, 19*, 37–54.

Section 3: Conclusions and Application— Power and Conflict in Your Family Experience _____

This chapter has introduced you to some theoretical conceptions of conflict and power, ideas about where our conflict management styles and strategies come from, information about conflict outcomes, and discussion of abuse and violence in family strategies. As you attempt to relate this information to your own life, you may need to begin by rethinking your concept of conflict. This will help you consider how you engage in conflict (the positive and negative), as well as thinking about the possibility of change for negative conflict patterns you might have or observe.

Changing the Way You Think about Conflict

One change that is hard for most people to make, when they learn about conflict theory and research, is to stop thinking of conflict as always a bad thing, and as a situation where one party must win and the other lose (or one party be right and the other wrong). As is indicated in this chapter, conflict is not about right and wrong. Conflict instead is about differences we perceive and how we interact in relation to those differences. Conflict is created in interaction between family members. Although the word *conflict* has negative associations, it is a natural part of our family processes. People are different from one another, thus it is natural that they will have different perceptions, desires, values, and so forth. Conflict is not only natural, but it can also be beneficial. Think about the last big positive change that happened in your family. Were there any conflicts associated with that change? It is likely that, big or small, there were. Often conflict is what encourages us to make change. At some point you may have expressed to your adult caregivers that your curfew (or some other rule) was too strict. This conflict may have resulted in a change of that rule (if you were lucky). When we express our points of difference in the family, it allows us to create changes and that is a growth process for the family and its members. This is the positive value of conflict.

Of course, conflict can at times be a negative experience. Due to the cultural differences in the perception of conflict and beliefs about conflict, engaging in conflict may be more problematic in some cultures than in others. Thus, we must keep in mind that, even though it is not always negative, conflict is not always positive for the interactants either.

When we can begin to think of conflict in this way, not as inherently negative or bad (nor always positive or good) but rather as an ubiquitous part of our family process, it may help us fear conflict less and attend more to how we engage in conflict. As noted by the many scholars referenced in this chapter, it is how we *manage* conflict that has the most effect on relational outcomes, not the amount of conflict itself. Thus, conflict is not something to be feared or simply avoided, but it is worthwhile to think about the ways that we deal with conflict as we interact with family members.

Considering How You Engage in Conflict

As with many other communication patterns, the way we handle conflict is likely due to a variety of factors. Researchers suggest that there are individual factors, cultural and family factors, and role factors that impact our management strategies.

One of the individual factors that researchers believe may be related to our ability to engage in conflict in a productive manner is cognitive complexity. This concept, based on constructivism, relates to the degree to which we think of others in multifaceted, complex ways. From this perspective, individuals who are more cognitively complex are able to create more person-centered messages; however, that doesn't mean they always will (sometimes they may not want to). The concept of complexity and how it relates to conflict management can be used to inform our interactions with others. It can help us understand why children, and even adolescents, may not be able to create messages that are compelling for the other. (Have you ever heard a 13-year-old try to argue with his or her parents based only on what he or she wants and not at all thinking about what the parents might be thinking or wanting?) It also may point to the issue of intentionality in conflict management. Even people who are capable of producing compelling person-centered messages may not always want to. This concept can provide us a lens of understanding for our own conflict choices and also those of others.

In addition to individual factors, the family culture and the larger societal culture impact the ways we interact during conflict. Family conflict patterns are developed through interaction, as members take on particular conflict strategies and roles. Considering the conflict roles exhibited in your family, as discussed by Hughes and Stow, may provide insight into how conflicts proceed in your family interactions, and some alternative role positions you may want to adopt in conflict management. Additionally, children in families learn the way to engage in conflict in part from their parents. When parents manage conflict in ways that are primarily constructive, their children are likely to learn to manage conflict in similar ways (and vice versa). As adults, this information should certainly influence how we engage in conflict with and in the presence of children, and also allows us to understand more about how we arrived at our own patterns of managing conflict.

The larger cultures in which the family is embedded also impact the way members engage in conflict management. Research suggests that gendered patterns, such as women nagging and men withdrawing, have something to do with our expectations of men and women and the relative power differences (and types of power) for the two groups. Scholars also indicate that cultural expectations about individuality, collectivism, and so on may impact our face management strategies in conflict (the extent to which we are concerned with preserving our own position or that of others). As in the Chawla article, culture can strongly impact the power bases held by members of families and who is allowed to use what conflict strategies. And when two cultures clash, conflict can be more difficult to manage due to differing positions and expectations. Thinking about cultural impacts and expectations provides us another method for understanding our own communication in conflict and that of others.

Although the most useful and constructive ways to manage conflict in any family or any particular situation depend on the aspects of that family and situation (and the participants), there seem to be some communicative behaviors that are more destructive than constructive in conflict. The research we addressed in this chapter suggests that some conflict management strategies are more effective than others, and result in better relational outcomes.

One conflict behavior that often seems to have negative repercussions is the refusal to acknowledge or engage in communication about the conflict when other relational partners are seeking to do so. This is discussed in this chapter in terms of demand–withdrawal patterns and the Avoider role discussed by Hughes and Stow. There are likely a variety of factors that impact why individuals engage in withdrawal from conflict. Some research suggests that men are more likely to withdraw from conflict in family settings because of cultural expectations that men should not discuss their feelings. Other individuals may avoid or withdraw from conflict because of a fear that conflict is bad, or because they see themselves as powerless in the conflict situation.

Another set of conflict behaviors that have been shown to have negative outcomes for relationships are those which represent extreme negativity (hostility, name calling, contempt, etc.). Negative affect behaviors in conflict have been shown to have poor effects on relational satisfaction as well as the emotional health of the relational partners. Of course, the extreme form of such negative behaviors is abuse and violence. As discussed in this chapter, cultural patterns are also related to the extent to which abuse is perpetrated in some families, and who is most likely to be the victim of abuse. Abusive relationships have extremely troubling outcomes for victims, abusers, and observers, as can be seen in Eckstein's article.

Some family patterns are extremely negative, but can be prevented or changed with effort. The writings of Chawla and Brule explicitly show how some family interactants have attempted to change or alter negative patterns within their family settings, and how difficult that can be. Additionally, the research studies included in this chapter point to the existence of more positive conflict management strategies that appear to have a more positive impact on relationships and relational interactants; for example, support-reassurance, expressions of caring, calm discussion, and problem solving. As family members, we may want to engage in increased use of such strategies in our interactions. It is important that we consider the ways that we deal with conflict in our families so that we can make changes where necessary in order to achieve the benefits of conflict interactions, but avoid the potential troubling outcomes for all family members.

Questions for Consideration and Discussion

1. In general, how do you think people feel about conflict in family settings? Where does this perception come from and how might we adjust it to be more functional for families?
2. In the most recent family conflict you experienced, what power did you have? What power did your relational partners have? Who do you feel had more power in the situation? Why?
3. Gottman and Fitzpatrick have developed typologies of couples with regard to their communication patterns, including conflict management. What do you see as the benefit of developing such typologies? What drawbacks might there be?
4. How does the larger culture in which you live impact the way your family engages in conflict? In what ways do you see your family corresponding to cultural expectations and in what ways do you see your family diverging? Why?
5. When conflict turns into family violence, it can be very detrimental to family members. As a society, how can we help families learn strategies to avoid and/or manage conflict that threatens to become violent or abusive?

Key Terms and Concepts _____

attribution theory
authoritarian parenting
authoritative parenting
coercive power
cognitively complex
conflict
conflict avoiding couple
conflict management

constructivist
demand–withdraw pattern
expert power
family violence
independent couple
legitimate power
permissive parenting
power

referent power
rejecting–neglecting parenting
reward power
separate couple
social construct
traditional couple
validating couple
volatile couple

7

Race, Ethnicity, and Family

Chapter Outline

Chapter Objectives

1. To be able to define race and ethnicity and understand the difference between them
2. To develop understanding of how race/ethnicity impact family culture and experience and thus family practice
3. To understand the relationship between socialization practices and racial/ethnic impacts on family
4. To critically address how messages about race/ethnicity have affected your understandings of self and others, as well as the family behaviors of self and others

Section 1: Overview of Issues of Race, Ethnicity, and Family

- If you were to casually describe yourself to someone you had never met, what descriptors would you use?
- If you were asked about your ancestry, what categories would you mention?
- If your college or university offered a scholarship program "based on race," would you assume yourself to be eligible? On what racial category or categories would you make that assumption?

Looking at your answers to these questions, did your racial/ethnic characteristics appear the same in answer to each question? Would you be more likely to think about yourself as belonging to a particular racial/ethnic group under some situations than others? Keep these thoughts in mind as you read this chapter and think about the complexity of race and ethnicity.

Defining Race and Ethnicity

The U.S. Census of 2000 asked respondents to select their race from the following categories (Grieco & Cassidy, 2001):

> White
> Black or African American
> American Indian or Alaska Native
> Asian
> Native Hawaiian and other Pacific Islander
> Some other race

Many of these categories had subcategory choices (i.e., Asian Indian, Chinese, Filipino, Japanese, Korean, Vietnamese, and Other Asian were subcategories for the race categorized as Asian). In addition to those choices, participants were asked to indicate whether they were Spanish, Hispanic, or Latino (this choice could then be combined with any previous option given). Individuals could also select more than one race or subcategory, allowing for many possible combinations of categories. It's a fairly complex system of attempting to capture how individuals understand their own race/ethnicity. Each time the census is conducted, the methods used to assess race are shifted somewhat in an attempt to more accurately capture citizens' beliefs about their racial category. After many years of conducting the census, these changes continue, and likely there will be some alterations in the race component for the next census. This is due to the difficulty of clearly defining the boundaries of racial categories and the labels that are appropriate to those categories.

Race as a Category of People Perception

Race and ethnicity are difficult terms to define because they signify so much that cannot be captured in a simple definition. But, for the sake of this reading, I provide definitions of

BOX 7.1 • *Internet Connection*

The U.S. Census Bureau Web site provides a variety of information about race, as well as a discussion of how race is defined and calculated in government surveys. You can reach the race page of the census site at www.census.gov/population/www/socdemo/race.html.

each here. Wilkinson (1999, p. 18) defines a **race** as "a category of people who are related by a common heredity or ancestry and who are perceived and responded to in terms of external features or traits." It is important to note in this definition that race is a social concept, not a biological one. What this means is that, although we often think about race as a genetic trait, there is no race gene. People of the same race have similarities in appearance because of evolutionary changes related to their location of national origin, not because they have a "White gene" or a "Black gene." It is important to understand this because it speaks to the idea of variability, similarity, and difference within and between races. Two people of the same racial category are as likely to be genetically dissimilar as two people of different racial categories.

This is not to say that race isn't "real." It is real, because it is a very real part of the way we respond to each other socially. Because racial division is based on external features and traits, race is a social marking that we use when communicating with and about others. We categorize others into racial groups, and apply beliefs about those groups to others as we attempt to understand them and their behavior. Thus, the experience of living life for individuals of one race is different from the experience of living life for individuals of another race, because those racial categories impact how others respond to us and what sort of opportunities are more and less available to us. How we think about race, and the categories into which people are divided based on external markers, are also related to issues of power. This is part of why, over the course of history, what has "counted" as a race has changed. At one point in U.S. history, Black men and women who had been enslaved and Black men and women who were free were considered to be of different races (Fields, 1990). Historically, in the United States and across the world, race has often been used as a way to keep some groups of individuals in power, while denying power to other groups. Negative racial stereotypes provide "justification" for treating one race as inferior in some way to others. Thus, even though race is not a genetic characteristic, it is certainly part of the reality of our experience as individuals and as family members.

Ethnicity as Culture of a Group of People

Ethnicity can generally be referred to as those cultural beliefs and behaviors that a group of people, originating at some point of their family history in a particular location, share, which make them distinct from other groups (Wilkinson, 1999). So, like race, ethnicity isn't biological. Ethnicity is largely an issue of shared culture that develops in a particular geographic region over a long period of time. As members of that culture leave and go on to other places, they and their families carry the traditions and beliefs of that culture with them. For example, Italian Americans are immigrants or descendants of immigrants who originally lived in Italy. In Italy, they or their ancestral family developed a culture, and then that culture has gone on with them (and been passed down to their children and grandchildren in somewhat altered forms) as they relocated. Ethnicity is not equal to race; the two represent different ideas, though they may be connected by location. This means that people within a particular race (e.g., White) can still be of different ethnic groups (like Irish or French).

"White" as Race

As noted by Walker (1993), Frankenberg (1993, 2001), Bonilla-Silva (2003), and other scholars, one issue with race is that people often forget that White is also a race. We often treat White as an absence of race. For example, if a politician is White, news stories about him or her will generally not mention race. However, if he or she is Black, that will often be mentioned in some way. The same is often true for stories about crime, where race is not mentioned if all of the involved individuals (perpetrators and victims) are White.

This tendency to view White as a nonrace happens both for individuals in everyday interaction and for family communication scholarship. Thus, thinking about the impact of race on family is largely focused on how non-White families behave. This is unfortunate, in that it may limit our scholarly understandings of race and ethnicity in family settings, but it is partly a reflection of the reality that families of color face. Individuals and families who are White are not without race; however, because White is so often seen as an absence of race, their race is not often a focus of attention, or prejudice, from others. Thus, race is a more salient issue in the experience of non-White family members. In addition, White families are disproportionately reflected in family communication research. Studies often involve subjects of a variety of racial groups (and are not, thus, *only* about Whites), yet the predominant race of participants is typically White. So, in some ways, it does make sense that research explicitly about race is largely focused on families that are not White. Even though that is the case, in this chapter the authors discuss research that considers individuals of a variety of races and ethnicities.

Difficulty of Discussing Race and Ethnicity

To engage in a discussion of race is not always easy, and may seem like it is an acknowledgment of difference in a way that is itself prejudicial. You've probably heard people say that they "never notice" race or that race is completely unimportant to them. This perspective likely springs from a good place (wanting to avoid any aspect of racism); however, it runs the risk of denying the real social and structural differences that occur on the basis of racial categorization. The attempt to be "colorblind" arises in part from a desire to avoid racism, and in part from a discomfort with "wrangling with" the complexity of race and the potential recognition that racial categories result in some individuals having more opportunities than others (Bonilla-Silva, 2003; Frankenberg, 1993; Knowles & Peng, 2005). However, to ignore race is not to avoid racism. Race is a fundamental part of our experience of humanity. Although racial categorization has been, and will likely continue to be, used as a way to oppress particular groups and empower others, a discussion of race and its impacts on our lives is not itself inherently racist. It is only through a frank consideration of race and ethnicity, and their impact on us, that we can hope to understand and avoid the potential negative outcomes of racial and ethnic categorization.

This section of the chapter discusses some of the ways that race and ethnicity relate to beliefs and interactions in family and the creation of family culture. Second, it addresses issues of racial/ethnic socialization in the family system. Finally, this section considers interracial and multiracial families.

Race, Ethnicity, and Family Culture

Early research in family process typically did not consider how race and ethnicity impact or relate to family interaction. Race was mentioned only as a demographic variable of the participants and little attention was given to how race is related to culture, family process, and thereby communication. In the past few decades, more family scholars have addressed the importance of race and ethnicity in the creation of family practices (Diggs & Socha, 2004; Kotchick & Forehand, 2002; Turner & West, 2003). This is important, Turner and West (2003) note, because without attention to these issues of diversity, the study of family is partial and makes a faulty assumption of homogeneity in family structure and process. Kotchick and Forehand (2002) note that, even more recently, researchers have begun to pay attention to within-group variations and the parenting strategies that represent particular strengths for that culture. Such a focus gives us a better sense of family experiences and successes, because a parenting style that works well in one culture may work less well in another. One example of this relates to parental discipline styles, as discussed in Chapter 6. Although many studies have found authoritative parenting to be most effective, some research has indicated that for particular ethnic/racial groupings, authoritarian styles may have more positive effects (for example, Chao, 1994; Lamborn, Dornbusch, & Steinberg, 1996). From this we can see the importance of thinking about how race and ethnicity contribute to family culture, and how that culture then relates to family processes and outcomes. It would be faulty to assume that what works for one family culture is best for all others, partly because of the family beliefs and values that develop from larger cultural influences, such as race and ethnicity.

Race, Ethnicity, and Family Values

Racial and ethnic culture impacts what families most value, and is the "glue" that helps sustain family togetherness. We learn in our cultural settings, including race and ethnicity, what is valued for individuals and for families. We are assessed by members of our cultures on the degree to which we are able or willing to act in a way that corresponds to those values. For example, in mainstream U.S. culture of the 1950s, divorce was considered a failure and an embarrassment. When parents were divorced, people looked askance at them and at their family because of this perceived failure to uphold the value of marital and family commitment. Today, that expectation has changed somewhat in mainstream culture, and we are less surprised or judgmental about families of divorce. Racial and ethnic culture has similar effects on our family values.

Families may hold particular values more strongly because of the influence of racial/ethnic culture. In a study of Mexican American families in California, Aoki (2000) found that participants focused on the importance of family in their lives and how family members must support and sustain one another even when they would rather not. Aoki's respondents also discussed the way that religion was an anchor point for the family. These

BOX 7.2 • *Did You Know?*

Living in nuclear family households is not the norm in all cultures. For example, in sub-Saharan Africa, about 50 percent of older adults live with grandchildren and/or adult children (Zimmer & Dayton, 2005). In northern Vietnam, 75 percent of newly married couples reside with the groom's parents (Hirschman & Nguyan, 2002). And, in Taiwan, 50 percent of young teens were raised in households with their grandparents (Yi, Pan, Chang, & Chan, 2006).

ideas, Aoki argued, served as forces that unified the family members and provided them with a strong sense of family identity, as well as ethnic identity. In a similar study, Mosely-Howard and Evans (2000) found seven prominent themes in the narratives of African American families: relying on family tradition to raise children, the value of kinship bonds, pride in cultural heritage, overt teaching about racism, negotiation between two cultures, education, and the role of spirituality. The authors argue that these themes indicate the value placed on relationships in these African American families.

Sometimes the values affected by racial/ethnic culture are general beliefs, and in other instances they may be more specifically related to beliefs about family responsibilities. For example, Burr and Mutchler (1999) considered how Black, Hispanic, and White participants felt about the provision of financial support and coresidence between adult children and their parents. The authors found that older Black and Hispanic respondents were more supportive of the idea that generations should live together when necessary than were older White respondents. These results were the case with regard to both adult children living with their parents, and parents living with their adult children. Black and Hispanic participants were also more likely to feel that adult children should provide financial support to their parents when needed than White participants. The three groups had more similar beliefs about parents providing financial support when necessary to their adult children. Lee, Peek, and Coward (1998) also found that older Black respondents believed that children had a greater obligation to help support and assist their parents than did older White respondents. The authors of these two studies suggest that these differences are likely related to cultural differences in ideas about family responsibility, particularly the responsibility of children to their parents. Such beliefs may impact the likelihood of intergenerational support being offered, and also affect how family members feel about it being offered. Family members from cultures where such support is considered an obligation may see it as a natural part of the family history. Family members from cultures where such intergenerational support is less valued may see it as more burdensome or have no model of how to engage in such exchanges.

Race, Ethnicity, and Family Behavior

In addition to affecting our beliefs about family and our values with relation to family issues, racial and ethnic culture impacts how we actually "do family." Penington (2004) studied mother–adolescent daughter pairs in Europen American and African American families. As you will see in Section 2 of the chapter, her research revealed many similarities between the pairs, but also differences that appeared to be related to how each racial group saw family and their role in it. Phinney, Kim-Jo, Osorio, & Vilhjalmsdottir (2005) considered similar issues of autonomy and connectedness in their analysis of independence, compliance, and assertion for adolescents and young adults in families. Their study involved European Americans, Armenian Americans, Mexican Americans, and Korean Americans. They found many similarities between the groups, as well as some differences. One major similarity that the authors noted was that the groups did not differ in terms of autonomy (independence) in their family relationships. One major difference was that the non-European participants were more compliant with parental requests or commands than the European participants. The authors argue that these differences are likely related to cultural expectations about family, children, and the process of becoming adult.

At times, we may see the intersection of race/ethnicity with other cultural factors, such as religion. Sherif (1999) argues that the rules of the Qur'an (the Islamic holy book) and Islamic culture impact how children are raised in Islamic families. Children are considered very important to the life of the family, and are brought into the adult social circle early in life. The interaction with adults produces a consistent emphasis on displaying gender-specific behaviors. Parents will correct young boys from an early age for displaying feminine behaviors, and girls are taught early to be soft spoken and dress modestly. Islamic children are also taught to respect their parents and not question the parents' decisions or argue with the parents. This extends into young adulthood and beyond with the selection of a major in college and even a spouse.

From these studies and examples, it seems clear that the cultures related to race and ethnicity impact the beliefs and values that families hold about their relationships and obligations. They also affect the behaviors that families engage in when interacting with one another. As the culture impacts the family, so the family creates and recreates the culture; within the family, socialization is provided with regard to family culture and racial/ethnic culture.

Race/Ethnicity Socialization

As we have discussed previously, one part of family life is socialization. Family members socialize each other with regard to both family expectations and the expectations of the larger culture. Through **race/ethnicity socialization,** parents pass on to their children the racial and ethnic cultural beliefs, values, and behaviors that they have learned. Children likewise affect their parents' understandings of self and culture.

At times, adults may offer specific explicit messages about race/ethnicity to their children. Frabutt, Walker, and MacKinnon-Lewis (2002) studied African American families with a young adolescent child. They investigated connections between the extent of explicit racial socialization messages a mother provided (ranking them as high, moderate, or low), and various family factors including warmth, negativity, and involvement. These researchers found that mothers who showed moderate racial socialization seemed to have the most involved, warm, and positive relationships with their children. Whereas this relationship may not be causal (that is, the researchers can't claim that the socialization leads to the relationship or vice versa), it is interesting to note that the research seems to suggest that moderate explicit racial socialization efforts (not talking about race with extremely high frequency, but not ignoring it either) were connected to the most positive family patterns. This study addresses the frequency of socialization efforts, but it focuses exclusively on explicit messages, and doesn't address how families felt about or experienced their own socialization processes. Other authors, however, have talked about these issues.

Members of families may believe passing on messages about race/ethnicity to be more or less important due to cultural expectations and the positioning of that race/ethnicity within larger social settings. Kawamoto and Cheshire (1999) interviewed American Indian mothers and preadolescents from Oregon. Though the families were living in an urban environment, the mothers indicated the importance of teaching the practices and beliefs of the culture. The researchers noted that the transmission of such information occurred in many ways, including observing cultural phenomenon (tribal dance), telling stories, and so on. The mothers felt that such efforts were vitally important in their cultural and family lives.

Similarly, other scholars have found that race socialization is particularly important in some family settings. Hughes and Chen (1997) found that African American families engaged in a variety of socialization about race issues. In their study, they indicate that families primarily attempted to teach children about African American culture. A second type of socialization that was common in the families related to preparing children for encountering racism and prejudice of others. Finally, they noted that only a small number of parents also provided their children with messages indicating that they should not trust people of other races (see also Garcia-Coll, Meyer, & Brillon, 1995). Marsiglia and Holleran (1999) consider the role of Mexican American mothers in passing along cultural socialization messages to their daughters. The researchers found that the mothers of their adolescent respondents were passing along traditional messages from Mexican culture, which prominently placed women in a subordinate yet morally superior role to men, but were also providing more feminist messages of independence and strength to their daughters. The families studied by all of these authors believed in the importance of passing on information about racial and ethnic culture. However, not all families feel the same need to explicitly socialize their children with regard to racial/ethnic issues.

As discussed earlier in the text, family stories are an important way that socialization messages are passed on. Bylund (2003) found both similarities and differences in family stories told by her European American, Mexican American, and African American participants. Although her study was too small to make generalizations, she noted that only the African American family explicitly stated that there were lessons about race, and racism, to be learned in family stories. Bylund noted that this is likely due to the family's history in the United States and the complex nature of Black–White race relations in this country.

Talking about race in very explicit ways may seem to be more important for families whose race/ethnicity is more "marked" within a larger social setting. McAdoo (2001) argues that socialization messages about race and ethnicity are vitally important. Parents have to walk a thin line between preparing their children for racial issues and overemphasizing the problems or dangers of race and discrimination. Because of the racial/ethnic stereotypes and prejudices that exist in the larger culture, however, most parents whose children are not of minority status do not feel the same need to expressly address issues of race with their children.

Family socialization can become particularly complex when the racial/ethnic culture of the family seems to be in contrast or conflict with the mainstream culture of the society it exists within. This is often the case in families where immigration has been recent. In some situations, families may change as they adapt to the new culture. Jain and Belsky (1997) considered the role of acculturation (adapting to and accepting the expectations of a new culture

BOX 7.3 • *Reading about Immigration and Family*

If immigration is something that is distant from your own experience, you may find it revealing to read autobiographical or fictional accounts of the intersections between family, race, and ethnicity within the context of immigration. Some titles to consider include:

The Namesake by Jhumpa Lahiri (2004)
On Gold Mountain by Lisa See (1996)
The Fortunate Pilgrim by Mario Puzo (1965)
American Chica by Marie Arana (2005)
Lost in Translation by Eva Hoffman (1990)
Crossing Over by Ruben Martinez (2002)
Children of Loneliness by Anzia Yezierska (1923)
The Plot Against America by Phillip Roth (2004)
Paper Fish by Tina DeRosa (1980)
Brown Girl, Brownstones by Paule Marshall (1959)

and interweaving those expectations into the previously existing cultural beliefs) in the fathering behaviors of Indian immigrants. They found that the acculturation process did have an impact on parenting behaviors. Fathers in the study who were more acculturated to the United States were more involved and engaged in child care than those who were not. The authors argue that this is because the Indian culture places virtually all responsibility for child care on the mother, whereas U.S. culture has shifted toward more shared responsibility. Thus, as the fathers adopted the U.S. culture in their lives, they also changed their parenting style.

The acculturation of the fathers in Jain and Belsky's (1997) study seems to have resulted in a positive outcome for the family (more involved parenting), but other studies related to the issue of immigration, family, and acculturation have pointed to the tensions that can arise as a result of cultural shifts. In Li's 2004 study of Chinese immigrant families living in Canada, he found that parents placed a heavy emphasis on learning and on the development of moral character. Additionally, the parents also promoted the idea that children should become culturally integrated into the larger Canadian culture in order to be more successful in life. Li (2004) notes that at times these two competing values (retaining of a traditional Chinese culture, while becoming part of the larger culture in Canada) caused tensions for the children in these families. In a similar study, Farver, Narang, and Bhadha (2002) considered the influence of families on the acculturation and ethnic identity (as well as psychological characteristics) of Asian Indian adolescents who had been born in the United States (but whose parents were immigrants). The authors found that those families who felt more marginalized, or less integrated into mainstream culture, and/or had not found a way to integrate their ethnic identity with their national culture, experienced more family conflict. Additionally, when parents and children had similar levels of acculturation, the adolescents had greater self-esteem and less anxiety than when there were differences between parent and adolescent integration into the culture. Aoki (2000) also found, in his study of Mexican American families, that changing socialization and acculturation of generations produced conflict for family members because children and grandchildren, as they became acculturated to the larger society, were less inclined to see the importance of a strong family connection or religion than their parents and grandparents were (see also Silverstein & Chen, 1999).

Socialization is an important, and in fact inevitable, part of family life. As discussed here, families may feel more or less urgency to impart specific messages to their children related to race. Studies seem to suggest that European American families (whose race/ethnicity is less marked) may stress racial/ethnic learning in the family less than non-White families. Cultural socialization in the family may be even more complex when there are different, and even contradictory, values, beliefs, and behaviors being promoted by the racial/ethnic cultures and by the larger culture in which the family is embedded. Issues of socialization and how to "deal with" race may be even more complicated for families that are composed of more than one race or ethnicity.

Interracial and Multiracial Families

The terms *interracial* and *multiracial* are used to designate families where members represent more than one racial grouping. This may be two White parents who adopt a Black child. It may be an African American parent and a Chinese American parent who together have children. There are endless variations of racial/ethnic composition we can find in family systems. Being in a family that is composed of multiple races presents unique challenges and opportunities for family members. There are many ways that a family may be multicultural (e.g., two religions, two ethnicities), but racial differences are somewhat unique in that they are apparent not only to those inside the relationship, but also to observers.

Interracial Couples

In the United States, interracial marriage was illegal or somehow limited in many states up until the 1960s. It wasn't until 1967 that the Supreme Court, in the case of *Loving v. Virginia*, ruled that antimiscegenation laws were unconstitutional. Although this forced all of the states that still had laws against interracial marriage on their books to retract them, it did not create an automatic acceptance of such relationships (for a discussion see Wallenstein, 2002). Even today, social sanctions against interracial relationships are a common occurrence in the United States. Thus, it may be harder for interracial couples and families to maintain happy and satisfying relationships in the face of both cultural differences and the disapproval of others.

Achieving a satisfying and stable relationship may be somewhat more difficult for interracial couples; however, research suggests that it is certainly possible. Leslie and Letiecq (2004) studied interracial couples (where one partner was Black and one partner was White). They found that partners who had a strong sense of pride in their own race, but were also willing to accept people of other races, were the most satisfied with their marital relationship. Foeman and Nance (1999) concur with this view, arguing that interracial couples who are able to go through a series of four stages of adjustment are more likely to be successful and satisfied. First, the relational partners must have an awareness of four perspectives on race: their own, their partner's, their racial group, and their partner's racial group. Communication about these perspectives helps partners develop this understanding.

Second, the couple must find a way to deal with the social perceptions of others in regard to race. They need to decide together how to respond to racial insults or slights. Third, the partners need to develop a way to understand and define themselves and their relationship that is not based on negative ideas or the downsides of interracial relationships. Perhaps they may reach a definition that allows them to see how much richness there can be in bringing together the rituals, beliefs, and values of two cultures. Finally, couples have to learn how to sustain and maintain their relationship with regard to race issues by returning to the discussion when they need to. Ignoring race and race issues does not make them go away; it is through communication that we manage problems related to race.

Children in Multiracial Families

As with adults in interracial relationships, discussion of race and race issues is also important for biracial or multiracial children. Fukuyama (1999) writes about her experience being a biracial (Japanese and Anglo American) child in the 1950s and beyond. She states that it was difficult for her, as a child and well into her adult life, to find a way to claim both cultural heritages, but that eventually doing so made her a more emotionally healthy person. Fukuyama says that discussions about race and racism were not a part of her childhood experience with her parents, and this made it difficult for her to develop a way to approach these issues (see also Williams, 1999). Stephan and Stephan (1991) and Suyemoto (2004) argue that, once biracial and multiracial children have developed this sense of positive self-identity, they may be particularly responsive and respectful of the diversity of others. Thus, even though some see biracial status as a negative for children, these authors argue that it can be a positive, if self-concept is strong.

Similar, yet different, issues may arise when parents and children do not share race/ethnicity. Galvin (2003) considers some of the particular challenges faced by families where a child or children is adopted **transracially** (across races) and internationally. Families in such situations (for example, when a Korean child is adopted by a set of White parents) face an interesting and complex set of dynamics. Galvin notes that issues of family identity development are affected by the transracial and international nature of the family. Among other concerns, families may need to deal with racism in attitudes of other family members, may not have creation stories to share with the child, need to be prepared to address the physical differences between the child and other family members both within and outside the family, and may struggle to define and describe their family cultural identity. Additionally, Galvin states that such families must discover how they will (or will not) discuss their adoption story with outsiders, and deal with incidents of racism from others. Finally, Galvin indicates that socialization may be particularly complicated

BOX 7.4 • *Family in the News*

Although recent stories about stars like Angelina Jolie have made transracial adoptions seem relatively commonplace, their history is more complex than you might think. The Adoption History Project offers information about transracial adoptions across time at http://darkwing. uoregon.edu/~adoption/topics/transracialadoption.htm.

in transracial international adoptive families, because families must decide how, when, and how much to expose the child to the culture of origin as well as the adoptive culture. This may be even more difficult because adoptive parents may have little firsthand knowledge of the child's culture of origin. Children who had been adopted transracially and their parents, interviewed by deHaymes and Simon (2003), supported Galvin's claims, noting that they faced criticism and comments from others, as well as making their own adjustments and deciding how to deal with issues of culture and socialization.

Multiracial families can be a site of opportunity to create unique cultural/ethnic identities; to explore the diversity of cultural attitudes, beliefs, and practices; and even to help others outside the family see race in more complex ways. Family members, however, do have to learn together how to cope with their differences and with the reactions they receive from others. This process occurs through communication.

Overall, in this section we have considered the definitions of race and ethnicity and how difficult it is to clearly define these concepts. Additionally, you read about some of the ways that race/ethnicity intersects with family beliefs and processes and how families participate in the socialization process with regard to race/ethnicity and culture. Finally, we've considered some of the situations that affect multiracial families. Section 2 discusses research examples that relate to how race and ethnicity are experienced in family settings. The first article considers racial and gender socialization in African American middle-class families. The second considers interactional patterns in mother–daughter relationships for Black and White families, whereas the third article addresses research about parenting in interracial families. Section 3 concludes with a discussion of how this material can be applied to your life.

References

Aoki, E. (2000). Mexican American ethnicity in Biola, CA: An ethnographic account of hard work, family, and religion. *Howard Journal of Communications, 11*(3), 207–227.

Bonilla-Silva, E. (2003). *Racism without racists: Color-blind racism and the persistence of inequality in the United States.* Lanham, MD: Rowman & Littlefield.

Burr, J. A., & Mutchler, J. E. (1999). Race and ethnic variation in norms of filial responsibility among older persons. *Journal of Marriage and Family, 61*(3), 674–687.

Bylund, C. L. (2003). Ethnic diversity and family stories. *Journal of Family Communication, 3*(4), 215–226.

Chao, R. K. (1994). Beyond parental control and authoritarian parenting style: Understanding Chinese parenting through the cultural notion of training. *Child Development, 65,* 1111–1120.

deHaymes, M. V., & Simon, S. (2003). Transracial adoption: Families identify issues and needed support services. *Child Welfare, 82*(2), 251–272.

Diggs, R. C., & Socha, T. (2004). Communication, families, and exploring the boundaries of cultural diversity. In A. L. Vangelisti (Ed.), *Handbook of family communication* (pp. 249–266). Mahwah, NJ: Erlbaum.

Farver, J. A. M., Narang, S. K., & Bhadha, B. (2002). East meets West: Ethnic identity, acculturation, and conflict in Asian Indian families. *Journal of Family Psychology, 16*(3), 338–349.

Fields, B. J. (1990, May/June). Slavery, race and ideology in the United States of America. *New Left Review,* 95–118.

Foeman, A. K., & Nance, T. (1999). From miscengenation to multiculturalism: Perceptions and stages of interracial relationship development. *Journal of Black Studies, 29,* 540–557.

Frabutt, J. M., Walker, A. M., & MacKinnon-Lewis, C. (2002). Racial socialization messages and the quality of mother/childhood interactions in African American families. *Journal of Early Adolescence, 22*(2), 200–217.

Frankenberg, R. (1993). *White women race matters: The social construction of whiteness.* Minneapolis: University of Minnesota Press.

Frankenberg, R. (2001). The mirage of an unmarked whiteness. In B. Brander Rasmussen, M. Klinenberg, I. J. Nexica, & M. Wray (Eds.), *The making and unmaking of whiteness* (pp. 72–96). Durham, NC: Duke University Press.

Fukuyama, M. A. (1999). Personal narrative: Growing up biracial. *Journal of Counseling and Development, 77*(1), 12–14.

Galvin, K. (2003). International and transracial adoption: A communication research agenda. *Journal of Family Communication, 3*(4), 237–253.

Garcia-Coll, C. T., Meyer, E. C., & Brillon, L. (1995). Ethnic and minority parenting. In M. H. Bornstein (Ed.), *Handbook of parenting: Biology and ecology of parenting* (Vol. 2, pp. 189–210). Mahwah, NJ: Erlbaum.

Grieco, E. M., & Cassidy, R. C. (2001). *Overview of race and Hispanic origin: Census 2000 brief*. Retrieved from the U.S. Census Bureau Web site: www.census .gov/prod/2001pubs/c2kbr01–1.pdf 1/1/2005.

Hirschman, C., & Nguyen, H. M. (2002). Tradition and change in Vietnamese family structure in the Red River Delta. *Journal of Marriage and Family, 64*, 1063–1079.

Hughes, D., & Chen, L. (1997). When and what parents tell children about race: An examination of race-related socialization among African American families. *Applied Developmental Science, 1*(4), 200–214.

Jain, A., & Belsky, J. (1997). Fathering and acculturation: Immigrant Indian families with young children. *Journal of Marriage and Family, 59*(4), 873–883.

Kawamoto, W. T., & Cheshire, T. C. (1999). Contemporary issues in the urban American Indian family. In H. P. McAdoo (Ed.), *Family ethnicity: Strength in diversity* (2nd ed., pp. 94–104). Newbury Park, CA: Sage.

Knowles, E. D., & Peng, K. (2005). White selves: Conceptualizing and measuring a dominant-group identity. *Journal of Personality and Social Psychology, 89*(2), 223–241.

Kotchick, B. A., & Forehand, R. (2002). Putting parenting in perspective: A discussion of the contextual factors that shape parenting practices. *Journal of Child and Family Studies, 11*(3), 255–269.

Lamborn, S. D., Dornbusch, S. M., & Steinberg, L. (1996). Ethnicity and community context as moderators of the relations between family decision making and adolescent adjustment. *Child Development, 67*, 283–301.

Lee, G. R., Peek, C. W., & Coward, R. T. (1998). Race differences in filial responsibility expectations among older parents. *Journal of Marriage and Family, 60*(2), 404–412.

Leslie, L. A., & Letiecq, B. L. (2004). Marital quality of African American and White partners in interracial couples. *Personal Relationships, 11*(4), 559–574.

Li, J. (2004). Parental expectations of Chinese immigrants: A folk theory about children's school achievement. *Race, Ethnicity & Education, 7*(2), 167–183.

McAdoo, H. (2001). Point of view: Ethnicity and family dialogue. *Journal of Family Communication, 1*(1), 87–90.

Mosley-Howard, G. S., & Evans, S. B. (2000). Relationships and contemporary experiences of the African American family: An ethnographic case study. *Journal of Black Studies, 30*, 428–452.

Penington, B. A. (2004). Communicative management of connection and autonomy in African American and European American mother–daughter relationships. *Journal of Family Communication, 4*(1), 3–34.

Phinney, J. S., Kim-Jo, T., Osorio, S., & Vilhjalmsdottir, P. (2005). Autonomy and relatedness in adolescent–parent disagreements: Ethnic and developmental factors. *Journal of Adolescent Research, 20*(1), 8–39.

Sherif, B. (1999). "Islamic Family Ideals and Their Relevance to American Muslim Families." In *Ethnic Families: Strength in Diversity*, ed. H. P. McAdoo. Newbury Park, CA: Sage.

Silverstein, M., & Chen, X. (1999). The impact of acculturation in Mexican American families on the quality of grandchild–grandparent relationships. *Journal of Marriage and Family, 61*(1), 188–198.

Stephan, W. G., & Stephan, C. W. (1991). Intermarriage: Effects on personality, adjustment, and intergroup relation in two samples of students. *Journal of Marriage and Family, 53*, 241–250.

Suyemoto, K. L. (2004). Racial/ethnic identities and related attributed experiences of multiracial Japanese European Americans. *Journal of Multicultural Counseling and Development, 32*(4), 206–221.

Turner, L. H., & West, R. (2003). Breaking through the silence: Increasing voice for diverse families in communication research. *Journal of Family Communication, 3*(4), 181–186.

Walker, A. J. (1993). Teaching about race, gender, and class diversity in United States families. *Family Relations, 42*(3), 342–350.

Wallenstein, P. (2002). *Tell the court I love my wife: Race, marriage, and the law*. New York: Palgrave Macmillan.

Wilkinson, D. (1999). Reframing family ethnicity in America. In H. P. McAdoo (Ed.), *Family ethnicity: Strength in diversity* (2nd ed., pp. 15–60). Thousand Oaks, CA: Sage.

Williams, C. B. (1999). Claiming a biracial identity: Resisting social constructions of race and culture. *Journal of Counseling and Development, 77*(1), 32–35.

Yi, C., Pan, E., Chang, Y., & Chan, C. (2006). Grandparents, adolescents, and parents: Intergenerational relations of Taiwanese youth. *Journal of Family Issues, 27*(8), 1042–1067.

Zimmer, Z., & Dayton, J. (2005). Older adults in sub-Saharan Africa living with children and grandchildren. *Population Studies, 59*(3), 295–312.

Section 2: Research Examples _____

"What Shall I Tell My Daughters That Are Black?": Oral History Reflections of Middle-Class African American Motherhood in a Culturally Diverse Community

Patricia S. Hill

> In Section 1, you read about the importance of race socialization for families whose race/ethnicity is particularly marked in their environment. In this article, Hill presents the results of research that considered this issue from the perspectives of mothers who needed to make decisions about socialization practices for their African American daughters, growing up in middle-class communities. Hill's work speaks to the intersections of racial, gender, and socioeconomic cultures, and how parents make decisions about which messages to provide their children, explicitly or implicitly about those issues. Whether we experience a similar life to the mothers discussed here, attention to intersections such as this, and their role in family socialization processes, is an important aspect of family communication study.
>
> *L.B.A.*

Rich (1970) notes that women are not only of women born but also of women reared. Research reinforces the centrality of the mother in the transmission of attitudes, values and culture, and the continuing importance of mother–daughter ties (Bergman, 1987; Mouton, 1985; Walsh, 1987). Such research reveals that interactions between mother and daughter have an effect on the daughter's development, and these "lessons learned" are vital to her functioning later as an adult. Further, literature on African American mothers' roles and their interactions with their daughters has called attention to the fact that African American mother–daughter relationships differ from patterns among non-African American women (Bell-Scott & Guy-Sheftall, 1991; Hine & Thompson, 1998; Wade-Gayles, 1993). Peterson (1992) suggests that the fact that African American mothers are often very influential in the upbringing of their daughters is not significant in and of itself. She notes that mothers in many cultures have the primary responsibility for child care, and are thus very influential. She maintains that what is *different* in African American motherhood is the fact that the bond between mother and daughter often lasts long past childhood and that "Black women continue to draw strength from their relationships with their mothers and grandmothers and speak of the strong lessons they learned which 'made' them the women they are" (p. 67).

When Burroughs (1969) asks in her poem, "What shall I tell my daughters that are Black?" she speaks to two important considerations. First is the significance of the lessons that need to be taught to African American daughters as a fundamental aspect of African American motherhood. Second is the assessment of what cultural prescriptions and creativity must be employed by the mothers to facilitate the transmission of skills and values to these daughters that they may be adequately prepared for the future. This is particularly relevant for middle-class families who reside in culturally diverse communities, where race, class, and gender oppression punctuate everyday experiences. As Close (1993) notes, a tragic paradox typifies these experiences—"the better the conditions, the more bitter the tone" (p. 37). For such households, prejudice as well as intergroup bias persist as what Benjamin (1991) considers "a final hurdle" (p. 291) for middle-class African American families. Feagin and Sikes (1994) note that in our contemporary society, middle-class African Americans are stereotypically viewed as "the prosperous examples of the success of equal opportunity and affirmative actions programs who have secured the promises of the American dream" (p. 64). They further maintain that there is little recognition of the sacrifice and hard work that go hand in hand in trying to achieve the American dream. This is evident in literature that acknowledges the stress and the psychological costs of economic success for many African American middle-class families (e.g., Bertaux & Thompson, 1997; Sellers, 2001).

A precarious accomplishment of African American middle-class mothers is that they are positioned between the social worlds of class and race in their communities. In such contexts, it becomes particularly salient for them to teach daughters adaptive capacities and perseverance (Barker & Hill, 1996). Collins (1990) calls this "a troubling dilemma" of African American motherhood because daughters with strong self-definitions and self-valuations, who offer serious challenges to oppressive situations, may not physically survive. African American mothers in these contexts "routinely encourage Black daughters to develop skills to confront oppressive conditions" (p. 124). The passing on of "ways of knowing" is a critical component of the everyday experiences of middle-class African American mothers residing in culturally diverse communities. Thus, this oral narrative investigation seeks to uncover the specific skills and values that are passed on to daughters as everyday lessons to sustain their survival in the context of this culturally diverse community. This work demonstrates the complexity of these issues, and illustrates the importance of exploring the experiences African American middle-class mothers as a useful area of study.

The examination takes a historical perspective in exploring the situation of African American women's experiences and how this frames their symbols, values, and ways of knowing. Central to the methodology of this study is the belief that the essential meanings of women's lives can be grasped only by listening to the women themselves (Collins, 1990; Hooks, 1984). To that end, the method of this study was that of oral history interviews with data analysis utilizing the constant comparative method (Glaser & Strauss, 1967) of qualitative analysis as informed by Black feminist thought (Collins, 1986, 1990).

Black feminist thought provides a synthesis of a body of knowledge that is crucial to putting in perspective the situation of African American women and their place in the overall society. As one of several feminist standpoint theories,[1] it provides a conceptual framework that acknowledges the everyday experiences of African American women negotiating their identities, their relationships with family, and the overall society. Black feminist thought revolves around an understanding of the basis of a shared oppression of African American women, with a recognition of the intersecting nature of race, class, gender, and sexual oppressions in their varied experiences (Dill, 1988).

For this study of African American motherhood in a culturally diverse community, oral history interviews were conducted with a snowball sample[2] of 25 African American women, who ranged in age from 25 to 77. All the women described their class status as middle class. Purposeful or criterion-based sampling (Merriam, 1988) was used in order to define a population situated in a specific context, from which to gain the most insight. To participate in the study, participants needed to meet two criteria: (a) self-identified as African American, and (b) lived in the community for a good portion of their lives (at least 10 years).

Oral history interviews were conducted solely by the author. Each interview session was loosely structured, with the average interview ranging between two to three hours. Participants were encouraged to talk in their own words about salient events and experiences and to describe feelings and thoughts they had about them. These life accounts allowed for the emergence of the participants' meaning as it is constructed in the present in relation to past realities. Because it was a women's story as she experienced it, and narrated it, tape-recorded oral history interviews were transcribed verbatim. Accuracy of the transcripts was verified by spot-checking the tapes against transcriptions. Although the data may not be replicated, they are considered valid in that they reflect women's everyday experiences.

The data were inductively analyzed aided by the assumptions of the constant comparison process of grounded theory (Glaser & Strauss, 1967). Yow (1994) suggests this approach is particularly useful when a new perspective on a situation is needed, as it shows explicitly how to code and conceptualize data as they flow in.

The first stage in the constant comparison process begins by "comparing incidents applicable to each category" (Glaser & Strauss, 1967, p. 106). A system of "open coding" was used whereby the data were examined line by line to initiate the process. The categories were generated according to recurrent phrases or key statements that were noted to symbolize an event or process. During this stage, color pencils were utilized to distinguish different indicators as they emerged in the narrative.

The second stage included integrating categories and their properties. When a new indicator emerged, it was compared with ones that had already been grouped in the same category in order to determine a "goodness of fit" (Lindlof, 1995, p. 223). These emergent categories were analyzed according to their relation to other data as well as alternative explanations in the data. Lincoln and Guba (1985) maintain that this step moves the analysts "closer to a particular construction of the situation at hand" (p. 343). During this stage of the data analysis, the study utilized the "cut-up-and put-in-folders" approach (Bogdan & Bilken, 1982, p. 166). Multiple copies of the data were made. The first copy was used for coding; the second copy was used for cutting and taping. After the categories were first marked to identify their origin in the data text, they were then cut and taped onto clean pages. These were placed into manila folders that were labeled with the categories. The units of data were then examined further for possible assertion.

The data analysis then moved to the third phase where the process attempted to categorize and "delimit the theory" (Glaser & Strauss, 1967). It was during this phase that the analysis attempted to achieve parsimony, where relatively few new data were needed. From the refined categories emerged "essential themes" (Lindlof, 1995). Black feminist thought informed the conceptualization of these thematic categories as well as the interpretation of the patterns of similarities and difference. These themes were considered critical in addressing the inquiry of this study. Moreover, they reflect the collective wisdom of the mothers in this context and lessons that they perceive are particularly important for the development of their daughters' ways of knowing.

Essential Themes

Peterson (1992) states that as long as institutional racism, sexism, and classism exist in this country, African American women realize that "at any given time, the doors of opportunity can slam in their faces" (p. 77). Such oppression positions African American women as outsiders or *others* in their community. As the signifiers of consciousness and cultural heritage (Vaz, 1997), African American mothers have historically helped daughters in the construction and reconstruction of their self-definitions through their talk. This is evidenced in three essential themes that emerged from the narrative of the women who participated in this study: (1) othered by sexism, (2) othered by racism, and (3) othered by classism. The following discussion illustrates these themes as lessons of middle-class African American motherhood in a culturally diverse community.

Othered by Sexism

According to Rothenberg (1995), the ideology of sexism refers to a system of beliefs and behaviors by which a group is oppressed, controlled, and exploited because of presumed gender differences. This ideology of sexism informs gender relations, and is manifested in individually held beliefs and social behaviors. A common concern shared by many of the women involved in this study was the need to prepare daughters to rise above manifestations of sexism. The oral narratives clearly spoke to issues and assumptions of sexual oppression in general and its manifestations in this community context as forming a basic current of their everyday experiences. A good example of this is illustrated when Tasha Greathouse[3] reveals what she perceives to be an important lesson passed down from her mother and grandmother about gender differences. She reported:

> I think my mother and grandmother taught me an understanding of knowing yourself as a female and not letting men push you around and treat you like dirt or make you feel less about yourself. That is a hard job, the media does a good job at making women feel useless. It is very difficult when a daughter comes into her own sexuality, for her to create her own self. That has to come through, make sure that comes through. I don't want my daughter to be mistreated by a man, because that could destroy her. That is not being anti-male, I don't want my son to be mistreated by a female. So very early on, I insisted that she never let a boy touch her unless he got her total permission from the bottom of her soul she has to feel that it is okay because everything out there says that it is okay to feel it, touch it, slap it, beat it and that is a very important concept to get across.

Another respondent, Freedom Kessler, who lived in this community context for over 40 years, spoke to the matter of sexism as a common factor that shapes African American women's identities and family relationships. She conveyed:

> There are differences in the things that we women have to do here and elsewhere, and how we have to handle things. We are not this great big thing standing there as a challenge, but

we are kind of gentle and direct in our ways and we try to win over people rather than bur-
geoning them down. We use strategies to get to where we want to go. Devious! I think
I came that way, because if you don't get what you want one way, you find another way.
I think that is a women's way.

The preceding examples are illustrative of a general consensus that as daughters
come into knowledge and understanding of the world in general and of their specific context, lessons of sexual oppression provide valuable insight. The narratives reveal that these
mothers do indeed address sexist oppression with the recognition of it, and with affirmation
of what it means to be a woman, a human being, and a citizen in this community.

Othered by Classism

Benjamin (1991) maintains that African American middle-class mothers often face the
task of preparing children for slights and obstacles that are the consequence of their middle-class status. According to Jackson and Curtis (1972), African American children have
encountered limited experiences with this issue in predominately European American,
middle-class settings. They argue that "the parents feel they should prepare their children
for a larger society that may not be as accepting of them" (p. 33). The oral history narratives identified many experiences with class issues ranging from majority-group insensi-
tivities to within-group animosities. Donna Brooks's narrative provides an exemplar of
some of the "incongruities" African American middle-class families face in this culturally
diverse setting, and the lessons that must be taught to reconcile conflicting perspectives.
She states:

> It is kind of like being exposed to a fountain of fortune and you have to teach the dose that
> you are able to take, and you are so happy about it that you want everybody to be as excited
> about it as you are. But you can't force it on people, they have to acclimate to their own
> dose. You know, the White kids have the cars, the trips, it is the class thing. I mean, that's
> why you go there, right, it is a suburb and it's got the quality education, great recreational
> facilities and you know, it has got beautiful homes the whole thing.

The women interviewed for this study described several strategies utilized to pass on
an awareness of status orientation. In many cases, the "birds of a feather flock together"
premise influenced choices for reference-group associations. Several women spoke to the
imperative of reinforcing daughters' exposure to individuals who were similar to them in
class status. Social clubs such as Jack and Jill and The Links were prominent as associations where African American middle-class children could participate in activities to reaffirm "middle-class values." Although Pearl Pressman defined both Jack and Jill and The
Links as "Black elitist groups," she elaborated on her awareness of their worth in guiding
daughters toward desired middle-class values. She recalled:

> Most of the kids' friends at that time were White, because it was the kids that they went to
> school with. They did have Black friends because they went to a Black church, and because
> of our family and old friends. They were also exposed to other Black children. I was in Jack
> and Jill and I guess I am not quite that kind of person, but I had joined it because I really felt
> a need to get my daughters exposed to other Black children.

However, the narrative recorded an intriguing heterogeneity in the perspectives of the women. Several shared that they were adamant about not supporting participation in, and in some cases, not being able to join "these exclusive clubs." These varied responses reveal important differences of motivation based on status orientation, but are shaped by the commonality of blackness in this community context. Such is the case for Gwendolyn Tate, who recalls:

> My daughter was in the junior council, it was a way for her to get exposed because I could not afford The Links and Jack and Jill and all of that, and it gave her a chance to meet some people that could have influenced her life.

Johari Cooper emphasized that contradictions of class have historically connected generations in the socialization of daughters in this diverse community. Recognizing that problematic intergroup relations continue to impact everyday experiences, she stressed this point:

> Class was a major thing when I grew up. It was predominantly upper middle class Blacks that lived on this street. We weren't allowed to be in Jack and Jill because my father was a plumber, and that is the thing that is so ironic about it, because my father made good money or else we would not have been here, because my father was not a White collar worker, we were not asked to be in the Jack and Jills, and I think still that is the case, and that has to be learned.

The narratives clearly indicate there is a common awareness that economic and social positions can be distressingly precarious. Status orientation is an important dilemma faced by the women in this context; and whatever strategy one endorses, it is incumbent upon the mothers to address sociohistorical, macro, and micro factors that shape both daughters' opportunities and constraints.

Othered by Racism

Hecht, Collier, and Ribeau (1993) suggest that certain factors of racism and discrimination "are shared by most people of color in America" (p. 197). These factors contribute to the "outsider status" (Collins, 1990) of African Americans in our contemporary society. Feagin and Sikes (1994) note that many African American parents in predominantly European American communities find it necessary to instill in their children "race pride" and "the race lesson" (p. 25). They further maintain that on one hand these parents imposed limitations because of race, and on the other hand they encouraged "unlimited aspirations and being equal as an American" (p. 27).

Racism was consistently discussed by the women in this study, alluding to a common inherited wisdom that gets passed on as how to overcome, make yourself as good as anyone else, achieve, accomplish, and celebrate blackness in oppressive conditions. What emerged out of these oral histories was clearly an affirmation of achieved material success. Yet, despite this success, ever-present was the subjective component of prejudice and racial discrimination that impacted everyday experiences. The oral history narratives reveal several strategies employed by mothers to help daughters develop racial understandings. For example, Marilyn Hale's account precisely delineates factors that must be overcome:

> I try to let my daughter know that no matter how stable the community and educational situation you grow up in, you are going to have to deal with problems of a racial nature, and

you can't get around that. I want her to understand the history of Black Americans and what our families have been through to know that she can also achieve her goals in spite of the prejudice and racism that she is bound to find when she gets out into the world.

It is apparent from the women's personal narratives that education was perceived to be the key not only to unlock the door to economic opportunity, but also to overcome oppressive racial obstacles. Thus, providing a good education was a strategy that would enable daughters to better compete in society. This is stressed by Betty Bazel, who recalled:

> We put our kids in a school system that we wanted them to get the best academic education that money could buy—that we could afford. We wanted them to be acceptable on all levels no matter where they went, and we didn't want them denied anything for any reason. Or we didn't want them to think that they were limited and couldn't do or compete with anybody because they were Black. . . . I think that the best anybody leaves behind are their children. That's the real gift that you give, and every mother thinks about this.

Many of the women who participated in this study expressed the importance of the lessons of racism "learned from concrete experience" (Collins, 1990). Such valuable lessons, they noted, could not be conveyed in the confines of academia. The narratives vividly signified the value of teaching by example as well as by mouth. For instance, many of the women elaborated on the importance of acting as role models. Others revealed that modeling strategies of resistance were utilized to confront racism in this community context as well as wider social environment.

Summary

The purpose of this work is to add to the body of literature that has emerged on African American motherhood and the centrality of the mother in the transmission of attitudes, values, and culture. From the traditions of Black feminist thought and narrative inquiry, three essential themes illuminated valuable insight into how African American mothers in this study are profoundly impacted by the subtleties of racism, sexism, and classism as a reality of their lives. Crenshaw (1991) argues that race, class, and gender intersect and shape African American women's lives in a multitude of ways. The current findings reinforce this notion. For the majority of the women interviewed in this study, race, class, and gender oppression are clearly dilemmas that impact their everyday experiences. Thus, the passing on of critical understandings of oppression to help mold and sustain daughters is perceived essential for generations to come.

Together, the three essential themes that emerged from this collective portrait reveal the complexities of lessons passed on to communicatively reinforce values and experiences that shape notions of motherhood. Further, the themes reveal that racism, sexism, and class issues are relevant realities, if one wishes to understand the complexities of African American mother–daughter relationships. They shape social location, opportunity, and structure interactions that characterize individual experiences.

Because African American mothers' experiences have been socially marginalized, their life stories cannot be isolated from their distinct and multiple perspectives, values, and roles. As scholarship on family communication continues to position African American motherhood within a framework of class, race, and gender, we can begin to give a voice and an audience for the telling of their lives.

Questions for Consideration and Discussion

1. Hill argues that the transmission of particular life skills and values are extremely important for African American families who live in middle-class, culturally diverse communities. Why is this the case?
2. This work points to the intersections between class, race, and gender in the experiences of these mothers. What other cultural groupings may intersect with race in a way that impacts family experience?
3. In this article, Hill refers to oppression as being "othered." What is meant by this term? What can it help us understand or attend to about oppression?
4. As legal systems have shifted with regard to race and equality, so too have the ways in which racism is expressed. In your experiences, what are the ways that you see racism being expressed today? How do you envision that changing over the course of your lifetime?
5. This work utilizes an oral history method of study. What might be the particular advantages of using oral history to study issues of racism, sexism, and classism?

Endnotes

1. For a review of feminist standpoint theory see Harding (1991) and O'Brien Hallstein (2000).
2. Snowball sampling is a special nonprobability method used when the desired sample characteristic is rare. Snowball sampling relies on referrals from initial subjects to generate additional subjects.
3. Pseudonyms were used to ensure confidentiality and anonymity of respondents.

References

Barker, N. C., & Hill, J. (1996). Restructuring African American families in the 1990s. *Journal of Black Studies, 27*(1), 77–93.

Bell-Scott, P., & Guy-Sheftall, B. (1991). Introduction. In P. Bell-Scott, B. Guy-Sheftall, J. J. Royster, J. Sims-Wood, M. DeCosta-Willis, & L. P. Fultz (Eds.), *Double stitch: Black women write about mothers and daughters* (pp. 1–4). New York: HarperPerennial.

Benjamin, L. (1991). *The Black elite: Facing the color line in the twilight of the twentieth century.* Chicago: Nelson-Hall.

Bergman, A. (1987). On the development of female identity: Issues of mother–daughter interaction during the separation-individuation process. *Psychoanalytic Inquiry, 7*(3), 381–396.

Bertaux, D., & Thompson, P. (1997). *Pathways to social class: A qualitative approach to social mobility.* Oxford, England: Claredon Press.

Bogdan, R. C., & Bilken, S. K. (1982). *Qualitative research for education.* Boston: Allyn & Bacon.

Burroughs, M. (1969). For Malcolm. In D. Randal & M. Burroughs (Eds.), *For Malcolm: Poems of the life and death of Malcolm X.* Detroit, MI: Broadside Press.

Close, E. (1993). *The rage of a privileged class.* New York: HarperCollins.

Collins, P. H. (1986). Learning from the outsider within: The sociological significance of Black feminist thought. *Social Problems, 33*, 514–532.

Collins, P. H. (1990). *Black feminist thought: Knowledge, consciousness and the politics of empowerment, perspectives on gender.* New York: Routledge.

Crenshaw, K. (1991). Mapping the margins: Intersectionality, identity politics, and violence against women of color. *Stanford Law Review, 43*, 1214–1299.

Dill, B. (1988). Making your job good yourself: Domestic service and the construction of personal dignity. In

A. Bookman & S. Morgan (Eds.), *Women and the politics of empowerment* (pp. 33–53). New York: Garland.

Feagin, J. R., & Sykes, M. P. (1994). *Living with racism: The middle class experience*. Boston: Beacon Press.

Glaser, B. G., & Strauss. A. L. (1967). *The discovery of grounded theory: Strategies for qualitative research*. Chicago: Aldine.

Harding, S. (1991). Standpoint theory for the next century. *Women & Politics, 18*(3), 93–102.

Hecht, M. L., Collier, M. J., & Ribeau, S. A. (1993). *African American communication*. (Vol. 2). Newbury Park, CA: Sage.

Hine, D. C., & Thompson, K. (1998). *A shining thread of hope*. New York: Broadway Books.

Hooks, B. (1984). *From margin to center*. Boston: South End Press.

Jackson, E., & Curtis, R. (1972). Effects of vertical social mobility and status inconsistency: A body of negative evidence. *American Sociological Review, 37*, 701–713.

Lincoln, Y., & Guba, E. (1985). *Naturalistic inquiry*. Beverly Hills, CA: Sage.

Lindlof, T. R. (1995). *Qualitative communication research methods*. Thousand Oaks, CA: Sage.

Merriam, S. B. (1988). *Case study research in education: A qualitative approach*. San Francisco: Jossey-Bass.

Mouton, R. (1985). The effect of the mother on the success of the daughter. *Contemporary Psychoanalysis, 21*(2), 266–283.

O'Brien Hallstein, D. L. (2000). Where standpoint stands now: An introduction and commentary. *Women's Studies in Communication, 23*(1), 1–15.

Peterson, E. A. (1992). *African American women: A study of will and success*. Jefferson, NC: Mcfarland.

Rich, A. (1970). *Of women born*. London: Virago.

Rothenberg, P. S. (1995). *Race, class, and gender in the United States: An integrated study*. New York: St. Martin's Press.

Sellers, S. L. (2001, Winter). Social mobility and psychological distress: Differences among Black American men and women. *African American Research Perspectives*, 117–143.

Vaz, K. M. (1997). *Oral narrative research with Black women*. Thousand Oaks, CA: Sage.

Wade-Gales, G. (1993). *Pushed back to strength: A Black women's journey home*. Boston: Beacon Press.

Walsh, M. R. E. (1987). *The psychology of women: Ongoing debates*. New Haven, CT: Yale University Press.

Yow, V. R. (1994). *Recording oral history: A practical guide for social scientists*. Thousand Oaks, CA: Sage.

The Mother–Adolescent Daughter Tug-of-War: Ethnicity's Impact on the Connection–Autonomy Dialectic

Barbara A. Penington

In Chapter 3, we addressed the dialectical perspective and considered the dialectic of connection and autonomy as related to family. In this article, Penington applies that concept to a study of relationships between mothers and their adolescent daughters. She considers the extent to which racial culture may impact how autonomy and connection are managed by mother–daughter pairs through adolescence. As college students, you have likely passed through the adolescent period, and Penington's work may provide you with insight into how culture affected your own management of this dialectic.

L.B.A.

During adolescence, individuals move from reliance on parents to a more mature independence or autonomy (McCandless & Coop, 1979; Steinberg, 1990, 1995). In recent years, however, scholars have recognized that adolescents do not simply move away from parental influence, but at the same time desire to maintain connection with parents (Santrock & Yussen, 1992). Youniss and Smollar (1985), for example, assert that although mothers and daughters confide in each other more than any other parent–adolescent dyad, the greatest amount of conflict also occurs between mothers and daughters (Montemayer, 1982). Pipher (1994) argues that "adolescent" daughters provoke arguments as a way of connecting and distancing at the same time . . . they struggle with the love for their mothers and their desire to be different from their mothers" (p. 286). The tension, stress, and uncertainty created by these contradictory yet interrelated forces represent common complaints arising in many mother–adolescent daughter relationships.

Although ethnicity plays a key role in how family members communicate and ultimately construct their family experience (McGoldrick & Giordano, 1996), family scholars have been slow to recognize the need for ethnically diverse samples (Socha, Sanchez-Hucles, Bromley, & Kelly, 1995). Research in family communication has used primarily European American middle-class participants (Dilworth-Anderson, Burton, & Johnson, 1993; Socha et al., 1995). This has promoted a Eurocentric view of the family that many medical professionals, social workers, clergy, and educators in our country have relied upon when counseling mothers and adolescent daughters of different ethnic backgrounds. This is especially disturbing given the fact that there are currently more immigrants living in the United States than at any other time in our history (Camarota, 2001), and birth rates that are dropping for Whites are increasing for racial and ethnic minorities (Smith, 2000). Thus, a crucial question that begs scholarly investigation arises: Do mothers and adolescent daughters of different ethnic groups experience and communicatively manage connection and autonomy in a similar fashion?

Theoretical Framework

Two theoretical frameworks informed this study. The first, symbolic interactionism (Blumer, 1969; Mead, 1956), asserts that individuals attach social meanings to their worlds and then act toward others on the basis of these meanings. To learn how individuals construct meaning in relationships, the symbolic interactionist approach encourages study participants to describe their experiences in-depth using their own words and style. The dialectical framework was also important as this study sought to better understand issues of connection and autonomy, two interrelated yet opposing needs that are present in all personal relationships. Baxter and Montgomery (Baxter, 1988, 1990; Baxter & Montgomery, 1996; Baxter & Montgomery, 1998) have been pioneers in highlighting the dialectical framework's ability to capture the complex nature of personal relationships. In the mother–adolescent daughter context, dialectical thinking helps us better understand how the contradictory needs of connection and autonomy can exist and be expressed simultaneously.

The Mother–Adolescent Daughter Relationship: Issues of Connection and Autonomy

Few researchers have studied how connection and autonomy issues are managed during adolescence. One exception is Vangelisti (1992), who found that older adolescents' accounts of communication problems with parents emphasized issues "related to the dialectical tension between individuality and connectedness" (p. 395). Other researchers have also used the psychoanalytic approach to explain connection and autonomy as it relates to gender. Chodorow (1978) and Gilligan (1982), for example, suggested that as young women reach adolescence, they begin searching for a personal identity apart from their mothers. This is often difficult, however, as daughters identify with mothers, whereas sons psychologically separate from their mothers because of the difference in sex.

Impact of Ethnicity

Although Baxter and Montgomery (1996) assert that all relationships experience issues related to connection and autonomy, one wonders if mothers and adolescent daughters of diverse ethnic groups experience this dialectic in a similar manner. Cross-cultural communication research models suggest that ethnic groups display variations in value orientations. Individualism and collectivism, for example, represent value orientations first identified by Hofstede (1980, 1983) that may be useful when examining issues of connection and autonomy. According to Hofstede, members of individualistic cultures put personal needs before the needs of their in-groups. They value freedom, self-reliance, and uniqueness. Collectivistic cultures, on the other hand, perceive group needs as primary and emphasize conformity, cooperation and harmony. Helms (1990) and Asante (1973) have suggested that

White individuals, as compared to other cultural groups in the United States, share a strong belief in the importance of individualism. Rotheram-Borus, Dopkins, Sabate, and Lightfoot (1996), investigating teachers' perceptions of students, found that Black students as compared to White students displayed more group orientation and respect for authority.

Unfortunately, for many years the majority of family-focused research studies used exclusively European American participants (Dilworth-Anderson et al., 1993). Socha et al. (1995), for example, counted the number of studies in communication journals from 1947 to 1994 that dealt with African Americans. Based on 231 family communication articles, only 5 addressed African American families, and not 1 of these studies focused on parent–child communication. Socha and Diggs (1999) attempted to "remedy this neglect" of an ethnic focus in family communication research in their edited text *Communication, Face, and Family: Exploring Communication in Black, White, and Biracial Families*. In this text, Daniel and Daniel (1999) discussed communication strategies used by Black parents to ensure their children's survival and success. In the same text, Diggs (1999), studying self-esteem in African American and European American adolescents, reported that "parents (generally mothers) were overwhelmingly identified as the source of positive feelings for Black and White adolescents" (p. 124). White adolescents in contrast to Black adolescents reported more frequently that friends impacted their self-feelings.

Studies such as these represent a starting point for developing insights about the impact of ethnicity on issues of connection and autonomy in the mother–adolescent daughter relationship, but a more thorough investigation is clearly needed.

Methodology

This study used qualitative methods, specifically in-depth interviews. Socha et al. (1995) have suggested that a study could be compromised when European American researchers collect data from African American families; thus, as the primary researcher in this study was European American, an African American research assistant also participated in the interview process and data analysis.

Participants

Fourteen mother–adolescent daughter dyads—seven African American and seven European American—were used as participants. Participants were obtained using a "snowball sampling" approach. The daughters ranged in age from 13 to 17 years; the mothers were from 34 to 48 years. All mothers were employed more than half-time, with eight mothers having full-time employment. Participants came from middle-class families, all of which had a father figure present.

Data Collection and Analysis

Mothers and their daughters were interviewed separately on two occasions. Specific areas probed were family roles, communication patterns, and conflict within their relationships.

Interviews were audio-recorded and later transcribed. Daughters' transcripts averaged 13 pages in length; mothers' averaged 18.5 pages. Two to six weeks following the initial interview, follow-up interviews were conducted where the researcher asked for clarification and elaboration on portions of participants' first interviews.

Results

Interview data demonstrated that both African American and European American mothers and adolescent daughters experienced tension related to their simultaneous needs for connection and autonomy. *AA* has been used to designate African American participants, and *EA* designates European American participants. The following excerpts from both an African American and a European American mother illustrate how participants described their relationships in terms of connection and autonomy.

> Sometimes it gets to the point where you just don't want to be bothered and it's like, "Oh God, I just can't wait for you to leave this house!" But then I think, I don't want you to go; I really don't want you to go.
>
> (Darcy, AA participant, talking about her 16-year-old daughter, Chandra)

> I mean I do want her to grow and expand, but at the same time it's like, oh, there goes your little girl.
>
> (Bev, EA participant, talking about her 14-year-old daughter, Hope)

Clearly, Darcy can't wait for her daughter Chandra to be out of the house, yet she doesn't really want her to go. Bev wants Hope to "grow" and become a well-rounded individual, but still feels a strong bond to her daughter as she refers to her as her "little girl." Mother participants, regardless of ethnic group, voiced their need to remain close to daughters. At the same time, they asserted that their primary role as mother was to foster a sense of independence and self-reliance in their daughters.

Daughters as well as mothers felt the tugs of connection and autonomy. Kate (EA) a 16-year-old, for example, prided herself on her involvement in various school and community activities. She was clearly developing an identity apart from her mother, yet she made the following statement:

> But usually, I couldn't go three weeks without talking to my mom. Like when my sister and brother were little she took them and flew to Texas, and I was almost crazy by the time she got back because you know, she and I have like an outlet where it's like, negative charges and positive charges and we equalize. It usually ends up working out that way. I usually have to talk to her, otherwise I get really, really stressed out.

Daughters of both ethnic groups, although conveying stories about disagreements and conflict, also identified their mothers as important confidants. Although participants of both ethnic groups demonstrated many similarities in the way issues of connection and autonomy were handled, the following text highlights some of the differences observed.

The Bedroom

The first difference between ethnic groups and how they managed issues of connection and autonomy involved use of participants' bedrooms. All European American daughters interviewed had their own rooms, whereas only one of the African American daughters roomed alone. As all participants in this study were from similar socioeconomic backgrounds and had homes of fairly comparable size, this suggested that European American participants valued privacy and the importance of having one's own space more than African American participants. Sandy (EA), who had one of the largest families in the study, related how she and her 15-year-old daughter built a bedroom in a corner of their basement. Sandy talked with pride about how they nailed up the drywall by themselves just so her daughter would not have to share a room with her sisters. Bev (EA), described her daughter Hope as "very independent . . . she's like me; she likes her time alone too. When she's in her room, she doesn't have anybody around to answer to." This comment, in light of Asante's (1973) and Helms's (1990) studies which found European Americans to value individualism, was representative of the European American participants. One's own room tended to reinforce a stance of autonomy in family relationships. European American mothers respected their daughters' desires to have time to themselves so they rarely went into their daughters' rooms uninvited. An African American daughter, on the other hand, always shared a room with either siblings, or in one case, her mother. This suggested a stronger tendency toward connection that is consistent with an ethnic group that favors a collectivistic orientation.

African American participants' comments also suggested a greater degree of connection than did their European American counterparts when they talked about the mother's bed as one of their favorite places to talk. Katherine (AA), for example, explained that both of her daughters had developed a pattern of crawling into her bed because their father worked long hours and got home very late at night. As she described:

> She [my daughter] comes in my bed . . . and we lay there and talk. She tells me everything that's going on with the other girls. . . . We are friends and I can tell her something that I would tell an adult and I would say you can't tell nobody, it's between mother and daughter, and she will hold the secret.

Keesha (AA), whose mother Veronica worked third shift as a correctional officer, mentioned that she often lies in her mother's bed with her to talk. For Keesha and Veronica, this is an excellent way for them to connect, as one is sometimes waking up while the other is going to bed: In addition, Keesha and Veronica read together in Veronica's bed, where they often discuss their favorite books. It would seem that African American adolescent daughters have found in their mothers' beds a cozy, quiet place that is conducive to communication, whereas only one of the European American dyads identified "Mom's bed" as an important place to talk.

Best Friends

African American and European American dyads also differed slightly in their perceptions of "best friend" and that in turn impacted the degree of connection and autonomy in their relationships. African American mothers and daughters often identified each other as their best friend. Deleasa (AA), for example, described her mother as her "running buddy" and a "good friend that I like hanging out with." Chandra (AA) insisted that she could tell her mother anything, "we're just real close and I'm real open with her." African American mothers echoed their daughters' characterization of the relationship. Katherine (AA), a social worker, emphasized mother and daughter as best friend when she said:

> I express to both of them, I'm your friend. You have friends, but I'm your best friend. I try to tell them that all the time. You are going to get hurt in life, and what you think isn't always what it is. Me and your daddy are your best friends.

Here, Katherine works to socially construct the "friend" role in her relationship with her daughter. Katherine consistently tells her daughter that she is her best friend. She also suggests that her daughter may get hurt in life if she puts her trust in other would-be friends. Like Katherine, Rhonda compares the trustworthiness of mothers to that of girlfriends in an attempt to socially construct "mother as best friend." Rhonda shared:

> You could say with all my girls, they're my daughters, but they're my best friends. So, just through experience, she's learned that you can tell a friend something [but she] goes and tells someone else and then the whole school knows what's going on. But, like I told them, the one thing about Mom, you tell Mom something, it's going to stay with Mom.

European-American mothers played the role of friend in their relationships with their daughters, but it was seldom the best friend role. Janna (EA), for example, stated:

> You can't always be friends. It has to be a mother–daughter relationship. And when we first started, I wanted just to be buddies, and you can't be buddies. It doesn't work that way.

Jessica (EA), a high school teacher, also discussed the issue of friendship with her daughter and related it to her own adolescent relationship with her mother:

> I don't think of myself as being a friend. I look at myself as being not in charge of things, but more as someone who will guide her through life. . . . I would make decisions for my mother or she would confide in me, but it would be things that I didn't want to know about. And I didn't want that type of relationship with my kid, and I guess maybe that's why I say that we're not friends. I don't want her to look at me as being her friend.

Compare this more autonomous philosophy to Katherine's (AA) comment provided earlier:

> We are friends and I can tell her [my daughter] something that I would tell an adult and I would say you can't tell nobody, it's between mother and daughter, and she will hold the secret.

European American daughters indicated that their peers, rather than their mothers, were their best friends. Kari (AA), for example, said: "I'm in a group of friends, and I can really talk to them about anything. . . . I don't like to tell my mom some stuff, but I can tell them anything, and they won't get mad." Kate (EA) has a boyfriend who functions as best friend. About her mother as a friend, Kate stated:

> I think my mom doesn't know as much about, you know, the things that go on in school. She doesn't know the names of the people that I go to school with, even though I mention

them several times, it sort of just goes in one ear and out the other, and so when I'm talking about school or when I'm talking about when my brother has problems . . . I usually end up talking to my boyfriend a lot about that, about the problems going on in our family, and he's you know, very supportive, and that helps a lot.

Perhaps the best friend issue is tangentially related to that of privacy. Several European American mothers refrained from asking their daughters about personal matters because they felt their daughters would broach the subject if they so desired. Bev (EA) shared:

I'm sure with girlfriends they talk about who likes who; most of the time those things don't go real smoothly with me. I guess its basically about how your day went in your classes, her school activities, we'll talk about that . . . sometimes I think friends mean more to her than we do; obviously they have more influence.

This remark tends to support Diggs's (1999) research suggesting that White adolescents in contrast to Black adolescents reported more frequently that friends impacted their self-feelings. The African American daughters' tendency to identify their mothers as best friends contrasted with the European Americans' tendency to have best friends as peers, supporting the notion that African American mothers and daughters demonstrate a higher level of connection whereas European Americans demonstrate a higher level of autonomy within their relationships.

Protecting Daughters

Finally, African American mothers differed from European American mothers in the degree to which they felt their daughters needed protection and the methods whereby protection would be accomplished. A communication strategy used by African American mothers that served this purpose was what Daniel and Daniel (1999) refer to as use of the "imperative mode." Use of the imperative mode was exemplified when African American mothers related stories of how they were often very direct with their daughters regarding what the daughters should or should not do, expecting their immediate obedience. Daniel and Daniel suggest that African American parents use this communication strategy as it has historically protected their children from a hostile environment where one wrong action or word could result in their immediate, unprovoked arrest or even physical harm. Sometimes the communication between the African American mother and daughter could be so blunt that it scared the daughter into obeying. Katherine (AA), for example, related this story of how she and her husband tried to teach Tanya to be very careful when jumping into cars to get rides:

Last summer we had relatives that lived two blocks down and a friend of ours came up, and her cousins came by to have some fun; they were playing ball and she [Tanya] jumped in the car to ride down the street to her cousin's house. And her dad just blew his top because you don't just jump in a car with nobody! To ride nowhere! And we used the example of the girl, here in the city, who was just riding in a car and two shots were fired and someone was killed. The next day they came back to get her. And they shot her and killed her because she saw who had shot the person the day before. It was a perfect example why we say you don't get in anybody's car. We use a lot of things like that as examples.

European American mothers didn't demonstrate the degree of control that the African American mothers did. And although the African American daughters in this study seemed quiet, respectful, and compliant in response to their mothers' orders, European American daughters often questioned their mothers' decisions and even "talked back" occasionally. Jory (EA), for example, stated:

> Like with friends you watch what you're saying more so you say it so it's nicer . . . not disrespectful, but with my mom I say a lot of disrespectful things. You know, I just don't think about it as much because I just spit it out, and just say what I want to say, because she [my mom] has to forgive me, you know; it's not like your friend who could be gone the next minute.

This supports the results of Kizielewicz's (1988) study that compared African American and European American adolescent daughters' communication with mothers.

Discussion

African American and European American mother–adolescent daughter dyads were similar in that both groups experienced struggles with issues of connection and autonomy. Generally, however, African American participants appeared to experience a stronger sense of connection than did European American mothers and daughters. This finding supported Cauce and colleagues' (1996) research with Black adolescent daughters that found that their relationships with their mothers were characterized by closeness and control. The African American participants' greater degree of connection could be a result of a proclivity toward collectivism as well as the African American mothers' need to protect their young daughters from a threatening environment. The close bond between African American mothers and adolescent daughters, however, did not preclude autonomy altogether. Rather, it seemed to put the emphasis on a future sense of autonomy. Darcy's (AA) comment is representative of what most African American mothers expressed about their hopes for their daughters' futures:

> I just want her to make it. I want her to make it where she is comfortable and where she just lives a good life. I want her to be really good in her profession. I want her to excel, and have everything that she wants. I don't want my life to emanate from her. I want her life to—I want to see her bud and her flower open up in whatever she's doing.

African American mothers' comments indicated that a heightened degree of connection during adolescence would help ensure their daughters' future success. European American participants tended to favor more autonomy in their mother–adolescent daughter relationships which is congruent with an individualistic orientation. Although European American participants generally described their relationships as close, they valued individual privacy. In addition, European American daughters relied more on friends as confidants than did African Americans. It appeared then that autonomy and connection were enacted more in a moderated form in the European American group. Because European American daughters experienced more autonomy in adolescence, mothers in that group seemed less concerned about adult autonomy, but more concerned about maintaining a "close" relationship with their daughters in future years.

Limitations

One limitation to this study may have been that it used a comparatively small, purposive sample of mothers and adolescent daughters. Thus, results cannot be generalized to an entire population as perhaps the results could have been if the sample had been large and randomly drawn. Yet, because the purpose of the study was to gain a deeper, more comprehensive understanding of communication in the mother–adolescent daughter relationship, thick description based on mothers' and daughters' accounts of their relationships was needed. Performing in-depth interviews to obtain this rich, descriptive data is a time-consuming process, and thus justifies the use of a smaller number of participants. Also, because the research attempted to examine the mother–daughter relationship in middle-class adolescents from two different cultural groups, participants had to be more carefully selected so that they represented the groups in which the researcher was interested.

Another limitation of qualitative studies, such as this one, is related to researcher bias or subjectivity. Quantitative studies that rely on statistical analyses of the data are thought by some to be more objective. Some might question, for example, if other researchers would present and interpret these data on mothers and daughters in the same way as I have done, where I had no choice but to use my own frame of reference for the task. In qualitative studies, the researcher is expected to put any preconceived notions about the topic on the "back burner," but at the same time, the researcher is an important part of the knowledge construction process creating a rendering of the data that is not only clearly expressed, but also true to the experience of the participants. When I returned to participants' homes for follow-up interviews, I specifically asked the participants if their interview transcripts were representative of their relationships and experience, and they all answered affirmatively.

There were other limitations that should be mentioned regarding this study. One limitation was that the study was cross sectional rather than longitudinal in nature. To truly understand the adolescent transition of the mother–daughter relationship and the experience and management of connection–autonomy issues, it should be studied over time and in relation to other life transitions. This study was also limited in type of family examined. Study participants were from the middle class where there was a father or father figure in the family. Although there is some transferability to mothers and adolescent daughters of other family types, results cannot necessarily be generalized to all mothers and adolescent daughters. Clearly single mothers, lesbian mothers, adoptive mothers, and stepmothers, to name a few, might have differences in the ways they experience and communicatively enact their relationships with adolescent daughters. Socioeconomic classes other than the middle class should also be examined. Finally, because this study suggested that ethnicity did impact connection and autonomy in the mother–adolescent daughter relationship, other ethnic groups should be included in future research on this topic.

One word of caution should be voiced. It was not my intention to evaluate participants and determine which ethnic group is more psychologically "healthy." We must be cautious in evaluating what degree of connection or autonomy is more beneficial. Boyd-Franklin (1989) points out, for example, that Black families differ from White families in degree of enmeshment. A psychologically healthy Black family, she asserts, may be viewed by the White therapist as being too enmeshed, as White families often do not have that degree of connection.

Thus, when we examine family relationships in different cultural contexts, our question should not be which group does it better, but how do they do it at all? Understanding rather than evaluation at this juncture is the most appropriate response to the results of this study.

Questions for Consideration and Discussion

1. What were your own experiences of negotiating the autonomy–connection dialectic in adolescence? To what degree were those experiences impacted by racial culture?
2. Penington interviewed both parents and adolescents for this work. What do you see as the primary differences in the experiences of parents and adolescents with regard to negotiating autonomy and connection? Similarities?
3. In addition to race, what other cultures may impact the experience of autonomy and connection in the teen years? How so?
4. In addition to the autonomy–connection dialectic, what other dialectics do you think may be impacted by racial culture?
5. This work compared the experiences of African American and European American parents and teens. What are the advantages of between-race comparisons? What are the potential drawbacks?

References

Asante, M. K. (1973). *Transracial communication.* Englewood Cliffs, NJ: Prentice Hall.

Baxter, L. A. (1988). A dialectical perspective on communication strategies in relationship development. In S. W. Duck, D. F. Hay, S. E. Hobfoll, W. Iches, & B. Montgomery (Eds.), *Handbook of personal relationships.* London: Wiley.

Baxter, L. A. (1990). Dialectical contradictions in relationship development. *Journal of Social and Personal Relationships, 7,* 69–88.

Baxter, L. A., & Montgomery, B. M. (1996). *Relating: Dialogues and dialectics.* New York: Guilford Press.

Baxter, L. A., & Montgomery, B. M. (1998). A guide to dialectical approaches to studying personal relationships. In B. Montgomery & L. Baxter (Eds.), *Dialectical approaches to studying personal relationships* (pp. 1–16). Mahwah, NJ: Erlbaum.

Blumer, H. (1969). *Symbolic interactionism: Perspective and method.* Englewood Cliffs, NJ: Prentice Hall.

Boyd-Franklin, N. (1989). *Black families in therapy: A multisystems approach.* New York: Guilford Press.

Camarota, S. A. (2001). *Immigrants in the United States—2000: A snapshot of America's foreign-born population.* Retrieved July 5, 2004, from the Center for Immigration Studies, Web site: www.cis.org/articles/2001/back101.html

Cauce, A. M., Hiraga, Y., Graves, D., Gonzales, N., Ryan-Finn, K., & Grove, K. (1996). African American mothers and their adolescent daughters: Closeness, conflict, and control. In B. J. R. Leadbeater and N. Way (Eds.), *Urban girls: Resisting stereotypes, creating identities* (pp. 100–116). New York: New York University Press.

Chodorow, N. (1978). *The reproduction of mothering: Psychoanalysis and the sociology of gender.* Berkeley: University of California Press.

Daniel, J. L., & Daniel, J. E. (1999). African American childrearing: The context of a hot stove. In T. J. Socha & R. C. Diggs (Eds.), *Communication, race, and family: Exploring communication in Black, White, and biracial families* (pp. 25–44). Mahwah, NJ: Erlbaum.

Diggs, R. C. (1999). African American and European American adolescents' perceptions of self-esteem as influenced by parent and peer communication and support environments. In T. J. Socha & R. C. Diggs (Eds.), *Communication, race, and family: Exploring communication in Black, White, and biracial families* (pp. 105–146). Mahwah, NJ: Erlbaum.

Dilworth-Anderson, P., Burton, L. M., & Johnson, L. B. (1993). Reframing theories for understanding race, ethnicity, and families. In P. G. Boss, W. J. Doherty, R. LaRossa, W. R. Schumm, & S. K. Stinmetz (Eds.), *Sourcebook of family theories and methods: A contextual approach* (pp. 135–163). New York: Plenum Press.

Gilligan, C. (1982). *In a different voice: Psychological theory and women's development.* Cambridge, MA: Harvard University Press.

Helms, J. E. (1990). Toward a model of White racial identity development. In J. Helms (Ed.), *Black and White racial identity: Theory, research, and practice*, (pp. 49–66). New York: Greenwood Press.

Hofstede, G. (1980). Motivation, leadership, and organizations: Do American theories apply abroad? *Organizational Dynamics, 9*(1), 42–63.

Hostede, G. (1983). National cultures in four dimensions. *International Studies of Management and Organization, 13*, 46–74.

Kızielewicz, N. (1988). A study of mothers and adolescent daughters in African American families. (ERIC Documents Reproduction Service No. ED326782).

McCandless, B. R., & Coop, R. H. (1979). *Adolescents: Behavior and development.* Chicago: Holt, Rinehart & Winston.

McGoldrick, M., & Giordano, J. (1996). Overview. Ethnicity and family therapy. In M. McGoldrick, J. Giordano, & J. Pearce (Eds.), *Ethnicity and family therapy* (2nd ed., pp. 1–30). New York: Guilford Press.

Mead, G. H. (1956). *On social psychology: Selected papers* (A. Strauss, Ed.), Chicago: University of Chicago Press. (Original work published 1934)

Montemayer, R. (1982). The relationship between parent–adolescent conflict and the amount of time adolescents spend alone and with parents and peers. *Child Development, 53*, 1512–1519.

Pipher, M. (1994). *Reviving Ophelia: Saving the selves of adolescent girls.* New York: Ballantine Books.

Rotheram-Borus, M. J., Dopkins, S., Sabate, N., & Lightfoot, M. (1996). Personal and ethnic identity, values, and self esteem among Black and Latino adolescent girls. In B. J. R. Leadbeater & N. Way (Eds.), *Urban girls: Resisting stereotypes, creating identities* (pp. 35–52). New York: New York University Press.

Santrock, J. W., & Yusseen, S. R. (1992). *Child development: An introduction.* Dubuque, IA: William C. Brown.

Smith, A. L. (2000). *Executive summary: A population perspective of the United States.* Retrieved July 5, 2004, from the Population Resource Center Web site: www.prcdc.org/summaries/uspopperspec/uspopperspec.html

Socha, T. J., & Diggs, R. C. (1999). At the crossroads of communication, race, and family: Toward understanding Black, White, and biracial family communication. In T. J. Socha & R. C. Diggs (Eds.), *Communication, race, and family: Exploring communication in Black, White, and biracial families* (pp. 1–24). Mahwah, NJ: Erlbaum.

Socha, T. J., Sanchez-Hucles, J., Bromley, J., & Kelly, B. (1995). Invisible parents and children: Exploring African American parent–child communication. In T. J. Socha & G. H. Stamp (Eds.), *Parents, children, and communication: Frontiers of theory and research* (pp. 127–145). Mahwah, NJ: Erlbaum.

Steinberg, L. (1990). Autonomy, conflict, and harmony in the family relationship. In S. Feldman and G. Elliot (Eds.), *At the threshold: The developing adolescent* (pp. 255–276). Cambridge, MA: Harvard University Press.

Steinberg, L. (1995). Commentary: On developmental trajectories and social contexts in adolescence. In L. Crockett & N. Crouter (Eds.), *Pathways through adolescence: Individual development in relation to social contexts* (pp. 245–253). Hillsdale, NJ: Erlbaum.

Vangelisti, A. L. (1992). Older adolescents' perceptions of communication problems with their parents. *Journal of Adolescent Research, 7*(3), 382–402.

Youniss, J., & Smollar, J. (1985). *Adolescent relations with mothers, fathers, and friends.* Chicago: University of Chicago Press.

Parenting in the Interracial Family: More Alike Than Different

Suzy Prentiss

Based on estimates from the U.S. census, as well as the work of population studies, multiracial families in the United States, and around the world, are becoming more common. From the standpoint of family communication studies, consideration of inter-racial and multiracial families is important for multiple reasons, including how such families are responded to by others, and the process of bringing together diverse cultures that occurs within such families. In this work, Prentiss examines the discourse of parents in interracial families, and considers the extent to which that discourse reflects concerns or issues specific to that family type. This work provides an exemplar of the idea that, whereas different family types may have distinct experiences, often the commonalities between family types are greater than the areas of divergence.

L.B.A.

Why should students of family communication study interracial families? Consider the following stories:

- An infant born without a completely formed skull died shortly after birth and was laid to rest in a local cemetery next to a family member. A few days later, the deacons of the church voted to have the child's body exhumed and buried elsewhere. What atrocity could that innocent newborn baby girl have committed during her few precious hours of life that was so horrendous it warranted removal from her eternal resting place?
- A female student is called a "mistake" to her face by the high school principal who then proceeds to threaten to cancel one of high school's most anticipated and revered traditions—the spring prom. The principal is fired, the school system sued, and the school burned down. The situation attracts the interest of the NAACP, the FBI, and the Ku Klux Klan. What could cause such a protest of a revered social event—gang violence, drugs, illegal activity? None of the above.
- A famous athlete faces one of the greatest challenges of his life. He is forced to sit idly by as leukemia ravages the body of his teenage daughter. Though this type of cancer is both rare and aggressive, a bone marrow transplant may save her life. However, due to her heritage her chances of finding a donor match are quite slim and no one in her family is a match. This baseball star loses his daughter despite a national campaign increasing the bone marrow donor registry, especially among minority donors.

All these stories have three things in common. First, they are all true. Second, they all occurred in the 1990s in the United States (1994, 1996, and 1995, respectively). Third, the female subject in each story is biracial—Black and White. In the first story, young Whitney Johnson's only "crime" was being born to an interracial couple; her mother is White and her father is Black. She was buried next to her White great-grandfather in a Georgia cemetery that had banned minority burials since before the Civil War (Kallestad, 1996). In the second story, ReVonda Bowen was called a mistake by her high school principal because of her biracial heritage. He threatened to cancel the spring prom because several interracial couples were to attend (Reed, 1994). Later, the school was burned, the principal fired (though lauded by many), and the school district sued. In the last story, baseball legend Rod Carew's daughter Michelle died from leukemia. A bone marrow transplant, often the only course of treatment in battling such an aggressive form of cancer as hers, was an unlikely option due to Michelle's biracial heritage and the fact that minority donors are very rare (Rosen, 1995).

As the world is becoming more integrated and diverse, the frequency of interracial romantic relationships and marriages is increasing (Besharov & Sullivan, 1996; Dainton, 1999; Qian, 1999; Roberts, 1994; Suro 1999). According to the 1980 U.S. Census, over one million interracial marriages were reported, 121,000 of which were Black–White couples (Glick, 1997). By 1995, according to census data, the number of Black–White interracial marriages had risen to approximately 328,000 (McNamara, Tempenis, & Walton, 1999; Rosenblatt, 1999). Consequently, the number of biracial children born of these unions is also increasing. The 1990 U.S. Census figures estimate the number of biracial (Black–White) children in this country at between 500,000 and 5,000,000 (Winn & Priest, 1993), with these numbers expected to grow. Though interracial marriages overall are relatively rare, accounting for roughly 1 out of every 1,200 marriages in the United States (Solsberry, 1994), marriages between Blacks and Whites are the most uncommon of all (Davidson, 1992; Solsberry, 1994; Wehrly, Kenney, & Kenney, 1999; Williams & Andersen, 1998). Still, rooted in America's history of slavery, the fury over miscegenation laws, and the prevalence of racism, it is these Black–White interracial relationships that cause the most uproar (Brown, 1989–1990; Roberts, 1994; Solsberry, 1994). As the number of these Black–White intermarriages increases, it is unfortunate that the innocent children of these unions potentially face the greatest challenges.

Any literature review on Black–White intermarriage and parenting will ultimately lead to information on miscegenation laws (legal measures prohibiting interracial relationships and marriage, most notably Black–White unions) and problems faced by the interracial couple at various stages of their relationship. There is also a substantial body of research addressing the self-identity (and racial identity) struggles experienced by biracial adolescents. There is a real void in the research, however, when it comes to parenting biracial children in interracial families and how the roles of parents are similar to or different from those in monoracial families. In fact, because interracial families are considered minority families, research on minority families may be useful in gathering information and creating questions for further study.

According to researchers Franklin and Boyd-Franklin, in their chapter addressing Black parenting perspectives (1985), it is the responsibility of parents and close family members to create "the social/environmental context for the child . . . [which may involve] exposing a child to his or her history, cultural heritage, and the impact of racism" (p. 202). It would seem that these are tasks or challenges that must be successfully managed by the interracial family, as well. Paramount to an accurate understanding of the internal and external processes influencing biracial children's self-identity development are their families. Recently, Orbe (1999) identified four communication options for the interracial family when discussing race: "(a) embracing the Black experience, (b) assuming a commonsense approach, (c) advocating a color blind society, and (d) affirming the multiethnic experience" (p. 170). Socha and Diggs (1999) echoed the important role played by family communication in the process of racial identity formation on the familial level and argued that this development is more complex and important in interracial (Black–White) families. The intricacies and nuances of the family communication dynamic take on additional significance when examined within the context of interracial families.

Extensive literature review makes it clear that this subject area is worthy of further investigation and study that needs to be explored in more depth. Though much scholarship has been written about miscegenation laws, the self-identity development of biracial adolescents, and interracial romantic relationships, a gap still exists with respect to the personal accounts of the parents of biracial, Black–White, children. It is necessary to capture and then appreciate the everyday experiences of those parents and their perceptions and expectations as they managed their parental roles and responsibilities. What are their struggles, their triumphs, and their challenges as parents? What have they experienced as a member of an interracial couple, and what impact have they had upon each of their lives? What do they hope for their children? What do they fear?

The methodology considered most appropriate for this study was qualitative research. It was deemed imperative that participants share their own stories in their own words. Ultimately, qualitative research strives to capture a broad, yet vivid picture of the phenomenon in question through the experiences of the participants (Taylor & Bogdan, 1984b). A primary focus within the qualitative paradigm is a profound respect for the participants and their experiences. This fundamental emphasis on respect and understanding influences each step of the study, from creation to completion to data analysis to conclusions.

For this study, information was gathered from 10 participants during semistructured long interviews lasting approximately 45 minutes to an hour and a half each (McCracken, 1988; Taylor, 1994). It is important to remember that the participants in a qualitative study do not serve as the spokespeople for everyone affiliated with their experiences, conditions, and qualifications; rather, they merely provide "an opportunity to glimpse the complicated character, organization, and logic of culture" (McCracken, 1988, p. 17). Ideally, in the case of this particular study, the long-interview format offered the participants an opportunity to share their parenting experiences in detail, discussing those memories and feelings that they deemed most important. In addition to the long interview, participants were asked to fill out a basic demographic data sheet that provided a basic framework of resources, such as education level, income, family size, and so on available to these families—to allow those reading the text to identify more closely with them and benefit from their wisdom and experience.

It is important to note that the participants in this study were one (or both) of the biological parents of biracial (referred to as African American and Caucasian or Black–White) children. As the principal investigator of this project is herself the mother of a biracial (Black–White) son, she was aware of a number of interracial families in the Knoxville, Tennessee, area. Initially, she contacted people she personally knew for participation in this study and then employed a snowball technique to solicit other participants (Babbie, 1995). This snowball technique involved finding potential or actual participants and then asking them to refer or introduce the principal investigator to others (Taylor & Bogdan, 1984a). The sample area was limited to the Greater Knoxville/ Eastern Tennessee area. A crucial consideration of this study was that varied family types be included in order to make the suggestions and experiences more applicable and, therefore, more meaningful to others.

It was hoped that any parent involved in the rearing of a biracial child or children reading this study would be able to identify with at least one of the participant's experiences.

Initially, an instrument consisting of three major areas of inquiry (the interracial relationship, raising a biracial child, and most challenging experiences as a parent) was developed as a guide and included possible questions, prompts, and points of discussion. Some of these included, but were not limited to:

- How have your family, relatives, and friends responded to your interracial relationship?
- How have they (those mentioned above) responded to your biracial child?

Based on the data collected during the first interview, additional follow-up questions were created. These included:

- How would your child describe himself/herself in terms of racial classification?
- How do you think "society" would classify him/her?
- During any stage of this journey (dating, pregnancy, child rearing) has the question: "What about the child(ren)?" ever been raised? If so, how did you respond?

Upon completion of the taped interviews, the tapes were transcribed and analyzed in depth. A comparative analysis of the transcribed data was used to examine and organize the information into common patterns or themes. These patterns were then grouped into categories that facilitated a better examination and analysis of common experiences and unique perspectives. The following excerpts reflect an exhaustive data analysis designed to accurately capture the experiences of the participants in their own words while providing thoughtful insight into and an understanding of their stories. As you read the responses of the participants, notice how their fears, concerns, triumphs, and joys are those of parents—not as Black parents, or as White parents, nor as the parents of biracial children, but just as parents.

Joys of Parenthood

According to one father, parenting is "the best thing we do." A single mother responded: "My son is my world." Another father described his rewards of family life excitedly and in greater detail. He reported:

> It's humbling [laughing] . . . [they are young] and they constantly show me that we can't control them. It's probably the most important part of our day—the effort and the time we spend with them and teaching them about who they are, about the fact we love them and they are worthy and precious and special. It's the best thing we do, outside of loving each other and keeping our private life, that relationship between us healthy and whole. That's the next thing, passing our love on to our kids.

For the parents profiled in this study, their children and family life are a great source of joy and pride.

Challenges of Parenting

The challenges faced by these parents (as leaders of their interracial families) about which they felt comfortable speaking addressed a number of issues on multiple levels. As parents, some were concerned with status—as a single parent or as a part-time or custodial parent. One mother reported that her biggest challenge was being a single parent. She stated:

> As a single parent . . . balancing both the mother and father [roles] and you want to be a friend to your child, you also want to be a parent, having to be . . . the good and bad guy in the same respect, especially when it comes to discipline situations. I have to be Mom and Dad at the same time.

A similar response was offered by another single mother who explained:

> Being a single parent is difficult. I wouldn't trade it for the world, but I think having to be the good person and the bad person, and having to do the discipline, and having to decide— every decision is made by you and your child's life is on that—I think is the most difficult. The easy part is the loving, the kisses, and the fun stuff, but the difficult stuff is the stuff you would normally share with another.

Two of the fathers participating in the study experienced custody issues; one now has custody of his son whereas the other father has visitation. To both of these men, the issue of custody was very much a concern and priority. One father described his struggle to get custody of his son and have him live in his household. He reported:

> I think the biggest challenge was with R [eldest child] because, up until two years ago, I did not have custody of him. So it was very hard dealing with the ex-wife. . . . I had to make a plan, to make a situation where I can get custody . . . so I work toward getting custody of him. . . . I think he needed to be moved to the right environment to develop correctly.

Most of the concerns of the mothers were typical and basic, issues and worries that may be felt by the majority of parents regardless of marital status, economic situation, or race. One mother remarked: "I have a really hard time with consistency, so with discipline, actually with anything, that's what I have the biggest challenge with is consistency." Discipline (one of the hallmarks of parental duties and concerns) was specifically mentioned by another mother. She stated: "The only [other] thing really we have had a problem with is discipline, not knowing how to discipline children to begin with."

For each of the four fathers, providing for their families (or children) was a primary concern. The first, profiled previously, was very concerned with the development of his son and the fact that, as the noncustodial parent, his influence may be limited. For another father, his biggest challenge was to provide financially for his family, another common concern. This man explained his situation. He remarked:

> I'd say the most challenging would be the loss of the house . . . because providing for a wife and two kids, it was pretty hard. Losing your house and having to move into an apartment, a small apartment, that's about the worst thing we have actually had to go through.

The third father described his need to provide security for and protect his family. He detailed his safety concerns, especially where his baby girl was concerned. The fourth father discussed his concerns to protect his child in a specific child care situation.

Each participant in this study discussed areas of parental concern such as status, custody, health, discipline, financial provisions, and safety. Though these are parents of biracial children, it seems that their concerns were very typical and had less to do with race and more to do with love.

Issues of Race

Many parents mentioned the challenge posed by standard forms that inquire about race ("check one"). This is probably the one area of concern that posed a challenge unique to interracial families and their biracial children, especially those forms that ask to "check one box" for identifying racial classification. This was a point not addressed by the interview protocol, but raised and discussed by many of the participants. In fact, each of the mothers specifically mentioned forms. One mother discussed her approach to the forms and how that now influences how her daughter completes them. She explained:

When we have to fill out forms it is very difficult to be able to do that and so I always put "Other" [figuring] if they want to have a discussion of what her race is [they will, but] nobody has taken me up on that. So she has seen that's what I do and that's what she does. Whenever she has to fill out a form she automatically puts "Other."

A second mother expounded upon her thoughts regarding the standardized forms and what relevance they may have. She stated: "I think that society, just from the forms I have had to fill out, will think of them in a category as being Black. Just because there is not a place [specifically] for them to check . . . not a lot of 'biracial' spaces to check."

Another female discussed her approach to completing the forms for her young children: If I'm in a certain mood I'll put "Other" or I'll put "Black/White." And sometimes I don't care I just want to get the form filled out, so I just put down Black. It really doesn't have a significance a whole lot to me. It just depends on how feisty I feel [when I am filling it out]. [laughing] If I want to make an issue of it or not, but no, overall no, I don't lose sleep over it.

The fourth mother offered a suggestion for a new racial category. She reported:

Unfortunately when they have to check the boxes [on forms], "Multicultural," that's what I'm hoping. And that's what I hope to see on forms. I think it is ridiculous the Census Bureau didn't have it on there; I would check it [laugh]. But I think multicultural. Some people say "mixed" but I don't like that term.

The last female participant detailed a recent experience:

I went the other day to fill out a form and it asked his [son's] background and they didn't have anything [correct], they had "Black," "White," "Asian," and "Other." The lady was like, "Why don't you just check 'other'?" I go, "My child is not an 'Other.' " She goes, "I know, but that will basically explain it." I go, "No." So I hit "Black" and I hit "White" and [now] they have to deal with it. I just think it is wrong, it is so limiting like that. I will not check "Other" for my child.

For most of us, questions about our racial or ethnic identity are not even raised; yet it is often assumed that for interracial families and their biracial children these issues will become obstacles and challenges on a daily basis (think about the question, "what about the children?"). This study suggests that, at least among these parents, race is not an issue of constant concern. However, it must be dealt with when society imposes the need for labels and racial identification, such as with school enrollment forms or job applications.

So, what does it all mean? The 10 parents of 13 biracial, Black, and White children had a lot to say about their romantic relationships, their challenges and rewards as parents, and their concerns and preparations for the acceptance of their biracial children by a society that certainly favors monoracial individuals. In some cases, religious differences and news of an unplanned pregnancy may have negatively compounded the reaction to the interracial romance, whereas in other cases, the birth of their children served instantly to dissolve barriers and mend bridges. The challenges faced by these parents of biracial children were similar to those traditionally voiced by parents of monoracial children and included their personal status (in terms of marriage and custody), their ability to provide a safe and financially secure environment, their concern for education, and their need to have healthy and well-adjusted children.

The race of their child(ren) posed a challenge with regard to completion of standardized forms and the resources available to the families. Race also became an issue with respect to the self-identity development of their child(ren) and how society views their child(ren) in terms of race. However, issues of race (whether the interracial nature of their romantic relationships or the biracial identity of their children) did not seem nearly as important to these 10 parents as the literature had suggested. They did not mention it as a challenge except when discussing standardized forms that have to be completed.

It could be argued that, on a daily basis, race may not even enter into the equation, but may rise only in response to certain specific instances or situations. Over time and as the tasks of daily living are managed, does the racial composition of the family rise to the surface of concern? Is it a fact that the family's identity, certainly with the passage of time, is more a result of its members, experiences, and memories than its diversity? Are incidents of prejudice and racism clear and objective or are they more a response to a perceived situation or attitude? It could also be argued, however, that these participants did not feel comfortable discussing racial incidents or that in an effort to "normalize" their families they chose not to discuss negative experiences that may be unique to interracial families. Consider this: Is parenting in the interracial family more alike than different?

Questions for Consideration and Discussion

1. In this study, Prentiss found that most of the issues mentioned by the participants were similar to the experiences of any parent, not specific to the parenting of biracial or multiracial children. What might this reveal about parenting generally and/or parenting in an interracial family more specifically?

2. One of the few race-related issues mentioned by these respondents was the difficulty they faced filling out forms that asked for the race of their children. Why do you think this particular issue was mentioned so frequently by the participants?

3. In 1967, the U.S. Supreme Court ruled that laws against interracial marriage were unconstitutional. In 2000, the last state, Alabama, repealed its antimiscegenation law. What consequences, socially, have there been as a result of these legal changes? How might these changes have impacted family life?

4. In the final page of her article, Prentiss offers several possible reasons for the limited discussion of race by these participants. Which of these reasons resonate most for you, and why?

5. Drawing from this study, what do you see as possibilities for future research regarding multiracial families?

References

Babbie, E. (1995). *The practice of social research*. Belmont, CA: Wadsworth.

Besharov, D. J., & Sullivan, T. S. (1996). One flesh: America is experiencing an unprecedented increase in Black–White intermarriage. *The New Democrat, 8*, 19–21.

Brown, P. (1989–1990). Black–White interracial marriages: A historical analysis. *Journal of Intergroup Relations, 26*, 26–36.

Dainton, M. (1999). African-American, European-American, and biracial couples' meanings for and experiences in marriages. In T. J. Socha & R. C. Diggs (Eds.), *Communication, race, and family: Exploring communication in Black, White, and biracial families* (pp. 147–166). Mahwah, NJ: Erlbaum.

Davidson, J. R. (1992). Theories about Black–White interracial marriage: A clinical perspective. *Journal of Multicultural Counseling and Development, 20*, 150–157.

Franklin, A. J., & Boyd-Franklin, N. (1985). A psychoeducational perspective on Black parenting. In H. P. McAdoo & J. L. McAdoo (Eds.), *Black children: Social, educational, and parental environments* (pp. 194–210). Beverly Hills, CA: Sage.

Glick, P. (1997). Demographic pictures of African American families. In H. P. McAdoo (Ed.), *Black families* (3rd ed., pp. 118–138). Thousand Oaks, CA: Sage.

Kallestad, B. (1996, March 29). Deacons back down on exhuming mixed-race baby. *Knoxville News-Sentinel*, p. A15.

McCracken, G. (1988). *The long interview*. Newbury Park, CA: Sage.

McNamara, R. P., Tempenis, M., & Walton, B. (1999). *Crossing the line: Interracial couples in the South*. Westport, CT: Greenwood Press.

Orbe, M. P. (1999). Communicating about "race" in interracial families. In T. J. Socha & R. C. Diggs (Eds.), *Communication, race, and family: Exploring communication in Black, White, and biracial families* (pp. 167–180). Mahwah, NJ: Erlbaum.

Qian, Z. (1999). Who intermarries? Education, nativity, region, and interracial marriage, 1980 and 1990. *Journal of Comparative Family Studies, 30*(4), 579–597.

Reed, S. K. (1994). Heat of the night. *People, 42*, 40–41.

Roberts, R. E. T. (1994). Black–White intermarriage in the United States. In W. R. Johnson & D. M. Warren (Eds.), *Inside the mixed marriage* (pp. 25–79). Lanham, MD: University Press.

Rosen, M. (1995). The game of his life. *People, 44*, 133–135.

Rosenblatt, P. C. (1999). Multiracial families. In M. E. Lamb (Ed.), *Parenting and child development in nontraditional families* (pp. 263–278). Mahwah, NJ: Erlbaum.

Socha, T. J., & Diggs, R. C. (1999). At the crossroads of communication, race, and family: Toward understanding Black, White, and biracial family communication. In T. J. Socha & R. C. Diggs (Eds.), *Communication, race, and family: Exploring communication in Black, White, and biracial families* (pp. 1–24). Mahwah, NJ: Erlbaum.

Solsberry, P. W. (1994). Interracial couples in the United States of America: Implications for mental health counseling. *Journal of Mental Health Counseling, 16*, 304–317.

Suro, R. (1999). Mixed doubles. *American Demographics, 21*(11), 56–62.

Taylor, R. (1994). Qualitative research. In M. Singletary (Ed.), *Mass communication research* (pp. 265–279). New York: Longman.

Taylor, S. J., & Bogdan, R. (1984a). In-depth interviewing. In *Introduction to qualitative research methods* (pp. 76–105). New York: Wiley.

Taylor, S. J., & Bogdan, R. (1984b). Introduction to qualitative methods. In *Introduction to qualitative research methods* (pp. 1–12). New York: Wiley.

Wehrly, B., Kenney, K. R., & Kenney, M. E. (1999). *Counseling multiracial families*. Thousand Oaks, CA: Sage.

Williams, S., & Andersen, P. A. (1998). Toward an expanded view of interracial romantic relationships. In V. J. Duncan (Ed.), *Towards achieving MAAT: Communication patterns in African American, European American, and interracial relationships*. Dubuque, IA: Kendall/Hunt.

Winn, N. N., & Priest, R. (1993). Counseling biracial children: A forgotten component of multicultural counseling. *Family Therapy, 20*, 29–36.

Section 3: Conclusions and Application—Issues of Race and Ethnicity in Your Family Experience

As you have read this chapter, have you been thinking about your own perceptions of race and ethnicity and how they relate to your family experiences? If you were to talk to other individuals who read the same material, the conclusions you drew about this issue would likely be very different, even for those who, on the surface, appear to share your racial and ethnic origins. This marks the complexity of the ways in which we respond to race and ethnicity. In this section, I address two primary ways that you may wish to use the material you encountered in this chapter in your own life. Principally, this relates to reflecting on your own family history with regard to race and ethnicity, and developing new understandings of and reactions to others.

Reflections on Your Family History

As you consider how race and ethnicity intersect with your own family experience, it would be helpful to begin by thinking about how you see race/ethnicity yourself. How often is your race a part of the way you understand yourself? How and in what ways do race and ethnicity enter into the way you think about others? Considering these questions will give you some insight into the ways that you understand race in terms of your own experience. Now the question becomes, where did you develop those views?

We all learn about race and ethnicity in some way within our family settings. As you read in this chapter, the extent to which race and ethnicity are explicitly discussed varies from one family to another. Research tends to suggest, as you saw in Hill's study, that families who have experienced more prejudice from others in regard to race/ethnicity may spend more time in conscious discussion of racial issues. Additionally, some races are more marked than others (that is, the race itself becomes more of a noticed identifier for individuals). Hill's respondents wanted their daughters to understand about the intersections between class, sex, and race so that they would be prepared to deal with the responses of others and would develop a healthy image of themselves as Black women. In White families, the need to discuss race may feel less intense. This is because, as noted early in the chapter, White is often considered an "absence of race." Thus, there may seem to be less to discuss. In some situations, families who are White will still attend to ethnicity in obvious ways; for example, Hispanic families may use more explicit messages about ethnicity than Eastern European White families. Even when racial or ethnic socialization does not occur explicitly, messages are still being provided. Never discussing race is to send a message about race and ethnicity. It may be a message that race/ethnicity doesn't matter if you are "like us," or that race/ethnicity is inappropriate or unimportant to talk about.

Considering this, think about the messages that you received about race and ethnicity in your family of origin. What sort of things did your parents or adult caregivers tell you about the qualities, behaviors, or beliefs related to your own race/ethnicity? What were the implied messages revealed in behavior (i.e., you know your family is Irish and you celebrated St. Patrick's Day, but never really talked about being Irish) or indirect talk ("we do xyz" with no clear discussion of who "we" are)? What messages did your parents, adult caregivers, and other relatives provide you about how others might see your family due to race/ethnicity? If you don't remember your family particularly talking about race/ethnicity in relation to the responses of others, what sort of implicit messages might you have learned? How were those messages provided through behavior or indirect talk? Perhaps your parents told you that a certain behavior would make others think that you were acting like a member of another race/ethnicity. Messages like this, although not directly indicating expectations for your race or ethnicity, indicate by comparison how you should be. Comparative messages such as this also indicate something about the race/ethnicity of others. Thinking about your years growing up, what explicit and implicit messages did your family provide with regard to the race/ethnicity of others?

Considering questions like these allow us to develop some insight into how our views were shaped by family experience, and also how we reshaped what we learned through our own encounters with others outside the family setting. This can also provide a way of thinking about how our family values, behaviors, and interactions may have been impacted by ethnic and racial culture.

As you read in this chapter, race and ethnicity has been shown to affect values related to family and family interaction. Thinking about your family of origin, can you locate a particular value or set of values that seemed to be a crucial part of "being" in that family? You might even want to ask some of your family members to see if together you can generate such a list. Now consider the extent to which you also see those values as being associated with your race/ethnicity. Do others in your racial/ethnic culture seem to hold those same values about family? Asking this sort of question can help us see how larger cultural settings, such as racial and ethnic culture, inform the beliefs and practices that we enact within our individual families.

As racial/ethnic culture affects our beliefs and values related to family life, so too does it affect our enactments of family. Penington's research, presented in this chapter, found some commonalities in the relationships of Black mothers and daughters and White mothers and daughters. But, she also found some differences that seemed to be at least somewhat related to racial culture and family expectations arising from that culture. Similar findings, noted in this chapter, have resulted from studies looking at parent discipline strategies, how parents socialize children to cultural sex role expectations, and the compliance of children with parental requests. Given that race/ethnicity can have cultural impacts upon us, and that culture seems related in many ways to how we behave in family settings, it stands to reason then that differences in race/ethnicity may result in differences in family behavior. So, how can you use this understanding in your own life?

As a child (or even now, as an adult), you may have sometimes wondered why your parents, adult caregivers, or other family members behaved in the way that they did. Thinking about how racial and ethnic culture impacts family behavior may give you some new insight into their behavior. In a family communication course, one of my students was bemoaning the fact that her parents had been so willing to allow her brother freedom to go where he wanted with his friends (as a teenager), but her behavior was very restricted, even though she was a better student and more inclined to follow rules. As the class discussed this issue, what seemed to be a pattern related to ethnicity emerged. The women in the room who felt their parents had been unnecessarily strict with them, but not their brothers, were from Italian American families. The women who had not experienced this difference were not from Italian American families. Does this mean that all Italian American families are more strict with their daughters than their sons? Absolutely not. But, in this conversation, the possibility that this behavior may have been related to a culture of ethnicity gave these women a new way to consider their parents behavior. This is an example of how considering the connection between race/ethnicity and family interaction patterns may provide us with new ways to think about our family.

In addition to giving us new ways to consider our own family experience, attention paid to racial/ethnic cultural effects can give us new understandings of the behaviors of others. We have all had times when we have been surprised by the behaviors of another family. Often, when we encounter a family who is behaving in a way that we find surprising, unusual, or odd, we tend to assign the cause of that behavior to the individual family members. Again, considering the roles of race and ethnicity may give us a new insight into that behavior. Although a particular pattern of interaction may seem surprising viewed through the lens of our own racial or ethnic culture, considering it through the lens of a different culture may make it easier to understand and appreciate the diversity.

A note of caution is important as we end this chapter. As we saw in Prentiss's study, the interracial families she studied were more similar to same-race families than they were different. Differences in race and ethnicity may sometimes create differences in family patterns, but we should not make an assumption that families will, or should, be very different from one another because the members have a different race or ethnicity (and we certainly should avoid assuming that one type of family will be "better" or "worse" than another due to race/ethnicity). All families exist within a web of multiple cultures, and cultures related to race and ethnicity are a part of that setting. Thinking about race and ethnicity as we consider our own familial values and behaviors and those of others may provide us with new insights. However, we should not forget that families are also impacted by socioeconomics, religion, regional cultures, national cultures, and individual factors, among other things. The multitude of ways for families to "be" families is staggering and affected by many factors both internal and external. Considering the role of race and ethnicity is but one way we can develop new understandings of the diversity of family life.

Questions for Consideration and Discussion

1. How would you describe the race (or races) and ethnicity (or ethnicities) of your family of origin? If you find it difficult to describe, why?
2. What are some of the ways that race and ethnicity have affected the beliefs, values, and behaviors in your family systems?
3. As considered in this chapter, we learn about race/ethnicity from family, and also from mediated messages. What information about race/ethnicity did you learn in your family settings and how did it correspond (or not) with media messages you encountered?
4. Demographically, the United States has increasing numbers of interracial and multiracial families. If this trend continues, how do you think it will change the way family "is done" and the expectations of family?
5. How might parents and other adult caregivers meet the simultaneous needs and desires to provide a positive image of family race/ethnicity and family history for children, while also avoiding making race seem the most important facet of self and family?

Key Terms and Concepts

ethnicity	multiracial	race/ethnicity socialization
interracial	race	transracial

8

Sexuality and the Family

Chapter Outline

Chapter Objectives

1. To become more cognizant of the role of sexuality in the family
2. To understand how covert and overt communication about sexuality in family settings impacts children and adolescents
3. To develop an awareness of particular issues faced by gay- and lesbian-parented families and families with gay/lesbian children
4. To use material to analyze communication in your own family of origin, understand the families of others, and plan for your future

Section 1: Overview of Family Communication and Sexuality

- If you were watching television at 8:30 on a Wednesday night, and you saw an advertisement that had a somewhat sexual overtone (a flock of women and one man following an attractive man with a diet soft drink), what kind of reaction would you have?
- If you saw a gay couple holding hands in front of their children, how would you respond?
- If you saw a mother and father kiss in front of their children, what would you think?
- If you heard a four-year-old child use the word *sex*, how would you react? What thoughts might go through your head?

The ways in which we respond to, and communicate about, issues of sexuality are certainly multifaceted. In these examples, some individuals might find themselves saying they would be more shocked or appalled by the four-year-old child saying "sex" than by the risqué advertisement on television during a time when children are likely to watch. Other people may not be particularly shocked that a four-year-old would speak about sex, but would be disturbed that a gay or lesbian couple might show physical affection in front of a child. Some individuals might not have a particularly strong reaction to any of these situations, whereas others might find them all inappropriate in some way. The responses we have to issues related to sexuality come from our histories in family cultures, friendship and romantic relationship cultures, and larger social settings.

Let's begin by addressing, generally, the role of sexuality and sexual communication in family settings. The family system is imbued with sexuality. Parents and adult caregivers enact their sexual relationship within the family setting. That relationship impacts their happiness and satisfaction, which then affects the family system. Parents and children socialize each other about sex-role/gender expectations (what it means to be male or female) in the family. This learning then becomes a part of their understanding of self that they carry with them, in some form, throughout their lives. Messages are given to children, in the family setting, about sexuality generally, sexual orientation, the appropriateness of particular physical behaviors, and how to respond to issues of sexuality. As children grow, and their own sexual nature becomes more apparent (though it is always there), children also communicate to family members about their own concerns, impressions, and values related to sex roles, sexual orientation, and sexuality. As we are all sexual beings, so too are families sexual entities.

In this text, we have already considered some information related to sex-role/gender socialization and sexual orientation. In this chapter, we focus on issues of sexuality in the family including adult sexuality and relational satisfaction, parent–child communication about sexuality, and parent and child sexual orientation.

Partner Sexuality and Relational Satisfaction

As we discussed in Chapter 2, the adult romantic/sexual relationship is often seen as the foundation of family. For most family settings, the adult caregivers are involved in a romantic/sexual relationship. In intact nuclear or blended families, the parents (and/or stepparents) maintain a romantic/sexual relationship with each other. In single-parent or solo-parent families, the parent may maintain a romantic/sexual relationship with a dating partner or partners. Though this relationship is about the adult caregivers, and not the family as a whole, because families are systems, the outcomes and interaction patterns in the marital/partner relationship reverberate throughout the family system. Sexuality is no exception.

Numerous studies have indicated a positive correlation between **relational satisfaction** (an overall happiness with the relationship) and **sexual satisfaction** (happiness with the sexual aspects of the relationship). That is, studies seem to indicate that as sexual happiness increases, so too does relational happiness (for discussion see Byers, 2005; Purnine & Carey, 1997). However, what isn't fully clear is the order of causation. Byers (2005) suggests a number of ways this relationship could be explained.

It could be that couples who are more satisfied sexually are more satisfied relationally. In a study of Chinese families, Guo and Huang (2005) found that the level of sexual satisfaction a couple had was predictive of their marital satisfaction, and concluded that greater education about sexuality is likely to produce more satisfying sexual relationships, and thus more satisfying marriages.

A second possibility is that couples that are more relationally satisfied with each other become more sexually satisfied. Young, Denny, Young, and Luquis (2000) examined sexuality and relational questionnaires completed by 641 married women. They found that relational satisfaction factors (general relationship satisfaction, satisfaction with the non-sexual elements of the relationship) were correlated with and predicted significantly the amount of sexual satisfaction experienced. The authors conclude that sexual interactions and satisfaction need to be considered within an understanding of evaluations of the relationship as a whole (see also Lawrance & Byers, 1995).

A third possibility is that the two factors impact each other. In a study of romantic couples, Sprecher (2002) found that there was a positive correlation between sexual satisfaction and relational satisfaction, such that when one improved, so did the other, and when one suffered, so did the other. But, in her study, which was done over five waves of data gathering in an attempt to look for temporal change, it was not clear that either variable "came first" in changing. Thus, Sprecher argues that it is possible that the two factors simultaneously impact one another.

Finally, it may be that a third factor contributes to both relational and sexual satisfaction. An increase in communication intimacy has been shown to be related to both relational and sexual satisfaction (Byers, 2005; Byers & Demmons, 1999; Cupach & Comstocks, 1990; Litzinger & Gordon, 2005). Litzinger and Gordon examined the relationship between these two factors in a group of 387 married couples. Their study indicated that both communication and sexual satisfaction were positively correlated with marital satisfaction. However, they also found that if couples are communicating well, this seems to be the primary factor of importance, and thus may lead to both relational and sexual satisfaction.

It is possible that there is not a single explanation for how relational and sexual satisfaction relate to one another. Based on the variety of studies that suggest different causality in this relationship, Byers (2005) suggests that the connection between sexual and relational satisfaction may vary based on the couple involved. What does seem clear is that there is some relationship between sexual happiness and relational well-being for romantic partners. And, given that we know that when parents have a happier relationship, there are

BOX 8.1 • *Internet Connection*

A television program that has received much interest in 2006 is *Strictly Dr. Drew*. The show, which has fared well in viewer ratings, focuses on ways that adults can increase their sexual satisfaction in relationships. Read more at http://health.discovery.com/fansites/dr_drew/dr_drew.htm.

positive results throughout the family system, this is indicative of the importance of sexuality in family settings.

Parent–Child Communication about Sex and Sexuality

Just as sexuality impacts on the parental/adult caregiver romantic relationship, so too does it reverberate through the parent–child relationship. Though the study of family communication about sexuality is a relatively new area of focus (Warren, 1992, 1995), a variety of studies in communication and other family fields have indicated that family communication can have an impact on the sexual beliefs, knowledge, values, and behavior of family members. It is important to note that families cannot "not communicate" about sex and sexuality. Family interactions inevitably "say something" about sexuality, even if the discussions are never explicitly held.

From the time a child is born, his or her parents or adult caregivers communicate with him or her about sex and sexuality. This occurs in a variety of ways. Parents communicate with children about sex through **sexual modeling** (the ways that they behave with one another or with other adult romantic partners in the case of single parents). Parents who are relatively open about their own nature as sexual beings (i.e., kissing in front of the children) may communicate to their children about the naturalness of sexual attraction. Parents who never touch at all in front of their children may communicate that physical affection and attraction are inappropriate, or to be hidden.

In addition to communicating via their behavior with each other, parents communicate with their children in how they respond to the behaviors of the child, and how they interact with the child or children. When fathers show less physical affection to sons than to daughters, as discussed in Chapter 5, this may send a message that physical intimacy between males is "off limits." When a parent or adult caregiver observes a child fondling his or her own genitals, the response of the parent tells the child something about sexuality (maybe that it is natural, maybe that it is "dirty," maybe that it is private). When a parent turns off the television if a scene shows sexuality in any form, that action communicates something to the child about sexuality.

Family communication that may seem to be unrelated to sex often is. For example, the tasks of raising a child, including diapering, toilet training, bathing, and so on, call for some degree of conversation about genitalia. And, children are naturally curious about their own body parts and the body parts of others. Thus, family **body talk** is a common occurrence.

Many families develop euphemisms with which to talk about genitalia ("wee-wee," "pee-pee," "down there"). Although the purpose of such talk may be about toilet training or learning body parts, it nonetheless communicates something about sexuality.

Of course, parents and adult caregivers may also communicate with children through **overt sexuality communication.** Whether this occurs in the context of a child-led discussion ("Mom, where do babies come from?"), casual comments, or "the talk," many families engage in some form of overt talk about sexuality. Thus, communication about sexuality in the family takes many forms. In this text, however, we focus on the obvious discussions of sexuality, as those have been more completely studied than the more "hidden" types of sex communication just discussed.

Overt Parent–Child Communication about Sexuality

Overt and ongoing communication about sexuality in the family is a relatively rare phenomenon, with some studies reporting that only around 10 percent of families participate in such discussions (Warren, 1992, 1995). Conversations that do occur are often limited to particular family dyads. Studies have often indicated that mothers and daughters are the family dyad that primarily engages in talk about sexuality (Fox, 1981; Heisler, 2005; Hepburn, 1983; Hutchinson & Cooney, 1998; Rosenthal & Feldman, 1999). Mothers and daughters talk more about sexuality in general, but other scholars have also found that fathers are more likely to be the ones speaking with their sons (Fisher, 1993). Taken together, this seems to suggest that boys receive less overall talk about sexuality from their parents and adult caregivers.

So, you might wonder, exactly what and how often are parents explicitly communicating to their children about sexuality issues. Work done by scholars such as Heisler (2005), Hutchinson and Cooney (1988), and Fox and Inazu (1980) suggest that, in most families, some explicit communication about sexuality does occur. However, their studies also indicate that some topics are harder for parents to discuss with their children. These scholars argue that parents are more likely to talk about general issues like relationships, morals, menstruation, pregnancy, postponing sex, and resisting sexual pressure (with most of that talk being done by mothers). Talk about topics such as sexually transmitted diseases (STDs) is less common, with Hutchinson and Cooney finding only half of mothers and less than one-quarter of fathers participating in such talks. Hutchinson and Cooney concluded that parents may be less comfortable discussing such issues than they are less sensitive concepts like menstruation. This type of finding has been replicated in other research, such as Jordan, Price, and Fitzgerald's (2000) study that indicated 20 percent of parents were "somewhat" or "very" uncomfortable talking about sexuality and that the more sensitive the topic, the less inclined parents were to discuss it (with topics like pornography, masturbation, and prostitution the least likely to be talked about) (see also Rosenthal & Feldman, 1999).

From these studies, we see that some parents do discuss sexuality issues with their children (though mothers do so more than fathers), but the topics discussed may be restricted and limited due to parents' (and possibly the teen's) discomfort with discussing particular topics. This understanding is important because of the potential effects of parent–child communication about sexuality on adolescent and young adult sexual behavior and health.

Family Communication about Sexuality and Impact on Child Behavior

Studies have indicated that the relationship between explicit parent–child communication about sexuality and adolescent behavior is very complex. Moore, Peterson, and Furstenberg (1986) found that when parents who had traditional or conservative attitudes talked to their adolescents about sex, teenage girls were less likely to be sexually active (see also Newcomer & Udry, 1985), but teenage boys were more likely to be more sexually active. On the contrary, Fisher (1989) found that increased explicit communication about sexuality seemed to be unrelated to the sexual behavior of adolescent males, but was positively correlated to the sexual behavior of adolescent girls (that is, more communication was associated with more sexual activity). She found this correlation for both liberal and conservative parents. Fingerson (2005) studied mother–adolescent relationships, mother–adolescent communication, and adolescent sexual activity. She found that when mothers and teens had a stronger relationship, the teens were less likely to have had sex. However, when mothers and teens talked more about sex, the teens were more likely to have had sex. From these studies, we can see that the connection between explicit communication about sexuality and adolescents' likelihood of becoming sexually active is complicated and hard to predict. Miller (2002) suggests that some of the difficulty may lie in addressing causality. Do adolescents whose parents talk more about sex have more sex, or is it that when parents suspect their adolescent is having or will have sex, they start talking more about it? It's not an easy relationship to untangle.

Though the effects of parent–child communication on amount of sexual activity and the age at which such activity begins is unclear, research has indicated somewhat more consistent results with regard to how talk about sexuality affects safe sex behaviors. Miller, Levin, Whitaker, and Xu (1998) found that when parents and adolescents had conversations about condom use before the adolescent's first sexual encounter, the adolescent was far more likely to use a condom during that encounter and to continue to practice condom use thereafter (see also Fisher, 1987; Handelsman, Cabral, & Weisfeld, 1987; Newcomer & Udry, 1985). Additionally, the quality of that talk is also important. Whitaker, Miller, May, and Levin. (1999), Booth-Butterfield and Sidelinger (1998), and Powell and Segrin (2004) found that when parents talk openly and comfortably to their children about sexual risks and condom use, those children, as adolescents, are more likely to discuss safe sex with their sexual partners and use condoms. Similarly, Warren (1995) and colleagues have argued that when parents approach sex communication with a supportive stance, and integrate that communication throughout the children's lives,

---

BOX 8.2 • *Family in the News*

A Centers for Disease Control and Prevention (CDC) report issued in late summer 2006 indicated that fewer high school students were having sex than in the early 1990s, the ones that were had fewer partners, and more were using condoms. The study findings can be seen at www.cdc.gov/HealthyYouth/yrbs/pdf/trends/2005_YRBS_Sexual_ Behaviors.pdf.

teens are more likely to discuss sex and birth control with their dating partners in a way that leads to safer sex behavior.

Overall, the evidence about the effects of sexual discussions with children are somewhat mixed; however, research does tend to indicate that, the more parents discuss sexuality with their children, the more the children's beliefs and values about these topics become similar to their parents. Additionally, the research supports the theory that parent–child communication about sexuality must occur over time, rather than being isolated to the teen years, and be supportive and open in nature if it is to result in better judgments on the part of teens with regard to safe sex behavior. Because communication is at the heart of the creation and negotiation of shared meanings, this claim certainly makes sense.

In addition to discussions of sexuality and the impact those have on family members, a second sexuality-related concept that has been studied in family communication research relates to the sexual orientation of family members. Although most studies in family communication studies have assumed a heterosexual orientation for parents (and rarely discussed the sexual orientation of children), more recently the issue of sexual orientation of family members has begun to be an object of interest in family studies.

Sexual Orientation and the Family

To discuss family in terms of sexual orientation is more difficult than it may appear at first. We tend to think of **sexual orientation** as being "fixed" (you are either homosexual or heterosexual and once you become sexual you know for sure which one), but research suggests that how individuals define themselves in terms of sexual orientation may be more fluid than that. It is not uncommon for an individual to identify himself or herself as heterosexual, and even marry, but then later identify as homosexual (Wyers, 1987). Thus, identifying which families have members who are gay or lesbian isn't always simple.

Allen and Demo (1995) analyzed over 8,000 articles published about family relationships between 1980 and 1993. They found that, in that time, families headed by gay or lesbian adults were extremely underrepresented in family research. These authors contend that one of the problematic issues in research and theory relating to gay and lesbian families is definitional. If a family has one gay or lesbian member, is it a gay or lesbian family? Does that label apply only if the parents/adult caregivers are gay or lesbian? Additionally, an individual may operate in a heterosexual family and a gay or lesbian family at the same time (where one is the family of origin and the other is the family of procreation/partnership). This further complicates the issue. These authors suggest that the label **gay/lesbian family** should be used for families where there are two adult partners who are gay/lesbian, with or without children, and families where there is one adult who is gay/lesbian raising at least one child. We will adopt this definition, and begin our discussion of sexual orientation and the family by discussing gay/lesbian families.

Gay/Lesbian Families

Culturally, in the United States there is public debate over gay/lesbian families. Some of this concern stems from religious or moral beliefs. Although this debate is certainly an important issue, it falls outside the purview of this text. Whether we condone or accept homosexuality as a life pattern, we cannot deny the presence of significant numbers of gay and lesbian individuals around the world. Thus, this discussion does not focus on whether individuals "should" or "should not" be gay/lesbian (or even whether sexual orientation is a matter of choice or a trait that is outside our control). Rather, we consider some of the specific issues under debate with regard to gay/lesbian families.

Before we begin discussing gay/lesbian families, you might be wondering how many families in the United States are parented by homosexual individuals. This isn't totally clear (partly due to the fluidity of sexuality discussed previously). However, the American Psychiatric Association (2000) estimates that between 1 and 4 million lesbian women are mothers. The number of children living in gay- and lesbian-parented households is estimated to be between 6 and 14 million (American Civil Liberties Union, 1999).

Concerns about gay/lesbian families tend to revolve around three particular issues. First is the idea that children who have gay or lesbian parents are more likely to be homosexual themselves. Second, individuals sometimes indicate concern that if a child does not have a parent of both sexes, he or she will not achieve appropriate socialization or have a satisfactory childhood. This is most often mentioned as a concern related to the sons of lesbian women. Third, because of a lack of acceptance for homosexuality in U.S. culture, there is question about the social stigma that may attach to the children of gay/lesbian parents. Let's consider these issues in turn.

The first concern often indicated about gay/lesbian families is that children raised in such families are more likely to be gay or lesbian. Of course, this is only an issue to the extent that we believe homosexuality to be a problem (that is, as a society, we aren't concerned if parents "pass on" heterosexuality to their children, but we are concerned that they may pass on homosexuality). We certainly learn many of our relational patterns in our families of origin, as discussed in previous chapters, but research does not indicate that sexual orientation is such a learned behavior. Allen and Burrell's 1996 overview of previous research related to the children of gay and lesbian parents concluded that they were no more likely to be homosexual themselves than children of heterosexual parents. Stacey and Biblarz (2001) similarly argue that their respondents, adult children of gay and lesbian parents, were no more likely to identify themselves as gay or lesbian; however, they were more accepting of homosexuality and nontraditional gender roles. Thus, it appears that, whereas children of gay/lesbian parents may be less troubled by the idea that they could possibly be attracted to someone of the same sex, they are no more likely to actually self-identify as homosexual.

The second concern about gay/lesbian families often mentioned is the lack of a father or mother figure in the family to provide socialization, and so on. Silverstein and Auerbach (1999), based on a large study of fathering across family forms, argue that "father absence" in lesbian families is not, in and of itself, detrimental to the children in those families. These scholars do note that father absence may at times result in a decreased socioeconomic status that could affect child outcomes. However, when socioeconomics are controlled for, having a household without a father does not result in an overall reduction in child well-being (see also Crockett, Eggebeen, & Hawkins, 1993; Phares, 1999). Silverstein and Auerbach's research indicated that children need at least one responsible parent who cares for them on a consistent basis in order to have positive outcomes. In homes where there are two parents, this may be easier to manage simply because when one parent is unavailable (emotionally or physically) to the child or children, the other parent is there. However, their research did not indicate a difference with regard to families where there were heterosexual or homosexual parents. Additionally, these authors and others note that children receive socialization from individuals other than their parents. It would be erroneous to assume that a child with lesbian parents would not have male family members (or close family friends) who would participate in the socialization process. The same is true for households headed by gay men.

The third concern mentioned that is often leveled against families headed by gay/lesbian parents is that children will suffer from the social stigma of having "two moms" or "two dads" and thus will have psychological and social adjustment issues. **Social stigma** exists when an individual has a characteristic or set of characteristics that are seen as significantly undesirable socially (Goffman, 1963; Link & Phelan, 2001). It is likely the case that children in families of gay/lesbian parents are sometimes teased by others, or questioned about their family life. There is social stigma related to being in a gay/lesbian household (Herek, 1991). However, this is a societal problem, not a problem of the families themselves. If homosexuality itself was not stigmatized in U.S. culture, children of gay/lesbian parents would not be teased, or worse, about their family situation. Although social stigma related to homosexuality is an important issue, Allen and Burrell (1996), in their review of various studies of children from gay/lesbian families, found that children of homosexual parents did not have poorer social or psychological adjustment than children of heterosexual parents. This suggests that, although stigma is likely present for such families, it does not seem to have a strong detrimental effect on the children. It would be better for children of gay/lesbian families to not be teased or bullied by others due to their family structure, but such problems can also occur for single-parent families, families who are of lower socioeconomic status, interracial families, and families where a member has a disability. Thus, the issue of stigma is not something that is unique to gay/lesbian families.

Even though the primary concerns that are often voiced regarding gay- and lesbian-parented families do not appear (based on research) to be as serious as we may have thought, there are some issues that occur in gay- and lesbian-parented families that do not occur in heterosexual families. One of these issues is disclosure, by the parents, of homosexuality (West & Turner, 1995). This issue is unique to gay- and lesbian-parented families because in a culture where heterosexuality is the assumed norm, children of heterosexual parents do not need to be told about their parents' sexual orientation. As previously discussed, social penetration theory (Altman and Taylor, 1973) and other interpersonal theories suggest that disclosure is an important part of the creation of closeness and connection between relational members. Research related to parental disclosure of homosexual orientation to children tends to suggest that there is a positive effect on the parent–child relationship after disclosure; however, homosexual parents indicate that knowing when, if, and how to disclose to children is often a struggle (West & Turner, 1995). This relates back to the privacy–openness dialectic considered in Chapter 3. Deciding when to be open, what information to share and what information to conceal, and so forth is an active dialectic in the issue of disclosure in gay/lesbian families.

Overall, research about gay/lesbian families suggests that those families are much more similar to than different from heterosexually parented families. Although there are issues that gay/lesbian families face that are distinct from heterosexual families, outcomes for children do not appear to be dramatically different. Of course, sexual orientation is not something that only adults in a family have. Gay/Lesbian adolescents, as they come to understand their sexual orientation, also face a number of challenges as they engage in the "coming out" process within the family setting.

Gay/Lesbian Adolescents and Family

Some scholars (for example Armesto & Weisman, 2001; Beaty, 1999) have discussed the difficulty involved for an adolescent or adult to come out to his or her family. **Coming out** refers to the times at which a gay or lesbian individual acknowledges homosexual orientation to his or her family, friends, peers, colleagues, or larger social groups. The process of informing family members of homosexual orientation can be difficult for many reasons, depending on the family situation, the age of the individual who is coming out, and characteristics of the family members and the family system.

One issue involved with the coming out process for adolescents is that the individual himself or herself must first be aware of and accepting of his or her own sexual orientation (Beaty, 1999; Troiden, 1989). This process occurs gradually, over time, and involves the development of understandings related to sexuality in general, heterosexuality or homosexuality more specifically, and self-identification. Because U.S. culture is heterosexually oriented, it may be difficult for the adolescent to accept that he or she is different from others (DiPlacido, 1998). In fact, many gay/lesbian individuals go though a period of denial related to sexuality, and also a period when they feel that their orientation is wrong or shameful. Thus, one reason that gay and lesbian preadolescents and adolescents may not tell their parents (or others) about their sexual orientation is that they are still working through the process of understanding it themselves. Once an adolescent is comfortable enough to come out to his or her family, the reactions of the family members become a concern.

Armesto and Weisman (2001) studied parental reactions to the coming out of a gay or lesbian adolescent. They found that parents who believed that homosexuality was controllable were much more likely to be rejecting of the child who parents who believed it to be uncontrollable. This is likely because parents who believe that their child has intentionally made what they see as a negative, or abnormal, life choice are more inclined to feel anger toward the child. Additionally, Armesto and Weisman found that when parents felt a higher degree of shame, they were more likely to be rejecting. But when they felt a higher degree of guilt, they were more likely to be accepting. **Shame** refers to a general negative feeling related to self-worth ("I am bad"), whereas **guilt** is a negative feeling related to a particular behavior ("That was wrong to do"). Parents who are more likely to experience shame may

BOX 8.3 • *Internet Connection*

Because hearing that a family member is gay/lesbian can be very difficult. Parents, Families & Friends of Lesbians & Gays (PFLAG) offers support groups, information about how to respond to coming out, information about sexuality, and more. You can find a PFLAG group or read their articles at www.pflag.org/.

see themselves as bad parents because their child is gay, or may see the child himself/ herself as a bad person for being gay. Parents who are more inclined to feel guilt, rather than shame, may feel some guilt about the situation ("Did I do something that caused my child to be gay?"), but that guilt doesn't transcend into beliefs about their personhood (or that of their child). Of course, parents who don't see homosexuality as particularly problematic are unlikely to experience either shame or guilt about the situation.

Parental and family acceptance of an adolescent or young adult's sexual orientation is important because, without acceptance, social support is unlikely to follow. As we considered in Chapter 5, research related to theories of social support indicate that it is linked with a variety of positive outcomes for individuals, and a lack of social support may contribute to negative outcomes. Fontaine and Hammond (1996) and other scholars have considered the higher rates of depression, suicide risk, anxiety, and substance abuse for homosexual adolescents who feel rejected by family and peers. D'Augelli (2002), in a study of 542 gay and lesbian adolescents, found that adolescents had more mental health problems, including suicide attempts, when both parents had a negative reaction to a child's homosexuality, or when the parents did not know because the child felt unable to tell them due to the anticipation of a negative reaction. Because gay and lesbian adolescents often experience rejection in peer settings (D'Augelli, 2002; Fontaine & Hammond, 1996), the support of family is even more important.

Whether considering homosexual men and women as parents, or the coming out process of gay/lesbian adolescents, sexual orientation is a part of family life. Although scholars have often "ignored" orientation, by assuming heterosexuality of all family participants, consideration of the role of sexual orientation and associated processes (familial and societal) has become a more prominent part of the study of family communication in recent years, and this trend will likely continue into the future.

In this section, we considered the parental sexual relationship, family talk about sexuality, and issues related to sexual orientation. Sexuality is a complex issue and communication about it is fraught with embarrassment, insecurity, confusion, and even fear. However, it is important to realize how much a part of family life such communication is. Section 2 discusses how to communicate with children about sexuality, and the construction of family identity in lesbian-parented families. Finally, in Section 3 we consider how information about sexuality and the family might impact your life now and in the future.

References

Allen, K. R., & Demo, D. H. (1995). The families of lesbians and gay men: A new frontier in family research. *Journal of Marriage and Family, 57*(1), 111–127.

Allen, M., & Burrell, N. (1996). Comparing the impact of homosexual and heterosexual parents of children: Meta-analysis of existing research. *Journal of Homosexuality, 32*(2), 19–35.

Altman, I., & Taylor, D. A. (1973). *Social penetration.* New York: Holt, Rinehart Winston.

American Civil Liberties Union. (1999). *Fact sheet: An overview of lesbian and gay parenting, adoption, and foster care.* Retrieved March 5, 2005, from the American Civil Liberties Union Web site: www.aclu.org/LesbianGayRights/

American Psychiatric Association. (2000). *Fact sheet: Gay, lesbian and bisexual issues.* Retrieved March 5, 2005, from the Body: The Complete HIV/AIDS Resource Web site: www.thebody.com/apa/apafacts. html

Armesto, J. C., & Weisman, A. G. (2001). Attributions and emotional reactions to the identity disclosure ("coming out") of a homosexual child. *Family Process, 40*(2), 145–161.

Beaty, L. A. (1999). Identity development of homosexual youth and parental and familial influences on the coming out process. *Adolescence, 34*(135), 597–601.

Booth-Butterfield, M., & Sidelinger, R. (1998). The influence of family communication on the college-aged child: Openness, attitudes and actions about sex and alcohol. *Communication Quarterly, 46*, 295–308.

Byers, E. S. (2005). Relationship satisfaction and sexual satisfaction: A longitudinal study of individuals in long-term relationships. *The Journal of Sex Research, 42*, 113–118.

Byers, E. S., & Demmons, S. (1999). Sexual satisfaction and sexual self-disclosure within dating relationships. *The Journal of Sex Research, 36*, 1–10.

Crockett L. I., Eggebeen, D. J., & Hawkins, A. J. (1993). Father's presence and young children's behavioral and cognitive adjustment. *Family Relations, 14*, 355–377.

Cupach, W. R., & Comstock, J. (1990). Satisfaction with sexual communication in marriage: Links to sexual satisfaction and dyadic adjustment. *Journal of Social and Personal Relationships, 7*, 179–186.

D'Augelli, A. R. (2002). Mental health problems among lesbian, gay, and bisexual youths ages 14 to 21. *Clinical Child Psychology and Psychiatry, 7*(3), 433–456.

DiPlacido, J. (1998). Minority stress among lesbians, gay men, and bisexuals: A consequence of heterosexism, homophobia, and stigmatization. In G. M. Herek (Ed.), *Stigma and sexual orientation: Understanding prejudice against lesbians, gay men, and bisexuals* (pp. 138–159). Newbury Park, CA: Sage.

Fingerson, L. (2005). Do mothers' opinions matter in teens' sexual activity? *Journal of Family Issues, 26*(7), 947–974.

Fisher, T. (1987). Family communication and the sexual behaviors and attitudes of college students. *Journal of Youth and Adolescence, 16*, 481–493.

Fisher, T. (1993). A comparison of various measures of family sexual communication: Psychometric properties, validity, and behavioral correlates. *The Journal of Sex Research, 30*(3), 229–238.

Fisher, T. D. (1989). An extension of the findings of Moore, Peterson, and Furstenberg (1986) regarding family sexual communication and adolescent

sexual behavior. *Journal of Marriage and Family, 51*(3), 637–639.

Fontaine, J. H., & Hammond, N. L. (1996). Counseling issues with gay and lesbian adolescents. *Adolescence, 31*, 817–830.

Fox, G. L. (1981). The family's role in adolescent sexual behavior. In T. Ooms (Ed.), *Teenage pregnancy in a family context* (pp. 73–130). Philadelphia: Temple University Press.

Fox, G. L., & Inazu, J. K. (1980). Mother–daughter communication about sex. *Family Relations, 29*(3), 347–352.

Goffman, E. (1963). *The presentation of self in everyday life.* Garden City, NY: Anchor Books.

Guo, B., & Huang, J. (2005). Marital and sexual satisfaction in Chinese families: Exploring the moderating effects. *Journal of Sex & Marital Therapy, 31*(1), 21–29.

Handelsman, C., Cabral, R., & Weisfeld, G. (1987). Sources of information and adolescent sexual knowledge and behavior. *Journal of Adolescent Research, 2*, 455–463.

Heisler, J. M. (2005). Family communication about sex: Parents and college-aged offspring recall discussion topics, satisfaction, and parental involvement. *Journal of Family Communication, 5*(4), 295–312.

Hepburn, E. (1983). A three-level model of parent–daughter communication about sexual topics. *Adolescence, 18*(71), 523–534.

Herek, G. M. (1991). Stigma, prejudice and violence against lesbians and gay men. In J. C. Gonsiorek & J. D. Weinrich (Eds.), *Homosexuality: Research implications for public policy*. Newbury Park, CA: Sage.

Hutchinson, M. K., & Cooney, T. M. (1998). Patterns of parent–teen sexual risk communication: Implications for intervention. *Family Relations, 47*(2), 185–194.

Jordan, T. R., Price, J. H., & Fitzgerald, S. (2000). Rural parents' communication with their teen-agers about sexual issues. *Journal of School Health, 70*(8), 338–344.

Lawrance, K., & Byers, E. S. (1995). Sexual satisfaction in long-term heterosexual relationships: The interpersonal exchange model of sexual satisfaction. *Personal Relationships, 2*, 267–285.

Link, B. G., & Phelan, J. C. (2001). Conceptualizing stigma. *Annual Review of Sociology, 27*, 363–385.

Litzinger, S., & Gordon, K. C. (2005). Exploring relationships among communication, sexual satisfaction, and marital satisfaction. *Journal of Sex & Marital Therapy, 31*(5), 409–424.

Miller, B. C. (2002). Family influences on adolescent sexual and contraceptive behavior, *Journal of Sex Research, 39*(1), 22–26.

Miller, K. S., Levin, M. L., Whitaker, D. J., & Xu, X. (1998). Patterns of condom use among adolescents: The impact of mother–adolescent communication. *American Journal of Public Health, 88*, 1542–1544.

Moore, K., Peterson, J., & Furstenberg, F. (1986). Parental attitudes and the occurrence of early sexual activity. *Journal of Marriage and Family, 48*, 777–783.

Newcomer, S. F., & Udry, J. R. (1985). Parent–child communication and adolescent sexual behavior. *Family Planning, 17*, 169–174.

Phares, V. (1999). *Poppa psychology: The role of fathers in children's mental well-being.* Westport, CT: Praeger.

Powell, H. L., & Segrin, C. (2004). The effect of family and peer communication on college students' communication with dating partners about HIV and AIDS. *Health Communication, 16*(4), 427–449.

Purnine, D. M., & Carey, M. P. (1997). Interpersonal communication and sexual adjustment: The roles of understanding and agreement. *Journal of Consulting and Clinical Psychology, 65*, 1017–1025.

Rosenthal, D. A., & Feldman, S. S. (1999). The importance of importance: Adolescents' perceptions of parental communication about sexuality. *Journal of Adolescence, 22*, 835–851.

Silverstein, L. B., & Auerbach, C. F. (1999). Deconstructing the essential father. *American Psychologist, 54*, 397–407.

Sprecher, S. (2002). Sexual satisfaction in premarital relationships: Associations with satisfaction, love, commitment, and stability. *The Journal of Sex Research, 39*, 190–196.

Stacey, J., & Biblarz, T. (2001). (How) does the sexual orientation of parents matter? *American Sociological Review, 66*(2), 159–183.

Troiden, R. R. (1989). The formation of homosexual identities. *Journal of Homosexuality, 17*, 43–73.

Warren, C. (1995). Parent-child communication about sex. In T. L. Socha and G. H. Stamp (Eds.), *Parents, children, and communication: Frontiers of theory and research* (pp. 173–201). Mahwah, NJ: Erlbaum.

Warren, C. (1995). Perspectives on international sex practices and American family sex communication relevant to teenage sexual behavior in the United States. *Health Communication, 4*(2), 121–136.

West, R., & Turner, L. H. (1995). Communication in lesbian and gay families: Building a descriptive base. In T. J. Socha & G. H. Stamp (Eds.), *Parents, children and communication: Frontiers of theory and research* (pp. 147–169). Mahwah, NJ: Erlbaum.

Whitaker, D. J., Miller, K. S., May, D. C., & Levin, M. L. (1999). Teenage partners' communication about sexual risk and condom use: The importance of parent–teenager discussions. *Family Planning Perspectives, 31*(3), 117–121.

Wyers, N. L. (1987). Homosexuality in the family; Lesbian and gay spouses. *Social Work, 32*, 143–148.

Young, M., Denny, G., Young, T., & Luquis, R. (2000). Sexual satisfaction among married women. *American Journal of Health Studies, 16*, 73–84.

Section 2: Research Examples _____

Communicating about Sex as a Daughter, Parent, and Teacher

Amber E. Kinser

> In Section 1, we addressed some of the difficulties that family members face in the attempt to talk overtly about sexuality. For this article, Kinser uses an autoethnographic approach (a study of self) to explore this issue from the perspective of the child in the family, the parent in the family, and a professor of family communication as well. This piece is an illustration of both the concepts we have discussed in this chapter and the power of carefully constructed autoethnography as a scholarly tool.
>
> *L.B.A.*

Family communication about sex is exceedingly complex. Research suggests most parents agree that talking with children about sex is important, but it also suggests that many parents speak with young people about sex at best indirectly, or ineffectively, from the point of view of the children. The purpose of this section is to explore some of the everyday life complexities of family talk, and other communication, about sex and the body. Using an autoethnographic approach (writing about the culture of the self), I explore here some of the multiple layers of sex communication by examining with a critical eye the practices in my family when I was growing up, in my family now that I am raising children, and in my students' families based on what they have shared in class. It is my hope that autoethnography's pointed focus on the frank and the particular of an individual perspective, in this case my own, might illuminate possible paths for inquiry and critique that can inform more general perspectives about family sex communication. Ideally, I would like to help lift some of the stigma and discomfort from family sex communication by sharing some of the intimacy, ambiguity, and humanity of my own story.

Sex Talk Metaphors

The metaphors we use to refer to conversations with children about sex are revealing. They reveal our discomfort about the topic, our insistence that the most important thing to know about sex is the science of it, our resistance to letting children in on the human relationship dimensions of sexuality, our fear of being or appearing sexually inappropriate, our dissatisfaction or guilt about our own sexual decisions, and our deficient preparation for handling sexual matters. Most people probably understand the phrase "the facts of life," for example, to represent discussion about "where babies come from," about how a female and male engage in sexual intercourse and how that often enough results in pregnancy, and consequently decisions about parenthood. It represents a focus on the clarity of seemingly indisputable biological "sexual urges" rather than the murkiness of passion, desire, choice, need, regret, guilt, and power. A discussion about sex that sticks to the "facts" is significantly easier to navigate for the discussion leader (usually the parent or parents), though its usefulness for the other participants in the discussion (usually the children) is limited. Its advantage, of course, is that it allows us to feel like we are talking about the important stuff of sex without actually having to talk about the important stuff. It is interesting to note that we find sexual matters important and central enough to warrant the status of the title The Facts of Life, yet not important or central enough to include with its discussions these murky and uniquely human dimensions. At the same time, we may discuss issues such as respect, obedience, integrity, race, justice, work, and love with our children, yet do not view these as important or central enough to warrant the status of The Facts of Life, even though they are probably no less so, and perhaps more so, than sex.

Talk about "the birds and the bees" is also revealing. Here again, we seek to reduce sexual matters to the biology and science of them alone. This metaphor has the additional advantage of keeping the discussion out of the realm of everyday human living altogether. Further, the images of the nonhuman animals conjured by The Birds and the Bees complicate our ability to focus on just what it is these birds and bees are *doing*. If we were able to picture these flying animals having sex, it is unlikely to pose the threat of leading to thoughts and mental images of *humans* having sex. It is no coincidence that we don't refer to sex talk as being about "the dogs and the horses;" too many people already know and have seen or can easily picture precisely what is going on there. The distance between picturing images of these animals and picturing similar images of human animals is a short one; if it weren't, we wouldn't take such note of, or be so embarrassed by, finding horses or dogs engaging in sexual behavior. If instead we used a metaphor like "the bottlenose dolphins and the bonobo chimps," we would be able to talk more clearly, for example, about same-sex behavior because these are among the minimally 10 percent of the animal kingdom that practice same-sex sexual behavior. But again, using our current metaphors allows us to *not* talk about much of anything. So birds and bees it is.

A third popular phrase for referring to sex communication, particularly to that taking place in families, is "the talk." This is probably understood by many to refer to a necessary but often discomfiting conversation that is withheld until a child reaches puberty, at which point, it is widely held, bodily changes threaten to awaken sexual awareness for the first time—or at least in more overwhelming and exigent ways than before. This metaphor makes clear the assumption that what a person needs to know about the sexual body not only can be *condensed* to a single talk, but also can be *learned* in a single talk. It suggests that the person who initiates The Talk will know when and how to give it at such a precise and identifiable single moment in another person's life. In fact, that someone is giving a talk makes clear its monologic nature: there is little conversational exchange going on, no reciprocity of listening or speaking. One person lacks the knowledge, now suddenly needs the knowledge, and the other person possesses, distills, and transfers it to her or him. The Talk suggests that a child has not been learning about sex and bodily intimacy since she or he was born; that years of messages about privacy, nudity, hugs, personal space, and kisses have not been about sexuality at some level; and that billboards, magazines, the Internet, peers, television, song lyrics, commercials, radio, and film have not been overwhelming the child with sexuality information for years. The idea of The Talk, though it may feel uncomfortable while it is going on, is in the long run for many parents a comforting idea. It simplifies the complexities of sexual matters, and helps parents feel powerful in an area where they are finally powerless: dictating their children's sexuality. This metaphor allows us to pretend that we really only have to talk about sexuality once, at which point we fortunately can invoke the facts of life and the birds and the bees, and talk very little about sexuality ever. So the first points of confrontation for us in studying family sex communication are the multiple alternatives already in place for sending a lifetime of messages about sexuality while never actually *talking* about it.

Talking and Thinking about the Body

The first time I asked my students to contribute to our discussion on the impact of language by sharing some of the ways their families talked about sex, I was surprised. Even now when I pose this question every semester, I am struck by their responses. One of the ways I begin this part of the module on language is to suggest that the way our parents talked about our bodies shaped in part how we have come to view our bodies and bodily intimacy; I ask them to share some of the terms that were used in their families to refer to body parts, specifically genitalia. Most often, no one responds to that question, which probably does not surprise you. I then suggest that surely their parents used *some* kind of terms when, for example, they were teaching about bathroom behavior like using the toilet or bathing. At this point, some students gradually recall, or gradually admit, what terms they were taught as children, usually with awkwardness. I am struck that they have a hard time getting comfortable with this conversation even as college adults.

They are embarrassed partly by the unique, sometimes comical, sometimes even bizarre terms their own families used and the terms they use even now. The mother of one of my students, for example, used the term "bug" to refer to female genitalia, whereas her father "never addressed sexuality ever." She is chagrined to realize that she ended up referring to her daughter's genital region as a "tootie." The family of another student used "bird-dog" and "pecker" to refer to the penis, and "goose" or "down there" to refer to "all the female sexual organs." My students also are uncomfortable partly because they never have thought about terms like these as a topic for open discussion. Still other students remember that their families did not use any names to refer to what are considered to be sexual body parts because there *were* no such references made in their home. They report that their parents did not talk about genitals, about sex, about reproduction, or about menstruation. My students can see how such silence communicated powerful sexuality messages that stuck with them. These class sessions strike me both because I know that healthy sexuality and identity are significantly influenced by family communication, and because my experiences with these issues in my own family are markedly different from those of my students.

I grew up in a home that was very comfortable talking about genitals, sex, reproduction, and menstruation. This is surprising given that my parents sent us to a religious school for years and were surrounded by friends and neighbors who had a twofold lesson about sex communication with their kids: don't talk about it and don't do it. I lived with my mother and father, then grew up from two years old on with my mother and stepfather, and maintained a good relationship with my biological father for a long time. It was largely my mother who taught me most of what I know about the body, including feeling comfortable talking about it. As I've explained in other writing: "She taught me to be bold about my body—to look at it, talk about it, ask questions about it. She taught me to be bold about my sexuality. She did not hide her sexual playfulness with my [step]father; she was unconcerned about other people's responses to the mirrors on her bedroom ceiling" (Kinser, 2004, p. 126). If I was not feeling like my usual self because I was menstruating, I could comfortably tell my stepfather that I had my period and he seemed fine with this openness. It was my father who drew the picture of the fallopian tubes, the ovaries, the uterus, and the vagina while he was explaining what getting a period means. My family used terms like "testicles" fairly easily, and when I asked my mother at a very young age what an "orgzm" was—I knew neither what it was nor how to pronounce it—she explained it to me without hesitation. Even though "climax" and "juices flowing" were not notions I could do much with at the time, what I learned in that conversation with my mother, and others like it, is that a person is entitled to know and understand her body and how it works and how that relates to other people.

My family was not without its hang-ups. We had our share of dysfunction and we were not comfortable talking about *everything*. I did not know what a clitoris was until my young adulthood, though I was unwittingly introduced to how it worked and how that felt when I was climbing up a pole to slide down it while on the playground in elementary school. I knew nothing of circumcision or foreskin until I became sexually active as a young adult; I knew of no terms to refer to the labia. Also in elementary school, it was my slightly younger cousin and not my parents who explained the bodily specifics of hetero-sexual intercourse, which she learned from her mother, my mother's sister. It was then, I think, that I learned the terms "penis" and "vagina." Though the memories would not sur-face until my young adulthood, I was unwittingly introduced to this too as a victim of sex-ual abuse by a man down the street when I was five years old. I didn't mention it to my parents until after several repeated incidents and I don't know quite why. There was no con-versation about birth control until after I already was sexually active. I don't recall conver-sations about STDs (sexually transmitted diseases). Although my parents, especially my mother, were direct and comfortable and honest in much of their treatment of family sex communication, we did miss some important components.

Even with these various complexities in my own family's sex communication, I am amazed at how many of my students report minimal or no concrete interactions about sex or the sexual body. Perhaps I should not be surprised then, even though I am, that my students typically "get the willies" at the thought of their parents having a sex life. I always have a small handful of people in class who are very clear that their parents are sexually active beings and who are quite comfortable with that, though they are uninterested in spending time talking or thinking about it, which makes sense to me. But a majority of my students shudder, physically, at the thought. They can never quite explain why they react this way. Somehow they manage to separate being a parent from having sex. Perhaps that is one reason the United States leads all other developed nations in unintended pregnancy (Warren, 1992). Here, too, my childhood was notably different from that of my students. My parents taught my two older sisters, my younger brother, and me that their bedroom was to be of no concern to us and that, for the most part, we had no business being in there. We also knew that when their door was shut they were off limits to us and we were clear on the fact that this was because they were having sex. I was annoyed in these moments at not having immediate access to my parents precisely when I wanted it, as I suppose most children would be; my sisters and I rolled our eyes at the thought. But I never got the willies about what they were doing behind that door. I imagine some of my students learned from their parents and developed the same head-in-the-sand approach to their parents' bodies that their parents seem to have developed about theirs. I find it interesting that my students critique their parents' puritanical attitudes regarding their sex lives, but display similar puritanical attitudes toward that of their parents.

Sex Communication and My Sexual Decision Making

The relative openness and honesty with which my family engaged in sex communication in large part enabled me to start having intercourse no earlier than I did at 16, and to make choices that were in my long-term best interest, like deciding, most of the time, to be sexual only with people I cared deeply about, using reliable birth control consistently, and seeking regular gynecological care where my decisions could be informed by health care expertise and where I could be checked for and treated for STDs. When my mother first discovered I had become sexually active upon finding a condom wrapper I had failed to throw away, her immediate response was about birth control. I was more concerned that she knew I was having sex and sobbed through that conversation; she was more concerned about my preventing pregnancy and kept asking me why I was crying. We set up a gynecological appointment and I started taking "the pill." At this time, we were not focused as a culture on STDs, and certainly not on AIDS/HIV, which had not yet touched the public nerve, so what talk there was with kids about sex tended to focus on birth control or abstinence.

Still, no one variable can determine an outcome; sex communication between parents and children is not the only variable that influences sexual decision making. Mine was influenced by multiple variables. For example, I was fortunate enough and, I like to think, smart enough to have usually dated young men who were equally prepared for long-term healthy decision making, and sometimes even more prepared than I was. One boyfriend refused to have sex with me because we were too young, and a later boyfriend would never have sex with me unless we used a condom or my diaphragm. Relatively healthy relationships, direct conversations with responsible partners, access to and the means to afford birth control, and the good fortune to have my birth control never fail so far, plus multiple other variables that I probably never will know about all worked together with my family's sex communication, resulting in my having two children at points in my life when I was ready and prepared to be a parent. Family sex communication can be a powerful predictor of the sexual decisions young people make, but it is not the only predictor (Nelson, 1997; Walters & Walters, 1983).

Sex Communication with My Children

Perhaps because I have recognized the limited role families might play in shaping sexual attitudes and behaviors, I have been mindful of sexual socialization since my first of two children, my daughter, was an infant. I have wanted badly to get right whatever role I might play. My parents set good examples in many ways and I want to continue in that tradition. I also have made a number of choices in this area that my parents would never have made. Sometimes I feel confident about those choices; other times I am not so sure. As a parent, I want to be open about and comfortable with sex and body talk in our home like my parents were, but I want to go even further than they did. I want to talk about birth control and STDs before my children begin sexual activity. I want to be more attentive to their personal body boundaries and more respectful of their personal space. I want to work harder to counter the negative messages in the various media when they portray sexual relations as grounded in manipulation, and portray sex as primarily about power. I want to counter the hateful and damaging cultural message that homosexuality is less human or less loving or less beautiful than heterosexuality. I want to teach them somehow that, as Eisler (1995) has argued at length, sex is both more important and less important than the culture would have us believe.

I think I have raised my daughter so far to feel comfortable with her body and talking about it. She knew the word for labia about as early as she learned the words for nose and eyes, and learned about clitoris and vagina, as the subjects arose, not long after that. It was a little tricky when she used these terms out loud at the grocery store, needless to say, because few people, I've discovered, share my commitment to open and direct family sex communication. In fact, few of my adult female friends at the time knew what my daughter was referring to when they overheard her say "labia," as do few of my students now. Since preschool, she has been different from her peers in sexual knowledge, and I guess I am comfortable with that.

My first direct conversation with my daughter about sexual behavior was prompted at three years of age when she walked in on her father and me having sex. We were caught by surprise, thinking we had locked the door. Despite my surprise, I was able to avoid shouting for her to get out and instead was able to focus calmly on the house rule about knocking on closed doors. I was conflicted by thoughts of telling her to go out, of picking her up and making it not such a big deal, and that this is one of the most monumental moments in a child's life that will have reverberations throughout it and I needed to handle it well. Plus, of course, I was trying to figure out just how long she was there and how much she saw. When she finally did leave the room, I followed her out into the hall and asked her if she was all right. To my unprecedented terror she asked me "How come Daddy was on you like that?" Now the interesting point for me as I write this story is that I truly thought, given how much I think and read and teach about this very kind of family sex communication, that I would have some earthly idea of how to respond to this question. But words seemed to fail me. Finally, I was able to tell her that her father "was loving on me," and that what she saw is one of the ways that moms and dads love on each other.

The conversation went on for a bit as I tried to adhere to two principles that I have come to see as critical components of parental sex communication: Do tell children what they want to know, and don't tell them more than they are able to handle at a given point in their development, which is quite often more than parents think. But I had a hard time in that moment sorting out what to tell her that honored both of those principles. In the end, we talked about love and affection, and that big people often love one another with their bodies, and that it is good and that it made her father and me happy and that everything was all right. It was a moment I will never forget. In retrospect, I am pleased that her first direct lesson about sex was primarily about love, affection, and intimacy, rather than "where babies come from," because the latter is but one of many components of sexual relations in general, and the former is what *most* sex *is* about. I think I did the best I could do in the moment in my daughter's sexual socialization, but I probably never truly will know.

As a family communication professor and feminist scholar interested in sexuality studies, not to mention book collector, I have an abundance of books and resources related to sex, most of which are in our home. Yet even with ready access to plentiful sexuality information, my preteen daughter sought out other, culturally sanctioned resources. When she took more than the normal amount of time to answer her bedroom door one evening, I suspected she was online on some site she did not want me to see. I asked her what she was doing and she said she was emailing. I said, "Well let's take a look at where you've been lately," and clicked on her online history. As I thought, she was checking out visual pornography sites. She was embarrassed and sheepish. I asked her why she was embarrassed and she didn't know. I told her there was nothing embarrassing about being curious—everyone is curious, especially about sex. I said, "Your dad, stepdad, and I have all looked at those sites out of curiosity. But there is nothing there worth seeing, finally. If you want to look at nude bodies and people being sexual there are images that are worth seeing and you won't find them on those sites. We have plenty of books here you can look at. If you want something of your own, I'll buy you a book of nudes rendered by artists. Some depictions of sex and the body are beautiful and enlightening and others are not. Expose yourself to the beautiful ones instead of that. Do something more intelligent with your mind." We continued to talk about what she saw online and it was a good conversation, I think. I suppose she has revisited those sites some, to my disappointment, but the lure of secrecy and the forbidden is lifted some, and she leaves her door open much more often than she used to. Sometimes I feel comfortable with how this interaction turned out. Other times I wonder about it.

Even though moments like these with my daughter have been tricky, I have discovered that body talk was easier for me with her than it is with my son. When he was three, their father and I divorced. When I started seeing someone else, I learned that my new partner lived, when he was a boy, with an adult female family member who had been sexually inappropriate with him and that it has greatly affected him to this day. So I have been particularly vigilant about my behavior with my son, wanting very much never to make him feel uncomfortable, but still wanting very much not to fail in my responsibility to help him understand his body. We have had conversations from the beginning, so that I was sure he knew how to care for his body; also, I know that he will look different from most of his peers and I wanted to begin early helping him feel comfortable with his body regardless of how other boys look. I learned from my own research that circumcision was medically unnecessary and his father and I decided that, for us, any choice about circumcision should be made by our son when he is capable of making it himself. One of the consequences of that decision is that my son and I often are in the position of talking openly and directly about things that are very personal and private for him. His father takes care of this when our son is at his house, and although my current husband, his stepfather, is willing to help me on this front, their relationship has not developed enough yet to keep such interactions from being more awkward than they already are. So my son and I are having more sexually sensitive discussions than most mothers and sons are having, I suspect. I wonder if fear or uneasiness with this discussion is why many families avoid it through circumcision. The topic never feels completely comfortable for me. I do know that the few times he has had concerns about his body, he has felt at ease enough to talk with me so we can take care of it. That never feels completely comfortable for me either, and I doubt it does for him.

Some Implications for Family Sex Communication Research

As an academic, and unlike most parents I suspect, I am familiar with the research about family sex communication and what thousands of adolescents, teens, college students, and parents are reporting about how their families communicate about sex and how that relates to the sexual behaviors of the young people in those families. What I wish is that I could read through these hundreds of studies and come to some definitive conclusions about how to interact with my kids in order to bring about the sexual attitudes and behaviors that I believe are important. I am willing to modify my current thinking and methods, and adopt some others that are proving to work. To my dismay, however, the research has not proven to be quite that conclusive.

Much of the difficulty, from a research perspective, in exploring how families socialize children about sexuality lies in the fact that families are communicating about sexuality even when they are not sitting down and discussing it. Issues of privacy and personal space, expectations for intimate contact with others, a parent shooting "a look" to a child in response to something he or she is wearing or has said or asked, what the children are allowed to watch on television and why are all oblique forms of sexual socialization. Family sex communication includes untold numbers of tiny messages, "unspoken, indirect, and nonverbal," that accumulate over a long time—12, 15 years and more—that represent parental attitudes and values (Fox, 1980, p. 22). These are nearly impossible to "research." Furthermore, parent-child interaction is only one of many variables influencing adolescent and teen behavior. Mediated messages, peer relationships and expectations, sex education in school, friendships, observations of parents' relationships, sibling relationships, fashion, individual personality, religion, and how the parents' parents addressed sexuality in their home all play a part in shaping a young person's behavior.

One of the important things to keep in mind about young people's sexual behavior is that the point in a child's life when the parents want most for the child to follow their teaching, is the point at which they are most likely to follow that of their peers. So if the parent–child conversation about sex and the body begins at puberty, it is too late to accomplish the parents' goal. I have argued for a long time in the classes I teach that if parents find themselves having The Talk, they have done it wrong. Nietzsche (1878) has argued that marriage is a long conversation. If it is true of marriage, it is no less true of parenting, and in particular of parenting about sexuality. Family sex communication begins in infancy when the child first learns about touch and need and the feeling of skin against skin. When a child *has* to give Grandma a kiss, for example, she or he learns, among other things, that other people get to decide how and with whom she or he will be intimate and how. If children have no space to call their own, designated for example by the right to close their bedroom doors and to expect that others usually will knock, they are learning here too about how little power they have to control their lives. Moments like these send important messages that reverberate throughout the child's sexual decision making.

We cannot expect that persons who have been taught that others control their body and space will feel empowered to make smart sexual decisions. We cannot expect that children will be willing to bring their sexuality concerns and questions to adults who have no time or patience to answer their other childlike questions. We cannot expect children to develop a healthy sense of their own sexuality when their every curiosity and intrigue is judged and corrected. I suspect that parents are spending too much time trying to figure out how to simplify and wrap up the sex conversation instead of embracing the fact that it has been going on since the child's first day. It neither started recently nor will end soon and it has taken and will take myriad forms, most of which do not look or sound like sex talk at all.

One of the most important contributions we could make to the sexual well-being of young people is to see more clearly the multiple and varied ways we are communicating about sexuality when we are *not talking* about it. Another important contribution would be to reexamine the multiple ways we have devised as a culture to claim we are talking about sexuality and appear to be doing so, but actually and conveniently avoid addressing the sexual matters that matter most. We need to find alternative metaphors for sex talk that, unlike The Facts of Life, The Birds and the Bees, and The Talk, get at the humanity of sex and actually confront its murkiness and ambiguities. Without these contributions, the stacks of research conducted on family sex communication since the mid-1960s will be of little use, and we will be no closer to discovering what is best for the sexual well-being of young people and the adults they will become than if we had never asked the research questions at all.

Questions for Consideration and Discussion

1. In this piece of work, Kinser discusses the metaphors facts of life, birds and the bees, and the talk with regard to family communication about sex. Which of these terms had you heard and/or used prior to this reading? What do these terms suggest to you about sexuality?
2. As noted here, families often construct their own terminology to use when describing genitalia and other body issues. Thinking back to your own childhood, what terms were used and how did those make you feel about your body? When did you first note that other people had different terms, and how did you feel about that?
3. Kinser discusses some hopes that she has for communicating about sexuality with her children. Looking back on your family experiences, what were the positive parts of the communication you received from your parents/caregivers? What do you wish they had done differently?
4. In this work, Kinser says that she hopes such writings will help reduce some of the discomfort or stigma of family communication about sexuality. Having read this piece, do you feel your attitudes about family sex communication have changed? Explain.
5. This work is autoethnographic in nature. What do you see as the benefits and drawbacks of an autoethnographic approach?

References

Eisler, R. (1995). *Sacred pleasure: Sex, myth, and the politics of the body.* San Francisco: HarperSanFrancisco.

Fox, G. L. (1980). The mother–adolescent daughter relationship as a sexual socialization structure: A research review. *Family Relations*, *29*(1), 21–28.

Kinser, A. E. (2004). Negotiating spaces for/through third wave feminism. *National Women's Studies Association Journal, 16*(3), 124–153.

Nelson, M. C. (1997). *Community and media influences on adolescent sexual abstinence.* (Doctoral dissertation, University Microfilms International). Dissertation Abstracts International, *58*(5), 2721. (UMI No.

AAM9734630). Retrieved August 24, 2004, from PsycINFO (1840-Current) database.

Nietzche, F. (1878). *Human, all too human: A book for free spirits.* Retrieved April 12, 2006, from www.public appeal.org/library/nietzsche/Nietzsche_human_all_too_human/index.htm

Walters, J., & Walters, L. H. (1983). The role of the family in sex education. *Journal of Research and Development in Education, 16*(2), 8–15.

Warren, C. (1992). Perspectives on international sex practices and American family sex communication relevant to teenage sexual behavior in the United States. *Health Communication, 4*(2), 121–136.

The Social Context of Lesbian Family Identity

Elizabeth A. Suter

Karla Mason Bergen

Karen L. Daas

As we discussed in Chapter 1, family has been defined in a variety of ways across time and subject matter. Generally, however, definitions have often focused on the legal union between a man and woman and their offspring. This means that some families, including gay- and lesbian-parented families, may need to work harder to be seen as family, or even to feel confident in their own family status. In this work, Suter, Bergen, and Daas discuss some of the strategies used by lesbian parents to construct family identity. As you read, consider how cultural understandings and expectations have contributed to the strategies noted here, as well as to your own family identity experiences.

L.B.A.

More children are raised in lesbian and gay households than ever before. Most estimates agree that in the United States today between 6 and 12 million children are being raised by gay parents (Patterson, 1995; Woosley, 2003). In the lesbian community, in particular, having children is so common that many refer to it as the lesbian baby boom (Chabot & Ames, 2004; Kershaw, 2000). In fact, somewhere between 1 and 5 million lesbians are now mothers (Johnson & O'Connor, 2002). Some lesbian mothers have children through previous marriages and heterosexual relationships, but many lesbians are now having children through artificial insemination by donor (Kershaw, 2000). As the number of lesbian families continues to grow, it is clear these understudied and less traditional families need to be studied.

Our study contributes to an understanding of lesbian family life by exploring how lesbian families use rituals and symbols to communicate they are a family. We explore how these lesbian families use rituals and symbols to communicate both external and internal family identity. Communicating an external sense of family identity refers to how families make clear that they are a lesbian family to others, including extended family, neighbors, and strangers. Communicating an internal sense of family identity refers to how families make clear that they are a lesbian family to one another, particularly to the child(ren).

Rituals and Symbols as Communicative of Identity

Rituals help families express their family identity. Family rituals include holiday celebrations, family traditions, and everyday patterned interactions (Wolin & Bennett, 1984).

Likewise, symbols help communicate family identity. Family symbols include objects and words that show family ties (Goffman, 1971).

Symbolic Interactionism

We use a symbolic interactionist perspective (Mead, 1943; Perinbanayagam, 2003) to help explain the ways lesbian families communicate that they are a family. Communication is the primary way identity is negotiated. In other words, individuals and families do not necessarily get to be who they want to be. Instead, they are defined through their interactions with others. Persons are uncertain if others will accept or reject the identity they present. Role is also closely tied to identity. The role a person performs, such as joint motherhood, partly defines who one is (Goffman, 1959). Therefore, the research question for our study was: How do lesbian families use rituals and symbols to create and negotiate their identity?

Method

We invited lesbian families to be a part of our study by making announcements at community groups and placing advertisements in public places. We interviewed 21 lesbian families in their homes. We analyzed the interviews in the qualitative tradition using a form known as constructivist grounded theory, which argues that there is not an objective reality to be "discovered," but rather that research provides "an *interpretive* [italics in original] portrayal of the studied world, not an exact picture of it" (Charmaz, 2002, p. 678). Our study focuses on 16 of these families who all had their children via donor insemination. However, we used data from all 21 interviews to create an educational brochure and Web site.

Findings and Discussion

We found that lesbian families use rituals and symbols to communicate family identity externally (to others) and internally (to themselves). We first discuss how lesbian families communicate their identity externally. We then discuss how these families communicate their identity internally.

We found that the symbols of last names and donor choice and the ritual of doing family helped these lesbian families communicate their family identity to others. We also found that the symbol of names for two mommies and the rituals of attending a same-sex parenting group and doing family helped these lesbian families communicate their family identity to one another, particularly to the children. In this section, we discuss how families used these rituals and symbols to show others that they are a family.

Externally Communicating Family Identity

Last Names.   We found that last names are one key symbol that communicates an external sense of family identity. In 12 families, the child's name included the last name of the nonbiological mother (the nonbirth mother). One family took the biological (birth) mother's last name as a shared family name. The remaining three families gave their children the biological mother's last name. Sharing a family name supports a family's identity, particularly when others use the family name (Suter & Oswald, 2003). For instance, Cami and Bray reported that receiving cards and packages addressed to their family name "Olson" validates their identity as a family. Cami explained, "It is traditional assessment that you're a family. . . . You have the same last name. People just click that that's a family."

Last names also make the lesbian family form clear to acquaintances and strangers (Suter, 2004). Robin described how "when we go places, the hospital or emergency room or something like that, when we say, 'This is Jacob Miller-Wilson' and then they go, 'Which one of you is the mom?', and we say, 'We are both the mom.'" The child's hyphenated last name highlights the connection both mothers have with their child and shows others that they are a family unit.

By contrast, Annette's hesitation to take her partner and child's last name serves as a powerful reminder of how easily these families' identities can be disconfirmed. Because of her family's lack of support, Annette is keeping her family name until her parents die, in hope that her parents will be there as grandparents for her and Jamie's son. Although Theresa and Brenda gave their child a hyphenated name, they did not merge their names because of the potential threat to Theresa's military job. This threat underscores the power last names have to communicate family to outsiders, which as these examples illustrate, can sometimes be positive and other times negative.

Last names also externally communicate roles to others. For instance, Angie and Lisa's twins' hyphenated name communicates their joint motherhood to others. Angie explained, "[The reason] we wanted to do hyphenated names was that it just showed, you know, maybe school administrators or doctors or whatever that they belong to both of us." For this family and others, sharing a last name helps show others that they are a family.

Donor Choice.　　We found sperm donor choice is a second key symbol that communicates an external sense of identity. Families chose donors from sperm banks, which provide families access to donor files that include descriptions of the donor's physical features, family medical history, level of education, and occupation. Some files also include photographs and personal essays.

Most families chose donors because of their physical appearance. Choosing a donor based on desired physical traits nonverbally communicates family by creating family resemblance. Families chose donors who had similar traits to the nonbiological mother to increase the likelihood that the child would look like a blend of the two mothers. Sandra explained, "So that we would all look related." Traits of importance included skin tone, eye color, hair color, and ethnicity. Jamie talked about how this is like what naturally occurs when heterosexual couples have a biological child, "Your heterosexual couples that have children have the biological connection and the physical characteristics." Looking related paints the picture of family.

A few families went beyond physical appearance and factored in nonphysical traits, such as values or personality characteristics they learned through the donors' essays. For Jenny, honesty was the most important value. She chose the donor she thought was the most honest because he admitted he had suffered a period of depression, whereas other donors claimed to be perfectly healthy. Likewise, Michelle and Susan chose a donor because they were won over by his personality. In his personal essay, he described himself as someone who likes to drink coffee on Sunday morning, a "regular guy."

Doing Family.   We found that a primary ritual that communicates family identity to others is patterned everyday interactions—ordinary family activities that happen regularly (West & Zimmerman, 1987 Wolin & Bennett, 1984;). Ellen described how, "when they see us together with her, I think they know automatically that we are a family. We don't act any different than any other family."

Families reported that everyday activities, such as shopping, family walks, interacting with neighbors, and attending church, expressed their family identity to others, who either accepted or rejected that identity. Carol identified shopping as a key ritual that announces familyhood to others. She said, "Shopping, because it doesn't matter where we go, somebody has to, they see the intimacy between the two of us, the three of us, really, and need to define it, and it happens a lot." Family walks can function in the same way. Sarah spoke about how being together on nightly walks shows familyhood. She explained, "It's a joining of all three bodies at one time doing an activity . . . the closeness and proximity of us together." Lynn recalled how they were "doing the stroller thing, the dog thing" and an interaction with a neighbor made clear "we, the whole group of us walking together, dog, child, live in that house over there. And you could see the wheels turning." Likewise, attending church services shows family identity to others. For example, Angie and Lisa's pastor asked them to speak during a Sunday service about life as a lesbian family. Angie and Lisa felt the parishioners' reactions supported their family identity. Angie recalled, "This young girl came up and told me, 'Thanks for being brave.'"

In summary, this section used the perspective of symbolic interactionism to explain how rituals and symbols help lesbian families show family identity to others. A shared family name signals that the two mothers and their child or children consider themselves a family unit, careful selection of donors' traits create physical resemblance, and everyday activities, like shopping or nightly walks, communicate family status. The negotiated nature of identity is illustrated when interactions with others either affirm or disconfirm lesbian family identity. We now discuss how the symbol of names for two mommies and the rituals of attending a same-sex parenting group and doing family communicate internal family identity.

Internally Communicating Family Identity

Names for Two Mommies.   We found that the names children call their mothers communicate internal family identity. Cami explained the importance of these names: "[At] one of our first meetings of our same-sex parenting group, everybody was like, 'What are you going to have your kids call you?' you know, because it's uncharted territory." Most families chose to use different variations of *mother*, such as *mom* and *momma* for both mothers. Other families drew a term from another culture such as *ama*, *nay*, or *aunee* for one mother. Some families chose parallel names, such as *Momma M* and *Momma R* or *Mama Tina* and *Mama Wanda*.

Choosing separate names for the two mothers helps clarify the child's internal sense of family identity. Michelle and Susan struggled over what to have their daughter call them.

Susan compared using *mom* for both mothers to naming two children the same first name. Likewise, Patty said, "We figured we had to distinguish so that our child wouldn't be so confused."

On one hand, others can support internal family identity by using the chosen mother terms. Maria and Robin have chosen to be called *Momma M* and *Momma R.* Maria explained, "Our names carry over through to preschool: the kids refer to us and they will say, 'Jacob, Momma M's here.'" By distinguishing between Momma M and Momma R, the preschool teacher and classmates support Jacob's family identity. On the other hand, others can confuse the child's internal sense of family identity. For instance, Pam described an interaction between her son and a child at day care. Pam explained how her son Drew said, "'I have two mommies; and then this one kid goes, 'You can't have two, you know, mommies.' He goes, 'Yes I can. I have 'Mommy' and 'Momma.'" This example illustrates how easily lesbian family identity can be rejected.

Same-Sex Parenting Group. We found that attending a same-sex parenting group was a key ritual that supports a family's internal sense of identity. Many families attend a group primarily so that their children can see and interact with other families with two mothers. Many parents go so that their children will not feel isolated. Wanda wanted to show her daughter "that she wasn't just the lone ranger at school with two moms." Families also go so their children do not feel that their family is abnormal. Sarah observed, "We are the only same-sex couple on this block of eight or ten houses. So, if you figure that and you want to base that as your norm, then we can appear abnormal to her."

Families hope that the group will create a set of friends that the children can rely on, if they are later teased, harassed, or shunned because they have lesbian parents. Sandra explained, "To have other kids as they grow that they can talk to and kind of have as a resource like you know. They are going to go through a lot of stuff that we didn't have to go through growing up."

Families also attend a same-sex parenting group to support the mothers' own sense of family identity. Interaction with other lesbian mothers provides support. As Holly said, "We benefit just having other people around that are going to be going through those same things." Interaction with a group that shares a similar family identity validates internal family identity.

Doing Family. We found that patterned everyday interactions (West & Zimmerman, 1987; Wolin & Bennett, 1984) were important family rituals that communicated family not only to others but also to the family members themselves. Recurring daily interactions, such as shared meals and bedtime rituals, help support internal family identity. Shannon and Ellen make eating dinner together every evening a priority because they feel family meals are a time and place to build family. Likewise, nightly bedtime rituals help lesbian families feel like a family. Maria revealed the almost-sacred quality of their family bedtime ritual. She stated, "If the phone rings, we don't answer it." Dina and Libby's nighttime ritual with Hannah includes lying in bed together and saying their prayers. Dina and Libby lead the traditional, "Now I lay me down to sleep . . ." and Hannah fills in the blanks at the end. She always adds "Mommy" and "Momma."

Families also discussed the importance of recurring weekly interactions. Maria and Robin described how their Sunday morning ritual of blueberry pancakes and sausages helps build a sense of family. Carol and Lynn stressed how passing down rituals they had grown up with creates familyhood. Carol grew up with music blaring in the background during Saturday morning house-cleanings. She said, "When we have the music on when we are cleaning the house, to me does feel like family because . . . Saturdays, when I was growing up, that's what we did. We had Barbra Streisand blaring in the background and we cleaned." Likewise, Michelle passes down a family ritual by singing her mother's special song to her own child. Singing this song carries on a tradition that established a bond between Michelle and her mother and now establishes a special bond between Michelle and her child.

In summary, we used the perspective of symbolic interactionism to explain how rituals and symbols help lesbian families construct their own family identity. Two distinct names for the biological and nonbiological mother help clarify the child's sense of family, seeing other children who also have two mothers may lessen a child's sense of social isolation, and everyday patterned interactions create a heightened sense of family. The negotiated nature of identity is illustrated when a child's family identity is challenged by another's child's questioning the possibility of having two mommies.

Conclusion

We studied rituals and symbols to understand how lesbian families communicate their family identity externally and internally. We found that families chose shared last names to show others they are a family. The parents in these families also selected donors who resembled them in order to nonverbally communicate family to others. Finally, these families interacted as families in public (shopping or taking walks together) to show others that they are a family. In addition to using symbols and rituals to show others they are a family, these families also reported using symbols and rituals to show each other, especially their children, that they are a family. Parents chose names for both mothers to communicate their parental roles to their children. Families also attended a same-sex parenting group so that they would be in contact with other families that resemble their own. Finally, families had everyday rituals, such as eating meals together, to show each other that they are a family.

Our study demonstrates how lesbian families use rituals and symbols to communicate family identity. In so doing, our study illustrates the symbolic interactionist claim that communication is the primary way identity is negotiated between self and other. Interactions with others shape the family's identity. Identity is a social process in which lesbian families negotiate acceptance or rejection of their family identities with others. Our study shows how others, particularly children's peers, can challenge lesbian families' identities.

In response to the finding that children from heterosexual families often challenge the family identity of children from lesbian families, we created and distributed resource materials for elementary school educators. Our desire to make a difference in the community led us to develop a brochure and Web site that address problems children of lesbian families may face in the classroom. We have received positive feedback from administrators and teachers who find the materials timely and practical.

Finally, our study shows the need for additional research on how speech acts such as teasing and questioning impact the children of lesbian and gay parents. Although Rankin (2003) documents the teasing, harassing, shunning, and verbal threats gay, lesbian, bisexual, and transgender students experience on college campuses, future research needs to gain access to elementary-aged children of lesbian and gay parents and understand the climate in schools from their perspective.

Questions for Consideration and Discussion

1. What particular cultural forces contribute to the need for lesbian families to communicate family identity to outsiders?
2. In addition to lesbian/gay families, in what situations might family names be important for the construction of internal and external family identity?
3. The authors note the importance of "doing family" for lesbian family identity. How might we apply these findings to the study of other family forms?
4. This study focuses on lesbian-parented families. Do you believe that families parented by gay men would be similar? What different identity issues might they face?
5. In this study, the participants were 16 lesbian-parented families, all of whom used donor insemination. How might this have affected the results of the study?

References

Chabot, J. M., & Ames, B. D. (2004). "It wasn't 'let's get pregnant and go do it'": Decision making in lesbian couples planning motherhood via donor insemination. *Family Issues, 53,* 348–356.

Charmaz, K. (2002). Qualitative interviewing and grounded theory analysis. In J. F. Gubrium & J. A. Holstein (Eds.), *Handbook of interview research: Context & method* (pp. 675–694). Thousand Oaks, CA: Sage.

Goffman, E. (1959). *Presentation of self in everyday life.* New York: Doubleday.

Goffman, E. (1971). *Relations in public: Microstudies of the public order.* New York: Basic Books.

Johnson, S. M., & O'Connor, E. (2002). *The gay baby boom: The psychology of gay parenthood.* New York: New York University Press.

Kershaw, S. (2000). Living in a lesbian household: The effects on children. *Child and Family Social Work, 5,* 365–371.

Mead, G. H. (1943). *Mind, self, and society.* Chicago: University of Chicago Press.

Patterson, C. J. (1995). *Lesbian, gay and bisexual identities over the lifespan.* New York: Praeger.

Perinbanayagam, R. S. (2003). Telic reflections: Interactional processes, as such. *Symbolic Interaction, 26,* 67–83.

Rankin, S. R. (2003). *Campus climate for gay, lesbian, bisexual, and transgender people: A national perspective.* New York: The National Gay and Lesbian Task Force Policy Institute.

Suter, E. A. (2004). Tradition never goes out of style: The role of tradition in women's naming practices. *The Communication Review, 7,* 57–88.

Suter, E. A., & Oswald, R. F. (2003). Do lesbians change their last names in the context of a committed relationship? *Journal of Lesbian Studies, 7,* 71–83.

West, C., & Zimmerman, D. H. (1987). Doing gender. *Gender and Society, 1,* 125–151.

Wolin, S. J., & Bennett, L. A. (1984). Family rituals. *Family Process, 23,* 401–420.

Woosley, L. (2003, March 9). Family ties. *Tulsa World,* p. D1.

Section 3: Conclusions and Application—Sexuality, Family, and You _____

In this chapter, you read about the parental sexual relationship and how it relates to marital satisfaction. From this review, it is clear that, although we can't be quite sure about the direction of causation, sexual satisfaction and marital happiness are linked for many couples. Thus, adult partner sexual interaction impacts the family system as a whole.

We also addressed how parents communicate about sexuality to their children, both implicitly and explicitly. You read about the impacts that parent–child communication about sexuality seem to have on adolescent behavior. These impacts are part of why it is so important for us to consider how parents and children talk about (or don't talk about) sexuality in the family.

The final major theme of this chapter was related to homosexuality in the family. Attention to the particular dynamics of sexual orientation in family interaction has been a relatively recent phenomenon in research. Additionally, the issue of gay/lesbian parents has become more of a point of societal focus in the last decade, with many public debates and strong feelings about the issue from a variety of viewpoints.

Now that you have read about these issues, how might they impact you in your life as a member of families? How might you use this information to understand families (yours and others)? In this section, I suggest three ways to utilize your new knowledge: to gain understandings of your family of origin and how it impacted you; to get insight into the experiences of others; and to think about how you might use these understandings and insights in your communication with others.

Sexuality Communication in Your Family of Origin

Who in your family talked to you about sexuality? Research would tend to suggest that, when parents do talk about sexuality, they talk to the child of the same sex. If that was not true in your family, think about why. One of your parents may have been more comfortable speaking about sexuality issues. Or, it may have been that one of your parents felt that talking about sexuality was largely unnecessary. As you read earlier in the chapter, girls are spoken to more explicitly about sexuality than boys. So, if you are male, it is possible that neither parent felt that a talk about sexuality was particularly important for you. If there were both male and female children in the family, comparison of how parents spoke to each might give you insight into why a particular parent or adult caregiver spoke to you about sexuality most often.

If your parents did explicitly talk to you about sexuality, what was the focus of the conversation? As discussed here, research tends to indicate that often explicit communication about sexuality centers on issues such as how conception occurs and contraception, and talk about issues such as masturbation and having a healthy sex life are rarely spoken of. Frequently, the discussion is about what not to do (i.e. "Don't have sex!"). Were your conversations about sexuality similar to this. If not, you might ask yourself why? Do you think your parents were more or less comfortable than "the average" parent in talking about sexuality? As Kinser discusses, even parents who have a desire to be open with their children about sexuality may experience discomfort when attempting to talk about sexuality with their children. Regardless of whether your conversations with your parents/adult caregivers were similar to what has been shown in research, consider the extent to which you felt satisfied with the information you received from your parents. Did you want more information? Less? Different?

In addition to thinking about how your adult caregivers communicated overtly to you about sexuality, consider how they communicated more subtly about this issue. As you grew up, how much exposure to sexuality were you allowed? If there was a scene in a television show or movie involving sexuality, did your parents turn it off? How did your parents/adult caregivers behave toward each other in your presence? Did you have a sense of their physical interest in each other, or was that largely hidden? As you ponder these questions, you can consider what you learned from these implicit messages.

Finally, think about what you learned in your family of origin about sexual orientation. Most parents and other adult caregivers proceed from the assumption that every child will grow up to be a heterosexual adult. As a child, you may remember being teased by adult family members about your cross-sex friends ("Oh, is he your little boyfriend?"). You may have had an adult say that you had a "crush" on someone of the opposite sex. In these ways, adults, without ever explicitly saying it, teach children that heterosexuality is normal, male–female relationships are about romance, and male–male or female–female relationships are about friendship. In many families, explicit conversations about homosexuality are rare. In some families, to be sure, discussion of sexual orientation is more open. If your family was one of those families, why? Were your parents particularly adamant in their views about homosexuality and thus wanted to be sure you understood? Is someone in your family openly gay or lesbian and that prompted more discussion of sexual orientation? Did cultural events occurring at that time that lead you to ask about homosexuality, or lead your parents to discuss it more?

Once you have thought about how you experienced communication about sexuality in your family of origin, you can apply those understandings to thinking about your own sexual behavior. Research suggests that talking about sexuality with children and adolescents has outcomes on their later sexual behavior and attitudes. Although it is hard to isolate the effects, because of the many other things that impact our sexual lives, it is likely that the way your family of origin dealt with sexuality had some impact on you as you grew up. Reflecting on the connections between family communication about sexuality and your own behaviors and attitudes may provide you with some interesting insights. In addition to helping you think about and understand your own experiences, this knowledge can also be applied to considering the experiences of others.

Understanding the Experiences of Others

As children, and often even beyond, the ways that our family interacts become so "normal" for us that when we see or hear others behaving in ways that are different, we may feel that they are doing it "wrong" or are "weird." That's natural, particularly when we are young, because our own experiences are really all we know. As we get older, and learn more about the diversity of family experience, it may help us appreciate the variations in families, including diversity with regard to communicating about sexuality.

Throughout life, you will develop relationships with people from many different families, and each one of those individuals will have his or her own attitudes and behaviors in relation to sexuality. At times, the behavior or beliefs of another may be hard to understand. If the person is an acquaintance, this may not present much of an issue. However, if a close friend or romantic partner seems to have very different ideas than you do about sexuality, it can cause confusion, or even conflict in the relationship. Understanding the role of family of origin in helping us develop our sexual selves can give you a way to think about these differences between people and accept them as not necessarily better or worse, just different.

Thinking about Your Future in the Family

As you continue on in your life, you will likely engage in long-term romantic relationships. The research that we considered here suggests that attention to the impact of sexuality on a romantic relationship is important. At times, we may feel that sexual happiness should just happen naturally. However, that is often untrue for couples, and knowing how sexual satisfaction relates to relational happiness may help you to work on your sexual relationship and seek help if and when needed.

Additionally, many of you either do have or will have children. Even if you do not plan to have children of your own, it is likely that you will interact with children as an aunt or uncle, or close family friend. As you continue to consider the role of communication about sexuality in the family, ask yourself how your knowledge may guide your future communication with children and adolescents in your life. Most adults would agree that they want the children they care about to grow up and become sexually healthy and well-adjusted adults. Will you talk to these children about sexuality? How will you? What do you wish your adult caregivers had said to you that they didn't? What did they say to you that you want to pass on to the children you are close to? Thinking about what you have learned in this chapter may help you understand how, even when you aren't talking explicitly with children about sexuality, you are teaching them about it. This may not be always comfortable, but such consideration can help us be more reflective adults in our interactions with children and therefore may lead to subsequent generations who have a good understanding of their own sexuality, and the sexuality of others, and can make wise life choices as they embark upon their own adulthood and their own relationships with future generations of children.

Questions for Consideration and Discussion

1. Reflecting upon your own experiences, how did family communication affect your sexual behavior as you became an adolescent and adult?
2. How do you think that culture (larger societal culture, racial/ethnic culture, religious culture) impacted your family of origin's communication about sexuality? What do you see as the positive and/or negative outcomes of that impact?

3. Kinser's article, as well as other research cited here, points to the complex nature of communicating with children about sexuality and the discomfort that may arise for both parents and children. Can you see any ways that parents might be able to lessen this discomfort for themselves and their adolescents?

4. As laws regarding homosexuality and gay/lesbian relationships change and evolve over time, how do you think this may affect gay- and lesbian-parented families?

5. Drawing from the work in this chapter, what specific recommendations would you make to new parents as they approach the issue of sexuality in their families?

Key Terms and Concepts

body talk
coming out
gay/lesbian family
guilt

overt sexuality communication
relational satisfaction
sexual modeling
sexual orientation

sexual satisfaction
shame
social stigma

Health, Disability, and the Family

Chapter Objectives

1. To develop an understanding of the interrelationship between family processes and drug and alcohol abuse

2. To recognize the various impacts that acute and chronic physical and psychological or mental illness and disability can have on family systems

3. To become aware of the basic principles of a social perspective of disability

4. To develop a critical awareness of the impacts of socialization on your own understandings and enactments of health issues and disability in family settings

Section 1: Overview of Family Health and Disability Issues _____

- What do you think the role of parents should be in presenting information about drugs and alcohol? Does that role change as the child enters adolescence?
- How did your parents or adult caregivers model alcohol and/or drug use for you? How did it affect you?
- If an older family member experienced poor health, what would you see as your responsibilities in the situation?
- If asked to explain disability to a child, what would you say?

Issues of Health and Disability as a Continued Part of Family Life

Issues of health and disability are a part of our being as people. In each day that we live in our bodies, we live in states of health and varying ability. Thus, these issues are interwoven continually into the fabric of family life. There are a variety of health and wellness issues that could be considered in relation to family settings. For example, in Chapter 8 we addressed sexual risk behavior, which is one health issue related to families. Here, we focus on three additional categories of health issues in family life: drug and alcohol use (and abuse), acute and chronic physical illnesses and disability (from the flu to cancer to visual impairment, etc.), and acute and chronic psychological illness/disorder (depression, schizophrenia, eating disorders, ADHD, etc.). Because we cannot hope to consider the innumerable ways these issues impact the family, or even the totality of research that has been conducted about any of the individual topics, this discussion will necessarily be partial. As you read through this chapter, consider the examples and research presented here while also thinking about other situations that have occurred in your life and the lives of other people you know and how the understandings gleaned from this body of research and theory can be applied to those situations.

Drug and Alcohol Use and Abuse

The use of mood-altering substances has been a part of human experience throughout recorded history. Most adults partake of some form of altering substance, whether it be caffeine, nicotine, alcohol, or other drugs. Whereas the use of any substance may affect behavior and impact family life (i.e., too much coffee can make me jittery and more likely to be impatient with my children; even having a few beers might lead to poor choice making on occasion), we are culturally more concerned with the consumption of illegal substances, or the consumption of such drugs to the point that they impact daily functioning. Thus, we don't worry much culturally about adults consuming caffeine; however, we are concerned about the use of crack or heroin by adults and we worry about the use of all restricted drugs and alcohol by adolescents (because for them, both are illegal).

BOX 9.1 • *Did You Know?*

As drug laws change, so too do our responses to drug use. Prior to 1875 in the United States there were no laws prohibiting drug use. The first drug prohibited was opium, in San Francisco, CA. Marijuana began to be heavily taxed in 1937; however, it was not formally illegal at a federal level. The 1937 act was struck down as unconstitutional in 1969. The following year, the Controlled Substances Act made marijuana illegal at the federal level, though all 50 states already had state laws doing the same.

Adolescent Use

Like concerns about sexual behavior of teenagers, worry about drug and alcohol use and abuse has become a part of our public consciousness, and much of the impetus for the "war on drugs." Though schools and the media provide children and adolescents with information about the dangers of drug and alcohol use, the family is also a place where communication of attitudes and information about drugs and alcohol, as well as the modeling of drug or alcohol use, occurs. As we discussed previously in the text, theories of socialization point to the family as one of the major socializing forces for individuals. Families communicate with children about their own family culture, as well as about the larger cultures in which the family is situated. Some of that communication is about alcohol and drug use. The effects of parental influence on childhood and adolescent substance abuse will never be totally clear, because there are so many other factors (including peer influences) that impact the use of such substances. However, scholars have developed some interesting theories with regard to this issue. Most studies focus on parental awareness of teen use, parental monitoring of teen behavior, and parent–child communication about drugs and alcohol.

The first question we might ask is: Do parents know when their children are using drugs and alcohol? Williams, McDermitt, Bertrand, and Davis (2003) studied the awareness of parents about their high school–aged child's use of drugs and alcohol. For the 985 adolescents they studied, they concluded that only 34 percent of parents knew about alcohol use and only 11 percent knew about drug use. You might wonder why this is important in our understandings of drug and alcohol use by adolescents. A study by Bogenschneider, Wu, Raffaelli, and Tsay (1998) sheds some light on this issue. In this study, they also found that only about one-third of parents were aware of their adolescent's alcohol use. Additionally, the study revealed that those parents who were more aware were more likely to believe that the adolescent's peers also drank, worry about the consequences of risky alcohol-related behavior, and discuss alcohol use with the adolescent. Thus, these researchers theorize that awareness of drug and alcohol use may relate to more parental response to the risk.

Awareness is not the only issue in parenting impact on adolescent substance use. **Parental monitoring** refers to the extent to which parents are aware of and have some control over where their children are and with whom. Monitoring of a child's behavior has been found to have a correlation with substance use. In a two-year study of fifth- to seventh-grade students, Jackon, Henriksen, and Dickinson (1999) considered the specific alcohol-related communication and monitoring behaviors of parents for their elementary school children and the subsequent alcohol use of those children as they entered adolescence. Their study indicated that when parental monitoring behaviors were lower, adolescent alcohol use was likely to increase (see also Richards et al., 2004). Additionally, when parents allowed the child or adolescent to consume alcohol in the home, he or she was more likely to engage in alcohol consumption generally. The reason that increased monitoring seems to be related to reduced alcohol use isn't totally clear. These scholars argue it may be that adolescents whose parents monitor them more have fewer opportunities to engage in use, or, it is possible that these adolescents are more concerned with the potential of being "caught" drinking or using drugs.

In addition to awareness and monitoring, specific communication about drugs and alcohol is another factor that may impact use in childhood and adolescence. Like communicating about sexuality, the number of parents who "should" talk with their children about substance use and the number who do so with frequency are not the same. Kelly, Comello, and Hunn (2002) found that most adolescents reported that their parents had talked to them at some time about problems of drug and alcohol use. However, only 12 to 15 percent reported that their parents had talked to them about those dangers within the previous year. This is important because, as Booth-Butterfield and Sidelinger (1998) found in their research, parental communication about alcohol use seems to be correlated with less risky alcohol related behaviors. When parents do talk to their children about drugs and alcohol, research suggests that both teens and parents believe the following would be helpful: that parents be honest (talk about their own experimentation); that parents be knowledgeable to present accurate information, rather than simply using scare tactics or being inaccurate; and that parents express their regrets regarding their own use when appropriate (Thorne, McLean, & Dasbach, 2004).

Scholars theorize that awareness, monitoring, and communication about drugs and alcohol decrease the risk of adolescent use overall, but there may be cultural or sex differences between groups of adolescents that impact how susceptible they are to drug/alcohol use, and how much impact parental communication will have. Barnes, Farrell, and Banerjee (1994) studied Black and White adolescents in New York City. They found that, for both groups, parental monitoring, communication, and support were important in helping reduce substance use. However, they did find some differences. For these adolescents, religiosity seemed to provide a protective factor against substance use for Black adolescents, but not for White adolescents. Additionally, the White participants seemed to be more impacted by peer pressure than the Black participants. The authors argue that the reason for the difference is likely cultural. African American culture has a focus on religiosity and the role of the church in day-to-day family life. Thus, it may be more influential in preventing drug/alcohol abuse. Additionally, culture may impact the extent to which adolescents are concerned about belonging to a particular social group, and therefore relate to peer influence.

In addition to racial culture, studies have indicated that there may be sex differences in how parental behaviors impact adolescent substance use. Engels, Vermulst, Dubas, Bot, and Gerris (2005) considered characteristics of adolescent men and women, and their families, in relation to alcohol abuse in adolescence and young adulthood. They found differences in patterns for men and for women. For young men, having more aggressive tendencies and lower levels of family functioning seemed related to greater alcohol abuse. For young women, however, problem drinking was more associated with low levels of parental control in combination with low levels of parental affection. These differences may relate to our different expectations of men and women (with relation to issues like aggression and affection, etc.) For the participants in Richards and colleagues' (2004) study, parents were more likely to monitor the behavior of female adolescents than males. However, it seemed that increased monitoring by parents had a greater impact on the male adolescents than the female adolescents. The authors suggest that parents may monitor girls more because they believe them to be more at risk of harm from others. However, they argue that boys may be more at risk for being affected by cultural influences that encourage aggression, drug and alcohol use, and delinquency.

Parental Use

Not only do parents have an impact on the substance use of adolescents, drug and alcohol use and abuse by parents themselves can also have an impact on families. Parental alcohol and/or drug abuse has been found by many scholars to have negative effects on children (Fals-Stewart, Kelley, Fincham, Golden, & Logsdon, 2004; Haugland, 2003, 2005; Johnson & Leff, 1999). Those negative effects take the form of both internalizing behaviors (depression, sadness, poor self-esteem) and externalizing behaviors (acting out, poor academic performance). The causes of these poor behaviors may be that parents who are abusing drugs and alcohol do not monitor their children as closely as parents who are not, such parents may engage in poor disciplinary practices, and/or the parental relationship may be very conflictual, thus impacting the children.

Drug and alcohol use and abuse can also impact the parents' relationships with each other. However, those effects are somewhat more difficult to assess because of differences related to when in the marital relationship the use began, whether only one or both marital partners are substance users, and how the marital system has developed in relation to the drug and alcohol use. Generally, however, we know substance abuse problems have been associated with more generally negative interaction patterns for partners (Floyd et al., 2006; Marshal, 2003), which may sometimes include emotional, physical, and sexual abuse (Field, Caetano, & Nelson, 2004; Maharajh & Ali, 2005; Marshal, 2003). Additionally, research suggests that there are negative outcomes for spouses of substance abusers in terms of physical health issues and mental health issues, including stress, anxiety, and depression (Howard & Howard, 1985; Hudson, Kimberly, Firely, Festinger, & Marlowe, 2002; Hurcom, Coppello, & Orford, 2000).

Recovery and the Family System

Generally, we might assume that drug/alcohol abuse is the problem of the perpetrator and the other family members suffer through no fault of their own. However, research suggests that, due to the systemic nature of relationships, there are behaviors that each family member engages in that may make recovery more difficult and serve to actually perpetuate and encourage substance abuse (Le Poire, 1995, 2004). Drawing from, and building upon, this idea, Le Poire and colleagues (Le Poire, 1995, 2004; Le Poire, Erlandson, & Hallett, 1998) have developed the **inconsistent nurturing as control theory.** This theory argues that, although family members want the drug/alcohol abuser to stop the behavior, they also simultaneously want to both control and nurture the abuser. Because family members wish to stop the behavior, they may engage in attempts to control the other (i.e., taking the car keys to prevent him or her from going to the bar). On the other hand, those same family members may have developed a role of caretaking for the other (i.e., tending to him or her after a binge, taking care of debts). Because this is the nature of the relationship the family has developed, members may wish to stop the substance abusing behavior, but at the same time be fearful that if it does stop, the relationship will be altered forever. So, they both control and nurture the other, on an inconsistent basis. Because of this, the control efforts may not be particularly effective in reducing or stopping the behavior and the total relational interactions may actually perpetuate the drug/alcohol abuse behavior.

From this review, we can see that substance abuse can have an impact on family members and their interactions, and the behaviors and communication patterns of family members also influence drug and alcohol use and abuse, in an extremely complex manner. Drug and alcohol use is, in theory, a choice (though addiction isn't that simple, as we have seen here). When a family experiences physical illness or disability, the choice of "having" the illness is not theirs, but they nonetheless have to negotiate the meaning of that illness or disability and also how to "adjust" their family system.

Negotiating Meaning of Illness and Disability

Before we begin to address some specific issues faced by families when a member or members have illness or disability, it is important to consider the way meaning of illness/disability are negotiated in family settings. To some extent, it may seem as if having an illness or disability is a matter of scientific fact, not negotiated meaning. However, it is not that simple. An individual may have a physical or psychological condition that is evident via medical testing and so on, but how family members assign meaning to that condition, and therefore respond to it, is a matter of communication and negotiation.

Various authors have described stages or steps that families and individuals may go through in the process of understanding and assigning meaning to illness and disability (see, for example, Fox, Vaughn, Wyatte, & Dunlap, 2002; Higgins, Raskind, Goldberg, & Herman, 2002; O'Connor, Young, & Saul, 2004). Though different scholars use different terms for the stages or steps in the process, the ideas tend to coalesce around three primary foci. Early in the process, there may be an awareness that something is "different" about the individual (different from self at a prior moment, or different from others at similar stages of development). That **awareness of difference** is accompanied by some negotiation of value/meaning for the difference (i.e., is this difference a "good" or "bad" thing . . . or maybe some of each). At some point, there is generally a stage of **labeling.** This typically occurs when family members are informed of a label or designation for the difference by medical, psychological, or educational professionals. Here, too, a process of meaning negotiation occurs. The label may be accepted, rejected, partially accepted, or substituted by family members. As the family communicates with and about the label, positive and/or negative meanings are associated with that label and its accompanying concepts. Usages for the label also begin to be negotiated here. Will we use this label only in "official" documents? Will we use this label to explain to family and friends? Will we use this label in family conversation? Another part of the process of meaning negotiation is the **integration** of this "bit" of meaning into the family's overall understanding of the individual and the family system. In this stage/step, the family members add their understandings of the illness/disability as it relates to the individual and the family to their other knowledge about that individual and the family. The disability/illness is seen as a part of a whole, not as the whole.

Although these "stages" may for some families be a fairly linear process, for other families they will not be. Some families may feel little awareness of difference before that difference is labeled by professionals (or even after). Some families may experience a sense of difference that they consider an illness or disability; however, it is never labeled officially. Other families may reject the idea of difference and the label in such a way that these bits of meaning never become integrated into the family understanding. Families may repeat stages across time, cycle through them as they encounter new phases in the life cycle, progress through them slowly or quickly, and so on. Throughout these stages, families may feel a variety of emotional responses, including grief, anger, denial, joy, frustration, and fear. Thus, the experience of illness and disability for each family is communicative at its root and completely unique.

In addition to how family members negotiate meaning for particular physical/psychological conditions in their own family experiences, we as a society also establish particular meanings for bodily and mental characteristics, and what counts as normal, healthy, able, or disabled. Much of our societal understandings of illness and disability are based on a medical model that presumes a particular type of body or mind as the norm and works toward achieving that norm, as much as possible, for everyone. Later in this section, you will read about an alternate way to understand the nature of disability.

Chronic and Acute Physical Illness and Disability

The distinction between physical illness and physical disability is not a clear division. Some conditions are considered illness, or disease, but may also be construed as disability (i.e., diabetes). Some illnesses "produce" or coexist with disability (i.e., macular degeneration, polio, rheumatoid arthritis). Thus, in this section I address research related to the impacts of physical illness and disability on family systems and their members and relate that research to the theoretical ideas about family communication you have encountered in the text.

Family Roles

As discussed in Chapter 3, role theories suggest that family members perform particular functions needed for the system; these are their family roles. When a family member becomes significantly ill or is diagnosed with a disability, some degree of role renegotiation, or even role relinquishment, may occur.

When a child becomes ill, or has a disability, role change may occur for parents and siblings. Algren (1985) studied the role of mothers whose child had been hospitalized. Algren found, in agreement with previous research, that these parents were uncertain of their roles when the child was in a hospital setting and were anxious to engage in more parenting/caretaking activities than they felt were allowed or promoted by medical staff. In a similar manner, Gallagher, Rhodes, and Darling (2004) found that parents whose children are diagnosed with disability may eventually come to see themselves as educators and advocates in the early intervention system. Thus, these parents are involved in a renegotiation of their understanding of their roles as parents when their child is seriously ill or has a disability.

The roles of other children in the family are also affected by the illness or disability of a sibling. Breyer, Kunin, Kalish, and Patenaude (1993) looked at the impact of serious childhood illness on siblings. We might suppose that the biggest problem healthy siblings would face is a lack of attention as parents focus on the ill child, but this was not what these children reported. The biggest worries they had related to the sibling's illness, and the thing they most wished was to be more (not less) involved in interaction and caretaking for the sibling who was ill. The children believed that their parents were keeping them away from their siblings in order to protect them from sadness or worry about the illness; however, this was not what the children wanted. In the face of the illness, these children wanted to engage in the typical roles of siblings (playing, talking, and caretaking their brother or sister). But, due to their parents' attempts to protect them from trauma, their roles as siblings had shifted in a direction they found unsatisfying.

Family roles are an important part of understanding family process and experiences. When an event occurs that significantly alters the behavior or status of one family member (including illness and disability), it is likely to impact the roles that the other members of the family feel they should fulfill, and do fulfill. Role renegotiation, role conflict, and role relinquishment may occur as the family system adapts to the situation.

Communication Patterns

As discussed in Chapter 2, family communication theorists have argued that families vary in terms of their orientation to conversation. Even though families develop particular communication orientations and patterns over time, illness or disability may create substantial differences in family patterns (Beach, 2002). As family members engage in discussion of illness, they negotiate how they will communicate about such issues. Sometimes, this may involve a temporary "laying aside" of their family roles to discuss the illness or disability in a more clinical or medical fashion, attempting to avoid the emotionally laden aspects of the issue. For example, Boehmer and Clark (2001) found that men who were experiencing prostate cancer did not engage in much communication with their wives about the cancer. When communication did occur, it was rarely ever about the feelings that the marital partners had about this life changing illness.

How much, and in what way, communication changes during illness depends in part on the length of time that the illness lasts. Lavee and Mey-Dan (2003) considered the impact of long-term childhood illness on the parental relationship. In their study, they found that there were both negative and positive relational outcomes over the course of the illness. For many couples, communication seemed to improve; however, satisfaction with sexuality in the relationship decreased. The authors noted that the length of the illness was a factor for parental relationships, as well. Overall relational satisfaction tended to be lower in the first year after diagnosis. For the second and third year, some increase in satisfaction was found. When children were ill for four or more years, deterioration in relational satisfaction was again seen. There could be a variety of reasons for such changes, including the effect of family stressors, changes in family roles and responsibilities, financial issues, and so on that point, once again, to the complexity of the family system.

As our family systems encounter issues such as disability and illness, how we communicate may be impacted. The communication patterns we develop over time arise from (and contribute to) the culture of the family system. Thus, it makes sense that issues like significant illness and disability will have effects on the family system that lead to changes in communication patterns.

Social Relations

In addition to impacting the relational processes within the family, illness and disability can also affect family members' relationships with others outside the family system. In one example of this phenomenon, DeJudicibus and McCabe (2004) found that children whose parents had multiple sclerosis had poorer social adjustment and more difficulty interacting with peers. As parents' negative emotions (depression, anxiety, etc.) increase, children's inability to get along with peer groups also increases. The authors suggest that there may be two primary reasons for this. First, children whose parents are ill may take on more of a caretaking role in the family. The assumption of this role may make it harder to interact with peers (because they become used to interacting with adults in a different way). Second, if parents have high levels of negative emotions their children may assume the type of communicative behaviors that are modeled by their tense, depressed parents.

As illness and disability can affect social relationships, so too can social relationships affect the health of the family member with illness or disability. In Chapter 5, you read about theories of social support in family settings. You also read how studies have indicated the positive impact social support can have on physical illness and disability. Research indicates that patients who have cancer (Ford, Babrow, & Stohl, 1996; Wright, 2002), arthritis (Holtzman, Newth, & Delongis, 2004), heart problems (Janevic et al., 2004; Pedersen, Van Domburg, & Larsen, 2004), and other health concerns may improve more easily when they have more social support. That social support can come from individuals outside the family system, but it can also come from those within the family. In their studies of the stories of families facing cancer, Anderson and Martin (2003) and Figueiredo, Fries, and Ingram (2004) found that, though serious illness can be very difficult to talk about in family settings, communication of support from family members is a crucial part of dealing with cancer. When family members are not supportive, there are negative outcomes on emotional functioning and social relationships for the cancer patient.

In some fashion, we carry our physical selves into every relationship that we have with others. Thus, it is reasonable that changes in our physicality, including illness and disability, impact and are impacted by the social relationships we forge with others.

The research discussed here indicates the complexity of effects of acute or chronic physical illness or disability. And, those effects go in both directions: the illness or disability impacts the family, and the family impacts the illness or disability. Similar processes occur in relation to psychological or cognitive illness and disability.

Chronic and Acute Psychological/Cognitive Illness and Disability

Psychological/cognitive illness and disability affects the lives of adults and children across the world. In this part of the chapter, we consider some of the findings or research related to the connections between family process and psychological/cognitive illness and disability. As in the previous section, we begin with a focus on children.

Some scholars have theorized that family communication and interaction patterns may be related to the development of psychological illness. As discussed in Chapter 6, violent and abusive family relationships have been associated with psychological issues such as depression (Arias, 2004; Bent-Goodley, 2004). However, even in families where abuse is not occurring, particular patterns of interaction have been argued to be related to psychological illness.

Of Children and Adolescents

One example of this connection between family patterns and psychological issue can be found in research about adolescent eating disorders. A variety of scholars have posited mechanisms through which family communication patterns contribute to eating disorders. Some scholars suggest that parental preoccupation, with weight and weight issues, and the ensuing communication that reflects that preoccupation can contribute to the creation of an eating disorder for the child or adolescent (see, for example, Park, Lee, Woolley, Murray, & Stein, 2003; Park, Senior, & Stein, 2003; Saarilehto, Keskinen, Lapinleimu, Helenius, & Simell, 2001). Other scholars have argued that other family processes, not obviously related to eating behaviors, may also be correlated with increased potential for adolescent eating disorders (Segrin, 1998; Waller & Calam, 1994; Wonderlich, 1992). Family characteristics that have been specifically connected to eating disorders include low family cohesion, extremely high-conformity orientation (Wechselblatt, Gurnick, & Simon, 2000), and extensive secrecy (Dalzell, 2000). Although scholars theorize a connection between these family communication patterns and eating disorders, causality is difficult to assign due to the myriad of influences (genetic and social) that impact upon an individual's psychological well-being. Eating disorders are but one example of how family interaction may be related to the development of psychological illness/disability. Other scholars have researched the role of family process in psychological conditions such as schizophrenia, depression, and suicidal ideation (Blatt & Homann, 1992; Bochner & Eisenberg, 1987; Miller & Day, 2002; Segrin, 1998; Slesnick & Waldron, 1997).

Regardless of the influence that family interaction plays in the development of psychological/cognitive illness or disability for a child, there are outcomes of the illness/disability for the family. Tunali and Power (2002) discuss the extent to which parents of children with autism may need to redefine their roles and role tasks as parents, as well as their expectations of the child following the diagnosis. For example, these authors found that mothers of children with autism began to believe more strongly that mothers of young children should stay home, rather than pursing a career (see also Shearn & Todd, 2000). This redefinition or renegotiation will likely be an ongoing process across the family life course. Similarly, Milliken (2001) spoke with parents of adult children who had been experiencing schizophrenia over an extended period. These parents indicated that they felt some degree of confusion about their roles as the child reached adulthood. They still felt the need to act in a parental fashion and caretake their child, but that child was legally an adult, and medical professionals, legal professionals, and

BOX 9.2 • *Internet Connection*

Because eating disorders are relatively common, you likely have a friend or family member who has been affected by them. To learn more about eating disorders and treatment, visit www.nationaleatingdisorders.org.

even the child himself or herself did not always acknowledge the parents' ongoing responsibility for the adult child (see also Pejlert, 2001). These research examples reflect the systemic nature of the family system (Chapter 3), and the way in which a change in one part of the system affects other parts, including the roles that are enacted by family members.

Of Parents and Adult Caregivers

When parents experience mental illness or disability, there are also impacts on the family system. Those impacts vary across families. Research suggests that some children may experience adverse emotional, social, or psychological effects related to a parent's mental illness (Oyserman, Mowbray, Allen-Meares, & Firminger, 2000; Thomas, Forehand, & Neighbors, 1995; Warner, Weissman, Mufson, & Wickramaratne, 1999). Smith (2004) argues that the cause-and-effect relationship here could proceed in a number of ways. There could be genetic predispositions that are a factor in both the mental illness of the parents and also the problems of the child. The genetic factors could be interacting with the environment created by a parent who is mentally ill. The mental illness of the parent could affect other things (such as the marital relationship, socioeconomic status, social isolation, etc.) which then impact the child. Or, the parent's psychological illness could create disruptions in the parenting process. Whatever the cause, research seems to suggest that many children are negatively impacted when parents have a chronic psychological illness. However, other children may prove more resistant to such impacts (Garber & Little, 1999; Mowbray et al., 2004). Tebes, Kaufman, Adnopoz, & Rocusin (2001) argue that when parenting behaviors are less disrupted due to the mental illness it may provide some protection for the child and increase his or her resilience. Other factors—such as a larger family social network (which may result in greater social support), higher socioeconomic status, less family stress, and a better parent–child bond—may also be related to why some children are more resilient and less prone to negative effects from parental psychological disorder.

Adults experiencing their own psychological issues may also have problems with role confusion or feeling that their roles as parents are being challenged by others. Sands, Koppelman, and Solomon (2004) studied mothers who were experiencing chronic severe mental illness. For many of these mothers, one or more of their children were living with extended family or had been taken into the social services system. Although these mothers still felt themselves to "be mothers" to the children, and retained the desire to parent them, they felt uncertain about their legal and social status with regard to their children and social service agencies were not providing that information to them. Many of the mothers were even uncertain of exactly where and with whom their children were living. Because these mothers were not fulfilling the social expectation of parenting, they were not seen as mothers by the individuals around them, and this diminished their ability to negotiate a way, even if not the typical way, to mother their children.

The aging process, and the mental changes that are sometimes associated with that process, is another family stage issue that may create changes in roles and behaviors. When a parent or grandparent begins to lose some mental acuity, due to Alzheimer's disease or similar cognitive changes, other family members may be called upon to fulfill some of the roles of that individual, or take on additional roles to meet the needs of the family. For example, Stephens, Townsend, Martire, and Druley (2001) found that adult daughters are often called on to take a caretaking role for elderly relatives. This is not likely related to the cultural expectation that women are better at, or more suited to, caretaking. Research suggests that caretakers often experience some degree of role shift and strain when faced with the addition of the caregiver role to the roles they already fulfill in the family (income production, spousal roles, child care, etc.). The ability to assume this role without suffering significant negative effects may depend on the resources, both inside and outside the family, the caretaking individual has available to him or her (see also Brody, 1990; Dautzenberg et al., 2000; Stephens & Townsend, 1997).

Psychological illness and disability, whether that of a child or a parent, can have a significant impact upon the family and its members. Dealing with such illness and disability in the family may require a renegotiation of family roles and expectations. Social expectations and beliefs about psychological "normalcy" and family roles affect the ways that family members experience psychological illness and disability.

Another Perspective on Disability

Most of the research we have been discussing takes what is called by some the **medical/individual model of disability.** From this perspective, disability is something that an individual has, due to his or her inability to perform "necessary" or "normal" life activities, or the "difference" in his or her body or mind. Research that proceeds from a medical or individual model often considers ways to cure, treat, or manage the deficiencies of the individual with disabilities (Oliver, 1996). The end goal, from this view, is to make the individual, and his or her life, as normal as possible. However, this is not the only way to understand or think about disability.

Social models of disability are based on the theory that the physical or psychological conditions of the person with impairment do not, in and of themselves, produce disability. Instead, the culture in which the individual lives and the physical and social conditions of that environment create the disability (Abberley, 1987; Oliver, 1990, 1996). Think about the buildings that you go into and out of each day. Those buildings were constructed to prioritize walking as the normal way to get from one place to another. Stairs are probably more common than ramps, restrooms are built for individuals who walk (except for special stalls for the "handicapped"), and elevators are often absent (or so limited that they certainly cannot accommodate the majority of individuals who enter the building). Under these circumstances, an inability to walk becomes a disability. In a similar fashion, school systems from kindergarten through college require that students stay in one location for long periods, concentrating on one topic, in a quiet atmosphere. In this scenario, ADHD becomes a disability. Theorists and researchers working from a social model investigate the social nature of disability, how disability is created through patterns of behavior and communication, and how communication can thus be used to change the way we think about ability and disability and empower individuals with a variety of abilities.

Though the social model of disability has become more common in research and theory, the medical/individual model is still most common in public conversations and media representations of disability (Coles, 2001). Television, magazine, and newspaper coverage of disability issues focuses attention on surgical or technological ways to "fix" disability; new medications are continually being developed for ADHD, ADD, and obsessive-compulsive disorder (OCD); and programs are promoted that help children with autism spectrum disorders behave more normally in social settings. This medical model of disability in our cultural representations

BOX 9.3 • *ADHD/ADD and the Family*

The increase of attention deficit disorder (ADD) and attention deficit hyperactivity disorder (ADHD) diagnoses over the past decade has been an issue of considerable public attention. It is extremely difficult to produce statistics regarding the number of children who have been diagnosed with ADD or ADHD (due in part to the increasing rates), but most scholars agree that between 3 and 7 percent of children in the United States are affected (with higher rates for boys than girls) (McCleary, 2002; Neven, Anderson, & Godber, 2002; Reid, Trout, & Schartz, 2005).

The impulsivity, focus difficulties, and distractibility often experienced by children diagnosed with ADD/ADHD have impacts not only on the child, but on the family system as well. One arena in which this may be the case is the parent–child relationship. Studies suggest that parents of children with ADD/ADHD are more likely to attribute negative behavior on the part of the child to internal characteristics than external factors, more likely to experience anger in the presence of their children, less likely to be generally responsive to the children, and more likely to overreact in discipline situations (Gerdes & Hoza, 2006; Johnston, Chen, & Ohan, 2006; Seipp & Johnston, 2005; Whalen et al., 2006). These issues may be related to the stress, social anxiety, and uncertainty sometimes felt by parents whose children have been diagnosed with these conditions and the resources these parents have for coping (McCleary, 2002). Thus, we can see how ADD/ADHD may have an impact on how both parents and children feel about their relationship and each other.

In addition to issues that occur within family relationships, children with ADD/ADHD and their families may also experience difficulties in their relationships with medical professionals, educational providers, and other social contacts. In a study of mothers of children with ADD/ADHD, Malacrida (2001) found that her participants had experienced feelings of being judged as poor parents; shame or guilt over their children being labeled or stigmatized; anger over the refusal of medial or educational officials to assist in diagnosis or accommodations; and worry about what others might think of them, their family, and their children. Such concerns may reflect, or create, social distance for families who have a child with an ADD or ADHD diagnosis.

Often, ADD and ADHD are treated using stimulant medications in an attempt to reduce the inattentiveness and impulsivity seen as the problem. However, more recently some professionals are recommending a multifaceted approach that emphasizes overall family wellness, and making sure that all members of the family are having their needs met (Neven et al., 2002; Reid et al., 2005). This type of approach involves an acknowledgment that both parents and children can be active participants in creating the most functional settings, interactions, and learning experiences for family members, and that medication is not the only option for children or adults with ADD/ADHD. Proponents of this view argue that such an approach is, in the end, good for all children because it places a focus on understanding different child development patterns, the role of culture in assigning value to child behaviors (i.e., what is good/bad), and empowers children and parents to make decisions that are best suited to individual needs.

presents disability as tragedy. Those who persevere "through their disability" and succeed in some way (seen as surprising for someone so tragically disabled) are heralded as heroes. People who have "triumphed over" disability and lived a full life are treated as unusual and astounding examples (i.e., Marlee Matlin, Ray Charles, and Christopher Reeve).

The social model of disability is an alternative way to think and talk about disability and how, as a culture, we respond to impairment. Because our understandings are developed through communication, this is an important part of the study of family communication with relation to disability.

In this section, you have read about alcohol and drug use and abuse in the family system, physical illness and disability, psychological illness and disability, and the social disability perspective. These issues are a part of all families' lives in one way or another. Section 2 examines the effects of parents on adolescent drug and alcohol use; the intersection between the experiences of families with children who are visually impaired and the ways these children are constructed in children's books; and the ways in which mediated messages reflect parents with disabilities. Section 3 discusses how this information about family health and disability can be used in your own life.

References

Abberley, P. (1987). The concept of oppression and the development of a social theory of disability. *Disability, Handicap and Society, 2*, 5–19.

Algren, C. (1985). Role perception of mothers who have hospitalized children. *Children's Health Care: Journal of the Association for the Care of Children's Health, 14*(1), 6–9.

Anderson, J. O., & Martin, P. G. (2003). Narratives and healing: Exploring one family's stories of cancer survivorship. *Health Communication, 15*(2), 133–143.

Arias, I. (2004). The legacy of child maltreatment: Long-term health consequences for women. *Journal of Women's Health, 13*(5), 468–473.

Barnes, G. M., Farrell, M. P., & Banerjee, S. (1994). Family influences on alcohol abuse and other problem behaviors among Black and White adolescents in a general population sample. *Journal of Research on Adolescence, 4*, 183–202.

Beach, W. A. (2002). Between dad and son: Initiating, delivering, and assimilating bad cancer news. *Health Communication, 14*, 271–299.

Bent-Goodley, T. (2004). Perceptions of domestic violence: A dialogue with African American women. *Health & Social Work, 29*(4), 307–316.

Blatt, S. J., & Homann, E. (1992). Parent–child interaction in the etiology of dependent and self-critical depression. *Clinical Psychology Review, 12*, 47–91.

Bochner, A. P., & Eisenberg, E. M. (1987). Family process: System perspectives. In C. R. Berger & S. H. Chaffee (Eds.), *Handbook of communication science* (pp. 540–563). Newbury Park, CA: Sage.

Boehmer, U., & Clark, J. (2001). Communication about prostate cancer between men and their wives. *The Journal of Family Practice, 50*(3), 226–231.

Bogenschneider, K., Wu, M., Raffaelli, M., & Tsay, J. C. (1998). Other teens drink, but not my kid. Does parental awareness of adolescent alcohol use protect adolescents from risky consequences? *Journal of Marriage and Family, 60*(2), 356–373.

Booth-Butterfield, M., & Sidelinger, R. (1998). The influence of family communication on the college-aged child: Openness, attitudes and actions about sex and alcohol. *Communication Quarterly, 46*, 295–308.

Breyer J., Kunin, H., Kalish, L. A., & Patenaude, A. F. (1993). The adjustment of siblings of pediatric cancer patients: A sibling and parent perspective. *Psycho-Oncology, 2*, 201–208.

Brody, E. M. (1990). *Women in the middle: Their parent-care years*. New York: Springer.

Coles, J. (2001). The social model of disability: What does it mean for practice in services with people with learning difficulties? *Disability & Society, 16*(4), 501–510.

Dalzell, H. J. (2000). Whispers: The role of family secrets in eating disorders. *Eating Disorders, 8*(1), 43–62.

Dautzenberg, M. G. H., Diederiks, J. P. M., Philipsen, H., Stevens, F. C. J., Tan, F. E. S., & Vernooij-Dassen, M. J. F. J. (2000). The competing demands of paid work and parent care: Middle-aged daughters providing assistance to elderly parents. *Research on Aging, 22*, 165–187.

DeJudicibus, M., & McCabe, M. (2004). The impact of parental multiple sclerosis on the adjustment of children and adolescents. *Adolescence, 39*(155), 551–569.

Engels, R., Vermulst, A. A., Dubas, J. S., Bot, S. M., & Gerris, J. (2005) Long-term effects of family functioning and child characteristics on problem drinking in young adulthood. *European Addiction Research, 11*, 32–37.

Fals-Stewart, W., Kelley, M. L., Fincham, F. D., Golden, J., & Logsdon, T. (2004). Emotional and behavioral problems of children living with drug-abusing fathers: Comparisons with children living with alcohol-abusing and non-substance-abusing fathers. *Journal of Family Psychology, 18*(2), 319–330.

Field, C. A., Caetano, R., & Nelson, S. (2004). Alcohol and violence related cognitive risk factors associated with the perpetration of intimate partner violence. *Journal of Family Violence, 19*(4), 249–253.

Figueiredo, M. I., Fries, E., & Ingram, K. M. (2004). The role of disclosure patterns and unsupportive social interactions in the well-being of breast cancer patients. *Psycho-Oncology, 13*, 96–105.

Floyd, F. J., Cranford, J. A., Daugherty, M. K., Klotz, M., Fitzgerald, H. E., & Zucker, R. A. (2006). Marital interaction in alcholic and nonalcoholic couples: Alcoholic subtype variations and wives' alcoholism states. *Journal of Abnormal Psychology, 115*(1), 121–130.

Ford, L. A., Babrow, A. S., & Stohl, C. (1996). Social support messages and the management of uncertainty in the experience of breast cancer: An application of problematic integration theory. *Communication Monographs, 63*, 189–207.

Fox, L., Vaughn, B. J., Wyatte, M. L., & Dunlap, G. (2002). "We can't expect other people to understand": Family perspectives on problem behavior. *Exceptional Children, 68*(4), 437–450.

Gallagher, P. A., Rhodes, C. A., & Darling, S. M. (2004). Parents as professionals in early intervention: A parent educator model. *Topics in Early Childhood Special Education, 24*(1), 5–13.

Garber, J., & Little, S. (1999). Predictors of competence among offspring of depressed mothers. *Journal of Adolescent Research, 14*(1), 44–71.

Gerdes, A., & Hoza, B. (2006). Maternal attributions, affect, and parenting in attention deficit hyperactivity disorder and comparison families. *Journal of Clinical Child and Adolescent Psychology, 35*(3), 346–355.

Haugland, B. S. M. (2003). Paternal alcohol abuse: Relationship between child adjustment, parental characteristics, and family functioning. *Child Psychiatry and Human Development, 34*(2), 127–146.

Haugland, B. S. M. (2005). Recurrent disruptions of rituals and routines in families with paternal alcohol abuse. *Family Relations, 54*, 225–241.

Higgins, E., Raskind, M. H., Goldberg, R. J., & Herman, K. L. (2002). Stages of acceptance of a learning disability: The impact of labeling. *Learning Disability Quarterly, 25*(1), 3–18.

Holtzman, S., Newth, S., & Delongis, A. (2004). The role of social support in coping with daily pain among patients with rheumatoid arthritis. *Journal of Health Psychology, 9*, 677–695.

Howard, D., & Howard, N. (1985). Treatment of the significant other. In S. Zimberg, J. Wallace, & S. Blume (Eds.), *Practical approaches to alcoholism psychotherapy* (pp. 137–162). New York: Plenum Press.

Hudson, C. R., Kimberly, C., Firely, M. L., Festinger, D. S., & Marlowe, D. B. (2002). Social adjustment of family members and significant others (FSOs) or drug users. *Journal of Substance Abuse Treatment, 23*(3), 171–181.

Hurcom, C., Copello, A., & Orford, J. (2000). The family and alcohol: Effects of excessive drinking and conceptualizations of spouses over recent decades. *Substance Use & Misuse, 35*, 473–502.

Jackson, C., Henriksen, L., & Dickinson, D. (1999). Alcohol-specific socialization, parenting behaviors and alcohol use by children. *Journal of Studies on Alcohol, 60*(3), 362–367.

Janevic, M. R., Janz, N. K., Dodge, J. A., Wang, Y., Lin, X., & Clark, N. M. (2004). Longitudinal effects of social support on the health and functioning of older women and heart disease. *International Journal of Aging & Human Development, 59*, 153–175.

Johnson, J. L., & Leff, M. (1999). Children of substance abusers: Overview of research findings. *American Academy of Pediatrics, 103*, 1085–1099.

Johnston, C., Chen, M., & Ohan, J. (2006). Mothers' attributions for behavior in nonproblem boys, boys with attention deficit hyperactivity disorder, and boys with attention deficit hyperactivity disorder and oppositional defiant behavior. *Journal of Clinical Child and Adolescent Psychology, 35*(1), 60–71.

Kelly, K. J., Comello, M. L., & Hunn, L. (2002). "Parent-child communication, perceived sanctions against drug use, and youth drug involvement," *Adolescence, 37*(148), 775–787.

Lavee, Y., & Mey-Dan, M. (2003). Patterns of change in marital relationships among parents of children with cancer. *Health & Social Work, 28*(4), 255–263.

Le Poire, B. A. (1995). Inconsistent nurturing as control theory: Implications for communication-based research and treatment programs. *Journal of Applied Communication Research, 23*, 1–15.

Le Poire, B. A. (2004). The influence of drugs and alcohol on family communication: The effects that substance abuse has on family communication and the effects that family members have on substance abuse. In A.

L. Vangelisti (Ed.), *Handbook of family communication* (pp. 609–628). Mahwah, NJ: Erlbaum.

Le Poire, B. A., Erlandson, K. T., & Hallett, J. S. (1998). Punisher versus reinforcing strategies of drug discontinuance: Effect of persuaders' drug use. *Health Communication, 10*(4), 293–316.

Maharajh, H. D., & Ali, A. (2005). Aggressive sexual behavior of alcohol-dependent men. *Alcoholism Treatment Quarterly, 23*(4), 101–106.

Malacrida, C. (2001). Motherhood, resistance, and attention deficit disorder: Strategies and limits. *Canadian Review of Sociology and Anthropology, 38*(2), 141–165.

Marshal, M. P. (2003). For better or for worse? The effects of alcohol use on marital functioning. *Clinical Psychology Review, 23*(7), 959–997.

McCleary, L. (2002). Parenting adolescents with attention deficit hyperactivity disorder: Analysis of the literature for social work practice. *Health & Social Work, 27*(4), 285–292.

Miller, M., & Day, L. E. (2002). Family communication, maternal and paternal expectations, and college students' suicidality. *Journal of Family Communication, 2*(4), 167–184.

Milliken, P. J. (2001). Disenfranchised mothers: Caring for an adult child with schizophrenia. *Health Care for Women International, 22*, 149–166.

Mowbray, C. T., Bybee, D., Oyserman, D., Allen-Meares, P., MacFarlane, P., & Hart-Johnson, T. (2004). Diversity of outcomes among adolescent children of mothers with mental illness. *Journal of Emotional and Behavioral Disorders, 12*(4), 206–221.

Neven, R. S., Anderson, V., & Godber, T. (2002). Rethinking ADHD: Integrated approaches to helping children at home and at school. Crows Nest, New South Wales: Allen and Unwin.

O'Connor, D. L., Young, J. M., & Saul, M. J. (2004). Living with paraplegia: Tensions and contradictions. *Health & Social Work, 29*(3), 207–218.

Oliver, M. (1990). *The politics of disablement*. London: Macmillan.

Oliver, M. (1996). *Understanding disability: From theory to practice*. Basingstoke, England: Macmillan.

Oyserman, D., Mowbray, C. T., Allen-Meares, P. A., & Firminger, K. B. (2000). Parenting among mothers with a serious mental illness. *American Journal of Orthopsychiatry, 70*(3), 296–315.

Park, R. J., Lee, A., Woolley, H., Murray, L., & Stein, A. (2003). Children's representation of family mealtime in the context of maternal eating disorders. *Child: Care, Health and Development, 29*(2), 111–119.

Park, R. J., Senior, R., & Stein, A. (2003). The offspring of mothers with eating disorders. *European Child & Adolescent Psychiatry, 12*(Suppl. 1), 110–119.

Pedersen, S. S., Van Domburg, R. T., & Larsen, M. L. (2004). The effect of low social support on short-term prognosis in patients following a first myocardial infarction. *Scandinavian Journal of Psychology, 45*(4), 313–318.

Pejlert, A. (2001). Being a parent of an adult son or daughter with severe mental illness receiving professional care: Parents narratives. *Health and Social Care in the Community, 9*, 194–204.

Reid, R., Trout, A. L., & Schartz, M. (2005). Self-regulation interventions for children with attention deficit/hyperactivity disorder. *Exceptional Children, 71*(4), 361–377.

Richards, M. H., Viegas-Miller, B., Wasserman, M. S., O'Donnell, P. C., Colder, C., & Williams, K. (2004). Parental monitoring mediates the effects of age and sex on problem behaviors among African American urban young adolescents. *Journal of Youth and Adolescence, 33*(3), 221–233.

Saarilehto, S., Keskinen, S., Lapinleimu, H., Helenius, H., & Simell, O. (2001). Connections between parental eating attitudes and children's meagre eating. Questionnaire findings. *Acta Paediatrica, 90*(3), 333–338.

Sands, R. G., Koppelman, N., & Solomon, P. (2004). Maternal custody status and living arrangements of children of women with severe mental illness. *Health & Social Work, 29*(4), 317–325.

Segrin, C. (1998). Disrupted interpersonal relationships and mental health problems. In W. R. Cupach & B. H. Spitzberg (Eds.), *The dark side of close relationships* (pp. 327–365). Mahwah, NJ: Erlbaum.

Seipp, C., & Johnston, C. (2005). Mother–son interactions in families of boys with attention-deficit/hyperactivity disorder with and without oppositional behavior. *Journal of Abnormal Child Psychology, 33*(1), 87–98.

Shearn, J., & Todd, S. (2000). Maternal employment and family responsibilities: The perspectives of mothers of children with intellectual disabilities. *Journal of Applied Research in Intellectual Disabilities, 13*(3), 109.

Slesnick, N., & Waldron, H. B. (1997). Interpersonal problem-solving interactions of depressed adolescents and their parents. *Journal of Family Psychology, 11*(2), 234–245.

Smith, M. (2004). Parental mental health: Disruptions to parenting and outcomes for children. *Child and Family Social Work, 9*(1), 3–11.

Stephens, M. A. P., & Townsend, A. L. (1997). Stress of parent care: Positive and negative effects of women's other roles. *Psychology and Aging, 12*(2), 376–386.

Stephens, M. A. P., Townsend, A. L., Martire, L. M., & Druley, J. A. (2001). Balancing parent care with other roles: Interrole conflict of adult daughter caregivers. *Journal of Gerontology: Psychological Sciences, 56B*, 24–34.

Tebes, J. K., Kaufman, J. S., Adnopoz, J., & Racasin, G. (2001). Resilience and family psychological processes among children of parents with serious mental disorders. *Journal of Child & Family Studies, 10*(1), 115–136.

Thomas, A. M., Forehand, R., & Neighbors, B. (1995). Change in maternal depressive mood: Unique contributions to adolescent functioning over time. *Adolescence, 30*(117), 43–52.

Thorne, A., McLean, K. C., & Dasbach, A. (2004). When parents' stories go to pot: Telling personal transgressions to teenage kids. In M. W. Pratt & B. E. Fiese (Eds.), *Family stories and the lifecourse: Across time and generations* (pp. 187–209). Mahwah, NJ: Erlbaum.

Tunali, B., & Power, T. G. (2002). Coping by redefinition: Cognitive appraisals in mothers of children with autism and children without autism. *Journal of Autism and Developmental Disorders, 32*(1), 25–34.

Waller, G., & Calam, R. (1994). Parenting and family factors in eating problems. In L. Alexander-Mott & D. B. Lumsden (Eds.), *Understanding eating disorders: Anorexia nervosa, bulimia nervosa, and obesity* (pp. 61–76). Philadelphia: Taylor & Francis.

Warner, V., Weissman, M. M., Mufson, L., & Wickramaratne, P. J. (1999). Grandparents, parents, and grandchildren at high risk for depression: A three-generation study. *Journal of the American Academy of Child and Adolescent Psychiatry, 38*(3), 289–296.

Wechselblatt, T., Gurnick, G., & Simon, R. (2000). Autonomy and relatedness in the development of anorexia nervosa: A clinical case series using grounded theory. *Bulletin of the Menninger Clinic, 64*, 91–99.

Whalen, C. K., Henker, B., Jamner, L. D., Ishikawa, S. S., Floro, J. N., Swindle, R., et al. (2006). Toward mapping daily challenges of living with ADHD: Maternal and child perspectives using electronic diaries. *Journal of Abnormal Child Psychology, 34*(1), 111–126.

Wonderlich, S. (1992). Relationship of family and personality factors in bulimia. In J. H. Crowther, D. L. Tennenbaum, & S. E. Hobfoll (Eds.), *The etiology of bulimia nervosa: The individual and familial context* (pp. 103–126). Washington, DC: Hemisphere.

Wright, K. (2002). Social support within an online cancer community: An assessment of emotional support, perceptions of advantages and disadvantages, and motives for using the community. *Journal of Applied Communication Research, 30*(3), 195–209.

Section 2: Research Examples _____

Talking with Your Children about Alcohol and Other Drugs: Are Parents the Antidrug?

Michelle Miller-Day

As addressed in Section 1, the connections between parent communication about drugs and alcohol and teen use are somewhat unclear. Nonetheless, parents want to be able to impact the odds of their teens experimenting with these substances. In this article, Miller-Day discusses research related to parent–child communication about these topics. As you read, consider the patterns of communication regarding drugs and alcohol in your own family of origin and how those may have related to your behavior as a teen.

L.B.A.

So, what is the problem? The problem is that alcohol and other drug use is linked to more than 40% of all academic problems among college students and 28% of all college dropouts. Of the nearly 12 million undergraduates in the United States, statistics indicate that 240,000 to 360,000 students will ultimately die from substance use–related causes (Eigen, 1991). According to the American Council for Drug Education (2005), more than 90% of college students say that drinking is a central part of social life and nearly half of all Americans over the age of 12 are consumers of alcohol, with as many as 4.5 million adolescents classified as alcoholics.

In terms of smoking tobacco products, the health risks to smokers include various smoking-related diseases such as lung cancer, emphysema, and heart attacks (Department of Health and Human Services [DHHS], 2001). Moreover, cigarette smoking is one of the leading causes of preventable death and results in over 400,000 deaths each year (American Cancer Society, 1996).

Yet, even when not abused, substance use is a problem. Experimentation with drugs alone may interfere with student's social skills, academics, sleep, and overall health.

But, what can parents do about their kids' use of alcohol and other drugs, especially when they are away at college? Organizations such as the Partnership for a Drug-Free America (PDFA) encourage parents to converse with their offspring about the risks of drug use. Slogans such as "Parents—the Anti-Drug" are exclaimed in a plethora of media to stimulate parental influence in adolescent drug prevention efforts. The goal of the Surgeon General of America (2000), National Institute on Drug Abuse (NIDA, 2000), and the PDFA (2002, 2005) is to empower parents to address issues of drugs and drug use *before* offspring are at highest risk for drug use and abuse. A report by NIDA (2000) suggests that parent–offspring interaction is an important predictor of offspring's negative drug attitudes, and that conservative drug use norms may protect youth against future risk of negative outcomes. Yet, according to PDFA (2005), results from its seventeenth annual tracking study of parents' attitudes toward drugs and teen drug use revealed that the current generation of parents—the most drug-experienced group on record—saw less risk in a wide variety of illicit drugs, and were significantly less likely to be talking with their teens about drugs, when compared to moms and dads in the early 2000s. This report also found that the number of parents who report never talking with their child about drugs has doubled in the past six years, from 6 percent in 1998 to 12 percent in 2004. Most parents believe it is important to discuss alcohol and other drug use with their children and say they would be upset if their child experimented with drugs; however, fewer than one in three teens (roughly 30 percent) say they've learned a lot about the risks of drugs at home (PDFA, 2005).

There has been a significant initiative in the United States in the early twenty-first century to encourage parents to talk with their elementary- through college-aged offspring about drugs and drug use. It is not clear, however, what these dialogues sound like. What is the content of parental talk about the risks of alcohol, tobacco, and other drugs? How do they occur? The following section reveals some of the central elements to parent–offspring *drug talks* as revealed in a series of studies by me and my colleagues.

What Do Parents and Their Offspring Recall about the Talk?

Of those parents and students who recall their drug talks, these talks can be classified into parental approaches of a *my* responsibility orientation, a *your* responsibility orientation, and an *our* responsibility orientation. According to Miller-Day (2002a), a "my responsibility orientation" contains strategies that are oriented toward the parent assuming most of the responsibility for monitoring and sanctioning a child's choices and emphasizes conformity rather than conversation. This orientation toward talking about drugs includes threatening punishment, establishing a no-tolerance rule, and rewarding offspring for nonuse. Conceptually, these strategies emphasized the power of the parent to establish standards, seek compliance, and provide rewards or punishments. A "your responsibility orientation" contains strategies that are oriented toward the child's responsibilities for his or her own drug use choices. These strategies encouraged offspring to use their own judgment and required them to pay for their own substances. By relegating the responsibility for drug choices to the child, the parent abdicates his or her responsibility. Finally, an "our responsibility orientation" contains strategies that are oriented toward mutual responsibility and discourse: talking together about the risks of drug use (unrestricted flow of information between parent and offspring) and merely "hinting" about expected behavior (restricted flow of information). Inherent in this factor is the parental assumption that he or she can make a contribution to the child's decision-making process and that messages of conservative drug use might contribute to that end. Although the parent may deliver these messages, it is implied in these strategies that the child will use the information contained in the messages to make his or her drug involvement choices. So, what are these messages? Both parents and offspring report that their talks about alcohol, tobacco, and other drugs typically frame drugs and drug use as a problem, with parents focusing on substantiating claims with evidence and providing both proscriptive and prescriptive information.

Framing Drugs and Drug Use as a Problem

As indicated in Miller-Day and Barnett (2004) and Miller-Day and Dodd (2004), in drug talks parents tend to frame drugs as problematic, emphasizing the negative effects of drugs, and provide offspring with two kinds of messages—warning of the dangers of drugs and messages of disappointment.

Warnings.   The most common warnings offered in these talks addressed the (il)legality of drugs, the effects of drugs on personal control, and health and safety consequences for use. Some parents emphasize the risk of incarceration for drug use and for other parents there was talk of jail terms and fines for parents who allowed their offspring to drink. The larger message was that "laws are meant to be obeyed." If they are not, there are potential consequences for the student's future.

Parents also warn that drugs and drug use could lead to feeling out of control, with potential consequences for health and safety. One respondent in Miller-Day and Dodd (2004) pointed out, "she reminded me that I could get addicted and I couldn't control it, it would control me." Another stated that "[the talk was to] remind me of what I could be like if I let alcohol control my life." One mother argued, "drinking could make a person lose control over their reasoning powers and allow a person to do something stupid."

Parents also warned about the consequences for losing control. The loss of control highlighted the importance of decision making and emphasized that "the choices [offspring] make during these years could influence [them] for their entire life." One parent in Miller-Day (2005) said:

> Subjects like these have always been discussed rather informally in our home. . . . The message we always tried to relate was threefold: laws were meant to be obeyed, you never know what can happen if you lose control, and substance abuse can destroy your future. (p. 15)

Interestingly, metaphors of "control" seem also to be important to adolescents who use drugs. Miller, Alberts, Hecht, Trost, and Krizek (2000) reported that in a study comparing language use of adolescents who were high risk for drug use (reported use or abuse) and low risk (no use and low intension to use), that high-risk youth tended to equate drugs with having a sense of personal control—gaining control in their life—rather than a loss of control. It was the low-risk youth who viewed drug use as a potential loss of control. Parents may be trying to address the attitude that drugs are about person control with these control-related prevention messages, making it clear that an individual chooses whether to use drugs or not and this choice might ultimately alter the direction of one's life.

The final control-related warning included threats to health and safety—in some cases victimization. Many parents in these studies report they warn their offspring about others spiking their drink or taking advantage of them. One student reported, "[My mom] told me to put a napkin over my drink or keep my hand over it, so that no one can drop something in it while I'm turned away." Parents emphasize the importance of monitoring intake because "whatever you take into your body has [health] consequences."

Other parents warn of potential harm to self and others when "under the influence." One father in Miller-Day and Dodd (2004) admitted his strategy was to convince his daughter that drug use "may lead to doing unwanted things and can even cause rape" (p. 77). Still other parents emphasize shared stories of how parents can be unintended victims for their offspring's use, such as parents held financially and legally liable for a car accident that occurred after the teen driver had been drinking in their home.

Conveying Disapproval.   Parents and offspring also report the use of expressing outright disapproval of drugs and drug use. In another study, Walker, Hamrick, McLaren and Miller-Day (2005) found that parents who conveyed disapproval fell into two groups: (1) those who conveyed disapproval to "get it on the record" that they talked with their child about the topic even though they were convinced he or she would experiment with drugs regardless, and (2) those clearly stated disapproval for drug use and outlined clear expectations for nonuse behavior. For those in the first group, parents would often claim disapproval of use but then articulate an expectation that alcohol and other drug use is normative. For example, one student in Miller-Day and Dodd (2004) recalled the following conversation:

> My dad tried to tell me that marijuana is a gateway drug into the worse drugs. But I told him that I wouldn't do anything else but marijuana. He told me he used to smoke weed, and sometimes he still does. But he told me to watch out for myself and to be a responsible person. He said that even though he's giving me this lecture. . . . He knows that this talk isn't going to stop me from smoking weed once in a while. He was absolutely right. But what the talk did do is . . . that every time I smoke, I think about what drugs this possibly can lead me into and I get grossed out hence I rarely ever smoke. Maybe once in a blue moon. (p. 78)

For the second group of parents, disapproval is often tied to parental disappointment *in* the child. If these parents' kids use drugs they express personal disappointment and dissatisfaction with the child as a person. Many offspring report that their parents would be personally disappointed in them if they were aware of their alcohol or other drug use because the expectation is that they do not use. Drug use for these parents is framed as a person failure or a character flaw. One student in Miller-Day and Dodd (2004) remembered, "[My mother] stated that if you ever want to kill me, then you will do drugs. Obviously, I wouldn't want that to happen so, I don't think I will ever try them" (p. 78).

In addition to problemitizing drugs in parent–offspring drug talks, *what* parents and offspring talk about often includes the use of evidence to support claims, and proscriptions and prescriptions for behavior. Here are a few examples of each that were found in both Miller-Day and Dodd (2004) and Walker et al. (2005).

Evidence

Use of Personal Examples.   In talking with their offspring about drugs, parents will often provide personal accounts of how their own life and the lives of friends and family members were affected by drugs or drug use. Clearly, most parents do want to protect their offspring from risk, but this becomes an awkward situation when the parent him or herself has used illicit substances in the past (or currently). As the PDFA (2005) survey points out, today's parents might not regard drug use as seriously as past generations of parents. So, they ask themselves what of their personal experiences they should or should not share with their children. One mother in Walker et al. (2005) said that she "told [her son] about many different things that happened in my life. I used to smoke and he knows that. He and his sister encouraged me to stop. I did tell him that I had never tried other drugs, even when it was popular" (p. 11). Personal examples of how difficult it is to stop smoking is a common personal example that may be particularly persuasive in these talks since many children witness the difficulty firsthand.

Experiences of family members and friends may also be utilized as evidence to support claims of the harmful effects of drugs. Stories of a relative's struggle with use or abuse provide illustrative material that tends to increase the immediacy of parental message. According to Parrott (1995), when a person pays attention to a personal story, he or she will expend more cognitive effort to process the message, thereby enhancing recall. Enhanced recall would increase the chances that offspring would retain the message and use it when faced with drug use situations. The finding that parents with a history of drug use take their offspring's use "less seriously" than parents of previous generations concerns prevention experts and many parent-training program developers appear to be unsure how to design intervention messages for parents who use or who have used drugs (including alcohol). Perhaps, as these data suggest, a strategy for these parents might be to integrate personal stories into the conversation rather than ignoring the issue or their own experiences.

Written Evidence.   Some parents use written materials, such as information they find on the Internet. For example, this mother's approach reported in Miller-Day and Dodd (2004), "My husband uses tobacco products that I disapprove of, but he is a grown man. David must make his own decisions. More than once I cut articles from the paper to show them BOTH the dangers of smoking to health" (p. 79). Reportedly, only 5% or fewer parents make use of written materials in their antidrug socialization (Miller-Day & Dodd, 2004; Walker et al., 2005). It appears that most parents rely on personal examples to support the messages they provide offspring.

The "Shoulds" and "Should Nots"

In addition to problemitizing drugs and providing evidence, parents also tend to offer advice about what offspring should or should not do or believe. This information falls into four primary categories: tools for healthy living, guidelines and rules, using your own judgment, and sanctions for violations.

Tools for Healthy Living.   Parents often provide their offspring with advice on how to get through difficult situations such as drinking and driving, peer pressure, and just making good decisions. As one mother said in Walker et al. (2005), "We impressed upon [our daughter] that she might not have control over the behavior of her friends, so we were relying upon her to have the common sense to walk away from a bad situation" (p. 13). This mother offered her daughter several "tools" for handling difficult situations. Another parent in Miller-Day and Dodd (2004) recalled:

> We talked about what I should do in situations where others are using drugs and what to do if I ever did decided to do drugs and how to handle friends and peer pressure and if they were to ever overdose in any other situations. (p. 79)

Guidelines and Rules.   There is evidence that some parents articulate a no-tolerance rule in their households, others provide guidelines. Some offspring are told to *never* drink, smoke, or do drugs or there would be negative consequences. Others are given more general guidelines, such as these students in Walker et al. (2005):

My mom told me that she expected me to act responsibly while in Canada and not to get out of control and drink too much. They also told me to act like they taught me and to be responsible and respectful. (p. 13)

If you are going to drink, don't mix alcohol with sweet drinks, it will make you sick. Eat substantial food before going out for the night, stick with tonic or water as mixers, or drink beer. Don't drink and drive or ride with anyone who has been drinking, walk to the parties with a friend and walk home with a friend. If you are ever in a questionable situation, call home, dad or I will come get you. (p. 14)

Generally, when there is talk of rules and guidelines, there tends to be more flexibility surrounding alcohol and tobacco use, especially as youth enter college—although illegal drug use (e.g., marijuana, cocaine, and inhalants) is generally pronounced as "against the rules."

Make Your Own Decisions.   As offspring move from adolescence into young adulthood, parents may rely more on the "your responsibility" approach and send messages about using good judgment and making wise decisions when it comes to alcohol and other drug use. The following account from a mom in Miller-Day and Dodd (2004) illustrates one parent's emphasis on making good choices:

My attitude as a parent was I started very early conveying attitudes about any drug use, or abuse, about over the counter drugs, prescriptions, etc. They were raised to make the decision and if a bad one take the consequences. Any discussion about substance abuse fit into the general scheme of things. No big deal was made, it was not made out to be any different than wearing a coat in sub zero weather. (p. 80)

Penalties.   If parents expect their offspring to abstain from use or to comply with the family rules regarding use (e.g., responsible moderation), there are often penalties associated with violating those expectations. But a small percentage of parents actually discuss these penalties. Penalties are often hinted at, but not directly stated in conversation. For example, one student in Walker et al. (2005) shared, "Although my parents never really sat down and talked with me about drugs, bit I know if I did I could kiss off ever getting a dime from them again" (p. 12).

Moving beyond the content of parent–offspring discussions, it is also interesting to examine how these talks occur. The following outlines findings regarding "how" these talks transpire.

How Do These Talks Transpire?

One of the most interesting findings in this line of research is the emergence of four dimensions that describe a *typology* of parent–offspring discussions—how these drug talks occur. The four types are ongoing direct and indirect and targeted direct and indirect.

Ongoing Talk

Direct.   The majority of parents and youth who do participate in drug talks seem to have done so across a period of time, often starting the talks in early childhood. This approach tends to be one where discussion of the topic is ongoing a part of the natural fabric of everyday life (Miller-Day 2002b). Direct verbal messages are shared that clearly articulate attitudes or expectations regarding drugs. The following excerpts illustrate this parental approach to antidrug socialization:

> My parents would always bring up the situation about tobacco use, drugs, or alcohol whenever it was on TV or brought up in another conversation. They did this to me basically from when I was in elementary school, until I left for college. (Miller-Day & Dodd, 2004, p. 81)

> Little comments here or there. A trickle of ideas that kind of got it soaked into her brain. (Walker et al., 2005, p. 13)

These exchanges tend to be casual, with an open flow of information between parents and offspring.

Indirect.   An alternative to weaving antidrug messages into the fabric of the daily conversation is to indirectly convey messages in daily interaction. These indirect messages include cues such as hints or nonverbal messages. Sometimes people refer to this approach as "walking the talk." Research is very clear that parental use of substances (e.g., alcohol or tobacco) increases the likelihood that offspring will also use (Henriksen & Jackson, 1998). So, it is not surprising that abstinence from substances and everyday behaviors that convey the message that use is unacceptable provide a strong message of nonuse to offspring.

Targeted Conversations

Direct.   Targeted conversations most closely resemble the "sit down let's have a talk" one-shot discussions advocated in some media campaigns and, again, are direct and also indirect in nature. Direct targeted conversations are explicit conversations or comments articulating rules, behaviors, attitudes, or expectations about drugs and drug use. These conversations tend to be inspired by upcoming events (e.g., before prom or before offspring goes to college), or in reaction to an event (e.g., finding drugs in the offspring's bedroom or knowledge of offspring's drunkenness). These targeted conversations focus expressly on the topic of alcohol or other drugs and are often specific to a particular event or situation.

Indirect.   Indirect targeted conversations are targeted at specific events or situations, but are less direct and rely more heavily on nonverbal messages of disapproval. For example, one student in Miller-Day and Dodd (2004) reported, "My father made comments like so and so's parents must be so disappointed, I know you would never do anything like that" (p. 78) and a student in Miller-Day (2002) recalled, "She saw me reach for the beer in the fridge and she just gave me 'that look' and so I reached for a can of Pepsi instead" (p. 612).

Despite the fact that communication may not be very clear, parents suggest that youth generally "get the message." Again, indirect targeted messages may be situational; that is, they occur only once or twice in specific memorable situations. This approach tends to establish drugs and drug use as a problem, but fails to provide evidence to support this problem orientation; nor does it provide guidelines for what offspring should or should not do in these situations.

Antidrug Socialization

Socialization refers to the deliberate shaping of individuals to conform to expectations. As the research illustrates, parental antidrug socialization efforts tend to be integrated into everyday life or targeted efforts. Parents who pursue integrated socialization efforts make a series of ongoing comments about drugs and integrate that talk into the fabric of the family's everyday life. When this kind of discourse is woven into daily interactions, the topic becomes "no big deal." Integrated approaches to socializing youth about family norms regarding drug use cast parents into the role of ongoing agents of socialization throughout a child's development. Targeted socialization efforts, however, tend to be limited to a particular point or few points in time during the offspring's development. As one student stated in Miller-Day and Dodd (2004), "one talk is better than no talk" (p. 86). These conversations happened typically before some kind of an event where the likelihood of drug use was increased, such as before prom or a party. "Drug talks" as characterized in many media representations fit into this approach, encouraging parents to sit down and share conversational partner's attitudes, expectations, and rules about drug use. Yet, the question remains—are parents the antidrug?

The research findings offer a number of different pathways for understanding parent–student drug talks. Based on the evidence in the Miller-Day et al. studies, certain pathways are currently being tested to assess effectiveness in preventing later drug use by adolescents. In this line of research the pathway predicted to be most effective is one in which there is ongoing discourse, by both parents with the youth, motivated by his or her health, that occurs proactively and reactively, at home, providing personal examples and offering tools for healthy living while also establishing clear guidelines and penalties for violations.

A typology of parent–offspring drug talks like the one presented here can guide parents in their antidrug socialization efforts, but the question remains—does it matter? Does any amount of talk really influence youth to abstain from alcohol, tobacco, or other drug use? If it does, are there developmentally appropriate messages to use when the child is in elementary school? Middle school? High school? And even college? These are family communication questions for the next decade; what do you think?

Questions for Consideration and Discussion

1. Statistics suggest that almost half of college academic problems and almost a third of dropouts are related to drug or alcohol use. How does this resonate with your experiences as a college student?
2. Some antidrug campaigns (i.e., Parents—the Anti-Drug) suggest that parental communication and monitoring have a significant effect on adolescent use. What do you see as the benefits and drawbacks, for parents, of such campaigns?
3. Miller-Day notes that parental communication often focuses on the negatives of drug and alcohol use. As someone who has likely experienced such communication, how do you feel teens respond to this negative focus?
4. Clearly, as a child grows from early childhood to late adolescents, communication about drugs and alcohol will change. How do you envision such talk changing over childhood?
5. Miller-Day suggests that this typology of parent talk could be used in a study of the effects of parent–child communication about drugs and alcohol. How might such a study be structured?

References

American Cancer Society. (1996). *Cancer facts & figures—1996*. Atlanta, GA: Author.

American Council for Drug Education. (2005). *American Council for Drug Education fact sheet*. Retrieved July 5, 2005, from www.acde.org/health/Research .htm

Department of Health and Human Services. (2001). *Testimony on tobacco before the Senate Committee on Labor and Human Resources*. Retrieved July 7, 2005, from www.hhs.gov/asl/testify/ t980210e.html

Eigen, L. D. (1991). *Alcohol practices, policies and potentials of American colleges and universities: An OSAP white paper*. Rockville, MD: U.S. Department of Health and Human Services, Office for Substance Abuse Prevention.

Henrickson, L., & Jackson, C. (1998). Anti-smoking socialization: Relationship to parent and child smoking status. *Health Communication, 10*(1), 87–101.

Miller, M., Alberts, J. K., Hecht, M. L., Trost, M., & Krizek, R. L. (2000). *Adolescent relationships and drug use*. Mahwah, NJ: Erlbaum.

Miller-Day, M. (2002a). *Parental strategies to prevent underage alcohol and other drug use: Parental communication orientation, and college students' reported drug use*. Paper presented at the National Communication Association Convention held in New Orleans, LA.

Miller-Day, M. (2002b). Parent–adolescent communication about alcohol, tobacco, and other drug use. *Journal of Adolescent Research, 17*, 604–616.

Miller-Day, M. (2005). U.S. parent-offspring discourse about alcohol and other drugs. *Language and Communication Journal, 10*, 10–18.

Miller-Day, M., & Barnett, J. (2004). "I'm not a druggie": Adolescents' ethnicity and (erroneous) beliefs about drug use norms. *Health Communication, 16*, 207–231.

Miller-Day, M., & Dodd, A. (2004). Toward a descriptive model of parent–offspring communication about alcohol and other drugs. *Journal of Social and Personal Relationships, 21*(1), 73–95.

National Institute on Drug Abuse. (2000). Developing successful drug abuse prevention programs. *NIDA Notes, 14*(6). Retrieved April 2, 2005, from www.nida.nih.gov/NIDA_notes/NNVol14N6/tear off.html

Parrott, R. (1995). Motivation to attend to health messages: Presentation of content and linguistic considerations. In E. Maibach & R. Parrott (Eds.), *Designing health messages: Approaches from communication theory and public health practice* (pp. 7–23). Thousand Oaks, CA: Sage.

Partnership for a Drug-Free America. (2002). *2001–2002 Partnership for a Drug-Free America annual report*. Retrieved April 2, 2005, from www. drug free.org/acrobat/PDFA_Annual_Report_2001_ 2002.pdf

Partnership for a Drug-Free America. (2005). *2004 Partnership Attitude Tracking Study (PATS)*. Analysis of National Center for Health Statistics by Child Trends. Retrieved April 2, 2005, from www.drug freeamerica.org/

Surgeon General of America. (2000). *Reducing tobacco use: A report of the surgeon general*. Retrieved April 2, 2005, from www.cdc.gov/tobacco/sgr/sgr_2000/ index.htm

Walker, A., Hamrick, K., McLaren, R., & Miller-Day, M. (2005). *Parent–offspring communication about alcohol and other drugs: A replication and extension*. Paper presented at the Southern States Communication Convention, Memphis, TN.

Disability in the Family: Stories Real and Imagined

Elaine Bass Jenks

Dena G. Beeghly

Reading (and being read to) is an important part of the childhood experience. As children experience literature, they see reflections of themselves, and reflections of others. Our understandings of life experiences, including the family experience, is impacted by what we see in fictional accounts of childhood. In this work, Jenks and Beeghly apply this understanding to an analysis of disability in children's literature. They compare representations of childhood disability, and in particular visual impairment, with the lived experiences of families with a visually-impaired child, and discuss the ramifications of the diffrences they find. This work indicates the importance of making connections between what we learn about self and others in literature of childhood, and our own lived experiences, understandings, and beliefs.

L.B.A.

Naomi knows when it's springtime (Kroll, 1993); Oscar has a secret code (Rau, 1998); Hershel makes beautiful cookies from images he sees dancing in his head (Goldin, 1991); Nellie can tell that her family is near the ocean before her brothers can (Condra, 1994); and Sarah doesn't bump into things when a blown fuse causes the lights to go out (Rodriguez, 2000). What Naomi, Oscar, Hershel, Nellie, and Sarah have in common is that they are children who are characters in picture books. And even though there are thousands of children who are characters in picture books, what sets apart these children is that all five are blind.

This article explores disability, specifically blindness and visual impairment, in the family. Much research has been done on the topic of children who are blind or visually impaired (e.g., Ammerman, Van Hasselt, Herson, & Moore, 1989; Baird, Mayfield, & Baker, 1997; Behl, Akers, Boyce, & Taylor, 1996; Dote-Kwan 1995; Dote-Kwan & Hughes 1994; Kekelis & Prinz 1996; Loots, Devise, & Sermijn, 2003; Masino & Hodapp, 1996; Nixon, 1988). This article focuses on children who are blind or visually impaired living in families where the other family members are fully sighted.

We approach the topic of children with disabilities from an interdisciplinary perspective. Jenks (2002, 2003, 2005) has researched communication and visual impairment in the family, and Beeghly & Prudhoe (2002) have researched children's literature in the classroom. For this study, we combine our interests and experience in comparing the narratives of parents raising children who are blind and visually impaired to the narratives of children who are blind or visually impaired that are depicted in children's books. We are particularly interested in the family relationships presented in each of these narratives. Before comparing the narratives, we briefly introduce the topics of communication and visual impairment, the inclusive classroom, and the research methods employed in this study.

Communication and Visual Impairment

There are two main reasons this topic of communication and disability, specifically blindness and visual impairment, has just begun to be studied (Thompson, 2000). First, the model of disability is changing from a medical model to a social model. The medical model of disability emphasizes changing the person to fit the environment, whereas the social model emphasizes changing the environment to fit the person (Quinn, 1998). The second reason is that we don't feel comfortable talking about the topic of communication and disability in the United States.

We are taught from a young age not to talk about disability. Actually, what we're taught is more than not talking about disability; we're taught to ignore disability, to pretend we don't see it, to pretend it doesn't exist. The irony here is that we're taught to ignore disability in the name of politeness (Goffman, 1959). We're taught, and we grow up to teach our children, that the polite choice when meeting people who are different is to not mention the way(s) in which that person is different. It's not that adults don't notice these differences. It's that adults have been taught that it's impolite to stare, ask questions, or mention differences of any sort.

Thus, children who are blind and visually impaired are being raised in families that live in a society in which the model of disability is changing from a medical model to a social model and in which individuals are taught to ignore differences. Families aren't given instructions on how to raise their children who are blind or visually impaired in a sighted world. And no one is given instructions on how to talk about disability.

Inclusive Classrooms

The Education for All Handicapped Children Act (U.S. Public Law 94–142) was passed in 1975 (Perkins-Gough, Snyder, & Licciardi, 2003) and the Americans with Disabilities Act (ADA) was passed in 1990 (Shapiro, 1994). These laws and their amendments prohibit discrimination on the basis of disability (Potok, 2002). Thus, in the past 30 years, more children with disabilities, including children who are blind or visually impaired, are being educated in general education classroom settings. However, teachers, just like family members, aren't taught how to talk about disability.

Schools are adjusting to the changing model of disability. Public schools are required to educate all children in the least restrictive environment. This means that students with and without disabilities now learn together in what are known as "inclusive classrooms." However, simply being together in the same classrooms doesn't automatically lead to an appreciation and acceptance of those with disabilities (Andrews, 1998; Guinagh, 1980).

If we are to have classrooms where all learners are valued and none are ignored, teachers must provide opportunities for students to learn about and talk about disabilities (Hudson, Reisberg, & Wolf, 1983; Mosio, 1994; Stoler, 1992.) All children benefit from using materials that are inclusive in terms of content and illustrations. When students with disabilities read and learn about children who look like them, do things they do, and have families like they have, it is plain that they belong and are a valued part of the classroom community. Children without disabilities who are exposed to inclusive materials also begin to understand that disabilities are part of the mix of life, and that all children should be equally valued.

Using children's literature is an effective way to begin conversations about differences and disabilities (Andrews, 1998; Bauer, 1985; Blaska & Lynch, 1998; Nasatir & Horn, 2003; Saunders, 2000; Smith-D'Arezzo, 2003). When stories with realistic, accurate portrayals of children with disabilities and their families are part of the curriculum, the message is clear: Disabilities are part of the world in which we live. We don't need to ignore them; we can talk about them.

Research Methods

Our research on the topic of communication and visual impairment is ethnographic in nature. For this project, we compared two cultural artifacts that tell stories about disability in the family. We worked from interviews with parents and teachers of children with disabilities collected over a seven-year period in both academic and social settings. These data, although filled with individual stories, tell a cultural narrative about actually living with disability. We also worked from children's picture books about blindness and visual impairment. The goal of this section is to compare narratives of experience with narratives of imagination found in texts available to teachers in inclusive classrooms and to parents in libraries.

The narratives of experience come from interview transcripts and observation notes collected over the past seven years (Jenks, 2002, 2003, 2005). This research on communication and visual impairment is not a traditional study in the sense of having a set time and place during which the research is conducted. Over the past seven years, stories have been collected at camps and educational institutions that children and adolescents who are blind and visually impaired attend, and at athletic events for individuals of all ages who are blind or visually impaired. These stories have been collected both formally, during interviews recorded on audiotape, as well as informally, during conversations recorded in fieldnotes.

The narratives of imagination come from children's fiction. We studied children's literature as objects of culture in which these children live. We chose to limit this report to children's picture books about blindness and visual impairment. Using suggestions from the National Library Service for the Blind and Physically Handicapped (www.loc.gov/nls), we closely read 18 children's picture books that appear on a list of "Books Featuring Characters Who Are Visually Impaired" found on the Web sites of the Iowa Braille School (2004) and the Texas School for the Blind and Visually Impaired (2004). We checked out these 18 picture books from our public library because we wanted to be sure we were looking at books that could actually be obtained by individuals who weren't writing book chapters on the topic. The following narrative comparison focuses on only 14 of these stories, as two of the books we read had seeing-eye guide dogs as the main characters (Lang, 2001; Rossiter, 1997) and two others depict main characters who are adults who are blind, not children (Gellman, 1992; Keats, 1971).

We were particularly interested in the messages about families that are communicated through these books. Using a previous study on young adult literature (Caroll & Rosenblum, 2000), we chose to focus on the realistic portrayal of disability depicted in these books. We read the books studying the accuracy of the information about blindness and visual impairment that is presented as well as the presence or absence of stereotypical or romanticized depictions of disability (Caroll & Rosenblum, 2000). Further, because we read children's picture books, we were also interested in the visual images present in these books.

We view the children's literature we've studied as a place where fully sighted individuals can learn about blindness or visual impairment. Reading stories about children with disabilities allows young people to both avoid their parents' rules of politeness (Goffman, 1959) in relation to disability and to begin to learn how to talk about difference.

After we read the children's picture books, we identified two main themes the children's fiction centered on in relation to the portrayal of visual disability—wearing glasses and being blind. Using these two themes, along with the third theme of family communication, we outlined how each fiction book portrayed each theme. After the thematic analysis of the picture books was complete, we searched for discussions of wearing glasses, being blind, and family communication in the interview transcripts and conversation fieldnotes. Using the stories told to us by parents and teachers of children who are blind or visually impaired, we then compared what the picture books portrayed to what the parents and teachers said they experienced. Thus, our assumptions about the accuracy of the information about blindness and visual impairment depicted in the children's books are based on the reported experiences of individuals who have daily contact with individuals who are blind or visually impaired. In the following narrative comparison, we describe how the details of each theme are presented in the picture books, followed by a description of how these same details are experienced in everyday life by parents and teachers of children who are blind and visually impaired.

Narrative Comparison

Wearing Glasses

Of the 18 children's picture books we read, we were initially surprised to find that 5 of these books focus on children getting glasses for the first time. In all five of these books (Brown, 1979; Goodsell, 1965; Raskin, 1968; Smith, 1991; Wild, 1992), glasses treat the child's vision problem and by the end of the story, the child has corrected vision. The reason we were surprised is that we obtained the list of books from libraries for the blind, and we assumed that all of the characters depicted would be blind or visually impaired. Most people who wear glasses are not visually impaired. Visual impairment is defined as "a limitation of function that is not correctable by standard methods" (Ettinger 1994, p. 178). And glasses are the standard method of correction for vision problems.

However, wearing glasses is a potential "difference that makes a difference" (Bateson, 1979, p. 76) to a child. So we begin our analysis by examining the realistic portrayal of a child getting glasses in these picture books. Four of these picture books show unclear vision visually (Goodsell, 1965; Raskin, 1968; Smith, 1991; Wild, 1992). By that we mean that these books show what the child who needs glasses can see before he or she gets glasses. And in every case, the books show the child seeing the world as blurry. Although these visual depictions may be useful for fully sighted children who can't imagine what it's like to not see clearly, these same pictures are useless to children who are blind or visually impaired.

The other three books (Brown, 1979; Goodsell, 1965; Wild, 1992) contain more realistic portrayals of the differences children who need glasses experience. The Goodsell and Wild stories both talk about the child not knowing that other people can see differently. Goodsell's story also notes that other individuals believe the child in her story who needs glasses is shy because she doesn't wave back when she's waved at because she can't see the people waving. This is an important point for children in elementary school classrooms who may not have considered the fact that others are perceiving the world differently then they are. This teaches the idea that a physical difference may be the cause of a behavioral difference. We've had both parents and teachers tell us that behavioral attributions are often made about children who are blind or visually impaired including the assumptions that they are snobbish, clumsy, vain, and unable to speak for themselves or move without assistance.

All five books show the child going to an eye doctor and two even show the child visiting an optician (Goodsell, 1965; Raskin, 1968). Most important, four of the five books (all but Wild, 1992) show the child having an initial negative reaction to the thought of having to wear glasses. Brown's (1979) character, Arthur, has the most detailed negative reaction to wearing glasses, first trying to lose his glasses, then later hiding his glasses in his lunchbox and telling his teacher he lost them. Arthur doesn't like being different from his friends and his family, none of whom wear glasses. Our discussions with parents and teachers of children with disabilities confirms this sensation of children having initial negative reactions to not only glasses, but to all sorts of visual aids, from large print or Braille books to telescopes, magnifiers, and the need to sit near the front of the classroom.

Even though these books do a good job portraying children's experiences of not knowing they are perceiving the world differently than others, of having to go through a medical process in order to get glasses, and in having an initial negative reaction to having to wear glasses, these books do contain unrealistic aspects of children wearing glasses. Wild's (1992) character, Kate, is not only not hesitant about wearing glasses, but is immediately excited about needing glasses and even has a sister tell her how lucky she is to be getting glasses. Brown's (1979) character, Arthur, after finally wearing his glasses is able to perform better in school and at sports, making him instantly popular. In fact, Arthur is so popular that by the end of the story that his friend Francine gets a pair of glasses with clear glass in the lenses, just to be able to wear glasses, too.

Being Blind

Nine of the 18 picture books we read were stories about children who were blind or visually impaired (Condra, 1994; David, 2000; Fraustino, 2001; Goldin, 1991; Kroll, 1993; Litchfield, 1977; Martin & Archambault, 1987; Rau, 1998; Rodriguez, 2000). These stories range from an extremely realistic depiction of a child going blind (Litchfield, 1977), to a poetic fable about a child with "blind sight" (Fraustino, 2001, p. 5). What these books have in common is that the main character is a child and, with the exception of the book by Litchfield (1977), the child is already blind when the story begins.

A Cane in Her Hand by Litchfield (1977) is the only book that focuses on visual impairment, not blindness. This book describes the experiences of a girl who already "can't see very well" (Litchfield, 1977, p. 2) when the story begins. This girl, named Valerie, senses her vision is getting worse and experiences pain in one of her eyes. After a trip to the eye doctor, the rest of the story focuses on Valerie learning to use a white cane with a special teacher in a resource room at school. Valerie's exact diagnosis and terms like "orientation" and "mobility specialist" don't appear in the story, but we were encouraged by the author's attempt to realistically depict what Valerie was experiencing. At the start of the story, when Valerie feels her vision deteriorating, she's teased by her sister and her cousins, one of whom says, after Valerie trips, "Look where you're going. You blind or something?" (p. 5). At the end of the story, a stranger who sees Valerie in a store says, "She's such a pretty little girl. Too bad she can't see," to which Valerie replies, "I'm not deaf!" as she runs out of the store (p. 27).

There are some unrealistic aspects of Valerie's experience in this story, particularly in the description of how children at school react to Valerie using her white cane in the halls for the first time. Valerie is concerned about how her friends will feel, but the story reads, "They understood. It didn't make any difference to them" (Litchfield, 1977, p. 23). Regardless of her friends' instant acceptance of her use of a white cane, this story teaches the very important lesson that people don't have to live in total darkness to be blind.

The other eight books (Condra, 1994; David, 2000; Fraustino, 2001; Goldin, 1991; Kroll, 1993; Martin & Archambault, 1987; Rau, 1998; Rodriguez, 2000) all feature children who have no visual acuity as the main characters in the stories. This, in itself, is inaccurate, because very few people who are blind have no visual perception at all. Of the 10 million people in the United States who are considered blind or visually impaired, only 130,000 of these individuals (1.3%) have no light perception (American Foundation for the Blind, 2001).

Even though the concept of people who are blind living in the dark is easy for fully sighted individuals to understand, the concept of visual impairment or some sort of visual acuity between full sight and total darkness is difficult to imagine. The vast majority of individuals who are legally blind have enough vision to read large print (American Foundation for the Blind, 1999; Shapiro, 1994). Further, there are a lot of differences in visual perception among individuals who are visually impaired (American Foundation for the Blind, 1999). By depicting all eight of these fictional characters as totally blind, these authors continue the stereotype that the only sort of visual impairment that is not correctable by glasses is a world of total darkness.

There are some realistic elements in these books about children who are blind, including Brian's difficulty finding a door that his brother left open (Davis, 2000) and Sarah's (Rodriguez, 2000) concern about people leaving things on the stairs that she might trip over. Two other examples from these books include a realistic depiction of sibling rivalry between two brothers in *Brian's Bird* (Davis, 2000) and an accurate description of a slumber party in *Sarah's Sleepover* (Rodriguez, 2000). But, overall, these books are filled with inaccurate stereotypes about blindness ranging from Naomi (Kroll, 1993) and Nellie (Condra, 1994) being able to experience nature more fully than sighted individuals to Oscar, who is blind, teaching his friend Lucy, who is sighted, to instantly read Braille (Rau, 1998). Myths about people who are blind having special insight are reinforced in stories by Fraustino (2001) and Martin and Archambault (1987), and in *Cakes and Miracles* (Goldin, 1991) when an angel visits Hershel who is blind and tells him that he will be able to make beautiful cookies from images he sees in his dreams which, of course, he does.

It's good for sighted children in classrooms to be exposed to stories in which the main characters have a disability and, although it's good for children who are blind or visually impaired to have characters like themselves depicted in picture books, only two of these nine books (Litchfield, 1977; Rau, 1998) show the child attending school. However, no one but Valerie (Litchfield, 1977) uses a cane and only Oscar (Rau, 1998) reads Braille, when all of these children would use white canes and read Braille in real life.

The issue of children who are blind and visually impaired attending school with, but reading differently from, sighted children is one of the most dangerous omissions in these books. The question of how to educate children with disabilities continues to be a difficult issue for the families and teachers we interviewed. Parents of children who are blind and visually impaired first have to choose whether to send their children to general education settings or to schools for the blind. Other parents choose schools for the blind to allow their children to learn in an environment with other children who are blind or visually impaired. Other parents choose general education settings to allow their children to learn in an environment where not everyone shares the same visual acuity. The connection between the parents and teachers we've interviewed, and the previous research, is that parents hope teachers will help their children make their way in the world from both types of educational contexts (Hatlen, 2002; Muhlenhaupt, 2002).

Seven of these nine books (Condra, 1994; David, 2000; Fraustino, 2001; Goldin, 1991; Litchfield, 1977; Martin & Archambault, 1987; Rodriguez, 2000) depict sighted family members interacting with the main character who is blind. The family members range from parents (Condra, 1994; Davis, 2000; Goldin, 1991; Litchfield, 1977; Fraustino, 2001; Rodriguez, 2000) to siblings (Condra, 1994; Davis, 2000; Fraustino, 2001; Litchfield, 1977) to cousins (Litchfield, 1977; Fraustino, 2001; Rodriguez, 2000) to grandparents (Davis, 2000; Fraustino, 2001; Martin & Archambault, 1987).

With the exception of some slight sibling discord in Brian's Bird (Davis, 2000) and *See the Ocean* (Condra, 1994), all of the family members in these picture books are depicted as supportive of the child who is blind. The most understanding family members are the grandparents found in *Brian's Bird* (Davis, 2000), *The Hickory Chair* (Fraustino, 2001) and *Knots on a Counting Rope* (Martin & Archambault, 1987).

Further, none of these books contain examples of families in which more than one individual is blind even though a number of causes of blindness are inherited (American Foundation for the Blind, 2001). Whereas some children who are blind or visually impaired are the only member of their families who is not fully sighted, other children who are blind or visually impaired live in families in which more than one individual has low vision.

The most accurate description of how visual acuity affects, or actually doesn't affect, children's behavior appears at the end of *Katie's Magic Glasses* (Goodsell, 1965), where the author writes, "This is the end of the story. Of course, if it were a fairy tale, it wouldn't end here. You know what would happen next, don't you? Katie's magic glasses would transform her into a perfect little girl with perfect manners who lived happily ever after. But this isn't a fairy tale, and Katie went right on being Katie: Sometimes happy, sometimes mad, sometimes good, and sometimes bad" (p. 42).

Family Communication

The family communication that occurs in these books is presented in contrast to communication with friends. That is, families are portrayed as supportive of the child's need to wear glasses and friends are shown as nonsupportive, primarily through teasing and insulting the child who needs glasses for being different.

This presentation of family members as completely supportive does not mirror the interviews we've conducted. Specifically, teachers have noted a lack of parental support for some of their students with disabilities and parents have noted a lack of support from other family members in relation to their child's needs. Further, the lack of discord within families of the children who were blind in these picture books strikes us as unrealistic. Divorce statistics are higher in families of children with disabilities than they are in the general population (Ziolko, 1991). Moreover, researchers have found that parents of children with disabilities go through stages of adjustment in order to accept their child's disability (Tuttle, 1986) and that families of children with disabilities face more practical problems than other families (Ziolko, 1991).

The family members of children who are blind and visually impaired we interviewed reflect this research, not the children's literature depictions. That is, these parents report all sorts of family communication challenges, especially between their child and his or her siblings and with their extended family members, particularly grandparents, the very individuals who are portrayed as exceptionally understanding in the children's literature. Showing all family members easily getting along in picture books about children who are blind or visually impaired perpetuates the myth that living with a disability somehow makes us better people. In fact, the children who are depicted in these storybooks are so well behaved they seem somewhat unreal.

Children who are blind or visually impaired are being raised at a time when the model of disability is changing from a medical model to a social model that has allowed many more children with disabilities to be included in general education settings. We found a number of inaccuracies in the realistic portrayal of living with blindness in the picture books we studied in comparison to the parents and teachers we've interviewed. We also found stereotypes and myths of blindness perpetuated in these children's stories. However, we are most impressed that all 18 books portrayed the child with a disability, or a child who needed glasses, as being able. That is, there were no depictions of children being sent away from home because they are blind or visually impaired.

Further, in all 18 books there were a number of depictions of children who are blind, visually impaired, or just in need of glasses, participating in activities in which fully sighted children might participate. For example, Valerie (Litchfield, 1977), Kate (Wild, 1992) and Nellie (Condra, 1994) are shown swimming. Brian (Davis, 2000) is shown taking care of a pet bird. Sarah (Rodriguez, 2000) has a sleepover and gets snacks out of the cupboard for her guests. And the boy in *Knots on a Counting Rope* (Martin & Archambault, 1987) rides a horse. This focus on ability is echoed in the research we've conducted with parents and teachers. In fact, sometimes parents and teachers used one another as the example of people who have to be convinced that children who are blind and visually impaired are able. Parents cite teachers and teachers name parents, and everyone mentions strangers, as the individuals who need to be taught that children with disabilities are capable of accomplishing a wide variety of tasks, including learning.

In relation to education, we are concerned that very little classroom interaction was depicted in these books. With the exception of *Arthur's Eyes* (Brown, 1979), no teacher–student communication is portrayed. In Brown's book, Arthur's teacher is the person who convinces Arthur to finally wear his glasses by showing Arthur that he keeps glasses for reading, glasses that look "just like Arthur's" (p. 24) in his pocket. There are, however, no examples of parent–teacher communication in any of these storybooks, even though the individuals we've interviewed, as well as the previous research (e.g., Harniss, Epstein, Bursuck, Nelson, & Jayanthi, 2001), find that parent–teacher or home–school communication is extraordinarily important for children with disabilities.

In relation to family communication, we are concerned that only happy moments of family life are portrayed in these books. However, we find that these books emphasize the importance of the role of family members in the lives of children with disabilities. The adjustment of a child with a disability is directly affected by the family's adjustment to the disability (Ziolko, 1991). The families in these children's picture books are depicted as extremely supportive. Whereas continuous, upbeat behavior is not realistic, family support is paramount to children with disabilities.

The lessons for children who are blind, sighted, and visually impaired who are exposed to these books are that it is wrong to make fun of other children for being different, that family members support one another, and that children with disabilities are not unable. What we have learned through our interviews and observations is that no one is given instructions on how to talk about disability—not parents, not teachers, not children. Using children's literature in the classroom is one way to begin this conversation. When we talk about a disability, we learn that the disability does not define a person. When we demystify the disability, we have an opportunity to get to know the person. And when we get to know the person, we understand that although we are different we are also alike.

Questions for Consideration and Discussion

1. Jenks and Beeghly note that we do not, culturally or in family, receive instructions on how to talk about disability. If we did, what should such instructions "sound like"?
2. Several of the books on the list the researchers obtained were about children getting glasses. Why do you think this might be?
3. Jenks and Beeghly consider how children with visual impairment are portrayed in children's books and how that diverges from the experiences of actual parents and teachers of children with visual impairment. How might children's book authors better represent visual impairment issues?
4. This work focused on visual impairment. Do you think books about other physical/cognitive disabilities of children would be similar, more realistic, or less realistic? Why?

Children's Picture Books Analyzed

Brown, M. (1979). *Arthur's eyes*. Boston: Little, Brown.

Condra E. (1994). *See the ocean*. Nashville, TN: Ideals Children's Books.

Davis, P. A. (2000). *Brian's bird*. Morton Grove, IL: Albert Whitman.

Fraustino, L. R. (2001). *The hickory chair*. New York: Scholastic Press.

Gellman, E. (1992). *Jeremy's dreidel*. Rockville, MD: Kar-Ben Copies.

Goldin, B. D. (1991). *Cakes and miracles: A Purim tale*. New York: Viking.

Goodsell, J. (1965). *Katie's magic glasses*. Boston: Houghton Mifflin.

Keats, E. Z. (1971). *Apt. 3*. New York: Viking.

Kroll, V. L. (1993). *Naomi knows it's springtime*. Honesdale, PA: Boyd's Mill Press.

Lang, G. (2001). *Looking out for Sarah*. Watertown, MA: Talewinds.

Litchfield, A. B. (1977). *A cane in her hand*. Chicago: Albert Whitman.

Martin, B., & Archambault, J. (1987). *Knots on a counting rope*. New York: Henry Holt.

Raskin, E. (1968). *Spectacles*. New York: Atheneum.

Rau, D. M. (1998). *Secret code*. New York: Children's Press.

Rodriguez, B. (2000). *Sarah's sleepover*. New York: Viking.

Rossiter, N. P. (1997). *Rugby & Rosie*. New York: Dutton Children's Books.

Smith, L. (1991). *Glasses: Who needs 'em?* New York: Viking.

Wild, M. (1992). *All the better to see you with!* Morton Grove, IL: Albert Whitman.

References

American Foundation for the Blind. (1999). *What is low vision?* Retrieved from www.afb.org/info_document_view.asp?documentid=213

American Foundation for the Blind. (2001). *Statistics and sources for professionals.* Retrieved from www.afb.org/info_document_view.asp?document id=1367

Ammerman, R. T., Van Hasselt, V. B., Herson, M., & Moore, L. E. (1989). Assessment of social skills in visually impaired adolescents and their parents. *Behavioral Assessment, 11,* 327–351.

Andrews, S. E. (1998). Using inclusion literature to promote positive attitudes toward disabilities. *Journal of Adolescent & Adult Literacy, 41,* 420–426.

Baird, S. M., Mayfield, P., & Baker, P. (1997). Mothers' interpretations of the behavior of their infants with visual and other impairments during interactions. *Journal of Visual Impairment & Blindness, 91,* 467–483.

Bateson, G. (1979). *Mind and nature: A necessary unity.* Toronto, Canada: Bantam.

Bauer, C. J. (1985). Books can break attitudinal barriers toward the handicapped. *School Counselor, 32,* 302–306.

Beeghly, D. G., & Prudhoe, C. M. (2002). *Litlinks: Activities for connected learning in elementary classrooms.* New York: McGraw-Hill.

Behl, D. D., Akers, J. F., Boyce, G. C., & Taylor, M. J. (1996). Do mothers interact differently with children who are visually impaired? *Journal of Visual Impairment & Blindness, 90,* 501–511.

Blaska, J. K., & Lynch, E. C. (1998). Is everyone included? Using children's literature to facilitate the understanding of disabilities. *Young Children, 53,* 36–38.

Caroll, P. S., & Rosenblum, L. P. (2000). Through their eyes: Are characters with visual impairment portrayed realistically in young adult literature? *Journal of Adolescent & Adult Literacy, 43,* 620–630.

Dote-Kwan, J. (1995). Impact of mothers' interactions on the development of their young visually impaired children. *Journal of Visual Impairment & Blindness, 89,* 46–58.

Dote-Kwan, J., & Hughes, M. (1994). The home environments of young blind children. *Journal of Visual Impairment & Blindness, 88,* 31–42.

Ettinger, E. R. (1994). *Professional communications in eye care.* Boston: Butterworth-Heinemann.

Gill-Williamson, L. M. (1991). The impact of a visually impaired parent on a family's decision making. *Journal of Visual Impairment & Blindness, 85,* 246–248.

Goffman, E. (1959). *The presentation of self in everyday life.* New York: Doubleday Anchor Books.

Guinagh, H. (1980). The social integration of handicapped children. *Phi Delta Kappan, 62,* 27–29.

Harniss, M. K, Epstein, M. H., Bursuck, W. D., Nelson, J., & Jayanthi, M. (2001). Resolving homework related communication problems: Recommendations of parents with children with and without disabilities. *Reading & Writing Quarterly, 17,* 205–225.

Hatlien, P. (2002). The most difficult decision: How to share responsibility between local schools and schools for the blind. *Journal of Visual Impairment & Blindness, 96,* 747–750.

Hudson, F., Reisberg, R. E., & Wolf, R. (1983). Changing teachers' perceptions of mainstreaming. *Teacher Education and Special Education, 6,* 18–24.

Iowa Braille School. (2004). Books featuring characters who are visually impaired. Retrieved from www.iowabraille.k12.ia.us/bibliography_of_blind.html

Jenks, E. B. (2002). Searching for autoethnographic credibility: Reflections from a mom with a note pad. In A. P. Bochner & C. Ellis (Eds.), *Ethnographically speaking: Autoethnography, literature, and aesthetics* (pp. 170–186). Walnut Creek, CA: AltaMira Press.

Jenks, E. B. (2003). Sighted, blind, and in between: Similarity and difference in ethnographic inquiry. In R. P. Clair (Ed.), *Expressions of ethnography: Novel approaches to qualitative methods* (pp. 127–137). New York: State University of New York Press.

Jenks, E. B. (2005). Explaining disability: Parents stories of raising children with visual impairments in a sighted world. *Journal of Contemporary Ethnography, 34*(2), 143–169.

Kekelis, L. S., & Prinz, P. M. (1996). Blind and sighted children with their mothers: The development of discourse skills. *Journal of Visual Impairment & Blindness, 90,* 423–436.

Loots, G., Devise, I., & Sermijn, J. (2003). The interaction between mothers and their visually impaired infants: An intersubjective developmental perspective. *Journal of Visual Impairment & Blindness, 97,* 403–418.

Masino, L. L., & Hodapp, R. M. (1996). Parental educational expectations for adolescents with disabilities. *Exceptional Children, 6,* 515–524.

Mosio, M. D. (1994). A survey of attitudes of undergraduate education majors toward inclusion. Bowling Green, OH: Bowling Green State University. (ERIC Document Reproduction Service No. ED376688).

Muhlenhaupt, M. (2002). Family and school partnerships for IEP development. *Journal of Visual Impairment & Blindness, 96,* 175–179.

Nasatir, D., & Horn, E. (2003). Addressing disability as part of diversity through classroom literature. *Young Exceptional Children, 6,* 2–10.

Nixon, H. L. (1988). Reassessing support groups for parents of visually impaired children. *Journal of Visual Impairment & Blindness, 82,* 271–278.

Perkins-Gough, D., Snyder, D., & Licciardi, B. (2003). ASCD community in action. *Educational Leadership, 61,* 94–95.

Potok, A. (2002). *A matter of dignity: Changing the world of the disabled.* New York: Bantam Books.

Quinn, P. (1998). *Understanding disability: A lifespan approach.* Thousand Oaks, CA: Sage.

Saunders, K. (2000). *Happy everafters: A storybook guide to teaching children about disability.* Sterling, VA: Stylus.

Shapiro, J. P. (1994). *No pity: People with disabilities forging a new civil rights movement.* New York: Random House.

Smith-D'Arezzo, W. M. (2003). Diversity in children's literature: Not just a black and white issue. *Children's Literature in Education, 34,* 75–94.

Stoler, R. D. (1992). Perceptions of regular education teachers toward inclusion of all handicapped students in their classrooms. *The Clearing House, 66,* 60–62.

Texas School for the Blind and Visually Impaired. (2004). *Books featuring characters who are visually impaired.* Retrieved from www.tsbvi.edu/Education/books.htm

Thompson, T. L. (2000). Introduction. A history of communication and disability research: The way we were. In D. O. Braithwaite & T. L. Thompson (Eds.), *Handbook of communication and people with disabilities: Research and application* (pp. 1–14). Mahwah, NJ: Erlbaum.

Tuttle, D. W. (1986). Family members responding to a visual impairment. *Education of the Visually Handicapped, 18,* 107–116.

Ziolko, M. E. (1991). Counseling parents of children with disabilities: A review of the literature and implications for practice. *Journal of Rehabilitation, 57,* 29–34.

Disability and Parenting: Representations of Consequence

Joy M. Cypher

Parents frequently turn to popular press material to provide advice on how to engage in parenting best practices, as well as to understand the parenting experiences of others. What they read or see in mediated messages informs their evaluations of their own lived experience, as well as how they might evaluate the experiences of others. Representations of parents with disability in mediated messages are relatively rare, though the reality is that many parents experience some form of disability during the life course. In this work, Cypher considers how parents may see parenting and disability discussed in popular discourse, and how this may impact them in a variety of ways.

L.B.A.

On Thursday, August 5, 2004, I watched a beaming Marnie Ruderman of New York hear her children's voices clearly for the first time. I was privy to this intimate moment through the power of television. Marnie and her family were the subjects of a brief segment on *Good Morning America* called "Medical Miracles Live." On this particular morning, I watched as Marnie used a new hearing aid that would allow this severely hearing-impaired mother of two to hear her children and husband. In a prefilmed interview, Marnie cried as she and her husband, Steve, described her inability to hear her children in the next room. She wanted to be a better parent, and hearing was a necessary component of that.

This story of Marnie and her quest to become a better parent by overcoming her disability offers a compelling example of the challenges involved with being a disabled parent. In this article, I will look at the representations of disabled parents like Marnie in an attempt to better understand how these images shape our ideas of parenting and disability, and the intersection of the two.[1]

Introduction

To many Americans, the word *disability* calls forth images of wheelchairs, seeing-eye dogs, and special parking spots. Not only are physical signifiers like these invoked, but so are personal or emotional traits such as weakness, limitation, and even suffering. Because such common assumptions of disability abound in North American culture, it isn't surprising that we seem to expect little from persons with disabilities. Yet there is an area of scholarship that views disability differently—disability studies. Unlike the assumptions described, disability studies does not presume that disabilities are natural occurrences resulting from physical or mental impairment. Instead, from this view disability is a consequence of our too stringent ideal of bodily norms (Albrecht, Seelman, & Bury, 2003; Davis, 1997; Finkelstein, 1980; Rogers &

Swadener, 2001; Scheer & Groce, 1988, Vernon, 1999). Thus, if someone fails to meet the standards, such as the use of her legs for walking or standing, then we attribute a weakness to her, even if she can successfully go about her business using a wheelchair. A common example used to explain this position is that of stairs: from a traditional view of disability (often called the medical model; see Oliver, 1990, or Coleridge, 1993) a person is considered disabled if he cannot walk up a flight of stairs. Disability studies scholars and activists argue that the person is disabled not by his body, but by the choice of society to mandate stairs as the only or best way to access the space. Thus, it is not legs that disable, but other people, their choices, and the assumptions that motivate those choices.

I first discuss one particular aspect of disability, the parent with a disability. As a disability studies scholar, I too believe that impairment alone is not the only, or even most significant, factor in a person's experience of disability. Thus, I analyze popular media discussions of disability (magazines and major newspapers) to understand the dialogue about disability in the public sphere. The discussion begins with a description of current themes and metaphors of disability and parenting. I then use these themes to address some of the consequences these representations have for the growing number of parents with disabilities and their families.

Methods of Analysis

Current popular discussions of disability in families almost solely focus on disabled children as well as strategies for parent advocacy and coping. Motivation for my current project arises instead from the question, "What about disabled parents?" Although originally intending to study parenting magazines, I found too few references to analyze. Thus, I expanded my search to include popular magazines in general.

This project is based on my assumption that popular images and representations form a crucial building block in the creation and fortification of cultural meanings (Barthes, 1972; Berger, 1972; Giroux, 1994). Because I am concerned with magazines available to the general population (and not just a specialized group) regardless of education or monetary privilege, I chose popular press easily available through free sources, specifically through Internet access available at public libraries. In short, Web sites that charged a fee or publications available only through purchase were exempted from this study. Additionally, periodicals geared toward academics or health care professionals were excluded due to their highly specialized language undesirable to popular press consumers. Thus, magazines and nationally available newspaper articles from 1996 through 2004 were included, as were online magazines from this same period. The year 1996 was the starting date for my sample because prior to that date, few magazines were published online.

In selecting articles for this study, I narrowed the field by using only texts that focused on a disabled parent or parents, and not simply disability or disabled children. This kept the articles in line with my research objective, and differentiated works on disabled parents from the more common works on the parenting of disabled children. Searches through Internet databases used the following key phrases: *disabled parent*, *disability and parenting*, *parents with disabilities*, *handicapped parents*, *parents and handicaps*, *parents with handicaps*, and *special needs parents*. From these searches, 16 articles were collected and analyzed for thematic similarities and differences; these were then compared and distilled into three final themes of Needy, Selfish, and Extra-ordinary as discussed in the following text.

There are numerous methods possible for studying communication about disabled parents, but I have chosen a textual analysis of popular representations due to the pervasiveness of popular texts in North American society. Because much of what we learn about families comes from not only private examples but also public discussion, popular culture texts provide another central source of our assumptions of family and disability. As such, family communication scholarship can be further elucidated through an analysis of public discourse such as this.

Themes of the Parent with a Disability

Neediness

The first theme culled from the articles is neediness. Articles presenting this view of disability emphasize disabled parents as requiring help from others, often children, to accomplish simple tasks. Thus, everyday parental activities are shown to be chores for which others were ultimately responsible. In the *Toronto Star* (2002) article "Blind Parents Donate Eyes of Drowned Son," we learn of the death of a six-year-old boy who held his family together. The article states, "they depended on Hassan to a great degree because he was the only family member who could see" (2002, p. A2). Readers are informed that Hassan not only guided both his sister and father in their public movements, but that he facilitated his mother's housework by sorting laundry and groceries for her (p. A2). Thus, what would otherwise have been a sad and all-too-early obituary for a young boy became instead (or, perhaps, simultaneously) a comment on the inner workings of Hassan's family and their reliance on him for necessary daily tasks. As readers, our pity and sadness are piqued; we are torn between pity for the six-year-old's burden to care for his disabled parents and sister, only later, sadness over his death. When his mother states "it's his presence we'll miss" (p. A2), it is possible to wonder whether we should also feel pity not simply for a family who lost a son, but perhaps more important, their caretaker.

An article printed in the *Wall Street Journal* (Bullock, 1997), and later in *Reader's Digest* (Bullock, 1998), similarly recalls the trials of a young boy forced to care for his father. The boy, now the adult author of the article, describes being a literal crutch for his father as he walked to work. Bullock further recalls that in bad winter weather, "my sisters and I would pull him through the streets of Brooklyn, New York on a child's sleigh to the subway entrance" (1998, p. 8) so that he could get to work. For readers, the poignant imagery of a grown man needing his children to carry him to a subway, then further carried by public transportation, creates the clear image of a man unable to accomplish basic tasks without the daily aid of his children. Like Hassan's obituary, a key focus of the article is the role reversal of a child caring for a needy parent.

Yet the most dramatic description of parental neediness was found in the *Redbook* article about "forgotten children" (Prose, 1999). The article speaks of HIV positive parents and mentally disabled parents who rely on their children for both physical and emotional caregiving. The scholarly concept of "parental child" (Aldridge & Becker, 1993; Winton,

2003), one who must take the role of parent within the family system, is strongly implied in this article. It is similarly invoked in the *Rosie* article "Sister Act" where a daughter asks after her mother's diagnosis of cancer, "Do I have to be the Mom now?" (Thompson, 2001). As scholars describe it, parental children or "child carers" are considered examples of borderline abuse, an idea echoed in one chilling tale of a boy who "took his barefoot mother by taxi to the hospital during one of her psychotic episodes" (Prose, 1999, p. 100). The neediness of the mother described here is clear to readers; we understand that she and her child have effectively switched roles between caregiver and one who needs care. This impression is heightened by the article's use of stigmatized identities—the uncontrollable psychotic, the diseased, dying parent—to incite not only sympathy and pity for the children, but also horror at the parental neediness imposed on them.

Selfishness

The second theme emergent from these articles was that of selfishness. Parallel in some ways to neediness, this theme repeatedly surfaced as parents with disabilities disregarding the welfare or futures of their children. Just as the *Redbook* article invoked the neediness of a parent with mental disabilities, the article later subtly directs the reader toward the "appropriate" response to these parents. Thompson (2001) describes the surprising display of humanity toward the mentally disabled mother partaking in a therapy session: "to an observer, one of the astonishing things about this session is the staffers' sympathy for Kevin's mother" (p. 100). From this statement, we learn that sympathy for a mother with disabilities is "astonishing." Presumably, our sympathy and concern are more appropriately limited to the children of such parents. Thus, when contrasting the selfless, caring Kevin with his needy and psychotic mother, we see selflessness against indulgence, care versus selfishness.

Yet interestingly, the majority of evidence supporting the theme of selfishness revolves less around needy parents with disabilities, and more around proactive parenting and medical decision making. A case study in *Pediatrics* debates the decision of deaf parents to withhold a hearing test for their newborn. Because both parents were deaf, they had no fear for the potential deafness of their child, thus no need to have a hearing test administered to their newborn. The physician, and author of the case study, wrote, "the refusal to test hearing seemed an unusual response in these knowledgeable parents" (Stein, 2001, p. 883). Dr. Stein further found the decision "baffling," due to his assumption of limited language acquisition by deaf children, asking, "Didn't I have an obligation to the child and her family to insist on the hearing test?" (p. 883).

Stein's response to the parents' choice to forgo a hearing test is complex. First, he suggests that "knowledgeable parents" don't make choices such as this; instead, they recognize the obligation to care for the potential impairment while it can still be treated. Thus, the choice to ignore the doctor's suggestion of a hearing test reflects a seemingly different set of priorities for the parents—perhaps a desire not to have a hearing child. Additionally, Stein reinforces the misconception that American Sign Language (ASL) is not a real language (although it is recognized worldwide by linguists or language specialists as such). From his interpretation of the parents' actions, then, they are choosing a negligent future of limited language skills and incurable impairment for their young daughter. Later in the article, he and other doctors commenting on the case agree that these parents view deafness as a cultural distinction (one that perfectly exemplifies the disability studies assumptions described earlier). Thus, the parents' choice embraced the deaf culture and not the medical view of deafness.

Although the Stein case study offers a somewhat balanced description of parental decision making regarding deaf children, other articles counter with one-sided and dramatic representations of such parents as selfish. The March 31, 2002, edition of the *Washington Post Magazine* presents the story of two deaf women intent on their child being born deaf. Numerous articles were written in response to the story, including the *Advocate* article "Children by Design." Author Jay Blotcher characterizes the debate over the parents' right to self-select deafness for their infant as based in the definition of "deafness as an identity, not a disability" (2002, p. 15). Here, as in Stein's case study, parents are critically questioned for choosing self-identity issues over the presumably more advantageous future of their child.

Charles Colson's "A Clan of One's Own" in *Christianity Today* goes further in its critique. Colson asks rhetorically, "Why would parents, especially ones who have themselves experienced the challenges of being deaf, wish this condition on their child? . . . The answer lies in the way many deaf people . . . view themselves. Increasingly, they see deafness with a capital D—not as a disability but as a culture" (2002, p. 156). Colson later correlates the choice of the two mothers to "the crassest form of self-centeredness: Deliberately visiting one's disadvantages on one's children" (p. 156). There is little ambiguity in Colson's argument against deaf parents making choices about the hearing, or as Colson prefers, "disability" status of their future children. The article posits firmly that deaf parents who wish for deaf children are simply irresponsible, selfish people. Moreover, readers should assume that a more appropriate response from the two women would be to rally against deafness, deny its significance in their lives, and hope for a time when they can live differently than they previously have. Colson's article suggests that their resistance to assimilation into a world that considers them "broken" is not indicative of a culture that discriminates against difference, but rather of a fundamental self-centeredness (and the crassest form, no less).

One of the few interviews granted by the mothers, Sharon Duchesneau and Candace McCullough, was published in the April 13, 2002, *Lancet*. In this article, we learn first that "congenital deafness is a contraindication to sperm donation," thereby preventing the births of deaf children. Surely, Colson, and perhaps even Stein would support this general rule. Yet as we examine these debates, we are left with a reasonable question regarding the reproductive choices of deaf parents. As Duschesneau and McCullough are quoted within the article, "Many Deaf People Marry Other Deaf People and Have Deaf Children, for the Same Reasons We Did" (McLellan, 2002, p. 1315). This insightful comment from the center of the debate leads us to ask: What of these other deaf parents? Are they equally unethical in their choices to procreate? Should we mandate their sterilization to prevent their unimpeded reproduction? What difference is there between these examples?

In each article addressing the "ethical" issue of Duschesneau and McCullough's parental choice, no author has asked these questions. If it is socially acceptable for parents to abort based on tests suggesting the possibility of a disability, why is it less ethical—or simply selfish—to *want* the child? And, more troubling in this debate is the implication about the deaf parents with deafness themselves: that they are, at best, selfish, and, at worst, inferior to the hearing population due to their deafness. By engaging only part of the complicated issue of reproductive rights of persons with disabilities, the hearing world seems oblivious to alternative voices.

Extra-ordinary

Whereas the previous two themes were highly charged and negative, the third, extra-ordinary, is significantly different. On the surface, this theme appears positive in its message about parents with disabilities. Similar to the disability studies idea of "supercrips" (Clogson, 1990), persons with disabilities as "characters who triumph over tragedy" (Barnes, Mercer, & Shakespeare, 1999, p. 195), the theme of extra-ordinary also emphasizes the atypical strength of disabled parents who go about their everyday lives despite challenges. What is heightened, then, is the assumption that "ordinary" parents presumably face no challenges in raising children.

Articles displaying this theme use descriptive language to set apart parents with disabilities from and above the rest of society. The *New York Times* describes the fortitude and courage of a disabled mother as "soldiering on" (Rehrmann, 2003, p. B6). A feature on disabled parents in the magazine *Mothering* similarly introduces the "exceptional mothers and fathers" who manage to be parents with disabilities ("When People See Us," 1999, p. 70). We learn of the exceptional "character traits needed by disabled women wanting children" in Nancy Perry-Sheridan and Ellen Seiden's article "I Was Told Not to Have Children" in *Parents* magazine (Perry-Sheridan & Seiden, 1995, p. 123). We also learn of Teri Lehner's courage against "unspeakable odds" (Martin-Morris, 2001, p. 50), giving birth despite her paraplegia.

Each of these examples portrays disabled parents as extra-ordinary and their experiences as atypical. When reading these descriptions, we are led to believe that a disabled parent is in fact going against the norm and heroically wrangling with the clearly assumed challenges that accompany their choice. We understand through these representations that a disabled person must struggle through the difficult activities of parenting with greater strength and courage than other parents.

Not only are disabled parents set apart as extra-ordinary because they became parents, but also because they lead fulfilling, dynamic lives. Robert Christy's (2001) article "Life with Cerebral Palsy" in *Maclean's* offers a common pattern in "supercrip" narratives: amazing life experiences. In this article, Christy describes his life, saying,

> I have traveled, stood on the Great Wall in China and cruised down the Yangtze River, through the Three Gorges. I've been on safari, swum in the Indian Ocean and played golf in Kenya. I've walked the beaches of Trinidad, stood in the main square of Lima . . . and prayed at the Western Wall of the Second Temple in Jerusalem. I paid for it all myself, through writing contracts, even though I have cerebral palsy. (p. 12)

Christy's words frame him as an enviable, amazing character. We consider his exciting adventures, his accomplishments as a parent and grandparent, and his rugged individualism ("I paid for it all myself") and we, the readers feel small in comparison. The compelling denouement of the tale comes at the end: he did it all "even though" he is disabled. To accomplish these tasks is commendable, yet Christy reminds us that he is a better man, an extra-ordinary man, for having done them with a disability.

The story of Michael May, as told in the *People* article "Learning to See," further exemplifies the extra-ordinary theme of disabled parenthood. Michael, blind for 43 years, successfully underwent a series of surgeries to restore his sight. We are privy to his experiences with transplant rejections, months of strong medication and painful treatments; yet as he reveals to us, "probably the biggest deal, though, is being able to play ball with my boys" (Harrington, 2003, p. 124). The bravery summoned to face pain, loss, and disfigurement all for the joy of playing with his children offers an undeniable image of a super-parent. As readers we might ask if we were willing to go through all of this for the same simple pleasures. We marvel, in awe at the "incredible journey" (p. 124) that is his life. And when he states humbly, "Life is a challenge—and a gift. Sight, for me, is something extra" (pp. 124–125), we are convinced that Michael's redemption from a 43-year darkness is well earned.

The three themes of disabled parents—needy, selfish and extra-ordinary—all offer some insight into the current conceptions of disabled parents. These themes echo other studies on images of disability (Clogson, 1990; Haller, 1995), suggesting that disabled parents are viewed through the general, cultural lens of disability. These representations are far from realistic, however. Each emphasizes a small, though dramatic possibility; yet, these possibilities exist among all parents, disabled or otherwise. Furthermore, these themes exaggerate that disability is the dominant factor in these parents' lives. For so many people, the birth of a child is world-changing; somehow, this commonality seems to be overshadowed by a parent's disability. Thus there exists little balance in these images of disabled parents. They are either presented as self-centered and childlike, or as exceptions to the norm of parents in general.

In my readings for this project, two articles failed to fit neatly with the rest. They offered no exaggeration, no subtle chastisement for pride, nor any fearful indictments of emotional or physical negligence. These articles provide a crucial reminder that parents, with or without disabilities, have similar concerns, although their methods of dealing with those concerns might be different. Sandra Gordon (2001) writes in her article "New Help for Disabled Moms" in *Parenting* magazine, that discrimination against mothers with disabilities often prevented women from "getting adequate prenatal and obstetrical care" (p. 23). Now, however, there are hospitals and programs to help mothers with questions about "everything from conception to parenting, with advice that's tailored to their specific needs and disability" (p. 23). Conception and parenting are regular topics in prenatal counseling, not something unique to parents with disabilities. The article's focus then is simply parenting issues—there are no metaphors of heroism, nor condemnations of weakness, only new parents with varied needs.

Similarly, in a question-and-answer section of *BabyTalk* titled "Talking Points," Anita Sethi (2002) provides a proactive counter to a previous discussion of deaf parents and their children. A concerned, deaf mother who fears that her hearing son, Toby, will have impaired speech due to her own deafness writes to Sethi asking for advice. Sethi states, "Toby has the very good fortune to grow up in a household where more than one language is used. . . . Deaf parents do as good a job raising hearing children as do hearing parents even though they often don't seem to realize it" (p. 29).

Rather than condemning the mother for using sign language in the home, encouraging fear of language acquisition delays, or highlighting the "challenges" of such a family system, Sethi encourages the mother to be confident in her skills and abilities. The acknowledgment of ASL as a legitimate language, and thus as the household as bilingual (Sethi, 2002, p. 29), suggests to readers that indeed, deaf parents have rich cultures to offer their children. Additionally, Sethi avoids exaggerating the strengths offered by a deaf parent when she says they do "as good a job raising hearing children as do hearing parents" (p. 29). No supercrip metaphors are used in her response, though Sethi still offers positive support to the concerned mother.

These two articles offer us an important reminder that although it is easy to exaggerate the strengths or weaknesses of disabled parents, such approaches ultimately miss the mark. When popular representations of disabled parents create caricatures of real-life issues, all parents suffer. For instance, if we presume that only disabled parents have needs met by simple actions by their children, then we overlook many everyday family interactions and responsibilities (consider a child's list of chores on the refrigerator). If we expect that only disabled parents make personally and culturally bound decisions regarding their children, then we misunderstand what it means to raise a child in a community. And if we believe that only disabled parents struggle with sacrifices, challenges, and difficulties, then we haven't seen the millions of parents among us who do so every day. I believe that a more productive understanding of families can emerge when we see images of parents, disabled and nondisabled, working toward the same goals with similar concerns. With this approach, common ground is built.

In this section, I have reviewed three themes of disabled parents as seen in popular press and suggested an alternative viewpoint that held the core image as "parent" rather than "disabled." By considering the consequences of our cultural representations of parenting and disability, we are better prepared to recognize and embrace those perspectives that offer opportunities rather than obstacles to the betterment of families and respect for bodily and cultural diversity.

Questions for Consideration and Discussion

1. Cypher notes that we have particular associations with the very word *disability*. Make a list of other terms that come to mind when you think of disability. What are the ramifications of these connections for our understandings of individuals with disability?
2. From a disability studies perspective, the primacy of stairs as a way to get from place to place creates disability. What are other examples of how cultural practices may create disability for particular individuals?
3. Cypher reveals three prominent themes seen in depictions of parents with disabilities. What do you think the outcomes of such images are in the way we understand and respond to parents with disabilities in U.S. culture?
4. One of the themes found here was the parent with a disability as extra-ordinary. Even though this is, in a sense, a positive stereotype, why is it problematic?
5. What do studies of popular press discussions of family bring to the study of family communication processes?

Endnote

1. For this chapter, I am using the theoretical assumptions of the social model of disability (as discussed in section 1). To apply this set of assumptions to language, we should consider current framing of disability when discussing people. In the US and Canada, it is considered culturally appropriate to use "people first" language—where the people being described are always the primary focus by placing them before the modifier. Thus, "parents with disabilities" places the parents first with the disability second to imply the appropriate way we as audience members should view them. According to the social model of disability however, this representation accepts without question the "fact" of disability as a true and legitimate problem. Thus, proponents of the social model of disability generally eschew such representations as well-meaning continuations of problematic social norms. Instead, the social model suggests a "forefronting" of the issue at hand—specifically the idea that disability is a result of social frames and not of

bodily differences. Thus, as is common practice in the UK, where the model has it origins, "disabled parent" is a political statement identifying a parent disabled by social and bodily norms, not an unreflective observation of a physical state of being. When the bodily state is meant to be directly described by those using the social model, the term "impairment" is often used.

As you read this chapter, please note the use of the social model of disability language. This language is used purposely to represent the ideology of the critique I offer, and to suggest the very fluid and dynamic nature of representation and social action.

References

Albrecht, G., Seelman, K., & Bury, M. (Eds). (2003). *Handbook of disability studies*. Thousand Oaks, CA: Sage.

Aldridge, J., & Becker, S. (1993). Children as carers. *Archives of Diseases in Childhood, 69*(4), 459–462.

Barnes, C., Mercer, G., & Shakespeare, T. (1999). *Exploring disability: A sociological introduction*. Malden, MA: Blackwell.

Barthes, R. (1972). *Mythologies* (J. Cape, Trans.). New York: Hill and Wang.

Berger, J. (1972). *Ways of seeing*. Harmondsworth, England: Penguin.

Blind parents donate eyes of drowned son. (2002, July 31). *Toronto Star*, p. A02.

Blotcher, J. (2002, May 28). Children by design. *The Advocate, 864*, 15.

Bullock, A. J. (1997, June 11). A good heart to lean on. *The Wall Street Journal*, p. A22.

Bullock, A. J. (1998, March). A good heart to lean on. *Reader's Digest, 152*, 7–8.

Christy, R. (2001, February 5). Life with cerebral palsy. *Maclean's, 114*, 12.

Clogson, J. (1990). *Disability coverage in sixteen newspapers*. Louisville, KY: Avocado Press.

Coleridge, P. (1993). *Disability, liberation & development*. London: Oxfam.

Colson, C. (2002, October 7). A clan of one's own. *Christianity Today, 46*, 156.

Davis, L. (1997). *The disability studies reader*. New York: Routledge.

Finkelstein, V. (1980). *Attitudes and disabled people: Issues for discussion*. New York: World Rehabilitation Fund.

Giroux, H. (1994). *Disturbing pleasures: Learning popular culture*. New York: Routledge.

Gordon, S. (2001, March). New help for disabled moms. *Parenting, 15*, 23.

Haller, B. (1995). Rethinking models of media representations of disability. *Disability Studies Quarterly, 15*(2), 26–30.

Harrington, M. (2003, November 24). Learning to see. *People, 60*, 123–125.

Martin-Morris, D. (2001, January). Little miracles. *McCall's, 128*, 48–51.

McLellan, F. (2002, April 13). Controversy over deliberate conception of deaf child. *Lancet, 359*, 1315.

Oliver, M. (1990). *The politics of disablement. A sociological approach*. New York: St. Martin's Press.

Perry-Sheridan, N., & Seiden, E. (1995, October). I was told not to have children. *Parents, 70*, 121–123.

Prose, F. (1999, July). The forgotten children. *Redbook, 193*, 96–100.

Rehrmann, A. (2003, December 23). Losing her legs, a mother soldiers on. The *New York Times*, p. B6.

Rogers, L., & Swadener, B. (Eds.). (2001). *Semiotics and dis/ability: Interrogating categories of difference*. New York: State University of New York Press.

Ross, S. (Executive producer). (2004, August 5). *Good Morning America* [Television broadcast]. New York: American Broadcast Company.

Scheer, J., & Groce, N. (1988). Disability as moral experience: Epilepsy and self in routine relationships. *Journal of Social Issues, 44*(1), 63–78.

Sethi, A. (2002, January). Talking points. *BabyTalk, 67*, 29–30.

Stein, M. T. (2001, April). Parental request to withhold a hearing test in a newborn infant of deaf parents. *Pediatrics, 107*, 883–887.

Thompson, T. (2001, October). Sister act. *Rosie, 128*, 88–90.

Vernon, A. (1999). The dialectics of multiple identities and the disabled people's movement. *Disability and Society, 14*(3), 385–398.

"When people see us together, they smile." (1999, January/February). *Mothering, 92*, 70–76.

Winton, C. A. (2003). *Children as caregivers: Parental and parentified children*. Boston: Allyn & Bacon.

Section 3: Conclusions and Application—Considering Health, Disability, Family, and Socialization _____

This chapter considered several issues related to health and disability in family settings. We discussed drug and alcohol use in family settings and how parental communication may contribute to or prevent use by minors. The Miller-Day and Dodd piece provided some evidence about the way that parents and adolescents do talk about drug and alcohol use. We considered health and disability issues in the family. Jenks and Beeghly compared how children with visual impairment are discussed in books for children and how parents and educators actually experience their lives with children who have visual impairment. Cypher addressed how cultural images portray parents with disabilities. We also considered the way in which we think about disability, including the extent to which impairment may be physical or psychological, but disability is social. All of these issues related to culture and socialization that occurs both within the family setting and larger cultural institutions. Considering how they are related can provide you with insight into your own beliefs and behaviors and those of others.

The Complexity of Socialization about Drugs and Alcohol

When you consider the ways in which your parents/adult caregivers communicated to you, explicitly and implicitly, about drug and alcohol use, you are thinking about a process of socialization. In your adolescent years, were the decisions you made in regard to the use of these substances affected by the family interaction patterns in your home? If you completely or generally avoided the use of drugs and alcohol as a teen, what factors led to that decision? Were parental processes, including communication about these substances, modeling, and monitoring, the primary reason for your decision, or were there other elements? If you did not avoid these substances in your teen years, what were the factors that contributed to your decision? How do you think that parental socialization process impacted the way that you feel about drugs and alcohol today? As we have discussed in this chapter, family processes do seem to be related to drug and alcohol use of adolescents and young adults. As Miller-Day and Dodd affirmed in their research, when parents and adult caregivers speak to children and adolescents about drugs and alcohol, they pass on their beliefs and attitudes. As parents engage in behavior related to these substances, including their own use and how they monitor and respond to the behavior of their children, they pass on their own beliefs and attitudes. The family is an important part of our socialization related to drugs and alcohol. However, these processes are not the only thing that contributes to socialization about these substances.

You grew up in a culture that also provided messages about the use of substances. Television shows, songs, and movies provide us with information about drugs and alcohol. Often, alcohol is shown as a necessary part of a fun or interesting evening for adults. Although drugs are less favored culturally than alcohol, they still appear in movies, music, and TV programs. How did the images that you saw or heard in the media with relation to substance use intersect with what your parents/adult caregivers taught you?

At the same time as you received media messages that seem to promote drug and alcohol use in some ways, you also likely got information from other social institutions, such as schools and religious organizations. Schools promote "Just Say No." Religious organizations also often speak in opposition to the use of such substances, particularly drugs, but even alcohol in excess. How did the conflicting information you received from the media and other social institutions affect you? Did you choose to pay more attention to one message than the other?

You also received communication from peers. Parents sometimes assume that peers are a negative influence ("peer pressure"); however, peers may encourage behavior that is beneficial or behavior that is harmful. The types of messages you received from your peers were likely affected by the peer group culture you spent the most time in. As noted in this chapter, research suggests that some adolescents are more affected by peer influence than others. How did your peers' attitudes and behaviors about drugs and alcohol affect you as a teen?

Considering the complexity of socialization about substance use indicates all of the different influences on children and adolescents. This information can help you more carefully consider how these messages impact you, as well as thinking about how what you model and say may impact others, including adolescents and children.

Illness, Disability, and Socialization

Illness and disability have very real impacts on family life, as we have discussed in this chapter. At some point, every family will experience illness or disability issues and will need to negotiate changes in the family system as a result. How we categorize and respond to physical and psychological conditions is an issue of socialization.

One example of this process at work can be seen with learning disorders. At this point, documented learning disorders like dyslexia and ADHD are categorized as disabilities. Individuals who have been diagnosed with learning disorders are protected under the Americans with Disabilities Act. Not all that long ago, this was not the case. At that time, some students were seen as just having a harder time learning than others. Some were diagnosed with hyperactivity and given medications. Still others were considered less intelligent, and little concern was given to their educational progress. The change that has occurred in the labeling and response to these individuals is a social change. Children growing up in a time when ADHD or ADD did not exist as labels to facilitate our understanding of learning difficulties were often socialized to believe that those who had a hard time learning, or got poor grades, were just not as smart as others. Now, children are being socialized to understand learning disorders as a phenomenon that exists outside of intelligence. As you might imagine, this has changed the social response to learning disorders. You might have read in the news that the rates of learning disorders are climbing. Some have even called it an "epidemic." Although some researchers argue that there may be environmental or other reasons for an increase, other researchers argue that differences in learning abilities have always existed, but because we have a way to label them now, more parents are seeking diagnosis for their children so that the children can receive an educational experience tailored to their needs.

As the social model of disability suggests, our understandings of what is an illness or a disability are a product of socialization and the communicative negotiation of labels and meanings. This idea isn't always easy to grasp. It is easier to understand how our responses to issues like ADHD have changed over time, but some would argue that a disability like being deaf is surely not socially constructed. As presented earlier in the chapter, and reinforced by the Cypher and Jenks and Beeghly pieces, even our understanding and responses to issues of physical impairment are created via communication. Being deaf is an impairment of one physical sense. However, it does not have to be a disability. I once attended a weekend conference for individuals with deafness and sign interpreters. For two and a half days, no one spoke, televisions had their volume down, and so on. In that environment, being deaf was in no way a disability. Lengthy philosophical conversations were carried on. Jokes were told and enjoyed. Television and movies were watched. Deafness becomes understood as a disability in a culture that places a premium on sound and on the power of the spoken word and is not well fitted to the use of other senses for communicating (even some major news channels remain without closed captioning).

So, just like our understandings about drug and alcohol use, our understandings and responses to illness and disability are socially constructed and learned through a process of socialization. How can and will you use this information in your life? Knowing more about how we are socialized to understand things in a particular way allows us the critical tools we need to be reflective about our own beliefs. Such self-reflexivity may result in a reaffirmation of the currently existing beliefs. However, it also positions us to be open to different ways to understand things like health and disability.

Questions for Consideration and Discussion

1. What are some of the barriers that may prevent parents from feeling comfortable or capable in talking to their children about drug and alcohol use?
2. Given the somewhat conflicting research on parental communication and adolescent drug and alcohol use, what do you think parents should do to help prevent their teenagers from using these substances?
3. In what ways have you seen illness and/or disability (physical or psychological) impact your family system, and how did the system adjust?
4. In recent years, the concept of learning disabilities has become more a part of the public consciousness. How do you think this has impacted society, the educational process, and family life?
5. What cultural barriers, if any, do you see in achieving a common understanding of disability as socially constructed? What are the limitations and benefits of this view?

Key Terms and Concepts _____

awareness of difference	integration	parental monitoring
inconsistent nurturing as control theory	labeling	social models of disability
	medical/individual model of disability	

10

The Family in Mediated Contexts

Chapter Objectives

1. To develop an awareness of the positive and negative impacts of media use for families
2. To understand the socialization impact of the media with respect to family images
3. To reflect on how media use and images of family in the media have impacted your own family experiences

Section 1: Overview of the Family in Mediated Contexts _____

- If you needed to give a family member airline information about a flight you were taking, would you do so via phone, instant messager, or email?
- When looking for information about an issue affecting your family (illness, taxes, vacation plans), where do you turn?
- When you sit down to watch a little "mindless" television, what sort of families do you expect to see? Why?
- Have the images you have encountered in the media regarding family ever made you feel better, worse, or different about your own family?

Family life clearly does not occur in a vacuum. It impacts and is impacted by the contexts that "surround" it. One of those contexts is media. Media—including print media (books, magazines, and newspapers), broadcast media (television, film, radio), and Internet media—all contain messages for and about family, and are used by family. Some of this has been touched on in previous chapters, for example in the Cypher reading in Chapter 9, and the discussion of media rules and Egan reading in Chapter 4. In this chapter, we focus more directly on mediated contexts and how they affect and are affected by our understandings and enactments of family life. Specifically, Section 1 focuses on two things: how media like television and the Internet are utilized by family members, and how mass media messages represent and create our understandings of family. Section 2 discusses three research reports related to these issues. Finally, in Section 3 we consider how you might utilize this knowledge in your own family life.

Media Use and Family Life

Some media theorists, like McLuhan (McLuhan & Fiore, 1967) and Postman (1993), suggest that the types of media we have available to us can impact and change the way we interact with those around us. The idea that media environments have a substantial impact on our human affairs is called **media ecology.** McLuhan argued that as media change, our interactions with family members and others in our social environment also change. It is not, he said, the specific messages of the media that change our interactions, but rather the presence of the media itself. Before the invention of printing machinery, books were extremely time consuming to make, and newspapers were nonexistent. Information and family histories were passed from one individual to another via oral communication. As you might guess, this called for a substantial amount of interaction. After books and newspapers became more widespread, information could be gleaned through reading and history could be passed down in the same way. However, reading is a very solitary process. It doesn't work well with more than one person. This, then, may have somewhat reduced and altered family interaction.

As you see, McLuhan and Postman are arguing that the format of media, and how the format changes over time, impacts the ways in which we interact with others, and the ways in which we seek and obtain information. Radio, television, and the Internet are media that have also impacted our social lives, including our lives as family members. Because of the ubiquitous nature of television, and the relative recency of the Internet as a communication medium, this section focuses on some of the ways that television and the Internet have affected or may affect family life.

Television in Family Life

As of the year 2000, over 95 percent of American families owned a television set and in the average household that television is on for over seven hours per day (Nielsen Media Research, 2000). With the prominence of television as a media form, it is important to consider how its use impacts family interaction patterns. Because TV use has been covered extensively in a variety of mass media texts (see, for example, Andreasen, 2001; Martini, 1996), and because the presence of TV impacts upon family communication, but the medium itself is generally not used as a part *of* family communication, we consider it rather briefly here.

McLuhan (McLuhan & Fiore, 1967) argued that the invention of new mediums impacts upon our relational interaction patterns. His theory would suggest, then, that family interaction patterns have likely changed as a result of the almost constant presence of television in American family homes. The frequency with which families view TV might be assumed to reduce the amount of communication family members have with each other. However, research related to this issue has produced somewhat conflicting results.

Some researchers have concluded that the mere presence of television in households decreases the time that family members will spend in actual interaction with one another. In a seminal piece of early research, Maccoby (1951) concluded that, when families engage in TV viewing, it becomes a **parallel activity** (people together engaging in the same activity, but not interacting with one another). More recent research has also found that television may, at times, reduce interaction, but that it does not seem to have negative impacts overall. For example, Martini (1996) found that having TV on during meal times does reduce the family interaction that occurs. Brody, Stoneman, and Sanders (1980) found that parents and children may talk less while the television is on, but they tend to touch more.

Taking this idea further, other researchers emphasize the idea that television may actually have a positive impact on family patterns. Schmitt, Woolf, and Anderson (2003) and Lull (1990) found that families tend to engage in other interactions while watching

BOX 10.1 • *Did You Know?*

Between 1950 and 1965, home ownership of televisions in the United States went from 9 percent to more than 90 percent!

Read more TV facts on the National Institute on Media and the Family Web site at www.mediafamily.org.

television, sometimes using the topic matter of the programs and advertising as a "jump start" to conversation. These authors have found that parents and children talked to each other, played, ate, and "snuggled" while watching TV.

Of course, neither set of theorists has to be "wrong" per se. Authors like Kubey (1990) have argued that, whereas television viewing may in fact reduce the amount of conversation between family members somewhat, it may increase their relational happiness or satisfaction. Additionally, **uses-and-gratifications theory** of media suggests that how media impacts us depends on how we use it, and we make choices about media use based on our own individual and systemic needs and motives (Katz, Blumler, & Gurevitch, 1974; Rosengren, 1974). Drawing from that, scholars like Lull (1990) and Alexander (1994) theorize that how family is impacted by television is related to how family members use the medium, and their motives for its use. Television can be used by family members to spur conversation or to avoid it. It may be used to bring people together, or to keep them apart. Similar complexities exist when we consider the impact of the Internet on the family system.

The Internet in Family Life

The Internet can offer benefits to family members in a variety of ways. But, with those benefits come associated drawbacks. We begin this part of the chapter by considering some of the advantages that the Internet has brought to family members. We follow that by addressing some of the associated problems that may result due to increased use of the Internet by family members.

One benefit that the Internet can offer to family members is the information and social support that can be gleaned from Web sites, email chains, and bulletin boards. As family members go through their days, there are times when they need information. That information may be relatively minor (directions to a restaurant) or more significant (completing research for a college class). The Internet provides a wealth of sites that offer information about an almost endless number of topics. This may enable family members to gather the information they need without leaving the home. It may also reduce the time required for information seeking, therefore providing more time for other family tasks. In addition to using Web sites for information, family members may also take advantage of Usenet groups or online bulletin boards. Arnold (2003, 2005) found that pregnant mothers and parents of large families use online bulletin boards for advice, as well as for social support. As parents gain the information and support that they need, this may make them feel more prepared to enact their parenting roles in the family. Presumably, such feelings of self-efficacy on the part of parents would have good impacts on family patterns.

BOX 10.2 • *Internet Connection*

Statistics on Internet use, as well as other web information, have been gathered by the University of Maryland on their WebUse site at http://webuse.umd.edu/.

Similarly, Dunham et al. (1998) notes that young single mothers, when provided with an online social support group in which to discuss their experiences and concerns, exhibited less parenting stress as they increased participation in the group (for additional work on social support in online venues, see Muncer, Burrows, Pleace, Loader, & Nettleton, 2000; Wright 1999, 2002). Thus, through communicating with people outside the family, through Web sites, bulletin boards, email groups, and so on, family members may gain both information and social support that contribute to the interactions within the family system.

A second benefit of home computers and the Internet to parents, stepparents, and adult caregivers and children is the ability to coordinate schedules and other information between family members. As we have discussed throughout the text, the family system is a complex unit and the behaviors of one member affect the other parts of the system. This means that family members often need to know what other family members are doing, not only within the family home, but also with regard to outside contexts. In larger family systems, or families who maintain more outside connections and obligations (for example, through children's extracurricular activities, parental work obligations, extended family, etc.) this need may be even more pronounced. Braithwaite, McBride, & Schrodt (2003) found that email is a common way for divorced parents and stepparents to communicate with regard to the children. Likewise, Trice (2002) found that first-year college students used email to contact their parents with regard to academic and social advice, as well as financial assistance, though the extent to which students used email for contact depended on the family communication culture that had been established before college. In these examples, we can see that the Internet provides family members with another mechanism for communication and coordination of schedules and information.

In relation specifically to computer use by children and adolescents, studies have found that there seem to be some other benefits of the increasing time spent using computer media. A study by the Kaiser Family Foundation (Rideout, Roberts, & Foehr, 2005), a national organization that researches family and family health issues, of over 2,000 children and adolescents between the ages of 8 and 18, found that 74 percent of the respondents had Internet access in the home, and over half of the participants were using computers every day, with close to one hour spent online each day. As the children got older, time spent online tended to increase. Some of the advantages of Internet use for children and adolescents may include increased information literacy gained through practice with computers and the Internet, slightly better academic performance possibly due to ease in research and the building of writing and other skills, and the ability to maintain contact with a wider array of friends through the use of instant messaging programs (Subrahmanyam, Kraut, Greenfield, & Gross, 2000; Wolak, Mitchell, & Finkelhor, 2002).

Although there are positives of computer use for children and adolescents, studies have also indicated some drawbacks of the extensive use of computer media. One disadvantage that often concerns parents and public policy makers is the potential of revealing information to the wrong online "friends." Research suggests this concern is not groundless. Finkelhor, Mitchell, and Wolak (2000) found that 1 in 5 of the 1,500 youths studied had received unwanted sexual solicitations online in the prior year. One in 17 respondents was threatened or harassed online. And, less than 10 percent of the unwanted sexual solicitations were reported to an Internet service provider, law-enforcement agency, or help hotline. In face-to-face settings, children and adolescents are somewhat more restricted in terms of with whom they can create relationships. Parents and adult caregivers often have some degree of control over those individuals that a child or adolescent is exposed to in a face-to-face realm, and are likely to discourage friendships with much older adults. In the cyber-world, the potential of creating a relationship with an older adult, even one who may be posing as a child online, is much greater. Child safe programs, such as NetNanny, can be used to help decrease this potential. However, it still exists.

In addition to the risk of victimization of children and adolescents due to Internet use, there are other potential problems. Time spent online may result in a lack of exercise and lead to associated obesity and health problems. Additionally, increased loneliness and depression, more aggression, and a decrease in ability to distinguish between reality and simulation have been correlated with increased time spent online (Subrahmanyam et al., 2000; Wolak, Mitchell, & Finkelhor, 2002). For some of these factors, it is unclear which is the causal agent (does more loneliness result in more time online, or vice versa?), but the connections are still problematic.

In addition to the downsides associated particularly with child or adolescent Internet use, there are other problems that can be related to online communication. Flaherty, Pearce, and Rubin (1998) looked at the extent to which mediated communication is an equal substitute for face-to-face communication. Probably not surprisingly, the researchers found that these two types of communication are not functional alternatives. Part of the reason for this is that face-to-face communication offers the possibility of immediate and nonverbal communication that is not really possible in Internet communication. Although emoticons and Internet acronyms show some emotion online, they are not a substitute for the experience of seeing someone laugh, or hearing sarcasm in a voice. This may be why the parents and stepparents in Braithwaite, McBride, and Schrodt's (2003) study utilized telephone or face-to-face contact more than email as a way of communicating. This may also be related to the fact that adolescents that are communicating primarily online, though they may have a wide circle of online acquaintances, may feel more depression and loneliness (Subrahmanyam et al., 2000).

Similarly, the seeming benefit of being able to accomplish more from home may also have some potential for negative consequences. Cassidy (2001) notes that advertisers and computer experts have claimed that the home PC has been, and will be, particularly useful for women in family settings as it allows them to accomplish more of their domestic labor (paying bills, ordering gifts, storing recipes, making greeting cards, etc.) without leaving the house. Additionally, advertisements and other writing with regard to PC use often tout the idea that mothers are well suited to **"cyber-commuting"**—that is, having a job, but doing most of the work from home so that they can continue to care for their children. The result of this is that mothers (or fathers or other adult caregivers who work from home) may find their social interaction narrowing as a result of spending large amounts of time in the home. Additionally, when parents or other adult caregivers attempt to simultaneously fulfill two roles (that of worker and parent) in the same setting at the same time, some of the role conflict and strain discussed in Chapter 3 may occur, and the individuals may feel as if they are not fulfilling either role adequately.

A final problematic aspect of increased computer use is that it actually may reduce the amount of communication that goes on within the home. As Morrison and Krugman (2001) note, using the computer is a one-person activity. When an individual is engaged in use of the home computer, he or she is less likely to be carrying on conversations with family members. As computers become more ubiquitous in family settings, to the extent that often various family members have their own computer in different rooms, use of the computer may facilitate separation of family members and decreased interaction. This may have negative consequences for family cultures and family systems.

There is no doubt that, for many of us, the Internet has become an omnipresent part of life. Online access is still somewhat divided by socioeconomic status, but every year an increasing percentage of families in the United States obtain Internet access. This means that the impact of this medium on family and family interactions seems likely to continue to be a strong part of our future.

Images of Family in the Media

The way that family members utilize media technology is not the only process through which media impact families. Approaches such as cultivation theory (Gerbner, Gross, Morgan, & Signorielli, 1986; Shanahan & Morgan, 1999) and cultural studies (Hall, 1977, 1980) suggest that mediated messages have an impact on the ways that we see and understand the social world. These theories do not suggest that what we see or hear in the media becomes, unreflectively, our beliefs about the world. That is, this work does not argue that we don't understand the difference between fiction and reality, or that we cannot reject or reinterpret what we see in media messages. Rather, scholars who work with such theories argue that mediated messages become a part of our body of knowledge, along with firsthand experiences, interactions with others, and so on, and that combination then creates our beliefs about social phenomena such as the family. Therefore, the **media portrayals of family** that occur are important to our individual and cultural experience of family.

Images of Family Types

Nuclear families on television are often portrayed in an extremely positive way. They are loving and kind; parents are wise; and problems can be solved with relative ease. Reep and Dambrot's (1994) study indicated that these messages about families, and in particular about parents, seemed to stick with the undergraduate students that they surveyed. Portrayals of families, however, are different based on the characteristics of the family. For example, Graves (1993) found that Black families, in comparison to White families, on television were more often shown as isolated from other families, characterized by frequent sibling conflict, and more likely to be either victims or perpetrators of violence. Socioeconomic class also plays a role in television programming. Butsch (1992) notes that middle-class families are shown as main characters with far greater frequency than working-class families. Additionally, these middle-class families are often quite successful in their careers,

BOX 10.3 • *Family in the News*

In late 2005, the comic strip *The Boondocks* hit television as an animated series on Cartoon Network. The series immediately elicited a vocal response. The debate over the show revolved around the characters, which some considered stereotypical and problematic, whereas others felt the portrayal was a realistic and humorous representation of the cultural and political issues facing families of color. Despite the controversy, as of this writing, the show continues enjoying good ratings and its run on Cartoon Network has been extended.

making enough money to live well, hire servants, travel, and work reasonable hours. Thus, whereas nuclear families generally are shown in highly positive terms, families that are not White or middle class may be shown in a somewhat less positive way.

Though nuclear families are largely shown positively, stepfamilies tend to be shown in either unrealistically negative or unrealistically positive ways. Leon and Angst (2005) considered the images of stepfamilies that appear in films. Their analysis of films from 1990 to 2003 showed that stepfamilies were often portrayed in a negative way, or in some cases, a mixed way with a focus on both negative and positive moments, but with little focus on the everyday "neutral" moments of family life. Other research has indicated that when stepfamily relationships are shown in a positive way, it is unrealistically positive, seeming to indicate that stepfamilies should have no problems adjusting to one another, and that there will be instantaneous love and support among family members (Coleman & Ganong, 1987; Ganong & Coleman, 1997). Such images of stepfamilies may encourage understandings of stepfamily life that either overemphasize the difficulties or make it appear that something is wrong in stepfamilies where the members do not immediately feel love for one another.

Portrayals of Mothers

Images of family displayed in media not only tell us something about the family as a whole, but also indicate understandings about the roles and characteristics of particular family members. Media images of motherhood often tend to be either extremely celebratory ("good mothers" as saints) or derogatory ("bad mothers" as abusers). Charles and Shivas (2002) conducted a study of magazine articles discussing the birth of the McCaughey septuplets and articles discussing the birth of children to mothers who use crack cocaine. Both the birth of higher order multiples (triplets and beyond) and the use of drugs during pregnancy are potentially detrimental to the baby/babies. However, the authors noted that, statistically, the likelihood of serious mental or physical damage for a septuplet is far greater than the likelihood of such damage for a baby due to mother's cocaine use (though sometimes cocaine use is connected with other factors that may lead to poor child outcome, like lack of good prenatal care, alcohol use, or low socioeconomic status). Not surprisingly, Charles and Shivas found that the media spoke of crack cocaine using mothers in almost entirely negative terms (frequently with discussion of how to prevent them from having more children), whereas the McCaughey situation was almost entirely spoken of in positive terms. These authors were not suggesting that using crack cocaine is a good idea for mothers. Instead, they point to the fact that, though multiple birth is actually more dangerous to the fetus than crack use, the mothers who used crack were positioned as horrible mothers, whereas the mother who elected to attempt to carry seven children was spoken of glowingly. The authors note that it is probably not surprising that articles about maternal drug use tend to focus on crack (which is actually less dangerous to the fetus than some other drugs), given that crack cocaine users tend to be from the lowest socioeconomic classes. Mothers who use fertility treatments, on the other hand, tend to be from higher socioeconomic classes.

In a similar finding, Smith (2001) studied portrayals of working mothers in magazines. She found that, again, mothers were divided into two groups. Working mothers of middle or upper class were primarily spoken of in relation to mothering, and child care was assumed to be unable to replace the quality of maternal care. For mothers of lower socioeconomic classes, articles most prominently spoke of them in terms of their status as workers, and any child care that provided them the ability to work was considered better than maternal care. Interestingly, mothers of middle or upper class are often able to obtain higher quality child care than mothers of lower socioeconomic classes. However, that fact does not seem to impact the portrayal of their mothering situations in these mediated messages.

As these research examples show, mothers are frequently shown in mediated messages as either very good or very bad. Of course, mothers aren't all good or all bad. Every mother makes some mistakes and virtually every mother does some things right. Positioning mothers as completely saintly or totally abusive may lead "real" mothers to feel bad about their mothering (if they can't live up to saintly, they must be abusive). This is even more problematic if mothers from low socioeconomic classes are often shown as the bad mothers.

Portrayals of Fathers

Images of fathers in mediated messages are also often stereotypical. Kaufman (1999) looked at images of fathers and mothers in television commercials. The author found that fathers were portrayed as not particularly involved in family life. These fathers were shown as passive, incompetent, and dependent upon their wives in the family realm. When interacting with children, men were mostly shown interacting with boys and were teaching, playing, or reading with the children. On the rare occasion when men were shown caring for children, the products they used (i.e., fast food, microwave meals) tended to suggest that they didn't really know what they were doing, and didn't need to know.

In sitcoms, working-class fathers are often portrayed as bumbling, confused men who really have little idea what they are doing and need their wives to save them from themselves (Sharrer, 2001). Examples of this can be seen in *The King of Queens* and *The Simpsons*. Middle-class or upper-middle class fathers, however, are shown as more capable, rational, and intelligent (Butsch, 1992; Sharrer, 2001), particularly in the stereotypic realms of work, household maintenance, and so on (e. g., *The Cosby Show*). Though this is the case, Sharrer (2001) argues that more recent sitcoms are likely to have even middle-class fathers as the butt of jokes because that has become a standardized form of humor (for example, *Everybody Loves Raymond*). Although fathers are portrayed as somewhat clueless in the family realm, they are also often shown on TV as having the final authority in the household (Olson & Douglas, 1997).

The images of fathers then are also, like images of mothers, stereotyped. Fathers are shown as the "nonexperts" in the family realm. They may be successful in work, but they are poor at caretaking behaviors, particularly with regard to children. Additionally, as with mothers, fathers from lower socioeconomic classes are shown in more problematic ways. They become the comedic bumblers who can do very little right and have to be saved. As with images of mothers, these images of fathering may have an impact on how people, even fathers themselves, understand fathering. Such images suggest that men should not even attempt child care because, of course, they will not be good at it. These images also position men from lower socioeconomic classes as failures in the financial realm, because they have not succeeded in lucrative careers, and in the family and social realms because they are inept.

Portrayals of Children

Images of adults are not the only portrayals of family members that are somewhat narrow and potentially troubling. In general, children appear far less on television and in films than would be truly representative. Additionally, in a study of prime-time comedies, Jordan (1995) found that the children shown in the programs were not much like typical children. These children interacted with adults far more than with other children. Additionally, they engaged in "parenting" type behaviors for adults. Adults confided their secrets and problems to the children, and the children were likely to engage in advice giving, and persuading of the grownups. As with portrayals of adults in family settings, if children are shown in ways that are not truly representational (i.e., acting like small adults rather than children), parents and other adult caregivers may feel that their own children are not living up to social expectations.

In total, research regarding images of family in the media tends to suggest that families are shown in ways that are stereotypical, narrow in focus, and certainly not representative of the full range of variation within family types. This does not mean that when an individual encounters such images he or she will automatically accept them as truth. As adults, we do see a difference between media portrayals and reality (though reality television is certainly straining that distinction). However, if, over time, these images are repeated enough, they can become a part of our social understanding of family and family processes. Think of it like drips of water on a rock. Each drip, by itself, has little impact on the stone. But if those drips continue to fall, one after another, over time eventually the very shape of the stone will be changed. That is the impact of media images of family in our lives.

In this section of the chapter, we have considered how television and the Internet are utilized by family members, and the positive and negatives of that use. We have also addressed the impact of media representations upon our understandings of family. Section 2 discusses studies related specifically to family use of the Internet, online bulletin boards as social support, and images of motherhood in print media. Then, in Section 3 we consider how the information presented in this chapter could inform your understandings and enactments of family, now and in the future.

References ___

Alexander, A. (1994). The effect of media on family interaction. In J. Bryant, A. C. Huston, & D. Zillmann (Eds.), *Media, children, and the family: Social scientific, psychodynamic, and clinical perspectives* (pp. 51–60). Hillsdale, NJ: Erlbaum.

Andreasen, M. (2001). Evolution in the family's use of television: An overview. In J. Bryant & J. A. Bryant (Eds.), *Television and the American family* (2nd ed., pp. 3–30). Mahwah, NJ: Erlbaum.

Arnold, L. B. (2003). Delivering empowerment: Women's narratives about the role of pregnancy bulletin boards. *Qualitative Research Reports in Communication, 4,* 45–52.

Arnold, L. B. (2005). Don't you know what causes that?: Advice, celebration, and justification in large families bulletin board. *Communication Studies, 56*(4), 331–351.

Braithwaite, D. O., McBride, M. C., & Schrodt, P. (2003). Parent teams and the everyday interactions of co-parenting children in stepfamilies. *Communication Reports, 16,* 93–111.

Brody, G. H., Stoneman, Z., & Sanders, A. K. (1980). Effects of television viewing on family interactions: An observational study. *Family Relations, 29,* 216–220.

Butsch, R. (1992). Class and gender in four decades of television situation comedy: Plus ca change. . . . *Critical Studies in Mass Communication, 9*(4), 387–399.

Cassidy, M. F. (2001). Cyberspace meets domestic space: Personal computers, women's work, and the gendered territories of family home. *Critical Studies in Media Communication 18*(1), 44–65.

Charles, S., & Shivas, T. (2002). Mothers in the media: Blamed and celebrated: An examination of drug abuse and multiple births. *Pediatric Nursing, 28*(2), 142–145.

Coleman, M., & Ganong, L. (1987). The cultural stereotyping of stepfamilies. In K. Pasley & M. Ihinger-Tallman (Eds.), *Remarriage and stepparenting: Current research and theory* (pp. 19–41). New York: Guilford Press.

Dunham, P. J., Hurshman, A., Litwin, E., Gusella, J., Ellsworth, C., & Dodd, P. W. (1998). Computer-mediated social support: Single young mothers as a model system. *American Journal of Community Psychology, 26*(2), 281–306.

Finkelhor, D., Mitchell, K. & Wolak, J. (2005). *Online victimization: A report on the nation's youth.* Retrieved May 10, 2005, from the National Center for Missing & Exploited Children Web site: www.unh.edu/ccrc/Youth_Internet_info_page.html

Flaherty, L. M., Pearce, K. J., & Rubin, R. B. (1998). Internet and face-to-face communication: Not functional alternatives. *Communication Quarterly, 46*(3), 250–268.

Ganong, L., & Coleman, M. (1997). How society views stepfamilies. *Marriage and Family Review, 26,* 85–106.

Gerbner, G., Gross, L., Morgan, M., & Signorielli, N. (1986). Living with television: The dynamics of the cultivation process. In J. Bryant & D. Zillmann (Eds.), *Perspectives on media effects* (pp. 17–40). Hillsdale, NJ: Erlbaum.

Graves, S. (1993). Television, the portrayal of African Americans, and the development of children's attitudes. In G. L. Berry and J. K. Asamen (Eds.), *Children and television: Images in a changing sociocultural world* (pp. 179–190). Newbury Park, CA: Sage.

Hall, S. (1977). Culture, media, and the ideological effect. In J. Curran, M. Gurevitch, & J. Woollacott (Eds.), *Mass communication and society* (pp. 332–333). London: Edward Arnold.

Hall, S. (1980). Encoding and decoding in the television discourse. In S. Hall, D. Hobson, A. Lowe, & P. Willis (Eds.), *Culture, media, language* (pp. 128–138). London: Hutchinson.

Jordan, A. (1995). The portrayal of children on prime-time situation comedies. *Journal of Popular Culture, 29*(3), 139–147.

Katz, E., Blumler, J. G., & Gurevitch, M. (1974). Utilization of mass communication by the individual. In J. G. Blumler & E. Katz (Eds.), *The uses of mass communication: Current perspectives on gratifications research* (pp. 19–32). Beverly Hills, CA: Sage.

Kaufman, G. (1999). The portrayal of men's family roles in television commercials. *Sex Roles: A Journal of Research, 9*(1), 439–458.

Kubey, R. (1990). Television and family harmony among children, adolescents, and adults: Results from the experience sampling method. In J. Bryant (Ed.), *Television and the American family* (pp. 73–88). Hillsdale, NJ: Erlbaum.

Leon, K., & Angst, E. (2005). Portrayals of stepfamilies in film: Using media images in remarriage education. *Family Relations, 54*(1), 3–23.

Lull, J. (1990). *Inside family viewing: Ethnographic research on television's audience.* New York: Routledge.

Maccoby, E. E. (1951). Television: It's impact on school children. *Public Opinion Quarterly, 15,* 421–444.

Martini, M. (1996). "What's new?" at the dinner table. Family dynamics during mealtimes in two cultural groups in Hawaii. *Early Development and Parenting, 5,* 23–34.

McLuhan, M., & Fiore, Q. (1967): *The Medium is the Massage.* New York: Bantam.

Morrison, M., & Krugman, D. M. (2001). A look at mass and computer mediated technologies: Understanding the roles of television and computers in the home. *Journal of Broadcasting & Electronic Media, 45*(1), 135–161.

Muncer, S., Burrows, R., Pleace, N., Loader, B., & Nettleton, S. (2000). Births, deaths, sex and marriage . . . but very few presents? A case study of social support in cyberspace. *Critical Public Health, 10*(1), 1–18.

Nielsen Media Research. (2000). *Report on television.* New York: Author.

Olson, B., & Douglas, W. (1997). The family on television: Evaluation of gender roles in situation comedy. *Sex Roles: A Journal of Research, 36*(5–6), 409–427.

Postman, N. (1993). *Technology: The surrender of culture to technology.* New York: Vintage Books.

Reep, D. C., & Dambrot, F. H. (1994). TV parents: Fathers (and mothers) know best. *Journal of Popular Culture, 28,* 13–23.

Rideout, V., Roberts, D. F., & Foehr, U. G. (2005). *Generation M: Media in the lives of 8–18 year olds—report.* Retrieved May 10, 2005, from the Kaiser Family Foundation Web site: www.kff.org/entmedia/7251.cfm

Rosengren, K. E. (1974). Uses and gratifications: A paradigm outlined. In J. G. Blumler & E. Katz (Eds.), *The uses of mass communications: Current perspectives on gratifications research* (pp. 19–32). Beverly Hills, CA: Sage.

Scharrer, E. (2001). From wise to foolish: The portrayal of the sitcom father, 1950s–1990s. *Journal of Broadcasting & Electronic Media, 45*(1), 23–40.

Schmitt, K. L., Woolf, K. D., & Anderson, D. R. (2003). Viewing the viewers: Viewing behaviors by children and adults during television programs and commercials. *Journal of Communication, 53*(2), 265–281.

Shanahan, J., & Morgan, M. (1999). *Television and its viewers: Cultivation theory and research.* Cambridge, England: Cambridge University Press.

Smith, A. M. (2001). Mass-market magazine portrayals of working mothers and related issues, 1987 and 1997. *Journal of Children and Poverty, 7*(2), 101–119.

Subrahmanyam, K., Kraut, R. E., Greenfield, P. M., & Gross, E. F. (2000). The impact of home computer use on children's activities and development. *The Future of Children, 10*(2), 123–144.

Trice, A. D. (2002). First semester college students' email to parents: I. Frequency and content related to parenting style. *College Student Journal, 36*(3), 327–335.

Wolak, J., Mitchell, K. J., & Finkelhor, D. (2002). Close online relationships in a national sample of adolescents. *Adolescence, 37*(147), 441–456.

Wright K. (2002). Social support within an online cancer community: An assessment of emotional support, perceptions of advantages and disadvantages, and motives for using the community. *Journal of Applied Communication Research, 30*(3),195–209.

Wright, K. B. (1999). Computer-mediated support groups: An examination of relationships among social support, perceived stress, and coping strategies. *Communication Quarterly, 47*(4), 402–414.

Section 2: Research Examples _____

Family Communication in the Age
of the Internet

Traci L. Anderson

Tara L. Crowell

Kevin Pearce

For many families, computers have become a ubiquitous part of life. Scholars we considered in Section 1, such as Postman, argue that the presence of a new media form will impact how we experience our lives and relationships. In this work, Anderson, Crowell, and Pearce consider how the Internet is used in family communication, and how family communication patterns may affect that use. As you read, consider the extent to which you incorporate computer-mediated communication in your family interactions, and how your family communication patterns may or may not be related to your Internet use choices.

L.B.A.

We learn our communication behaviors and attitudes first from our parents/caregivers and how we learn to communicate with family members has a profound effect on our future interpersonal relationships. For example, research has shown that married couples whose communication patterns are more similar tend to have less conflict and be more satisfied (Fitzpatrick, 1983). Communication patterns also determine in what ways and how frequently we choose to speak to our family members. They even affect how we use technology (Krcmar, 1998). In short, family communication patterns influence many different aspects of our communicative behavior.

The way in which families communicate has evolved over time as changes in society and the introduction of new technologies have changed both our cultural values and expanded the ways in which we communicate with one another. Psychologists argue that new technologies such as the Internet and its various applications (e.g., chat rooms, instant messaging) have altered the amount of face-to-face communication we have with our family and friends (Kraut, et al., 1988). According to Nielson/NetRatings (n.d.), as of March 2004 over 204 million Americans access the Internet from home, log on approximately 19 times a month, and spend more than 10 hours a month online; this type of use changes how often and in what ways we communicate. Thus, this article explores how and to what extent people use the Internet to communicate with family members. Additionally, it examines if family communication patterns impact family members' use of the Internet to communicate with one another.

PC and Internet Demographics

As stated earlier, 204 million Americans access the Internet from home and a Pew Internet and American Life Tracking Survey (Fallows, 2004) shows that, as of 2004, 61% of all women and 66% of all men in the United States were using the Internet. Additionally, 78% of 18- to 29-year-olds were using the Internet and the younger a person was the more likely she or he was to go online. Looking at household computer use, in 1999, 68% of family households with children had computers and 41% had Internet access (Stranger & Gridina, 1999). Roberts, Foehr, & Brodie (1999) reported that as of 5 years ago, 16% of children (primarily older children) had a computer in their bedrooms; that number has undoubtedly increased over the last few years. Thus, many people have personal computers and Internet access, and their purpose for using each varies.

There are numerous reasons why people use the Internet. According to Papacharissi and Rubin (2000), who examined motivations for using the Internet, people reported that communication was the second most common reason for using the Internet (after informa-tion seeking). This means that people are using the Internet to participate in online discus-sions and debates; stay in touch with family and friends; and freely express thoughts, feelings, and ideas (something that the relative anonymity, or pseudonymity, of the Internet fosters).

In another Pew study (Madden, 2003), 85% of the people surveyed felt that the Inter-net is a good way to communicate or interact with others and 75% claimed it was a great way to conduct everyday transactions. This Pew report notes that of those people who are online, 90% use email and 45% use various forms of instant messaging (or "chatting"). When the Pew researchers examined exactly how people used the Internet for communica-tive reasons, 79% said they used the Internet to communicate with friends and family. Inter-estingly, 17% said that online communication was their primary method of communicating with friends. Fifty-two percent sent greeting cards or invitations online. Additionally, 46% of people surveyed use the Internet to plan group functions and 26% went online to search for a romantic relationship. Thus, people are spending a great deal amount of time online communicating with others.

Families, Computers, and Internet Use

As the importance of computers in our day-to-days lives increases, so too does the understanding of its influence on the family unit. Over the past few years, the role com-puter technology plays within the home and family life has sparked interest in this topic for many researchers. Scholars have begun to question the possible impact that com-puter technologies have on the family unit in much the same way as they investigated the impact of television on family life. For example, scholars consider topics such as how children use home computers for game playing and educational purposes (e.g., Wartella & Jennings, 2001) and parental concerns about children's Internet use, such as exposure to pornographic material (e.g., Okrent, 1999). In addition, researchers have started to examine specifically how new technologies (such as computers, cell phones) function in the home. Morrison and Krugman (2001) conducted a study in which they examined the role that different forms of technology played in the home. They found that home computers are usually located in more isolated areas and this tended to limit family socialization in what they labeled as "high technology" homes. However, it did foster other kinds of interaction. When people gained information online, they in turn shared the information with other family members and, in the process, increased their interaction. Morrison and Krugman found that computers in the home did not alter the amount of interaction per se, but they did alter interaction that revolved around other technologies such as television.

Morrison and Krugman (2001) also looked at the use of the Internet to facilitate communication. They found that members of high-technology homes with online access were able to maintain, extend, and form relationships through the use of email and the computer. However, much of this interaction was with people outside the family. What we do not know specifically is how family members use new technologies to facilitate family interaction; or, how new technologies are used to communicate with other family members.

Family Communication Patterns and Computer-Mediated Family Communication

Based on existing research, it appears that Internet access in the home promotes family socialization to some extent and lends itself to communicating with others outside the family unit. However, we are unsure to what extent and in what ways family members utilize Internet access to communicate with one another. Additionally, to date, no research has been published on whether family communication patterns influence use of online technologies for family interaction.

As you have read earlier in this book, family communication patterns refer to the ways in which family members interact (parents and children); specifically, the degree to which conformity and/or conversation are encouraged influences greatly the beliefs that family members hold about how to communicate (Ritchie & Fitzpatrick, 1990). The concept of conformity orientation refers to the degree that family members defer to, and agree with, the values and beliefs that are encouraged within the family. Interactions within families that are high in conformity orientation stress harmony and conflict avoidance; thus, parents in these families expect and encourage children's obedience. In contrast, the concept of conversation orientation refers to extent to which open discussion and diversity of opinion about most issues are encouraged within the family. For families that are high in conversation orientation, communication transactions are guided by principles such as "look at all sides of an issue," "be open with your emotions," and "talk openly and freely among family members."

Past research has revealed that family communication patterns have a large impact on family TV viewing habits and practices. For example, mass media researcher Krcmar (1996) found that children in high conformity orientation families, who are expected to follow television viewing rules and to watch television in the same way as their parents, were more likely to attempt disobeying parents rules about TV viewing if such an opportunity presented itself. In another study, children from families with a high conformity orientation were found to be more likely to argue with their siblings about television viewing (Morgan, Alexander, Shanahan, & Harris, 1990). Conversely, children in families with a high conversation orientation tended to be more selective about their television viewing, less satisfied with television, and more considerate of other people's viewing habits (Lull, 1980). It can be reasoned that if family communication patterns impact one type of media use, they may impact another, more interactive form of media. Yet, we do not know if family communication patterns affect this particular kind of media use within the family. Thus, the purpose of this research was to answer the following two broad questions:

RQ1: How, and with what frequency, do family members use the Internet to communicate with one another?

RQ2: Do family communication patterns impact family members' use of computer-mediated family communication and, if so, how?

Method and Results

Procedure and Participants

Students enrolled in undergraduate communication courses at two East Coast universities voluntarily completed questionnaires about their families and Internet use. A total of 184 students participated in this study. Of these 184 participants, 101 (54.9%) were women and 83 (45.1%) were men. Participants ranged in age from 17 to 37 with an average age of 20. Thus, the sample's age may be characterized as that of the "typical" college student. The size of the participants' immediate families ranged from 2 to 11 with an average family size of 4.

All but 4 participants' families had at least one home computer. Thus, 180 participants (97.82%) had computers in their parents' homes. The number of computers in a home ranged from 1 to 7 and the average number of computers in the parents' homes was approximately 2. Of these PCs, 380 (92%) had Internet access. Additionally, 173 participants (94%) had their own personal computers, whereas only 11 (6%) had no PC.

Not surprisingly, as you can see in Figure 10.1, many individuals in this age cohort have been using the Internet for quite a few years. All but two participants said they had been using the Internet for 3 to 15 years, with an average use of approximately 7.5 years. One hundred seventy-six participants (95.65%) reported using email ranging from 1 to 200 minutes a day (mean [M] = 16 minutes) and 165 participants (89.67%) reported using instant messaging (IM) from 1 to 360 minutes a day with an average chat time of 56 minutes. Online discussion boards, or newsgroups, were used the least frequently; only 58 participants (31.52%) reported using newsgroups. Surprisingly, 16 participants (8.70%) said they did not use the Internet to surf the Web, although the remaining 168 participants (91.30%) browsed the Web 1 minute to 8 hours a day with an average browsing time of about 36 minutes. Twenty-seven participants (14.67%) reported going online for other reasons such as blogging (Web logging, or maintaining an online diary) and game playing (such as The Sims Online).

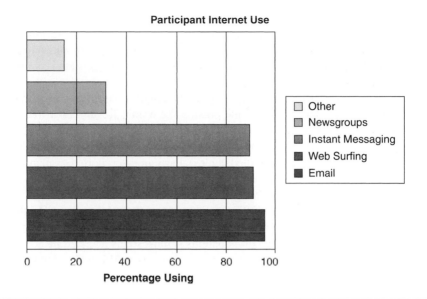

FIGURE 10.1 *Participant Internet Use.*

Research Findings

We first examined how, and with what frequency, family members use the Internet to communicate with one another. Using a 7-point Likert-type scale (1 = never and 7 = always), participants indicated the extent to which they sent and received email from various family members. Participants reported that they received email from mothers the most frequently with an average score of 2.75. Sibling (mutual) exchange of email was the second most frequent with an average score of 2.29. Sending email to mothers closely followed sibling exchange of email, with an average score of 2.27. The least reported email exchange was with fathers; participants received email from fathers ($M = 2.03$) more than they sent email to fathers ($M = 1.89$). These means indicate that the average frequency of email with *any* family member is relatively low.

Although email exchange among family members was relatively low, results indicate that some family members were using IM more than email with their immediate family members. When asked about their familial IM activities, participants reported chatting with siblings more minutes per day, on average, than with mothers or fathers. According to participants, the greatest amount of daily IM time occurred with brothers ($M = 5.5$ minutes) and the second highest amount of IM time was with sisters ($M = 4.92$ minutes). Instant messaging with mothers was third highest, with an average of 3.5 minutes per day. As with email, the least amount of IM took place with fathers (just over a minute a day, on average). Given these relatively low numbers, we also decided to examine only those participants who used IM and, after excluding those who did not chat with family members at all, found that the average time per day spent instant messaging with family drastically increased. Overall, 56 participants used the IM function to communicate with family members and the number of minutes per day these participants spent chatting with brothers and with sisters was relatively similar at 13.79 and 13.73, respectively. Participants also reported chatting with mothers for an average of 12 minutes and with fathers for about 7.5 minutes per day. As with email, participants reported chatting with mothers more than fathers.

We then determined how frequently email is used to communicate with family members that traditionally reside outside the home. Results of a frequency distribution indicated that most participants (81 participants [44%]) exchanged email with their cousins. The next family member with whom email was exchanged most was one's uncle (37 participants [20.1%] emailed uncles). Participants reported exchanging email the least with grandparents. Only 22 participants (12%) exchanged email with grandmothers and 12 participants (6.5%) exchanged email with grandfathers. Although it may seem as if grandparents are "left out of the loop," it is important to keep in mind that senior citizens are less likely to have home computers and online access than younger persons; thus, the rate of email exchange with grandparents is most likely affected by access issues.

Participants also reported using the Internet to IM with extended family members. Results of a frequency distribution indicate that 105 participants (57%) chatted with cousins, 37 (20.10%) chatted with aunts, and 15 (8.15%) chatted with uncles. Again, online communication with grandparents occurred the least frequently. Only 8 participants (4.3%) chatted with grandmothers or grandfathers.

Overall, when examining Internet communication with family members, we found that although more participants used email than IM to communicate with extended family members the opposite was true for immediate family members. Participants communicated with immediate family members more with IM than email. Thus, different modes of computer-mediated communication may be more (or less) suitable for different types of relationships. For example, email is an asynchronous form of communication, which means people write and read messages at separate times and do not have to be online at the same time to communicate with one another. Instant messaging is a synchronous form of communication in which people communicate simultaneously (in "real time") and must be online at the same time in order to communicate with one other (Walther, 1994). In general, synchronous forms of computer-mediated communication allow for more interactivity and are more similar to face-to-face and telephone communication than asynchronous forms. In synchronous computer-mediated communication a person can respond immediately to her or his conversational partner and is likely to ask and answer direct questions (Rice, 1986). Thus, people may be more inclined to use instant messaging with immediate family members (e.g., mom, brother) because it is a more interactive form of communication and lends itself to closer, more intimate relationships than does email. On the other hand, email, which is more "distant" in part because of its lack of real-time interactivity, may be a better method to stay in touch with extended family members to whom people generally are not quite as close (at least in the U.S. culture). Additionally, it is interesting to note that our results show more computer-mediated family communication takes place with women than with men, regardless of the sex of the adult child. That is, both daughters and sons emailed and used IM more with their mothers than fathers, and more with aunts than with uncles.

In this study, we also investigated whether family communication patterns impact family members' use of computer-mediated family communication and, if so, how. To assess participants' family communication patterns we used Ritchie and Fitzpatrick's (1990) Revised Family Communication Patterns (RFCP) scale to measure the perceived dimensions of conformity orientation and conversation orientation within participants' families. According to Ritchie and Fitzpatrick, conversation-oriented items tap into "whether the child is encouraged to develop and express autonomous opinions and ideas" whereas conformity-oriented items tap into whether the child is encouraged to "pursue relational objectives by conforming to parental authority" (p. 524). Previous research has indicated the RFCP scale is reliable (Ritchie & Fitzpatrick, 1990). In this study the mean score for conversation orientation was 4.63 (on a scale of 1 to 7) and for conformity orientation the mean was 3.54. Thus, according to participants' responses, overall their families are higher in conversation orientation than in conformity orientation.

To examine the relationships between these dimensions of family communication and frequency of computer-mediated communication with family members, we ran correlations among the two orientations and the frequencies of email use and IM with immediate family members. Results identify six statistically significantly correlations, all between conversation orientation and the amount of email and IM between various family members. We found that for participants, as conversation orientation increased the frequency with which email was sent to mothers increased and the frequency mothers sent email to participants increased ($r = .234, p = .001$). Additionally, as conversation orientation increased the frequency with which email was sent to fathers increased ($r = .216, p - .003$) and the frequency fathers sent email to participants increased ($r = .234, p = .001$). Furthermore, there is also a small but significant, positive relationship between conversation orientation and time participants spent instant messaging with their mothers ($r = .178, p = .015$) and time participants spent instant messaging with their fathers ($r = .154, p = .038$). Thus, child–parent use of email and IM increased as the families' conversation orientation increased. No statistically significant relationships were found between conformity orientation and Internet use.

Conclusion

In the age of rapidly changing and advancing technology it is no wonder that an increasingly large number of people are utilizing the Internet for communication purposes. In this article, we explored some of these uses by uncovering how and with what frequency people use the Internet to communicate with family members and whether family communication patterns impact family members' use of the Internet to communicate with one another. Although this study is exploratory in nature and further research must be conducted in this area, based on survey responses from 184 undergraduates we have uncovered some interesting preliminary findings.

Specifically, we found that almost all individuals in this age cohort not only owned a computer, but also had Internet access and used it daily for both email and IM purposes. However, less than one-third used discussion boards and newsgroups, and even fewer used it for basic Web surfing, blogging, and online game playing. Similarly, participants reported less overall frequency of emailing immediate family members than might be expected, with the most email exchange occurring with mothers. However, those who *did* use instant messaging with immediate family members reported using IM more than email. In contrast, participants reported greater frequency of emailing than chatting with extended family members (e.g., cousins, aunts, uncles, grandparents). Thus, depending on the family member, different computer-mediated activities appeared to be more or less suitable as communication channels for our participants. We recommend further exploration of this phenomenon.

As for the relationship between family communication patterns and Internet use, we found some significant positive relationships between family communication patterns and Internet use. Specifically, there was a positive relationship between high conversation orientation and engaging in parent–child emailing and instant messaging. In light of the fact that families who are high in conversation orientation encourage open communication and the sharing of ideas and among parents and children, it is not surprising that members of these families would feel comfortable communicating online because they are comfortable communicating in general (in face-to-face settings). We also found that both men and women exchanged more email and used IM more often with female members of the family as opposed to men; this is consistent with the (historically) traditional role of women in the family. Specifically, women have been socialized to be the caretakers within families and this often leads to greater frequency of communication and higher levels of intimacy within communication transactions.

Due to the criteria for external validity/generalizability (sample and replication), results of this study need to be interpreted with caution. There is a need for further research on family communication patterns and computer-mediated communication using a larger, more diverse sample. For example, researchers may want to obtain data from both children and parents. This would allow researchers to obtain dyadic data—the perceptions of communication patterns from two different "viewpoints"—thus allowing us to gain a better indicator of each family's family communication patterns. Additionally, although the use of college-aged children was useful for this project because it allowed us to examine the extent to which adult children who are away from home maintain contact with family members, younger children still living at home should be included in future studies to examine the role that online family communication plays in their lives.

Overall, this study provides valuable preliminary results of young adult children's Internet use and the relationship between this use and their family communication patterns. Just as technology is ever changing, we know that so, too, are family dynamics. For now, research indicates that technology has not replaced face-to-face communication but for some families—especially those higher in conversation orientation—has introduced an additional channel of communication when face-to-face is not possible. Understanding the relationship between family communication patterns and the use of technology will become increasingly important given that today's children will never know a world without the Internet.

Questions for Consideration and Discussion

1. Given the increasing frequency with which people are utilizing the Internet to communicate with friends, family, and romantic partners, what are the potential impacts of "downtime" associated with network failure and so on?
2. This study was completed on the East Coast of the United States. In what ways, if any, might this have affected the subject composition or results?

3. Ninety-eight percent of the participants in this study had a family computer and most of those had Internet access. What do these demographics suggest about this particular group of individuals?

4. Anderson, Crowell, and Pearce found that participants used email more for extended family, but used IM more for immediate family. How does this resonate with your own experiences? If it does, why do you think these patterns exist? If this finding is not similar to your experience, why not?

5. The authors suggest that future research is needed to more fully understand how IM and email are used in family interaction. If you were designing a study to do that, what would your research questions (or hypothesis) be? What methods might you use?

References

Fallows, D. (2004). *The Internet and daily life.* Retrieved September 2, 2004, from www.pewinternet.org/PPF/r/131/report_display.asp

Fitzpatrick, M. A. (1983). Predicting couples' communication from couples' self reports. In R. Bostron (Ed.), *Communication yearbook* (Vol 7, pp. 49–82). Beverly Hills, CA: Sage.

Kraut, R., Patterson, M., Lundmark, V., Kiesler, S., Mukophadhay, T., & Scherlis, W. (1988). Social implications of the Internet. *American Psychologist, 53,* 1011–1031.

Kremar, M. (1996). Family communication patterns, discourse behavior, and child television viewing. *Human Communication Research, 23,* 251–277.

Kremar, M. (1998). The contribution of family communication patterns to children interpretations of television. *Journal of Broadcasting & Electronic Media, 42,* 250–265.

Lull, J. (1980). Family communication patterns and the social uses of television. *Communication Research, 7,* 319–334.

Madden, M. (2003). *The changing picture of who's online and what they do.* Retrieved March 19, 2004, from www.pewinternet.org/pdfs/PIP_Online_Pursuits_Final.PDF

Morgan, M., Alexander, A., Shanahan, J., & Harris, C. (1990). Adolescents, VCRs, and the family environment. *Communication Research, 17,* 83–106.

Morrison, M., & Krugman, D. M. (2001). A look at mass and computer mediated technologies: Understanding the roles of television and computers in the home. *Journal of Broadcasting & Electronic Media, 45,* 135–162.

Nielsen Ratings/Netratings.com report. (n.d.). Retrieved October 1, 2002, from www.nielsen-netratings.com/hot_off_the_net.jsp

Okrent, D. (1999, May 10). Raising kids online: What can parents do? *Time,* 38–49.

Papacharissi, Z., & Rubin, R. (2000). Predictors of Internet use. *Journal of Broadcasting Electronic Media, 44,* 175–196.

Rice, R. E. (1986). *Computer-conferencing.* In B. Dervin & M. J. Voigt (Eds.), *Progress in communication sciences* (Vol. 7, pp. 215–240). Norwood, NJ: Ablex.

Ritchie, L. D., & Fitzpatrick, M. A. (1990). Family communication patterns: Measuring intrapersonal perceptions of interpersonal relationships. *Communication Research, 17,* 523–544.

Stranger, J. D., & Gridina, N. (1999). *Media in the home 1999: The fourth annual survey of parents and children.* Norwood, NJ: Annenberg Public Policy Center of the University of Pennsylvania.

Walther, J. B. (1994). Anticipated ongoing interaction versus channel effects on relational communication in computer-mediated interaction. *Human Communication Research, 40,* 473–501.

Wartella, E., & Jennings, N. (2001). New members of the family: The digital revolution in the home. *Journal of Family Communication, 1,* 59–70.

Social Support and Empowerment for Mothers on a Pregnancy Bulletin Board

Lorin Basden Arnold

> As we have considered throughout the text, family communication is not just about what happens within the family. Our communication with others is impacted by, and impacts, our family patterns and our feelings and beliefs about family roles and characteristics. Similarly, we have addressed the role of social support in family processes. In this work, I address these issues within the context of an online bulletin board for pregnant women. Although you may not have experienced pregnancy, consider how your online interactions with nonfamily may have been interrelated with your own family processes.
>
> *L.B.A.*

Pregnancy is a time of a woman's life when many changes are happening, and the potential for problems seems large. Pregnancy is also an experience that, particularly the first time, nothing can really prepare a woman for. For these reasons, among others, pregnant women may feel a need to seek additional information about childbirth and pregnancy to supplement that provided by their doctors, midwives, nurses, and family members. In the past, women may have sought that information by talking to friends. However, now the Internet has become an additional place to begin searching for information about pregnancy (Madonna, 1998a, 1998b; Zelzer, 1995). Online bulletin boards for pregnant women allow them to communicate with a larger number of other expectant parents than they would probably have in their face-to-face social circles. An additional advantage to such bulletin boards, over childbirth classes or local mothers' groups, is that they can be accessed from home, work, or anywhere with Internet access. In the study reported here (previously discussed in Arnold, 2003), I researched the use of an electronic bulletin board by pregnant women. I wanted to understand what led these women to participate in an online pregnancy bulletin board, how they experienced their participation in the board, and the outcomes they saw from that participation. Based on the responses of the women I interviewed, I concluded that they felt more empowered and capable as mothers due to the information and social support that they received from the bulletin board. Thus, this "nonfamily" communication contributed to their role enactment as family members.

To talk about this study, let's start briefly with the idea of empowerment. Empowerment, as it sounds, has to do with the belief that one has the ability to make choices and take courses of action (Surrey, 1991a). Some scholars believe that, for women, empowerment is often a product that comes partly from social relationships in which members show each other support and empathy (Jordan, Kaplan, Miller, Stiver, & Surrey, 1991; Liang et al., 2002; Rubenstein & Lawler, 1990). Because of this, Surrey (1991a), Liang et al. (2002), and other scholars believe that an individual's empowerment needs to be understood within the relationships that he or she has, including community relationships. Belonging to a community of individuals makes a person feel valued and important to others, and helps him or her feel that he or she is similar to others (Liang et al., 2002). Within such groups, Surrey (1991b) argues, members help each other feel mutually empowered by responding to each others feelings and providing communication that those feelings are understandable, normal, and valid. This mutually empowering relationship then helps the participants feel capable and confident to make choices and take actions in their lives. For the members of the bulletin board I studied here, empowerment happened through this type of mutually supportive community, and the exchange of information between members of that community.

The Expecting Club

During this study, I interviewed a group of women who had participated in a pregnancy bulletin board located on a Web site called ParentsPlace.com. I initially asked more than 100 bulletin board participants to take part in the study. Of that group, 23 women, aged 26 to 41, agreed to be interviewed. For the interview process, I asked the women to discuss their experiences on the bulletin board through a series of open-ended questions. The interviews were accomplished in a variety of ways, including email, phone, and in person. Although the specific questions I asked each woman depended on how that particular conversation progressed, the initial set of questions addressed what caused them to participate in the bulletin board, what their experience with the bulletin board was like, how that experience affected them both during and after the pregnancy, whether and how the bulletin board affected their relationships with their medical caregivers (doctors, nurses, and midwives), and what functions they believed the board to have for them during and after pregnancy.

After I completed the interviews, I analyzed the answers provided by these women, looking for common ideas and themes mentioned by the participants (for a discussion of thematic analysis see Glaser & Strauss, 1967; Meyer, 1997; Langellier & Sullivan, 1998; Owen, 1984). Though each interview was unique, and the group as a whole discussed many aspects of their experience with the bulletin board, including both positive and negative elements, the two most prominent themes that were presented in their talk related to empowerment. The empowerment discussed by these women seemed to come from two primary sources. First, they felt empowered by the information that they gathered through board interaction. Second, the relationships they had with the other members created a sense of empowerment.

Knowledge and Empowerment

When women become pregnant, they often experience some loss of control over their lives and their bodies. The very nature of pregnancy itself is a loss of control: Weight is gained; the body changes; and physical needs and requirements shift. These things are largely outside the control of the pregnant woman. In addition to the physical loss of control, the way that pregnancy is treated by medical practitioners also may make women feel that they have little choice. In the interest of a healthy newborn, doctors have established "rules" for pregnant women including the types of tests and exams they need to have, what sorts of nutrients they must consume, and what behaviors or foods they must avoid. Frequently, women are presented with only one choice about a particular aspect of pregnancy, and are not told that there are other options available to them (Markens, Browner, & Press, 1997). The result is that women may feel that they don't have many choices during pregnancy (Bird, 1994). The use of pregnancy bulletin boards may be one way women can take control of the pregnancy experience. Bird noted that, when women talk together about pregnancy, it may give them a sense of control by suggesting things that the women can "do" and choices that they can make during the pregnancy. Some of the activities and choices discussed may be relatively significant (the use of natural labor induction rather than using drugs for induction), whereas others may be more for the sake of entertainment ("old wives tales" about how to tell whether the baby is a boy or a girl). But, Bird argues that it doesn't matter whether the women actually engage in the behaviors discussed, and it doesn't matter whether the behaviors are serious or frivolous. What is important is that women are empowered by sharing knowledge with one another and thus feel more like they have some control over pregnancy.

For this group of women, sharing of information about the pregnancy experience was a prominent part of the bulletin board activity. As the women spoke to each other in this electronic forum, they gave each other advice based on their own past and current experiences with pregnancy. Of course, friends and family members also engage in this type of sharing with pregnant women. However, the bulletin board gave this group of expectant mothers a larger store of knowledge and experience to draw from.

Sue[1] (participant in second pregnancy, first birth) stated:
The wealth of information that I learned from the other moms (especially the more experienced moms who had already been pregnant and delivered a baby) is amazing.

Renee (participant during first pregnancy/birth) agreed, saying:
It was great to have many different experiences that I could ask for advice and help. There are so many times that you don't want to ask your friends or family such 'silly' questions, but on the board it is no big thing to ask questions and then to find out that many other people have gone through or are going through the same thing that you are asking about. That made me feel like my [pregnancy] was going normally.

As you can see from the answers of Sue and Renee, they found that information they got in the personal stories from the bulletin board, from women who had been or were going through the pregnancy experience, was very valuable to them. As humans, we tell stories to one another to share information, but we also do so in order to understand and provide interpretation for the events that we encounter (McCall, 1990). The stories that the women told to each other provided them with ways of understanding and thinking about their individual experiences. Communication scholar Kenneth Burke calls such communication "equipment for living" (Burke, 1974). The stories that these women told each other also helped provide them with a feeling of confidence regarding their experiences. Gail3, who participated on the bulletin board during her third pregnancy, but first birth, said:

[The board] gave me so much confidence and reassurance through factual knowledge. You hear so many "old wives tales" that you don't know what to believe. I feel as though I wouldn't have been informed through just reading books and articles.

Gail and others participants stated that the talk they engaged in with the other members of the bulletin board increased their confidence about pregnancy. Many of the participants also indicated that the increased confidence and knowledge they had impacted how they interacted with their doctors, nurses, and midwives. Oldermom (participant during second pregnancy, first birth) said:

> I felt more educated and informed. I was able to ask more intelligent questions when visiting the doctor. The result was that I participated more in the decision-making when it came to medical decision.

Similarly, Samantha (participating during her first pregnancy) said:

> I felt more like an equal with my Dr. I didn't feel that he was this all knowing person while I knew nothing and had to rely on him. I think since I didn't have to call him with all of my questions, I came across to him as more calm so that if I was worried about something I felt that maybe he took me more seriously than if I worried about every little thing (I could be wrong—this is just my perception). I learned to trust my gut instincts about the baby earlier than I would have without the board.

As in Samantha and Oldermom's responses, many of the participants indicated that their experience in this online group had impacted how they interacted with their medical personnel. Their stories don't indicate that they disregarded their doctors or midwives because of what they learned on the board. However, the information and advice provided by those medical caregivers was compared to and discussed in conversations that took place on the bulletin board. Thus, as the board gave these pregnant women information, it also provided them with talk that made them feel more confident and justified as they made medical decisions during their pregnancies.

The information that was shared on the bulletin board between these expectant mothers provided them with additional knowledge, gave them more confidence regarding their pregnancy experience, and impacted their relationships with medical care providers. In these ways, that information was empowering for the participants in the bulletin board. In addition to information, members of this board also offered relational support to one another, and that too lead to greater feelings of empowerment.

Relational Support and Empowerment

As women talk together about pregnancy, they establish what Bird (1994) calls "social pregnancy." Social pregnancy is what occurs when others begin to relate to the woman as an expectant mother. Generally, Bird notes, the process of attaining social pregnancy happens as an increasing number of female friends become aware of the pregnancy and begin to interact with the pregnant woman on the basis of that understanding. At first, only family and very close friends may know about the pregnancy and thus participate in the social pregnancy. However, as the pregnancy becomes more physically noticeable, other women notice and engage in communication about the pregnancy experience. This circle of communication about pregnancy then provides the pregnant woman with a community of peers and can contribute to that woman's sense of personal empowerment.

Because women who interact on an online bulletin board often are not in face-to-face contact with the other participants, physical markers of pregnancy (the rounded stomach) are not necessary in order to be "seen" as pregnant. Many of the participants in this study joined the bulletin board in the earliest weeks of their pregnancies, some even before they had seen a doctor to confirm the pregnancy. Thus, the bulletin board experience allowed the women to become "socially pregnant" and obtain a supportive community through the circle of women's discourse about pregnancy more quickly. As they responded to my questions, it was clear that the members viewed such relational support as a crucial aspect of the bulletin board. Momof4, who participated during her fifth pregnancy and fourth birth said:

> My experience with the pregnancy board has been an extremely positive one. The support throughout the pregnancy was overwhelming. It seemed like someone had or was going through the same things I was which was very comforting.

Many of the mothers I interviewed talked about the support they received in this group. They discussed the supportive comments, "hugs" that were exchanged between members, the positive thoughts that were sent out in problem times, and the genuine affection that was displayed in this online forum. Frequently, participants referred to each other as friends, and sometimes made note that the bulletin board friends were more supportive, in many cases, than their face-to-face friends and family. This is reflected in the responses of DB02 (participating during her second pregnancy) and Louise (participating during her second pregnancy and first birth):

> I made some incredibly supportive and wonderful friends that will listen to every single whine, complaint and triumph. They make you feel that everything is normal and ok!

> The most important thing for me was being able to discuss things 24 hours a day, seven days a week. I could communicate from home or work and was able to ask anything I wanted. I loved the semi-confidential nature of the Internet. It enabled me to ask questions I may not have done from my doctors and friends and family. No one judged my questions or said I was "silly" or "stupid." My fears were always supported and not pushed aside. I also always found someone who had an experience in life of something, however major or trivial.

Several participants discussed thinking that their family and face-to-face friends might get "sick of" discussing the pregnancy, or think that the only interest the woman had was the pregnancy. Other women indicated that their friends and family were simply not available enough to talk about all of the good and bad parts of pregnancy. One participant, Betty Jean, said that a coworker had specifically asked her to not talk about the pregnancy at work. So, for these participants, the bulletin board gave them a place not only to gather information about the pregnancy experience from others, but also to share their own stories of pregnancy. As they talked about their pregnancy within this supportive group of peers, they were able to work through their own experiences and decisions. For some board members, this was even more important because they felt isolated from others in the "real world," as seen in the comments of Gail (participant during first pregnancy) and mdes (participant during second pregnancy):

> At a time when I had little to no social life at one of the most important times in my life, I found the need to find people who were going through the same thing . . . or at least closely the same thing. By finding the bulletin board, I found a whole group of women who were pregnant and due at the same time I was. I found their wisdom and support unmatchable and have referred many many people to partake in the same experience.

> I am not living in my native country and have felt particularly isolated during pregnancy because of that, so to befriend a group of women from around the world who are in a similar situation has been a godsend. My experience has been overwhelmingly positive.

Some participants, like Gail and Andes, talked about feeling alone before they found the bulletin board. For some of them, this was because they were physically away from their close families and friends. For others, because they were stay-at-home mothers, they felt isolated from peers. The circle of friends provided by this bulletin board helped decrease their loneliness.

As you can see from the examples given here, this online bulletin board provided relational support and the development of empathetic relationships for members. Participants talked about the general support they received, the advantage of having readily available friends with whom to discuss pregnancy, and how the supportive environment of the group decreased the sense of isolation. As they developed these empathetic relationships with one another during pregnancy, the members of the board were empowered in their roles as women and mothers.

It is important to note that this study is an analysis of the narratives of a small group of women about their experiences with a pregnancy bulletin board. Thus, there are some important limitations to this work. The results cannot be generalized to women in general. Additionally, though all of the women interviewed here had healthy babies at the end of their pregnancies, we can't assume that the empowerment they obtained through board participation played a causal role. It is possible, however, that feelings of empowerment lead to concrete behaviors that then impact pregnancy outcome. A connection between knowledge, good choice making, and positive pregnancy outcomes has been suggested by some research (American College of Obstetricians and Gynecologists, 2000; Sundari, 1993). Other scholars have argued that supportive relationships in pregnancy may be related to positive pregnancy outcomes, such as a pleasant birth experience, a healthy baby, and less postpartum depression (Collins, Dunkel-Schetter, Lobel, & Scrimshaw, 1993; Norbeck & Tilden, 1983; Norr, Block, Charles, Meyering, & Meyers, 1977). Based on this research, it is possible that the empowerment through knowledge and empathetic relationships gained from this board and others like it could contribute to positive outcomes in pregnancy; however, additional research will be required to establish such a connection.

So, what have we learned here? Though this study was limited in scope, the narratives of these women indicate that pregnancy bulletin boards may be more than simply something to pass the time. They can help create increased empowerment through both the knowledge shared between women and the empathetic relationships created. Based on previous research, it is possible that such empowerment could even lead to positive pregnancy outcomes. However, regardless of any practical physical results of participation in an online pregnancy bulletin board, these women told of feeling increased confidence during their pregnancy because of the bulletin board experience, and that, in and of itself, is a positive result. As we continue to study the impact of Internet use on family interactions and enactments, it is important that we attend to how "outside the family" experiences (such as seeking information regarding family issues online, participating in online bulletin boards related to family issues, getting social support from online groups with regard to psychological and health issues, etc.) interact with our "in the family" enactments and our "of the family" beliefs and understandings.

Questions for Consideration and Discussion

1. This work utilizes the concept of empowerment with regard to pregnant women. In addition to pregnancy, at what other times in family life might empowerment be seen as very important?
2. Here we can see how information functioned to provide empowerment. Have you experienced information as empowering? In what ways?

3. Why is social support a part of empowerment?
4. This article centers around the use of online bulletin boards for pregnancy. What other family events might encourage the use of Internet support or information forums?
5. What characteristics of this particular group of respondents may have affected the results found in this analysis?

Endnotes

1. Names used here are pseudonyms chosen by each participant during the study.

References

American College of Obstetricians and Gynecologists. (2000). *Encyclopedia of women's health and wellness.* Washington, DC: Author.

Arnold, L. B. (2003). Delivering empowerment: Women's narratives about the role of pregnancy bulletin boards. *Qualitative Research Reports in Communication, 4*, 45–52.

Bird, S. E. (1994). It's the talking that's important: Pregnancy folklore as women's discourse. *Women's Studies in Communication, 17*(2), 45–68.

Burke, K. (1974). *The philosophy of literary form: Studies in symbolic action* (3rd ed.) Los Angeles: University of California Press.

Collins, N. L., Dunkel-Schetter, C., Lobel, M., & Scrimshaw, S. C. M. (1993). Social support in pregnancy: Psychosocial correlates of birth outcomes and postpartum depression. *Journal of Personality and Social Psychology, 65*(6), 1243–1258.

Glaser, B. G., & Strauss, A. L. (1967) *The discovery of grounded theory: Strategies for qualitative research.* Chicago: Aldine.

Jordan, J. V., Kaplan, A. G., Miller, J. B., Stiver, I. P., & Surrey, J. L. (1991). *Women's growth in connection: Writings from the Stone Center.* New York: Guilford Press.

Langellier, K. M., & Sullivan, C. F. (1998). Breast talk in breast cancer narratives. *Qualitative Health Research, 8*, 76–95.

Liang, B., Tracy, A., Taylor, C. A., Williams, L. M., Jordan, J. V., & Miller, J. B. (2002). The Relational Health Indices: A study of women's relationships. *Psychology of Women Quarterly, 26*, 25–35.

Madonna, D. (1998a). The Internet: Birthing by email. *The International Journal of Childbirth Education, 13*(2), 40–41.

Madonna, D. (1998b). The Internet: What we already know. *The International Journal of Childbirth Education, 13*(3), 36–38.

Markens, S., Browner, C. H., & Press, N. (1997). Feeding the fetus: On interrogating the notion of maternal–fetal conflict. *Feminist Studies, 23*(2), 351–372.

McCall, M. M. (1990). The significance of storytelling. *Studies in Symbolic Interaction, 11*, 145–161.

Meyer, J. C. (1997) Humor in member narratives: Uniting and dividing at work. *Western Journal of Communication, 61*(2), 188–209.

Norbeck, J. S., & Tilden, V. P. (1983). Life stress, social support, and emotional disequilibrium in complications of pregnancy: A prospective, multivariate study. *Journal of Health and Social Behavior, 24*(1), 30–46.

Norr, K. L., Block, C. R., Charles, A., Meyering, S., & Meyers, E. (1977). Explaining pain and enjoyment in childbirth. *Journal of Health and Social Behavior, 18* (3), 260–275.

Owen, W. F. (1984). Interpretive themes in relational communication. *Quarterly Journal of Speech, 70*, 274–287.

Rubenstein, H., & Lawler, S. K. (1990). Toward the psychosocial development of women. *Affilia: Journal of Women and Social Work, 5*(3), 27–38.

Sundari, T. K. (1993). Can health education improve pregnancy outcome?: Report of a grassroots action-education campaign. *The Journal of Family Welfare, 39*(1), 1–12.

Surrey, J. L. (1991a). Relationship and empowerment. In J. V. Jordan, A. G. Kaplan, J. B. Miller, I. P. Stiver, & J. L. Surrey (Eds.), *Women's growth in connection: Writings from the Stone Center* (pp. 162–180). New York: Guilford Press.

Surrey, J. L. (1991b). The self in relation: A theory of women's development. In J.V. Jordan, A. G. Kaplan, J. B. Miller, I. P. Stiver, & J. L. Surrey (Eds.), *Women's growth in connection: Writings from the Stone Center* (pp. 51–66). New York: Guilford Press.

Zelzer, D. D. (1995). Weaving a web of birth information. *Midwifery Today and Childbirth Education, 36*, 42–43.

Where Are the Mommies?: A Content Analysis of Women's Magazines

Deirdre D. Johnston

Debra Harvey Swanson

Beliefs about the characteristics required of family members are learned in family settings and also in our cultural communication. Therefore, images of family in the media are important to our family understandings. In this piece, Johnston and Swanson explore the ways motherhood is discussed in popular women's magazines, to consider how such images may affect mothers views of self, and the beliefs of non-mothers about mothering. While you read this piece, reflect on the media images of mothering you have seen in the last few months, and how those resonate with what is discussed here.

L.B.A.

In contemporary society, mothers are confronted with two polarized stereotypes of what constitutes good mothering (Buxton, 1998). "Super mom"—a chic dresser and career woman, driving her SUV, drinking a latte, and negotiating a deal on her cell phone, is en route to dropping her children (dressed in designer outfits with matching hats, tights, and shoes) at day care. "Earth mother"—in capris and sandals, a gaggle of toddlers wrapped around her legs, freezing small portions of organic pureed carrots in ice-cube trays, is simultaneously nursing a baby and offering instructions to a gifted preschooler building a geodesic dome out of newspapers on the kitchen floor. Our research suggests that mothers actually internalize these stereotypes of mothers who have made employment decisions different than their own (Johnston & Swanson, 2004a, 2004c). In our research we argue that the perpetuation of these stereotypes contributes to the cultural "mother wars" that pit at-home and employed mothers against each other in a crazed competition for "Best (or Worst) Mother of the Year" (Johnston & Swanson, 2004c).

These caricatures of mothers are exaggerated and have little basis in reality. Researchers have noted how teenage mothers, older mothers, single mothers, lesbian mothers, and mothers of color reside outside the cult of "good motherhood" as defined by the culture. For example, Solinger (1994) writes that Black single mothers are labeled deviant by the culture, whereas White single mothers are viewed as troubled, but redeemable.

The traditional expectations that mothers should not work outside the home clearly privileges White middle-class married mothers who can financially afford to make that choice. Those same privileged mothers hire working-class women and women of color, who are often mothers themselves, for child care or housekeeping. It's okay for lower socioeconomic or non-White mothers to work; indeed we denigrate less financially privileged mothers if they do not seek employment, while simultaneously applauding the "good" middle-class mother for staying home full-time.

The cult of domesticity that establishes the expectations of "good mothering" is defined by the culture (Chang, 1994). The cult of domesticity promotes consumerism, home decorating, preparation of trendy family home-cooked dinners, knowledge of the latest child-raising theories, and an obsession with the micro-management of children. The micro-management of children promotes a particular child raising ideology, one Hays (1996) describes as an era of intensive mothering expectations. These expectations promote a child-centered, expert-guided, emotionally absorbing, labor intensive, and financially expensive childrearing philosophy. Mothers are positioned as the sole source of child guidance, nurturance, education, and physical and emotional sustenance. All aspects of baby's experience must be carefully orchestrated to promote proper development. At a recent conference on mothering research Fox, author of *Dispatches from a Not-So-Perfect Life* (2003), told a story of a mother who was accosted at the neighborhood playground for giving her daughter organic yogurt in a tube. The critical mother charged that the sugar content was too high, and that she, the better mother, removed half of the flavored yogurt by syringe and replaced it (by syringe) with unflavored yogurt. Hays (1996) argues that no mother can achieve and maintain these intensive expectations as there is always some area in which she will be inadequate.

One source of cultural role expectations and ideology is the media. We are particularly interested in the messages presented in women's magazines. Women's magazines are seductive: They present glossy full-color images of beautiful women. Women's magazines are pervasive. Even if a mother doesn't subscribe to these magazines she is confronted with their messages and images in doctors' offices and grocery store check-out lines. Women's magazines are highly utilized by women as a source of advice on domesticity, motherhood, and what it means to be a woman. Consider the names of these magazines: *Better Homes and Gardens* and *Good Housekeeping* create expectations of domestic success. *Family Circle* and *Family Fun* encourage family unity and joy. *Self, Ms., New Woman,* and *Working Woman* promote an identity. Although not the only source of identity information for mothers, magazines are pervasive and seductive sites of ideological representation. Whether or not a woman models or resists the ideology represented in magazines, the images and articles create a reality that limits what we think is "real" and limits our imagination of what we think is possible (Corrigan & Sayer, 1985).

Studies of magazine content reveal that despite dramatic changes in women's representation in the labor force, there has been little change in the portrayal of women in women's general-interest magazines over the second half of the twentieth century. Murphy (1994) describes the world created by magazines filled with women who are White, middle to upper-middle class, domestic, beautiful, and consumed by materialistic quests. Murphy also analyzed new nontraditional women magazines (e.g., *New Woman, Working Woman,* and *Lear's*) and concluded: "It may now be acceptable to be independent, politically involved, sexually active, committed to a career, even to be over forty. But it's only acceptable if you look right and have the right accoutrements" (p. 126). Murphy and other researchers have concluded that women's magazines continue to perpetuate gender myths and are far from an accurate reflection of women in society.

If women continue to be portrayed in traditional gender roles in magazines, how then are mothers portrayed? Kaplan (1990, 1992) concluded in her analysis of popular culture films that motherhood and employment continue to be presented as mutually exclusive: women were presented as sexual and career-oriented, or mothers, but seldom both. One of the few studies of mothers in magazines was conducted by Keller (1994). She analyzed themes of mother portrayals in traditional women's magazines, and found a progression from a traditionalist ideology in the 1960s, to a feminist ideology in the 1970s, to a neotraditionalist ideology (i.e., quit employment, return to home and hearth) in the 1980s. Her research, however, stops with the analysis of 1980s magazine content.

Finding no current analyses of the representation of mothers in women's magazines, we decided to conduct a content analysis (Johnston & Swanson, 2003a, 2003b). Our research is based on a sample of five different magazines. The two magazines with the highest subscription rates for women between the ages of 25 and 45 are *Good Housekeeping* and *Family Circle*. We included these two magazines in our sample because this is the prime childbearing age for women. *Parents* magazine was included because it has the highest subscription rate for mothers of preschool children. Because of our interest in the portrayal of employed women, we also included *Family Fun* and *Working Mother* which have the highest percentage of total subscribers who are employed women. The months selected were March, June, September, and December to ensure that we had one issue per quarter and to avoid months that might overrepresent mother-related content, such as Mother's Day articles in the month of May. We analyzed the entire content of each publication: articles; advertisements; letters and testimonials; columns; and short take-out boxes. Each of the 1,383 text units was coded on a number of variables pertaining to the way the mother was represented in the text or image.

Where Are the Mommies?

We found that women's magazines continue to promote traditional representations of mothers (Johnston & Swanson, 2003a). Mothers are presented as White, at-home mothers primarily confined to the home. An analysis of women (both mothers and nonmothers) in advertisements revealed that 60% are White and 40% women of color. When we analyzed only those women represented as mothers, the women of color disappear: 95% of mothers presented in the home and 89% of employed mothers were White. This biased representation perpetuates stereotypes that only Whites value family, motherhood, and parenting.

Employed mothers were absent from magazines as well. Although, according to Census data, 62% of mothers of preschool children work full- or part-time outside the home, only 12% of all mothers portrayed in these magazines had an employment identity. Considering that 62% of preschool mothers are balancing home and employment, it is astonishing that only 3% of the topics addressed in the articles, letters, sidebars, or ads in these magazines referenced employment-related issues.

What Are the Messages to Mommies?

An analysis of these five magazines revealed a plethora of double-bind messages directed to mothers. Double binds are messages that promote two mutually exclusive self-presentations. To identify with one self-presentation is to invite condemnation for not living up to the alternative self-presentation. The most obvious double bind for mothers is choosing whether to stay home or work outside the home. If a mother chooses to stay home she is devalued by an economic culture for lack of social contribution and financial worth. If a mother chooses to work outside the home she is ridiculed for being selfish and a bad, neglectful mother. No matter what choice a mother makes in response to a double bind, she is undermined and made to feel guilty and inadequate.

Literature and research on motherhood suggest four maternal double binds in our culture: (1) mothers are selfish/selfless; (2) mothers should foster independence/dependence in children; (3) mothers fail/succeed in public/private spheres; and (4) mothering is natural/in need of expert help. We analyzed magazine content for evidence of these double binds in messages to women.

Selfish/Selfless Identity

The selfish/selfless double bind suggests that mothers who stay home with their children are selfless and self-sacrificing because their children are more important to them than their needs for money or success. The flip side of this double bind suggests that mothers who work outside the home are selfish because they put their own needs and aspirations before the needs of their children. This is a double bind because to achieve either role expectation (at home or employed) invites a condemnation. For example, women who are employed are lauded for being independent and valued for their economic worth, but condemned for being selfish mothers. In turn, women who are at home are lauded for being "good mothers," but not valued by society.

We analyzed whether this double bind was present in contemporary women's magazines. The analysis of magazine content revealed many examples of at-home mothers portrayed as self-sacrificing and selfless, but no examples of employed mothers portrayed as selfish.

In any article, letter, or advertisement there is an implied motivation as to why the reader should take a particular course of action—to be a good mother, to be a good wife, to be good to your family, or to be good to yourself. The motivation presented to at-home mothers was almost exclusively to be a good mother and never to be good to self. In one magazine example, buying condensed milk is all about being a good mother: "For not insisting bunny slippers are shoes. For leaving Blankie behind. For actually getting out of the car. I'll risk spoiling your dinner" and make "Welcome Home" brownies for you with condensed milk.

At-home mothers were also defined exclusively through their relationship with their children. For example, one letter to the editor promotes the maternal bliss myth—the source of happiness is motherhood, and if you are not happy, there is something wrong with you. The letter started out with the sentence "The key to being a good mothers is simple: happiness" and goes on to suggest that if you are not happy, you are a failed mother who should attend to managing your time with your kids. The letter clearly assumes a selfless self-sacrificing mother knows better than to pursue her happiness through an identity outside of motherhood.

Employed mothers, in contrast, were targeted with motivations to "be good to self and family." For example, a Campbell's soup ad states: "If dinner has to be in the oven by

6:00, you better make darn sure you're home by 5:55." Employed mothers were also more likely to have multiple identities—suggesting that one need not sacrifice all of one's identities for motherhood. In one Oldsmobile advertisement we see a woman looking into the camera and the text reads, "Saturdays at noon, I am a soccer mom. It's not Saturday. It's not noon." This advertisement highlights the mom's relational identity with her family by describing her as a soccer mom. The traditional soccer mom is a devoted mother to her children, present and cheering at all the games, bringing treats to the team, standing there rain or shine, supporting her child in his or her activities. In this particular example, she refers to her Saturday-soccer-mom "good mom" status, but declares an identity independent of her mother-relational identity by "today is not Saturday." This example illustrates a theme in the magazine content we analyzed to present employed mothers as devoted mothers as opposed to selfish career-obsessed workers.

Independence/Dependence Relationship to Child

The independence/dependence double bind is defined by a mother's relationship to her child. Stereotypes suggest that at-home mothers are overly enmeshed with their children and engender dependence, whereas employed mothers are equally criticized for pushing their child to be too independent.

In our analysis of magazine content we once again found evidence of the at-home mother double bind, but found no criticism of employed mothers. Consistent with stereotypes of mothers, there were more portrayals of exaggerated needs for connection among at-home mothers. This portrayal is made clear in a recent article "Why Toddlers Cling" (*Parents* magazine, November 2004). The opening sentence reads "Goodbyes are never easy. But for some toddlers, leaving Mom's arms feels like a tantrum-worthy tragedy." Later in the article, the author attempts to let mothers know what their toddlers are thinking when being separated. Some of these toddler thoughts include: "Saying goodbye to Mommy means my world is ending. Maybe she'll forget about me. If I cry when she's about to leave, she'll stick around longer." These thoughts can easily evoke paranoia in mothers reading *Parents* magazine by suggesting that separation from children is traumatic and unnatural and by extension "bad mothering." The good mom never leaves, and especially not for selfish employment reasons.

A 2004 State Farm Insurance advertisement depicted a working mother helping her son put on his shoes on. Dressed in a suit, the mother clearly works outside the home, but still has time to take care of her son's needs. The caption on the page reads, "We never met a mom who wasn't working: It's pretty simple, really. Your family depends on you to be there." The overall advertisement implies healthy levels of dependence and independence between mother and child. The child is clearly dependent on his mother to help him get his shoes on, yet the mother and child are not so dependent on one another that they cannot separate. The mother is talking on the phone independently from her son while helping him put his shoes on, and it is clear to the onlooker that mother and child are preparing to spend the day apart. This positive portrayal of working mothers shows movement away from the neglectful mother and absent mother associations to mother child separation found in 1980s popular culture by Kaplan (1992).

Success/Failure in Private Sphere versus Public Sphere

The success/failure double bind is associated with stereotypes that employed mothers are successful in employment, but failures at home, and at-home mothers are successful at home, but failures outside the home. The analysis of magazines showed that, not surprisingly, at-home mothers are targeted in messages promoting "success" in the home. What is surprising is that at-home mothers were also depicted as incompetent at home in 21% of their representations. One article presents a mother talking on the phone with a screaming baby on the hip, while dinner is burning in the saucepan on the stove. In another magazine article an at-home mother confesses: "I had slipped the new diaper on without removing the old one. She'd been sitting in the same soggy diaper for hours."

Less than 10% of all representations of mothers presented mothers as competent in both the public and domestic spheres, and less than 1% presented mothers as competent in the performance of their public sphere identity without also commenting on their competence as mothers. So, although employed mothers were not often represented, they were represented as more competent than at-home mothers. A Stouffer's lasagna advertisement suggests "Nothing brings a family together like a home cooked meal." The mother in the picture is serving lasagna to her family gathered around the table. She is still in her office clothes. The father, in his shirt-sleeves and tie, is helping by handing out dishes. The parents are obviously equally involved in getting table on the dinner for the family and equally committed to the delusion that frozen lasagna constitutes a home-cooked meal. As is typical in the context of these magazines the mother's competence in the public sphere is never at issue—if she wears a suit, her competence is implied. The employed mother's competence as a mother is always in question and presents a sort of literary tension—will she pull it off this time? The magazines do, however, resolve this tension with portrayals of employed mothers as successful in the domestic sphere.

Natural/Unnatural

The natural/unnatural double bind reflects a cultural stereotype that mothers are naturally endowed with an innate ability to be good mothers. This is often used as a justification for why mothers, not fathers, should stay home full-time with children. Feminists have argued that the nurturance of children is natural for both mothers and fathers, or that nurturance is a learned behavior that can be learned by both males and females. There are cultural stereotypes of employed mothers characterize them as unnatural mothers incapable of nurturing and bonding with their children. The unnatural mother needs advice and expert help because she does not possess the innate qualities and intuition of a good mother.

What we found surprised us: Employed mothers are portrayed as natural mothers in the majority of their portrayals, but at-home mothers are presented as natural mothers in less than half of their portrayals. At-home mothers are more likely to be portrayed in need of expert help in order to fulfill even the simplest mothering functions.

Whereas cultural stereotypes present employed mothers as frazzled, too busy, and stressed, magazines portray them as innately nurturing and wise. For example, a Ford advertisement says: "At Ford, we always listen to our mothers . . . 30 of the Windstar Product Development Team members happen to be moms." Not only are these employed mothers natural at mothering and working, but their domestic roles (as mothers) inform their public role (on the Windstar Development Team)—their mother knowledge actually makes them more valued employees.

At-home mothers, however, are often presented in need of expert help. A *Parents* article is headed in bold letters that reads "My son fell out of a second-floor window." The mother in the article was an at-home mom cooking dinner and not paying attention to her two sons while they were playing upstairs. Certainly a natural mother would not have let this happen to her children while she was at home! Just a few pages later, we see mothers in jeans and sweatshirts, talking on their cell phones and drinking coffees, obviously pushing strollers to the parks are bombarded with "Stroller do's and don'ts." The expert advice given in this article is so simplistic it is hard to believe any mother would not have the common sense to abide by these rules. In each example, the photo of the mother shows her distracted or inattentive, the child obviously close to an accident.

The portrayals of at-home mothers as incompetent in meeting domestic success expectations, combined with portrayals of at-home mothers in need of instruction to perform simple mothering tasks, create a reinforcing cycle. "When at-home mothers are made to feel incompetent, they are more likely to seek expert help and advice" (Johnston & Swanson, 2003b, p. 260). This drive to overcome characterizations of incompetence by seeking expert help is likely what keeps these magazines flying off the grocery store racks.

Conclusion

Although we expected to find double binds undermining both at-home and employed mothers, we found that the four double binds we analyzed in magazine content are targeted to at-home, but not employed, mothers. At-home mothers—the primary target for most of these magazines—were patronized and reduced to one-dimensional caricatures. Employed mothers—whom we expected to be denigrated in women's magazines—were presented, without exception, as successful competent women and mothers. The double binds associated with the portrayals of at-home mothers were explicit in the text and images in the magazine content. Employed mothers, however, are confronted with an implicit double bind in these magazines: they are presented positively, but they are seldom presented. This creates an impression that women can be mothers and employed workers, but very few do. The ratio of at-home to employed mother representations was more than 9:1. Rich clearly articulates this problem of invisibility; "when someone with authority . . . describes the world and you are not in it, there is a moment of psychic disequilibrium, as if you looked into a mirror and saw nothing" (1986, p. 199).

This research suggests that women's magazines promote a particular mother identity and simultaneously condemn the promoted identity. Employed mothers may be confident and successful, but their relative absence in these magazines suggests that not many can make this work. Frequent but negative portrayals of at-home mothers and infrequent but positive portrayals of employed mothers likely have the effect of undermining the confidence of both groups.

This research has implications for our understanding of the current mother wars (Buxton, 1998). Foucault (1978) argued that power systems, such as patriarchy, create expectations that can be fulfilled by the dominant group, but ensure the failure of the subordinate group. Magazine content, as one source of cultural expectations for motherhood, contributes to a climate in which mothers feel inadequate in meeting the cultural expectations of good mothering. Inadequacy breeds defensiveness and a need to justify one's own mother-work identity by demeaning the mother-work identity choice of other mothers.

To change the cultural climate, mothers must be empowered. All mothers need to be supported in their decisions to make the employment choice that best meets their own and their family's needs. For the sake of our children, as well as for the sake of mothers, it is in the best interests of the culture to help mothers reach their mothering potential. The mother wars rhetoric promotes a binary mothering ideal; people either identify with the good at-home mother–bad employed mother or the good employed mother–bad at-home mother. When we use the phrase "good mother" we imply that there are "bad mothers." To transcend these polarized constructions of motherhood we must recognize that there is more than one way to mother successfully. We must make employment status irrelevant to the evaluation of mothering. There are good employed mothers and there are bad at-home mothers. Employment choice doesn't predict mothering abilities and qualities. Only when we honor multiple and varied mothering ideologies will we, as a culture, be able to provide the necessary support and resources to empower mothers to be the best mothers they can be.

Questions for Consideration and Discussion

1. Johnston and Swanson discuss two stereotypes of good mothering, super mom and earth mother. What stereotypes of bad mothering have you seen in media messages?
2. This work analyzes women's magazines, which are more prevalent in U.S. culture than men's magazines. Why do you think this is the case?
3. The analysis revealed that very few mothers shown in the magazines were women of color. What reasons might be behind this and what are the potential ramifications?
4. How would you recommend that writers and editors avoid the doublebinds discussed by Johnston and Swanson?
5. The authors argue that double binds create guilt for mothers. Why might guilt be a problematic emotion for effective parenting?

References

Buxton, J. (1998). *Ending the mother war: Starting the workplace revolution.* London: Macmillan.

Chang, G. (1994). Undocumented Latinas: The new "employable mother." In E. Glenn, G. Chang, and L. Forcey (Eds.), *Mothering: Ideology, experience and agency* (pp. 259–285). New York: Routledge.

Corrigan, P., and Sayer, D. (1985). *The great arch: English state formation as cultural revolution.* Oxford, England: Blackwell.

Foucault, M. (1978). *The history of sexuality* (Vol. 1). New York: Pantheon.

Fox, F. (2003). *Dispatches from a not-so-perfect life: Or how I learned to love the house, the man, the child.* New York: Harmony Press.

Hays, S. (1996). *The cultural contradictions of motherhood.* New Haven, CT: Yale University Press.

Johnston, D., and Swanson, D. (2003a). Invisible mothers: A content analysis of motherhood ideologies and myths in magazines. *Sex Roles, 49*(1/2), 21–33.

Johnston, D., & Swanson, D. (2003b). Undermining mothers: A content analysis of the representation of mothers in magazines. *Mass Communication & Society, 6*(3), 243–265.

Johnston, D., & Swanson, D. (2004a). *Defining mother: The experience of motherhood ideologies by work status.* Paper presented at the annual meeting of the North Central Sociological Association, Cleveland, OH.

Johnston, D., & Swanson, D. (2004b). *Impact of mother in the construction of adult daughter's worker–mother identity.* Paper presented at the Feminism and Mothering meeting of the Association for Research on Mothering, Toronto, Canada.

Johnston, D., & Swanson, D. (2004c). Moms hating moms: The internalization of mother war rhetoric. *Sex Roles, 51*, 497–509.

Kaplan, E. (1990). Sex, work and motherhood: The impossible triangle. *The Journal of Sex Research, 27*, 409–425.

Kaplan, E. (1992). *Motherhood and representation: The mother in popular culture and melodrama.* New York: Routledge Kegan Paul.

Keller, K. (1994). *Mothers and work in popular American magazines.* Westport, CT: Greenwood.

Murphy, B. (1994). Women's magazines: Confusing differences. In L. Turner & H. Sterk (Eds.), *Differences that make a difference: Examining the assumptions of gender research* (pp. 119–127). Westport, CT: Bergin & Garvey.

Rich, A. (1986). *Blood, bread, and poetry: Selected prose 1979–1985.* New York: Norton.

Solinger. R. (1994). Race and "value": Black and White illegitimate babies, 1945–1965. In E. Glenn, G. Chang, & L. Forcey (Eds.), *Mothering: Ideology, experience, and agency* (pp. 287–310). New York: Routledge.

Section 3: Conclusions and Application—The Media as Part of Your Family Life _____

Think back on the last 24 hours of your life. In how many of those hours were you exposed to some sort of media: radio, television, film, Internet, magazines, books, billboards, and so on? If you are like most people, the answer would be a relatively significant proportion of that 24-hour period. The media are all around us. We are exposed to them in a variety of ways throughout the day. In this chapter, we considered how mass media interact with family. We discussed the use of media, including television and the Internet. We also considered the images that the media provide of family and family interaction. Though we might like to think that the media do not affect our attitudes and our behaviors, research and even common sense tell us that the media do have an impact on us, in a variety of ways.

Media Use

As we discussed at the start of the chapter, and as considered by Anderson, Crowell, and Pearce, and Arnold, the types of media that we have available to us, and that we use in and outside our family settings do affect the ways that we engage in social interaction with one another. Television is a good example of this.

Prior to the advent of the television, families obtained most of their news from newspapers and their entertainment from books, newspapers, and the radio. Newspapers and books are solitary pursuits . . . they don't bring people together to engage in conversation and they often are read only by one person (unless an adult is reading to a child or another family member). Radio, however, did hold the potential to bring the family together. Family members would join each other to listen to their favorite radio program. Though they needed to focus their listening on the program, they were free to engage in other pursuits with their eyes. In addition to conversing during the breaks, they could knit, play cards, and so forth while listening to the show. Because they had to use their imaginations to understand the stories at hand, family members may have engaged in more discussion about what the characters looked like, or what that sound was in the background. Thus, though they were occupied by the medium, they could maintain family communication and connection during the show. When television arrived on the scene, things changed. Families still came together in the evening to enjoy their favorite programs. But now, the medium occupied all of their senses. Enjoying the programming required listening and looking. Less discussion of what was happening in the stories was necessary because the program indicated visually and in the auditory channel what was going on. So, although the family was still together, interaction was changed.

Thus, the very presence of the medium is what changes the interaction patterns. It isn't just the precise messages that are transferred in that medium, but how it is used by people that create the changes. As discussed in Section 1 and in the article by Anderson, Crowell, and Pearce, the Internet has also produced changes in family interaction patterns. As communication technology continues to change, so too will social interactions.

Think about the future of technology. Cell phones now send pictures and text messages along with being used for oral conversation. Cell users can read the news, enjoy video reviews, and check the train schedule from their phones. Computers are getting smaller and smaller. Notepad computers allow people to check their email from any "hot spot" without carrying a hefty laptop. How will the changes of the future impact social interaction and the family? That is uncertain. What is clear is that, as we adopt new technology and enjoy new media, we need to be mindful of the changes it may cause in our social interactions with friends and family. Will it make us closer? Will it drive us further apart? Will it make us more connected to the workplace and thus cause greater amounts of role strain? If we can consider the changes, both good and bad, that a particular technology will make on our social interaction, we can make wiser choices about what technology to adopt and what media to allow in our lives and in our homes. Choices may include the consideration of convenience, but should go beyond that if we want to truly understand the ramifications upon the interactions with the people we care about.

Media Images of Family

The forms of media that we use are not the only things that impact family. The images that we encounter on various media also affect our understandings of family. As noted in Section 1 and the reading by Johnston and Swanson, mediated images of family rarely reflect the complexity of family forms and roles. When the media oversimplifies portrayals of any type of individual, they contribute to a social understanding of that type of person as unidimensional, or at least limited in variation.

Think about the portrayal of gay men on television today. The number of gay characters, even on cable programs, are limited and certainly do not reflect the percentage of people that are, in fact, homosexual. Shows such as *Will and Grace* and *Queer Eye for the Straight Guy* utilize strong stereotypes of homosexuality for humor. Gay men are often shown as relatively shallow, concerned mostly with appearance and sexuality, and very "unmasculine." So, how might this impact gay men who would like to, or who have adopted a child? What sorts of attributions will be made about their parenting ability and seriousness? As we discussed earlier, some individuals have an objection to gay or lesbian parents that springs from a religious conviction about that sexual orientation and lifestyle. Others, however, object because they believe that gay men and lesbian women will not be good parents. Research does not support this argument. And yet, it persists. Why is that? Could it be that images we see of gay men in television and movie programming impact our understandings of who they are and therefore how they can parent? Mediated images always have some impact on us, but the portrayals of people, cultures, or ideas that we haven't had much exposure to face-to-face may have even more impact.

As a wise consumer of media, you are in a better position to critically analyze the images and portrayals that you encounter, and think about how they affect you, and how your beliefs have been influenced by those mediated messages. In Chapter 9, we considered how a more critical and reflective stance on our own worldview can produce the opportunity to become familiar with different positions and different understandings of the world and the people in it.

Additionally, you are a member of at least one family system. Chances are, at some point you will enter at least one more family system. Within each family system that you are a part of, you occupy particular roles based upon the functions you fulfill and how you interact with others. The responsibilities associated with different family members and the functions that particular family members are expected to fulfill are a product of socialization within the family and within the culture. Media are a part of that socialization process. If the media present a particular image related to your family role, say, for example, if you are a mother or a father, and you do not see yourself matching up to that role, how might it make you feel? What sort of assessments might you make about yourself? Once again, a more critical position about mediated messages can help you to avoid some of the detrimental effects of being a media consumer.

The media are a part of our lives. Very few people in the United States can say that they have totally avoided media in their lives. The media, in and of itself, aren't bad, but we need to think carefully about how we use them and what they say to us, and about us, as we interact as family members and members of the larger culture.

Questions for Consideration and Discussion

1. What type of media do you use on a daily basis? How do they improve your life? What are the drawbacks that you see to their use?
2. Research indicates that many young adults use the Internet almost daily. How has being in college affected your use of the Internet? How has your Internet use impacted your communication with family members?
3. As media continues to evolve, how do you see family interactions being affected by things such as cell phones, text messaging, and so on?
4. This chapter addresses the images of mothers in media. Adult children, adolescents, and children are also reflected in media messages. How have you seen your family roles reflected in the media? To what extent do those portrayals adequately reflect you and your life?
5. To what extent do you believe it is the responsibility of media programmers to accurately reflect family life or to consider the impacts of messages on images of the family?

Key Terms and Concepts _____

cyber-commuting	media portrayals of family	uses-and-gratifications
media ecology	parallel activity	theory

Conclusion: Family Communication Research and Theory—Past, Present, and Future

In this text, we have considered a considerable body of family communication research, and we have really only skimmed the surface of the research that has been conducted regarding communication processes and the family. The field of family communication study is almost unlimited in potential arenas of focus, as the unique aspects of communication about and within families change and shift across cultures and time periods.

As you have read this book, and encountered a wide variety of findings and theories regarding family communication, you have probably sometimes felt that there is too much to fully organize into your brain! And the fact that research takes varying approaches, depending upon the worldview of the scholars (more social scientific or more humanistic) and the necessities of methodological approaches, probably does not diminish that feeling that there is an almost overwhelming amount to think about. However, reflection about the theories and research that have been presented in this text can reveal some underlying understandings that I believe permeate our field of study and the findings we have discussed. Let's return to those fundamentals here.

First, family and culture are intertwined. It is in our family settings that we first become socialized to the cultural expectations that will be brought to bear on our lives. It is from our culture that we draw the beliefs and expectations that come to comprise the standards for family behavior and understanding. Regardless of the area of analysis, the theory in discussion, or the finding under examination, we must continually return to culture as a lens through which to view family interaction. Even theories and research premised upon genetic tendencies have a cultural base. To study whether shyness is hereditary begins with a set of culturally created assumptions about what shyness is, and a body of cultural knowledge that indicates the impacts of shyness in social interaction.

Second, family cannot be understood without a focus on communication phenomenon. It is through the process of communication that we create families (we meet, we court, we wed, we procreate, etc. through communication) and it is through communication that we maintain them. Communication with one another allows us to fulfill our family roles and expectations, maintain our relationships, socialize our young, create and sustain our rules, and so on. Family is communication.

Third, families are systems (and contain systems, and are embedded within systems). Whether a scholar takes an explicitly systemic approach or not, family communication research is based on the idea that the different parts of a family system impact each other, the family is something beyond just the individual members added together, the behaviors of today affect the system of tomorrow, and change is continual yet pattern is present. These are basic system ideas that form an important part of the family communication field of study.

With an eye toward these three ideas, and a background in the theories and research presented in this book, you are well positioned as a beginning family communication scholar to approach this field of study in all its variations. This foundational learning can become a launchpad for thinking about where family communication study will go from here.

As field of study that really began to come into its own in the 1970s, family communication study continues to grow and develop as we move through this early part of the twenty-first century. As scholars of family communication, it is interesting to think about where we are now, and where we may go from here.

One issue that will likely continue to be important to the field of family communication study is the generation of true "family communication theories." As you have seen throughout this text, many of the theories used in family communication study are theories developed to understand communication processes more generally, small-group processes, or interpersonal interaction. There are only a few exceptions to this, including family communication patterns theory and inconsistent nurturing as control theory. As the field of family communication continues to grow and develop, we are likely to see more theories established that spring directly from the examination of communication in and about family.

A second important issue that presents itself to family communication scholars of the present and will in the future is the role of technology in family interaction. Already, we have seen an impact from the Internet in middle- and upper-middle-class American family culture. As more people have access to the Internet, its impact is likely to grow. Family communication scholars will need to examine how this medium affects families across relationships, in different dimensions of the family system, and across culture. In addition to Internet use, the growing prominence of cell phones is another technological change that will need attention from family communication scholars. How is parenting changing in cultures where children and adolescents regularly carry cell phones? How are extended family relationships being affected by greater ease (and decreased expense) of long-distance calling? And what about Internet phone capabilities (like Skype) that allow us to both talk to and see family members at great distances? How will that technology affect us? Thus, we can anticipate that attention to technological changes will be an important part of our field of study in the coming years.

Third, given the importance of culture in our family beliefs and enactments, as cultures continue to change over time, our field of study will need to follow those changes in an attempt to understand the impact upon families. In the United States we are watching family forms undergo a variety of changes, as multiracial families continue to increase, gay- and lesbian-parented families become a more visible presence, marriage laws continue to be negotiated, maintenance of a living wage on one income becomes more and more difficult, and cultural acceptance of blended families and single-parent families increases. To understand family communication processes means a continual reexamination of how issues like these impact the lived experience of family members.

Fourth, as medical and scientific advances continue around the world, the life of families will be impacted in ways we can only begin to apprehend. In industrialized nations, longevity continues to increase as medical breakthroughs are made. How will this affect our family relationships and our understanding of what it means to be elderly? Likewise, the ability to save the lives of infants born extremely early or with previously fatal conditions continues to grow. However, this miraculous technology also leaves us asking how the lives of such infants will unfold, how those lives will impact the families in which they are raised, and how that will affect the larger culture in which those families live.

These are but a few of the issues that will continue to impact the study of family in the coming years. Family communication research is an infinite area of study, as the unique properties of families across time, across cultures, and across individual experiences are infinite. This may, at times, befuddle us with the complexity of even attempting to understand, but it points to the excitement of studying family and family communication.

As you leave this text, it will be your task to determine how you can utilize the knowledge gained here in your own life. Will you use what you have learned to help understand and critically analyze your own life and the lives of those around you? Will you use this information to plan your future family interactions in your family of origin, extended family, and/or families of cohabitation or procreation? Will you continue to study family communication phenomena as a scholar? Will you pull this information into another field of study or occupation (elementary education, nursing, child psychology) to enhance your knowledge there? It is my hope that, however you decide to utilize the material presented in this text, you will find it useful in your life and will continue to be invigorated, in one way or another, by the experience of studying family and family communication.

Appendix A

How to Read a Scholarly Research Article

If reading scholarly work is new to you, it may seem somewhat difficult or confusing. However, once you get accustomed to the form and style of such work, it really isn't as difficult as it might appear at first. In this appendix, I introduce you to the "genres" (general types) of work you see represented in this text, and some of the terminology that is used in scholarly work, as well as considering the typical parts of a research report. Although the articles in this text have been written specifically for you, the undergraduate student, you will likely read other articles directly from scholarly journals and this information will help guide and inform that reading.

Worldviews: Social Science and Humanism/Interpretivism

One area of distinction between types of research in communication relates to the perspective, or worldview, of the researchers. Some researchers proceed from a *social scientific* view, whereas other scholars adopt a more *humanist* or *interpretive* perspective.

The difference between social scientific scholars and humanist/interpretive scholars begins in how they understand the nature of truth and reality. In general, social scientists believe that there is a Truth (a *fundamental reality*) and that reality can be found through research if that research is done carefully and repeatedly. Humanist/interpretivist scholars argue that there are truths (*multiple realities*) and that reality can be understood only through the lens of our own experiences.

Following on this difference in understanding of reality, these two types of scholars understand human behavior in different ways. Social scientists believe in a concept called determinism. *Determinism* reflects a belief that human behavior is determined by a combination of genetic factors and environmental factors. Thus, if we know enough about people's heredity and environment, we can predict behavior. Humanist/interpretivist scholars don't believe in determinism. Instead, they argue that human behavior is fundamentally affected by *free will*. As humans we make choices about our behavior (and can chose to do things that seem contradictory to both heredity and environment). So, humanists/interpretivists do not try to make predictions about human behavior.

Because these types of scholars have different viewpoints on truth and human behavior, they also have different primary values in terms of research. Social scientists value *objectivity* in their work. Being certain that a piece of research is carefully done and doesn't reflect any bias—that is, is objective—is very important from a social scientific stance. Given that humanist/interpretivist scholars don't see Truth as accessible, but rather seek truths, they value work that emancipates ideas, voices, and people. *Emancipation* refers to freeing. Thus, humanist/interpretive scholars hope to free new ideas, hear voices that are not typically heard, and increase the power and visibility of people often rendered silent or invisible.

All of these differences lead to a distinction in the end goal of these groups of scholars. Social scientific scholars hope to be able to reach *general statements of relationships* between one variable of human experience and another. The more people these statements can be applied to, and the more situations in which they can be seen to apply, the better the results are. Each bit of research done about a topic has the potential to contribute to these general statements of relationship (sometimes called "covering laws"). Interpretivist/humanist scholars hope to provide *new understandings*. They want to be able to show something about human experience that is new and compelling. The finding may apply to a small group of people or a large group, a very specific situation or more general sets of situations.

A final difference that can be seen between these two groups of scholars is how research is conducted. Social scientific research is typically done using *experimental design* or *surveys*. Humanist/interpretive research is usually accomplished through *ethnographic study* (studying a group of people closely in an attempt to understand their culture), or *textual analysis* (carefully looking at communicative phenomenon in an attempt to see themes, patterns, etc.).

So, why is it important for you to understand these differences? First, because in order to really understand a piece of research, it is best to know from what worldview the researchers are operating. Although research can have elements of both stances, most research is identifiable as being primarily one or the other. Having a clear understanding of the beliefs that ground the research will help you fully appreciate the claims being made by the authors (and also prevent some confusion).

Second, a clear understanding of the stances taken by communication researchers will allow you to be better prepared to engage in critical analysis of the work. When reading research, it is most fruitful to critically analyze and assess its quality by comparing it to the standards of the stance it represents. Assessing social science based on humanist/interpretive standards will not really help critique it fairly because those are not the standards of the researchers. Likewise, assessing humanist/interpretive work on the basis of social scientific standards will get in the way of your ability to see its value for what its authors were attempting to do.

You may find that one or the other of these approaches is more appealing to you, and that's fine. But knowledge of both will equip you to really grasp the material you are presented with in communication scholarship.

Quantitative and Qualitative Methodology

A second distinction that can be made between types of research relates to the methods that scholars use to study the phenomenon they are interested in. The two types of methods you will encounter in this text are *quantitative methods* and *qualitative methods*. Interpretivist/humanists most commonly use qualitative methods, and social scientists often (but not always) use quantitative methods, but the two methodological categories can cross the two worldview categories previously discussed.

Before we turn to the differences between the two types of methods, there is a set of terms you will need to understand when reading either quantitative or qualitative research: *reliability* and *validity*. Not all researchers discuss these things, and some humanist/interpretive scholars would argue that they are not of real concern to them. However, these terms are still important for you to know.

The *reliability* of a finding reflects the extent to which, if the same experiment was performed in the same way a number of times, the results would be the same. If I completed a study of how much my children liked tofu, and when they tasted it, all of them were repulsed, but when I repeated the study one hour later only one third of them were repulsed, that study wouldn't be very reliable. We can also talk about intercoder reliability. *Intercoder reliability* refers to agreement between the different researchers who are analyzing the data. When a study has more than one researcher doing analysis of the material gathered, we want them to analyze it in the same way. Measures of intercoder reliability are a way to show that this is happening.

Validity is that the values in the study represent what they are trying to represent. *Internal validity* means that, within the study, measurements are indeed assessing what they were designed to assess. If I was attempting to study how much my children liked tofu, but I had soaked the tofu in wasabi soy sauce, my study would not have good internal validity because it could be the sauce, rather than the tofu, that they were responding to. *External validity* means that the measurements within the study represent the phenomenon outside the controlled analysis that they mean to represent. If my children ate tofu happily during the study (because they were being studied) but then would never eat it again, that measurement would have poor external validity.

Although these terms are used by scholars conducting various types of communication research, discussions about qualitative and quantitative methods also have their own particular terminologies and understanding some of those ideas will help clarify what the writers are saying.

Qualitative methods are those that consider the qualities of a particular communicative phenomenon, rather than doing numerical analysis. Qualitative methodology can be done in a number of ways. Frequently, qualitative analyses involve looking for themes, or patterns in communication. Often, the terms used with regard to qualitative methods are relatively self-explanatory (or easy to understand with a brief discussion). However, to get you started, let us consider two concepts often present in qualitative research reports.

Inductive analysis is an attempt to look at a body of communicative data (interviews, texts, etc.) and from that find the themes or patterns that seem to emerge in the discourse. Rather than beginning with a set of categories that are applied to the communicative phenomenon, the researchers allow the discourse itself to drive the creation of categories or particular understandings. As *thematic analysis* occurs, researchers return to the discourse again and again as they create the categories, themes, and so on to be sure that those ideas really represent the phenomenon.

Observational role is another idea that is often important to qualitative research. When engaging in ethnographic (study of the cultural practices of a particular group) or other naturalistic studies, scholars must decide how they will interact with the individuals being studied. Generally, there are four possible positions of observation. First, the researcher may be a *complete participant*. This means that he or she functions fully as a member of the group under study, and the group members are not aware that he or she is conducting research (this sometimes happens because the scholar was or is part of the group first and only later decides to analyze that group). Second, the researcher may be a *participant-observer*. This means that he or she participates as fully as possible in the group, but the members of the group are also aware that they are being studied. Third, the researcher may be an *observer-participant*. In this role, he or she would mostly just observe the individuals under study and try to stay out of the way for the most part, but there would sometimes be interactions. Finally, the researcher may be a *complete observer*. In this case, he or she would not interact with the members of the group at all, but would only observe them. Understanding what observational role the researcher assumed in the study will help you comprehend how he or she gained understanding of that situation.

Quantitative methodologies are those that rely on numerical computations in the accomplishment of research. In this text, you will see several examples of quantitative methodology being used. Quantitative methods are sometimes daunting to students because they don't understand the equations or what the numbers mean. The exact numerical analyses completed and the way that those are reported depend on the nature of the study. Thus, the scholars who have written for this text have attempted, in each article, to explain clearly the numerical analyses that are important for you to understand their findings. But, for now, we will address two basic terms to get you started.

One term you will commonly see in qualitative analysis is *correlation*. A *correlation* is a relationship between two values (numbers assigned to some variable). As one value changes, so does the other (in some way). A *positive correlation* means that as one number goes up or down, so does the other number. If the amount of hours I exercise is positively correlated to the amount of ice cream I eat, that means that the two will both go up or down together. A *negative correlation* means that as one number goes up, the other number goes down. If the amount of hours I exercise is negatively correlated to the number of pounds I weigh, that means that as one increases the other decreases. Correlations are written from a 0 (no connection between the numbers) to a + 1 or a − 1. A correlation of +1 means that the two numbers move in the same direction at exactly the same rate. So, if I exercise for 1 hour, I eat 2 bowls of ice cream; if I exercise for 2 hours, I eat 4 bowls of ice cream. A correlation of −1 means that the two numbers move in opposite directions at exactly the same rate. If I exercise for 2 hours, my weight decreases by 8 oz; if I exercise for 3 hours, my weight decreases by 12 oz. It is important that you note that correlation doesn't mean causation. Because two variables are correlated, that does not mean that one causes the other (and certainly not that we know which one causes the other). It could be the case that I eat more ice cream because I'm hungry after exercising. Or, it could be the case that when I eat more ice cream I feel guilty and exercise. Or, it might be that my gym has an ice cream shop where the ice cream is really good. So, the more often I go to the gym, the more often I exercise and the more often I eat ice cream.

Finally, researchers using quantitative methodology will often speak of *statistical significance*. Whether or not a correlation is statistically significant depends on a variety of factors. The computation of statistical significance is complex, so I won't go into it here. What you need to understand is that when researchers say that a measure is statistically significant, what they mean is that it is unlikely that the connection between the two variables is simply due to chance, so this is a connection we should pay attention to in the findings. Correlations that are not statistically significant might still be connections, but it isn't quite clear whether they are or whether the connection that was seen is accidental.

This is an introduction to a few terms that you might see in quantitative and qualitative research. As you read the research sections in this text, you will encounter other terms. Read carefully and look for the definitions, and you will find that they are not as difficult as they may appear on the surface.

The Parts of a Research Report

As you read reports of research, you will find that there are typically several parts represented in the work. The organization of those parts varies depending on the work itself (social scientific work tends to follow a more regular format, whereas humanistic/interpretive formats are more varied). However, regardless of the organizational structure, there are elements that are usually present.

Introduction to the Topic

Reports of research begin with some introduction to the topic. This clarifies for you what is being studied in the piece of research. It also points out why this particular phenomenon is important to study.

Review of Other Research or Theory

In the writing, you should expect to see the scholars referring to previous research that has been done about the topic, or theoretical concepts that are related to the issue under study. This may appear at different points in the writing (usually after the introduction in social scientific work, but sometimes dispersed throughout in humanistic/interpretive work). The *literature review* gives you a sense of where this piece of research is positioned within the larger field, provides background information that you need in order to understand the work, and also points you to other articles that you might want to read for further discussion of the topic.

Research Questions or Hypothesis

At some point in the article, you can expect to find a statement of the research questions or hypothesis that the researchers had going into the work. These may be stated in various ways. What the research questions and hypothesis tell you is the purpose for doing the research, what the researchers hoped to answer, or the concepts that they wanted to test with the study.

Methods

The methods of the research will also be described in some way. This is the "who, where, and how" of conducting research. The researcher typically describes the people or texts that were studied and possibly address how those were selected. How and where the research was conducted generally also are considered in the writing. It is important for you to know how the research was conducted because this will help you contextualize the results.

Results and Discussion

Eventually, the work addresses what the authors found in their research. In quantitative research, this is often divided into *results* (which present the results of the statistical analyses that were run with the data) and *discussion* (which is the interpretations that the researchers made of those statistical findings). When reading research presented in this way, you may find that the results section seems kind of confusing at first, particularly if your background in statistics is limited. If this is the case, you may wish to read the discussion first (so you understand how the authors interpreted those numbers) and then go back to the results section. In qualitative research these two can be combined or separate. The results and discussions section or sections tell you what the researchers concluded from their work and what they find most important for you to know. Often researchers also discuss both the benefits and the liabilities of their particular study, and what studies they feel should be done in the future about this topic.

As previously stated, research reports won't always follow this format exactly, but most of these elements will exist somewhere in the writing. Looking for them as you read will help you organize your understandings of what the authors are saying.

Scholarly research writing is an acquired taste. There is no doubt that it is more difficult than reading *USA Today*, or a nice Stephen King novel. However, reading reports at research can be interesting, exciting, challenging, and confirming. If you persevere, it is worth the effort.

Appendix B

Sources for Family Communication Research and Information

Journals

Although this list is not exhaustive, it suggests some of the main venues for family communication research. However, it should be noted that frequently family communication scholars publish work in journals that are not specifically communication journals, but more generally related to family process.

Adolescence
American Communication Journal
Asian Journal of Communication
Atlantic Journal of Communication
Australian Journal of Communication
Canadian Journal of Communication
Communication & Critical/Cultural Studies
Communication Monographs
Communication Quarterly
Communication Reports
Communication Research
Communication Research Reports
Communication Studies
Communication Theory
Communication Yearbook
Critical Inquiry
Critical Studies in Media Communication
Cultural Studies
Discourse & Society
Discourse Studies
Electronic Journal of Communication

European Journal of Communication
European Journal of Cultural Studies
Family Process
Family Relations
Feminist Studies
Human Communication Research
Information, Communication & Society
International Journal of Cultural Studies
Journal of Adolescence
Journal of Aging Studies
Journal of Applied Communication Research
Journal of Asian Pacific Communication
Journal of Child and Family Studies
Journal of Communication
Journal of Communication Inquiry
Journal of Computer-Mediated Communication
Journal of Contemporary Ethnography
Journal of Family Communication
Journal of Family Issues

Journal of Family Practice
Journal of Family Psychology
Journal of Gender Studies
Journal of Health Communication
Journal of Marriage and the Family
Journal of Religion and Popular Culture
Journal of Social and Personal
    Relationships
Journal of Social and Political Thought
Journalism & Communication Monographs
Kentucky Journal of Communication
Language & Communication
Marriage and Family Review
    Media, Culture & Society

Ohio Communication Journal
Qualitative Inquiry
Qualitative Research Reports in
    Communication
Quarterly Journal of Speech
Research on Aging
Sex Roles
Southern Communication Journal
The Howard Journal of
    Communications
The Review of Communication
Western Journal of Communication
Women's Studies in Communication

Books

There are many books that relate to family communication processes, but here are some that might be a good start for research.

Boss, P. G., Doherty, W. J., LaRossa, R., Schumm, W. R., & Steinmetz, S. K. (Eds.). (1993). *Sourcebook of family theories and methods: A contextual approach*. New York: Plenum Press.

Braithwaite, D., & Baxter, L. A. (2005). *Engaging theories in family communication: Multiple perspectives*. Thousand Oaks, CA: Sage.

Bryant, J., & Bryant, J. A. (Eds.). (2001). *Television and the American family* (2nd ed.). Mahwah, NJ: Erlbaum.

Fitzpatrick, M. A. (1988). *Between husbands and wives: Communication in marriage*. Newbury Park, CA: Sage.

Floyd, M., & Morman, M. T. (2005). *Widening the family circle: New research on family communication*. Thousand Oaks, CA: Sage.

Guerrero, L. K., & Floyd, K. (2005). *Nonverbal communication in close relationships*. Mahwah, NJ: Erlbaum.

McAdoo, H. P. (Ed.). (1999). *Family ethnicity: Strength in diversity* (2nd ed). Newbury Park, CA: Sage.

Pratt, M. W., & Fiese, B. E. (Eds.). (2004). *Family stories and the lifecourse: Across time and generations*. Mahwah, NJ: Erlbaum.

Sabourin, T. C. (2003). *The contemporary American family: A dialectical perspective on communication and relationships*. Thousand Oaks, CA: Sage.

Sigel, I. E., McGillicuddy-Delisi, A. V., & Goodnow J. J. (Eds.). (1992). *Parental belief systems: The psychological consequences for children*. Hillsdale, NJ: Erlbaum.

Socha, T. J., & Stamp, G. H. (Eds.). (1995). *Parents, children and communication: Frontiers of theory and research*. Mahwah, NJ: Erlbaum.

Stone, E. (1988). *Black sheep and kissing cousins: How our family stories shape us*. New York: New York Times Books.

Vangelisti, A. L. (Eds.). (2004). *Handbook of family communication*. Mahwah, NJ: Erlbaum.

Weston, K. (1991). *Families we choose: Lesbians, gays, kinship*. New York: Columbia University Press.

Web Sites

Great care must be taken when using online material for research because the quality may be compromised. Below are a few sites that contain statistical data and other information about families that you may find useful.

Administration for Children and Families
www.acf.dhhs.gov/

American Academy of Child & Adolescent Psychitry's Facts for Families and Other Resources
www.aacap.org/info_families/index.htm

The Australian Institute of Family Studies
www.aifs.gov.au/

Child Trends
www.childtrends.org

Families and Work Institute
www.familiesandwork.org/

Forum on Child and Family Statistics
www.childstats.gov/

The National Center for Missing and Exploited Children
www.ncmec.org/

National Clearinghouse on Child Abuse and Neglect Information
www.calib.com/nccanch

The National Communication Association
www.natcom.org

National Council on Family Relations
www.ncfr.com/

National Institute on Media and the Family
www.mediafamily.org/

National Parent Information Network
http://npin.org/

PFLAG (Parents, Families & Friends of Lesbians and Gays)
www.pflag.org/

The Urban Institute's National Survey of American Families
www.urban.org/center/anf/nsaf.cfm

The U.S. Census Web site
www.census.gov/

Appendix C

Author Information

Editor/Author

Lorin Basden Arnold (PhD, Purdue University) is a professor at Rowan University where she teaches courses including family communication, interpersonal communication, and communicating gender. Her research interests focus primarily on the intersection of diversity (of various types) and family life. She has published in journals such as *Communication Studies, Qualitative Research Reports in Communication,* and *Women and Language,* as well as writing text chapters for books related to feminist mothering, teaching public speaking, and diversity issues. Her interest in family springs in part from her experiences raising Jacob, Devin, Abbigael, Benjamin, Nathaniel, and Emmeline with her partner, Derek.

Contributing Authors

Tamara D. Afifi (formerly Golish, PhD, University of Nebraska–Lincoln) is an assistant professor at the University of California–Santa Barbara. She teaches graduate and undergraduate courses in family communication, interpersonal communication, and research methods. Her research involves studying how families negotiate communicatively the challenges they face during various life transitions including information regulation and communication processes in postdivorce families (and other stressful circumstances). She has published in numerous journals, including *Human Communication Research, Communication Monographs,* the *Journal of Marriage and Family,* and the *Journal of Social and Personal Relationships,* as well as in edited volumes.

Traci L. Anderson (PhD, University of Oklahoma) is an assistant professor of communication at Bryant University where she teaches courses such as interpersonal communication, communication and gender, and computer-mediated communication. Her research interests focus on how computer-mediated interpersonal communication facilitates the development and maintenance of online relationships, and family communication between parents and adult children. She has published in the journals *Communication Studies, CyberPsychology and Behavior,* and *Communication Research Reports.*

Dena G. Beeghly (EdD, University of Georgia) is a professor of literacy at West Chester University where she teaches Multicultural Issues in Literacy, Children's and Young Adult Literature, and Literacy Theory and Practice. She is the coauthor of *Litlinks: Activities for Connected Learning in Elementary Classrooms,* McGraw-Hill Teacher Resource Series. Her most recent work is on electronic discussion and may be found in the *Journal of Adolescent and Adult Literacy.*

Karla Mason Bergen (PhD, University of Nebraska–Lincoln) is an associate professor at the College of Saint Mary, a private all-women's college in Omaha, Nebraska, where she teaches a basic oral communication course, interpersonal communication, and gender communication. Her primary research interest is how women communicatively negotiate unconventional identities. She has studied identity issues relating to female college professors, lesbian couples and families, and women in commuter marriages, and has published articles in the *Journal of Social and Personal Relationships* and the *Journal of Family Communication.*

Nancy J. Brule (PhD, University of Nebraska–Lincoln) is an associate professor in the Department of Communication Studies at Bethel University in Minnesota. Her research areas include adolescent-to-parent abuse, high-risk adolescent and parent communication, and parent–teen conflict. She has published in the *Journal of Applied Communication,* the *Western Journal of Speech Communication, Journal of Religious Communication, and Communication Teacher,* and has written numerous book chapters. She is executive producer of the educational documentary *Color of Hope: Exploring Adolescent-to-Parent Abuse.* She teaches undergraduate and graduate level classes in interpersonal communication, family communication, gender, persuasion, research methods, abusive relationships, and communication theory.

Leah E. Bryant (PhD, University of Nebraska–Lincoln) is an assistant professor in the Communication Department at DePaul University. She teaches undergraduate and graduate courses in interpersonal, family, gender, and small-group communication as well as relational problems. Her research interests include family, relational, and instructional communication. Her current research focuses on communication in stepfamilies formed following the death of a parent. Her work has been published in the *Journal of Social and Personal Relationships, Communication Studies, Communication Research Reports,* and *Qualitative Research Reports.*

Devika Chawla (PhD, Purdue University) is an assistant professor in the School of Communication Studies at Ohio University, where she teaches undergraduate and graduate courses in family communication, cross-cultural communication, interpersonal communication, and qualitative methods. Her study of Indian women's experiences in Hindu arranged marriages was awarded the 2005 Kramarae Outstanding Dissertation Award by the Organization for the Study of Communication, Language, and Gender. She has published essays on family history, mother–daughter relationships, interpersonal relationships, and family identity in *Cultural Studies-Critical Methodologies, Qualitative Inquiry, Radical Pedagogy*, and contributed book chapters in edited volumes.

Tara L. Crowell (PhD, University of Oklahoma) is an associate professor at the Richard Stockton College of New Jersey where she teaches courses including interpersonal communication, health communication, and organizational and quantitative research methods. Her primary research interest focuses on the role of interpersonal communication in the context of health-related issues, with a secondary interest in instructional communication research. She has published in journals such as *Journal of Health Communication, Communication Studies, Communication Research Reports*, and numerous book chapters in the area of safer sexual communication and online data collection.

Joy M. Cypher (PhD, Purdue University) is an associate professor at Rowan University, works in disability studies and communication. She has researched interpersonal constructions of disability between friends and the popular framing of families with disabilities. Recent scholarship in family communication revolves around scholarly discourse of the disabled parent as well as the representations of disabled parenting in popular magazines. Her chapter, "Representations of Consequence," was part of the Top Papers in Disability Studies panel of the National Communication Association (2005).

Karen L. Daas (PhD, University of Nebraska–Lincoln) is an assistant professor at the University of Texas at San Antonio where she teaches courses including interpersonal communication, communication theory, and cultural theory. Her research focuses primarily on how women's personal and relational identities are constructed and negotiated through communication. Some of her work has appeared in the *Journal of Personal and Social Relationships* and the *Journal of Family Communication*.

Marianne Dainton (PhD, Ohio State University) is a professor of communication at La Salle University. She teaches interpersonal communication, group communication, and communication theory. Her research focuses on relationship maintenance. She is the author of two books: *Maintaining Relationships through Communication* (coedited with Dan Canary) and *Applying Communication Theory for Professional Life* (coauthored with Elaine Zelley). She has published in *Communication Monographs*, the *Journal of Social and Personal Relationships, Family Relations, Western Journal of Communication, Communication Quarterly, Communication Reports*, and *Communication Research Reports*, as well as numerous book chapters.

Chrys Egan (PhD, Florida State University) is an associate professor of communication at Salisbury University in Maryland. Her research centers on the intersection of interpersonal and mass communication: how individuals uniquely consume media, and how media impact people's personal lives, including family media use and rules. She has published several pedagogical texts, academic articles in journals such as *Studies of Popular Culture* and *Iowa Journal of Communication*, and numerous newspaper and magazine articles. Her own family consists of her husband, John, a biology professor, and their adopted son, Liam.

Autumn P. Edwards (PhD, Ohio University) is an assistant professor of communication at Western Michigan University where she teaches courses in interpersonal communication and research methods. Her work has appeared in journals including *Communication Studies, Health Communication*, and *Communication Research Reports*, and as book chapters on topics including health communication, work–family issues, and third-wave feminism.

Kory Floyd (PhD, University of Arizona) is an associate professor of human communication at Arizona State University. He is also director of the communication sciences laboratory. He has published more than 65 book chapters and journal articles (in journals such as *Communication Monographs, Human Communication Research*, and the *Journal of Communication*) as well as 5 books. His research focuses on the communication of affection in families and other intimate relationships, and on the interplay between communication, physiology, and health. He is currently editor of *Journal of Family Communication*.

Annette L. Folwell (PhD, University of Oklahoma) is an associate professor in the Department of Psychology and Communication Studies at the University of Idaho. She teaches communication research methods as well as gender, aging, and family communication courses. Her scholarship centers on the older adult relationships, particularly marital, sibling, and grandparent– grandchild relationships. Her research has been published in *Journal of Social and Personal Relationships, Journal of Language and Social Psychology*, and *Journal of the Northwest Communication Association*.

Elizabeth E. Graham (PhD, Kent State University) is a professor in the School of Communication Studies at Ohio University. Her research and teaching interests include relationship transition, particularly in family settings, and research methods. Her work has been published in the *Journal of Family Communication, Communication Monographs, Communication Research Reports,* and other communication outlets. In addition to several book chapters already published, she is currently coediting a book titled *Communication Research Measures*. In addition, she serves as the University Ombuds at Ohio University and has held that position since 2002.

Jo Anna Grant (PhD, University of Oklahoma) is an associate professor of communication studies at California State University–San Bernardino. Her research interests are in communication and aging, interpersonal relationships, family relationships, and health communication. She has published articles examining the perceptions of power and closeness in family relationships across the life span in journals such as *Journal of Cross Cultural Gerontology* and *Journal of Social and Personal Relationships*. She teaches courses in interpersonal communication, health communication, small-group communication, and research methods.

Patricia S. Hill (PhD, Bowling Green State University) is an associate professor in the School of Communication at the University of Akron, where she teaches courses including public speaking, and interpersonal and intercultural communication. Her research interests include gender, race, and critical pedagogy. She has published book chapters and numerous articles in various journals, such as *Women and Language, The Gerontologist, Journalism History*, and *The Electronic Journal of Communication*. She implements her interests in interpersonal, intercultural, and critical pedagogy via interactive classroom methods to increase critical thinking skills. She is involved in initiatives for recruitment and retention of students of color.

Sherry J. Holladay (PhD, Purdue University) is an associate professor of communication at Eastern Illinois University, Charleston, Illinois. Her research interests concern issues related to communication and aging as well as organizational communication. With respect to communication and aging, she focuses on intergenerational communication, especially the development and maintenance of relationships between grandparents and grandchildren and relationships between age-discrepant friends. Her work has appeared in *International Journal of Aging and Human Development, Management Communication Quarterly, Journal of Communication, Communication Studies,* and *Handbook of Communication and Aging Research.*

Patrick C. Hughes (PhD, University of Denver) is an associate professor in the Department of Communication Studies at Texas Tech University. His research interests include family communication and how religious and cultural influences impact marital communication. His publications have appeared in *Journal of Family Communication, Communication Research Reports, Southern Communication Journal, Western Journal of Communication, Argumentation and Advocacy,* and *The Sourcebook for Family Communication*: Sage. (Eds., Turner and West) in addition to other journals and texts.

Elaine Bass Jenks (PhD, Pennsylvania State University) is a professor of communication studies at West Chester University where she teaches courses in interpersonal, friendship, family, and health communication. She uses an ethnographic approach to studying communication about and among individuals who are blind, sighted, and visually impaired. Her most recent work has appeared in the *Journal of Contemporary Ethnography, Expressions of Ethnography,* and *Ethnographically Speaking.*

Deirdre D. Johnston (PhD, University of Iowa) is a professor in the Department of Communication at Hope College. She has published work on media representations of mothers in *Sex Roles: A Journal of Research* and *Mass Communication and Society.* She has published research on the social construction of mothering ideology and identity by at-home, part-time employed, and full-time employed mothers in *Sex Roles: A Journal of Research* and the *Journal of the Association of Research on Mothering.* In 2005 her research was nominated for the Elizabeth Ross Kantor Award for Excellence in Work–Family Research.

Amber E. Kinser (PhD, Purdue University) is an associate professor of communication and director of Women's Studies at East Tennessee State University. She was awarded a Top Paper in Family Communication by the National Communication Association for her work on partnership issues in pregnancy. She is editor of an anthology titled *Mothering in the Third Wave* from Demeter Press. Her work has appeared in articles in *Women and Language* and *National Women's Studies Association* journals, and book chapters in *Feminist Mothering* by SUNY Press and *Mother Knows Best* by Demeter Press.

Ascan F. Koerner (PhD, University of Wisconsin) is an associate professor of communication studies at the University of Minnesota, where he teaches courses in marital and family communication, conflict, persuasion, social cognition, and communication theory. His research focuses on the cognitive bases of relationships and their influence on interpersonal communication, mainly in the context of family communication. His research has appeared in journals such as *Communication Monographs, Communication Theory, Human Communication Research*, and the *Journal of Family Communication*, as well as in publications such as *The Handbook of Family Communication, The Handbook of Conflict Communication*, and *Engaging Theories in Family Communication*.

Joy Koesten (PhD, University of Kansas) is assistant dean of the graduate school at the University of Kansas. Her research has focused on family communication, adolescent development, and risk behavior. She has published in *Communication Monographs, The Journal of Family Communication, The Applied Journal of Communication Research, Communication Education, Communication Studies, The Journal of Sociolinguistics*, and *The Journal for Financial Planning*. Dr. Koesten's work on stress and burnout in the financial planning industry won a national award for cutting-edge research in practice management at the Financial Planning Association Annual Conference and Exposition in San Diego, California.

Dennis Alajandro Vegas Leoutsakas (PhD, University of South Florida) is an assistant professor at Salisbury University where he teaches a broad range of interpersonal courses in the Department of Communication and Theatre Arts. His primary interest is applied work focusing on health and social issues. He has worked with orphan, intercultural, HIV, and substance abuse issues in such remote areas as South Africa, Estonia, and Ecuador. He has presented multiple storytelling concerts and workshops and published in journals such as *Drugs and Society: A Journal of Contemporary Issues*; *AIDS Education and Prevention: An Interdisciplinary Journal*; and the *South African Children's Book Forum*.

Laura Maki (MA, University of Minnesota) is a graduate student in the Department of Communication Studies at the University of Minnesota. Her research focuses on family communication and has been presented at conferences of the International Communication Association and the International Association for Relationship Research.

Michelle Miller-Day (PhD, Arizona State University) is an associate professor of communication arts and sciences and faculty affiliate with the Center for Human Development and Family Research at Pennsylvania State University. She has been conducting substance abuse prevention research for over 15 years and is the author of two books, *Communication among Grandmothers, Mothers, and Adult Daughters* and *Adolescent Relationships and Drug Use*. Her scholarly work has appeared in journals such as *Journal of Family Communication, Journal of Adolescent Research*, and *Health Communication*. She has also published in venues designed to help family practitioners with substance abuse work.

Mark T. Morman (PhD, University of Kansas) is an associate professor of communication studies at Baylor University, where he serves as faculty advisor for the Lambda Pi Eta communication honor society. His research focuses on affectionate communication within families and close relationships and on persuasive messages relevant to men's health issues. He has published several articles in both regional and national communication journals, is currently chair of the Family Communication Division of the National Communication Association, and serves on the editorial boards of *Journal of Family Communication* and *Journal of Social and Personal Relationships*.

Kevin Pearce (PhD, Kent State University) is an associate professor of communication at Bryant University. He has published scholarly articles on topics including the Internet, family communication, and written communication in journals such as *Communication Quarterly, Communication Research Reports,* and *Written Communication Quarterly*. His primary areas of research include family communication, mass communication, and instructional communication. He teaches a number of courses at Bryant University including Media Effects, Mass Communication, Global Communication, Argumentation and Persuasion, and Studies in Film and Video.

Barbara A. Penington (PhD, Marquette University) teaches Interpersonal Communication, Listening Behavior, and Cross Cultural Communication at the University of Wisconsin–Whitewater. Her most recent publications in family communication include "The Communicative Management of Connection and Autonomy in African-American and Euro-American Mother–Daughter Relationships" in the *Journal of Family Communication,* and "Playground or Training Ground: The Function of Talk in African American and European American Mother–Adolescent Daughter Dyads" coauthored with Lynn Turner in P. M. Buzzanell, H. Sterk, and L. H. Turner (Eds.), *Gender in Applied Communication Contexts*.

Suzy Prentiss (PhD, University of Tennessee, Knoxville) is a lecturer in the Communication Studies Department at the University of Tennessee, Knoxville, teaching Business and Professional Communication, Intercultural Communication, and First Year Studies. Her research/professional interests include speech anxiety and apprehension, family communication within interracial families, and diversity issues. She is currently collaborating on a project at a local middle school focusing on reducing bullying/hate speech and promoting tolerance among adolescents. She has published work in venues such as *Communication Teacher, Teaching Ideas for the Basic Communication Course*, and the *Journal of Intergroup Relations*.

Shirley A. Staske-Bell (PhD, University of Illinois at Urbana–Champaign) is a professor of communication studies at Eastern Illinois University where she teaches courses in interpersonal communication, including family communication, interpersonal conflict, intercultural communication, and courses in social interaction. She has used Conversation Analysis to study close relational partners' emotional communication and conflict interaction as well as family members' negotiation of identities and relational ties. She has published such studies in journals such as *Research on Language and Social Interaction* and *Symbolic Interaction*.

Chelsea A. H. Stow (MA, Texas Tech University) is a PhD student in human communication studies at the University of Denver. Her research explores communication in families and centers on family conflict, the family life cycle, the engagement/wedding process, and identity negotiation after a miscarriage.

Elizabeth A. Suter (PhD, University of Illinois at Urbana–Champaign) is an assistant professor in the Department of Human Communication Studies at the University of Denver where she teaches courses in family communication, relational communication, and gender and communication. Her research interests focus on the critical intersections of gender, race, and sexuality as families and individuals negotiate their identities with others. She has published in *Journal of Family Communication, Journal of Family Issues, Journal of Social and Personal Relationships, Women and Language, The Communication Review, Journal of Lesbian Studies, The Qualitative Report*, and *Sex Roles*.

Debra Harvey Swanson (PhD, Catholic University of America) is a professor at Hope College, teaching courses including Introduction to Sociology and Social Problems, Sociology of Gender, Race and Ethnic Relations, and Balancing Work and Family. Her research focuses on the social construction of mothering and she hopes to expand her work to include international mothers. She has published several articles with her colleague, Deirdre Johnston, in *Sex Roles,* as well as in *Journal of the Association of Research on Mothering* and *Mass Communication and Society*. Her research interest in mothering is driven by interest in her own children, Emma and Tyler.

Index